The Year of the Pageant

Andrew Swift & Kirsten Elliott

THE YEAR
OF THE PAGEANT

Andrew Swift & Kirsten Elliott

AKEMAN PRESS

Published by Akeman Press, 58 Minster Way, Bath BA2 6RL
www.akemanpress.com

ISBN: 978-0-9560989-00

Front cover: The Masque of Bladud from the 1909 Bath Pageant.

Back cover: Edwin Fagg's design for the head-dress of Ladye Bath
and costume designs for children in Episodes I and V of the Bath
Pageant.

Title Page: One of Henry VII's heralds from the Bath Pageant.

Printed by Short Run Press, Exeter

CONTENTS

ACKNOWLEDGEMENTS

First and foremost, thanks must go to Bruce Crofts, whose notes and research on the Bath Pageant, going back many years, provided not only the inspiration for this book, but also a good deal of the information contained in it, as well as a number of the photographs. The chapters on 'Street Life' and 'Memories of Larkhall', in particular, would have been impossible without material collected by him. We also have Bruce to thank for the excellent plan of the Pageant Ground reproduced on pages 584-5.

Thanks also go to: Andrew Ayers for information on his ancestor Mrs Ursula Cazalet Bloxam; Vic Chivers for information on his grandfather, Samuel Hallett, and memories of Beechen Cliff; Roger Eades for information on London Road and Sturge Cotterell's house at Lodge Style; the Fashion Museum, Bath for help and guidance on fashion in 1909; Chris Mees of Research Design for information on artists involved in designing costumes and properties; Victor Rosenburg for his memories of Edwardian Bath; Derek Rowe for information on Bath Street and the New Royal Baths; Brian Wates for the material on Reginald Ainsworth in Chapter 24; and Julian Landau for the lyrics from 'Skeleton Store Detective.

Special thanks also go to those institutions and individuals who have given permission to reproduce the following photographs and documents, which have been so valuable in conveying a sense of Edwardian life: Bath Record Office: 50, 113, 138 (both), 146 (right), 288, 313 (top), 316, 318 (both), 320, 334 (top), 400 (top two), 531, 541 (all), 544 (both), 545 (bottom), 546 (both), 547, 557, 564, 570 (top), 572 (top), 639, 641 (all), 648 (bottom two), 651 (top), 652 (top), 653 (bottom); Museum of Bath at Work: 60 (both), 257, 438 (top three), 439 (top), 440 (top two), 441, 470 (bottom), 471; Museum of Bath at Work (Mike Williams collection): 33 (top), 64, 78, 135, 313 (bottom); Somerset Record Office: 238; Harry Barstow: 326; Paul De'Ath: 369 (bottom), 371 (centre), 378 (top & bottom right), 458 (both), 459 (both); Jackie Douglass: 163 (bottom); Mr & Mrs EJ Fry: 89; Nigel Gillard: 686 (left centre); Colin Hamilton: 372, 373; Alan Keevil: 631, 621 (bottom); Steve Lord: 74 (both), 469, 484, 485 (both), 685; Frank McGarry: 163 (top); Anne Scott: 410, 424, 440 (bottom two), 442 (both).

A photograph from 1901, the very beginning of the Edwardian era: a soldier from the North Somerset Yeomanry rides past the Bath & County Club as elderly ladies, dressed in black to mourn the late Queen, with parasols raised against the sun, walk by.

CHAPTER 1

THE DAWN OF THE MODERN AGE

Asked to pick the year which saw the dawn of the modern age, many people would, I suspect, pick 1901 – the year Queen Victoria died – or 1914, when the First World War broke out. We would like to suggest another candidate, however – 1909.

An odd choice, you might think, and you'll probably struggle to think of anything significant that happened. Admittedly, no one famous died and no wars broke out; none the less, there were some important landmarks.

The welfare state was created. Old Age Pensions removed the spectre of the workhouse as a final destination for millions of working-class people. National Insurance, sickness and unemployment benefit, labour exchanges – all came on line in 1909. Lloyd George's 'people's budget' represented the most dramatic redistribution of wealth ever envisaged; the House of Lords' refusal to ratify it started the process of constitutional reform that continues today.

The first Model T Fords started to appear on the roads, heralding the age of mass motoring. A mere six years after the first powered flight, Bleriot flew across the English Channel, establishing aeroplanes as a viable form of transport.

The Housing and Town Planning Act, passed in 1909, was the first legal step towards controlled urban development.

Today, it is impossible to conceive of society without a welfare state, mass motoring, air travel or town planning, but a century ago they were all daring and often unpopular innovations. And all can be said to have their genesis in one year – 1909.

Bath, too, celebrates an important centenary in 2009. On 27 March that year, a meeting was held to protest against the demolition of Bath Street. It marked the beginning of the campaign to save Bath from the developers that continues today.

At the time, though, it was overshadowed by one of the most extraordinary events in the city's history. All but forgotten today, the Bath Pageant of 1909 was an extravaganza on a scale never attempted before or since. A century on, the logistics of it still defy the imagination.

There were over 3,000 performers, most of them in costumes made specially for the event. Just about everyone – certainly all the great and good – took part. The King's brother, assorted members of parliament, lord mayors, mayors and dignitaries from all over the country, travelled down to see the Pageant in special trains; there were representatives from twelve towns called Bath in the United States and two in Canada. The spectacle, akin in scale to the set of a Hollywood epic, lasted for over three hours and was repeated every afternoon for a week.

The format was straightforward – a series of episodes illustrating events from Bath's history. Yet, while celebrating the past, it also had an eye firmly on the future. The Bath Pageant was intended to re-establish Bath as one of the country's most fashionable tourist destinations. It was an expression of civic pride and a demonstration of what the people of Bath could do. Other towns and cities in Britain and the USA had had their pageants – but none was as grand as Bath's.

The phrase 'Edwardian England' is one that conjures up an image of almost impossible elegance and refinement, blasted into oblivion by the horrors of the Great War. And what of Edwardian Bath – that sepia-toned city where the strains of Elgar's *Chanson de Matin* accompanied the clink of teacups in the Pump Room, nothing moved faster than a Bath Chair and the sun always shone? In the quiet streets and hidden corners the shadows of Beau Nash and the beaux of days gone by still lingered; apart from an occasional train puffing reassuringly in the distance, the modern world hardly impinged. It is a compelling picture and one that was fostered by contemporaries.

In 1909, the 68-year-old naturalist and travel writer WH Hudson published *Afoot in England*, in which he described a visit to the city:

'Tis so easy to get from London to Bath, by merely stepping into a railway carriage which takes you smoothly without a stop in two short hours from Paddington, that I was amazed at myself in having allowed five full years to pass since my previous visit. The question was much in my mind as I strolled about noting the old-remembered names of streets and squares and crescents. Quiet Street was the name inscribed on one; it was, to me, the secret name of them all. The old impressions were renewed, an old feeling partially recovered. The wide, clean ways; the solid, stone-built houses with their dignified aspect; the large distances, terrace beyond terrace; mansions and vast green lawns and parks

2

and gardens; avenues and groups of stately trees, especially that unmatched clump of old planes in the Circus; the whole town, the design in the classic style of one master mind, set by the Avon, amid green hills, produced a sense of harmony and repose which cannot be equalled by any other town in the kingdom ...

To sit on some high hill and look down on Bath, sun-flushed or half veiled in mist; to lounge on Camden Crescent, or climb Sion Hill, or take my ease with the water-drinkers in the spacious, comfortable Pump Room; or, better still, to rest at noon in the ancient abbey – all this was pleasure pure and simple, a quiet drifting back until I found myself younger by five years than I had taken myself to be. I haunted the abbey, and the more I saw of it the more I loved it. The impression it had made on me during my former visits had faded, or else I had never properly seen it, or had not seen it in the right emotional mood. Now I began to think it the best of all the great abbey churches of England and the equal of the cathedrals in its effect on the mind. How rich the interior is in its atmosphere of tempered light or tender gloom! How tall and graceful the columns holding up the high roof of white stone with its marvellous palm-leaf sculpture! What a vast expanse of beautifully stained glass! I certainly gave myself plenty of time to appreciate it on this occasion, as I visited it every day, sometimes two or three times, and not infrequently I sat there for an hour at a stretch.

This, of course, is territory familiar from *The Country Diary of an Edwardian Lady, Pot Pourri from a Surrey Garden, The Wind in the Willows*. But this Laura-Ashleyfied, National-Trust-sanctioned view is only part of the picture: Bath in 1909 was far less comfortable, far more turbulent – and far more interesting – than Hudson's account suggests.

The Edwardian age was one of radical, unprecedented change. It was the crucible in which the modern world was born. At the same time, high society, led by Edward VII – the Prince of Pleasure – recaptured much of the hedonistic allure that had not been seen since the days of the Regency. Bath, though, did not partake of this reversion to the pleasure principle. The city which had once been a philandering paragon of fashionable excess had metamorphosed into a maiden aunt, infirm and of advanced years, wrapped in a fox stole, smelling of mothballs.

It was Monte Carlo, Cannes, Marienbad and Biarritz that picked up where Bath had left off a century earlier. In England,

One of the most striking differences between Bath today and Bath a century ago is the number of motor vehicles. Above, a solitary car trundles into Queen Square as a dog scuttles across the road; below, a nursemaid pushes a pram across Raby Place, now one of Bath's busiest junctions.

Among Bath's glories, then as now, are its parks and open spaces. Above, a view of Hedgemead Park, opened in 1889 after the houses on the site slid down the hill; below, a distinctly rural view of the lawn in front of the Royal Crescent.

Ascot, Henley, Cowes, Goodwood and the country houses of the fast set were the places to be seen, not Bath. What contemporaries thought of the Queen of the West can be gauged by a passage in John Galsworthy's *Man of Property* (1906):

> Aunt Ann turned her old eyes from one to the other. Indulgent and severe was her look. In turn the three brothers looked at Ann. She was getting shaky. Wonderful woman! Eighty-six if a day; might live another ten years, and had never been strong. Swithin and James, the twins, were only seventy-five, Nicholas a mere baby of seventy or so. All were strong, and the inference was comforting. Of all forms of property their respective healths naturally concerned them most.
>
> 'I'm very well in myself', proceeded James, 'but my nerves are out of order. The least thing worries me to death. I shall have to go to Bath.'
>
> 'Bath!' said Nicholas. 'I've tried Harrogate. That's no good. What I want is sea air. There's nothing like Yarmouth. Now, when I go there I sleep.'

The Pageant was an attempt to transform Bath from a place that even grumpy old men wrote off as a holiday destination. Before we look at how it was done – and how far it succeeded – we will take a look at Bath in 1909. But, just as the Pageant needs to be seen in the context of what was happening in Bath, so what happened in Bath needs to be seen in the context of what was happening on the wider stage. What follows is not intended to be a comprehensive survey of 1909, but an impression of what that extraordinary year might have looked like from the point of view of someone living in Bath.

Present-day Bathonians will find many parallels with and pre-echoes of current concerns in the accounts of what preoccupied their counterparts a century ago. Not only were there fierce battles between conservationists and developers; criticism of the council's policy of spending ratepayers' money on visitor facilities was as intense as it is today; and there was even an ongoing debate as to whether rugby should continue to be played on the recreation ground.

For all the parallels, though, the world of 1909 was profoundly different to that of 2009. The similarities serve not only to reinforce our kinship with the folk of a century ago, but also to underline the differences and to indicate how far and how fast we have travelled. Yet the continuity of our concerns is inescapable, and the repercussion of decisions made in 1909, as Bath stood on the brink of the modern age, can still be felt today.

CHAPTER 2

WAKE UP, BATH!

In 1901, the Prince of Wales – the future George V – gave a speech at the Guildhall in London in which he coined the phrase, 'Wake up, England!' Taken up by reformers on both sides of the political debate, it echoed like a clarion call through the ensuing decade. In 1909 it was taken up – and rephrased – by those who wanted to drag Bath kicking and screaming into the twentieth century.

The 'Wake Up, Bath!' campaign was spearheaded by progressive forces within the council. For them, Bath's salvation lay in a ruthless process of modernisation; they saw sentiment and heritage as the enemies of economic and social development. They were supported by a 'Wake Up, Bath!' campaign in the *Bath Chronicle*, with public meetings and council debates taking place against the backdrop of vigorous correspondence, for and against, on a daily basis. If this all sounds wearily familiar today, a century ago it was uncharted territory – and little did those councillors suspect that one of their most lasting achievements would be to 'wake up' the conservation lobby.

One of the most heated topics – then as now – was the extent to which Bath should invest in improving facilities for visitors. On one side were those who believed it was a solid investment and would boost the city's economy; on the other were those who wanted investment to be for the benefit of residents. In 1902, Charles Langston had published a pamphlet attacking the council in the form of a poem called *The Denunciad Up to Date: A Satire in Two Parts*. This contained the lines –

> *The residents our Aediles now ignore,*
> *The visitors are always to the fore.*
> *For them they build, pull down, and suffer loss,*
> *For citizens they do not care a toss*

– which neatly summed up one side of the argument.

Many also believed that spending money on visitor facilities would be counterproductive. Low rates were, they argued, one of the most attractive features for prospective residents; they even featured in official publicity material. If money was spent on visitor facilities,

Left: An Edwardian view of the Lower Promenade in the Roman Baths.
Right: This extension to the baths opened in 1889 on the corner of Stall and York Streets.
Although part of the building still survives further down York Street, this corner block
has been rebuilt in a style reminiscent of the quadrants at the end of Bath Street and now
houses a gift shop.

rates would rise, thus putting off the very people the council wished
to attract.

Bath's reinvention as a tourist resort in the late nineteenth and early
twentieth centuries – a process in which the Pageant was to play
a crucial role – relied heavily on the promotion of its Roman and
Georgian heritage. But it was still the spa waters that were the main
focus of attention. In 1889, a new suite of baths – known as the Aix
le Bains Massage Douche Baths, and incorporating features found in
spas on the continent – had been built on the corner of York and Stall
Streets. This had boosted visitor numbers, as had the opening of the
Roman Baths and the building of a Concert Hall as part of the Pump
Room extension in 1897. But still Bath seemed to be punching below
its weight. One correspondent in the *Chronicle* believed this was an
image problem:

> In my opinion, one of the things which seems to bar our city
> becoming popular as it ought is the impression one hears
> everywhere away that Bath is relaxing and a very oppressive place
> to stay at or live in. Could not something be done to remove that
> impression, as I am certain the impression is erroneous? Bath has

never been properly advertised. The advertisements which have appeared in various magazines certainly filled up space, but they were never attractive or likely to 'pull' ... One of the phrases of the bygones was 'Go to Bath', and if an enterprising committee tendered that invitation by letting the world know that there was something worth coming for – the best mineral waters in Europe, a round of uplifting entertainment, delightful walks and drives in most charming scenery, and every possibility of affording visitors a memorable holiday and change – the advice would be accepted and people would come.

Other people felt, however, that the problem lay deeper. For a start there was the look of the place. Austin King, secretary of the Bath Chamber of Commerce drew attention to the 'unsightly appearance' of the many unoccupied houses in the city, with their 'dirty windows' and the 'large numbers of agents' bills with which windows and railings are placarded'. He called for a bye-law limiting 'for sale' or 'to let' signs to one per property.

Then there was the problem of getting about. March 1909 saw heavy snowfalls which 'rendered pedestrianism in many parts of the city extremely difficult'. The problem was made worse, according to Dr Preston King, by people putting salt on pavements after snow or frost. He described it as a 'wicked practice' which made people's feet 'like refrigerators', and called for it to be made 'a penal offence'.

Even without the snow, many of the city's pavements were in a parlous state. Great Pulteney Street was in particular need of attention. In February, councillors were told that repaving the street with pennant stone would cost £3,000, although patent or destructor stone would cost half that. Another option was to relay and reface the existing stones, but several councillors pointed out that around two-thirds of the stones were damaged or would break if lifted. It was decided to defer repaving the street for five years. This created such an outcry that, at the end of April – mindful, perhaps, of the crowds that would use the street to visit the Pageant events in Sydney Gardens – it was announced that it would be repaved with Brook's Perfecrot Paving Flags at 4/3 per yard.

One of the main complaints from visitors, however, was not the state of the pavements but the amount of noise. A correspondent who signed himself 'Sleepless One' called for the council to 'stop hooters at factories in the early morning. I have known three [people] who would have taken big houses in Bath but could not put up with such a noise. After a sleepless night it is annoying to be awakened

A study in contrasts:

Above: Great Pulteney Street was a vision of tree-lined civility in 1909 – although then as now it was advisable to look out for uneven and cracked paving stones.

Left: Traffic congestion at the top of Broad Street as an electric tram swings round into the Paragon. The rumble of the trams, combined with the clip-clop of horses' hooves and the rattle of iron carriage wheels, was a constant source of irritation to those seeking rest and recuperation.

early by factory nuisances.' A Mr Bateman from Abingdon, who was suffering from a 'painful ailment' and had come to Bath seeking 'rest, recuperation and recreation', found himself imperilled by the 'Demon of Noise'. He was woken at 5.30 every morning by the first tram of the day, 'thundering past at ten times the speed of horse trams and a hundred times noisier'. Apart from the trams, which ran past every few minutes until midnight, 'huge ponderous traction engines and monstrous and hideous motor buses' added to the 'intolerable din'. These were supplemented by 'musical interludes of ear-piercing din from street hawkers, vendors chiefly of coke and kippers, neither of which are necessaries of life to Bath invalids', and the shouts of paperboys who either 'assume the majority of the population are very deaf, or try to make them so'.

Another – anonymous – gentleman, wrote to say that he had lived in Bath, on and off, for 40 years, but, after having been away for nine years, was 'aghast at the state of noise':

> Even traction engines pass through any street that suits the driver's whim. They should not be allowed on roads hollowed out underneath by cellars. Worst of all is the incessant sharp whistling of errand boys, coo-eeing to one another, banging bones, tins, railings, etc. Boys shout and scream until 9pm in streets within ear of the Circus. Everyone knows noise is dangerous to the nervous system. It prevents the operation of delicate instruments in observatories. It stops the propellers of submarines. It is one form of electricity the waves of which spell disaster. The police, teachers and clergy must do more to teach citizens and boys how to behave.

And then there were the street musicians. For one correspondent, these constituted the biggest nuisance of all:

> The only real complaint I have to make – and it is a substantial one – is that you permit beggars and wandering minstrels and street singers! Just imagine such a thing at a continental 'cure'. It is very, very trying to the nerves and patience of an invalid suffering from nervous pain to have a couple of wretches yelling, screaming, bawling at the top of their voices the words of some hymn for a quarter of an hour in the street in front of the house. That your Watch Committee permits this sort of thing, and people with flutes, cornets and organs, is an absolute amazement to me.

So much for Hudson's vision of quietude.

The city was also far dirtier and smokier than it is today. One writer to the *Chronicle* exclaimed, 'Oh, the smoke! Two clean collars a day!' One source of pollution was the destructor works. At a meeting of the Sanitary Committee in June, Councillor Timmins said that he had been playing at Bath Lawn Tennis Club, but, when water was thrown on clinkers cleaned out of the plant, it was impossible to continue, 'the air being so thick with smoke from the destructor'.

The gasworks were also a source of complaint. During a debate, Councillor Green reported that, although one doctor thought the smell would just cause nausea, another believed it could affect people with delicate chests. Councillor Miller replied that he thought it was supposed to be healthy. When the Council Surveyor, Charles Fortune, said that the stench from the gasworks made the men at the destructor works ill, his comments were greeted with laughter. He was not impressed and told the councillors that, if they had to take their meals there, they would be 'far from delighted'. He also told them that, when he visited the gasworks, he had to rinse his mouth out afterwards, and his tongue was like sandpaper.

For the governors of King Edward's School in Broad Street, it was smoke from the tramway chimney in Walcot Street that was a bone of contention. The council accepted that their grievance was 'a very real one', but, after an official had kept the chimney under observation for four weeks, decided that there was 'no ground for complaint', as the company 'had every appliance to prevent black smoke'.

Compared with nuisances on this scale, some complaints seem rather trivial. A constant source of friction was 'householders beating mats and sweeping down fronts of houses after 9am', which was not only 'very offensive and undesirable' but also in contravention of a bye-law. Nevertheless, the council took the matter sufficiently seriously to prosecute offenders. One who fell foul of the law was Kate Price, who was fined five shillings for sweeping the footway in front of 2 Canton Place, Walcot after 9am on 15 March despite having received two warnings.

Some people had a very clear idea what needed to be done to attract visitors to Bath. One of them was Harry Hatt – not, despite his name, a stand-up comic, but a hairdresser and perfumer in the Corridor, who later became Mayor. In a letter to the Chronicle he outlined his list of desiderata:

> Remove the two houses on the east side of Orange Grove that
> obstruct the view of the Institution Gardens;

Above: Sweeping the pavement outside the Old Farmhouse on Lansdown Road – if you got caught doing this after 9am you risked a fine. The Old Farmhouse had been rebuilt in 1892 in an Arts & Crafts-inspired style – half-timbered gables jostling with Bath-stone mullions – and was one of the best-appointed pubs in the city. The shop next door was a post office when this photograph was taken, but by 1909 the business had moved across the road to 23 Belvedere.

Left: Institution Gardens, as Parade Gardens were known a century ago, were the subject of several grandiose regeneration schemes.

Carry a broad terrace from the roadway down to the gardens;
Move the bandstand to face the new terraces;
Beautify the gardens with fountains;
Build winter gardens on the site of the old Bath Chronicle offices
   on Kingston Parade;
Put one large roof over the winter gardens and the Roman Baths,
   creating a building capable of holding up to 2,000 people;
Provide an up-to-date bathing establishment.

The tollgate on North Parade Bridge.

There were numerous complaints about the tolls levied on North
Parade and Cleveland Bridges. JW Tranter, an insurance agent from
Pierrepont Street, pointed out that 'of Bath's ten bridges only three
are free of toll', and went on to list the benefits that would ensue
if tolls were abolished – the working classes would be able to get
home for lunch, traffic would be better distributed, cab fares would
be reduced, as would 'profane language'.

It was estimated, however, that taking the bridges into public
ownership would cost in the region of £24,000, and there were
suggestions that building new bridges would not only be cheaper
but also more beneficial. There were calls for 'an ornamental
footbridge connecting the Institution Gardens with the recreation

ground … providing invalids and others with views of wooded eminences, church towers, spires and stately buildings'. Opponents argued that the scheme was impractical because of the risk of flooding, to which one correspondent retorted that, when Major Davis 'intended to put a mammoth hotel on the Recreation Ground [he] made provision for lifting it above the flood level'. No new bridges were built and Bath had to wait another 20 years before tolls were finally abolished. A century on, a footbridge to the recreation ground is still a project that raises its head from time to time.

Also yet to be built – despite many campaigns over the years – is a concert hall. A correspondent in 1909 entered the 'Wake Up, Bath!' debate by calling for

> a big hall with an organ, on the Newmarket Row site, something after the style of Colston Hall, Bristol. This would be most useful, and it is what Bath sorely needs. Here, refined and up-to-date entertainments could be held and would be most central.

Some proposals were even more radical:

> I have amused myself with imagining what a foreigner would do with the city if he had his chance of 'making it'. I can see in imagination all houses round the abbey and baths swept entirely away, the colonnade carried round and the vacant plot made into a charming garden. I can see too his building a funicular railway to the top of Beechen Cliff and then erecting a splendid hotel on the high lands – such an hotel as would equal any of the fair Harrogate hotels of which there can be no comparison at Bath.

In September, the *Bath Chronicle* featured a lengthy interview with 'a boarding house keeper in one of the best streets of Bath', who highlighted the problems facing the tourist industry:

> The whole point is whether the people of Bath are content to allow things to go on as they are, or whether they are prepared to attempt to take a fresh source of profit by making the city a pleasure resort as well as a health resort. I acknowledge that the great bulk of the people who come to my house don't care twopence about attractions. They simply want Bath treatment, and with that they are very well pleased and entirely satisfied.
>
> What we want to do is to attract others as well as invalids, and if we are to do that we must give them facilities for spending the time pleasantly. The elderly ladies who come here fill up their time by spending a good deal of it in bed, by seeing the

The sort of thing a young man could expect if he came to Bath for treatment. The masseur's patience with the photographer seems to be wearing a little thin in the second photograph.

doctor, by taking the treatment, by receiving massage and by grumbling about the weather. But suppose you, as a young man, had a touch of rheumatism, and you had been ordered here for treatment. The doctor would, perhaps, prescribe a bath every other day. How would you spend the rest of your time? For a few days you would pass the time well enough in inspecting the beauties and the architectural features of the city. But you would soon want a change, and if your rheumatism prevented you from playing golf, what would you do with yourself?

It is the lack of attractions that accounts for the fact that we get so few male visitors. In the boarding houses I should say that the proportion of lady visitors to gentlemen is something like fifty to one.

Some of the visitors who now come to Bath become bored for the lack of something to do, and if we are to attract visitors of another class, we must unquestionably provide more entertainment. The provision of something in the nature of winter gardens or Kursaal, such as has been suggested, would undoubtedly be a step in the right direction. But any place of amusement of that kind must be centrally situated – it must be as near the Pump Room as possible. I believe that there are thousands of people who would come to Bath if we offered the right kind of attractions. At present we do not touch those people at all. They go to places where there is more going on. Look at the attractions Bournemouth provides and look how that place is going ahead. Our Pump Room concerts do not greatly appeal to one visitor out of fifty. The ordinary person wants something more free and easy.

In the same month, the *Onlooker*, a London magazine, looked at the question of why fashionable society chose to visit continental rather than English spas. They concluded that English spas were 'too dull' and highlighted the anomaly of Bath being 'a winter spa without winter gardens':

Fashionable society flocks, in accordance with the convention of the day, to foreign spas and disburses its shekels of gold and silver for the increment of foreign competition. This, from many points of view – economic as well as social – is a pity ... An incalculable quantity of healing waters must in this country run year after year to waste, while patients and invalids who should benefit by them go year after year to the expense of a troublesome and tedious journey abroad to spend the money which, other things being as equal as the waters are, should be circulated to the profit of their own countrymen, amid, often enough, uncongenial surroundings for the enrichment of foreign rivals ...

The reproach, valid enough at one time, that the equipment of the English bathing establishment is conspicuously inferior to those of similar institutions abroad, no longer holds good. At Bath, any part of you can be sprayed and syringed as efficiently as it can be at Nauheim ... There is no reason to suppose that the bathing establishments of the more progressive of our British spas and health resorts are in the matter of material or personnel one whit behind the most formidable of their foreign rivals.

It seems to us that sufficient attractions – that is to say, attractions that really attract the class of visitors whose presence it is profitable to encourage – are, as a rule, the weak point. The local authorities are very slow in exploiting the natural advantages that are at their hand, and far too unenterprising in making them known. The average local improvement association might take with advantage a leaf out of the book of the Kurverein [tourist office] of the smallest German spa in catering for the entertainment of its 'cure guests', and in giving publicity to its programmes ... For the 'cure guest' looks not only be cured but to be amused and entertained in the interval. In a country still overweighted by the gloom of Puritanism, it is too much to hope for the mild flutter which makes the 'petits chevaux' of the Villa les Fleurs such an attraction to Aix, but something more entertaining than a perfunctory concert or a golf competition might well be arranged.

In late October, the 'Wake up, Bath!' lobby organised a public meeting in Argyle Chapel. Frederick Maddox proposed the motion: 'That the successful results of the progressive policy adopted by the

Town Council during the last 15 years warrants a continuance and development of a similar policy of progress in the future.' He started by tackling the issue of whether priority should be given to visitors or residents:

Bath's success or failure, it seems to me, has to be regarded mainly from her standing as a health resort, although at the same time I freely admit the welfare of the city is embodied in the comparative well-being of the greatest number of her citizens.

He went on to examine progress to date:

Fifteen years ago there was one concert given a week in the old Pump Room, and beyond that the old popular attractions in the city were provided by private enterprise. In referring to the progress that has been made I will divide it into two parts – that made on behalf of visitors and that made on behalf of residents ... For the former there is the excavation of the Roman remains, the building of the Grand Pump Room annexe, the Art Gallery and Reference Library, the Grand Parade and the development of the Institution Gardens. For the latter there is the building and equipment of the Technical Schools, the purchase of the electric-light works, the improvement of the water supply, the better equipment of the bathing establishment, the provision and upkeep of Victoria Park, Hedgemead Park, Henrietta Park and Alexandra Park, the building of Oldfield Park schools, the improved condition of the voluntary schools and the medical inspection of schoolchildren ... Our streets are better lighted and kept, sanitary conditions are improved and there are more open spaces.

It was, he concluded, an impressive record, but much more remained to be done, for both visitors and residents:

I would suggest a winter garden, open all day, a large, comfortable lounge such as places like Harrogate possess. I would recommend improvements in the bathing establishments, especially with regard to electrical treatment, also a free library and a school for defective children.

The motion was opposed by a Mr Blake, in a speech which, according to the *Chronicle*, 'consisted chiefly in disjointed remarks, delivered facetiously'. He argued that raising rates by nine pence in the pound was not progress, and said that, if the baths were running at a loss, prices should be lowered to attract more people. He was

The Concert Hall, now the ticket office for the Roman Baths.

also against the idea of a winter garden if it were to be paid for out of the rates. 'The only way,' he concluded, 'to make Bath up to date is by reducing the rates.'

It was left to Councillor Alfred Wills to take Mr Blake to task and demonstrate that his proposals were illogical. He then went on to compare the concerts in the Pump Room annexe to one he had attended in Germany a few months earlier:

> I was very much surprised and awakened to see the way they did the thing at Wiesbaden. They had a concert room there to which the annexe could only be compared to a back scullery. If we want to attract visitors to continental resorts to the city of Bath, we must bear in mind that we have to compete with places where they do those things upon this lavish scale.

The motion was carried unanimously and six weeks later another public meeting, called by the Mayor, was held in the Guildhall. Major Simpson, the city's Master of Ceremonies, who was to be elected Mayor two months later, explained why the meeting had been called:

> I have recently been approached by influential citizens who are desirous of developing the advantages that the city possesses, and who suggest that the Concert Hall at the Roman Promenade should be used periodically for concerts and dances for visitors and their friends during the winter season.
>
> As I see it there are three priorities: first, the bringing of visitors more into touch with one another; secondly, the provision of additional amusement for the young people who accompany the invalids who come to take the baths and the waters, and third, to attract more visitors to the city.
>
> The proprietors of the lodging houses, hotels and boarding establishments of the city look to the authorities to further increase the attractions of the city. If I were persuaded for one moment that such a movement as this would prove detrimental or damaging to the existing attractions, I would be very chary of giving countenance to it, but I am of the opinion that the more we excite the palate or taste for amusement, the more amusement will be sought after, and one attraction will be the means of inducing people to seek other attractions. I do not think that such a scheme as is now proposed will interfere with the audiences at the Theatre Royal, Palace, Assembly Rooms and other places. I would ask you never to forget that Bath

The dining room of the Pulteney Hotel, one of the largest and most fashionable hotels in the city.

is not going ahead as it should do. Many of you from time to time keep on impressing the fact that Bath must go ahead, but there seems to be some clog on the wheel, and there is always opposition put forward when we try to go ahead. I think it is time for us to do something more for visitors to the city.

Councillor Percy Jackman, part-owner of the Pulteney Hotel in Laura Place, supported the proposal:

We have visitors from all parts, and we have the most magnificent suite of rooms that it is possible for any city to have in the shape of the Concert Hall and the Roman Promenade. It is not so much for those who come for treatment that something needs to be done, as for the younger members of their families. They want some recreation and amusement provided in the evening. We have one of the finest bands for its size in the kingdom, and all that the citizens of Bath require is the energy to back it up. I suggest that a weekly dance for visitors should be held at the Roman Promenade, say from nine to midnight, and it should not be confined to visitors, but open to residents as well, with the Master of Ceremonies laying down certain rules as to dress and conduct. I also suggest that the matter should be taken off the backs of the Corporation, and that a committee of citizens be formed.

Art Nouveau decoration in the Concert Hall

Dr Charles Curd, a surgeon from 6 Gay Street, said that the scheme would be welcomed by 'all the medical men practising in Bath':

One of the greatest drawbacks we have to deal with is what to tell our patients to do when they are not bathing. I have had many patients come here with their families once, but they seldom come again. If they do come again, they come alone, leaving their boys and girls to stay at home. I strongly support the idea of providing some amusement which will be a great inducement for them to come here. They not only want dancing, but various other amusements such as cards and light music.

Mr Charles, who introduced himself as 'one of the younger members of the Bath Attractions Committee', said that he was 'glad to think that Bath is at last going to wake up':

It has been my misfortune or privilege to live for the last 14 years in one of the city's residential hotels, and I have got to know a good many of the people passing through. Nowadays they are nearly all old people. I remember some young people, but I have only seen them once; they have never come again. They say that Bath is too flat for them altogether. Our rival at Cheltenham is one of the greatest dancing centres existing, and Bath must wake up to that.

Christopher Thring, a solicitor, then spoke on behalf of the Assembly Rooms Company, saying that he agreed with everything that had been said, but thought the Assembly Rooms a far better venue than the Concert Hall. He suggested the council should either buy the Assembly Rooms or do a deal with the company that owned them and hold concerts and dances there. Among those who took exception to Mr Thring's remarks was Councillor Charles Long:

If we are going to have private enterprise thrown against us every time, we might as well close our doors altogether. I see no reason why we should hold such gatherings at the

Assembly Rooms when we have our own rooms, erected at great cost and magnificently furnished.

Mrs Stanley Moger also criticised Mr Thring, objecting 'to private interests being brought into the discussion, and to the introduction of a cliquey spirit'. Despite this note of disharmony, a committee was appointed to draw up a scheme for taking the suggestions forward.

The growth of Bath's tourist industry over the last century has been accompanied by what many could not have foreseen at the time – its virtual eclipse as a health resort. There are still complaints, though, that there is nothing to do in Bath in the evenings. As for the winter gardens, it was another of those ideas that – perhaps fortuitously – never got off the ground.

The council didn't just content itself with holding meetings to discuss the visitor question. In January 1909, they advertised for a 'Director of the Hot Mineral Baths & Pump Room & Publicity Department' at a salary of £350. The post was filled by John Hatton, who was only 27, but had been manager of Buxton Thermal Mineral Baths and Pump Room since 1905. During that time he had set up an information bureau and carried out extensive improvements, following visits to the major spas in England, France, Germany and Austria. Under his management, the number of visitors to the baths in Buxton had risen by 20%; receipts had risen 26%. He moved to Bath in April 1909, taking a house at South View on Beechen Cliff.

In February 1909, the council asked the Local Government Board for permission to borrow £500 to buy a warehouse in Swallow Street to enlarge the engine house for the baths. After a public enquiry in May, the loan was agreed and the work went ahead. Far more publicity was generated, however, by the plan to pipe spa water into Institution Gardens. This was carried out by Frederick Amery, a builder from Grove Street, and cost £128. The water was piped to a fountain in the colonnade below the Empire Hotel and was served to the public at twopence a glass. The counter over which customers were served was made from part of the Melfort Cross that had stood in the Cross Bath until its removal in 1743.

At the opening ceremony, Dr Richard Carter of the Circus explained why the fountain had been built:

It is desirable to develop further in the direction of making Bath a summer spa. We have an autumn and a winter season, but that is not enough, for other spas are attracting visitors in the summer by provisions for drinking outside, and for enjoying all sorts of amusements.

Guest of honour at the ceremony was Sir Malcolm Morris, an eminent surgeon and authority on spa treatments. The speech he made to Bath's councillors, after a sumptuous repast in the Guildhall, was not the platitudinous message of congratulation many of them were expecting, however. After the usual pleasantries and 'some chaffing observations' he moved on to the substance of his discourse:

> I have a message to make to you, and that is a message from the medical men, not only of Bath, but of this great country – that you, the Corporation of Bath, should do your duty for the benefit of your fellow creatures, not by dawdling on year after year … but do it, and do it quickly. If you will take that message from me, Mr Mayor and Corporation, and don't be so slow in your improvements, you will rival the great spas of Europe in a way that no other place can do. But you always think, and you talk for hours and hours upon ways and means. You spend your time considering as to whether this thing will pay or that thing will pay, and I tell you as an outside medical man you have a public duty to perform to the nation and not to your one town only. You have no right to let millions on millions run to waste every summer; your duty is to use it. If the water contains some material (I know not what it is) of benefit to human beings, you have no right to let it run to waste into your river. It is your duty to use it, and quickly. You have all the things to your hand here. Why in heaven's name can't you do it, and do it properly, and at once! I am an outsider – I have nothing to do with Bath and its rates, or with your inside petty jealousies and squabbles, which I take it exist in every provincial town in the world; but you have a national debt to perform. You possess, and heaven knows why you possess it, but you do possess it – the Almighty has given you a remedy for the cure of chronic diseases, and yet you don't supply a sufficient amount, and sufficient attractions for the people who should use it!

Egbert Lewis, chairman of the Chamber of Commerce, responded by neatly shifting the blame away from the Corporation:

> The Mayor and Corporation of any city have to suffer severe criticism from those who sent them to power – the ratepayers – and although Sir Malcolm has suggested the city should go forward and expand in their policy as to the baths, there are such

things as ratepayers, who are always objecting to the raising of the rates … Those who sit on the Corporation are doing a great work and are very greatly criticised by people outside who know nothing of their difficulties or of the things that have to be considered before schemes can be undertaken.

I regard it as the duty of every citizen in any town to take a certain share in the public work of his town, and every man in a city like Bath should, as far as possible, so long as it is not to the detriment of his business, do something to press forward the interests of the city. They cannot all go into the City Council, and some do work perhaps as good elsewhere – but there are unfortunately a number who stand outside and criticise the Mayor and Corporation, who would be doing better work if they came forward and undertook a position in which they could do some good. I am aware that entrance to the City Council is always by election, and that generally political feeling runs very high. The ideal system in my opinion would be to have no politics in municipal contests; it would be far better if it were possible that a man should be elected for citizenship, and for the value of his services than because he belonged to this or that political party.

After the applause had died down, Frederick Wardle, the Town Clerk, thanked Sir Malcolm for his comments, stressing how crucial it was for progressive forces in the city to be given their head:

I for one welcome Sir Malcolm's message … It is one which directs our eyes to the future, and of late we have been somewhat urgently approached – I might almost say assailed – by those who desire that we should concentrate our attention on the past. Some think that Bath should be preserved as a sepulchre of traditions that have gone by some time; I, being rather limited in my horizon, prefer to keep my attention on what must come. I think we can indulge both interests to a reasonable extent, but there must be a little conflict now and again, and when this arises we have to consider the future of the city as being pre-eminent to the sentiment associated with a not too remote past.

The debate he was referring to – one that marked the birth of the Bath heritage movement – was the first of the great battles still being fought today, to preserve Bath from the forces of change. The battlefield was a site now acknowledged as one of Bath's architectural showpieces – the colonnades of Bath Street.

Looking east along Bath Street in the mid-nineteenth century, with a billiard hall on the left and the golden globes of a pawnbroker at the far end on the right.

CHAPTER THREE

THE BATTLE OF BATH STREET

In 1867, the White Hart Inn, facing the entrance to the Abbey Church Yard on Stall Street, one of the oldest – and once one of the grandest – inns in the city, was demolished, after standing empty for six years. Two years later, the Grand Pump Room Hotel opened on the same site. In 1870, the Corporation built the New Royal Baths behind the southern wing of the hotel, and separated from the buildings on the north side of Bath Street (built in 1791 by Thomas Baldwin) by an alleyway. In 1888, the Baths were extended westwards towards St Michael's Place.

A booklet published by the council around 1900, entitled *Bath as a Health Resort*, described the New Royal Baths

as a handsome and convenient bath of fine proportions, and admirably appointed in all respects. The dimensions are 80 feet by 35, and the depth of water is graduated from five to three feet. The usual temperature, maintained by admixture with cooled mineral water, is 84 degrees. When filled this bath contains 40,000 gallons. It is used by ladies and gentlemen on alternate days. The charge is one shilling ... The entire suite, which cost the Corporation £12,000, was opened for public use in 1870, but though additions, with numerous new appliances, have frequently been made, the whole resources of this magnificent establishment are often found inadequate to the requirements of the public.

In 1902, the owner of the hotel died and, as a result of the litigation that followed, the hotel closed. The hotel company entered into negotiations with the Corporation for a new lease, offering the basements and ground floors of the buildings in Bath Street which formed part of the original lease to the Corporation, so that the New Royal Baths could be extended. They failed to reach an agreement and the following year the hotel was put up for sale.

In April 1903 it was acquired by Mr Waring (of Waring & Gillow's), who proposed spending £30,000 on improvements and entered into negotiations with the Corporation. In 1904, Alfred Taylor, a local architect, drew up plans for a southward extension

Two views of the Grand Pump Room Hotel in Stall Street.

of the New Royal Baths, which involved the demolition of the north side of Bath Street. The new main entrance to the baths, with a ticket office, was to be in the curved quadrant at the east end (and curiously similar in layout to the entrance to Thermae Bath Spa, built a century later at the south-western end of Bath Street), with a separate entrance for wheelchairs. The extension was to consist of suites of rooms equipped with wondrous – but to modern ears distinctly alarming – devices: steel, acid and electrical reclining baths, Aix massage baths, and 'd'Arsonyal high-frequency electrical treatment'. The plans were exhibited in the hotel, but negotiations soon reached stalemate and the scheme was dropped.

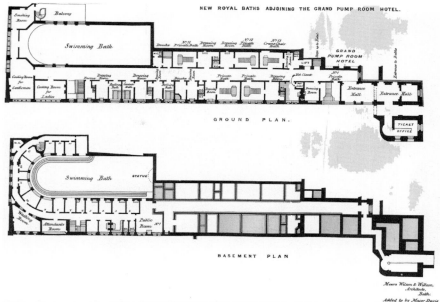

A plan of the New Royal Baths.

Five years later, the hotel was still closed and nothing had been done to improve facilities at the New Royal Baths. Then, at the beginning of 1909, it was announced that the scheme was being revived and the north side of Bath Street would be demolished. One of those who wrote to the *Chronicle* to express his 'profoundest regret' at the news was the architect and architectural historian, Mowbray Green.

Mowbray Green's *Eighteenth Century Architecture of Bath*, published five years earlier, marked a turning point in attitudes to the city's Georgian heritage. The Victorians had regarded eighteenth-century buildings not only as outmoded and insanitary, but also as an embodiment of the moral and religious laxity of the age. Towards the end of the nineteenth century, however, attitudes began to change. Extensions to the Guildhall and the Pump Room, designed to harmonise with the originals, marked a movement towards a rehabilitation of classicism in the city. Books such as William Tyte's *Bath in the Eighteenth Century* (1903) and A Barbeau's *Life and Letters at Bath in the Eighteenth Century* (1904), as well as books on the city's historic houses by Robert Peach and John Meehan sparked a reawakening of interest in the period. Lewis Melville's *Bath under Beau Nash*, published in 1907, included the reflection that, 'It is sad to see historic landmarks

Above: Inside the New Royal Baths. Below: A gentlemen's cooling room.

neglected as they are at Bath, where Londonderry House has been converted into cheap shops, and the house at which Beau Nash died into a furniture warehouse; Sydney House stands decaying, and Ralph Allen's city home is let out in tenements.'

It was Mowbray Green's lavishly-illustrated tome, though, which not only catalogued the city's Georgian treasures in meticulous detail but also established an aesthetic framework within which to evaluate them, that was crucial. When a range of old buildings on the north side of the Orange Grove was swept away in 1900 to make way for the Empire Hotel there was hardly a murmur of protest. Some of the buildings were good, some were indifferent, but together they were a compendium of building styles in the city over several centuries – one of them may even have been by John Wood. But the almost universal feeling was that what replaced them was a great improvement.

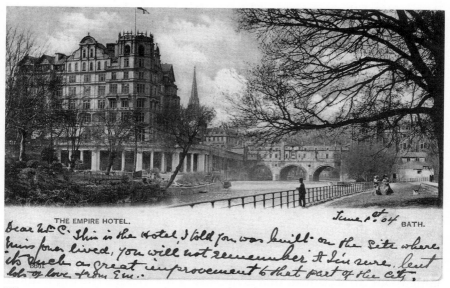

THE EMPIRE HOTEL.

The sentiments expressed on this postcard of the Empire Hotel, sent to Southampton in June 1904, summed up many people's attitude to the replacement of old buildings a century ago: 'This is the hotel I told you was built on the site where Miss Jones lived. You will not remember it, I'm sure, but it's such a great improvement to that part of the city.'

Nine years later, it is likely that many councillors anticipated a similar lack of reaction when they announced the plans for Bath Street. Little could they have suspected that the storm of controversy they would stir up would provide a benchmark for planning debate for over a century.

On 13 February, Waring & Gillow submitted a plan for an extension to the New Royal Baths and the Grand Pump Room Hotel, which involved rebuilding the whole of the north side of Bath Street. On Tuesday 2 March, a deputation headed by Prebendary Sydney Boyd, Rector and Rural Dean of Bath, presented a 400-signature petition opposing the scheme and asking the council 'to reconsider the plans submitted and consent only to such alterations as will preserve intact this unique piece of work'.

The Chamber of Commerce, which was keen to see the hotel reopened, met the protestors to see if an agreement could be reached. Councillor James Colmer, Chairman of the Corporate Property Committee, explained that the plans had already been approved, subject to the Sanitary, Surveying and Property Committees being satisfied. 'With all due respect to the deputation,' he continued, 'a great deal of fuss has been made over a little. Is not the Grand Pump Room Hotel the property of Messrs Waring, and are they not to be allowed to rebuild that property according to their own plans, so long as the interests of the various committees are not interfered with? So far as I am concerned I am not an admirer of this supposed ancient specimen of architecture. I fail to see any beauty in it whatsoever. As a matter of fact it would be a great improvement if the whole thing were cleared away. If you take the south side of the street at the present time it is little more than a bill-posting station, and it is rather a disgrace to the city. I certainly hope the council will not fall in with the suggestions of the deputation.'

It is curious how similar this sounds to speeches made almost a century later when Newark Works on the Lower Bristol Road was under threat.

Councillor Benjamin John said that he hoped a compromise could be reached to save the pillars, adding that the original plans showed the pillars intact. He moved that the committee should endeavour 'to secure all that is necessary for Messrs Waring without destroying the pillars in Bath Street'. After the motion was seconded, Alderman Charles Oliver rose to oppose it, saying that, as far as he was concerned, 'the issue is whether we should retain Bath Street or have the new hotel and improved baths. If the columns in Bath Street had proportion that would be a different thing, but they have actually columns three feet longer at one end than at the other. Necessity compels the removal of the pillars. Nassau House was demolished for public improvement and the same applies in this case. Messrs Waring are anxious to get on and tenders are being sent out. I have a letter from them in which they state: "We appreciate equally with your proudest citizens the unique character of this street and the value of such a feature of interest to the city of Bath, but it must be obvious to anyone giving the matter a moment's thought that it is highly unreasonable to ask for its perpetuation in the present old-world but dilapidated and wasteful condition. The retention of this arcade is really impossible, for it would not only add vastly to the cost of the work and produce a gross incongruity of appearance, but it would spoil our best letting rooms by narrowing the street,

Above: Nassau House in the Orange Grove, 'demolished for public improvement'.

Below: Councillor Harry Hatt ran a hairdresser's, perfumer's and wig maker's in the Corridor.

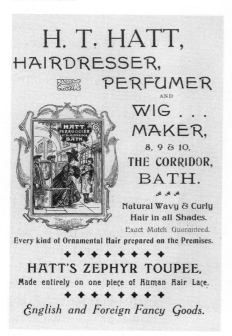

and so minimising the access of sunshine and air, while it would darken the ground floor so as to render it useless for the purpose of the new suite of baths which the Corporation are installing." I would add that I sincerely hope the matter will not be referred back.

'Do I understand,' asked Councillor Alfred Fortt, 'that if it is sent back to the committee it is likely to postpone the opening of the hotel?'

'That is so,' replied Alderman Oliver.

'Then I shall vote against it going back,' said Mr Fortt.

As the debate continued, it transpired that Waring & Gillow had not submitted detailed plans to the committee. In Alderman Oliver's own words, all they had provided were 'rough sketches'.

Among those who used humour to hold the deputation up to ridicule was Councillor Harry Hatt – perhaps trying out a new stand-up routine: 'The other day I noticed that one shop owner had draped one of the pillars with several yards of flannel, while at the present moment some of them are pasted with posters. It seems curious that all the lovers of architecture in Bath who go down there and drink in the beauties of the structure, have so far raised no objection to the pillars being put to such base uses as this. I am ready to believe that the deputation have had the advantage and advice in opposing the recommendation of the most eminent architects in Bath, and that they have been persuaded we should be destroying one of the finest specimens of Georgian architecture we have. I am equally sure, however, that it would be possible to get architects of equal eminence who would say that in a city like Bath, which possesses so many splendid specimens of architecture of the same period, the pillars are not of great architectural beauty and ought not to be preserved. There is for example John Ruskin, the author of *The Seven Lamps of Architecture*. If those who are opposed to the plans were to examine the street by the light of the lamp of truth they would find it condemned by Ruskin.'

Ruskin was a strange champion for Mr Hatt to choose. What he didn't point out was that Ruskin would have hated just about all the buildings in Bath. For him, Gothic was the pinnacle of architectural achievement; Palladio, and all that he engendered, was

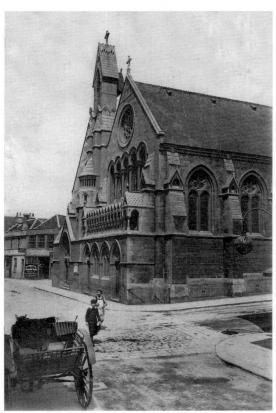

St Paul's, Monmouth Street, now Holy Trinity.

anathema. Ruskin's hatred of symmetry and proportion influenced generations of architects, bearing fruit, for example, in the ill-advised exuberance of the Empire Hotel. The ecclesiastical hotch-potch of St Paul's Church (now Holy Trinity) on Monmouth Street, by the local firm of Wilson, Willcox and Wilson (and probably influenced by Bassett Keeling's groundbreaking design for St George's, Camden Hill), was another building that owed an enormous debt to Ruskin. By the early twentieth century, however, Ruskin's star was waning and classicism was being reassessed by a generation eager to escape from the stern, unbending, humourless creed he, and others like him, had espoused. A century later, Ruskin, although still read and still admired, is, as far, as the history of architecture is concerned, generally acknowledged to have got it wrong; Palladio's reputation, on the other hand, has never been higher. His historical analysis may have been as off-key as Ruskin's, but the classical revival it inspired is now seen as one of the major turning points in architectural design.

That week's *Chronicle* carried, alongside a report of the debate, a poem supposedly written by John Wood:

> *I dreamed that an architect rose from the dead*
> *And listened in silence to all he heard said.*
> *He read through the papers, then wrote to the press*
> *As being the best means to voice his distress:*
> *Dear Editor, Sir – With my feelings I strive*
> *And can but feel thankful I am not alive.*
> *I beg of your kindness to let me have space*
> *To state what I think of this most modern race.*
> *'Tis vastly amazing and fills me with scorn*
> *To learn of its beauties Bath is to be shorn.*
> *My father and I, we both laboured and planned*
> *To build you a city, the best in the land.*
> *The work was not easy, the labour was great,*
> *And we and Ralph Allen worked early and late;*
> *We gave of our money, we gave of our brain,*
> *And built all our houses of stone of hard grain.*
> *But now comes a stranger who loves not the town,*
> *With plans of a building that brings our work down;*
> *Though we rose your status, and still bring you gains,*
> *Most wanton destruction we get for our pains.*
> *'Tis monstrous insulting, I'd have you know that*
> *Before your Town Council I kept on my hat.*
> *Mr Editor, Sir, I remain as I should*
> *Your very obedient servant, John Wood.*

On Friday 5 March, three days after the petition was handed to the council, Prebendary Boyd held a meeting at Abbey Church House at which it was agreed to form an 'Association for the Preservation of Houses, Place and Objects of Architectural, Literary or Historical Interest'. This was later renamed the Old Bath Preservation Society. The membership fee was a shilling and Prebendary Boyd was appointed its first president. The bandwagon was now well and truly rolling. On Wednesday 11 March, the committee of the Royal Institute of British Architects (RIBA) held a special meeting in London to consider what they could do to stop the council's plans. A few days later they notified the council that they were strongly opposed to 'any interference with the buildings in Bath Street and public attention was being directed to the proposed vandalism'.

On Thursday 25 March, a public meeting at the Assembly Rooms

The Rev Sydney Boyd, Rector and Rural Dean of Bath and Prebendary of Wells.

was addressed by DS MacColl, Keeper of the National Gallery, A Beresford Pite FRIBA, Professor of Architecture at the Royal College of Art, AM Broadley, an eminent writer and historian, and Prebendary Boyd. 'The attendance of all citizens and others interested in the preservation of this unique street' was requested, and a large crowd turned up to give its support.

On the same day, a letter from Ernest George, the President of the RIBA, condemning the scheme, was published in the *Times*. Two days later, under the heading 'Bath and the Philistines', a *Times* leader took up the cause:

The buildings are threatened, we understand, because it is proposed to put up a monster hotel in their place, which must, of necessity, destroy the character and proportion of the whole street. Bath Street, as Mr George remarks, 'is part of a scheme laid out with design and dignity in Georgian days' ... and he adds that we have few such examples of studied architectural treatment in our cities. For that reason it is the more important that we should preserve those which we do possess ... Those who have never seen a stately and well-planned street are not likely to grow impatient with the meanness and disorder of most modern streets ... The conception of a street planned as a whole, and composed like a picture, never enters their heads; and they would consider it mere sentimentality to sacrifice any individual profit or convenience to such a plan.

But the authorities at Bath have not this excuse. They are familiar with the dignity and beauty of their city; and their familiarity seems to have ended in contempt. Mr George tells us that, if a monster hotel is built, the Corporation of Bath will obtain an increased rent for the ground which it will occupy, and, no doubt, the Corporation will hold that they ought to make the best possible bargain for the citizens. Unfortunately, public bodies too often seem to assume as a matter of course that they ought to consider only the most material interests and the meanest ideas of those whom they represent. Whether or not they are Philistines themselves, they appear to regard themselves as the representatives of Philistines, and, therefore, as tied down to a Philistine policy. But even from the Philistine point of view a Philistine policy is not always the best, as the people of Bath may discover to their cost if they allow this act of destruction to be committed ... [Bath] has lately recovered from a long period of neglect, during which it was only a city of memories and ghosts, and this recovery is no doubt responsible for the project of the monster hotel. But Bath is now attracting visitors because of its charm, and it does not seem a wise policy to destroy that charm with the object of providing more accommodation for visitors. It is likely enough that, if the accommodation is provided at so great a sacrifice, the visitors will fail to make use of it.

On 8 April, Alfred Goodridge, the son of Henry Edmund Goodridge, entered the lists with a letter to the *Bath Chronicle*:

I humbly put this forth as the senior architect in the city, being now retired from practice, after upwards of half a century, and my father before me from 1819, having myself studied the art side of architecture, not only in the metropolis, but abroad. My membership of the RIBA is, I find, the oldest on the register. It is for others I write, as it cannot much affect me ...

Bath is an exceptional city, at any rate in this country. The better parts of the city are laid out architecturally, and date from the eighteenth century. The streets, crescents, squares, piazze and parades are planned with a strong classic feeling in the renaissance style, parts of it Palladian. Whoever built in those days, not only was bound to conform to approved drawings, in plan and elevation, and to obtain one connected and consistent character throughout ... but the whole was in the hands of a competent architect. It has attained its position and unique character by this arrangement from the beginning. It is well known as a very ancient Roman resort, and the remains are most interesting. But it is the Bath of the eighteenth century that draws so many to visit it, and reside here; also its surrounding beauty.

Now, if modern ideas of this day, occupied with commercial schemes, are to alter this, and modern requirements are to sweep, bit by bit these, many of them clever and pleasing features, away for commercial ends and purposes, as if we were in America, then you destroy the Bath of the eighteenth century, and in the end it will progress the wrong way, and it will cease to be frequented by well-to-do people, and, commercially, it would take no place at all. It would go down, except for its waters and antiquity, which would prove a failure commercially.

Therefore, it is of the first moment to maintain the eighteenth-century city, and to see that nothing is done to rob the city of its architectural character, handed down to us by those who made it what it is. And further, that everything is done to improve it, without destroying anything of its interesting character and beauty in doing so. You modernise an hotel, and at the same time help to damage the city, and drive away those who might otherwise come to it ...

I call to mind opportunities lost, in years past, for great architectural improvements, because the works were not done under competent architects. I greatly value the work of a land or borough surveyor, but it is not architecture, and architectural work should be in the hands of a properly educated architect. Take the sham jerry-built battlements on the wall, fit for a fort, at Camden Crescent, with three-inch ashlar and bars in the embrasure. It is bad in design and in execution. What have such battlements to do with Camden Crescent? A nice balustrade, in harmony with the crescent, drawn by an architect, would have been a pleasing architectural feature on the slope. A flight of wide steps from the centre of Camden Crescent to London Street, and the whole maintaining a superior character – what an improvement to the whole neighbourhood, carried out under a competent architect! The way in which the last house in Gay Street is finished, going into the park, is a caricature of architecture – balusters in the frieze of the entablature! Because it was not done by an architect. The old bridge – a stone bridge – ought to have been finished with a stone parapet and would have been a nice architectural feature, if done by a qualified architect ... Half a century since there were but two or three smoke stacks in the city, now upwards of a dozen, which ought never to have been allowed within the borough, especially the three electric light ones. Manvers Street, why was it not much wider, and of the character of the parades, forming a good impression on entering the city, built only on the west side, and pleasure grounds opposite.

Architecture is an art, and how can they, who have never been brought up to it, or are acquainted with it, be able to decide on the architectural features of a city? The treatment of open spaces and streets, planting trees, lamp pillars, signs, etc, should be under the direction of an architect in a city. The lamp pillar in Cleveland Place, the fountain in Laura Place stopped, decorated with small shrubs in flowerpots, and lately partly whitewashed, though built of best Portland stone and granite, the trees in Pulteney Street, do not these things show that there is want of proper professional direction in such matters in the city? ...

I would suggest to the Corporation to have a gratuitous advisory committee of not more than five – two educated architects, an artist, a man of travel, and one fond of building and the arts – and let them refer all these things to them to give advice. It is so done in many large cities, and with advantage. Some educated advice should be sought on aesthetic matters.

For the councillors, under attack on all sides, it was time to take the offensive. A couple of days before Goodridge's letter was published, the Mayor announced that a statement clarifying the legal position of the council would be made before the next council meeting. He warned, however, that most of Bath Street belonged to Waring & Gillow, 'who alone have the right to make alterations subject to their contract with the Corporation'. It was they, he suggested, who 'should be approached rather than the Corporation by those desiring to modify the scheme'. He closed his remarks with a dismissive comment to the effect that 'many have not taken the trouble to acquaint themselves with the facts'.

Three weeks later, the council issued a public statement:

The Bath Corporation having been held up to public odium as vandals and philistines in connection with the proposed enlargement of the Grand Pump Room Hotel (which involves the demolition of the colonnade on the north side of Bath Street) desire to place upon record a statement of the facts which have led to the present position.

Having stated their belief that the hotel would not reopen unless substantial alterations were made, they pointed out that plans for the rebuilding of Bath Street had been exhibited at the Grand Pump Room Hotel in February 1904 and that, when local newspapers had covered the story, 'not a single voice was raised to object to the scheme on antiquarian grounds'. They then printed a 'Schedule of Inaccuracies and Misrepresentations – statements made by opponents of the scheme that were 'not in accord with the facts'. This hilarious document is reminiscent of the scurrilous lists of 'Celebrated Untruths' published by the *Bath Figaro* in the 1830s:

That Bath Street is 'a time honoured structure which association has endeared or tradition made venerable'.

That the Corporation are 'animated by a flagrant kind of commercialism which reverences nothing ancient or beautiful, but pursues a wanton course of a ravening lion seeking whom he may devour'.

That Bath Street was 'part of the scheme for the building of Bath'.

That Bath Street is 'one of the most beautiful streets of Bath'.

That 'the scheme if carried through would be a deadly blow at the heart of Georgian Bath'.

That 'if the alterations are permitted one of the most beautiful cities in the world will be eventually sacrificed to the greed of money'.

That Bath Street is 'one of the best streets of the town'.

That the Corporation painted the stone columns to represent granite.

That the Corporation proposed to throw bridges across the street.

That the Corporation 'sold a portrait of a former Master of Ceremonies by Gainsborough'.

That this portrait belonged to the Corporation.

That 'no one has been allowed to know what the proposed building will be like'.

That Bath Street is part of Bath before Wood.

That Bath Street is 'a good and in Bath a unique survival of Roman architecture'.

That Bath Street is 'one of the finest examples of Palladian eighteenth-century architecture'.

There followed a statement from an eminent Bristol architect, Frederick Bligh Bond, who had been called in by the Corporation:

Two early-twentieth-century views of the north side of Bath Street.

I have made a careful examination of the houses on the north side of the street. I find that these were originally built in a most unsubstantial manner, and their construction is radically unsound. The whole front over the colonnade is a mere shell of the flimsiest nature, consisting of ashlar work barely six inches thick made out internally with lath and plaster on light studding to appear as a 21-inch wall – the vacuity being 14 inches. These walls run about 26 feet wide in the clear to each house, and their height is about equal to the width, but they appear to have no internal ties except the very light party walls which are carried out over the covered walls, and which, I believe, are but six inches thick. Each section of front contains six windows, one of which (first floor centre) has a heavy pediment. These front walls rest upon a wooden bressemer laid along the columns, and this is beginning to show signs of crushing. Some of the party walls show signs of subsidence. The ashlar fronts are all bulging outwards, as might be expected, and three at least of them are held up by iron bands and rivets ... The joists of the first floor run outwards, and appear to share in the support of the front wall and bressemer, as they rest (cantilever fashion) on the inner wall of the colonnade; but this wall has, at least for a part of its length, no foundation, being built in the air, so to speak, along the crown of a cylindrical vault which lies below. A more hazardous method of building it would be difficult to conceive. The western angle of this wall has recently developed a settlement of a serious nature, which is still opening. Internally the premises are not only, for the most part, in grievous disrepair, but are showing signs of subsidence in all directions, They hardly appear of a nature to repay renovation.

Frederick Bligh Bond had been an architect since 1888. He was not an expert on the eighteenth century, however. As well as designing public buildings in Bristol, he oversaw the restoration of several churches and was acknowledged as an authority on the history of church architecture. In 1908, the Church of England appointed him director of excavations at Glastonbury Abbey; he gave a lecture on his work there at Walcot Church Hall in January 1909. Although he had an office at 16 Brock Street, he did little work in Bath.

His outward appearance as a paragon of professional decorum belied his true nature, however. He was a member of the Society for Psychical Research; in 1919, ten years after advising Bath Corporation on the state of Bath Street, he published a book called *The Gates of Remembrance*, in which he described how he had used psychic methods to guide him in the excavations at Glastonbury. He was dismissed from his post and became editor of the magazine *Psychic Science*, later moving to the USA to become education secretary of the American Society for Psychical Research. Presumably Mr Bligh Bond did not feel the spirit of John Wood – or Thomas Baldwin – breathing down his neck when he was in Bath – or, if he did, he chose to ignore it.

It took a couple of weeks for Prebendary Boyd's Association to respond to the council's statement. When they did, they declared it 'chiefly remarkable for two features – its studious evasion of the main issue and its laborious refutation of trifling errors, several of them due to inaccurate reporting by the press':

In this superb fashion the Corporation of Bath, aided by one local expert outside their body, brush aside accumulated testimony to the value of Bath Street from the Royal Institute of British Architects, the Society of Antiquarians, the Society for the Protection of Ancient Buildings, the National Trust for Places of Historic Interest, and the judgement of an art critic of European fame like Mr DS MacColl, and an architectural critic of such acknowledged authority as Professor Beresford Tite ...

The fact seems to be forgotten that the Corporation exists for the citizens, who are perfectly entitled to criticise its actions and to take such steps as they may deem necessary to prevent wrong ...

The plans of the present proposals have never been publicly exhibited; have not been submitted to the judgement of the council itself; and ... no single person outside that body has been permitted to see them. At a meeting of the council on 16 February 1909, questions were asked by Alderman Rubie and Mr Councillor John as to 'what was intended to be done with the colonnade in Bath Street, in view of the alterations and extensions of the baths'. Thus, at a late stage in the proceedings, hardly anything was known by important members of the council of Messrs Waring's proposals. The assertion that the plans showing the present proposals were publicly exhibited and explained in 1904 ... is distinctly inaccurate. It is true that drawings showing extensive alterations to the hotel and the houses in Bath Street were prepared and exhibited by Messrs Waring in 1904, and that elaborate descriptions of the scheme appeared in the local press at the time; but the scheme then under consideration differed in many important particulars from that now put forward...

The Corporation are not entitled to assume that there was no opposition to the scheme of 1904. As a matter of fact, at the time the plans were exhibited the attention of several members of the Corporation were directed to the ruinous effect even this modified mutilation would have upon the street ...

The contention of the defenders of Bath Street has all along been that the prosperity of the city depends upon the preservation of its old-fashioned character which, in the judgement of many, has already been unnecessarily sacrificed.

Readers are invited to draw their own parallels between claims that the Bath Street plans were inadequately publicised and similar claims, almost a century later, concerning Churchill House. It is interesting to note that both the official statement from the council and the objectors' reply concentrated on the 1904 proposals, which were subsequently altered. When the original petition was laid before the council on 2 March, however, the Town Clerk was asked 'when plans were submitted which showed the removal of the pillars'; he replied that they had 'come before the committee on 24 May 1907 and were adopted by the council on 4 June 1907'.

On 23 June, a leader in the *Times* once again drew the nation's attention to the threat to Bath Street. After demolishing the council's arguments as to the supposed deficiencies of its design, it drew their attention to 'expert opinion on the subject':

It is true that we have heard expert opinions only on one side; but for the good reason that none seem to have been expressed on the other ... If the Corporation persist in their project it will be plain to all the world that they do so because they are indifferent to everything except profit. They may try to excuse themselves on the plea that they are seeking profit not for themselves but for their city. It remains to be seen whether the citizens of Bath will be pleased by the implied assumption of their representatives that they care nothing for the beauty of their city or for its historic associations.

On 27 July, there came an unexpected development. It was announced that a less ambitious rebuilding scheme would be adopted and that 'communication with the Bath Street houses will not be maintained'. When it was claimed that this was to meet the wishes of antiquarians, there were cries of 'rot'. This was not, however, the end of the saga.

On 30 September the *London Standard* reported that 'the controversy over the proposed extension of the Grand Pump Room Hotel at Bath is being revived in an acute form', and featured an interview with Mr Waring:

The question which has arisen is one which profoundly interests me from many points of view, As proprietors of the hotel the development of our scheme of extension has been delayed by the agitation which has arisen to spare Bath Street. As a firm possessing a reputation for work of artistic distinction whose aim has consistently been to revive the appreciation of beauty in domestic and civic art, we have been pained by an unwilling association with proposals which involved the destruction of a piece of architecture which was held in high esteem not only by the citizens of Bath, but by a large and influential body of architects and antiquarians representing the best artistic sentiment of the day. As you are aware, the blame has not been directed at my firm, but at the members of the Corporation of Bath for sanctioning the plans, and we were really under no obligation to modify the plans in the least. These plans, of course, gave us the maximum space for extending the hotel by the addition of the largest number and biggest possible rooms [sic], but we felt obliged, notwithstanding the loss, to bow to the wave of feeling which has been evoked, at least to the extent of deferring the demolition of the colonnaded houses until the question had been thoroughly debated.

The matter, however, has not progressed in the least, so we have gone to an eminent architect, whose name carries great weight in the profession, and he has prepared a design which retains the arcade, which is the distinctive feature of Bath Street, and the essential characteristics of the Georgian façade, by means of a coupled colonnade, out of which spring arches supporting the walls of the upper floors of the buildings. The introduction of a double colonnade was necessary to sustain the extra weight of the new superstructure.

The architect they engaged was Frank Atkinson, a leading proponent of the Edwardian baroque style, exemplified by Waring & Gillow's store in Oxford Street, which he had designed three years earlier. Whatever the merits of the style, Bath may count itself fortunate he did not get his hands on Bath Street. The council threw the scheme out.

At this point, the waters get decidedly murky. Several previous accounts have suggested that the objectors scored a total victory, with the buildings on the north side of Bath Street saved for posterity – at least until they burnt down in 1986, leaving only the facades. They did survive, but, for a time at least, it looked as though they were not going to.

After the council threw out the plans to rebuild the north side of Bath Street, a revised plan, which entailed the removal and rebuilding of the upper two floors, was approved. The council also served a notice threatening legal proceedings if work did not start by 20 November. Shortly before the deadline, contractors moved in to begin demolition.

On 22 November, at a meeting of the Surveying Committee, Councillor Hatt asked 'if there is any necessity for the hoarding erected in Bath Street to come right across the road into Stall Street? It seems to be taking up the whole of the street.'

The surveyor replied that 'the removal of the two upper floors in Bath Street is a very awkward job ... I have not given the contractors permission to maintain the hoarding at any particular place. I have only given temporary permission to erect the hoarding and it must be moved back as the floors come down.'

'Are they going to begin at the Stall Street end?' Mr Hatt asked. 'Yes.'

Councillor Bush then asked, 'if the committee has any control over the outside of the hoarding? If so, I should suggest they cover it with some art paper or illustration of agreeable design and colour. That would improve it very much.'

Two days later, on 24 November 1909, the Old Bath Preservation Society met to pass another resolution:

> This committee, observing that a portion of the north side of Bath Street is now being prepared for demolition, expresses its surprise and indignation that the Corporation of Bath should not only have failed to interfere to prevent this injury to the city, but should actually have brought pressure to bear on Messrs Waring to proceed with the scheme ... The committee further resolves to communicate this resolution to the Corporation, to Messrs Waring and to the national and provincial press, in the hope that the mischief may even yet be averted.

It was not the Society's eleventh-hour plea that saved Bath Street, however, but a dispute over one of the buildings in Bath Street. In mid-December, the Town Clerk received a letter from Messrs Waring's solicitor:

> Dear Sir,
> I duly received your letter of the 3rd inst, which I have submitted to my client. He instructs me to say that he has commenced the work of demolishing the Bath Street houses, and it is being proceeded with preparatory to the work of reconstruction. As to the question of the reconstruction of Bath Street, it is impossible at the present time to do that as a whole, because No 10 has not been acquired. It seems quite clear that the Corporation

have not performed their part of the contract in reference to No 10 Bath Street. They ought to have taken steps to acquire that immediately on the signing of the contract. They agreed to do so, and to apply for compulsory powers if necessary. Instead of doing so, they do not now seem one bit nearer acquiring that property than they were at the very beginning. In fact, you have expressly stated in writing that they will not go further with it, although that is an integral part of the contract, and absolutely integral to the carrying out of the scheme.

Alderman Oliver replied that it was a lie to say the council had done nothing about No 10. They had offered to sell it to Waring's for £2,000, but they had said it was not worth anything like that. However, No 10 – as the solicitor had pointed out – did not belong to the Corporation; although they owned the rest of the street, this one building belonged to St John's Hospital.

Unbelievably, after all that had happened, this dispute derailed the whole process. Work stopped, the hotel was quietly refurbished, the plans for Bath Street shelved and forgotten. Frankly, it all seems a little too convenient, with each side managing to save face – while blaming each other – and walking away from a project that had blown up in their faces. While avoiding the ignominy that would have ensued had they simply given way to the protesters, it begs the question of why the problem over No 10 was not raised before – and why neither side could be bothered to pursue the issue.

As for the Old Bath Preservation Society, it continued to campaign and grow. In 1945 it merged with the Bath Preservation Trust, founded eleven years earlier to fight proposals for a new road through the city centre.

The threat to the north side of Bath Street did not disappear completely. The Grand Pump Room Hotel maintained the lease on the buildings and various plans were put forward over the years to incorporate the upper rooms into the hotel, none of which was ever realised.

The quadrant at the east end of Bath Street was used for a time as a 'Zander Institute'. Jonas Gustav Wilhelm Zander was a Swedish physician who invented a therapeutic method of exercise – a forerunner of Pilates – using equipment suitable for 'women, older people, and "weakly" people of either sex'. In 1910 the Corporation bought some Zander appliances and set up an exercise suite linked to the Baths.

In July 1917, Alfred Taylor, who had drawn up the plans for the baths extension in 1904, came up with another plan for 'temporary additional rooms' on the north side of Bath Street. The new extension covered the same area as the one originally proposed, but the facilities planned were much more basic, consisting mainly of bathrooms and dressing rooms. The plan was revised in this modified form in 1917 because of the large number of wounded soldiers who were coming to the city for treatment. Once again, though, the plans came to nothing. In 1934, Alfred Taylor drew up further plans, to extend the baths southward into the western quadrant of Bath Street; this time the scheme was adopted.

The Grand Pump Room Hotel was demolished in the 1950s, and Arlington House built on the site. In 1963, the north side of Bath Street was rebuilt as council offices, retaining the façade. The New Royal Baths survived until 1978. In 1986, after plans to redevelop the north side of the street had stalled, partly due to the question of joint ownership, it was gutted by fire. The façade survived, however, and was held up by scaffolding until a commercial unit was built behind it a couple of years later. So, although the northern side of Bath Street did survive, after a fashion, it was a very close run thing.

Returning, for a moment to Bligh Bond's assessment of the way Bath Street was built – dismissed out of hand by the Old Bath Preservation Society, who ascribed its condition to poor maintenance and inappropriate alterations – it is worth quoting a more recent appraisal. In the 1960s, Cyril Beazer was engaged to demolish and reconstruct part of the south side of Bath Street, largely unaltered since it had been built. His report makes illuminated reading:

> The front façade is constructed on columns over the top of which was a nine by eight pitch pine beam carrying the whole of the front façade, and comprised one single skin of ashlar stone from the beam to the top of the parapet. Not only was it carrying this weight in stone but the floor joists were morticed into this six-inch ashlar wall as well as the plate at roof level carried on the internal face of the wall and the spread and thrust of a span roof against the wall. The nature of this structure was such that over the years the beam had rotted causing the front wall gradually to move out of the vertical towards the street to such an extent that in many places the wall had completely left the joists and they were hanging in mid-air … I called the building inspector in and when we had opened up the floors and commenced preparations for demolition he agreed the only thing we could do in the

interests of public safety was to close the street immediately. He went on to say there must be something wrong with the force of gravity in the area because it should have fallen into the street years before.

The preservationists may have got it wrong over the quality of the building, but, a century on, should we be grateful that they managed to save the north side of Bath Street? Michael Forsyth, in the new *Pevsner Architectural Guide to Bath*, describes Bath Street as part of 'the finest piece of formal planning in Bath ... a perfect piece of design made especially attractive by its modest, easily manageable size'. Further comment seems unnecessary.

If the saga of Bath Street showed the council at its most rampantly progressive, the saga of Laura Chapel showed it at its most inert and smug. In the eighteenth century, every up-market development had a private or proprietary chapel. Although the city's churches were rebuilt to attract fashionable visitors and residents, they were also patronised by artisans and members of the lower classes. Worse still, to get to them one needed to go through the streets. Going through the streets on a Sunday morning was not for the faint-hearted. It was the only day most working people had off, and, although pubs had to close during the hours of divine service, they could stay open until just before them – which meant a load of bevvied-up boozers were discharged onto the streets as respectable folks were making their way to church.

By the early twentieth-century, legislation and a general improvement in the manners of society had largely eradicated the problem. By 1909 only two proprietary chapels – All Saints below Lansdown Crescent and Kensington on the London Road – still operated. Laura Chapel in Henrietta Street had been built in 1795 by Thomas Baldwin, who also designed Bath Street. It accommodated 1,000 people and was, according to a contemporary observer, 'warm and comfortable in the winter season by fires in its recesses'. It was frequented by, among others, the Austen family; sermons preached there were sometimes published in pamphlet form. Declining attendance and the rising cost of maintenance, however, had seen it close in 1890.

By 1909 the ruinous state of Laura Chapel was a cause of grave concern. Councillor Thomas Plowman, Secretary of the Bath & West & Southern Counties Society, who lived at 69 Great Pulteney Street, was anxious that something should be done. When he raised the matter at a meeting of the Sanitary Committee on 25 February, he was

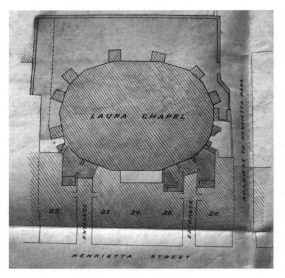

A plan of Laura Chapel.

told that it was hoped to settle the matter soon.

'That is not good enough,' he replied. 'It is a scandal to the neighbourhood. The place is extremely unsafe, the drains are exposed where the entrance has tumbled down and it is overrun with rats.'

'So is half Bath,' rejoined Councillor Evans.

On 11 March, it was announced that a decision on the chapel was expected by the end of the month. The difficulty was that the nominal owner was 'a vicar near Reading'; Captain Forester's trustees were also involved. At this point some wag suggested that the matter should be referred to the Old Bath Preservation Society, which had been formed six days earlier, 'as a fine specimen of eighteenth-century architecture'. This was intended as a put-down and, indeed, nobody, during the ensuing months, was to speak for Laura Chapel. It was the unloved face of Georgian Bath.

By early May, when the state of the chapel was raised at a meeting of the Surveying Committee, negotiations were no further forward. Charles Fortune, the City Surveyor, said that, 'if it falls at all it will fall inwards. That being the case, I have no power to step in.' In June the chapel's 'nominal owner', the Rev Alfred George Law of Fosbury near Hungerford, was tracked down. In a somewhat unexpected twist to the tale, when confronted with a deed showing he had purchased it in 1892, he said that he had 'never agreed to purchase the said chapel'. Nevertheless, he was persuaded to relinquish his interest in it.

At a meeting on 15 July, Dr Preston King, councillor for Lansdown, suggested that the Inspector of Nuisances should take the Medical Officer with him to the chapel and see if any more of the roof was likely to fall in.

'I visited it yesterday evening,' the inspector replied, 'and heard many expressions of approval from people keeping fox terrier dogs, who have had a fine time since the roof fell in'. After the laughter had died down, 'there is no danger,' he asserted.

Councillor Alfred Fortt was not amused, however. 'It won't be dangerous,' he shouted, 'until about three people are killed, and then all you people will wake up to the fact that it ought to have been demolished long ago. I would like to see some scientific opinion as whether the place will fall inwards or outwards.'

'I shouldn't think it requires a great amount of brains,' Mr Fortune replied, 'to see at once that a circular building will not fall outwards unless there are great indications of it doing so. There are none in this case. If it falls at all it will fall inwards.'

The clerk wound up the discussion by saying that, as the building was neither legally dangerous nor a nuisance they could do nothing.

Eventually, though, the council had a change of heart and on 29 November the demolition of the chapel began 'to the great relief of neighbouring residents'.

The name of the chapel can still be seen, chiselled above the former entrance.

Houses backing onto the river at Widcombe, many of which discharged their sewage directly into it.

CHAPTER FOUR

THE SEWAGE CRISIS

Although proposals to demolish old buildings and replace them with new ones was – and still is – controversial, you might think that, when it came to modernising Bath's sewage system, greater unanimity would have prevailed. Sadly, it did not. In this case, protests were prompted not by a sentimental attachment to the discharge of untreated sewage into the river; as with opposition to improving visitor facilities, it was a question of money.

Bath's sewage system had developed piecemeal as the city had grown. If, in the more salubrious parts of town, things were at least tolerable, down among the tenements and lodging houses around Avon Street, it was a different story.

During an outbreak of cholera in August 1849, the river was drained and accumulated mud removed. Some of the sewers that were exposed were found to be in a very bad state, with no current to carry off the 'accumulated soil'. In the same year, the City Engineer reported that 'the whole of the suburbs of the city [are] without any system of sewage and cesspools afford the sole means of drainage available'.

In 1857, under the provisions of the City of Bath Act, the council set up a committee to look into the problem of the sewers. Seven years later, the City Engineer put forward plans for intercepting the discharge of waste into the river and building a treatment plant outside the city. The council turned them down on grounds of cost.

By the 1870s the city had 148 sewage outfalls into the river. In 1892 residents presented a petition to the council calling for action. Once again, the council asked the City Engineer to draw up plans; once again they were rejected on grounds of cost. By 1905, things had got so bad that Somerset County Council told Bath it would take legal action if nothing was done.

Four years later, despite expressions of good intent, nothing had happened. What finally galvanised the council into action was the government inspector's response to an application to extend Bath's boundaries. Before the application could be considered, the council had to 'produce a complete scheme for sewerage and have it executed; make the waterworks efficient, improve the slaughterhouses, various insanitary areas and houses, and extend the refuse destructor'. This, according to the report in the *Chronicle,* 'caused great dejection and disappointment'.

The boundaries issue was, perhaps, the most important one facing the council in the first decade of the twentieth century. The city boundaries, established by royal charter in the reign of Queen Elizabeth and enlarged by the Municipal Corporations Act of 1835 and a Boundaries Commission ruling of 1868, excluded many areas that had been developed in the late nineteenth century and were now served by electric trams. To all intents and purposes they were effectively part of the city; but, although they used many of its services, they were not governed by or represented on the city council, nor did they contribute to it financially. The areas proposed for absorption into the city were the whole of the parishes of Bathampton, Charlcombe, Monkton Combe and Twerton, and parts of the parishes of Batheaston, Claverton, Swainswick and Weston.

Faced with the county council's ultimatum, the city council decided to push ahead with a sewage treatment scheme in the teeth of opposition from traditionalists both within the council and outside. Opponents of the scheme seized every opportunity to discredit it. On 11 January 1909, for example, when the Sanitary Committee reported that no infectious diseases had been notified during the previous week, Alderman Thomas Vincent said that this showed what a waste of money it would be. By 2 March, when the government inspector's decision was debated at a council meeting, tempers had risen alarmingly. When the Mayor moved that  the matter should be referred to the committee set up to deal with the boundaries issue, Councillor Sydenham rose to oppose the resolution 'on public grounds', declaring that, 'This matter which is so serious to the city has been a disgrace in the eyes of the whole nation.'

Amid cries of assent and dissent, Councillor Harry Hatt rose to make a point of order. The Mayor asked Mr Sydenham if he 'thought it patriotic to say such things, which were calculated to do so much harm to the city'.

'I beg to move that the matter be not referred to the Boundaries Committee,' he replied, 'I move that it be debated now.'

Councillor Valentine Evans – who had been so amused by the rats at Laura Chapel – then intervened, saying that it showed 'a shallow perception on the part of those prosecuting the matter to bring it forward now. Look at the list of things required by the local government board – you have got to do the sewage, construct an abattoir ...'

At which point he was drowned out by shouts of 'No'.

The Mayor then told him that 'Any member is entitled to debate the motion they move, but it is not within the province of the council to debate the amendment. You are not in order to second the amendment, but you can speak to the general motion.'

'I say it is a most serious matter,' said Mr Evans, 'involving an expenditure of about a million of money.' This was greeted with laughter, but he continued, 'Where are you going to get it from? The credit of Bath is not worth a sheep's head.'

Amid the general confusion, Mr Sydenham asked if his motion was out of order, to which the Mayor replied that it was the amendment that was out of order. Alderman Phillips was rising to make an observation, when Mr Evans muttered, 'I say, damn the chair!'

The uproar that followed, with shouts of 'Order' and 'Withdraw', lasted several minutes. When it had died down, Councillor Sydney Bush rose and said he wished to 'protest most earnestly against the remark that has just been made. One can afford to treat certain remarks with absolute indifference, but one cannot pass over such a disgraceful remark as this.'

There were shouts of 'Hear hear' and 'Withdraw', then the Mayor said, 'I did not hear the remark.'

After Mr Bush had repeated it, the Mayor said that he hoped Mr Evans would 'see fit to withdraw it. When he uses a remark of that kind with relation to the chair,' he continued, 'I think his own sense of decency ought to make him withdraw.'

'I will withdraw the remark,' said Mr Evans, and, after further debate in a more subdued manner, the resolution to refer the matter to the committee was carried.

Eventually, on 6 July, the council voted to spend £215,000 on a new sewage scheme 'to avoid polluting the river'. But if they thought that would be the end of the story, they were wrong. The funding may have been agreed, but the details had still to be settled. On 9

September, the inspector overseeing the project appeared before the council. One of those who grilled him was Alderman Edward Peacock, who owned a fishmonger's and poulterer's in Union Street, and was a vigorous opponent of the scheme.

'Do you think,' he asked the inspector, 'that the effluent after it is treated with all your chemicals will be any purer than the river is now at a normal time?'

'I think the sewage effluent will be purer than the crude sewage that now passes into the river; whether the effluent will be purer than the river water I cannot say.'

'I'm not talking of crude sewage.'

'There is no doubt the river will be very much purer opposite Bath than it is now.'

'That question doesn't affect the matter at all.'

'We want to make the river at Bath purer than it is now.'

At this point Alderman Peacock 'created some amusement' by producing a bottle containing 'water taken

Alderman Peacock's fishmonger's and poulterer's was one of the best known in the city.

from the river in the centre of the city'. Holding it up, he asked his colleagues to note its clarity.

'I could bring some worse than this,' said the inspector.

'I know this morning you could. This morning the river is in the same state as it was in 1896, when the county council sent a communication to Bath about the state of the river. The water they sent then did not come from the city at all, but from outside.'

Alderman Peacock proceeded to pour the water into a glass which he handed to the inspector, saying, 'You may drink it. It will not hurt you. I'll give you my word for that.'

The inspector took a sniff but declined the offer.

'I'll drink it then,' said Alderman Peacock, and took a mouthful, exclaiming, 'if you are going to find any purer effluent than that I'll forgive you. That is the state of the water unless there is a storm water such as there is today. You spoke about the water being aerated over a weir at the outfall – we have a weir with a seven foot drop here and another at Twerton, so the whole of the water is aerated twice over.'

'We don't propose to turn crude sewage into the river,' replied the inspector.

'I say we don't turn crude sewage into it,' replied Alderman Peacock. 'All the sewage is treated with any amount of water, independently of the flushing that passes through the stream. It is purer than any water going from your works, after being allowed to stand with the sewage in it a long time.'

Alderman Peacock was not the only one who thought the scheme pointless. Mr RF Chapman, a monumental sculptor from Widcombe, said he had known the river for nearly 70 years, saw no problem with the current system and was 'very seriously opposed' to the scheme.

Then there were those who, while not opposed to the scheme in principle, did not want it on their doorstep. The sewage works was originally going to be built in the meadows below Newton St Loe. Opposition from residents downwind of the plant forced a relocation to the meadows north-east of Saltford, opposite Swineford. This naturally upset the biggest local landowner, Major-General Inigo-Jones of Kelston Park, who told the inspector that there was 'a lot of land suitable for building around Kelston, Newton, Upton and Swineford – can I have a guarantee that the sewage works won't be smelt from there?'

When the inspector declined to give any such guarantee, the major-general asked him whether 'a whole district [was] to be made poisonous and uninhabitable in order to please Bath?'

'The city is not anxious to offend anyone,' said the inspector.

'I'm sure of that, but they bring this nuisance to us.'

'They regret it.'

'Why should you not go down to Hanham? You put it in the middle of a ring of villages where they may build.'

'There are no sites lower down which would be better.'

'I maintain then that you should follow the course of the river out to sea, below Bristol.'

'It is too expensive to take it into the sea. That alternative was considered; we should have to go through Bristol, and the Bristol people objected to it by vote; they went to a poll.'

Eight days later Alderman Peacock addressed a well-attended protest meeting in the Guildhall. Saying that he knew the river as well as the road to his house and was convinced that the scheme was unnecessary, he held up another glass of river water and assured the audience that he could take a sample of water from under each of the bridges in the city, and would find it very little less clear than the water in his glass. 'At present,' he affirmed,

'Bath has got the best system of sewage disposal of any town in the world, and it does not cost a penny to work it.'

Councillor Evans, who had called for a referendum on the grounds that at least eight out of ten residents were against the scheme, said it was all down to retaliation. 'The city council has determined to extend its boundaries, and Somerset County Council has retaliated by requiring the council to take its sewage out of the river.'

'Let them pay their debts first,' shouted a voice from the audience.

'I quite agree with you – we should pay our existing debts before going further into debt. I do not deny that improvement is necessary, but there are other means which might be adopted. The river could be dredged. Spending this large amount of money is a criminal waste. I move: "That this public meeting of ratepayers views with alarm the ever-increasing large expenditure of its council, and protests against its actions in endeavouring to proceed with the schemes of sewage disposal and boundary extension, without first consulting the wishes of the ratepayers, because we are certain at least four-fifths of them are strongly opposed to such a course of action. We are therefore compelled in the interests of the ratepayers to demand a poll of the city before anything more is done with reference to the sewage disposal scheme."'

Councillor Joseph Crook seconded the resolution, adding that, 'I do not always agree with Mr Evans in his observations in the council chamber, because I regard him as rather an Ishmaelite. But in this instance I support most cordially. I contend that the money might be spent in a much more useful manner than in the carrying out of the sewage scheme. Many improvements, for example, might be carried out in St James's Ward. I certainly think the citizens ought to demand a poll.'

Tom Stone, who had a paint, oil and glass merchants in Weymouth Street, congratulated Alderman Peacock 'for the energy he has displayed in connection with this agitation. I have lived in Bath for 37 years, and for part of that time have lived very close to the river, but I feel quite well today. A good many of the councillors to whom I have spoken on the subject have said that they hope the scheme will not be carried out.'

Mr G Shellard, a stonemason from Dahlia Place in Odd Down said that the 'Lunacy Commissioners' should be 'asked to come down and enquire into the state of mind of three-quarters of our town council'.

After the laughter had died down, Mr Chapman said that, rather than pay an extra shilling on the rates for the sewage, he would leave the city.

George Walker, a coal merchant who owned steam mills in Avon Street and was described as 'a familiar figure at public meetings of a contentious character' spoke next. He hadn't been given the nickname 'Stir-pot' for nothing, he said – adding that 'the more I can stir things up the better I like it'. His complaint, in this instance, was against the navigation of the Avon. He suggested that the Corporation's main should supply current to Mr Carr's mills at Twerton as an auxiliary power, adding – 'with considerable emphasis' – that he paid 7½d a ton in tolls for his barges. When Alderman Peacock pointed out that the Great Western Railway Company controlled the navigation of the Avon, Mr Walker asked him why the Corporation did not bring pressure to bear on the railway company. When Alderman Peacock failed to reply, he strode up to the front of the meeting and took him by the arm.

'You're the Corporation,' he told him pointedly, and, when Alderman Peacock asked him to let go of his arm, said 'you can't stop me.'

Protest meetings, then as now, have a habit of spinning off in directions unforeseen by their organisers. Alderman Peacock was no doubt relieved to bring matters to a speedy conclusion, especially if, having imbibed a little too freely of the waters of the Avon, he needed to use the Guildhall's commodious facilities. And in case you're wondering, it doesn't seem to have had any immediate ill-effects; Alderman Peacock died in 1913 at the ripe old age of 76.

In the end, the protests achieved nothing and the new sewage works at Saltford was inaugurated on 17 June 1914.[1] Almost a century on, we can rest assured that – thanks to the foresight of Edwardian councillors – we have a sewage treatment system that preserves the purity of the river – or can we? Wessex Water is currently investing £28 million in a scheme to 'greatly reduce the volume of stormwater and untreated sewage discharged via overflows into the River Avon [and] minimise the amount of sewage related debris discharged to the river.' The £215,000 spent on the sewage system almost a century ago represents an expenditure of around £16 million in today's terms; now another £28 million is being spent to make good the deficiencies of the original scheme. At least we should be grateful there are no modern-day Alderman Peacock's telling us that the system's fine as

1 A large celebratory photomontage of the opening can be seen at the Museum of Bath at Work.

The pumping station and Dortmund tanks at the sewage works at Saltford, opened in 1914.

it is and quaffing tumblers of contaminated water at rabble-rousing public meetings.

It is astonishing how blasé supposedly intelligent people were a century ago when it came to lapses of hygiene or sanitation which we would regard as criminal today. The problem was that a lot of the ideas concerning public health were 'new-fangled', and many of those who had got along quite nicely up to then saw no reason why they should pay them any attention. Many people still believed, despite scientific evidence to the contrary, that diseases such as cholera were airborne and contracted not by drinking contaminated water but by breathing 'miasma' or bad air. Florence Nightingale – who was still alive in 1909 – was a strong advocate of this theory.

Tuberculosis is another case in point. A century ago it was a virulent killer and would remain so until the advent of antibiotics after the Second World War. Sanatoriums, such as the one at Winsley, just over the border in Wiltshire, which opened in 1904 and had treated over a thousand people by the end of 1909, catered almost exclusively for patients with tuberculosis.[2] Scientists had gone a long way towards identifying the source and trying to control the spread of the disease; the problem was that many people, including those in positions of authority, did not want to listen.

In 1898, the Royal Commission on Tuberculosis confirmed that milk from tuberculous cattle was one of the principal causes of tuberculosis in humans, but, over ten years later, many local authorities had failed to take any action as a result. In 1909, for example, 23 of the 36 districts in the county of Middlesex reported

2 The sanatorium was set up by Dr Lionel Weatherly, believed to be the brother of one of Bath's most celebrated residents, Frederick Weatherly, who wrote the words of 'Roses of Picardy', 'Danny Boy' and other well-known songs. Lionel also established an asylum at Bailbrook House in 1886. He was a founder member of the Bath Amateurs, which later became the Bath Operatic Society. The site of Winsley Sanatorium is now a retirement village.

that 'no veterinary examinations of cows were made on behalf of the local authorities'. Citing these figures, a writer in the *British Food Journal* concluded 'that these 23 districts, in a county with about one million inhabitants, are governed, so far as sanitary matters go, by people who consider themselves qualified to hold opinions diametrically opposed to those held by experts and based on the best scientific evidence at present available'.

Bath had its fair share of self-styled experts as well. One of the most vociferous was Alderman Alfred Taylor, who owned

New Bond Street, Bath.   *Tel. 103.*

the Old Red House Bakery in New Bond Street. On 10 September 1909, he was present at a meeting of the Markets Committee when a new Tuberculosis Order was being discussed. Among its provisions was a requirement for cattle suffering from the disease to be destroyed. Alderman Taylor was appalled – 'those who drafted it,' he declared, 'are old women who have become very infirm and simple-minded. I hope,' he continued, 'that they might be impregnated with the germs so they will get off to the better country.' His bon-mot was greeted with laughter, and he brushed aside Councillor Horatio Green's attempt to explain that the order would reduce the incidence of the disease in children caused by impure milk. Unfortunately – for Alderman Taylor at least – it was not those who had framed the legislation who were about to embark on a journey to a better land. He died less than three months later, at the age of 68.

Alderman Peacock and Alderman Taylor are, perhaps, extreme examples of the kind of institutionalised inertia that will uphold the status quo, no matter how convincing the arguments against it, when vested interests are involved. We should be on our guard, though, against adopting too superior an attitude to such antediluvian attitudes. Despite many improvements, some things are little better, some are actually worse than they were a century ago. We may have eradicated the problem of streets clogged and smeared with horse manure; we have acquired, in the process, constant and often stationary queues of traffic, with some of the most polluted streets in the country and ever-increasing rates of allergy and asthma. Then there is the issue of waste.

A century ago, there was – compared with today – remarkably little rubbish. People consumed less and what they did consume was unlikely to come pre-packaged. Even so, waste was a growing problem. The Public Health Act of 1875 laid down that local authorities had to arrange for the removal and disposal of household waste, which householders had to keep outside in a 'movable receptacle' – and so the dustbin was born. The act also laid down that waste should be collected on a weekly basis. Early corporation dustcarts were open, two-wheeled affairs drawn by a horse. At the side was a ladder which the dustman climbed to tip the contents of dustbins into the cart. On windy days, as can be imagined, much of it ended up blowing along the street.

In Bath, a contractor was appointed to collect the rubbish and deposit it in two yards – one on the Upper Bristol Road, where the waste disposal depot still is today, and the other by the river in Twerton. According to Alfred Wills, who was responsible for improving waste disposal facilities in Bath in the early twentieth century, these sites were 'indescribably filthy and insanitary. No attempt was made to separate the soft core from the hard and during the process of decay it was disturbed by pigs, poultry and children, who earned a livelihood in picking up unconsidered trifles.'

The situation grew so bad that the High Court stepped in to force the contractor to screen the waste when it arrived at the yards and take the soft core away for disposal. In 1886 the council decided to take waste disposal into its own hands and acquired a plot of land at Midford, to which rubbish was sent by barge along the Somersetshire Coal Canal, until the Rural Council obtained an injunction prohibiting its use as a tip. Faced with the problem of increasing piles of rubbish and nowhere to dispose of them, the council opted, as many others had done, to build an incinerator or 'destructor plant'. The first destructor was built in Nottingham in 1874; during the next 30 years, 250 destructors were built in Britain. Although they produced steam for generating electricity, and fine ashes screened from the clinker could be sold to make mortar and paving slabs, destructors were unpopular not only because of their smell but also because of the ashes, dust and charred paper which fell in the surrounding area. Not surprisingly, there were soon calls for a more environmentally friendly solution.

In 1890, the British Paper Company was established to make paper and board from recycled materials. Some local authorities, too, started to introduce recycling schemes. A national association of 'cleansing superintendents' was formed to take the initiative forward. In 1907 a spokesman for the organisation said that 'the biggest change in municipal work would be the change from destruction to salvage in the near future'. Rubbish was sorted by hand and anything saleable put to one side. Records from 1913 show that Bath council sold unburnt tins for 21/- a ton, waste paper pressed into bales for 22/6 a ton, old carpets for 25/- a ton, bagging for 37/6 a ton, light scrap iron at 20/- a ton and galvanized scrap iron for 10/- a ton; annual income from the sale of these goods was estimated at £170.

Telephone No. 303.

Bath Urban Sanitary Authority's

DESTRUCTOR WORKS.

FOR SALE—AT WORKS—
Machine-Ground MORTAR, made from Best
hydraulic Lime and hard burnt Ashes only.
Concrete Paving Slabs.
A Large Assortment always on hand.
STEPS, LANDINGS, &c., Made to Order.
SCREENED ASHES in Stock.
Apply J. BARTER, Superintendent, at Works.

Then as now, though, there was still the problem of the rubbish that couldn't be recycled – and it grew year by year. Bath's first destructor started work in 1895, at the Upper Bristol Road site. It was enlarged in 1899 and converted for high-temperature operation in 1902. With the extension of Bath's boundaries in 1911, it could no longer keep up with the rising tide of rubbish, and a new destructor was inaugurated two years later.

When incineration fell out of favour during the twentieth century, what replaced it was not salvage but landfill. The only goods train leaving Bath today – although its days are apparently numbered – is one that transfers Bath's waste to a landfill site at Calvert in Buckinghamshire. Recycling, it is true, is creeping up the political agenda, but we still generate an amount of waste that would have left our Edwardian forebears speechless. And now – to the despair and fury of Green campaigners – there are plans to build a new mass-burn incinerator at Avonmouth, although Bath & North East Somerset Council has pulled out of the scheme. According to the government's audit commission, incinerators are the only long-term solution to the growing mountain of waste because recycling alone cannot deal with the problem.

Which brings us back, more or less, to where we were a century ago. Only the piles of rubbish are far, far higher.

Plus ça change, plus c'est la même merde.

The old fire station behind the Guildhall.

CHAPTER 5

NO FIRES BEFORE SEVEN

Fires were more prevalent a century ago than they are today. Mills and malthouses were particularly at risk – and Bath had plenty of both. Measures for dealing with fires, though, were unbelievably antiquated, even by the standards of the day. Not surprisingly, there was pressure for facilities to be improved – pressure that was as firmly resisted as calls for the sewage works had been.

The first fire brigades had been set up by insurance companies, but by the end of the nineteenth century control had passed to local authorities. In 1889, the West Of England Fire & Life Assurance Company disbanded their brigade in Bath and donated their engine and equipment to the Corporation. Two years later the Bath Fire Brigade augmented this manual appliance with a steam-powered one. These two machines – both drawn by horses – were still in use in 1909. There was also a hand-drawn hose cart with a 40 foot ladder, and seven more hand trucks in outlying parts of the city. Initially, the brigade was a voluntary force, made up of three officers and between 15 and 20 men. In the early 1900s, the council decided to create several full-time posts; by 1909 the brigade consisted of a chief fire officer, who received £100 a year, a senior fireman, who received £70 a year, three other firemen, a driver and a switchmen, who each received £65 a year. When not engaged on brigade duties, firemen had to work as porters in the Guildhall. There were also 17 voluntary firemen who received a retainer of two guineas a year. When attending fires, they were paid two shillings for the first hour and one shilling for every hour thereafter.

Many of those who grew up with horse-drawn fire engines later remembered them with affection, in much the same way that people wax lyrical about steam trains today. Here is Walter Macqueen-Pope recalling their appeal in the 1940s:

One of the big thrills was a fire-engine. This was not a motor affair but drawn by two fine, plunging horses, eager and speedy, who seemed to know themselves the urgency of their journey. The firemen sat along each side of it, wearing gleaming brass helmets

A fire engine similar to that used in Bath.

and brass shoulder-straps like plaited mail. As they went they shouted 'Fire, Fire, Fire!' and one rang a bell.

At the end of the engine was a large brass boiler with a funnel. This belched smoke and dropped red-hot cinders as the fire-engine dashed along. It was something of a sensation to see the fire brigade turn out. The horses dashed to their places on each side of the shaft pole, the harness fell on them from above, nimble fingers fixed it in a twinkling, the men leapt on, and the thing was off with a dash and a gallop and a grand amount of noise which the modern engine can never equal. It is all much quieter and more dingy today, and it is not all that quicker either.

The engine would be pursued by a running crowd and cyclists would speed in its wake to the scene of the fire. Nobody could resist it. It could be traced by the trail of cinders.

But time can cast a golden glow over the most dubious things. The reality, for the men who had to operate them – or who relied on them to extinguish fires – was somewhat different.

In July 1908, while attending a fire near Englishcombe, one of the engines had overturned on Pennyquick Hill; the Chief Fire Officer had subsequently died as a result of his injuries. In January 1909, however, the brigade was in the headlines for a different reason – the length of time it had taken them to get to a fire at Myrtle Place near Walcot Buildings. One observer claimed that it was 37 minutes after the alarm was raised before they were on the scene. From the fire station – then at the back of the Guildhall – to Walcot Buildings was no more than three-quarters of a mile – a 15-minute walk.

One of the problems was that the horses that drew the engines were only at the station between 7pm and 7am. They belonged not to the Corporation but to a private owner, to whose stables they returned during the day, for use on other duties. This not only caused delay – it also meant there was always a possibility no horses would be available at a given time.

An enquiry by the council's Brigade Committee established that firefighters had been on the scene much sooner than claimed. The alarm had been raised at 6.45pm and the hand-drawn truck had been sent on with two men at 6.46pm. They had a hose connected up by seven o'clock – 15 minutes later. The horses were telephoned for immediately, arrived at the station 15 minutes later and were despatched shortly afterwards.

This failed to impress one eye-witness who wrote to the *Chronicle* claiming that, if it had not been for the prompt action of a police officer who arrived from Weymouth Street with a hose at 6.50pm and, with the help of several bystanders, had it connected up by 6.53pm, the building would have burnt down before the fire brigade got there.

Another correspondent attacked the horse-hire policy:

It is time the brigade possessed a horse. It is most painful to see our local firemen running about the town with an obsolete hand truck … I am surprised that our worthy councillor, Mr Norris, is not aware of the fact that no fires are permitted until after the hour of 7pm, this being the time that hired horses are brought to the station. May I suggest that the appliances of the fire brigade form part of the proposed historic pageant. The period would be as near as possible to the time of the great fire of London.

The fire at Myrtle Place had highlighted the deficiencies of Bath's fire service and, in response to the wave of criticism that followed, the council asked the Brigade Committee to submit a detailed report. After due consideration they concluded that 'in many respects alterations are necessary to bring the brigade up to a modern standard':

The horsed escape and tender is of a pattern which is now completely superseded and is quite unsuitable for the purpose for which it is required, namely, to attend promptly at the scene of a fire in order to save life (if in danger) and to get a delivery of water on the fire in its early stages.

The vehicle is exceedingly cumbrous, weighing, when fully equipped 2 tons 11¼ cwt, and it is impossible to get it to a fire which involves the mounting of a comparatively slight gradient: in such a case the escape has to be detached and thus one of the main uses of the appliance is done away with. Even without the escape it is very difficult to get the tender up any of the hills surrounding the city.

The pair of horses required for the fire engine and escape are obtained from neighbouring stables (between 7am and 7pm) and by night are stabled in the fire station. The position of the stables is unsuitable, and if it is decided to continue the use of horses for a first turn-out some rearrangement should be made in this respect and a thoroughly up-to-date system of harness provided.

In case of a call by day there must necessarily be a delay of between 10 and 15 minutes caused by telephoning for the horses and awaiting their arrival. The result of this is that the brigade have to start to a fire with a small hand-truck and escape, three or four men running through the streets drawing this truck, and if the fire is any distance away the men arrive totally exhausted and unfit for hard work.

It has recently been the practice during the day to take a taxi-cab with a few necessary appliances, leaving the heavier apparatus to follow when the horses arrive, but it is very undesirable that the brigade should have to depend upon being able to obtain a taxi-cab in order to get to a fire.

The committee recommended the purchase not of horses but of a 'motor fire escape and tender ... together with a 36ft escape, two hand chemical extinguishers, 1,000 feet of hose, and one additional folding Pompier ladder'. This would cost around £800, with annual running costs of around £30-£35, compared to the £80 it would cost to keep two horses. It was the speed of the motor engine – 25 mph on the flat and 7 mph up a 1 in 8 hill – that was the real clincher, however. The committee's recommendations were accepted by the council with one vote against – from Alderman Alfred Taylor (who had also opposed the culling of tuberculous cattle). Incredibly, he stood up in the council chamber after the evidence had been presented and stated his belief that 'they were doing, and could do, just as well under present conditions as they could with the motor', adding that he thought it 'a waste of money'.

A few weeks later, it was reported that 'certain gentlemen on the council had visited Bristol to see the petrol motor machine, and were exceedingly surprised at the quick manner in which they were able to get to and fro'. The committee suggested that 'two or three prominent makers of fire-fighting appliances should attend at Bath and make themselves acquainted with the special circumstances having regard to the hilly nature of the locality, and that they submit their own special recommendations and prices'.

While the council was deciding what to do, however, Bath suffered two disastrous fires. The first occurred at around 4.45pm on the afternoon of Saturday 15 May at the Standard Bakery in Arlington Road, Oldfield Park. A corrugated-iron and wooden hay store caught fire shortly after a boy was seen running away from the building. Fanned by a breeze, the fire soon took hold. Workers at the bakery rushed to lead horses stabled in part of the building to safety before the flames reached them. The first firemen arrived – by taxi – with a hose and other apparatus ten minutes later. The roof fell in soon afterwards and the firemen set to work demolishing the rest of the building to stop the fire spreading. By six o'clock it was nearly out. In what was reckoned to be the 'most disastrous fire in this district for

The fire at the Standard Bakery in Oldfield Park.

20 years', damage was estimated at between one and two thousand pounds. Two boys later owned up to having climbed onto a trolley and thrown a lighted bolt of paper through the loft door.

The other major fire, at Batheaston Mill on 14 November, received extensive – and graphic – coverage in the *Bath Chronicle*:

For miles around the misty darkness of a November night was dispelled by a lurid glare. A remark made by Chief Officer England ... will give a simple yet effective idea of the outburst. When called by the alarm from the fire station he ran out of his house to the railings of the Institution Gardens and he says: 'It looked as if huge flares were burning in Bathwick near the bottom of Pulteney Street. It was impossible to believe it was a fire in Batheaston, so high were the flames, and so vivid the light.' When Mr England took this rapid look it was probably just as the roof of the mill had gone in, and the flames were shooting up to an extraordinary altitude. A keen and strongish east wind was blowing when the outbreak occurred, and this carried the smoke in dense clouds over the city and up the hills of Bath. So thick, pungent and penetrating was the volume that it entered houses innumerable, and many Bathonians awoke in alarm, fearing that their own domiciles were alight, and anxious and speedy tours of inspection were made by householders in the small hours of Sunday morning. Anxious enquiries were made from windows to the obliging policemen on their rounds, to be assured that the danger was as far distant as Batheaston.

Though the fire does not seem to have been discovered until 2.45am, or even later, there can be no question that the mill must have been burning for a long while before that hour ... Indeed, a Bath policeman, who was on duty in the Lansdown Road district, tells us that at 1.30 he noticed a strong smell of smoke, and so informed his inspector just afterwards, but they could not locate any fire ...

The mill was a tall, long, narrow structure, with five floors, a width of about 24 feet, and probably 100 feet in length. Adjoining the mill proper, to the eastward, was a lower, square, and more ancient store, and further to the east, stables and lofts still lower. The mill is driven by turbines, but in the adjoining store is a gas engine, used for supplementary power purposes, while Mr Elston had equipped the premises with valuable and comparatively modern grain-grinding machinery. In the upper floors were large quantities of wheat, while the lower stores were heavily stocked with flour.

It was about 2.45, as far as we can ascertain, that anybody first realised that a devastating fire was raging within the mill ... All could see the mill was doomed; it resembled a roaring furnace at white heat. Mr Elston [the miller], with assistance, managed to rescue some of the books from the office ... and attention was

Batheaston Mill before and after the fire.

directed to the horses in the stables. These, eight in number, were got out and taken up to the London Road out of harm's way …

The first alarm to the Bath Brigade sounded in their quarters at 2.54. It came by phone, and said the Batheaston mill was burning. Who gave it is not recorded. Within five minutes many more messages to the same effect were received. By 3.05 the steam engine was off, and many residents along the London Road will remember the dash our fire extinction corps made to their destination. It was a memorable sight to see the two Belgian black horses, with their long flowing tails, going at a swinging gallop with the bright steamer harnessed to them, the sparks and cinders from the firebox leaving a glowing trail along the tram track.

As far as can be gathered, the engine was at the bridge by 3.20. They had a narrow escape from a frightful calamity as they gained the scene of the fire. Tearing along the road they swung down the slope, Driver Francis Tugnett handling the steeds in splendid fashion. Chief Officer England saw, at a glance, what was the best position for the steamer (in order that it might draw up the water), and he shouted, 'Make for the bridge!' The blaze was then in full play, the roof had gone in, and nothing could be seen inside but the roaring flames, while huge tongues of fire leapt up from the mighty furnace. As the brigade dashed onto the bridge a floor inside the mill collapsed, causing the flames to shoot out from the lower windows, and almost lick the faces of the terrified steeds. They reared and plunged, and it seemed as if nothing could prevent the careering, maddened animals from dashing over the bridge and carrying the engine, firemen and all into the river, for the comparatively frail parapet would not have offered any effectual barrier to such a weight. But, providentially, when the worst threatened, one of the horses, slipping on the roadway, went down, and brought its companion to a standstill.

Before the brigade arrived some others had been rendering aid to those in the immediate locality. These included two Bath constables, who, seeing the blaze while on duty at Grosvenor, jumped into a taxicab which was going eastwards, and Mr SW Alexander, who first noticed the fire when he was cycling home from his duties at the post office …

By 3.30 quite a considerable crowd had assembled, many of them being Bath postal officials, who, like Mr Alexander, were leaving duty about 3am. It was a vivid, lurid, yet weird scene proceeding along the roadway to the fire. The Avon valley was illuminated brilliantly by the terrible blaze, which was fanned by the piercing wind that speedily blew the smoke towards the city. Above the body of glowing flame would be carried up now and again clouds of glowing sparks, which circled round in fiery eddies, and then, when the gust that had carried them aloft subsided, slowly floated to the ground, where the ashes lay quite thick, like a stygian snowfall, and scrunched crisply underfoot for many hundreds of yards westward of the fiery vortex, whence they had wafted. One passing impression will always remain, and that was how vividly Wood Dene (the mansion built not long ago on the rising ground above the London Road) stood forth in the glare ...

To save the mill was a task impossible when the brigade arrived; had they been on the spot with apparatus fixed when the alarm was given any such effort would have been equally hopeless ... The adjacent store was also beyond recall, and Mr England concentrated the work of the brigade on saving the stables and the steam tractor, while the fire in the mill was left to burn itself out ...Such ominous cracks appeared in the walls, and so ominously did they bulge, that orders had to be issued to the brigade to keep as clear of the mill proper as their work would allow. The engine worked splendidly. It sucked water up from the Avon in great volume and four deliveries were soon gushing out ...

Between 4.30 and five o'clock the masonry began to fall with resounding crashes, It was a rather unique spectacle when the triangular gable-end at the south side topped outwards. Much of the red-hot freestone plunged into the river, creating an impromptu geyser, the water splashing to a great height, while the steam rose up in a dense cloud. Later on, the firemen obtained a tall ladder and, throwing ropes across, pulled down more of the wall at this end, which was obviously dangerous ... By 5.15 the fire had sunk down to such small dimensions that the spectators went home to a premature breakfast and bed ...

It was 12.55pm before the steamer arrived back at the station, and then two firemen were left on duty. All through Sunday the debris in the bottom of the gutted mill was smouldering and smoking, and seemed likely to do so for some time to come. Despite the wet weather large numbers of people made their way to the mill, or rather all that is left of it; and, if the fire did nothing else, it gave a fillip to the tram traffic on the Bathford route.

The following day: directing water onto the smouldering remains; and surveying the damage.

On Monday the heaps of charred grain were still smouldering and firemen were still on duty. One of the regrettable consequences of the fire is that 15 or more men are thrown out of work.

John Elston, the miller, who lived at nearby Echo Villa, said he had no idea how the fire had started – all had been safe at six o'clock when the office was locked up and no one was about the premises as far as he knew. He estimated the damage at around £8,000.

Fires in mills were extremely common – Mr Elston had previously been the tenant of Upper Widcombe Mill in Prior Park Road and Bathampton Mill, both of which had been gutted by fire. Just over two months later, on 19 January 1910, the historic paper mills at Bathford were destroyed by fire, putting 60 more men out of work. The company went into liquidation and the site was bought by Henry Tabb, who engaged Hayward & Wooster to rebuild the mill. By 1913, Bathford Paper Mills Company was once again in full production.

January 1910 also the end of the road for Bath's antiquated horse-drawn fire engine and the arrival of a 50-horsepower, chain-driven Merryweather engine. With a maximum speed of 30 mph, it could get up Widcombe Hill, fully loaded, in seven minutes – a climb that had taken the horse-drawn engine 40 minutes. Only four months after its introduction, however, it overturned while descending a steep hill and was out of action for four months. It was a lorry from the tramways company that was hired to carry the brigade around town in the interim, however – there was to be no return to the days of horse-drawn tenders and taxis.

Although some parts of Bath have changed little in the last century, others have been transformed beyond recognition. St James Street South, seen above, now lies under Marks & Spencer's; the double-page spread overleaf shows a whole swathe of the city lost to bombing and redevelopment. The houses in the foreground on Holloway, the warehouses on Broad Quay, and virtually all the buildings in the middle distance, including St James's Church, have gone.

CHAPTER SIX

TOWN AND COUNTRY

The population of England & Wales grew, during the nineteenth century, from nine million to 32.5 million – an increase of over 250%. Over the same period, Bath's population grew from 33,000 to 49,839 – an increase of less than 50%. And, while the country as a whole experienced sustained growth, Bath's population, after rising steadily in the first half of the nineteenth century, declined thereafter. In 1851, it stood at 54,000; by 1891 it had dropped to 51,844, with a further decline by 1901.

These figures are slightly misleading, as there had been significant development outside the city boundaries, especially in Lower Weston and Twerton. By the time of the 1911 Census, the number of people recorded as living in Bath had risen slightly, to 50,721; later that year, the city's boundaries were extended, taking the figure up to 70,893. Nevertheless, Bath – whose population had grown six-fold in the eighteenth century – was a city in relative decline. What had sustained Bath's growth in the eighteenth century was leisure, and specifically the leisure of the elite. Despite grandiose plans drawn up in the early nineteenth century, that market could not go on expanding indefinitely – and as soon as the leaders of the *beau monde* decided that Bath was no longer the place to be, it was left to its fate, with nothing more substantial than the memories of past glories to sustain it.

While Bath struggled to stand still, the country as a whole experienced a seismic shift, from a rural economy, where wealth was based on land, to an urban one, where it was based on manufacturing. At the beginning of the nineteenth century, over 80% of people lived in the countryside; by 1851, the percentage had dropped to 50%; by 1901 it was down to 23%. Given the massive growth in population, the actual decline was nowhere near this dramatic – 9 million people lived in the country in 1851, falling to 7.5 million by 1901 – but the collapse of the rural economy was nevertheless devastating. To take one example, a 700-acre farm in Wiltshire which had sold for £27,000 in 1812 went for a mere £7,000 in 1892. In 1905, out of 34 farmers in Corsley in Wiltshire, twelve had subsidiary occupations, such as bakers, coal merchants or carriers.

The percentage of the population engaged in agriculture, forestry and fishing fell from around 15% in 1871 to 7% by 1901. Even in a rural county such as Somerset, less than a quarter of the male workforce was engaged in agriculture by the beginning of the twentieth century. In just 30 years, the acreage under crops in England & Wales had fallen from 24 million to 19.5 million, while wheat production had fallen by 50%. Every year, 45,000 acres had gone out of cultivation – half to rough grazing, half to non-agricultural use.

The reason was something we tend to think of as a modern curse – globalisation. Imported grain from North America had sent grain prices in this country tumbling. By 1894, wheat prices were the lowest they had been for 150 years; although they rose slowly thereafter, many British farmers found it impossible to compete with their transatlantic rivals. It was not only arable farmers who suffered. The introduction of refrigerated ships in 1884 meant that meat could be imported from New Zealand and Argentina more cheaply than it could be produced here. By 1914 over half of all Britain's food – and three-quarters of its grain – came from overseas.

By the early twentieth century, Britain was the most industrialised nation in the world, accounting for 35% of the world's trade. But, while the manufacturing sector prospered, the agricultural economy, left to the mercies of the global market and unprotected by state subsidies, collapsed. In no other country was the process so radical: in the United States and Germany, despite their reliance on manufacturing, a third of the population still lived and worked on the land. In Germany, three times more people worked on the land than in England; in France, four times more. At the time, Britain's reliance on food imports was not really a problem – except for those forced off the land, of course – but, when war broke out in 1914 and Britain found itself isolated, its shipping prey to U-boat attacks, the policy brought the country to the brink of starvation and defeat.

By the beginning of the twentieth century, the great manufacturing centres – London, South East Lancashire, Merseyside, the West Midlands, West Yorkshire and Tyneside – accounted for over 40% of the population of England & Wales. In 1909, however, it was estimated that nine out of ten families in the larger conurbations had migrated there from the countryside within three generations. The rural population was not only declining, it was ageing as well. Most children – especially the more ambitious ones – left to work in towns and cities.

Surveying the Condition of England in 1909, Charles Masterman, a Liberal cabinet minister, wrote that

> outside the exuberant life of the cities, standing aloof from it, and with but little share in its prosperity, stands the countryside. Rural England, beyond the radius of certain favoured neighbourhoods, and apart from the specialised population which serves the necessities of the country house, is everywhere hastening to decay.

The economic balance of power had tipped decisively in favour of business and manufacturing. The landed gentry had been displaced by the captains of industry, the farmhand by the factory hand. Arthur Gibbs, who chronicled life in the Cotswolds, thought that the land was 'going back to its original uncultivated state – the whole country seems to be given up to hunting'. Reading the pastoral poetry or the illustrated topographical books so popular in the early twentieth century, the overwhelming sense is one of picturesque decay. One writer, looking back many years later, recalled that the English countryside was 'never more beautiful or quiet – the great uncut hedges, abundant with flowers and small animals, arching over the empty lanes: the beauty of decay'. Life had drained out of the villages, agricultural depression weighed heavily upon the land, traditions survived, if they survived at all, among the old. When they died, a way of life that had evolved over countless generations was lost for ever.

A Somerset vicar, quoted by Charles Masterson in 1909, described how desperate country life had become:

> There is no social life at all. A village which once fed, clothed, policed and regulated itself cannot now dig its own wells or build its own barns. Still less can it act its own dramas, build its own church; or organise its own work and play. It is pathetically helpless in everything … As things go on now, we shall have empty fields, except for a few shepherds and herdsmen, in all the green of England. Nomadic herds will sweep over the country, sowing, shearing, grass-cutting, reaping, and binding with machines: a system which does not make for health, peace, discipline, nobleness of life … England is bleeding at the arteries, and it is her reddest blood which is flowing away.

A year earlier, JJ Hissey had described a drive from Podimore to Muchelney, on the Somerset Levels:

> After a time we dropped down from a breezy eminence to a low-lying, level, drowsy land of deep green meadows watered by sluggish streams, wherein for miles we met only a farmer's waggon crawling slowly along, the meeting of which but served to accentuate the general loneliness of the prospect, a prospect that stretched far away into a mysterious distance of misty blue. Densely populated as England is, gridironed all over with railways, yet there are districts in it the very abode of loneliness, where the centuries come and go with little outward change, and the country looks much the same as it did in the days of the Stuarts, or even before their time. In some parts of the country I even fancy the population is decreasing. Pasturage has taken the place of ploughed fields, as corn-growing is no longer profitable ; so less labour is required, and less labour is to be had if required, for the call of the town has been too strong for country folk to resist ; the sturdy yeoman, too, is fast disappearing, all of which bodes no good for the future of the land.

Many of those who left the land went not to the industrial conurbations but abroad. Between 1900 and 1914 around 5% of the population emigrated. They were overwhelmingly young, and a high percentage were male. Opportunities for ambitious young men – from town or country – were good. If Bath followed the national trend, around 2,500 people would have left the city to live abroad in that fifteen-year period. Although there are no records of how many did emigrate, a somewhat melancholy indicator of how great the exodus was comes from Great War casualty records. No less than 68 Bathonians serving with commonwealth forces were killed – one with the South African Infantry Brigade, three with the New Zealand Expeditionary Force, 15 with the Australian

Opportunities abroad appeared regularly in the Bath Chronicle's Situations Vacant column.

Expeditionary Force and 49 with the Canadian Expeditionary Force. These figures bear out a national trend: Canada was the favourite destination for emigrants, followed by Australia. Some countries took stands at shows and special events to induce people to try something a bit more challenging; at the Bath Horse Show in September 1909, for example, 'everyone interested in colonial farming, ranching and mining' was invited to 'visit the Rhodesia Stand'. It might have seemed a tempting prospect in 1909 – somewhat less so perhaps today.

Comparing the 1911 Census figures for Bath with those for the country as a whole, there are some wide divergences from the norm. For example, the city had the second highest proportion (after Devonport) – 518 per 1000 – of families with less than four people, and the lowest proportion – 115 per 1000 – of families with over six people, while 13% of people in Bath lived in single-person households, compared to only 5.3% for the country as a whole.

Women outnumbered men, making up 59% of Bath's population.[1] However, there were wide variations across the city. In Lansdown Ward, women accounted for 73%, and in Bathwick for 69%. The lowest percentage was in Lyncombe & Widcombe, where women accounted for 55%. Nationally, women made up 52% of the population.[2] Only three out of the 97 towns in England & Wales with a population over 50,000 had a higher percentage of women than Bath – Hastings and Southport (in each of which women made up 59%), and Bournemouth (where they made up 62%). What Bath held in common with these three towns, of course, was its desirability as a place of residence for ladies, especially spinsters and widows, in their declining years. That does not fully account for the high percentage of women, however.

If we turn to the figures for the different age groups, we find that, in the under-15 age group, which accounted for almost a quarter of the city's population, there was very nearly the same

1 All percentages have been rounded to the nearest whole figure.
2 The census report for 1911 explains the slightly higher number of females thus: 'Although more boys are born than girls (the average proportion in England and Wales during the last 75 years was 1,040 boys to 1,000 girls), this initial predominance of the male sex is soon lost, and the relative proportions of the sexes transposed, as the mortality of males is greater than that of females in infancy and in adult life. This natural excess of females is further accentuated by the temporary absence of men abroad serving as soldiers or seamen, etc, and by the great excess of the emigration of males over that of females.'

number of boys as girls (6,001 against 6,132). This was line with the national average. For all other age groups, however, the number of females was much greater than the number of males:

Age Group	Males	Females
15 to 29	5001 (38%)	8080 (62%)
30 to 44	4295 (41%)	6261 (59%)
45 to 59	3151 (39%)	4970 (61%)
60 to 74	1860 (35%)	3399 (65%)
Over 74	442 (28%)	1129 (72%)

The reason for this was the high number of servants in Bath compared to the national average. There were 3,824 female domestic indoor servants working in private houses in the city, plus another 494 in hotels, lodging and eating houses – 9% of the total population. The 1911 Census report summed it up succinctly: 'The highest female proportions of all are met with in certain health resorts ... in which large numbers of domestic servants are employed, and to which the unoccupied classes (preponderantly female) resort for residence.'

This is borne out by another statistic – the percentage of native Bathonians in the city. In 1911, 56% of male residents had been born in Bath, but the figure for women was only 44%. Women of independent means came to Bath to live, and female domestic servants came to the city to work for them. Men, on the other hand, were not only less likely to move to the city; many who grew up in Bath left to find work elsewhere or joined the army or navy.

Despite its reputation as a place where people came to die, however, the average age of the population of Bath was much lower in 1911 than it is today. A third of the population were under 20; half were under 30. Only 13% were 60 or older.

CHAPTER SEVEN

BATH AT WORK

Work is of two kinds: first, altering the position of matter at or near the earth's surface relatively to other such matter; second, telling other people to do so. The first kind is unpleasant and ill paid; the second is pleasant and highly paid.

Bertrand Russell

There were 42,813 people aged 10 or more in Bath at the time of the 1911 Census – 16,866 men and 25,947 women. 80% of the men and 40% of the women were in employment.

For the 10,446 women in work, the range of employment was, with very few exceptions, extremely limited: 3,824 were engaged in domestic service; 1,832 worked in the fashion or clothing trade (as drapers, milliners, seamstresses, hairdressers, etc); 1,265 worked in hotels, lodging houses, inns or eating houses; 1,070 worked in other service industries (cleaning, working in laundries

A postcard published by Lewis Bros, photographic publishers and artists of 1 Seymour Street, Bath, and believed to show their premises. Lewis Bros were the official photographers to the Bath Pageant. As can be seen, division of labour between women and men was very marked – and would have been reflected in rates of pay.

or hospitals, etc); 388 were teachers; 387 were nurses or midwives; 344 worked in the textile industry; 310 worked in the food trade; and 172 were commercial or business clerks. A few companies had started to employ women as typists, but this was still very much the exception. A Remington typewriter could cost over £21 – a vast sum in those days – and most firms still employed male clerks to write their correspondence by hand. There was just one woman doctor.

When we come to the 13,426 men in work, the range of occupations was much wider: 1,1719 worked in building and associated trades (plumbing, painting and decorating, etc); 592 worked in the cabinet making and allied trades; 686 were in general engineering, with a further 216 working as cycle or car makers and mechanics.

1,332 worked in the food trade (as milkmen, butchers, bakers, grocers, etc); 701 were in the clothing trade, with a further 219 in textile manufacture. 276 worked

Top: Women working at Twerton Steam Laundry.
Centre: Young mechanics outside a Bath garage.
Bottom: Porters at the Royal Mineral Water Hospital.

on the railways, 180 were quarrymen, 212 were printers, and 324 were carters or carriers

351 were commercial or business clerks; 249 were merchants, agents or accountants; 274 worked for national government (most of them in the Post Office), and 173 for local government. There were 70 doctors or surgeons, 114 clergymen, 70 barristers or solicitors, 101 law clerks and 124 teachers. 94 worked for the gas, water and electricity services, and 52 for the sanitary services.

647 were messengers, porters or watchmen; 357 were in outdoor service, with only 79 in indoor domestic service. 364 were gardeners 'not in domestic service'. 524 were listed as general labourers, with 73 costermongers and hawkers and 30 newsboys.

Comparing the pattern of employment in Bath with that of the country as a whole, the most striking difference is the low percentage of men engaged in manufacturing (22% against 33%). The percentages in building, cabinet making, printing and transportation, however, were higher than the national average.

Of those who were not in work, 871 men and 333 women were retired and living on pensions, while 256 men and 2,399 women were living on private means. That left 2,313 men and 12,769 women, who were either at school or college, unemployed, sick, or, in the case of the women, working as housewives. Perhaps the most telling figure is those 2,399 women of independent means – amounting to 9% of all women aged 10 or over in the city.

Mrs Layard's gardener at East Hayes House, Upper East Hayes.

For those in work, conditions were very different to those today. A typical working week was 60 hours – eleven hours a day plus a half day on Saturday. The legal maximum in shops – but only where young persons were employed on the premises – was 74 hours including meal times. In 1911, carters in London went on strike to secure a maximum working week of 75 hours. Servants' hours could be longer still. Employment legislation was in its infancy. Mandatory compensation for employees injured at work had only been introduced across the board as recently as 1906, and employers could dismiss workers more or less at will. Except in trades where there were skill shortages, there was always someone available to take the place of a worker whose attendance record was less than exemplary, one prepared to stand up for his or her rights or one who was a bit slow. Throughout the Edwardian era, the average unemployment rate was 4.5%, but in 1908-09 it rose to around 8%.

The slump of 1908-09 (they didn't have the phrase 'credit crunch' in those days) hit Bath, with its high percentage of building workers, especially hard. In March 1909, Bath Stone Firms' half-yearly report acknowledged that, 'in common with all businesses dependent on the building trade, the company has again suffered from reduced sales and keen competition … Comparatively few building contracts have been let and speculative building has been almost at a standstill.' In October 1909 the *Bath Chronicle* reported 'fears that in the approaching winter distress through unemployment in Bath may be more accentuated in the building trade. Business is slack. In one important local industry, many hands are on three-quarters time.' Other businesses were affected as well. In April 1909, Evans & Owen, who had a large department store fronting onto Bartlett Street, St Andrew's Terrace and Alfred Street, reported a 'considerable drop in profit' – £5,930 against £7,003 for the same period the previous year – 'due to the general depression in trade in the United Kingdom'.

In the days before unemployment benefit, being laid off was a very different proposition to what it is today. In 1905, the Conservative government had brought in an Unemployed Workmen Act, which required local councils to set up committees to help unemployed men find work. Bureaus – an early form of employment exchange – were set up in many towns and cities, including Bath, but they achieved only limited success. When recession hit the British economy in 1907 and deepened over the next two years, it was clear that something more was needed.

C. WIBLEY,
Builder & General Contractor,
STEAM SAWING
Planing, Moulding and Joinery Works and
Retail Timber Yard,
10 & 39, JAMES STREET, WEST,
BATH.
Telegrams—WIBLEY, BUILDER, BATH.　　Telephone No. 37.

Estimates Furnished for Every Description of New Buildings,
Alterations and Repairs, also Railway Work.
Painting, Decorating, Glazing, Modern Sanitary Work, Drainage,
Plumbing and all Branches of the Building Trade.
Funerals Economically Furnished.
Cheapest House in Bath for Plate Glass Windows and Shop Fronts.
GROUND MILL MORTAR FOR SALE ⎫ FRESH DAILY
ALSO WHITE SAWDUST　　　　　⎭
Residence—11, NORFOLK BUILDINGS.

*Wibley's of James Street West was one of
over 70 building firms listed in the 1909 Bath
Postal Directory; another — seen below — was
JW & EJ Fry's of 3 Dover Terrace on the
London Road, later demolished as part of the
redevelopment of Snow Hill.*

In 1909, WH Beveridge (remembered today as the author of the 1942 Beveridge Report) wrote a book in which he argued that the unemployed were actually the 'casually employed'. It was largely due to his influence that the Liberal government set up a national network of labour exchanges and a National Insurance scheme a year later.

Casual work was a soul-destroying business for most of those forced to resort to it. In the absence of permanent employment, many men took whatever work they could to try to make ends meet. Often they answered an advertisement for a boy's place – at a substantially lower wage – rather than not work at all. Unscrupulous employers took advantage of this, advertising for boys when they wanted men, to keep labour costs down. Many firms hired men by the day, to tide them over busy periods, paying no more than 3/- or 3/6 for a ten or eleven hour shift. Things got so bad in the winter of 1908-09, however, that the council decided to take urgent action.

The first week of 1909 brought a particularly cold snap, with a heavy fall of snow. The council responded

Chivers' Carpet Soap Factory in Albany Road, Twerton, and the company's stand at the 1907-8 Grocers' Exhibition in the Royal Agricultural Hall.

by hiring unemployed men to clear the streets, with the result that the centre of the city was clear within a few hours, at a cost of £171.12.6. The Board of Guardians, who ran the Workhouse, however, reported that 'many unemployed were offered work but refused to take a shovel when it was placed into their hands'.

On 18 February, it was reported that 453 men and boys – a record number – were registered as unemployed in the city. The council said that they would like to set them to work building a public bowling green, but no suitable site was available. A couple of weeks later, the Mayor wrote a letter to the citizens of Bath appealing for them to come forward with offers of work. He was very sorry, he said, that there had been such an increase in the number of unemployed workmen. 'Many are superior men,' he continued, 'but their resources are practically exhausted and much suffering and actual want of food exists. The Corporation have found much work for labourers, etc, but it is impossible to provide for the large number of skilled men now on the books.'

Bath Cabinet Makers' Company factory in Bellott's Road, Twerton.

Foremost among Bath's companies was Stothert & Pitt's. The extension of 1905 shows up clearly with its lighter stone and gives an idea how wonderful Newark Works would look if it were cleaned. To the right is Beyer's Corset Factory and Camden Flour Mills, while goods wagons can be seen in the Great Western goods yard. Victor Rosenburg recalls that 'Stothert & Pitt was the main industrial employer ... Its foundry employees worked from 6am to 6pm. There was no hooter, but a large bell was tolled when work was due to begin and end.' The terraced houses nearest the camera, in Magdalen and Park Avenues, were newly built in 1909.

91

When the council Unemployment Committee met on 5 March, the number of unemployed had risen to 537 – an increase of 84 in two weeks. Several initiatives were suggested – someone said that people should start employing male rather than female servants, someone else suggested that household refuse could be collected more than once a week, while a painter suggested that the Guildhall ceilings could do with a bit of attention. In the end a motion 'to attempt to raise funds' was passed with only one vote against (from Councillor Evans) and it was decided to hold a public meeting.

The meeting took place in the Guildhall on the afternoon of 15 March, with the Mayor in the chair:

We are met [he began] in consequence of what is a very serious state of things in the condition of the labour market in Bath. A few weeks ago I was much struck, in looking over the lists of unemployed, to notice the great change which has taken place. Not only has the number largely increased, but the character of the men registering is exceedingly different from previous years. They are men who have been almost constantly employed – many of them members of friendly societies and personally known to be men thoroughly deserving. After visiting the office of Mr Sheppy, the enquiry agent of the Voluntary Unemployed Committee, I was so convinced of the need for immediate action, that I inserted a letter in the papers, asking that persons should endeavour to find work for men out of employment. The response to that letter was considerable and very encouraging.

I do not ask the citizens of Bath to do anything in the way of charity. Unemployed men are opposed to that too. The working men of this city recognised very early in the winter that there would be a lot of unemployment, and made a voluntary arrangement with their employers, by which they sacrificed a

Situations Vacant.

Established 55 Years.
Under Royal, Noble and Distinguished Patronage.
MRS. WALDRON,
Families' and Servants' Registry and Governesses Institute.
Respectable Servants Always Required.
All Letters Requiring a Reply should Contain Stamped Envelope.
14, YORK STREET, BATH 97—TO
Hours of Business—10.30 a.m. till 6.30 p.m.

WANTED, APPRENTICE to the Dressmaking. Small Wage given from commencement.—Miss Manning, 4, Walcot Terrace, Bath. 77—9.23

PROVISION TRADE.—YOUTH, just left school. Required, to Help in Office and Learn the Business.—Huntley, 1, Milsom Street. 61

WANTED, Married Couple as CARETAKERS for Pageant House.—Apply in first instance by letter, W. Jeffery, 2, Northumberland Buildings. 75

A Situations Vacant column from January 1909 with an advertisement for caretakers for Pageant House.

quarter of a day every day, in order to provide work for those out of employment. The result has been that where employers previously employed nine men, they are able to employ ten. But the number of unemployed has increased.

So far almost £50 had been donated to the appeal, as a result of which 18 men have been put on to work – £12 was paid to them in the first week. All money provided will be paid for actual work done. There is a great deal of useful work in Bath that needs to be done but which doesn't come within the scope of the Corporation.

It was suggested that roads not hitherto adopted by the council and in a bad state of repair, such as Beckhampton Road, could be put in order, and Englishcombe Lane widened. The seats and shelter in Henrietta Park could be painted. Tennis courts and bowling greens could be laid out. Someone suggested that bad housing could be improved, at which someone else shouted out – to considerable applause – that bad houses should be bought up and pulled down. Somewhat more ambitiously, a Mr Mead suggested buying land and building a thousand cottages for the working classes.

Two weeks later the Surveying Committee, with the Mayor once again in the chair, met to determine how the money should be spent. The road from the Workhouse to Bloomfield Road would be improved, the footpath on the Upper Bristol Road west of Marlborough Lane (which would see increased traffic during Pageant Week) would be widened, and the footpath between Elm Place and Bloomfield Park would be lowered. This last suggestion was opposed by Councillor Strange, who argued that it would 'lose the country view' and might be a temptation to build houses on the land. Furthermore, the householders opposite were opposed to the plan. Councillor Hatt said that the footpath was only 200 yards long and the work should go ahead. It was decided there should be a site visit before a decision was taken.

On 8 April, the Mayor thanked those who had contributed to the appeal, which had now raised £175. He was also happy to announce that the number of unemployed was down to 400. In June, the Surveying Committee announced that 'unemployment expenditure' had ceased for the time being, and that many men were now employed on the Pageant. They were considering job creation schemes for the coming winter, however, including increasing the accommodation at the Technical College, rebuilding Sydney College, building tennis courts and bowling greens in Sydney

Gardens, putting up new houses in Dolemeads and building an abattoir on the outskirts of the city.

It was this last suggestion that proved most controversial. Councillor Young pointed out that such a facility would cost at least £20,000, Alderman Taylor said the effect on the rates would be unacceptable, while Alderman Peacock said that the way butchers slaughtered their animals was far better than at any abattoir unless there were inspectors working there all the time.

When the Unemployed Committee met at the Guildhall on 29 October, there were 203 registered unemployed, against only 134 at the same time the previous year. It was pointed out, though, that a large number of men had been working for the council the previous year. In a bizarre twist of logic, it was claimed that this showed conditions were really no worse than they had been a year earlier.

Except that 69 more men were out of work.

The enquiry bureau came under attack from Mr Harvey, who complained that job seekers who obtained casual work as sandwich-board men from the bureau were being paid 1/6 a day, while the firm who employed them received 3/- for the contract on each board. He said that anyone who offered a man work for 1/6 a day ought himself to be starving. He also drew attention to the case of Martin Warren, who was refused work by Mr Sheppy, the enquiry agent at the bureau, and whose name was struck off the books because he would not take a particular job when it was offered to him. He proposed a resolution that Mr Sheppy's services should be dispensed with.

Called to account for his actions, Mr Sheppy explained that 'Warren came to my office and asked for work. The only work available was road work or pick-and-shovel work and I told him so. He replied, "That is no use to me", and walked out of the office. I struck his name off the books not because he refused the work that was offered him but because he was not eligible for the work that was in hand.' The proposal recommending that Mr Sheppy's services should be dispensed with was heavily defeated.

As autumn turned into winter, the number of men roaming the streets looking for work rose dramatically. As in the previous winter, the sector that was hardest hit was the building trade. With construction virtually at a standstill, the only major project was the controversial redevelopment of Bath Street, due to start in late November. On the day demolition was due to start, a large group of men turned up in Bath Street, only to be told there was no work to be had. They then headed for the Guildhall 'in the hope of persuading the Corporation of finding them some work' and asked to see the Mayor. He was not available and they had to make do with Mr Sheppy, who told them the Committee sympathised with their plight and would see what could be done. The lack of jobs at Bath Street seems another indication that the company – along with the council – was not serious about the project, and were merely going through the motions, preparatory to the deadlock over No 10 being disclosed and work coming to a standstill. But, just as every cloud has a silver lining, so every rose has a thorn. The preservationists may have been delighted at the lack of progress and the ultimate abandonment of the scheme; the men who had banked on it providing them with a steady income in the run up to Christmas and well into the new year must have viewed Bath Street's salvation with rather different emotions.

The women's and men's day wards at the Royal Mineral Water Hospital.

CHAPTER EIGHT

COUNTING THE COST

A 1911 survey divided the population of Great Britain & Ireland into three groups, each of whom earned a third of the national income:

The Upper and Upper-Middle Classes
Households with an income of over £700 per annum. Total: 1.4 million people (3.1% of the population).

The Middle Classes
Households with an income of between £160 and £700 per annum. Total: 4.1 million people (9.2% of the population).

The Working Classes
Households with an income of less than £160 per annum. Total: 39 million people (87.6% of the population).

Stark though these statistics are, to appreciate the full scale of the inequality that existed in Edwardian England we need to turn to commentators like the industrialist and social reformer, Benjamin Seebohm Rowntree. 'That in this land of abounding wealth,' he wrote in 1901, 'during a time of perhaps unexampled prosperity, probably more than one-fourth of the population are living in poverty, is a fact which may well cause great searchings of heart.' Three years later, Montagu Crackanthorpe, KC, another social reformer, echoed his words:

So wide and so deep is the gulf which at this hour separates the rich from the poor ... that many ... have come to look on poverty more as a curiosity than as a trouble. When some half-clad, emaciated, foot-weary dosser from the East End slinks along the street curb amid the palaces of the West End, they instinctively avert their eyes, or else turn them on him as if he were a visitant from another planet ... It is no exaggeration to say that the worship of wealth in England has now reached a point beyond anything that has gone before. To have accumulated it insures for a man the highest consideration and esteem. To be allied to money, to bring it in by marriage or association, is to be 'on the make'.

More recently, Peter Laslett, Reader in Politics and the History of Social Structure at Cambridge University, concluded in 1961 that 'the distribution of incomes in Edwardian England was just about as unequal as it has ever been anywhere'.

It became more unequal as the decade wore on – with prices rising but wages remaining the same. In 1914, the Board of Trade estimated that real wages had fallen, on average, by 13% between 1906 and 1913, while the *Yearbook of Social Progress* for 1913-14 estimated that the pound of 1896 had come to be worth 18/5 by 1900 and 16/3 by 1912 – 'figures which are sufficiently serious to account for some of the prevailing unrest'. Much of the blame for inflation was put down to the influx of gold into the world's economic system from South African mines, but, whatever the reason, things got progressively worse for the majority of the population – and they were pretty bad to start with. 1909, with unemployment at record levels, must have been for many one of the worst years of all.

To understand the cost of living a century ago – given the massive inflation that has occurred since – it helps to give present-day equivalents for wages and prices. This is not as straightforward as it may seem. There are several ways of measuring relative worth: in the UK, the principal ones are the Retail Prices Index and the Average Earnings Index. Using the Retail Prices Index, £1 in 1909 was worth £74.70 in 2007; using the Average Earnings Index, £1 from 1909 was worth £393.67 in 2007 – an enormous discrepancy which highlights how significantly average wages have risen in the last hundred years. To indicate purchasing power, however, I have opted to use the Retail Prices Index as a standard multiplier, which will at least give an idea of how affordable things were for average wage earners in 1909. Wages and prices cited from now on will, therefore, be accompanied by the approximate present-day equivalent in brackets

In employment terms, the most striking differences between 1909 and 2009 are the enormous disparity between the wages of white and blue collar workers back then, and the relative wages of men and women. The average income of a male salaried worker was £340 per annum (£25,500 today), while the average income of a male industrial worker was £75 (£5,625 today); a female industrial worker received, on average, only £32 (£2,400 today). A report in 1901 cited an upholstery firm where a female worker received 18/6 a week for doing the same work as a man who received £2-2-0 a

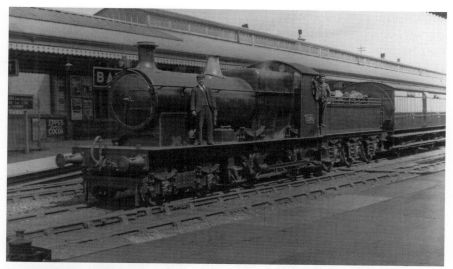

Above: A train on one of the centre roads at Bath GWR station. An engine driver could earn up to £110 a year, a fireman up to £75. Left: A photograph by Herbert Foster, a Bath photographer, of a lad working on the Great Western Railway. The starting salary for a job like this would have been around £20 a year.

week. Such inequality was by no means untypical.

At the time of the 1911 census, 77.7% of working men earned less than £100 a year. For women the percentage was much higher: only 1.3% of working women earned over £100 a year. A third of the population – 14.7 million people – earned £50 per annum (£3,750) or less.

A survey of typical wage rates in different trades and professions in 1909 gives a clearer idea of how much workers in these sectors fared. A post office superintendent or police chief inspector could earn £300 (£22,500), while a teacher could earn up to £200 (£15,000) and a bank clerk up to £145 (£10,875). A factory foreman, however – a man at the top of his profession – would be lucky to receive more than £120 (£9,000); a railway engine driver could expect to earn £110 (£8,250). In the building and allied trades, annual earnings averaged between £90 and £100 (£6,750-£7,500). A cabinet maker

99

took home around £85 (£6,375) a year, while a railway clerk or tram driver took home £80 (£6,000). Bakers, boot and shoe workers, tram conductors and locomotive firemen received between £70 and £75 (£5,250-5,625) a year.

These figures are all for men with good employment records and several years experience; starting salaries were much lower. Postmen, for example, who could earn up to £70 (£5,250) a year

School photographs from Twerton and Combe Down. While male teachers could earn up to £200 a year, top salaries for their female counterparts were around £130. In addition, male teachers could marry and have families; female teachers had to resign if they married.

started at a mere £39 (£2,925). Office boys generally started on £20 (£1,500) a year or less. Unskilled labourers earned between £40 and £60 (£3,000-4,500) a year. Agricultural labourers earned even less. The average wage for an agricultural labourer in the West of England was 13/8 a week – equivalent to £35 10s (£2,662.50) a year, although they were often laid off at quiet periods.

The most a women could hope to earn was around £130 (£9,750) a year as a schoolteacher, although this would only be after several years experience – something many female teachers failed to achieve, as they had to resign if they got married. Pupil-teachers in elementary schools had four years training from the age of 14. They worked five and a half days a week for 6/- (£22.50), attending lessons at secondary school on their half day off. If they passed the examinations at the end of that time, their starting salary would be £70 (£5,250) a year. Apart from that, top rates for female clerk-typists were around £75 (£5,625); nurses could earn up to £50 (£3,750), telephonists up to £45 (£3,375) and textile factory hands up to £40 (£3,000). Female shop assistants generally earned only around £30-35 (£2,250-2,625), while waitresses could earn as little as £13 (£975).

Another major difference between 1909 and 2009 is the number of people in domestic service. In 1909 it was the biggest single occupation, employing 2.6 million people, 2.1 million of them women. In a world without labour-saving devices – for washing, cooking, cleaning, heating and countless other domestic chores – servants were essential. For working-class housewives, running a home was a full-time job; this was partly due to the incessant trial of having to make ends meet against overwhelming odds, but it was also because everything had to be done by hand. Middle and upper class families not only lived in larger houses but also regarded many more things as indispensable to their well-being. Running their households would have been impossible without paid labour. Things were changing in the Edwardian era – and changing fast – but it would be a long time before the middle-class household without at least one live-in servant was the norm.

At the top end of the market – in mansions on Weston Road or Bathwick Hill, for example – a butler could earn £100 (£7,500) a year, a cook-housekeeper £80 (£6,000), and a governess £75 (£5,625), with living accommodation and food provided. Such salaries were the exception, however. In a house in one of Bath's Georgian terraces, with around five servants, a manservant, earning around £50 (£3,750) would take the place of the butler,

Staff at the Royal Mineral Water Hospital.

while the cook would earn around £30 (£2,250). The kitchen maid would earn around £16 (£1,200), the first housemaid around £20 (£1,500) and the second housemaid around £16 (£1,200).

The inevitable question is 'how far did the money go?' The answer, as far as most people were concerned, is 'not very far'. In 1899, it was estimated that a family of two adults

Female shop assistants generally earned less than £35 a year.

Let or Sold.

TO be LET or SOLD, 11, HAMPTON VIEW, Claremont, with immediate possession.—Apply 3, Frankley Buildings, Camden Road. 1C0—6-13

TO BE SOLD OR LET.

TOP OF BATHWICK HILL, in CLAVERTON PARISH.

Near Golf Club Links, Hampton Down.

NEWLY-BUILT SEMI-DETACHED HOUSE.

Rooms, large Entrance Hall, Bathroom, Hot Water System, Linen Cupboard, Usual Offices & Long Garden.

Drains connected to City Sewers.

With or without Ground Rent.

Particulars from principal House Agents, or

ERWOOD & MORRIS,

Builders, Railway Place. 370

TO be Let, Unfurnished, centre of the City, Good Part, HOUSE, containing 2 Sitting Rooms, 4 Bedrooms, Rent £25-£28, according to term. — Apply, Powells, Bath. 636—6-13

OVERLOOKING the Victoria Park. — To be Let, Unfurnished, an excellent and up-to-date GENTLEMAN'S RESIDENCE in good repair, containing ; 4 Reception Rooms, 8 Bedrooms. Bath (h. and c.), Offices, Dinner Lift, Garden. Immediate possession. Rent £120 or offer.—Apply Powells, Bath. 636—6-13

CIRCUS.—To be Let or Sold, an excellent up-to-date RESIDENCE in excellent repair, containing : 5 Reception Rooms, 8 Bedrooms, Bath (h. & c.). Electric Light, etc. Open to offer.—Apply Powells, Bath. 636—6-13

TO LET, Good STABLES and COACH-HOUSE at back of Pulteney Street. Rent £10 per Annum. Apply Powell and Powell, Bath. 100—T.C.

PERRYMEAD.—To be SOLD, Pleasantly-Situated RESIDENCE, containing Eight Rooms and Offices. Garden. Immediate Possession. Free of Ground-Rent. At the Small Price of £450. — Apply Powell and Powell, Estate Agents, Bath. 669—3-10

37 WELLS ROAD.—7 Rooms, Kitchen and Scullery, Washhouse, Coalhouse, Arches, Gardens. £21 Yearly, Exclusive.—Apply, 48, Wells Road. 252—23 6

TO be LET, a FULLY-LICENSED, HOME-BREWED HOUSE doing an excellent trade, going by Valuation only. Early possession may be arranged.—Apply Henry Mortimer, Brewers' and Hotel Valuer, Midland Depositories, Bath (Telephone No. 143). 526—23-6

TO LET, in rear of 21, Broad Street. — TWO good LIGHT FLOORS, about 45 feet by 24 feet, suitable for Warehousing ; Athletic Club, &c —G. H. Tucker, 4, Prince's Buildings. 440 T.C.

TO LET. — 2, BURLINGTON STREET. This Convenient House, newly decorated, Twelve Rooms, Kitchen, &c., Bath and Lavatory, h. and c., hot cupboard, &c. Rent £40.—Apply to G. H. Tucker, 4, Prince's Buildings, or the principal agents. 441—T.C.

22. — 21, WELLS ROAD, 1, WARWICK PLACE. Covered Entrance. Stable. Suit Tradesman. Close Station. Trams pass. — Keys 76, Hampton Park, Bristol. 343—2-N6

To Let

FORTT, HATT & BILLINGS,
HOUSE AGENTS AND AUCTIONEERS.

ROYAL CRESCENT.

TO BE LET FURNISHED for the Season.—A well Arranged and comfortably Furnished Residence, replete with every modern convenience, including Electric Light and Lift.—Rent and further Particulars of the Sole Agents. FORTT, HATT, and BILLINGS, 3, Burton Street, Bath.

SION HILL.

TO BE LET.—A pleasantly situated Residence with excellent views ; 3 Reception-rooms, 5 Bedrooms, Kitchen and usual Offices. Good Garden in rear. Rent Furnished, 2½ Guineas a week ; or Unfurnished. £35 per annum.—Keys of Sole Agents FORTT, HATT and BILLINGS, 3, Burton Street, Bath.

RUSSELL STREET.

TO BE LET UNFURNISHED, one of the best of these Houses, well appointed and arranged, with 3 Reception-rooms, 7 Bedrooms, Bathroom, Kitchen, Housekeeper's-room, and usual Offices. Modern conveniences. Rent £65.—Orders to View of the Agents, FORTT, HATT and BILLINGS, 3, Burton Street, Bath. 667

14 TRIM STREET.—8 Rooms. Rent £16.—Apply Mr. Shore, shop adjoining. 655—6-20

TO LET, Small VILLA, 105, Newbridge Road, Bath. Furnished and Attendance.—Apply 15, Bladud Buildings, Bath. 638

TO LET, 8, MILES'S BUILDINGS. Central. Eight Rooms. Good Repair. Suit Professional Gentleman.—Apply 7, Percy Place, Grosvenor. 633

UNFURNISHED FLAT, Two Good Newly Decorated Rooms, every Convenience (no attendance). Very Cheap Rent to one Lady.—B 32, Journal Office, Bath. 610—30-6

22 UPPER CAMDEN PLACE.—Seven Rooms (Large) Bathroom, Gardens, Beautiful View. Sanitary Certificate. — Keys at Mellvish's, Grocer, Opposite. 611—30-6

TO be LET, Well - Furnished HOUSE. Three Reception-Rooms, Five Bedrooms, Bathroom, Electric Light. Every Convenience. £2 12s. 6d. per week.—B 27, Journal Office. 396—90-13

£30. — UPPER WESTON, BATH. BELTON HOUSE (Detached). Private, Pleasant, High, Dry, Sloping Lawn. Gardens. Stable, Coach-Motor House.—76, Hampton Park, Bristol. 343—2-N6

*Houses, flats and rooms to let and
for sale in Bath in 1909.*

and three children needed 21/- (£78.75) a week to survive. Unfortunately, this was more than the average wage for male workers, who earned just under a pound a week – in towns that is; in the countryside, the average wage was considerably less – just 15/-.

In 1903, Seebohm Rowntree did the sums again and came up with a similar figure – the minimum wage which could support a family of five was £57 per annum (£4,275 today). This was an absolute minimum, however. 'A family living upon the scale allowed for in this estimate,' he warned,

> must never spend a penny on railway fare or omnibus. They must never go into the country unless they walk. They must never purchase a halfpenny newspaper or spend a penny to buy a ticket for a popular concert. They must write no letters to absent children, for they cannot afford to pay the postage. They must never contribute anything to their church or chapel, or give any help to a neighbour which costs them money. They cannot save, nor can they join sick club or trade union, because they cannot pay the necessary subscriptions. Their children must have no pocket money for dolls, marbles, or sweets. The father must smoke no tobacco, and must drink no beer.

Around a quarter of the population had a standard of living similar to or worse than that outlined by Rowntree. Recent government figures estimate the present-day poverty line as £299 a week (£15,548 pa) for a couple with two children. In relative terms that is over three and a half times the figure Rowntree came up with in 1903. That is a measure of how far we have come in the last 100 years.

In 1909, 80% of people rented living accommodation from a private landlord, with only 10% owning their own home.[1] At the bottom end of the scale a room in an inner-city slum tenement could be had for as little as 6/- a month (equivalent to £22.50 today), while a 4 bedroom house in a leafy suburb cost around £2 a month (equivalent to £150 today).

The biggest item on many people's agenda was food. The list opposite gives a rough idea of prices – all drawn from specific examples – for selected staples, together with a few

---

1 To put this in perspective, in England in 2003, 71% of homes were owner-occupied, 10% were privately rented and 19% belonged to housing associations or local authorities.

luxury items. More expensive and, in some cases, cheaper versions were also available. Prices of items like bread and potatoes also fluctuated widely because of good or bad harvests.

While some prices are comparable with those of today, there are some surprises. Perrier and other bottled waters, which seem a very modern affectation, were popular a hundred years ago – among those who could afford them. That should not be too surprising, given the threat of disease from polluted water supplies. It is also interesting to note that items like tomato ketchup and baked beans were still luxury items.

Cost of Typical Items of Food and Drink

		2009 equivalent (approx)
Loaf of bread	5d	£1.56
Tea (lb)	1/-	£3.75
Coffee (lb)	10d	£3.13
Butter (lb)	1/1	£4.06
Margarine (lb)	7d	£2.19
Lard (lb)	5d	£1.56
Cheese (lb)	10d	£3.13
Eggs (six)	7d	£2.19
Beef/Mutton (lb)	10d	£3.13
Back bacon (lb)	8d	£2.50
Sliced ham (lb)	2/4	£8.75
Potatoes (7 lb)	4½d	£1.41
Sugar (lb)	2d	63p
Baked beans (tin)	9d	£2.81
Tomato ketchup	9½d	£2.97
Rice (3 lb)	6d	£1.88
Jam	6½d	£2.94
Milk (pint)	1½d	47p
Perrier water (bottle)	5½d	£1.72

Most people's choice of food was extremely limited. This lack of choice ran through their lives. Take, for example, the guidelines on the next page, published in the early 1900s, on how to furnish a one-up/one-down house for twelve guineas. They give an idea of what the quality of life was for many people. There was no electricity or modern conveniences, of course. But it is not just that. This was life on the breadline – no frills, no luxuries, just the bare necessities.

Furnishing a One-up/One-down House for Twelve Guineas

		2009 equivalent (approx)
Leather sofa	£1-6-0	£97.50
Hardwood armchair	9/6	£35.63
Hardwood rocking chair	9/6	£35.63
Four kitchen chairs	15/6	£58.13
Table	10/6	£39.38
3½ x 4 yard oilcloth	14/-	£52.50
Cloth hearth rug	4/9	£17.81
Kitchen fender	6/6	£24.38
Kitchen fire-irons	4/6	£16.88
Ashpan	2/11	£10.94
Brass bedstead	£1-12-6	£121.88
Mattress	14/6	£54.38
Bed bolster & pillows	16/6	£61.88
Dressing table	£1-15-0	£131.25
Washstand	£1-9-0	£108.75
Two cane seat chairs	7/-	£26,25
2½ x 4 yds oilcloth	10/-	£37.50
Two bedside rugs	3/10	£14.38
TOTAL	£12-12-0	£847.55

Apart from food and furniture the other main item of expenditure for the working classes was clothes. Nothing exemplified the gulf between rich and poor in Edwardian England more than their dress. Working-class families relied on hand-me-downs and many a Sunday-best suit made a weekly trip to the pawnbroker's.

A working man could get a pair of boots for around 5/- (£18.75), a shirt for 2/- (£7.50) and a second-hand coat for around 3/6 (£13.13). Women's boots cost around 3/- (£11.25) while shawls and hats cost 1/- (£3.75) each.

Many a Sunday-best suit made a weekly trip to the pawnbroker's.

At the other end of the scale advertisements appeared in society magazines for 'petticoats at all prices up to £50 each' (£3,750) or 'evening confections at £200' (£15,000).

To put these figures in some sort of context, here are three budgets, drawn from contemporary sources, showing just how a typical upper-middle family and two working class families lived.

Annual Budget of an Upper-Middle Class Family: husband, wife, three teenage daughters, two grown-up working sons

		2009 equivalent (approx)
Income	£2,000	£150,000
Rent, rates, taxes	£300	£22,500
Boy's allowances (£50 each)	£100	£7,500
Governess & classes for girls	£100	£7,500
Husband & wife's allowance	£200	£15,000
Wine	£50	£3,750
Coal and light	£45	£3.375
Wages: Manservant	£50	£3,750
Cook	£30	£2,250
Kitchen maid	£16	£1,200
First housemaid	£20	£1,500
Second housemaid	£16	£1,200
Sewing Maid	£25	£1,875
Washing @ £2 a week	£104	£7,800
House bills (food, etc)	£437	£32,775
Garden & stable expenses inc. wages of two men, one boy & upkeep of two cobs	£300	£22,500
TOTAL	£1,793	£131,103

Leaving £207 (£15,525) for doctor's bills, holidays, etc.

A middle-class home.

*Eight-weekly Budget of York Lorry Driver earning £1 a week
Recorded by Seebohm Rowntree in 1903*

		2009 equivalent (approx)
Income		
Wage	£8	£600
Overtime	4/6	£16.88
Wife's earnings: cleaning	10/-	£37.50
Total	£8-14-6	£654.38
Expenditure		
Food	£3-19-6	£298.13
Rent & rates	£1-4-0	£90
Coal & wood	£1-1-3	£79.69
Oil, matches & candles	2/8	£10
Soap, etc	1/5½	£5.47
Sundries	2/3½	£8.60
Sick Club	8/3	£30.94
Burial Insurance	6/5	£24.06
Clothes	8/9½	£36.72
Boots	5/10½	£22.01
Doctor's bill	9/9	£36.56
Repayment of debt	5/-	£18.75
Total	£8-14-9	£660.93

*Weekly budget of printer's labourer, married with six children
Recorded by Maud Pember Reeves in 1913*

		2009 equivalent (approx)
Average wage	24/-	£89
Rent	8/-	£30
Burial insurance	1/8	£6.25
Boot club	1/-	£3.75
Soap, soda, blue	4½d	£1.40
Wood	3d	£1
Gas	8d	£2.50
Coal	1/-	£3.75
Food	7/0½	£26.40

The most striking item in the two working-class budgets is burial insurance. A century ago, a pauper's funeral – arranged by the local workhouse – was the ultimate degradation, to be avoided at all costs. Yet one in five people ended up in a pauper's grave and for many it was something that could be avoided only by membership

The fleet of funeral carriages owned by Small & Son's — undertakers, cabinet makers and timber merchants — on Midland Bridge Road. Sainsbury's now occupies this site.

of a funeral club. Even if doctors could not be called in or medicines bought when members of the family were ill, this was one area where economies were unthinkable.

The cheapest funerals cost £5 for an adult and £2 for a child. At a time of high infant mortality – one in six babies died in their first year – failure to join a funeral club could create a burden of debt that would last for years. Maud Pember Reeves recorded the financial impact of an infant's death on one working-class family: £1.12.0 for the funeral, 1/3 for a death certificate, 2/- for gravediggers, 2/- for hearse attendants, 2/- for a woman to lay the infant out, 1/- for the insurance agent, 6d for flowers, 1/- for a black tie for the father. The child was buried in a common grave with three others. The child's illness had cost the family 10/-, most of which had been spent on special food. The parents had insured her for 2d a week and received £2. The family lived on reduced rations for two weeks in order to get straight again. The father's wage was 24/- a week, every penny of which he gave to his wife.

In dealing with poverty, we are getting ahead of ourselves. Poverty in Edwardian England merits – and gets – a chapter to itself. For the time being, we will leave the final word to the poet John Davidson, who was well-qualified to write about the struggle to make ends meet. Despite critical acclaim, he made little money from his poetry. At 6.30pm on 27 March 1909, after years of financial worries, battling against ill-health and depression, he left his house in Penzance and disappeared. His body was discovered by fishermen six months later. This is taken from his most famous poem, 'Thirty Bob a Week':

> *I couldn't touch a stop and turn a screw,*
> *And set the blooming world a-work for me,*
> *Like such as cut their teeth – I hope, like you –*
> *On the handle of a skeleton gold key;*
> *I cut mine on a leek, which I eat it every week:*
> *I'm a clerk at thirty bob as you can see.*
>
> *But I don't allow it's luck and all a toss;*
> *There's no such thing as being starred and crossed;*
> *It's just the power of some to be a boss,*
> *And the bally power of others to be bossed:*
> *I face the music, sir; you bet I ain't a cur;*
> *Strike me lucky if I don't believe I'm lost! ...*
>
> *But the difficultest go to understand,*
> *And the difficultest job a man can do,*
> *Is to come it brave and meek with thirty bob a week,*
> *And feel that that's the proper thing for you.*
>
> *It's a naked child against a hungry wolf;*
> *It's playing bowls upon a splitting wreck;*
> *It's walking on a string across a gulf*
> *With millstones fore-and-aft about your neck;*
> *But the thing is daily done by many and many a one;*
> *And we fall, face forward, fighting, on the deck.*

CHAPTER NINE

ALL A BLOOMIN' SHAME

'Few people seem to realise how nearly the lives of the poor reach the limits of human endurance'

Reginald Bray, *The Town Child*, 1907

We can imagine what the lives of Bath's upper and middle classes were like a century ago from the houses they lived in, many of which are still standing. With the poor, it is a different story. To get some idea, walk up Broad Street and take a right turn into Broad Street Place. This was originally known as Gracious Court, after its eighteenth-century builder, Gracious Stride. In the mid-nineteenth century, the council renamed several of the more notorious courts and alleyways around the city in a futile attempt to improve their image – hence Gracious Court's change of name. Today, shaded by trees, with the YMCA on one side and a row of specialist shops on the other, it's an oasis in the heart of the city; a century ago, though, few people would have ventured down there if they didn't have to.

Standing in the little square, turn to look back towards Broad Street and at the traces of walls and fireplaces on the wall of the building to the right of the passageway. These are the remains of one of Bath's many rows of back-to-backs. It stretched the length of the court, ending at the top of the steps down to Walcot Street. There was a similar row on the other side. Some of the rooms were no more than six to eight feet square; some of them housed entire families. Many would have been in a parlous condition; as late as the 1920s the *Bath Chronicle* featured a family who lived in a single room here with no roof – just a canopy to keep out the worst of the winter weather. The only toilets were a row of a privies to the right of the steps. Water came from a communal pump.

Broad Street Place was not some aberration, some unaccountable blot on the city's otherwise exemplary housing stock. Back-to-backs are now so rare that the National Trust has preserved a court of them in Birmingham. A century ago it was a different story. Walk down the steps to Walcot Street and look over at the cattle market car park. Behind a row of shops, demolished in the 1960s, was a maze of little courts – worse, if anything, than Broad Street Place: tiny, insanitary hovels, with water running down the walls, rats running through the yards, and, when it flooded, the river running through the houses.

For flooding, though, it was Dolemeads that took the palm. This working-class estate, thrown up in the early nineteenth century on a flood plain, was notorious. It would flood at least once or twice a year; when there were serious inundations, the residents had to be rescued from the upper floors of their houses by boat or by ladders stretched across from the railway viaduct. By 1909, though, something had started to be done to improve the estate, with new artisan housing, raised high above the flood plain, constructed by the council to replace the old buildings. Much of the old Dolemeads had already been swept away; the rest was replaced in the 1920s. In contrast to the houses they replaced, the new 'model' houses are still commodious, still comfortable and still sought after. The same could not be said for those they replaced.

Above: Old houses in the Dolemeads.
Below: Gallaway's Buildings in the early twentieth century.

Some working-class housing does remain, however – Gallaway's Buildings, for example, the court facing Sally Lunn's. Built by Thomas Jelly around 1749 as lodging houses for the gentry, it was renamed North Parade Buildings in the mid-nineteenth century, for the same reason that Gracious Court was renamed.

Like many once-genteel streets in the lower part of the city, North Parade Buildings provided lodgings not for the rich but for the poor. Instead of lords and ladies taking a suite of rooms for the season, entire families would crowd into single rooms whose elegant décor, battered and worn though it was, only served to underline the contrast between then and now. The building on the corner – No 11 – housed a pub, with its own brewery in the yard at the back. There were once three other beerhouses in this short street before the council closed them down. It is hard to imagine just how many hundreds of people once lived here, jostling up against each other, with rooms here and there pressed into service as knocking shops, to the despair of the more respectable residents, until the authorities found out and locked their operators up.

Most of the streets that suffered a similar reversal of fortunes were demolished during the twentieth century, although a few, such as Kingsmead Square and St James's Parade, have survived. The most notorious was Avon Street, which stretched from Kingsmead Square down to the river. Built in the 1730s as lodging houses for the gentry, it was abandoned after only a few seasons because it flooded with monotonous regularity. Before long, it had acquired the reputation it retained until well into the twentieth

The back yard of 49 Avon Street.

century. An official report in 1842 summed up the general view when it concluded that 'all the scum of Bath – its low prostitutes, its thieves, its beggars – are piled up in the dens rather than houses of which the street consists'.

But this was doing the street's residents an injustice. Those who lived on the wrong side of the law assumed, as they always will, a far higher profile than those who try to maintain respectability. Vice, as tabloid journalists know only too well, is more interesting than virtue, and tales of the 'undeserving poor' will always be more popular than stories of those whose lives are blameless. The problem is that this concentration on the seamier side of life leads to an assumption that exceptions to the norm are the norm itself. It still happens today – read some newspapers and you'd think that everyone who lives on so-called 'sink estates' is a feckless welfare scrounger or petty criminal, whereas the reality is, more likely than not, that the majority of residents are trying to get by as best they can in the face of overwhelming odds, and bearing the brunt of antisocial behaviour from the ASBO-dodging monsters beloved of the tabloid press. If our view can be so distorted today, how much more likely is it that we will accept stereotypes of working-class life from a century ago. The common perception of old Avon Street, for example, is that it was a hotbed of crime, prostitution, violence and drunkenness. All those things existed, of course, and regularly featured in the *Bath Chronicle*'s court reports, but they were only one side of the picture. The vast majority of Avon Street's residents – who never appeared in the paper – were decent people trying to lead decent lives. Often hungry, often cold, ill-shod, ill-clad and – if they could find employment – overworked, under-appreciated and underpaid – to add to those indignities going down in history as feckless layabouts seems a cruel form of injustice.

So, bearing these caveats in mind, what was working working-class life like in Bath a century ago, and how widespread was the poverty? In 1903, Seebohm Rowntree estimated that 10% of the population of York lived in primary poverty and could not maintain 'merely physical efficiency', while 18% lived in secondary poverty, able to 'meet physical efficiency, were it not for some other expenditure either useful or wasteful'. In other words, almost a third of York's population could not afford a diet adequate to sustain a normal day's work. He thought that the figure was at least as high in other towns and cities. His findings were borne out by Charles Booth, a Liverpool shipping magnate, philanthropist and social reformer, who published a multi-volume survey of the *Life and Labour of the People in London*; he concluded that at least 35% of people in the East End of London were living in 'abject poverty'.

Bath may have been better than the East End of London, but the 1911 Census shows that, apart from minor variations due to people of independent means retiring to the city, in demographic terms it followed the national trend. Which means that just under a third of the people in the city were living below the poverty line. Families would have crowded into one or two rooms; vermin were a constant problem – 'houseflies and bluebottles swarmed every kitchen alive', recalled Robert Roberts,

> sticky foul-smelling paper traps dangled about, dark with their writhing bodies. And the bed bugs! With the warm days they appeared in battalions, first in the hovels, then in the better class houses, where people waged campaigns against their sickening sweet-odoured presence. Through summer days one saw the 'fever van' carrying off some child, who only too often would be seen no more.

Down towards the river especially, rats were another constant menace.

It was not uncommon for a family with three or four children to sleep together in one room. The poorest families lived in rooms furnished with orange boxes and slept under coats rather than blankets. This is Maud Reeves' description of a typical one-room tenement in the East End of London:

> The single room inhabited by this family is large – 15 feet by 13 feet – and has two windows. Under the window facing the door is the large bed, in which sleep mother, father and two children. A perambulator by the bedside accommodates the baby, and in the further corner is a small cot for the remaining child. The second window can be, and is, left partly open at night. At the foot of the bed which crosses the window is a small square table. Three wooden chairs and a chest of drawers complete the furniture, with the exception of a treadle machine purchased by the mother before her marriage on the time-payment system. The small fireplace has no oven, and open shelves go up each side of it. There are two saucepans, both burnt. There is no larder. On the floor lies a loose piece of linoleum, and over the fireplace is an overmantel with brackets and a cracked looking glass. On the brackets are shells and ornaments. Tiny home-

made window-boxes with plants in them decorate each window. The whole aspect of the room is cheerful. It is not stuffy, because the second window really is always open. The overmantel was saved for penny by penny before marriage, and is much valued. It gives the room an air, as its mistress proudly says.

Even worse than the appalling living conditions was the constant hunger and the poor quality of what food was available. In 1939, Sir Jack Drummond, a distinguished nutritionist, wrote that 'the opening of the twentieth century saw malnutrition more rife in England than it had been since the great dearths of medieval and Tudor England'. Although his claim has been challenged, that such a distinguished commentator could have reached this conclusion indicates the level of deprivation. At the turn of the century, 40% of the men who volunteered to fight in South Africa were rejected because they were unfit, many suffering from conditions caused by poor nutrition such as rickets.

In most towns and cities, including Bath, there were soup kitchens where soup and a slice of bread could be obtained for ½d. One was at the bottom of Chatham Row, off Walcot Street, in a building that still survives. They were run by charitable institutions; the soup was made from scraps of meat and bones provided by butchers and vegetables provided by greengrocers. When Noël Streatfield recalled soup kitchens in the 1950s, she expressed astonishment at how attitudes had changed:

> Neither the tradesmen who provided the materials for the soup, nor those ladies who served it, appeared to think it wrong in a rich country that families could be in such want that they would queue with jugs for a pennyworth of soup. There was nothing wrong with the people of that date, they were just as kind-hearted and easily moved as we are today, it was that the way they thought was different; poverty was something that happened – just as some people were born cripples, you helped, but you did not expect to cure them – indeed there were many who supposed that it would be upsetting God's purpose if you did.

Soup kitchens were for those who were desperate, but there were many others – who would not have been seen dead in such places – whose diet was little better. Shopping on Saturday evening for scraps of leftover meat displayed on trays outside butcher's shops, haggling with market traders over the price of vegetables, squeezing every last drop of nourishment out of everything they bought, trying to cook over a meagre fire – and then, along with their children, still feeling hungry, theirs was not an enviable lot.

Seebohm Rowntree described the plight of

a woman, now in fairly comfortable circumstances [who] told one of my investigators something of the struggle which she had gone through during the years when her husband was only earning 17/- a week. To make both ends meet with that sum for a large family of children was no easy matter. Each week, she said, as soon as she received the 17/- she put aside the money required for rent, and then planned out exactly how she could spend the remainder to the best advantage. The family never had a joint of meat, but occasionally she managed to afford 6d for a sheep's head or to buy 6d worth of 'meat pieces'. At the birth of a child she employed a woman for a week to nurse her, to whom she gave 5/- and her board. As soon as she knew that a child was coming she began saving odd coppers until the 5/- was collected, and so she was always able to pay the woman before she left the house. During the time she was nursing her children she lived chiefly upon bread and tea. Who can wonder that some of her children died during their first year?

Astonishingly, public opinion – among those who had the power to do something about such conditions – was only just coming round to the idea that malnutrition was a bad thing. In the eighteenth century, hunger was seen not only a natural state, but also a necessary one, since it spurred people who might otherwise be idle into working. Adam Smith and Thomas Malthus had debated whether the emerging market economy would eradicate hunger or whether it depended on it, but both agreed that the market should be left to produce plenty or want without intervention from the state.

In 1788, the Rev Joseph Townsend, who regularly preached at the Countess of Huntingdon's Chapel on the Vineyards in Bath and later became rector of Pewsey in Wiltshire, published his *Observations on Various Plans for the Relief of the Poor* in which he attacked the system of outdoor relief and promoted hunger as the most effective weapon against the aspirations of the working classes. 'The wisest legislator,' he wrote,

will never be able to devise a more equitable, a more effectual, or in any respect a more suitable punishment, than hunger is for a disobedient servant. Hunger will tame the fiercest animals, it will teach decency and civility, obedience and subjection to the most brutish, the most obstinate, and the most perverse ... It is universally found, that where bread can be obtained without care or labour, it leads through idleness and vice to poverty.

As James Vernon, the author of *Hunger: A Modern History*, points out, 'it was only in the second half of the nineteenth century that this view was first challenged, when hunger was discovered as a humanitarian issue, that reflected the failure of the state to protect its citizens from economic downturns over which they had no control'. One of those who helped to bring about this change in attitude was Friedrich Engels. 'The habitual food of the individual working man varies according to his wages,' he wrote in *The Condition of the Working Classes in England* in 1845:

Descending gradually we find animal food reduced to a small piece of bacon cut up with potatoes; lower still, even this disappears, and there remain only bread, cheese, porridge and potatoes, until on the lowest round of the ladder, among the Irish, potatoes form the sole food. As an accompaniment weak tea with perhaps a little sugar, milk or spirits is universally drunk. But all this presupposes that the workman has work. When he has none, he is wholly at the mercy of accident, and eats what is given him, what he can beg or steal. And, if he gets nothing, he simply starves ... Such a way of living unavoidably engenders a multitude of diseases.

It is remarkable how similar this is to much of what of Rowntree and Booth were to write over half a century later. Attitudes might have been changing, but they were taking an inordinately long time about it.

Given the lack of food, and lack of hygiene, it is not surprising that illness was prevalent. Exposure to germs did, of course, build up a certain immunity, but many people lived appallingly unhealthy lives. The level of ignorance about common diseases, even among the medical community, was staggering. Many believed that appendicitis was contagious, for example; nobody knew that rickets – still a major problem – was caused by dietary deficiencies. Coughs and colds were a constant problem for people in crowded, damp, unheated houses. A well-known cure for whooping cough was to go down to the gasworks and inhale the fumes. This was probably as effective as most of the patent medicines available at the time for 6d or 1/- a bottle. Aspirin had gone on sale in 1905, but, with many still swearing by remedies long since forgotten today, was far from achieving its later popularity. Many home-made remedies were based on onions and vinegar. To prevent colds, some children were sewn into brown paper vests smeared with thick lard or goose fat which they kept on all winter. The itchiness – and the smell – is best not pondered on. The misery of gastro-enteritis compounded by having to trot outside to use a communal privy – and the likelihood of having to queue – is something else best not pondered on too deeply either.

Working-class people only consulted a doctor in an emergency. Even then, the doctors they could afford to consult were often those who could not attract richer patrons – and with good reason. A well-known doctor in Avon Street at the turn of the century was Dr Nash – known to all and sundry as Dr Pill Box. He had originally had a practice in Great Pulteney Street, but was, apparently, rather too fond of the bottle. There were also dispensaries where poor patients could go for a free consultation, and a limited number of free hospital beds, but these were reserved for the most serious cases.

There were, of course, those, then as now, who put the ills of the working classes down to fecklessness and, in particular, to a weakness for alcoholic beverages. In 1909, each adult consumed, on average, 216 pints of beer or cider. That represented a significant drop from the 275 pints people had been getting down their necks 30 years earlier, but it was still too high for many social reformers. Despite all the stories of a chronically inebriated underclass, however, it was reckoned that only around 5% of working-class families included a regularly drunk parent.

At the bottom of the heap, though, the proportion was much higher – partly because drunkenness led to people falling to the bottom, partly because their circumstances were so dire that the temporary escape offered by alcohol was that much more tempting. For a slum dweller, the local pub had the home comforts so conspicuously lacking at home – warmth, bright lights, cheerful company, room to move about. For people who lived in cramped, squalid conditions, drinking in a warm, convivial space was often their only solace – with alcohol deadening the realisation that not only were you hungry, but your family was hungry as well, and, if you were one of the lucky ones who survived till a ripe old age, you'd end up, as likely as not, in the workhouse.

Beer was relatively cheap, at around 2d to 2½d a pint (equivalent to 63p-79p today), although it was possible to find it for as little as 1½d. Cider cost even less, starting at 1d a pint(equivalent to 31p today). Spirits were only drunk by the more affluent – whisky was the most popular tipple and cost around 3/- a bottle (£11.25 today), with gin available at 2/4 a bottle (£8.75 today) and brandy at 4/8 (£17.50 today). Wine, which was only drunk by the middle and upper classes and would never have been seen behind the bar of the ordinary pub, started at around 1/3 a bottle (£4.69 today).

Rowntree's remark about poorer working-class families not being afford anything beyond the bare necessaries was allied to an awareness that some men would stop off at the pub after getting paid and blow a sizeable hole in their week's wages. A packet of 20 cigarettes cost 6d (£1.88 today) – add to that the price of eight or so pints and you're well on the way to spending between 2/6 and 3/- – a hefty chunk out of a wage of less than a £1.

One of the reasons the powers that be were exercised about excessive imbibification of alcohol among the lower classes was – then as now – because of the amount of aggravation they caused. In February 1909, the licensing justices reported that there had been 87 cases of drunkenness in Bath in the previous twelve months – 52 men and 35 women – of which 76 were convicted. Surprisingly, over 30% of the miscreants came from outside Bath. Some, though, were persistent offenders, well known to the authorities. Rose Weeks, a flower seller from 5 Avon Street, sentenced to a month in prison for being drunk and disorderly on 19 January 1909, had 83 previous convictions. When Samuel Rowe, an ex-miner of no fixed abode, was brought before the magistrates in March 1909 for being drunk and disorderly in the High Street, it was revealed that he had been in prison no less than 130 times. He had just come out of Shepton Mallet prison after three weeks hard labour for begging in Bath. He had been a tramp for 29 years and said he now wanted to be sent to the workhouse so he could begin to think about the next world. He also said that he was resolved to become an abstainer.

'How did you manage to get like this?' the magistrate's clerk asked him.

'Well, sir, I'm a very good beggar,' he replied.

There was general laughter in the courtroom before he was sentenced to another month's hard labour.

Not surprisingly there was a widespread determination to stamp this sort of thing out. The temperance movement was strong in the early years of the twentieth century, and appealed particularly to children. Elsie Sealy, born in Bath in 1887, recalled that 'there was very little entertainment for the teenagers in Bath [so] we used to attend the Band of Hope, organised by the Grand Templar, whose grandson was Richard Dimbleby.' The International Order of Good Templars, who organised Band of Hope meetings for young people, as well as temperance meetings for adults, held at least twelve meetings a week in and around the city, where hymns and cautionary fables were interspersed with songs written to promote the cause, such as the perennial tearjerker, *Come Home Father*:

> *Father, dear father, come home with me now!*
> *The clock in the steeple strikes three;*
> *The house is so lonely, the hours are so long*
> *For poor weeping mother and me.*
> *Yes, we are alone, poor Benny is dead,*
> *And gone with the angels of light;*
> *And these were the very last words that he said,*
> *'I want to kiss Father good night'.*

There were eight other temperance societies in Bath in 1909 – the Bath Temperance Association, two branches of the Church of England Temperance Society, the Women's Total Abstinence Mission, the Bath Wesleyan Temperance Society, the West of England Temperance Friendly Society, the Independent Order of Rechabites Temperance Friendly Society, who met at Widcombe Temperance Hall, and the Sons of the Phoenix Help-in-Need Lodge, who met at the Star Coffee House in Kingsmead Square.

The temperance movement was a force to be reckoned with. Decades of lobbying had culminated in the Liberal government elected in 1906 adopting temperance as a main plank of its legislative programme. The prospect of a dry – or nearly dry – nation was no longer a dystopian fantasy, but a chilling reality. The Liberal government also had workhouses in its sights. These were set up by the Poor Law Amendment Act of 1834, which aimed to end the practice of providing 'outdoor relief' to the able-bodied poor – in other words, supporting them in their own homes. Parishes were grouped into Poor Law Unions, each with its own Union Workhouse. Bath Workhouse – now St Martin's Hospital – was on the Frome Road. Outdoor relief was considered too soft an option, and so, to discourage all but the absolutely destitute from applying to the workhouse, the regime was made as harsh and degrading as possible. 'Everyone there was dressed in a uniform,' one person who knew them recalled, 'the men in thick navy suits and the women in thick navy dresses; you always knew where they lived the moment

The staff at Frome Road Workhouse.

you saw them – their clothes gave them away. I have known many an old person who struggled to exist on a few shillings a week rather than go there. I don't think they were badly treated. It was the indignity of it that was so hard to bear, and people as poor as these had their pride.'

If an able-bodied man entered the workhouse, his family had to go with him; once through the gates, they were separated and only allowed to see each other for a short time on Sundays. Food consisted of thin porridge or gruel and rough bread with a bit of hard cheese. The able-bodied were given hard, monotonous, soul-destroying work such as breaking stones or picking oakum – old ropes soaked in tar – apart. People slept in communal dormitories and were bathed, under supervision, once a week. Many ended up in the workhouse because they were sick – and conditions such as these were a breeding ground for disease. Tuberculosis was especially rife.

The workhouse regime was terrible – almost beyond our imagining – but for the old it was especially cruel. People kept going as long as they could, taking up less demanding, poorly paid work, as their strength slowly ebbed away. Once past this, they slipped into a twilight world of extreme poverty, hunger, cold and darkness. By the age of 70, one Edwardian in five was a pauper; by 75, the proportion had risen to one in three. The spectre of the workhouse is one that has all but faded from our communal memory, but 100 years ago the poor dreaded it with a dread we cannot begin to comprehend. It was, to all intents and purposes, like looking forward to a prison sentence in your declining years. Once the gates had closed behind them, couples were separated; they spent their days sitting around in miserable day rooms or sick wards, all dignity gone, companionless, with nothing to occupy them and few if any visitors allowed. It was, if nothing else, a powerful disincentive to a long life. Laurie Lee, in *Cider with Rosie*, described the effect the workhouse had on Joseph and Hannah Brown, an old couple living in the village of Slad, near Stroud. They had lived in the same house for 50 years, then one day the 'authorities' decided they were too frail to look after each other any longer and should be moved to the workhouse:

> Hannah and Joseph thanked the Visiting Spinsters but pleaded to be left at home, to be left as they wanted, to cause no trouble, just simply to stay together.
>
> 'You'll be well looked after,' the Spinsters said, 'and you'll see each other twice a week.' The bright busy voices cajoled with authority and the old couple were not trained to defy them. So that same afternoon, white and speechless, they were taken away to the Workhouse. Hannah Brown was put to bed in the women's wing, and Joseph lay in the men's. It was the first time, in all their fifty years, that they had ever been separated. They did not see each other again, for in a week they both were dead.

Even if they were not paupers, a surprising number of our ancestors spent their last days in the workhouse, simply because the workhouse infirmary was the only place they could go when they could no longer be cared for at home. When they died, the workhouse medical officer would certify death and their bodies would be reclaimed by their families to make the funeral arrangements.

If the family was felt to be in a position to support elderly relatives in the workhouse, the Board would apply for a court order to make them pay. On 9 January 1909, Albert Reynolds, a market gardener from 8 Daisy Bank, Lyncombe, was summoned before ten magistrates at Weston County Police Court for non-payment of 1/- per week towards the maintenance of his mother in Bath Union Workhouse. He had paid nothing since last summer. When questioned, he admitted that his means were larger than when the order had been assessed, 'otherwise we would not have lived'. When the magistrates issued a distress warrant giving the Board of

Guardians power to enforce the order, 'I only wish I could comply with the order,' he told them, 'I suppose I can apply for a ticket for the workhouse for me and my family? I'll never work any more.'

It is perhaps no coincidence that Albert Reynolds was a well known socialist, a thorn in the side of many in the council and the establishment – no doubt including some of those who sat in judgement over him that day. One can only speculate as to what extent they relished the moment. At any event, he was back in court less than six weeks later. The staunchly Conservative *Bath Chronicle* reported that 'the well known Bath socialist' had failed to pay the 1/- a week and the distress warrant had been returned marked 'no effects'. It noted further that he was paying £11 per annum rent for his house, having lost the two acres of land that went with it. A lady had offered to help him out but he had refused to accept.

'You are setting yourself against all law and order,' the chairman of the bench told him, 'we will send you to prison for three weeks.'

'You will have to keep my wife and children now,' he replied, 'I will never do any more.'

Despite the policy of discouraging outdoor relief, with extra legislation passed at various times throughout the nineteenth century, it continued – partly due to a lack of accommodation, but largely because it was far cheaper to administer. In 1907, a survey concluded that there were nearly 800,000 paupers in the United Kingdom – over 2% of the population – but that over 1.7 million people had received relief during the previous year, only a third of whom were inmates of workhouses.

In May 1909, there were 615 people in Bath Workhouse – down seven from the number the previous Christmas; although some of these were from parishes outside the city boundary, making an exact calculation impossible, this represents 1.2% of Bath's population. On top of this, 91 children were in Cottage Homes, where they received a rudimentary education; 25 people for whom there was no room in the workhouse were boarded out; and 292, classified as lunatics, were in the County Asylum at Wells. In the first two weeks of May 1909, 736 'outdoor paupers' were relieved at a cost of £94. This very high figure indicates the level of unemployment at the time. Many of these outdoor claimants would, however, have had to carry out tasks such as stone breaking or picking oakum.

It is hardly surprising that some of those forced to endure the indignity of workhouse life kicked against it; upon these ungrateful wretches, however, did the full weight of official displeasure

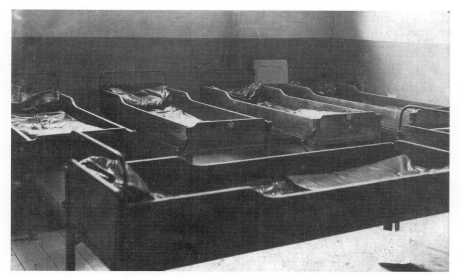

A casual ward in a workhouse.

descend. It is not recorded why Thomas King, stableman, an inmate of the casual ward at the workhouse, was so disgruntled, but in January 1909 he was charged with tearing off his clothes – 'everything except his shirt' – in a fit of rage. He was told that he could be supplied with a new suit 'on condition that he worked out its value' but declined the offer. The chairman of the Board of Guardians said that ratepayers could not be expected to pay for clothing in this way. He was given a month's hard labour. In September, a 43-year-old labourer was charged with refusing to carry out a job given him and going into the workshop reserved for men unfit for heavier tasks. He had been at the workhouse for 14 months, along with his wife and three children, all of which had cost over £60. He had worked under the head gardener for eleven months, including three as a carter, although he had been relieved of carting duties after beating the horse unmercifully – allegedly because it bit him. He was given three months hard labour.

Then there were those who ended up in the workhouse because they were mentally ill. In March 1909, the master of the workhouse reported the case of Mrs Pond, a 50-year-old woman who had been brought to the workhouse infirmary and died there after being refused entry to the Royal United Hospital. They had refused her admission because she was a 'noisy case'. A doctor had seen her at home and advised that she should be removed to hospital. On arrival she was found to be in an 'acute maniacal condition', 'rambling in

125

her talk' and 'very noisy', and had to be restrained by two porters. As she was 'unfit to be admitted to a general ward' and as her husband could not have her at home, the workhouse infirmary was the only place. 'There are a lot of patients at the Royal United Hospital,' a spokesman said at the inquest, 'and the presence of a noisy maniac there would be serious.' The coroner was not impressed, telling him that the hospital should provide a suitable place, but his explanation for shunting the unfortunate woman onto the workhouse was nevertheless accepted.

It is hard to comprehend the level of misery that many people had to endure as a matter of course a century ago. Even those lucky enough to be in good health and to live in a family where the breadwinner had a decent job with good prospects must have been aware how thin was the ground they walked on, and how deep the abyss beneath their feet. Charles Masterman wrote in 1909 of the 'vision of pitiful poverty far below … into which, at any time, any unfortunate worker may be precipitated; rarely, henceforth, to rise into the clear of intelligible life … a settled mass of congested poverty shivering through life upon the margin below which life ceases to endure'. Take the case of William Bally of 11 Perfect View, twelve years a gardener for the council, 'hardworking and respectable', who died suddenly at the age of 39 leaving his wife with six children. On 21 October 1910, Colonel Arnold Davies, the Chairman of the Pleasure Grounds Committee appealed to the public for funds to assist his widow and family who were, he said, 'practically destitute'.

Council gardeners in the nurseries at Royal Victoria Park.

Some stories open a window into a world that seems impossibly remote today. In the early twentieth century there were tens of thousands of tramps wandering the country. Some of them were women. On 29 January 1909 the coroner dealt with the case of Jane Feltham, aged 79, who had died in the Royal United Hospital four days earlier. On 23 January, Mary Budgeman of 89 Avon Street, who was going from house to house 'selling things', heard moaning coming from the coal cellar at 49 Combe Park. When she went to investigate, she found a women with 'her clothes all over her head [and] wearing men's boots'. From her appearance it seemed likely that she had been there for two or three days. She could not speak and her clothing was wet and dirty. She was given hot milk and then removed to hospital. She later said she came from Devonshire and had no relations. Mrs Pearce of Brookfield, Weston Road, said she had called at her home on 20 January, saying she had walked from Bristol and her feet were very bad. She had given her a penny. When the workhouse at Bristol was contacted, their records showed she had last stayed there in July. The verdict was that she had died from exhaustion, accelerated by exposure and starvation.

The annals of crime from a century ago are, as often as not, the annals of desperation in the face of overwhelming odds. When Tom Mitton, a chimney sweep from 3 Little Corn Street, was hauled before the bench on 9 February 1909, he was charged with begging in James Street West. When arrested, he had asked PC Gregory to 'make it as light as possible' as he had a wife and two little children at home. Chief Inspector Bence said the family was practically starving. Owen Restarick, the Police Court Missionary, said he sympathised with the prisoner. He had been put on probation in September for stealing a bicycle. He had been found several jobs but was not strong enough for regular work. He was discharged on promising to take his wife and children to the workhouse.

Some petty crimes were so petty, the wonder is that the police bothered to pursue them. Fred Robinson of Sladebrook Avenue, Twerton, for example, was charged with stealing two duck eggs – value 3d – at Englishcombe on 10 May. PC Ingram had put two marked eggs into a nest and concealed himself till the accused was seen to take them. He followed him, approached him and took the eggs from his pocket. Found guilty, the accused was bound over for twelve months.

Desperation expressed itself in different ways. On 7 March 1909, an unbearably sad little drama was played out in a courtroom in Bath. Nellie Howlett, aged about 25, was charged with attempting suicide the previous day. She sat in the courtroom, neatly dressed in a black costume and black hat, listening to the proceedings 'with great composure'. Thomas Miller, an ex-Mayor of Bath, who lived at Clan House in Bathwick, said that he had heard shouts at around 5pm the previous day near Cleveland House and had gone down to find two men dragging the accused to the bank. She had cried, he told the court, 'let me back again'. The prisoner said she had been employed at Bristol but given notice after a week. She walked from Bristol on Friday looking for friends in Bath. On Friday night she had slept in a fowl house at the bottom of Pulteney Road near the railway arches, and somewhere else on Saturday night – she wouldn't say where. On Sunday she walked near the canal trying to muster up the courage to jump into the water and some boys had thrown stones and mud at her. 'I had tried somewhere else but could not do it just there,' she said. She had left two books on the bank when she jumped in – the Bible and a novel called *Private and Confidential*. In the cells that morning she had apparently said, 'I'll do it again the least chance I've got.'

She was held on remand and made a written statement swearing that she wouldn't do it again. When recalled to court the following week, she was told that she might have been sent for trial to the Quarter Sessions and severely punished, but in view of her statement they would deal with her leniently.

'You know,' said the chairman, 'that your mother has made arrangements for you to go into a home?'

'Yes, sir.'

'Are you willing to go?'

'Yes.'

She was bound over for the sum of £5 to be of good conduct for six months and was told that, if she conducted herself well she would hear no more of it.

But, just in case you're about to go away with the idea that all Edwardian criminals were victims of circumstance, here, to end, is the story of two likely lads who were called up before the county magistrates in January 1909. Frederick Huet and Alfred Spencer from Cardiff were charged with stealing a silver watch worth £5 from Thomas Ellett, the landlord of the *Mason's Arms* at Combe Down. The accused went into the pub carrying a roll of lino about six feet long and nine inches wide. They told the 'untrue tale' about having been to a house to lay the floor and having this bit left over to sell. The prosecutor said the roll-of-linoleum story was about as old as the Book of Genesis and ranked with the 'Spanish prisoner' swindle.

The police station and magistrates court at Lower Weston. The building was demolished many years ago and until recently a garage occupied the site, which has now been earmarked for a convenience store.

He was surprised that no one seemed able to invent another story. While attempting to persuade the landlord to look after the lino for them they cut off his watch – 'but the deed was noticed'. After a struggle the two prisoners were overpowered, 'the house being in an uproar'. They were remanded in custody for a week, at which Spencer – you've got to admire his cheek – asked if they could go from the court in Lower Weston back to the police station by tram – 'as he did not like to walk through the streets handcuffed'! He said he would pay the fare. His request was accepted. When the case came up again they both got six weeks hard labour.

The trees were just saplings when this mother and toddler rested on the grass in Alexandra Park. The park, opened in July 1902, was named in honour of Edward VII's queen.

CHAPTER TEN

BUT TO BE YOUNG . . .

'An Edwardian childhood' – the phrase summons up images of long summer holidays, with the sun always shining, sailor suits and spinning tops – or perhaps Edith Nesbit's Railway Children, touched by misfortune, it is true, but with the consolation of steam trains at the bottom of the garden and an ultimate happy ending. For middle-class children it probably was a golden age, and there were plenty of middle-class children in Bath. There were plenty of schools to cater for them as well: King Edward's, of course, where fees ranged from £2 a term in the preparatory department to £3-10-0 a term for boys over 14, plus 2/- a term for stationery and 2/- for games; then there was Grosvenor School, established in 1849, and designed to prepare boys 'for the universities, the army, the navy and civil service and for commercial life', which cost from nine to twenty guineas a year for day pupils and from 50 to 75 guineas for boarders. Girls' schools included Grosvenor College, Bath High School in Portland Place, Bathwick Ladies' School at 45-46 Great Pulteney Street, and the Convent on Pulteney Road, which also took boys up to the age of twelve.

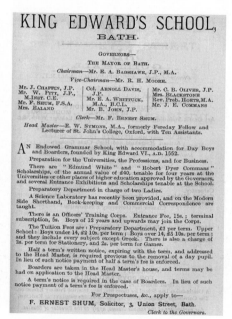

Such schools, though, were for the few; for the vast majority, there were council and non-provided (i.e. church) schools, which since 1902 had all been under the control of the local education board. The school-leaving age was twelve, although a small – but slowly increasing – number of promising children went on to secondary school – if their parents could afford it. Many could not.

Above: The Convent de la Sainte Union School in Pulteney Road.
Below: Children at Twerton Parochial School.

It was, as in so many other things, a question of the haves and the have-nots.

A century ago, working-class children looked very different from their upper and middle-class counterparts. It wasn't just their clothes, although ill-matched, threadbare and ill-fitting hand-me-downs would, of course, have set many of them apart. In 1900, the average height of a 15-year-old public schoolboy was five feet five inches; the average height of a working-class 15-year-old, who would almost certainly have been at work for several years by this time, was five feet one inch. Many working-class children simply did not eat enough to develop properly, and this also meant their lives were shorter. Average life expectancy was a mere 46 years for men and 50 years for women. Many children – as many as one in three – died in their first year. Again, this was largely due to lack of food. Their mothers, who had to nurse them through their critical early months, often subsisted on a diet of no more than bread and tea – hardly a recipe for bonny, bouncing babies. And, because they were so weak, the smallest ailment could be enough to carry them off. In the East End of London 55% of children died before they reached the age of five. In the richer West End, the figure was only 18%.

Many mothers, because of lack of nutrition, were unable to breast feed. Babies were given skimmed condensed milk, totally unsuitable for them because of its lack of fat. Many developed weak bones and deformed bodies as a result. If milk was not available, they were given mashed-up flour and water, but flour was difficult for babies to digest and many died of stomach disorders as a result. When they were ill, they were given mixtures like Godfrey's Cordial – a mixture of alcohol, opium, treacle and water – while teething babies were given chews laced with opium. It kept them quiet, but it was easy to overdose and babies sometimes died in their sleep from the effects of Godfrey's cordial.

Infant mortality reached a peak in 1899. It was acknowledged that many of the deaths were preventable and the late nineteenth and early twentieth centuries saw a raft of measures designed to improve the survival rate. In 1902, the Midwives Act made it mandatory for midwives to be trained and registered; in 1907 the Notification of Births Act laid down that the local medical office of health had to be informed as soon as possible after a birth, so that a health visitor could call on the mother and explain to her how to safeguard her child's health. These measures had a dramatic impact: between 1906 and 1910 infant mortality fell from 138 per 1000 to 117 per 1000.[1] The Royal United Hospital's annual report for 1909 recorded that, of 862 children born in the previous twelve months, 82 had died in infancy – equivalent to 95 per 1000, significantly better than the national average – a reflection of the higher than average number of middle-class households in the city. The report also recorded that health visitors had made 3,363 visits – which they reckoned to be an average of six per child. The condition of the infants was as follows: 'healthy and clean', 388; 'doubtful',

1 The rate today is about 5 per 1000.

123, 'dirty', 14, 'with eye inflammation', 23.[2] Accommodation was mostly good although 30 rooms were 'damp but clean', 22 were 'fairly clean', 18 were dirty and eight were insanitary.[3]

Children were born at home, in primitive and often unhygienic conditions. In the absence of painkillers, midwives often prescribed gin. Childbed fever was common; many women suffered from internal complaints after giving birth but could not afford to visit a doctor. They regarded it as something they had to bear. In 1907, Lady Florence Bell, a social reformer who made a detailed study of the working classes in Middlesbrough, described the effect of childbirth on young mothers:

> One's heart aches at seeing a girl of 24 or 25, when she ought to be at her best, most joyous, most hopeful – at the age when the well-to-do girl, in these days apt to marry later, is often still leading a life of amused irresponsibility and enjoyment – already appearing dulled, discouraged, her form almost shapeless, her looks gone … The time when existence seems to press most hardly is during the first 12 or 14 years after marriage, when there is usually a family of young children, who have to be provided for and who cannot earn; and the wife is constantly, before and after every birth, in a condition in which she cannot fulfil her duties with efficiency. It is not until later that the husband's wages are supplemented by odds and ends of work on the part of the wife, when she has a daughter old enough to leave in charge of the house, and also by earnings of one kind or another from sons and daughters employed in other callings.

After the agonies of childbirth, the loss of an infant in circumstances such as those that befell Emily Stone of 4 Abbey Green must have been heartbreaking. Her son, whom she christened Albert, was born late in 1908, and was a sickly child from the start. The midwife told her to give him brandy and water three times a day. On the morning of 3 January – a cold, miserable day – she woke and fed her children before going back to sleep at around a quarter to seven. When she woke again at around nine o'clock, Albert was blue. She sent for the doctor but he sent a message telling her to get someone else. She took him to the midwife who prescribed more brandy. This had little effect, so

---

2 Eye problems seem to have been a major problem: in June 1909, out of 136 infants at Christ Church School, 49 had 'squint' – an exceptionally high proportion which, apparently, was even commented upon by 'the London papers'.
3 The breakdown does not tally with the figure of 862 births, but is given as reported.

Children outside the Cross Bath.

she took him to the hospital where he was pronounced dead on arrival. At the inquest the house physician said that he thought the midwife was right to have prescribed brandy, that the death was due to deficient respiration, and the child had probably never breathed properly.

There were, however, appalling cases of child neglect among families who, cowed by the miseries of a life without hope, had more or less given up. One of the most harrowing was brought to court by the NSPCC a few weeks after the death of Albert Stone. Ellen Davis was summoned for neglecting Alice, age seven, and Gladys, age three and a half. She had first come to the attention of the NSPCC while living with a man called Walker in St James's Parade. There she had shared a bed not only with her partner but also with the two children; two older children had already been removed to a Cottage Home. When visited there, the children were found to be verminous, and it was apparent that their mother went out for hours at a time leaving the children locked in. She then moved to a tenement in Cross Lane which was described as 'indescribably filthy'. She supported herself by doing a spot of cleaning, but after doing a couple of hours work she would go off and spend the money on drink, returning home when it had all gone. In November 1908 she moved to what could euphemistically be described as a basement flat, but was in fact a disused coal cellar, quite unfit for human habitation, in Somerset Street. There her partner died from consumption. One of the children also developed consumption. When the inspector visited, he found a cold, damp room, lit by one small window half below ground, with the floor littered with empty beer and spirit bottles. He was 'almost overpowered by the stench'. Ellen Davis was found guilty and given four months hard labour. The children were taken into care and the police were instructed to see that the room was not used for human habitation in the future.

Elementary education had been compulsory since 1880, but many poor children worked as well as or instead of going to school. A report in 1901 estimated that at least 300,000 children of primary-school age worked part-time. Among the examples they cited were: a boy who helped a milkman from 4.30am until he went to school and again from 5pm to 9pm; a boy who worked 60 hours a week selling newspapers; a boy who worked as a 'lather boy' at a barber's from the time he came out of school to ten o'clock at night; a boy who delivered heavy groceries and was paid 3d for six hours work; a ten-year old girl who worked at a dairy from 6am to 9am and from 4.30pm to 7pm – 'her bare feet like two pieces of frozen meat' – for 1/9 a week; and a boy of eleven who worked in an undertakers, where his jobs included measuring the corpses. Robert Sherard, writing in the *London Magazine,* cited the cases

of a lad in Finsbury ... who works 68½ hours a week by running errands out of school hours for 3/-; of a boy in the same district, who, by selling papers in the street for 63 hours a week, earns the same amount ... The burdens which their taskmasters lay upon the child-slaves of England are heavy indeed ... I have heard of boys to whom a load of three-quarters of a hundredweight has been allotted ... One meets constantly in these depths with children who have been literally deformed and twisted out of shape by the loads which have been laid upon them.

In 1909, Bath Education Authority, using powers granted by the Children's Act, decided to come to grips with the problem of verminous children. An inspection found that between 10%

and 60% of children at elementary schools in the city had verminous heads, which could be dealt with by nurses. Around 20 children, however, were found to have verminous bodies. Although this only represented 0.3% of the total, it was a far more serious problem, and a cleansing station was set up in Milk Street to deal with it.

The cleansing station in Milk Street.

Children identified by the health visitor were picked up at school in an old horse cab and driven to Milk Street, where their clothes were piled into a steam disinfector and they were given a bath. While this was going on, inspectors went round to their homes to take their bedding away to disinfect it and spray the rooms. After their baths, the children were given a cup of cocoa and a piece of bread and butter. Once reunited with their disinfected clothes, they were driven back in the disinfected cab to their schools.

To deal with children who were falling through the educational net the government had, as long ago as 1857, set up industrial schools, to which children between the ages of seven and fourteen were referred by local magistrates. Initially, they were intended solely for children brought before the courts for vagrancy, but the

Above: The brigade band at the Sutcliffe Industrial School. Below: Christmas dinner in the school canteen.

Among the other charitable institutions in Edwardian Bath was a 'Home for Cripples' at Prospect Place, Camden Road.

'A large number of the poorer children of the city will be made happy by a visit from Santa Claus this afternoon ... The Mayor will give the "parcel-man" a send-off from Messrs Allen's warerooms in Dorchester Street at 1.45. The time is a little earlier than usual, but this is necessary, owing to the fact that there are some 400 additional children to be visited. Of course, the extra children have entailed additional expenditure, and the committee would be glad to receive donations towards the expense thus incurred.'

Bath Journal, 24 December 1909

criteria was later extended to include children found begging or 'in the company of reputed thieves', children guilty of a criminal offence or children whose parents declared them to be beyond their control. They aimed to remove children from bad influences, teach them a trade and prepare them for the world of work. They rose at six in the morning and went to bed at 7pm, their day consisting of basic schoolwork, learning a trade, housework, religious instruction, mealtimes and three short playtimes. Boys learnt trades such as gardening, tailoring and shoemaking; the girls learned knitting, sewing, housework and washing Parents were supposed to contribute to the cost, but this was clearly out of the question in many cases. By 1909, the weekly cost of keeping a child in an industrial home was 7/-, between 2/- and 5/- of which came, in the absence of parental support, from the government, with the local authority making up the rest. There was considerable unease about the system, with many considering it too great a drain on the public purse. There were three industrial schools in Bath – the Somersetshire Certified Industrial School for Boys on the Lower Bristol Road, the Bath Certified Industrial School for Girls at 16-18 Walcot Parade and the Sutcliffe Industrial

139

School in Walcot Buildings, founded by William Sutcliffe in 1848. The Sutcliffe Industrial School was smaller than the others, with an average of 30 boys.

Another institution for children was Magdalen Hospital School on Holloway. Under the management of the Municipal Charity Trustees, it provided accommodation for 30 'lunatic children' – 15 girls and 15 boys. When the Lunacy Commissioners visited in April 1909, they found it warm and well-ventilated, and the children – none of whom, they noted, was in bed – 'happy and contented'. There was an asphalted playground with 'a new and commodious shelter'. The children were occupied in making baskets, mats and woollen articles, as well as receiving instruction in handwriting.

Among the boys sent to an industrial school in 1909 was William Emery, age 10, of 7 Lucklom Buildings, Larkhall. In January he was charged with breaking into 12 Eldon Place and stealing a handkerchief, a tape measure, a money box and 3½d – total value 8½d. His father was a mason who had been out of work for four months, with three younger children. He said that his son had been getting into bad company and started playing truant. He had no objection to him going to an industrial school, but he would rather he wasn't sent to the Somersetshire Industrial School as he knew some boys there that might get him into trouble. The clerk asked him if he would mind him going to a ship – another option – but he said he didn't care where he went. In the end he was sent to Harborne Industrial School in Birmingham, with his father paying 1/6 a week towards his keep.

Although getting sent away to a special school for a spot of petty crime may seem draconian, by the standards of the time William Emery got off relatively lightly. Not so thirteen-year-old Charles Bulbeck, who stole a lump of coal in Haywards Heath, Sussex. Although it was his first offence, he was sentenced to six strokes with a birch rod and seven years' detention in a reformatory. The magistrates later relented, transferring him to Portland Industrial School, but his parents appealed to the Home Secretary, Winston Churchill. The case generated considerable public interest and when Churchill announced that, in his opinion, the birching was sufficient punishment and he should be sent home there was loud cheering in the House of Commons.

Corporal punishment was the rule rather than the exception at the majority of schools – and not just for bad behaviour. When Elsie Sealy started as a pupil-teacher at East Twerton Infants School in 1911, she 'felt the head teacher at my new school to be too brutal in flinging young ones across the floor in anger at poor work, incorrect sums and smudgy writing'. Today a teacher like that would be arrested, placed on a register, banned from teaching and probably receive a custodial sentence; a century ago such behaviour was commonplace. Charlie Chaplin's description of the regime at the orphanage he was sent to in Hanwell gives an even more graphic illustration of how serious assault was accepted as normal:

> For minor offences a boy was laid across the long desk, face downwards, feet strapped and held by a sergeant, then another sergeant pulled the boy's shirt out of this trousers and over his head, then pulled his trousers tight. Captain Hindrum, a retired Navy man weighing about 200 pounds, with one hand behind him, the other holding a cane as thick as a man's thumb and about four feet long, stood poised, measuring it across the boy's buttocks. Then slowly and dramatically he would lift it high and with a swish bring it down across the boy's bottom. The spectacle was terrifying, and invariably a boy would fall out of rank in a faint ... The strokes were paralysing, so that the victim had to be carried to one side and laid on a gymnasium mattress, where he was left to writhe and wriggle until the pain subsided.

Orphans had no one to speak for them; Isaac Billett, a twelve-year-old scholar at Kelston School, had his father, however, and when the Rector of Kelston turned up at the school to give him a good thrashing, his father was so incensed that he brought charges. So it was that, in November 1909, the Rev Ernest Walter Poynton found himself in the dock at Weston Police Court. Mr Basil Dyer spoke for the prosecution:

> It appears that on 4 November the defendant went to the school and asked certain questions of some of the children as to whether something had been said about his cook. On 5 November the defendant returned again, and told five boys to stand up, and asked them if they had said something to his cook when they had been in his garden. This they all denied. The defendant then took hold of Billett, laid him across a form, and told one of the other boys in the school to come and hold him. He also called an assistant mistress at the school to come and hold his head. The defendant then took a cane, and for some minutes thrashed the boy unmercifully. It appears that the defendant's excuse was that abusive words had been made to his cook by one of the boys. It appears that some of the boys had been employed by the

The Rev EW Poynton appeared as the Abbot of Bath in Episode III of the Bath Pageant.

defendant in his garden and orchard to pick up apples and sticks, and for this they were rewarded with pence, and sometimes given apples to take home. The allegation was that the defendant's cook had come out and asked the boys to shut the gate, and that Billett had replied, 'Shut the gate yourself.'

The punishment cannot be justified because in committing this assault upon the boy the defendant had not the excuse of provocation which the law allows him. The clergyman must have nursed his wrath for two days. If the boy used a bad word it had nothing to do with the school, and this parson had no right to punish the boy in the school. After the assault was committed, the boy went home and his father saw his condition. There were 13 or 14 large weals and from some of these blood was coming. The attack was a very brutal one and the punishment was such as ought under no circumstances to have been inflicted. The superintendent of police has also seen the boy, and says he would never permit such punishment to be inflicted on a prisoner ordered by the magistrates to be punished. I charge the defendant with gross and brutal assault.

At this point, Mr Dyer 'checked himself in his statement' and accusing the rector of laughing, a claim which was refuted by the rector's solicitor. After various witnesses, including two policeman and an NSPCC inspector, had corroborated the story, the solicitor for the defence argued that the rector had been justified in his actions – on the grounds that he was 'entitled to give half an hour's religious instruction daily' at the school – and that thrashing a boy for a misdemeanour came under the heading of religious instruction. He went to say that the rector 'had determined to punish this boy severely, because previous experience had told him that leniency had no effect on the boy. He had punished the boy for his good.' The chairman of the magistrates said that, regardless of whether or not thrashing came within the scope of the religious instruction, the caning was excessive and the rector was fined £1 to cover costs. The rector's solicitor asked for it to be placed on record that he was extremely disappointed by the judgement, as it sent 'the wrong sort of message'.

As with so much, attitudes were changing, but only slowly. Government legislation was, nevertheless, addressing the problem. In 1906, local authorities were given power to provide school meals for children from poor families, but, as it was optional, many did not use it – on grounds of cost. The following year the government introduced a system of medical inspections in schools. In February 1909 came the Children and Young Persons Act, under which children became protected persons. Parents who ill-treated or neglected their children could be prosecuted under the act; they also became liable for fines imposed on their children. It also banned the sale of alcohol to children and banned them from licensed premises. Cigarettes or cigarette papers were not to be sold to children under 16; a constable or park-keeper finding someone under 16 smoking could seize their cigarettes. They also had the power to search boys – but not girls – for cigarettes. Cigarette machines in public places were acknowledged to be a problem, but if a cigarette machine was 'found to be excessively frequented by children', the magistrates could order the owner to take steps to prevent them using it.

The first case under the new act was heard at the Guildhall on 3 April. Henry Lee of 38 Avon Street was summoned for allowing his son, Thomas, age 9, to beg. PC Kirkham had seen the boy outside the Palace Theatre on the Sawclose at 10.45 at night asking people leaving the theatre for their programmes, which he could then resell. When he realised he had been spotted he ran home, but PC Kirkham followed him, entered the house and found him hiding under his bed. There were four programmes in his overcoat pocket. PC Kirkham said that there was no food in the house and, when asked, the boy's mother could produce none. The chief constable said that the boy had frequently been seen near the Palace Theatre in the evenings. His father, who was described as 'of bad character' with convictions for begging himself, said he had no control over his son and had not sent him out to beg. He was discharged with a caution; his son was sent to an industrial school.

A week later, Walter Boswell, a carter from 38 Avon Street, was charged with allowing two children – Leonard Boswell, age 3, and Richard Cross, age 4 – to beg. He pleaded guilty and said he had been singing a hymn to try to get some bread for his children. Richard

Cross's father said he was unaware his son had been with Boswell, who had a previous conviction for begging. Boswell was given one month's hard labour; the Mayor observed that he was determined to stamp out the practice of using children to beg.

On 16 December, Thomas Grant, age 15, of 28 Peter Street, was charged with begging in Dunsford Place. PC Marshall had seen him going from door to door and asked him what he was doing. He repled that he was 'selling postcards'. No postcards were found on him, and on inquiry at one of the houses it was found that he had been asking for money. His mother said that he 'had been at work at the box factory, but they had told her that he was not sharp enough; in fact, they thought he was not quite right'. He was placed under the care of the police court missionary and the case was adjourned.

On 4 September, no less than five women were summoned for supplying children under the age of seven with beer contrary to the Children's Act. Eva Stoneman from 4 Albert Terrace, Widcombe had been seen giving beer to a two-and-a-half year old outside the Crown Brewery in New Orchard Street. When PC Earl asked her if she knew it was against the law, she said she didn't mind because it wasn't her child. With her was Charlotte Cannings from 19 Longmead Street, Twerton, who had also given beer to two children under five. When cautioned, she responded, 'they want a drink as well as we do.' They were both fined 5/-.

In 1901, 89.3% of children between five and eleven attended school; in the twelve to fourteen-year-old age group the percentage dropped to 41.5%. Above that, in the 15 to 18-year-old age group it fell to a mere 0.3%. As regards university education, in 1901 there were only 20,000 university students in the entire country. Although this number had increased somewhat by 1909, with two new universities – Belfast and Bristol – opening that year, it would be a long time before university education was for any but the privileged few – or the prodigiously gifted and determined.

It is salutary to compare government spending on education then and now. In 1900, just £12.2 million was spent – equivalent to £549 million today. By 1997, the figure had risen to £36,984 million – over 67 times more in real terms. Even so, there were those in 1909 who thought expenditure on education was spiralling out of control. When the Education Committee in Bath announced in June 1909 that the government was planning to increase the space requirement for children in school from eight to ten square feet, Councillor Plowman declared it was ridiculous. 'When I was at school,' he said, 'we got nothing like ten feet – any extra expense must not be encouraged.'

Economic concerns also saw off Bath's answer to Clifton College. Bath College, which occupied the building that is now Bath Spa Hotel, was described in Ward Lock's *Guide to Bath* as 'one of the great schools of England ... modelled after Clifton College'. By 1909, however, it was in serious financial difficulties and appealed to the council for a subsidy of £8,000. Some councillors were in favour, but there was strong opposition in the city. It was argued that the presence of a school like Bath College made Bath a more attractive place for people with children to settle, and, for a time, it seemed as though the college would be saved. But the thought that Bath's ratepayers, at a time of recession, when so many businesses and individuals were struggling, should subsidise the education of the privileged few was anathema, and, after a packed protest meeting in the Guildhall, the college was left to its fate.

Bath College.

By now, some readers may be growing uneasy at what they might see as an undue and unjustified emphasis on life at the sharp end. Some of the examples and statistics quoted have come from the East End of London – or York – or Middlesbrough, for goodness sake! Bath may have had its problems, but they were surely nowhere as bad as that, I seem to hear them say.

Well, I'm sorry, but they were. Documentary evidence may be scant, but there is one memoir that tells us exactly what growing up at the bottom of the heap was like in Bath a century ago. It was written by a remarkable lady called Louie Stride. She was born in the Old Gaol in Grove Street in 1907. Her mother was unmarried; who her father was she never knew. From Grove Street her mother moved to a court – long demolished – behind the *Hat & Feather* in Walcot Street. From there she did a moonlight flit (a common

The Old Gaol in Grove Street, the birthplace of Louie Stride.

Children get in the way of an Edwardian photographer in St James Street South.

enough practice if you couldn't pay the rent) to Walcot House, paying sixpence for use of a cart to move her few belongings. Her mother cleaned shops in Northumberland Passage for sixpence an hour – but she also stole linen and pawned it. The next move was to Holloway, but it didn't last long – the morning after their arrival, 'the women in the surrounding cottages attacked my mother verbally and in person, called her a scarlet woman and threw her goods out in the yard – "coming to live amongst a lot of decent people with a bastard" – they weren't going to tolerate that and they didn't.' This was, Louie recalls, 'one of the most humiliating days of my life'. And so it was back to Walcot, where her mother turned to prostitution to make a little extra money:

> I was on the breast till I was three years old, and running about, and it was more or less my only means of sustenance. One thing I have omitted to say is the continual hunger we endured. The rent used to be 1/6 to 2/6 a week and the few shillings my mother earned charring did not give adequate sustenance, just sporadic meals of bread and tea, so I was in a perpetual state of hunger and would do anything for food. At the school I would steal from younger children, can you imagine it – me four years old or so,

grabbing an infant's piece of bread and running into a lavatory to eat it. Of course, I was pounced upon by their older brothers and sisters, and called names and treated badly as only children can. I was known as Lulu No Drawers, which I suppose was a fact ... My head was cropped like a boy's because of lice – most children had them then! Also very early in the morning if we had threepence I would have to get up at six or sevenish to go to the bakeries for stale bread. There would be an army of kids all ages and sizes and we would wait patiently in the rain and cold! The first stop would be Red House in Walcot Street – if no stale bread there we would all rush down to Fortt's in Green Street, and if none there we would have to go down to the main bakery in Manvers Street, such a long way for little tired legs and hungry bellies.

By the age of five, after many evictions and moonlight flits, she was at 22a Broad Street, on the corner of Broad Street Place (which we visited at the beginning of Chapter 9). Here, 'the agent of the owner of the house, instead of having the rent, had goods in kind!' – a common practice at the time:

Sometimes I went to school and sometimes I didn't, perhaps I had no footwear or most likely was ill for want of food and I stayed home ... We subsisted on a bit of boiled rice and bread if lucky. Sometimes when we were in the money – ie sixpence – I would be sent down to Old Charlie's in Walcot Street. He had a little huckster's shop-cum-café. I think he did all the ostlers' meals at the *Saracen's Head*, and the draymen's, also the farmers and men who worked at the cattle market just opposite on market days. Here I would get a top of a cottage loaf for 2d, ½d of skimmed milk, ½d of tea, 1d of sugar, ½d of St Ivel's cheese, ½d worth of firewood ... And so I grew up, scavenging food where I could, in the gutter pretty often – surprising what one can find edible. I ran wild during the day and was locked in at night ... I took in any cat for company in the evenings when my mother went out on the streets, as she called her 'spare job'. Sometimes she came home with 1/6, that was the fee, and mostly without anything to eat. I was a marvel to survive the malnutrition as I did ...

While not implying for one moment that such things were in any way typical, this was one poor little mite's experience of Edwardian Bath.

CHAPTER ELEVEN

CLASS WAR

At this stage, after mentioning them in passing on several occasions, we really must turn to consider the extraordinary series of reforms initiated by the Liberal government, and the constitutional crisis of 1909 which they provoked. To deal with the issues properly would require a separate book; indeed, to do them justice here would require far greater space than we can give. But even to begin to understand the tensions that made 1909 so pivotal requires a basic knowledge of the political scene, so – bearing in mind that, if you want to know more, there are plenty of excellent studies available – here is a whirlwind tour of the events of that momentous year.

1909 was the year in which the House of Commons and the House of Lords reached deadlock over who should govern the country. Looking back, it seems obvious that it should have been the Commons who would ultimately win – perhaps it was obvious at the time – but one thing was sure: the Lords were not going to go down without a fight. Their defeat marked a watershed in British constitutional history.

The roots of the conflict went back many years. In the late nineteenth century, as the Liberal party started to shake itself free of Whig control, Whig grandees distanced themselves from the party. Things came to a head in 1886, when, in protest at Liberal support for Irish Home Rule, some Liberals set up a new party, the Liberal Unionists. This breakaway party supported the Conservatives, forming a coalition with them in 1895, but retained its own identity until 1912, when a complete merger was agreed.

The other main issue which divided Conservatives from Liberals at the time was free trade. Failure to impose tariffs on imported goods had led to the collapse of the agricultural economy; on the positive side, this meant that food was cheaper than it would have been had a protectionist policy been adopted. In other words, what was bad for farmers was good for the urban poor.

The free trade consensus that had existed in Britain since the repeal of the Corn Laws in 1846 was broken by Joseph Chamberlain, a Liberal Unionist sitting as a member of the Conservative cabinet. In 1903 he resigned from the government, taking many of his supporters

Joseph Chamberlain

with him, to campaign for Imperial Preference – preferential trade with the empire. This split weakened the Conservative/Liberal Unionist government to such an extent that it lost overwhelmingly to the Liberals in the 1906 general election.

In 1906, the Liberals won 377 seats, which gave them an overall majority of 132. Bath followed the national trend, contributing to the Liberal landslide. At the time the city still returned two Members of Parliament. Six years earlier, in 1900, they had elected Colonel Wyndham Murray, a Conservative, and Edmond Wodehouse, a Liberal Unionist. In 1906, Murray defended his seat, but Wodehouse's place was taken by a Conservative, Lord Alexander Thynne, the third son of the Marquess of Bath. They were both roundly defeated by the two Liberal candidates, Donald Maclean and GP Gooch.

In 1906, it was not a case of a party that had previously been in power taking up the reins of government once again; there was to be no return to Gladstonian Liberalism. The General Election of 1906 marked a sea change in British politics. It was not just the Liberals who wanted to change the world; there were other new kids on the block as well – 29 Labour MPs plus 14 miners' representatives. Joseph Chamberlain spoke of the 'Labour earthquake', while Arthur Balfour, the defeated Conservative leader, believed that 'It is quite obvious that we are dealing with forces not called into being by any of the subjects about which parties have been recently squabbling, but rather due to a general movement of which we see the more violent manifestations in continental politics … This new development … will end, I think, in the break-up of the Liberal Party, and, perhaps, in other things even more important.' Sir Wilfred Laurier, Prime Minister of Canada put it in even starker terms:

The recent elections have undoubtedly opened a new era in the history of England. The England of the past may survive partially yet for a few years, but it is a democratic England which now takes its place. The Labour element will count henceforth as a very important factor, and it is difficult to foresee exactly to what extent, but certainly to a very large extent, it will control legislation.

Looking back, 21 years later, on the events of 1906, the Liberal historian, GM Trevelyan, concurred with these views:

Sir Henry Campbell-Banerman

Herbert Asquith

The overturn, which took everyone by surprise, was significant of a greater tendency to mass emotion in the large modern electorate, bred in great cities, and less tied up by party traditions than the old ... A new generation had arisen, wanting new things and caring more about 'social reform' at home than about 'Imperialism' in Ireland, South Africa or anywhere else.

The new prime minister was Sir Henry Campbell-Bannerman; he resigned on 3 April 1908 and was replaced by Herbert Asquith, who held office until 1916. The key players in the extraordinary events that unfolded during 1909, however, were David Lloyd George and, to a lesser extent, Winston Churchill. What they sought to achieve was not only a fundamental redistribution of wealth but radical changes to the constitution and the economic basis of power – so radical that, a century on, their aims are yet to be fully realised.

Our view of Churchill is so dominated by the image of him as the British bulldog standing firm against the evils of Nazism, it is difficult to see him as a young man, crusading – despite his aristocratic background – on behalf of the working class. He had already resigned from the Conservative party in 1904 in protest against its anti-free-trade stance. In 1908 he became President of the Board of Trade in the Liberal government, setting minimum wage rates, establishing labour exchanges and introducing National Insurance. A clue to what drove him comes in the form of an

Winston Churchill

aside made to his private secretary during a visit to a working-class district of Manchester: 'Fancy living in one of these streets, never seeing anything beautiful, never eating anything savoury, never saying anything clever.'

But it was Lloyd George, whom Churchill took over from at the Board of Trade when he became Chancellor of the Exchequer, who was the real catalyst for change. His speeches, even today, have the power to shock, couched as they are in the language of class war rather than conventional parliamentary debate. At the time they were dynamite.

'All down history,' he declared in 1906, 'nine-tenths of mankind have been grinding corn for the remaining tenth and have been paid with the husks and bidden to thank God they had the husks.' When the Pensions Bill was going through parliament, he made no bones about his total rejection of established notions of state responsibility:

> The provision which has been made for the sick and the unemployed is grossly inadequate in this country, yet the working classes have done their best during 50 years to make provision without the aid of the state … These problems of the sick, of the infirm, of the men who cannot find the means of earning a livelihood are problems with which it is the business of the state to deal.

When he went down to Limehouse in East End of London to canvass support for his plans, his language was so unrestrained that it caused 'a state of great agitation and annoyance' in the King:

David Lloyd George

When the Prime Minister and I knock on the door of these great landlords and say to them, 'Here, you know these poor fellows who have been digging up royalties at the risk of their lives, some of them are old, they have survived the perils of their trade, they are broken, they can earn no more, won't you give us something towards keeping them out of the workhouse?' they scowl at us. We say, 'Only a halfpenny, just a copper.' They retort, 'You thieves.'

When his 1909 Budget proposals were attacked, 'this is a War Budget,' he retorted, 'it is for raising money to wage implacable war against poverty and squalidness.' He can be forgiven a bit of hyperbole, for it was Lloyd George that laid the foundations for the welfare state. Admittedly, policy had been moving in this direction for some time. Some wanted a more equitable distribution of resources on grounds of natural justice; some wanted it to stave off the threat of socialist revolution; but things would almost certainly not have moved so far or so fast without Lloyd George. His talk of war was not an idle metaphor; he got a war, all right – a constitutional war, with the Lords opposing the right of the Commons, sanctioned by precedent and tradition, to run the country. The outcome of that battle had – and continues to have – profound implications for the way Britain is governed.

The main provisions of the 1909 Budget were: income tax to be held at 9d in the pound, but with a higher rate of 1/- on incomes of £2,000 or more, and a 'super tax' of 6d on the amount by which incomes of £5,000 or more exceeded £3,000; petrol to be taxed at 3d a gallon and cars to be taxed according to their horsepower; duty on tobacco and alcohol to be raised, along with stamp duty and estate duty; a tax on liquor licences plus a reform of the licensing system.

Most controversial, however, was a package of land taxes: 20% would be levied on the unearned increment of land values, payable when land changed hands by sale, gift or inheritance; there would be also be a capital tax of ½d in the pound on the value of undeveloped land and minerals; and a 10% reversion duty would be charged on the financial recompense which came to a lessee at the end of a lease. Lloyd George, in his celebrated (or notorious, depending on your point of view) Limehouse speech, spelled out why land should be taxed:

> The landlords never deposited the coal in the earth. It was not they who planted those great granite rocks in Wales. Who laid the foundations of the mountains? Was it the landlord? And yet he, by some divine right, demands as his toll – for merely the right for men to risk their lives in hewing those rocks – eight millions a year ... Why should I put burdens on the people? I am one of the children of the people. I was brought up amongst them. I know their trials; and God forbid that I should add one grain of trouble to the anxieties that they bear with such patience and fortitude.

Not surprisingly, these proposals caused an outcry. Under the heading, 'The Socialist Budget: How it Will Affect the Building Trade', the *Bath Chronicle* highlighted the likely impact of the new land tax:

> It is admitted by all parties that the country has been passing through a period of very serious trade depression for the past two years, but the fact is somewhat lost sight of that the building trade has not only suffered in this limited period of general depression, but that it has been depressed for a period of many years, and that there are no signs of any improvement in its condition. This being the case, it is apparent that this trade is highly susceptible to any adverse influences, and it is especially important to those connected with it to be assured that the Finance Bill does not contain any such adverse influences.

Others were less equivocal in their condemnation. Lord Hardinge said the Budget was 'cunningly devised as a vehicle for the socialist revolution', while Lord Northcliffe claimed the Budget was 'so alien to the spirit of England that it represented a sort of treason against all that the country stood for'. The Duke of Northumberland lamented that 'our ancestors kept the political power of the state in the hands of those who had property ... but their successors have destroyed that system, and placed political power in the hands of the multitude, and we must take the consequences.'

While landowners railed against the proposed land tax, working people were more concerned about proposed duties on tobacco and alcohol. In August 1909, a roving reporter from the *Standard*, a national newspaper supporting the Conservatives, came down to North Somerset to find out what working people thought about the Budget. His report – naturally heavily biased against the proposals – nevertheless provides a fascinating social document, and one that contains pre-echoes of more recent outcries against duty hikes:

Out at Priston ... I discovered in a couple of old radicals what I believe to be a living protest against the socialistic tendencies of their leaders. They confessed that since the Budget was put forward they had given up the habit of smoking, and one, who preferred whisky to his native cider, had 'got to the end of the road', to use his quaint agricultural phraseology ... His father and his grandfather before him had voted Liberal [but] he should not vote at all! There you have the silent protest of the country.

Among the adherents of the opposition there is no mistaking the attitude taken up. The very name Lloyd George is anathema, and the increased tobacco tax is the one iniquity with which they are obsessed. They regard the tax as a personal affront, and when one considers that tobacco is often the only luxury which these men can enjoy one can get down to the level of their argument and understand.

Dunkerton is an important parish, including as it does the Dunkerton Colliery, which employs more than a thousand hands. It is not to be expected that among these miners the government has made many friends. Than the miner of average intelligence it is doubtful if you can find a politician more professedly independent of either of the two great parties. The failures of the one they regard with an air of indifference, as though they were inevitable; the triumphs of the other they treat with an unmistakable air of contempt. Among these Dunkerton miners I discovered a tendency towards something uncommonly like selfishness. Situated, as they are, right in the midst of an agricultural district, they are inclined to treat with condescension the humble farm labourer who earns 15/- or 16/- a week. You see it in the throw of their heads as they push their way into the village inns and order their spirit with a quick glance at the sunburnt man in the corner who is quenching his thirst with cider and building up his muscles on a hunk of bread and a morsel of cheese. They pay the extra charge for the spirit

Miners returning home at Westfield, Radstock

with the mannerism of men who are proud that they can afford it: and they do not care the toss of a coin whether or not the man in the corner drinks cider from choice or necessity.

The district, as a whole, is decidedly radical, with a pronounced leaning towards socialism. It was something of a revelation, therefore, to find how attentive they were to Mr Mowbray when he addressed them from the Conservative van. They listened to his arguments against the Budget without once attempting to interrupt, and long after the meeting was closed they continued to debate among themselves. It was not difficult to see that the majority have not yet drunk deeper than the froth of the Budget, and it is only by sending those political vans on tour that the opposition can hope to reach the country.

The people do not welcome the politician because of any insatiable desire to hear politics; the majority look upon his visit much as the townsman might regard a new attraction at the theatre. This is not written in a spirit of cynicism. Only those who go down into these hidden hamlets and live among the people can have any idea of the lives they live. There is something intensely tragic in the day's programme of one old fellow to whom I talked at Englishcombe. When I ventured to express surprise that he knew absolutely nothing of politics, and that his last acquaintance with a politician was when 'a carryvan pitched yonder, look! twenty year an' more agone', he pushed his old felt hat back from a brown, wrinkled brow, and told me why he had 'nothin' to do with them'. He rose every morning at 4.30, walked three miles to the farm where he was employed, had breakfast at seven, dinner at 12.30, tea at 5.30, left the farm at 6.30, excepting at harvest time, walked the three miles back home, and went to bed at eight or 8.30. The only luxury he allowed himself was half an ounce of tobacco a day, and he had cut the allowance down by half since the cost was increased. He did not know who had been responsible for the increase, but if it were a Liberal he should vote against him at the next election – if it wasn't that his father had always been a Liberal!

With the landowners on one side and the smoking classes on the other, the Liberals had a tough battle on their hands. Rallies, such as a mass demonstration in Hyde Park on 24 July 1909, were an essential part of the campaign. We are so used to rallies in London organised by opponents of government policy, it is something of a culture shock to realise that this was a demonstration organised by the government, in support of government policy. The difference between then and now is that this was a government fighting for the right to govern. Having quoted at length from a Conservative newspaper, it is only fair that we should turn to a Liberal one – the *Northern Echo* – for an account of the rally:

> The great demonstration at Hyde Park, London, on Saturday, in favour of the land clauses of the Budget, received enthusiastic support from all parts of the country, and it is estimated that 250,000 Liberals gathered round the platform.
>
> The procession from the Thames Embankment to Hyde Park took about an hour to pass through Trafalgar Square, where the traffic got badly 'hung up'. Some of the marchers were suburbanly smart, and there was an occasional silk hat, while other contingents had the appearance of the unemployed. The trade unionists, with their painted silk banners flapping in the breeze, made the best show.
>
> The resolution forming the text for the speakers was, 'That this meeting heartily welcomes the important provisions contained in the Budget for taxing monopolists and socially created wealth, and particularly for securing a complete

valuation of all land in the United Kingdom, holding this to be essential to any policy of land and social reform.'

It further hoped that 'the government will firmly resist any mutilation of their proposals dictated by selfish interests, and will seek an early opportunity for so extending them as to secure the best use of the land, which must result in increased employment, better housing for the people, and greater prosperity for our national industries'.

It was a bad day for the banner-bearers, owing to the stiff wind, and the flagmen who had fixed their colours to wagonettes or antique omnibuses had the best time of it. 'Cobden stood for free land'; 'Tax land, not food'; 'Shall those who own the land rule the people? No!'; 'The Budget must be law'; 'Tax the idlers – not the workers'; 'Right, not robbery'; 'Land for the landless' and 'Hurrah for Lloyd George' were a few of the mottoes displayed.

During the afternoon some 70 contingents with about eight bands arrived on the Thames Embankment from all parts of the Metropolis – a fine piece of organisation by the Budget League.

Despite the campaigning, however, the Lords threw the Budget out – as Lloyd George knew they would. The Lords had thrown out bills before – and would do so again – but throwing out a Budget breached an unwritten but long-established parliamentary rule. Not since the seventeenth century had the Lords challenged the right of the Commons to raise money. The Conservative peer Lord Ridley justified the veto as follows:

The mistaken impression of many people that the House of Lords could not touch finance was founded on a resolution of the House of Commons passed centuries ago. The Lords had hitherto acquiesced to decisions of the House of Commons because government had been conducted by sane men, but there was now a House of Commons controlled by madmen and they had to take a different view.

Asquith saw it in somewhat different terms, however:

The real question which emerges from the political struggles in this country for the last thirty years is not whether you will have a single or double chamber system of government, but whether when the Tory Party is in power the House of Commons shall be omnipotent, and whether when the Liberal Party is in power the House of Lords shall be omnipotent.

In the absence of electioneering photographs from Bath, this shows the Keynsham headquarters of Joseph King. Although Bath returned to the Conservative fold in 1910, King held North Somerset for the Liberals in both elections that year.

Asquith was left with no option but to call an election, appealing to the electorate not only to show their support for free trade and the initiatives his government had embarked on, but also for a mandate to challenge the House of Lords veto. The election, which was held in January 1910, produced a hung parliament. Bath returned to form, with both Liberal MPs losing their seats, by a narrow margin, to the Conservatives. With the support of Labour and Irish Nationalist MPs, however, Asquith was able to form a government. A second general election was called, in December 1910, as a result of the death of Edward VII; this too failed to produce an overall majority for either party, but the Liberals remained in power with the support of the Irish Nationalists.

Although Asquith was now leading a minority government, in 1911 the Parliament Act was introduced. This aimed to prevent the Lords from vetoing budgets or finance bills, and to limit their power to delay other bills to three parliamentary sessions. It also sought to reduce the maximum time between elections from seven to five years and introduce payment for members of parliament. Conservative peers were, understandably, unhappy about this, but, after King George V (who had succeeded his father a year earlier) agreed to create 250 new Liberal peers if the bill was not passed, they reluctantly agreed to pass it.

Concessions were, however, wrung out of the government and some of the provisions of the 1909 Budget were watered down or abandoned before they became law. Chief among these were the proposals concerning land tax. A century on, what many still regard as the central plank of Lloyd George's reforms is still 'unfinished business'. Lloyd George was influenced, in drawing up the Budget, by the work of an American tax reformer called Henry George, who argued that a tax system based on income would perpetuate economic and social injustice and inequality. George's ideas continue to influence political debate in the UK. A Liberal Democrat Group, ALTER (Action for Land Taxation and Economic Reform) – whose vice presidents include Nick Clegg and Vince Cable – is still seeking 'to rekindle the spirit of 1909'. Meanwhile, Tony Vickers, Chairman of the Liberal Democrat 1909 Group, has issued a rallying cry for the twenty-first century that draws heavily on the past:

It is uncanny how the same issues of embedded economic and social injustice which our forbears planned to tackle 100 years ago still haunt us. A century of Socialism and Monetarism has failed humanity. It is time we rediscovered our liberal economic traditions and stopped arguing about whether social and economic liberalism are 'left' or 'right'. The Land Question was answered 100 years ago – or more. The answer – Land Value Tax – brings the two wings of politics together harmoniously: you get an entrepreneurial but just society, which we call Liberal Democracy. Add green to the mix and there was never a better time to resurrect Land Value Tax and address other structural economic inequities, and the hereditary peers are not around to stop us this century! It is time we planned finally to complete Lloyd George's 'Unfinished Business'. As successors to his Liberal Party, it is down to Liberal Democrats to take this initiative.

Despite Lloyd George's failure to force through the central plank of his legislation, by any standards the Liberal government elected in 1906 achieved an enormous amount. Among the acts passed in 1909 was a Town Planning Act – the first attempt to really tackle this issue, outlawing, among other things, the building of back-to-backs – and the Children and Young Persons Act, which we looked at earlier. Perhaps the most far-reaching, though, was the introduction of Old Age Pensions. It has been said – it was said at the time, by some Labour MPs – that the act was more than a little timorous, and gave limited relief to only a handful of people. Comparing the provisions with those of today, it does indeed seem niggardly. To be eligible for a pension you had to have been a British subject for at least 20 years and be at least 70 years old. Anyone who had 'habitually failed to work' or been in prison in the past ten years was not eligible. You were also ineligible if you had not made payments, for at least ten years up to the age of 60, to a friendly society, insuring against old age and sickness. The pension was also means tested. To receive the full amount of 5/- a week (equivalent to around £18.75 today) you had to have an income of no more than 8/1 a week. If you had more than that coming in, you received progressively less, until, if you had more than 13/1 a week, you got nothing.

The point, though, is that it was a start, something on which to build; the welfare state could not be created overnight, and, even with such modest beginnings, there were those who saw the writing on the wall. Typical of the old guard was Sir Charles Crosthwaite, author and former governor of the North West Provinces of India, who wrote to the *Times* in support of workhouses:

Sir

However the Ministers may attempt to hide it, we are in fact in the presence of the universal outdoor relief scheme divested of the restraining provisions of the present Poor Law. How can any prudent man contemplate such a situation without dismay? The strength of this kingdom, in all its past struggles, has been its great reserve of wealth and the sturdy independent character of its people. The measure which is being pushed through the House of Commons with haste and acclaim will destroy both sources. It will extort the wealth from its possessors by unjust taxation. It will distribute it in small doles, the most wasteful of all forms of expenditure, and will sap the character of the people by teaching them to rely, not on their own exertions, but on the State.

Few were in any doubt that it marked a watershed in English life. Lord Roseberry, for example, believed that 'the most significant piece of legislation passed by the English parliament since the Reform Act of 1832, is the Old Age Pension Act of August 1, 1908.'

When the first pensions were paid out on 1 January 1909, 903 people in Bath, Twerton and Weston received them at a cost of over £350. Of the 188 who attended the main post office in York Buildings, 149 received the full amount, 14 received 4/-, 21 received 3/- and four received 1/-. 'An alarming number,' the *Chronicle* reported, 'could not write their names.' Illiteracy was not the only problem facing claimants. Many could not prove their age; the problem was especially acute in Ireland, where registration of births had been introduced later than in Great Britain. Many had to resort to entries in family bibles; one lady produced a bundle of love letters 50 years old which was accepted as proof. One Irishwoman testified that she recalled the killing of an exceptionally large pig over 70 years earlier – an event still celebrated in local folklore – 'although', it was noted, 'her ancient appearance was the determining factor'.

A year after the introduction of pensions, the government opened the first labour exchanges. The government's other major initiative was a National Insurance Act, under which employees and employers – along with the government – contributed to an insurance scheme which paid out when workers were sick or unemployed. Lloyd George made sure that everyone knew, as he steered the bill through parliament, how revolutionary the changes were:

> You have never had a scheme of this kind tried in a great country like ours, with its thronging millions, with its rooted complexities; and everyone who has been engaged in any kind of reform knows how difficult it is to make way through the inextricable tangle of an old society like ours. This is, therefore, a great experiment ... These are problems with which it is the business of the state to deal; they are problems which the state has neglected too long.

One reform which the Liberals failed to implement, and which was watered down into the hefty increases on alcohol duty in the 1909 Budget, was an emasculation of the licensed trade. The gulf between Conservatives and Liberals was nowhere wider than in their attitude to drink. The Conservatives, supported by powerful brewing interests, supported the status quo; the Liberals, on the other hand, committed to social reform and wedded to temperance ideals, wanted to wage war on binge drinking. The Licensing Bill introduced in 1908 proposed the immediate suppression of over 30,000 public houses – around a third of the UK total. Licences would be retained on the basis of one for every 750 people in towns and cities and one for every 400 people in rural districts.

Bath would have been particularly badly hit. With one pub for every 208 people, it would have lost around two-thirds of them under the government proposals. Local licensing authorities would have been responsible for selecting the pubs

Above: George Miles, seen here with his wife and children, took over the New Inn on Juda Place around 1910 and was landlord until the mid-1930s. If the Liberals had had their way, around two-thirds of Bath's pubs would have closed. The New Inn survived until 1966, when it was demolished to make way for the Snow Hill redevelopment.

Below: Eliza Beard, Bath's longest-serving landlady, outside the Royal Oak in Twerton with her daughter and grandchildren. She ran the pub from 1876 to 1931. After a long period of closure, the Royal Oak reopened in 2005; the local branch of the Campaign for Real Ale voted it pub of the year in 2007, 2008 and 2009.

to close; failure to do so would have meant a national licensing commission acting in their place. Local authorities would also have had the option of revoking more than the statutory number of licences 'if they thought fit'.

Vested interests in the licensed trade – especially the big brewers – saw off the Licensing Bill. The number of pubs was already falling – Bath lost on average five pubs a year between 1906 and 1914 – but, by and large, this was with the support of the licensed trade. Small, old-fashioned, insanitary pubs in inner-city areas where the population was declining were replaced by large new pubs in the suburbs. Brewers and licensing authorities worked together to broker the best deal for the trade, while closing pubs that posed the greatest threat to public order. The Licensing Bill threatened to blow this largely amicable arrangement out of the water – and that is why it was defeated. Out of that defeat, though, came the determination to inflict the maximum amount of damage in the 1909 Budget. Or so at least it seemed to the chairman of Bath's Licensed Victuallers when he addressed them in March 1909:

> There are men in the cabinet mean enough to say, 'You have beaten us on the Licensing Bill; now we'll stick a woman's hatpin in your back through the Budget, so that you cannot fight it.' That is the meaning of it; and that a man who is smart and clever, but not great and statesmanlike – Mr Lloyd George – can say such a thing in almost the same words, and that an erratic political sky-rocket like Mr Churchill should in effect say the same, is a lowering of the position of ministers of the government. If it is right that further taxation should be imposed on the trade, let it be done, but it should not be carried out just because the government has been beaten over the Licensing Bill … They are going to punish the trade by increased taxation, and rule them out of existence in that way because they could not kick them out in the other.

If the Liberals had got their way over the Licensing Bill, who knows what may have happened? Britain might have been set on an irrevocable course towards prohibition, which many Liberals were already advocating. Thankfully, it never happened, although restrictions placed on the licensed trade, under the pretext of national emergency, seven years later, together with far-reaching social and demographic changes later in the twentieth century, saw alcohol consumption plummet, until, with pressure for reform no longer on any political agenda and the temperance movement effectively consigned to history, it began to rise again. Today we find ourselves – or so some alarmists would have us believe – in the grip of a binge-drinking crisis every bit as grave as that of the Edwardians. Another unfinished bit of Lloyd George's reforms, perhaps?

CHAPTER TWELVE

WE WILL BE FREE!

Coal mining may seem a world away from the refined excesses generally associated with Georgian Bath, but, during the period of its greatest glory, Bath was at the hub of a major coalmining area. The closest mine was some three miles out of town, at Newton St Loe. This closed around 1880, but others a little farther off operated until well into the twentieth century. Carts loaded with Somersetshire coal were a familiar site in the city streets; it was the smoke generated by that coal which turned Bath stone from gleaming white to sooty black within just a few years.

Although there may have been mining in north-east Somerset in Roman times, the first record of coal extraction dates from the fifteenth century. It was not until 1763, however, when the Old Pit was sunk at Radstock, that the exploitation of the coalfield began in earnest. By the end of the eighteenth century, output had grown to such an extent that the Somersetshire Coal Canal was built to carry coal to Bath. The coalfield continued to expand; in the second half of the nineteenth century, railways gradually took over from the canal, which eventually fell into disuse. In the early twentieth century the Great Western Railway acquired the canal and built a line along it, which we will be visiting later. Coal production in the Somerset coalfield reached its peak in the early years of the twentieth century, with an annual output of around 1,250,000 tons.

In the towns and villages that sprang up in the coalfield there was, inevitably, friction between mine owners and the men that worked the coal. In 1817 a 10% reduction in wages led to riots that had to be quelled by the Royal Lancers and the North Somerset Yeomanry. In 1864. there was a 'great clamour' for a miners' union; the Somersetshire Miners' Association was formed eight years later. There were major strikes in 1874, 1889, 1893 and 1904, the last three of which went on for over four months.

But it is the Dunkerton Strike of 1908-9 that sticks in the memory of the men of North Somerset – and with good reason. Dunkerton Colliery, despite its name, was just outside the village of Carlingcott, over a mile south-west of Dunkerton. It had a working life of only about 20 years, but during that time it acquired

Two views of Dunkerton Colliery, once the largest in Somerset.

the distinction not only of being the largest colliery in Somerset but also the one with the worst reputation. The contract for sinking the first shaft was signed on 11 May 1903; the first coal was extracted two years later. The mine's reputation was due to the company's policy of extracting coal as quickly and as cheaply as possible. Corners were cut, with scant regard to safety; seams which proved hard to work were abandoned in favour of seams where coal was plentiful. The mine owners had little interest in its long-term viability; they wanted to make the maximum amount of money in the minimum amount of time. Conflict with the workforce was inevitable and it wasn't long in coming.

By April 1907, there were around 200 carting boys employed at Dunkerton, dragging coal out of the mine by means of that notorious device, the guss and crook. This had been devised because the steep, narrow seams of the Somerset Coalfield made the use of tubs impracticable. It consisted of a tarred rope which the carting boy wore round his waist; to this was attached a chain, at the other end of which was the crook. This was hooked onto a putt – a sledge filled with coal – which the carting boy would then drag up out of the mine, crawling along on all fours, with the chain between his legs. New boys would find their waists rubbed raw after a day at work; they were advised to rub their own urine into the sores to toughen up the skin. They were paid 1d per ton for the first 50 yards covered and ½d for every 50 yards after that. They complained that the roads were rougher at Dunkerton than at other collieries and the putts heavier, and put in for a pay rise, asking for 1d for every 50 yards covered. The company dismissed the claim. The dispute rumbled on for eighteen months until, on 29 October 1908, they came out on strike. Four hundred men came out in support, leaving only about 50 at work, who, because there were no boys to carry coal, were assigned to exploratory and maintenance duties.

Strike pay was 10/- a week for the men, 5/- for the boys and 1/- for each child of a collier. There was, inevitably, widespread hardship and, as the striking miners shivered and froze through the long months of a Somerset winter, feeling against those who had stayed at work intensified. Men, forced to desperate measures, were hauled up before the magistrates. William Day, a miner from Wellow, was fined 10/- for poaching rabbits at Rainbow Wood on land owned by Igdaliah Gale. In January, Sidney Bull and Bessie Down from Radford were brought before the magistrates charged with begging on Wellsway in Bath 'by means of a petition'. The money they were collecting was to go towards a party for the children of striking miners. A medal was to be struck to commemorate the strike and each child would receive one. Edward Phillips, JP, who lived at Sydney House in Bath, declared that their actions amounted to 'downright unmitigated tyranny. It's not like the real unemployed.' They were bound over to keep the peace and their petition was confiscated. A correspondent in the *Bath Chronicle* was outraged when he read about the incident:

> Bath is earning an unenviable name for being overrun with mendicants, mendacious cadgers, noisy street musicians and other nuisances. Things have come to a pretty pass when the Bath public are solicited for contributions to provide medals for children to commemorate the regrettable stupidity of their fathers, brothers and uncles going on strike at a time when the charitably inclined are pestered with petitions to relieve distress among the unemployed.

Feelings were running high, and nowhere more so than between the striking miners and those who were still working at the pit. On 22 January 1909, with the strike almost three months old, resentment flared into open conflict, and three men were admitted to the Royal United Hospital with gunshot wounds. The following week's *Bath Chronicle* admitted, in its report of the incident, that 'there are conflicting views as to what occurred'. A century later, with the dust well and truly settled and the participants in that brief but bitter battle all dead, it is still impossible to determine exactly what happened on the fateful night.

The chief protagonists at least agreed on the main outline of the story. On the evening of Friday 22 January 1909, after darkness had fallen, between 150 and 200 strikers gathered and set off from the colliery to Carlingcott, singing two songs written specially for them. The first, by an unknown author, was the 'Dunkerton Carting Boys Song':

> The men and boys of the Dunkerton pit
> Came out on strike, you see –
> For one 'alf-penny,
> And mean to have that 'd'.
> They won't go back till they've got the advance
> And won the victory
> So boys – join in – sing this song with glee:
>
> Chorus
> We're the Dunkerton carting boys,
> Just the Dunkerton carting boys,
> We're the Dunkerton boys. Oh! So true;
> Tho' we're poorly and plainly dress'd,
> We're as honest as one of the best,
> We'll all stick together, whatever the weather,
> The Dunkerton carting boys.

The second was written by Mr SH Whitehouse, the agent:

> We'll claim our rights, we will be men,
> We will not be enslaved again;
> The cry shall sound from sea to sea,
> We will be free, we will be free!
> No tyrant's frown, no false friend's smile,
> Shall henceforth our footsteps beguile,
> And every day, in every thing,
> We'll speak, and act just as we sing.

As they approached Vernal House, the home of Charles Heal, the colliery manager, two shots were fired from the house into the air. As the marchers continued along the public highway, further shots rang out from the house and several men in the crowd shouted out that they'd been shot. The police, who were close by, intervened at this point to prevent, according to their report, 'what might have been a rush on the house'. The *Bath Chronicle* takes up the story:

Great excitement prevailed, amounting, said an informant, almost to a panic, and there were cries for Mr Heal. It is rumoured that whoever was in the house made their escape, and the thoughts of those present were diverted, for the time being, to their injured comrades. Messengers were sent in search of doctors, and in other

The old Beehive at Carlingcott, where some of the injured were taken.

cases conveyances were procured, and the injured parties driven to doctors in the district, there being no medical man within a radius of two or three miles ... Some of the men were taken to a shop, others to the *Beehive* public house. First aid was rendered by the doctors, but it was found necessary to send three men, John Parfitt, Charles Moon and Tom Davis, to Bath Hospital.

James Bartlett, a carting boy, said that, after the shots were fired,

blood was flowing freely from me in several places. My friends got a car and drove me to Timsbury where I was seen to by a doctor. He pulled a shot from the back of my neck. He didn't pull the other ones out. There were four wounds in my arms and six in my legs, so small spreading shot must have been used in the gun.

He was too ill to say much more, but his older brother, who was a coal-getter, said that there hadn't been much of a demonstration:

There are a few who we call 'bosses', who didn't come out when we went on strike, and there's been a bit of trouble over them, but no violence. As far as the shooting goes, there were between a hundred and two hundred of us marching to Carlingcott singing our songs, and when we reached the manager's house there were shouts of 'Are we downhearted?' to which we shouted back 'No!' and then we were fired upon.

'Did any of the marchers fire at the house first?' the *Chronicle* reporter asked him.

'Absolutely not!' he replied, 'none of the men had any fire-arms with them. We were fired upon seven or eight times.'

Charles Heal, the colliery manager, gave a somewhat different version of events:

On Friday, at about two o'clock, when the men came out of the pit, between three and four hundred men and women, who'd assembled together, followed them – seven of them in all – to their homes. They hustled them about the roads, and had it not been for police protection, no doubt the men would have been most seriously handled. They then turned their attention to their cottages and began to smash their windows ... This continued until between 3.30 and 4, when the crowd dispersed to their homes, and things seemed fairly quiet. At about 6.15 they again collected in Carlingcott and passed through the street, smashing in the window of Albert Brock. There was a crowd of between two to three hundred. They then made their way to my house. I was out, but my wife, son and daughter, and a brother-in-law who had come on a visit, were sitting in the house talking when they heard a mob coming off the main road into the lane. A minute or two later stones began to come against the house.

Edgar, my son ran out of the back door with his revolver and fired it into the air twice – this being all the cartridges he had in his revolver. He thought the shooting would have the effect of preventing the crowd from coming into the house. But it seemed only to infuriate them, and the crowd came on, still throwing stones at the house and at my son, as he was standing in the recess near the back door. He rushed into the house, picked up my shotgun, put three or four cartridges into it and fired into the legs of the crowd in self-defence, as they were swearing they would take his life. This dispersed them for some time and enabled my wife and my son and daughter to escape from the house. My brother-in-law remained in hiding in the house. Just as the crowd was dispersing I drove home from Radstock, and on my going into the house found that my wife, daughter and son had all gone. My brother-in-law came rushing down the stairs asking me if I had seen the crowd, and he said that they had been smashing the windows and that Mrs Heal and my son and daughter had escaped.

As he was speaking to me we heard the noise as though the crowd was coming back to the house, and so he escaped and left me on the premises. My wife, son and daughter went to his sister-in-law's home at New Town, Carlingcott for shelter. My wife persuaded my son to get clean away as she was afraid they would take his life if they got hold of him.

Tom Davis, aged about 30, was one of the men shot by Edgar Heal. Interviewed in hospital, he gave the following version of events:

There were about 200 of us altogether, and we were on the road leading to Camerton, but some distance from Mr Heal's house. We stood there singing strike songs – 'Britannia's Sons' and 'The Dunkerton Boys'. We were about 60 yards from Mr Heal's house when two shots were fired. I don't know whether they were fired into the air or not. They may have been fired to frighten us. We had not intended going down to the house, but it was a high road, and when the shots were fired we went on. We walked along toward the house for 25 or 30 yards, and then we stopped and sang again. We were on the high road which runs at the back of Mr Heal's house near to the spot where a by-lane joins the road. One of the chaps said he could see the man by the light of a window, standing in between a couple of outhouses at the back of the main building. Several more shots were fired. I said, 'He's firing blanks,' but just then a young chap called Ted Stock was shot in the leg, and started to run away.

At the same moment, I felt a pain in my legs, and knew I had been shot. I caught hold of Ted's coat and said, 'Don't run away – I'm shot.' After running several yards I fell down. Someone took me to a house, and then I think I must have fainted off. After a doctor had seen to me I was taken in a trap to the Bath Hospital, where I arrived about half past nine.

At a special sitting of the Weston Police Court on the following Monday, Edgar Heal was charged with unlawfully and maliciously wounding Tom Davis and others. A large group of miners was present. The case was remanded to 8 February and Edgar Heal was released on £50 bail.

Carlingcott and Dunkerton remained on high alert. The following week the *Chronicle* reported that 'extreme precautionary measures are being taken. As well as a contingent of mounted police a county magistrate is in the vicinity each night, fortified with a copy of the Riot Act.' Retribution was not long in coming. On 6 February, twelve men were summoned on the instigation of Charles Heal and charged 'that on 22 January [they] did unlawfully, notoriously and tumultuously assemble together with intent to assist each other in an unlawful object – to wit, to prevent certain persons from doing work which they had a legal right to do, namely to work at Dunkerton Colliery, and afterwards in a violent manner, to the terror of the people, threatened the above mentioned and did damage to two dwelling houses.'

It was alleged during the trial that, when the workers left the pit, there were cries of 'Kill them!' and 'Get them down!' Other threats were used and trays beaten by the crowd. It was also alleged

After the incident at Dunkerton, the authorities didn't take any chances. This formidable body of policemen was drafted in to keep the peace in Radstock when miners there went on strike three years later.

that some were armed with sticks and stones. A police sergeant said that they were led by a group of women, one of whom carried a rough cross wrapped in crepe. Three police constables had been carried off their feet by the mob.

Frank Wilcocks of the Grove, Peasedown St John, a bailiff at the colliery, was escorted by police when he left work on 22 January. He hadn't heard any threats because of the noise made by the women. He had not gone to work since because of the ordeal.

The case was referred to the Somerset Assizes and was heard on 26 February. Two of the men were discharged, seven received three months' imprisonment with hard labour, three received six months' imprisonment with hard labour. On 20 March, Edgar Heal appeared before the Somerset Assizes and was found not guilty. The following day, ten more miners appeared before the Assizes. One received nine months' hard labour, two received seven months' hard labour, two received four months' hard labour; the rest were found not guilty.

The strike had already ended, the men and boys having returned to work on 18 February pending arbitration. A court appointed by the Board of Trade met at the Royal Hotel in Bristol on 5-6 March. After due deliberation they decided that the carting boys' rates of pay were fair and should not be increased. As for Charles Heal, he resigned as manager of Dunkerton Colliery in

December 1909 after six years service and moved to Mells to be manager of the colliery there.

Although Dunkerton Colliery closed in May 1925, mining continued at other sites in the Somerset Coalfield for almost 50 years. The last pit – Lower Writhlington, a couple of miles to the south – closed in 1973. Some of the colliery buildings at Dunkerton can still be seen, as can the batch – now covered with trees – where the spoil was dumped; for the most part, though, the scene today is one of green fields, rolling hills, clear streams and quiet lanes – rural England at its undemonstrative best. Even though most vestiges of mining have disappeared, however, memories of that black day in January 1909 – like the memory of the dreadful guss and crook – are still very much alive.

Also remembered – albeit for very different reasons – is an incident that happened nine months earlier at Norton Hill Colliery in Midsomer Norton. It was one that those who fulminated so self-righteously at the couple collecting funds for the children of striking miners might have done well to bear in mind.

A century ago, coal was the basis of Britain's position as the pre-eminent world trading power. In 1907, the value of the coal produced in Britain was twice that of the cotton industry and three and a half times that of the iron and steel industries – yet miners' wages fell by 10% between 1900 and 1911. Despite improvements in safety and conditions, working down a mine was still one of the most dangerous and difficult ways to make a living. In the early twentieth century, a miner who had worked in the pit all his life would had survived a one-in-twenty chance of being killed. Around a thousand men a year were killed by roof falls, flooding, explosions or other accidents. On 16 February 1909, 168 men and boys were killed at West Stanley Pit in County Durham. Eyewitnesses described standing near the pithead after a muffled explosion rocked the mine; the engineer looking down to see a red glow at the bottom of the shaft, before a red ball of fire shot from the pit and was sucked back down again. On the same day that a mass funeral was held for the victims, 267 miners at Mainsforth Colliery in County Durham were summoned for breach of contract for striking for two days and fined 10/- each with costs. In July 1909 the government brought in the Coal Mines Regulation Act, limiting the time men could work underground to eight hours; mine owners responded by cutting wages. Miners in Wales, for example, were told their wages would be cut by 7.5%.

Above: Norton Hill Colliery.
Below: A postcard published in Midsomer Norton to commemorate the disaster.

The Somerset Coalfield, although small in relative terms, employed 4,017 men in 1911 – 3.2% of the county's workforce. It had seen its share of casualties, including several major disasters – twelve men and boys killed at Wellsway Pit, Radstock in 1839, eleven killed at Newbury near Coleford in 1869, seven killed at Upper Conygre in Timsbury in 1895. Norton Hill Colliery, just east of the Somerset & Dorset station at Midsomer Norton, originally opened in the 1840s but closed around 20 years later. Around 1896 the site was acquired by Frank and Louis Beauchamp, who already owned other mines in the area. When it reopened it was the largest colliery in Somerset, acquiring the nickname Beauchamp's Gold Mine. It had a workforce of around 380 and soon acquired a reputation as one of the most up-to-date pits in the area. Then, at around ten o'clock on the night of 9 April 1908 there was a large explosion deep underground, which was heard over much of the town. A large crowd soon gathered at the pithead, and rescue parties were quickly organised to go down the pit. Twenty-nine men had gone down on the night shift; ten of them died. The heroism of the rescuers, and of the men underground, was extraordinary, and received nationwide coverage, so much so that, in the following year, it was announced that the Prince of Wales would be visiting Midsomer Norton to honour those who had risked their lives trying to save their friends and comrades.

The visit was scheduled for 23 June 1909. The royal progress through the area began at Shepton Mallet, where the Prince's car drove up Town Street and High Street to continuous cheering, before meeting Duchy of Cornwall tenants in Collett Park. The fire brigade of the Anglo Bavarian Brewery acted as guard of honour and over 2,000 children from the surrounding parishes sang 'God Bless the Prince of Wales'. After speeches, the Prince planted an oak tree and left for lunch at Longleat.

Light rain was falling when the Prince set off after lunch, but by the time he reached Frome 'the weather was brilliantly fine'. The people of Frome 'had caused the principal thoroughfares to be gaily decorated, and the enthusiastic cheering which arose on all hands as the royal motor car proceeded through the streets must have convinced its occupants of the deep loyalty of the picturesque market town'. Schoolchildren lining Bath Street waved flags and sang 'God Bless the Prince of Wales'; a band took up the same tune in the Market Place. Outside the Bull Inn was 'an effective naval device, the boys of the National School having manned a gatling gun on a platform from which salutes were fired as the royal cars moved through the square.'

Frome left behind, the Daimler cars 'took up a good pace' as they made their way to Laverton. They travelled at around 25 miles an hour, and the motors 'took the hills quite easily without showing any appreciable difference in pace'. Then it was on to Norton St Philip – more decorations, more flag waving, more cheering – and 'on the corner turning into the Hemington road the car slowed down

Local children parading through Shepton Mallet and the Prince of Wales in Collett Park.

while their Royal Highnesses took an interested look at the venerable *George Inn*'. On the bank outside the parish church, another group of schoolchildren broke into 'God Bless the Prince of Wales'. Then it was on through Faulkland and down into Radstock:

> The reception at the top of the hill leading to Radstock was particularly vociferous and spontaneous, several hundreds of people and children being grouped at this point. Coming into the town there was a salvo of artillery, or what sounded like it, from the anvils in Lord Waldegrave's colliery carriage works.

The town was one mass of decoration ... Up to the Wells Road and along past the block of colliers' cottages, the demonstration of loyalty was maintained as keenly as anywhere, and there was not a household, however humble, which did not display flags or garlands of flowers or royal photographs ... When coming into Midsomer Norton, below the Somerset & Dorset Railway arch the royal visitors were greeted with a salute of fog signals, the echo of which resounded throughout the pretty valley. Needless to say, the quaint little town made the most of its royal visit. History, or, perhaps, to be more correct, legend, states that the last royal visitor to honour Midsomer Norton was Charles II. At the entrance to the town the Prince was met by an escort composed of the Bath troop of the North Somerset Yeomanry ... who looked exceedingly smart in their blue and white uniform, and were well mounted.

They made their way, not to the colliery where, deep underground, the men had died, but to Norton House, Major Beauchamp's home, in front of which a dais had been erected.

'It is a great pleasure,' the Prince began, as he surveyed the crowd, with the heroes of that dreadful night sitting in the front row,

to be present here today and to visit this district in which is situated considerable property belonging to the Duchy of Cornwall, and to have the opportunity of seeing some of my tenants. As Grand Prior of the Order of St John of Jerusalem in England, I am especially glad to be able to present medals and other awards of the Order to some of your miners, who, on the occasion of the colliery explosion at Norton Hill on 9 April 1908, displayed that highest form of courage in risking their own lives to save those of their fellow creatures. I have also learned that there were others who performed acts of great self-sacrifice and devotion, and you recognise with gratitude the untiring and invaluable professional assistance rendered to your entombed colleagues by Dr Pollard.

Major Beauchamp then thanked the Prince and read a short address:

The names of the men receiving medals are Herbert Attwood, John Sims and William Gould. Herbert Attwood, within a few minutes of the explosion, descended the mine, and, as an obstruction caused by the explosion prevented the cage reaching the landing, he got out of the same and, at great risk to his life, slid down the greasy iron guide to the landing, which was 100 yards above the shaft bottom. He then took steps to restore the ventilation and travelled a long distance alone trying to reach the district of the explosion and where men had been working. Eventually he reached two men who had been killed. Driven back by after-damp he met Gould and Sims, who by this time had reached the landing, and he with them attempted to reach,

Above: A postcard commemorating the royal visit to Midsomer Norton.
Below: The Prince's progress through Paulton.

Above: The service in the ruins of Glastonbury Abbey.
Overleaf: Driving through Wells – a souvenir postcard printed with the wrong date.

by another route, the men who were known to be working in the district where the explosion occurred. After travelling some distance in their efforts to reach the men they were themselves overcome by after-damp and were found insensible by later relief parties.

The certificates have been awarded to the doctors and relief parties of colliery managers and miners, who, at great risk to their lives, volunteered to go down the mine with them to render all possible assistance, and succeeded in rescuing Attwood, Sims and Gould, the three men previously referred to. These acts of bravery are proofs of the manner in which miners always willingly risk their own lives in trying to save the lives of their comrades.

The Prince then awarded medals to the three men before getting back into his car and heading off, via Paulton, to a millenary service in Wells and another in the ruins of Glastonbury Abbey to celebrate the restoration work carried out by Frederick Bligh Bond.

ROYAL VISIT TO WELLS. T.R.H. Leaving for GLASTONBURY June 22 1909. No 24

180

CHAPTER THIRTEEN

IN PURSUIT OF SPRING

Four years after the Prince of Wales made his royal progress – by car – from Frome to Shepton Mallet, someone far less celebrated made a similar journey by bicycle and recorded what he saw.

Edward Thomas's *In Pursuit of Spring* is the record of a Eastertide journey from London to the Quantocks. It provides a vivid evocation of the countryside, towns and villages through which he passed on the eve of the Great War.

As one drives through the countryside south of Bath today, it might appear that it has not changed, in its essentials, for centuries. Yet, while much of what Thomas described is still recognisable, at times he might be writing about an unknown land, so much has been lost, so much gained, in the last century. Things commonplace to him – elm-lined roads, gypsy caravans, horse-drawn ploughs, coal carts – are, for the most part, not even fading memories today. This was a world when a car was an event, and country life, for all its vicissitudes, still followed the same rhythms it had followed for centuries; a world innocent, for a little while longer, of trading estates, supermarkets, dual carriageways, by-passes, executive homes and factory farms, where one could stop and stare – and listen to birdsong – without getting mown down by a ceaseless flow of traffic.

The importance of *In Pursuit of Spring* goes beyond this, however. When he cycled through Wiltshire and Somerset, Edward Thomas was a relatively unknown 35-year-old literary critic and nature writer. When the book was published, a friend of his, the American poet Robert Frost, told him that it was full of poetry, 'but in prose form where it does not declare itself'. He selected four paragraphs and told Thomas to rewrite them 'in verse form in exactly the same cadence'.

He took Frost's advice, experimenting with verse forms, and wrote his first true poem, 'Up in the Wind', a few months later, on 3 December 1914. Less than five weeks later, on 8 January 1915, he wrote 'Adlestrop', one of the most celebrated poems in the English language. It was based, like many of his poems, on an incident that he had earlier recorded in prose; he readily admitted that his poems were 'quintessences of the best parts of my prose books'.

In July 1915 he enlisted in the Artist's Rifle Corps and in December 1916, despite his age, volunteered for service overseas. He wrote his last poem, 'The Sorrow of True Love', on 13 January 1917, at an army camp in Kent shortly before leaving for France. At 7.36 on the morning of 9 April 1917 – Easter Monday – he was killed by a shell blast at the start of the Arras offensive. Despite the shortness of his poetic career and the slenderness of his *Collected Poems* – running to just 142 poems – he is not only one of twentieth-century's best-loved poets but also one of its most respected. In 2002, the Poet Laureate, Andrew Motion, asked to choose the ten greatest volumes of poetry in English, placed Thomas's *Collected Poems* alongside works by Chaucer, Shakespeare and Wordsworth.

All of that lay in the future that Eastertide when he cycled westward down dusty roads, through a landscape about to be transformed for ever.

His route is not easy to follow, even though, for the most part, he kept to main roads. He was uncharacteristically reluctant to tell us where he stayed the two nights he spent on the borders of Wiltshire and Somerset. This was almost certainly deliberate. He knew the area well; a year earlier he had stayed with Clifford Bax, the brother of the composer Arnold Bax, at Monkton House near Broughton Gifford. He had also stayed at Dillybrook Farm near Rode, and it is likely that he stayed there in 1913. It has been suggested that he had had a romantic liaison while staying at Monkton or Dillybrook – possibly one that was revived in 1913 – which would provide ample reason for him throwing up a smokescreen. If nothing else, it certainly adds to the mystery.

Although the journey took place in 1913 rather than 1909, little would have changed in the intervening four years – and a similar journey (although without references to the Titanic) could have made by anyone cycling through the countryside south of Bath in 1909. By any standards, it is an extraordinary account; with the benefit of hindsight it is more extraordinary still. We know two things its author did not – that he would come to be regarded as a major poet and that he would be killed in battle four years later. If you're familiar with Thomas's work, you will pick up many pre-echoes of his poetry in this account. The Edwardian age was one of great transformations; Thomas's journey, heading westward, was not only one of discovery but one that laid the foundations for his transformation from a jobbing writer to one of the greatest poets of the century.

The following, heavily-edited extracts from *In Search of Spring* can give no more than a flavour of the book. We make no excuse for including such a long extract: it provides what no amount of analysis and conjecture could hope to – a vivid evocation, based on close observation and long acquaintance, of what rural England was like a century ago. And, after so long spent in contemplation of the less savoury aspects of Edwardian life, we really do deserve a few days in the country.

We join Edward Thomas just before two o'clock on the afternoon of Easter Sunday, 23 March 1913. He had left Dunbridge, a few miles east of Salisbury, early that morning, and has just passed through Tilshead, travelling north towards Devizes on what today is the A360:

It is a hedgeless road, with more or less wide margins of rough grass, along which proceed two lines of poplars, some dead, some newly planted, all unprosperous and resembling the sails of windmills. A league of ploughland on either hand was broken only by a clump or two on the high ridges and a rick on the lower. As it was Sunday no white and black teams were crossing these spaces, sowing or scarifying. The rooks flew back and forth; the pewit brandished himself in the air; the lark sang continually; on one of the dead poplars a corn bunting delivered his unvaried song, as if a handful of small pebbles dropped in a chain dispiritedly. Nobody was on the road, it being then two o'clock, except a young soldier going to meet a girl. The rain came, but was gone again before I reached Joan-a-Gore's. The farmhouse, the spacious farmyard and group of irregular, shadowy thatched buildings, and the surrounding rookery elms, all on a gently sloping ground next to the road – this is the finest modern thing on the Plain. The farm itself is but a small, slated house, grey-white in colour, with a porch and five front windows, half hid among elm trees; but the whole group probably resembles a Saxon chief's homestead. The trees make a nearly continuous copse with the elms and ashes that stand around above the thatched cart lodges and combined sheds and cottages at Joan-a-Gore's cross. No hedge, wall, or fence divides this group from my road or from the ridgeway crossing it, and I turned into one of the doorless lodges to eat. I sat on a wagon shaft, looking out north over the ridgeway and the north edge of the Plain. Where it passed the cart lodge the ridgeway was a dusty farm track; but on the other side of the crossing it was a fair road, leading past a new farm group towards Imber.[1] Chickens pecked round me in the road dust and within the shed. Sparrows chattered in the thatch. The bells of sheep folded in neighbouring root fields tinkled. In the rookery the rooks cawed. The young soldier had met his girl, and was walking back with her hand in his. The heavy dark sagging clouds let out some rain without silencing the larks. As the sun came out again a trapful of friends of the

cottagers drove up. The trap was drawn up alongside of me with a few stares: the women went in; the men put away the horse and strolled about. Well, I could not rest here when I had finished eating. Perhaps Sunday had tainted the solitude and quiet; I know not. So I mounted and rode on north-westward.

The road was beginning to descend off the Plain. The poplars having come to an end, elms lined it on both sides. When the descent steepened the roadside banks became high and covered in arum, parsley, nettle, and ground ivy, and sometimes elder and ivy. No hedgerow on the left hid the great waves of the Plain towards Imber, and the fascinating hollow of the Warren close at hand. The slabby ploughland sinks away to a sharp-cut, flat-bottomed hollow of an oblong tendency, enclosed by half-wooded, green terraced banks all round except at the entrance, which is towards the road. This is the Warren, a most pleasant thing to see, a natural theatre unconsciously improved by human work, but impossible to imitate entirely by art, and all the better for being empty.[2]

---

1 The road is still there, but Imber is now in the middle of an army firing range. The village and the land surrounding it were commandeered by the government in 1943. It has been out of bounds, apart from occasional access days, ever since.
2 The Warren is still there, although the trees have grown up since Thomas passed this way.

Nearing the foot of the descent the road on the left is blinded by a fence, so that I could hardly see the deep wooded cleave parallel to me, and could only hear the little river running down it to Lavington. Very clear and thin and bright went this water over the white and dark stones by the wayside, as I came down to the forge at West Lavington and the *Bridge Inn*.[3] West Lavington is a street of about two miles of cottages, a timber-yard, inns, a great house, a church, and gardens, with interruptions from fields. All Saints' Church stands upon a steep bank on the left, a towered church with a staircase corner turret and an Easter flag flying. Round about it throng the portly box tombs and their attendant headstones, in memory of the Meads, Saunderses, Bartlets, Naishes, Webbs, Browns, Allens, and the rest. Among the Browns is James Brown, shepherd 'for thirty-nine years', who died in 1887, and was then but forty-six. The trees and thatched and tiled roofs of the village hid the Plain from the churchyard.

Dauntsey Agricultural College.

Instead of going straight on through Potterne and Devizes, I turned to the left by the Dauntsey Agricultural College,[4] and entered a road which follows the foot of the Plain westward to Westbury and Frome. Thus I had the north wall of the Plain always visible on my left as I rode through Little Cheverell, Erlestoke, Tinhead, and Edington. The road twisted steeply downhill between high banks of loose earth and elm roots, half draped by arum, dandelion, ground ivy, and parsley, and the flowers of speedwell and deadnettle; then up again to Little Cheverell. Here I mounted a bank of nettles and celandines under elm trees into the churchyard, and between two pairs of pollard limes to the door of the church, and

3 The *Bridge Inn* is still there, as is the stream, but there is no sign of a forge today.
4 Now renamed Dauntsey's School.

'I had the north wall of the Plain always visible on my left ...'

walked round it and saw the two box tombs smothered in ivy, and the spotted old carved stones only two feet out of the ground. Behind the church rises Strawberry Hill. A cow was lowing in the farmyard over the road. Fowls were scratching deeper and deeper the holes among the elm roots on the church bank.

Then for a distance the road traversed hedgeless arable levels that rose gently in their young green garments up to the Plain. I looked back, and saw the vast wall of the Plain making an elbow at West Lavington, and crooking round to a clump on a straw-coloured hill above Urchfont, the farthest point visible. Before me stretched the woods of Erlestoke Park, crossing the road and slanting narrow and irregular up and along the hillside, lining it with beech and fir for over a mile, under the name of Hill Wood. The road dipped steeply through the grounds of the park, and its high banks of gray sand, dressed in dog's mercury and ivy, and overhung by pine trees, shut out everything on either hand. Several private bridges crossed the deep road, and a woman had stopped that her child might shout, 'Cuckoo! Cuckoo!' under the arch of one of them. Emerging from these walls, the road cut though a chain of ponds. Erlestoke Park lay on both sides. On the right its deer fed by the new church under a steep rise of elms and sycamores; on the left rooks cawed among the elms and chestnuts scattered on lawn that sloped up to Hill Wood.[5]

A timber-yard, a *George and Dragon*, and many neat thatched cottages compose the wayside village of Erlestoke.[6] Water was flashing down the gutters. Quite a number of people were on the road, but no one could tell me the meaning of the statuary niched on the cottage walls. It must have come from 'some old ancient place,' they said. An old man who had dwelt for eighteen years in one of the cottages thus adorned, and had worked as a

5 In 1950, Erlestoke Manor was damaged by fire and converted to a prison. Many new buildings were added and a high perimeter fence constructed around the park. The bridges across the road have disappeared.
6 The *George & Dragon* and the cottages are still much as Thomas found them.

boy with old men that knew the place, could tell me no more. Some of the figures were nudes – one a female, with the coy hands of Venus, rising from her bath – others classical, and symbolic or grotesque: all astonishing in that position, ten feet up on a cottage wall, and unlikely to have come from the old church in Erlestoke Park.

Not a mile of this road was without cottagers strolling with their children or walking out to see friends in the beautiful weather. But just outside Erlestoke I met two slightly dilapidated women, not cottage women, with a perambulator, and twenty yards behind them two weatherbeaten, able-bodied men in caps, better dressed than the women. As I went by, one of them gave a shout, which I did not take as meant for me. He continued to shout what I discovered to be 'Sir' in a loud voice until I turned round and had to get down. They advanced to meet me. The shorter man, a stocky fellow of not much past thirty, with very little nose, thin lips, and a strong, shaven chin, hastened up to me and inquired, in an unnecessarily decided manner, the road to Devizes, and if there were many houses on the way. The taller man, slender and very upright, with bright blue eyes, had by this time come up, and the two began to beg, telling rapidly, loudly, emphatically, and complainingly, a combined story into which the Titanic was introduced. One of them pointed out that he was wearing the button of the Seamen's Guild. They wanted me to look at papers. The two women, who were still walking on, they claimed as their wives. The more they talked the less inclined did I feel to give them money. Though they began to call down a blessing on me, I still refused. They persisted. The shorter one was not silent while I mounted my bicycle. So I rode away out of reach of their blessings without giving them anything. I tried to explain to myself why. For sixpence I might have purchased two loaves or three pints for them, and for myself blessings and possibly some sort of glow. I did not know nearly enough of mankind to condemn them as mere beggars; besides, mere beggars must live, if any one must. But they were very glib and continuous. Also they were hearty men in good health – which should have been a reason for giving them what I could afford. The strongest reason against it was probably alarm at being given some responsibility at one blow for five bodies in some ways worse off than myself, and shame, too, at the act of handing money and receiving thanks for it. My conscience was uneasy. I could not appease it with sixpence, nor with half a sovereign, which might have been thought generous if I had told the story. If I was to do anything I ought to have seen the thing through, to have accompanied these people and seen that they slept dry and ate enough, and got work or a pension. To give them money was to take mean advantage of the fact that in half a mile or so I could stow them away among the mysteries and miseries of the world. Too late I concluded that I ought to have listened to their story to the end, to have read their papers and formed an opinion, and to have given what I could, because in any case I should be none the worse, and they might be the better, if only to the extent of three pints between them. I made a resolution – a sort of a resolution – to give sixpence in future to every beggar, and leave the question of right or wrong till

> When the Archangel's trump shall sound
> And slumbering mortals bid to rise,

and the schoolmaster's expectation is answered. Nevertheless, I was uneasy – so uneasy that the next beggar got nothing from me. It was simpler to pass by with a helpless 'Que sais-je?' shrug, than to stop and have a look at him and say something, while I felt in my pockets and made the choice between my coppers and my smallest silver.

Thus I rode uphill though more steep banks of gray sand draped in ivy, overhung with pine trees. Dipping again, I came to a park-like meadow, a pond, and a small house above rather stiff, ineffectual green terraces, on my right; while on the left the wall of the Plain was carved from top to bottom by three parallel even rolls like suet puddings, and these again carved across horizontally. A little farther on Coulston Hill was hollowed out into a great round steep bay which had once been a beech wood. Now all the beeches were lying anyhow, but mostly pointing downward, on the steep where they had fallen or slid, some singly, some in raft-like masses. Not a tree remained upright. The bared, blackish earth and the gray stems – of the colour of charred wood and ashes – suggested fire. The disorder of the strewn debris suggested earthquake. All was silent. A stiff man of fifty was endeavouring to loiter without stopping still in the road while his daughter of eighteen tried to keep her distance behind him by picking anemones without actually stopping.

Before Tinhead there were more vertical rolls and corresponding troughs on the hillside, and at the foot again three or four wide terraces, and below them a cornfield reaching to the road. To the low, dark-blue elm country away from the Plain – that is, northward – and to the far wooded ridge on its horizon, the westering light was beginning to add a sleeplike softness of pale haze. Over the low hedges I saw league after league of this lower land, and the drab buttresses of Beacon Hill near Devizes on its eastern edge. It had the appearance of a level, uninhabitable land of many trees. Several times a hollow cleft in the slope below the road – a cleft walled by trees, but grass-bottomed – guided the eye out towards it. All along good roads led down to the vale, and an equal number of rough roads climbed the hillside up to the Plain. I was to go down, not up, and I looked with regret at the clear ridge and the rampart of Bratton Castle carved on it against the sky, the high bare slopes, the green magnificent gulleys and horizontal terraces, the white roads, and especially a rough cartway mounting steeply from Edington between prodigious naked banks. For I had formerly gone up this cartway on a day so fine that for many nights afterwards I could send myself to sleep by thinking of how I climbed, seeing only these precipitous banks and the band of sky above them, until I emerged into the glory and the peace of the Plain, of the unbounded Plain and the unbounded sky, and the marriage of sun and wind that was being celebrated upon them. But it was no use going the same way, for I was tired and alone, and it was near the end of the afternoon, though still cloudily bright and warm. I had to go down, not up, to find a bed that I knew of seven or eight miles from Tinhead and Edington.

These two are typical downside villages of brick and thatch, built on the banks of the main road, a parallel lane or two, and some steep connecting lanes at right angles. When I first entered them from below I was surprised again and again how many steps yet higher up the downside they extended. From top to bottom the ledges and inclines on which they stand, and the intervening spaces of grass and orchard, cover about half a mile. Tinhead has an *Old George Inn* of an L shape, with a yard in the angle. Edington, almost linked to Tinhead by cottages scattered along the road, has a *Plough* and *Old White Horse.*[7] They were beginning to advertise the Tinhead and Bratton inns as suitable for teas and weekend parties. Hence, perhaps, the prefix 'Old'. For hereby is the first station since Lavington on the line that goes parallel to the wall of the Plain and a mile or two below the road, all along the Pewsey vale to Westbury.

I turned away from the hills through Edington, which has a big towered church among its farm-yards, cottage gardens, and elm slopes – big enough to seat all Edington, men and cattle. Like Salisbury Cathedral, this church looks as if it had been made in one piece. All over, it is a uniform rough gray without ivy or moss or any stain.

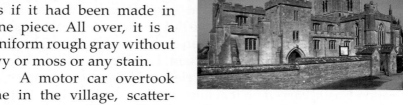

A motor car overtook me in the village, scattering a group of boys. 'Look out!' cried one, and as the thing passed by, turned to the next boy with, 'There's a fine motor; worth more than you are; cost a lot of money.' Is this not the awakening of England? At least, it is truth. One pink foxy boy laughed in my face as if there had been iron bars or a wall of plate glass dividing us; another waited till I had started, to hail me, 'Longlegs'.

Rapidly I slid down, crossed the railway, and found myself in a land where oaks stood in the hedges and out in mid-meadow, and the banks were all primroses, and a brook gurgled slow among rush, marigold, and willow. High above me, on my left hand, eastward, was the grandest, cliffiest part of the Plain wall, the bastioned angle where it bends round southward by Westbury and Warminster, bare for the most part, carved with the White Horse and with double tiers of chalk pits, crowned with the gigantic camps of Bratton, Battlesbury, and Scratchbury, ploughed only on some of the lower slopes, and pierced by the road to Imber. The chimneys of Trowbridge made a clump on ahead to my right. In the west the dark ridge of the Mendips made the horizon.

I turned out of my way to see Steeple Ashton. It has no steeple, being in fact Staple Ashton, but a tower and a dial

7 All three inns have closed. The only one still open in the two villages is the Lamb at Tinhead.

The market cross and lock-up at Steeple Ashton.

on a church, a very big church, bristling with coarse crockets all over, and knobby with coarse gargoyles, half lion and half dog, some spewing down, some out, some up. It is not a show village, like Lacock, where the houses are packed as in a town, and most of the gardens invisible; but a happy alternation of cottages of stone or brick (sometimes placed herring-bone fashion) or timber work, vegetable gardens, orchard plots, and the wagon-maker's. On many a wagon for miles round the name of Steeple Ashton is painted. It is on level ground, but well up towards the Plain, over the wall of which rounded clouds, pure white and sunlit, were heaving up. Rain threatened again, but did no more. The late afternoon grew more and more quiet and still, and in the warmth I mistook a distant dog's bark, and again a cock's crowing, for the call of a cuckoo, mixed with the blackbird's singing. I strained my ears, willing to be persuaded, but was not. I was sliding easily west, accompanied by rooks going homeward, and hailed by thrushes in elm trees beside the road – through West Ashton and downhill on the straight green-bordered road between Carter's Wood and Flowery Wood. I crossed the little river Biss and went under the railway to North Bradley. This is a village built partly along the road from Westbury to Trowbridge, partly along two parallel turnings out of it. The most conspicuous houses on the main road are the red brick and stone villas with railings and small gardens, bearing the following names: The Laurels, East Lynn, Cremont, Lyndhurst, Hume Villa, Alcester Cottage, Rose Villa, and Frith House, all in one row. On a dusty, cold day, when sparrows are chattering irresolutely, this is not a cheerful spot; nor yet when an organ-grinder is singing and grinding at the same time, while his more beauteous and artistic-looking mate stands deceitfully by and makes all the motions but none of the music of a baritone in pain.[8] To the outward eye, at least, the better part of North Bradley is the by-road which the old flat-fronted asylum of stone faces across a small green, the church tower standing behind, half hid by trees. I went down this road, past farms called Ireland and Scotland on the left, and on the right a green lane, where, among pots and pans, a gypsy caravan had anchored, belonging to a Loveridge of Bristol. Venus, spiky with beams, hung in the pale sky, and Orion stood up before me, above the blue woods of the horizon. All the thrushes of England sang at that hour, and against that background of myriads I heard two or three singing their frank, clear notes in a mad eagerness to have all done before dark; for already the blackbirds were chinking and shifting places along the hedgerows. And presently it was dark, but for a lamp at an open door, and silent, but for a chained dog barking, and a pine tree moaning over the house. When the dog ceased, an owl hooted, and when the owl ceased I could just hear the river Frome roaring steadily over a weir far off.[9] Before I settled into a chair I asked them what the weather was going to be like to-morrow. 'Who knows?' they said, 'but we do want sun. The grass isn't looking so well as it was a month ago: it's looking browny.' Had any eggs been found? 'Not one; but we've heard of them being found, and we've been looking out for plovers' eggs.' I asked what they did with the song birds' eggs, and if they were ever eaten. The idea of eating such little eggs disgusted every one over fifteen; but they were fond of moorhens', and had once taken twenty-two from a single nest before the bird moved to a safe place. Yes,

8 Thomas would struggle to recognize the main road through North Bradley today and an organ grinder would stand very little chance against the constant roar of traffic.
9 Probably the weir at Tellisford, just over half a mile west of Dillybrook Farm, which Thomas was to visit two days later.

they had plenty of chicks, and some young ducks half grown. The turkeys were laying, but it was too early to let them sit ... Again I heard the weir, and I began to think of sleep.

Once in the night I awoke and heard the weir again, but the first sound in the morning was a thrush singing in a lilac next my window. For the main chorus of dawn was over. It was a still morning under a sky that was one low arch of cloud, a little whiter in places, but all gray. Big drops glistened on the undersides of horizontal rails. There had been a white frost, and, as they said, we seldom have many white frosts before it rains again. But not until I went out could I tell that it was softly and coldly raining. Everything more than two or three fields away was hidden.

Cycling is inferior to walking in this weather, because in cycling chiefly ample views are to be seen, and the mist conceals them. You travel too quickly to notice many small things; you see nothing save the troops of elms on the verge of invisibility. But walking I saw every small thing one by one; not only the handsome gateway chestnut just fully dressed, and the pale green larch plantation where another chiff-chaff was singing, and the tall elm tipped by a linnet pausing and musing a few notes, but every primrose and celandine and dandelion on the banks, every silvered green leaf of honey-suckle up in the hedge, every patch of brightest moss, every luminous drop on a thorn tip. The world seemed a small place: as I went between a row of elms and a row of beeches occupied by rooks, I had a feeling that the road, that the world itself, was private, all theirs; and the state of the road under their nests confirmed me. I was going hither and thither to-day in the neighbourhood of my stopping place, instead of continuing my journey.

At a quarter-past nine it drizzled slightly more, but by ten the sky whitened, the grass gleamed. Over the broad field where the fowls and turkeys feed, and a retriever guards them, the keeper was walking slow and heavy, carrying a mattock, and after him two men, one in gaiters. While they were disappearing from sight in the corner where the field runs up into the wood, the chained retriever stood and whined piteously after them. I understood him very well. And somehow the men setting out thus for a day's work in the woods prophesied fine weather. Yet at half-past ten the gray thrust the white down again to the horizon, where the elms printed themselves against it.

The sun came out in earnest at eleven, and shone upon a field of tall yellow mustard and a man loading a cart with it, and I ceased to bend my back and crook my neck towards violet, primrose, anemone, and dog's mercury in the blackthorn hedges, and I let the sun have a chance with me. I was trespassing, but, alas! no glory any longer attaches to trespassing, because every one is so civil unless you are a plain or ill-dressed woman, or a child, or obviously a poet. So I came well-warmed to Rudge, a hamlet collected about a meeting of roads and scattered up a steep hill, along one of these roads. The collection includes a small inn called the *Half Moon*,[10] a plain Baptist chapel, several stone cottages, several ruins, solid but roofless, used solely to advertise sales, and a signpost pointing to Berkley and Frome past the ruined cottages, to Westbury and Bradley downhill from the inn, through the woods about the river Biss, and uphill to Rode and Beckington. Southward I saw the single bare hump of Cley Hill five miles away, near Warminster: northward, the broad wooded vale rising up to hills on the horizon. I went uphill, between two bright trickles of water. The steep roadside bank, strengthened by a stone wall, was well-grown with pennywort and cranesbill, overhung by goose grass and ivy, and bathed at its foot by grass and nettles. The wall in one place is hollowed out into a cavernous, dark dip-well or water-cupboard. The rest of the village is built upon the banks. First comes a Wesleyan chapel, a neat, cold, demure little barn of the early nineteenth century, having a cypress on either side of its front door, and a few gravestones round about. One of these caught my eye with the verse –

> *And am I born to die,*
> *To lay this body down,*
> *And must my trembling spirit fly*
> *Into a world unknown?*

– and the name of Mary Willcox, who died in 1901 at the age of eighty-eight. A cottage or two stand not quite opposite, behind gardens of wallflowers, mezereon, periwinkle, and tall copper-coloured peony shoots, and a wall smothered in

10 Either Thomas's memory was playing him tricks or the inn has since been renamed the Full Moon.

snow-on-the-mountains or alyssum. On the same side, beyond, a dark farm-house and its outbuildings project and cause the road and water to twist. The bank on that side, the left, covered with celandines and topped with elms, now carries a footpath of broad flagstones a yard or two above the road. Where this footpath ends, the road, still ascending, forks, and at once rejoins itself, thus making a small triangular island, occupied by a ruinous, ivy-mantled cottage and a cultivated vegetable garden. At the lower side a newish villa with a piano faces past the ruin uphill. At the upper side, facing past the ruin and the villa downhill, is a high-walled stone house of several gables, small enough, but possessing dignity and even a certain faint grimness: it is backed on the roadside by farm buildings. I saw and heard nobody from the *Half Moon* to this house, except a chicken.

I returned and went some way along the road to Beckington. A few people were walking in towards Rudge, children were picking primroses from both sides of the hedges, watched silently and steadfastly by a baby in a perambulator, not less happy in the sun than they. For the sun shone radiant and warm out of a whitewashed sky on the red ploughlands and wet daisy meadows by Seymour's Court Farm, on the teams puffing chain harrows and pewits plunging round them, and on the flag waving over Rode Church as if for some natural festival. I found my first thrush's egg of the year along this road, in which I was fortunate; for the bank below the nest had been trodden into steps by boys who had examined it before me.

I went downhill again through Rudge and took the road for North Bradley, keeping above the left bank of the river Biss and commanding the White Horse on the pale wall of the Plain beyond it. This took me past Cutteridge, a modest farm, all that remains of a great house, whose long avenues of limes, crooked and often as dense as a magpie's nest, still radiate from it on three sides. This is a country of noble elms, spreading like oaks, above celandine banks.

Turning to the right down a steep-sided lane after passing Cutteridge I reached the flat, rushy, and willowy green valley of the Biss. The road forded the brook and brought me up into the sloping courtyard of Brook House Farm. On the right was a high wall and a pile of rough cordwood against it; on the left a buttressed, ecclesiastical-looking building with tiers of windows and three doorways, some four or five centuries old; and before me, at the top of the yard, between the upper end of the high wall and the ecclesiastical-looking building, was the back of the farmhouse, its brass pans gleaming. This is the remnant of Brook House. What is now a cowshed below, a cheese room above, has been the chapel of Brook House, formerly the seat of Paveleys, Joneses, and Cheneys. The brook below was once called Baron's Brook on account of the barony conferred on the owner: the family of Willoughby de Broke are said to have taken their name from it. The cows made an excellent congregation, free from all the disadvantages of believing or wanting to believe in the immortality of the soul, in the lower half of the old chapel; the upper floor and its shelves of Cheddar cheeses of all sizes could not offend the most jealous deity or his most jealous worshippers. The high, intricate rafter-work of the tiled roof was open, and the timber, as pale as if newly scrubbed, was free from cobwebs – in fact, chestnut wood is said to forbid cobwebs. Against the wall leaned long boards bearing the round stains of bygone cheeses. Every one who could write had carved his name on the stone. Instead of windows there were three doors in the side away from the quadrangle, as if at one time they had been entered either from a contiguous building or by a staircase from beneath. Evidently both the upper and the lower chambers were formerly subdivided into cells of some kind.

The farmhouse is presumably the remnant of the old manor house, cool and still, looking out away from the quadrangle over a garden containing a broad, rough-hewn stone disinterred hereby, and a green field corrugated in parallelograms betokening old walls or an encampment. The field next to this is spoken of as a churchyard, but there seems to be no record of skeletons found there. Half a mile off in different directions are Cutteridge, Hawkeridge, and Storridge, but nothing nearer in that narrow, gentle valley.

The afternoon was as fine as Easter Monday could be, all that could be desired by chapel-goers for their Anniversary Tea. It was the very weather that Trowbridge people needed on Good Friday for a walk to Farleigh Castle, for beer or tea and watercress at the *Hungerford Arms*. As I bicycled into Trowbridge at four o'clock the inhabitants were streaming out along the dry road westward.

I am not fond of crowds, but this holiday crowd caused no particular distaste. Away from their town and separated into small groups they had no cumulative effect. They were for the time being travellers as much as I was. In any case, a town like Trowbridge is used to strangers of all kinds passing through it: it would take a South Sea Islander in native costume to make it stare as a village does ...

I did not stop in Trowbridge. Its twenty chimneys were as tranquil as its tall spire, and its slaughterhouse as silent as the adjacent church, where the poet Crabbe, once vicar, is commemorated by a tablet, informing the world that he rose by his abilities. In fact, the noisiest thing in Trowbridge was the rookery where I left it. Like nearly all towns – market towns, factory towns – Trowbridge is girdled by villas, chestnuts, and elms, and in the trees rooks build, thus making a ceremoniously rustic entrance or exit. While the rooks cawed overhead, the blackbirds sang below.

As far as Hilperton and the *Lion and Fiddle*,[11] houses and fields alternated along the road, but after that I entered a broad elmy country of young corn and new-ploughed land sweeping gradually away on my right up to grass slopes, and to the foot of dark Roundway Down and pale Beacon Hill, above Devizes. Far to the left the meadow land swelled up into the wooded high land above Lacock, Corsham, and Bath. Under elms near Semington the threshing-machine boomed; its unchanging note mingled with a hiss at the addition of each sheaf. Otherwise the earth was the rooks', heaven was the larks', and I rode easily on along the good level road somewhere between the two.

Motion was extraordinarily easy that afternoon, and I had no doubts that I did well to bicycle instead of walking. It was as easy as riding in a cart, and more satisfying to a restless man. At the same time I was a great deal nearer to being a disembodied spirit than I can often be. I was not at all tired, so far as I knew. No people or thoughts embarrassed me. I fed through the senses directly, but very temperately, through the eyes chiefly, and was happier than is explicable or seems reasonable. This pleasure of my disembodied spirit (so to call it) was an inhuman and diffused one, such as may be attained by whatever dregs of this our life survive after death. In fact, had I to describe the adventure of this remnant of a man I should express it somewhat thus, with no need of help from Dante, Mr A C Benson, or any other visitors to the afterworld. In a different mood I might have been encouraged to believe the experience a foretaste of

11 Still open today.

a sort of imprisonment in the viewless winds, or of a spiritual share in the task of keeping the cloudy winds 'fresh for the opening of the morning's eye'. Supposing I were persuaded to provide this afterworld with some of the usual furniture, I could borrow several visible things from that ride though Semington, Melksham, and Staverton. First and chief would be the Phoenix 'Swiss' Milk Factory where I crossed the Avon at Staverton.[12] It is an enormous stone cube, with multitudinous windows all alike, and at the back of it two tall chimneys. The Avon winding at its foot is a beautiful, willowy river. On the opposite side of the road and bridge the river bank rises up steeply, clothed evenly with elms, and crowned by Staverton's little church which the trees half conceal … This many-windowed naked mass, surmounted by a stone phoenix, immediately over the conspicuous information that it was burnt on November 5, 1884, and rebuilt on April 28 of the next year, is as big as a cathedral, and like a cathedral in possessing a rookery in the riverside elms behind it. With the small, shadowed church opposite, I feel sure that it would need little transmutation to fall into the geography of a land of shades. But the most beautiful thing of all was the broad meadow called Challimead on the west of Melksham, and the towered church lying along the summit of the gentle rise in which it ends. I bicycled along the north-west side of it immediately after leaving Melksham on the way to Holt. Elms of a hundred years' growth lined the road, some upright, most lying amid the wreckage of their branchwork far out over the grass. Parallel with the road and much nearer to it than to the church the Avon serpentined along the meadow without disturbing the level three furlongs of its perfect green. The windows of the church flamed in the last sunbeams, the tombstones were clear white. For this meadow at least there should be a place in any Elysium. It would be a suitable model for the meadow of heavenly sheen where Aeneas saw the blessed souls of Ilus and Assaracus and Dardanus and the bard Musaeus, heroes and wise men, and the beautiful horses of the heroes, in that diviner air lighted by another sun and other stars than ours.

But our sun was fading over Challimead. The air grew cold as I went on, and the pewits cried as if it were winter. The rooks were now silent dots all over the elms of the Trowbridge rookery. A light mist was brushing over the fields, softening the brightness

12 The factory, much expanded, was until recently owned by Nestlé.

of Venus in the pale rosy west, and the scarlet flames that leapt suddenly from a thorn pile in a field. Probably there would be another frost to-night ... People were returning to the town in small and more scattered groups. At corners and crossways figures were standing talking, or bidding farewell. I rode on easily through the chill, friendly land. Clear hoofs hammering and men or girls talking in traps were but an added music to the quiet throughout the evening. I began to feel some confidence in the Spring.

I went out into the village at about half-past nine in the dark, quiet evening. A few stars penetrated the soft sky; a few lights shone on earth, from a distant farm seen through a gap in the cottages. Singly and in groups, separated by gardens or bits of orchard, the cottages were vaguely discernible: here and there a yellow window square gave out a feeling of home, tranquillity, security. Nearly all were silent. Ordinary speech was not to be heard, but from one house came the sounds of an harmonium being played and a voice singing a hymn, both faintly. A dog barked far off. After an interval a gate fell-to lightly. Nobody was on the road.

The road was visible most dimly, and was like a pale mist at an uncertain distance. When I reached the green all was still and silent. The cottages on the opposite side of the road all lay back, and they were merely blacker stains on the darkness. The pollard willows fringing the green, which in the sunlight resemble mops, were now very much like a procession of men, strange primeval beings, pausing to meditate in the darkness.

The intervals between the cottages were longer here, and still longer; I ceased to notice them until I came to the last house, a small farm, where the dog growled, but in a subdued tone, as if only to condemn my footsteps on the deserted road.

Rows of elm trees on both sides of the road succeeded. I walked more slowly, and at a gateway stopped. While I leaned looking over it at nothing, there was a long silence that could be felt, so that a train whistling two miles away seemed as remote as the stars. The noise could not overleap the boundaries of that silence. And yet I presently moved away, back towards the village, with slow steps.

I was tasting the quiet and the safety without a thought. Night had no evil in it. Though a stranger, I believed that no one wished harm to me. The first man I saw, fitfully revealed by a swinging lantern as he crossed his garden, seemed to me to have the same feeling, to be utterly free of trouble or any care.

A man slightly drunk deviated towards me, halted muttering, and deviated away again. I heard his gate shut, and he was absorbed.

The inn door, which was now open, was as the entrance to a bright cave in the middle of the darkness: the illumination had a kind of blessedness such as it might have had to a cow, not without foreignness; and a half-seen man within it belonged to a world, blessed indeed, but far different from this one of mine, dark, soft, and tranquil. I felt that I could walk on thus, sipping the evening silence and solitude, endlessly. But at the house where I was staying I stopped as usual. I entered, blinked at the light, and by laughing at something, said with the intention of being laughed at, I swiftly again naturalized myself.

I awoke to hear ducklings squeaking, and a starling in the pine tree imitating the curlew and the owl hunting. Then I heard another chiffchaff. Everything more than a quarter of a mile away was hidden by the mist of a motionless white frost, but the blackbird disregarded it. At a quarter to eight he was singing perfectly in an oak at the cross roads. The sun had melted the frost wherever it was not protected by hedges or fallen trees. Soon a breeze broke up and scattered and destroyed the mist, and I set out on a warm, cloudy morning that could do no wrong. As I was riding down the halfway hill between Trowbridge and Bradford, where the hedge has a number of thorns trimmed to an umbrella shape at intervals, they were ploughing with two horses, and the sun gleamed on the muscles of the horses and the polished slabs of the furrows. Jackdaws were flying and crying over Bradford on Avon.

I dismounted by the empty *Lamb Inn*,[13] with a statue of a black-faced lamb over its porch, and sat on the bridge. The Avon ran swift, but calm and dull, down under the bridge and away westward. The town hill rises from off the water, covered as with scales with stone houses of countless varieties of blackened gray and many gables, and so steep that the roofs of one horizontal street are only just higher than the doorsteps of the one above. A brewery towers from the mass at the far side, and, near the top, a factory with the words 'For Sale' printed on its roof in huge letters. And the smoke of factories blew across the town. The hilltop above the houses is crested with beeches

13 The *Lamb* was later demolished and replaced by a mill, itself now derelict but with plans for conversion.

The bridge at Bradford on Avon

and rooks' nests against the blue. The narrow space between the foot of the hill and the river is occupied by private gardens, a church and its churchyard yews and chestnuts, and by a tall empty factory based on the river bank itself, with a notice 'To Let'.[14]

Opposite this a small public garden of grass and planes and chestnuts comes to the water's edge, and next to that, a workshop and a house or two, separated from the water by rough willowy plots, an angle of flat grass and an almond tree, and private gardens. Behind me the river disappeared among houses and willows.

As I sat there, who should come up and stare at the chapel on the bridge and its weather-vane of a gilded perch[15], but the Other Man.[16] Surprise sufficiently fortified whatever pleasure we felt to compel us to join company; for he also was going to Wells.

14 The large empty factory, Abbey Mills, is now retirement flats.
15 Actually a gudgeon, an early Christian symbol, which has given the town its motto: 'Under the fish and over the water'.
16 The 'Other Man' is a recurring feature in Thomas's prose writings and also appears in his poetry.

Farleigh Hungerford.

We took the Frome road as far as Wingfield, where we turned off westward to Farleigh Hungerford. In half a mile we were in Somerset, descending by a steep bank of celandines under beeches that rose up on our right towards the Frome. The river lay clear ahead of us, and to our left. A bushy hill, terraced horizontally, rose beyond it, and Farleigh Hungerford Castle, an ivied front, a hollow-eyed round tower, and a gateway, faced us from the brow. From the bridge, and the ruined cottages and mills collected round it, we walked up to the castle, which is a show place. From here the Other Man would have me turn aside to see Tellisford. This is a hamlet scattered along half a mile of by-road, from a church at the corner down to the Frome. Once there was a ford, but now you cross by a stone footbridge with white wooden handrails. A ruined flock-mill and a ruined ancient house stand next to it on one side; on the other the only house is a farm with a round tower embodied in its front.[17] Away from this farm a beautiful meadow slopes between the river and the woods above. This grass, which becomes level for a few yards nearest the bank, was the best possible place, said the Other Man, for running in the sun after bathing at the weir – we could see its white wall of foam half a mile higher up the river, which was concealed by alders beyond. He said it was a great haunt of nightingales.

17 Both house and mill have been restored. A turbine has been installed in the mill to generate hydro-electricity.

The bridge at Tellisford.

And there was also a service tree; and, said he, in that tree sang a thrush all through May ...

Thanks, I suppose, to the Other Man's conversation, we took the wrong road, retracing our steps to Farleigh instead of going straight on to Norton St. Philip. However, it was a fine day. The sun shone quietly; the new-cut hedges were green and trim; neither did any of the prunings puncture our tyres. Near the crossing from Woolverton to Freshford and Bath we sat down on a sheep trough and ate lunch in a sloping field sprinkled with oak trees ...

We had not gone a mile from this stopping-place when the Other Man got off to look over the *George* at Norton St. Philip, another show place, known to its proprietor as 'the oldest licensed house in England', and once for a night occupied by the Duke of Monmouth. It is a considerable, venerable house, timbered in front, with a room that was formerly a wool market extending over its whole length and breadth under the roof. In the rear of it crowded many pent-houses and outbuildings, equivalent to a hamlet, and once, no doubt, sufficient for all purposes connected with travel on foot or horseback. The Other Man was scared out of it in good time by a new arrival, a man of magnificent voice, who talked with authority, and without permission and without intermission, to any one whom neighbourhood made a listener. After a wish that the talker might become dumb, or he himself deaf, the Other Man escaped.

Above: The George – 'another show place'.
Below: 'We glided down the street' – houses round the well at Norton St Philip.

We glided down the street to a little tributary of a tributary
too pleasantly to stop at the church below, though it had a grand
tower with tiers of windows. The rise following brought us up
to where a road crosses from Wellow, and at the crossing stands
a small isolated inn called *Tucker's Grave*. Who Tucker was, and
whether it was a man or a woman buried at the crossing, I did not

Tucker's Grave, still open and still much as it was a century ago, one of the least-altered pubs in the country.

discover. The next village was Faulkland, a mile farther on. It is built around a green, on one side of which a big elm overshadows a pair of stocks and a low, long stone for the patient to sit upon, and at the side a tall one like a rude sculptured constable. A number of other great stones were distributed about the village, including two smooth and rounded ones, like flat loaves, on a cottage wall. The children and youths of the village were in the road, the children whipping tops of a carrot shape, the youths of seventeen or so playing at marbles.[18]

From this high land – for since rising up away from Norton St Philip we had always been over four hundred feet up, midway between the valleys of the Frome on the left and the Midford brook on the right – we looked far on either side over valleys of mist. The hollow land on the right, which contained Radstock coalfield, many elm trees, and old overgrown mounds of coal refuse, was vague, and drowsed in the summerlike mist: the white smoke of the collieries drifted slowly in horizontal bands athwart the mist. The voices of lambs rose up, the songs of larks descended, out of the mist. Rooks cawed from field to field. Carts met us or passed us coming from Rode, Freshford,

18 The stocks and stones are still there, although you'd be unlikely to find the local youths playing marbles in the road.

Frome, and other places, to load up with coal from the store by the side of the road, which is joined to the distant colliery by a miniature railway, steep and straight. But what dominated the scene was a tall square tower on the road. Turner's Tower the map named it. Otherwise at a distance it might have been taken for an uncommon church tower or a huge chimney. The Other Man asked twenty questions about it of a carter whom we met as we came up to it; and the carter, a round-eyed, round-nosed, round-voiced, genial man, answered them all. He said it had been built half a century ago by a gentleman farmer named Turner, as a rival to Lord Hylton's tower which we could see on our left at a wooded hilltop near Ammerdown House. Originally it measured two hundred and thirty feet in height. Mr. Turner used to go up and down it, but it served no other purpose, and in course of time more than half fell down. The long hall at the bottom became a club-room, where miners used to drink more than other people thought good for them. Finally Lord Hylton bought it: the club ceased. About a hundred feet of the tower survives, pierced by a few pointed windows above and doors below, cheap and ecclesiastical in appearance. Attached to it is a block of cottages, and several others lie behind.[19]

We crossed the Frome and Radstock road, and raced down a straight mile that is lined on the left by the high park walls of Ammerdown House, and overhung by beeches. At the bottom only an inferior road continued our line, and that dwindled to a footpath. For the descent to Kilmersdon by this direct route is too precipitous for a modern road. We had to turn, therefore, sharp to the left along the road from Writhlington to Mells and Frome, and then curved round out of it to the right, and so under the railway down to Kilmersdon.[20] Before entering the village the road bent alongside a steep wooded slope littered with ash poles. The bottom of the deep hollow is occupied by a church, an inn distinguished by a coat-of-arms, and the motto, 'Tant que je puis' and many stone cottages strung about a stream and a parallelogram of roads. The church tower has three tiers of windows in it, and a blue-faced clock, whose gilt hands pointed to half-past three. There is a venerable and amusing menagerie of round-headed and long-headed

19 Turner's Tower and the cottages attached to it have disappeared, although the cottages that stood behind it are still there. Foxcote Coal Depot, linked to the collieries by tramway, was 500 yards west of Turner's Tower.
20 The road still follows this route today.

Above: The church at Kilmersdon, with the Jolliffe Arms on the right.
Below: JM Fry's fleet of carriages lined up outside the post office at Stratton-on-the-Fosse.

gargoyles, with which a man could spend a lifetime unbored. Inside as well as outside the church the Jolliffe family, now represented by Lord Hylton, predominates, amid the Easter scent of jonquil and daffodil.

Out of Kilmersdon we walked uphill, looking back at the cottage groups in the hollow, the much-carved green slopes, and the high land we had traversed, all craggy-ridged in the mist. As steeply we descended to another streamlet, another hollow called Snail's Bottom, and the hamlet of Charlton and a rookery. Another climb of a mile, always in sight of a stout hilltop tower very dark against the sky, took us up to where the Wells road crosses a Roman road, the Fosse Way, now the road from Bath to Shepton Mallet. We chose the Fosse Way in order to see both Shepton and Wells. Thus we went through Stratton-on-the-Fosse, a high roadside village that provides teas, and includes a Roman Catholic college and a new church attached to it – that church whose tower we had been admiring so as it stood up against the sky. The flowering currant here was dressed in blossom.

A mile farther on we were seven hundred and twenty feet up, almost on a level with the ridge of the Mendips, now close before us. Running from that point down to Nettlebridge and its rivulet, and walking up away from them, was the best thing in the day. The gradient of the hillside was too much for a modern road. The Fosse Way, therefore, had been deserted and a new descent made, curving like an S; yet, even so, bold enough for a high speed to be attained before we got down to the *George*[21] and the loose-clustered houses of Nettlebridge. The opposite ascent was also in an S. At the top of it we sat on a wall by the larches of Harridge Wood, and looked back and down. The valley was broad and destitute of trees. Gorse scrambled over its sides. Ducks fed across the turf at the bottom. Straight down the other side came the Fosse Way, denoted by its hedges, and round its crossing of the brook was gathered half of Nettlebridge. The rough, open valley, the running water, the brookside cluster of stone cottages, reminded me of Pembrokeshire. There is no church.

From that bleak and yet pleasant scene I turned with admiration to a farmhouse on the other side of the road. It stood well above the road, and the stone wall enclosing its farmyard followed the irregular crown of the steep slope. This plain stone house, darkened, I think, by a sycamore, and standing high, solitary, and gloomy, above Nettlebridge, seemed to me a house of houses. If I could draw, I would draw this and call it 'A House'. For it had all the spirit of a house, farm, and fortress in one, grim without bellicosity, tranquil, but not pampered.

Presently, at Oakhill, we were well up on the main northern slope of the Mendips. The *Oakhill Inn*, a good inn, hangs out its name on a horizontal bar, ending in a gilded oak leaf and acorn. I

21 Still open today.

had lunch there once of the best possible fat bacon and bread fried in the fat, for a shilling; and for nothing, the company of a citizen of Wells, a hearty, strong-voiced man, who read the *Standard* over a beefsteak, a pint of cider, and a good deal of cheese, and at intervals instructed me on the roads of the Mendips, the scenery, the celebrated places, and also praised his city and praised the stout of Oakhill. Then he smacked his lips, pressed his bowler tight down on his head, and drove off towards Leigh upon Mendip.[22] I was sorry not to have arrived at a better hour this time. The village is no more than the inn, the brewery, and a few cottages, and a shop or two, in one of which there was a pretty show of horse ornaments of brass among the saddlery. I almost counted these ornaments, crescents, stars, and bosses, as flowers of Spring, so clearly did I recall their May Day flashing in former years. It was darkening, or at least saddening, as we rode out of Oakhill along the edge of a park which was notable for much-

'Unprepared as I was, I expected to meet my end in the steep conclusion of this descent': the entrance to Shepton Mallet along Waterloo Road.

twisted, dark sycamores on roots accumulated above-ground like pedestals. At the far side gleamed the water, I imagine, of the brewery reservoir. We reached the main ridge road of the Mendips soon after this, and crossed it at a point about nine hundred feet high. Shepton is five hundred feet lower, and but two miles distant; so that we glided down somewhat like gods, having for domain an expanse that ended in the mass of Selwood Forest twelve miles to our left, level topped, huge, and dim, under a cloudy sky. Unprepared as I was, I expected to meet my end in the steep conclusion of this descent, which was through narrow streets; and my brakes were bad ...

The market cross stands at the turn. It is a stone canopy, supported by six pillars in a circle, and one central pillar surrounded by two stone steps or seats, and the south side wears a dial, dated 1841. To know the yards of the *Red Lion, George* and

---

22 The *Oakhill Inn* is now run by Charlie and Amanda Digney, who also run the *Garrick's Head* and the *King William* in Bath. Although lunch today would set Thomas back somewhat more than a shilling, the traditional fare would probably be much to his liking.

Bunch of Grapes,[23] and all the lanes and high-walled passages between Shepton and the prison, would be a task (for the first ten years of life) very cheerful to look back upon, and it would be difficult to invent anything more amusing and ingenious, as it would be impossible to invent anything prettier than the ivy, the

Shepton from the church tower, with the market cross on the left and the yard of the Red Lion on the right.

ivy-leaved toadflax, and that kidney-leafed cressy white flower growing on the walls of the passages. There are no public lights in Shepton, so that away from the shop lamps all now was dark in the side streets and edges of the town. The stone prison and all its apertures, like a great wasps' nest, was a punishment to look at in the darkness. But night added grandeur to the many round arches of the viaduct on which the railway strides across the valley.[24] At this, a sort of boundary to Shepton upon the east, I turned back, and ended the day at a temperance hotel. Its plain and not old-looking exterior, ordinary bar and public room, suggested nothing of the ancientness within. I found a good fire and peace in the company of a man who studied Bradshaw. With the aid of maps I travelled my road again, dwelling chiefly on Tellisford, its white bridge over the Frome, the ruined mill and cottage, the round tower of Vaggs Hill Farm, and the distinct green valley which enclosed them, and after this, the Nettlebridge valley and the dark house above it.

23 All gone.
24 The prison and the viaduct are still there, although the railway closed in 1966.

210

CHAPTER FOURTEEN

A NORTHSTOKE TRAGEDY

Six miles north-west of Bath, at the end of a tangle of narrow lanes, is the village of Northstoke. It is not the sort of place you are likely to stumble on by accident, or on the way to somewhere else. You have got to want to go there, but even then it is likely to prove somewhat elusive. Which explains why so few people know the village. Admittedly, there is not much there – no pub, no post office, no shop – and there never has been. It has got a population of just 97; a century ago there were 126 people in the village. Today, most of its residents commute to Bath or Bristol. A century ago its population consisted mainly of landowners, small farmers and farm labourers.

But, while it is one of the least known and least visited places in the area, it has an illustrious past. It may have slept away the centuries, but its dreams have certainly been colourful. The astonishing thing about Northstoke is its sense of continuity, the sense that this is an ancient place. Northstoke has probably always been much the same size as it is today, but its history has been a gradual decline from dubious eminence to virtual obscurity.

Although early tribes may have settled here, and may even have regarded it as a holy place, it was the Romans who really put it on the map. The church contains fragments of Roman material, indicating it probably stands on the site of a Roman temple. It is Church Farm, just below it, that sets Northstoke apart, however. It started life as a Roman villa, and, although the original buildings are long gone, it still retains that characteristic shape, of a square built round a central courtyard. In AD758, the farm was granted to Bath Abbey, at its foundation, by Kenulf, King of Mercia, as a monastic grange. Despite the title being contested by Modbert de Stoke in 1120, it continued as such until the Reformation, when the manor passed first to Paulet Lord St John and then to the manor of East Greenwich. It is extraordinary to think that a working farm, more or less the same size as it is today, has stood on this site for almost 2000 years.

It wasn't such an out-of-the-way place for the Romans, though. It lay on the Roman road from Aquae Sulis (Bath) to Portus Abonae

(Sea Mills). It was a road the legions would have marched along, on their way to the fortress of Caerleon, on the other side of the Bristol Channel. And, on a summer's day at least, it is possible to imagine the villa's owners, as they gazed out across the verdant hills and valleys, with the sea glinting in the distance, being reminded of the view over the Roman campagna from Tivoli. Today, the Roman road is just a muddy footpath and Northstoke is on the road to nowhere. Its only other near-brush with history came on 4 July 1643, when Parliamentary troops camped near the church on the night before the Battle of Lansdown.

The present church was built by the Normans in the eleventh century. The mighty yew in the churchyard dates from around the same time. At the base of the steps leading up to the church (presently closed for safety reasons) is a well fed by a spring from the hills above the church. The water is so rich in limestone that objects left in it for any length of time calcify and come out looking as though they are made of stone. Petrifying wells were viewed as sacred by the Celts, suggesting that there may have been a religious settlement here before the Romans. The church's most remarkable feature is a massive rectangular font, possible Roman in origin, with three Celtic heads carved on it. There was originally a fourth, but this was filed down – possibly because the font was pre-Christian and started life as a ceremonial or sacrificial table, and the fourth head was removed so that the remaining three could represent the Holy Trinity.

Northstoke is a place of many secrets and many ghosts, although their presence is a generally benign one. There is one ghost, however, much closer to us than the Celts or the Romans or the medieval monks, whose spirit does not lie so easy.

At the far end of the village – a couple of hundred yards from the church – is an imposing house called Stonecross. It was built as a rectory in 1828 by the Rev Henry Hayes. Its wide lawns slope gently down to a ha-ha; at the end of the field beyond it the land drops steeply away, commanding a magnificent prospect of the Avon valley. When you consider that the rector who moved here in 1904 had a stipend of £157 a year and only 126 people to minister to, you might think he would have regarded himself as fortunate indeed. But the Reverend Shadwell Keen was not one for counting his blessings.

He was born in Ireland in 1863. After his ordination he worked at Exeter, Blaenavon, Swimbridge and Kilve before becoming a curate at Bath, with responsibility for Priddy, in 1901. That same

Northstoke Rectory as it would have appeared in 1909.

year he married Katherine Latham, four years his junior, in Croydon, and the couple settled at Arnwood on Lansdown Road in Bath. The marriage was doomed from the start. Mr Keen realised he had made a terrible mistake and felt that he had been trapped into marrying Katherine. Her mother, he later claimed, had told him that if he did not marry her 'her reason would suffer'. Within a few weeks, the threats and physical violence which would characterise their marriage began. There were constant arguments and he took to drink, which made matters worse. He was chairman of the Bath Abbey Men's Club and, so he said, spent most of his evenings there, although on at least two occasions he came home blind drunk and was violently ill. The black eye he gave to his wife after one of his binges put her in bed for a week, as she was too ashamed to be seen in such a state. Less than a year after moving to Bath this unhappy union was blessed with a child, born prematurely, amid claims – from Mr Keen – that he was not the father.

And so it went on, until in 1904 he was appointed rector of Northstoke. The previous incumbent, Frederick O'Melia, who had been rector of the parish for 24 years and overseen the restoration of the church by Major Davis, was retiring at the age of 70. Like Mr Keen, he was originally from Ireland and it is possible, given their shared ancestry, he had taken the younger man under his wing. For a couple whose marriage was so clearly in deep trouble, however, moving from the social round of Bath to a remote village was a recipe for disaster – and so it proved. Initially the Keens employed only one servant, a maid called Alice Taylor, but in December 1906, when Mrs Keen was four months pregnant with her second child, they hired a governess to look after their first son. The governess took her meals with the Keens and, as the time of Mrs Keen's confinement approached, Mr Keen spent more and more time alone with her. He was soon smitten, but instead of improving his temper this made matters worse; slowly but surely the situation spiralled out of control.

Early in May 1907, as Mrs Keen was in the last stages of her pregnancy, she was kneeling on the hearthrug in the living room when her husband pushed her by the shoulders and threw her on the floor. She gave birth to her second son a few days later, on 14 May. A couple of weeks later a nurse called Elizabeth Bright was hired to look after the baby. On 13 June Mr Keen sent his father-in-law an extraordinary letter:

> Dear Sir,
> Can you spare time to meet Drs Benson and Aubrey on the subject of your eldest daughter's mental condition. Dr Benson is confident that there is insanity in her family, and Mrs Latham must have known something when she told me that, unless I married her, her reason would probably suffer. I am confident that unless you send her to someone who can control her she will do, sooner or later, serious harm. She certainly cannot be allowed to remain here.

At around this time, Mr Keen was having supper in the dining room one evening with the governess. When Mrs Keen came in, he told her she was not wanted there and ordered her to go. When she refused he grabbed her by the hair, threw her violently on the floor and threatened to horsewhip her. When he started to hit her with his fists the governess intervened. Mrs Keen ran upstairs closely followed by the governess and they locked themselves into the nursery with the nurse. Mr Keen followed them, kicked the door down and threatened his wife.

The next day she went away to Reading to stay with her sister, leaving both her sons – and the governess – at the rectory with her husband. The governess wrote to her regularly, keeping her informed of how things were, and she returned in early August. The governess showed her a letter Mr Keen had written to her, in which he declared that 'I have now made up my mind not to have any more wine or whisky in the house … I have been giving myself a talking to for my want of control under provocation, and if I don't improve I must give up preaching to others, but I mean to have a good try.'

Mrs Keen went away again, taking her elder son and the governess with her, and leaving her younger son with the nurse. On 22 August 1907, Mr Keen wrote asking her to return home, which she did a few days later. For a few weeks life went on without any major upsets. The governess went home for Christmas and, as it was uncertain whether she would return, Mrs Keen engaged someone else in her place. Mr Keen tried to persuade her to give the new governess notice and get the other one to return. She refused, not only because she thought the previous governess had earned a holiday, but also because the new governess was very good with the baby. When the new governess fell ill and went home, however, the previous governess was recalled.

The night of Friday 6 March 1908 was a particularly stormy one, with the wind whistling round the house. It was growing late and Mrs Keen, who had been in the nursery, came down to the drawing room to find her husband. The door was ajar and, with the noise of the wind, he did not hear her coming. When she entered the room she found her husband and the governess sitting close to the fire. The governess had her arms around her husband's neck and seemed to be kissing him.

'What are you doing?' she shouted.

They jumped to their feet.

'Doing, why nothing,' said Mr Keen.

When his wife told him what she had seen, he denied that the governess's arms had been around his neck and asked how she could be so wicked to think such a thing.

The governess, in a state of shock, said, 'I feel faint, fetch me some water.'

Mr Keen fetched her a glass of water and explained that he had just come into the room and found the governess in 'a fainting condition'. Mrs Keen ordered the governess to her bedroom and asked her husband if he had done anything else to her. He fetched a Bible and swore he hadn't, denying again that he had kissed her. Mrs Keen insisted that the governess should leave the next day, although in the event she didn't leave until the following Monday, three days later, as Mrs Keen thought it would look better if she went quietly. Over the weekend, Mrs Keen interviewed the governess, who eventually admitted that she had committed adultery with her husband. When she confronted her husband, he maintained his innocence. When the governess left on the Monday morning, it was with the greatest difficulty that Mrs Keen prevented her husband running after her carriage to say goodbye.

On the following Friday evening, there was another row. Mr and Mrs Keen were alone in the drawing room when he threatened to 'bash her head in' with the poker. 'Don't be so stupid, Shadwell,' she told him, but took the precaution, as he picked up the poker, to ring for the maid. When the maid entered he smiled and said, 'You see I am going to stir the fire, Alice.' Two days later, as the result of another threat from her husband, she called her doctor, Dr Aubrey, to help her search the house for a revolver, which they found – loaded – in Mr Keen's bedroom. On the following Thursday she left the rectory and went to her sister's at Reading.

Having taken legal advice, she filed for divorce on the grounds of cruelty and adultery. The case was heard in the Divorce Court in London over three days in May 1909 before Mr Justice Bargrave Deane and a jury. Naturally there was intense media interest in the trial, not only in Bath but nationally as well. Despite the taboos governing what could and could not be discussed in polite society, and the restrictions imposed on playwrights and novelists, trials such as this were reported almost verbatim in the *Times* and the *Bath Chronicle*. It is hardly surprising that children were forbidden to read newspapers. One of the turning points of Ford Madox Ford's novel *The Good Soldier*, published in 1915, comes when the innocent Nancy Rufford – who 'hardly knew what a divorce case was' – comes upon a divorce report in a newspaper and, as she reads it, suddenly realises that she has unwittingly become embroiled in an eternal triangle. Curiously, the case featured bears an uncanny resemblance to that of Mr and Mrs Keen and the governess – is it possible that Ford Madox Ford recalled the case when he wrote the book?

It is difficult to overestimate the sensational nature of the trial. Mr Keen would have been well known to many people in Bath, including some of its most respectable – and respected – citizens. The fact that he was a clergyman made it even more shocking. And when the servants entered the witness box it really must have seemed that the world had turned upside down. The first to be called was the nurse, Elizabeth Bright. The prosecuting counsel asked when she had started working at the rectory:

'I first went into the service of Mrs Keen in June 1907. I was with her about four months.'

'Did you hear the rector threaten Mrs Keen?'

'Yes, it was one evening in June. He wanted her to go upstairs and he told her if she did not go he would horsewhip her. I heard him walking along the passage, as though he was coming for the whip. Then I met Mrs Keen coming upstairs. Her hair was hanging down over her shoulders and she seemed very frightened. Later on, the governess and Mrs Keen came into the nursery. Both of them looked very frightened. They fastened the nursery door. Then the rector came and tried to open it. When he found it was locked he punched it open. Part of the fastening and the bolt gave way. He stood over his wife and said some very unpleasant things. That wasn't the first time I'd heard him not being very polite to his wife, and she'd only had her baby a month earlier. He shouted at her and I could see she was very frightened of him. It was very bad for her in her condition.'

The prosecuting counsel then asked about Mr Keen's relationship with the governess.

'I remember him coming in very late one night and sending for her.'

'What time was this?'

'About eleven or half past.'

'Did you see the governess?

'Yes.'

'How was she dressed?'

'In her dressing gown.'

'Did you say something to her on that occasion?'

'Yes.'

'How long was she with the rector?'

'I don't know.'

'Did the rector make a habit of coming in late?'

'Yes.'

'Who received him?'

'Generally, the governess was there.'

'Were you aware of the governess taking tea to the rector in his bedroom in the mornings?'

'Yes.'

'Did she stay in his room for any length of time?'

'Yes, sometimes for ten minutes or so.'

'Were there any occasions on which they were alone together?'

'One time they went out after supper to post a letter. They were away about two hours.'

'Two hours to post a letter?'

'They went to Lower Weston, that's about three-quarters of an hour's walk away. It was while Mrs Keen was away.'

She was then cross-examined by Mr Bayford for the defence:

'Do you remember Mrs Keen going away with one of the children in August 1907?'

'Yes.'

'Did she take the child without her husband's knowledge?'

'Yes.'

'Was he angry about it?'

'Yes.'

'Did he mention bringing a charge of abduction?'

'Yes.'

'Did you ever see any familiarity between the governess and the rector?'

'No.'

'You claim she took tea to the rector's bedroom. Was there not a maid employed to this?'

'Yes. The governess did it when there was no maid.'

'And how often was there no maid?'

'Last summer, for about a fortnight.'

'And that was the only time?'

'As far as I know, yes.'

'You claim that she was in the habit of staying in the rector's bedroom for about ten minutes.'

'On at least one occasion.'

'Did you see her go in and come out?'

'No.'

'But you heard her go in and come out?'

'I heard her come out.'

'Didn't you hear go in?'

'No. She walked very quietly.'

Mr Bayford then asked her about the arguments between Mr and Mrs Keen:

'There was another argument the last week I was there.'

'Do you remember what was said?'

'No, all I could hear was Mr and Mrs Keen talking loudly.'

'They were both shouting? Mrs Keen as well?'

'Yes, but the rector's voice was louder than Mrs Keen's.'

'But you couldn't make out what either of them was saying?'

'No.'

'Did Mrs Keen get cross with the rector sometimes?'

'I don't know.'

'When these rows were going on was she talking as loudly as the rector?'

'There were so many – I did not hear them all.'

The next witness to be called was Alice Taylor, the maid. Mr Bayford, for the defence, asked her what alcohol was kept in the house.

'The rector kept a little wine in the pantry.'

'Did the rector drink to excess?'

'Not while I was there.'

'Did Mrs Keen get cross with the rector sometimes?'

'Yes.'

'And she would raise her voice?'

'Yes.'

'And this used to upset the rector, did it not? It troubled him'

'Yes, it did.'

'What did Mrs Keen say on the occasion when the rector threatened to "bash her head"?'

'I heard her say, "Don't be so stupid, Shadwell."'

'She was not frightened?'

'She seemed frightened when I went in.'

'Yes, but did she, from the tone in which she spoke, seem to be frightened?'

'I know what she said.'

'What did she want when she rang the bell?'

'She wanted me to see that the rector had the poker in his hand.'

The third witness was a young lady who was not called by name. The prosecuting counsel handed her a slip of blue paper on which a name was written. Looking at the paper, she said, 'that is my name and address,' and it was passed to the judge. The counsel for the prosecution opened the cross-examination:

'We have heard from Mrs Keen that you went to her as a nursery governess in December 1906.'

'Yes.'

'During the time you were with her, how did her husband treat her?'

'He was most rude and cruel.'

'Do you remember a time in June 1907 when you and the rector were in the dining room and Mrs Keen came in?'

'Yes.'

'Tell me what he said to her.'

'He ordered her upstairs.'

'And what did he do when she refused to go?'

'He told her would push her out of the room if she did not go. He dragged her by the hair onto the ground and said that if she did not go he would turn her up and horsewhip her. She was standing at the time. He went and fetched a hunting-crop from the hall. I shouted out for the nurse. I am sure he would have hit her with the hunting-crop if I hadn't seized it and told her to hurry upstairs.'

'What happened next?'

'I held him. It was terribly hard work and I was much bruised in the struggle. My chest became quite raw. The skin was broken. He was very excited. After Mrs Keen had gone upstairs I ran after her. We both went into the nursery and I locked the door. The rector came up, tried to open the door and then burst it open with his foot. When he got into the room he made a lot of horrible remarks to Mrs Keen.'

'Did you hear him use strong language to his wife on other occasions?'

'Yes.'

'Was he always a temperate man?'

'No.'

'What have you seen him doing with regard to alcohol?'

'I have seen him drinking a lot of whisky, sometimes wine, and occasionally brandy. At meals, however, he had water unless there was company, and then he took wine occasionally. He was very much excited after brandy.'

'Did you ever see any signs of mental aberration on Mrs Keen's part?'

'Never.'

'How did she treat him?'

'As well as she could under the circumstances. He was always rude to her.' Then, before the prosecuting counsel could continue, she turned to face the rector and announced loudly, 'he is looking at me now with horrible eyes!'

'What do you say?' asked the judge.

'She complains, my lord, that he is looking at her in a way she does not like,' replied the prosecuting counsel.

The foreman of the jury rose to his feet and said, 'I have noticed this on several occasions and would like to call attention to it.'

'Thank you, sir,' said the prosecuting counsel, as several of the rector's friends, sitting with him at the back of the court, remonstrated with him. Some tried to induce him to leave the court. He insisted on remaining but turned his face away from the lady in the box. The prosecuting counsel gave her a short time to compose herself, then asked if she wished to continue. She nodded.

'With regard to the other part of the case,' he explained, 'you need not give evidence unless you wish.'

'I know,' she replied.

'Are you willing to do so?'

'Yes.'

'Do you remember the occasion when Mrs Keen says she came into the room on 6 March – and found you with the rector?'

'Yes.'

'She says she found you with your arms round his neck.'

'I don't know what I was doing. My arms may have been round his neck.'

'Is it true your arms were round his neck?' asked the judge.

'I am not sure. I hardly know what I was doing then.'

'Answer yes or no,' said the prosecuting counsel.

'Yes.'

'Is it a fact that Mr Keen committed adultery with you?'

'Yes, he compelled me.'

'Do you remember Mr Keen coming to your home?'

'Yes.'

'Did you see him?'

'Yes, it was on Easter Eve.'

'Did you see him alone?'

'Yes.'

'What did he say in reference to this matter?'

'He said he was very sorry for all he had done. It made him feel what a mean wretch he was, and he wanted to do what was right. What should he do? When he stood by the dead body of his mother, it all came over him how very bad he had been.'

'Had she just died?'

'He had been to her funeral.'

'How long before.'

'I don't know – just a few days, I think.'

'And he asked you what he should do?'

'Yes, and I told him to tell Mrs Keen all that had happened. I asked him to go to my mother's room – she was very ill upstairs – and confess all to her.'

'What did he say?'

'He said, yes, he would go, and I took him up to the room, and left him there about five minutes.'

'Your mother has died since?'

'Yes.'

'Did he tell you what passed between him and your mother?'

'No, but when I took him to the room, I heard him say, as he went in, "your daughter is not to blame at all. I was the one to blame." He also asked mother what he should do.'

'Did you hear any more of what he said to your mother'

'Mother told him she had brought us up very carefully, and he replied, "Yes, too carefully." He said it would have been a good thing if I had known more of the world when I went to the rectory. He asked mother if, in the event of Mrs Keen asking for a divorce, and he let it go through undefended, would she give me to him. Mother indignantly replied, "No."'

'Did you see him when he came down?'

'Yes, he wanted something to eat. I gave him some tea. He stayed a few minutes. My mother told him if he did not get out of the house my father would be home soon, and if he found him there he would kill him. He begged to see mother again, but she would not see him.'

'We were told yesterday that on the morning you left the rectory, Mr Keen came to speak to you behind the screen in your room. What did he say?'

'He told me that if ever he had the chance he would marry me. He added that he was going to Scotland shortly. I told him he need say no more.'

'On the morning you left, had you received your salary?'

'Yes, I received a month's pay.'

'Who paid you?'

'Mrs Keen.'

'What did you do with it?'

'I lent it to Mr Keen.'

'How came you to do that?'

'He asked me to lend it to him.'

'On what date was that?'

'I can't remember. I had only had it a few days.'

'Had he ever borrowed money from you before?'

'A great many times.'

'I do not know what you had a month.'

'Do you wish me to tell you?'

'What I want to know is how much he borrowed?'

'Sometimes the sums were very small, sometimes a few shillings, and sometimes a pound.'

'Did he pay you back again?'

'No – at least not after the first few months. As soon as he knew I had money he borrowed it. He also used my stamps and notepaper. In fact,' she continued, bowing her head, 'he robbed me of everything I had – my honour, and character, and everything, and he hastened my mother's death.'

'However, I think you are engaged to be married now?'

'Yes.'

'And the gentleman knows all about it?'

'Yes. He knew all about it before he asked to marry me.'

The counsel for the defence then rose to cross-examine the witness, taking his cue from the prosecuting counsel's final question.

'When did you become engaged to be married?'

On Whit Sunday of last year,' she answered with a smile.

'When did you say Mr Keen first misconducted himself with you?'

'Shortly before Mrs Keen's baby was born – the second child. It might have been the end of April or the beginning of May 1907.'

'Do you say it happened frequently or not?'

'Rather frequently.'

'During the whole time?'

'I went away with Mrs Keen in the summer and it happened again when I came back.'

'Did you know that this was wrong?'

'The rector told me it was not. I could not help myself. At the beginning he had a horrible power over me. He stared at me and stared at me until I did not know what I was doing. He fixed his eyes on me for ten minutes at a time.'

'Couldn't you have given up the position and gone away?'

'I had not any money to go away. He borrowed it all.'

'You were paid £18 a year, were you not?'

'For the last three months I was paid at that rate. Before that £15 a year.'

'Were you paid monthly?'

'Yes.'

'You had a good many opportunities to get a ticket then, between May 1907 and March 1908?'

'As soon as I had the money he got it from me. Sometimes he asked me for it before I got it.'

'It would have been possible to make a statement to Mrs Keen at any time?'

'I was afraid to do so. I was afraid of him. His temper was very violent, and when he lost his temper I was afraid he would kill me. He threatened both Mrs Keen and me sometimes.'

'In the year 1907 there was an occasion in June, I think, when the rector ordered his wife upstairs?'

'Yes.'

'What was the trouble about on that occasion?'

'I can't remember what the quarrel was about on that occasion. He often told her he hated the sight of her.'

'Was she hot-tempered at times?'

'No, she was always very calm, even when he was most rude.'

'Would it be true to say that on the occasion he struck Mrs Keen?'

'I did not say he struck her. I said he dragged her down by the hair.'

'I appreciate you said that. Then it would not be true to say that he struck her?'

'No, but he was just in the act of using the hound crop when I seized it.'

The governess by this point appeared on the point of collapse and the usher handed her a glass of water. When she seemed a little calmer, the counsel for the defence asked about the other quarrel she had witnessed.

'There were so many quarrels,' she replied, 'and I can't remember them all. I do know that Mr Keen always started them. If she was reading, the turning over of the leaves annoyed him, and if she was sewing the noise of the needle irritated him, and that would start a quarrel. He would order her away, and naturally she refused to go.'

'Did she stop sewing when he asked?'

'No. She would say that I was sewing and making the same noise and why should she stop if I didn't?'

'Haven't you been engaged to be married before?'

'Never. I was attached to somebody and we had both promised never to marry anybody else without each other's consent. We were both too poor and could not afford to marry.'

'Had your parents objected to the match?'

'No, because they did not know there was anything between us. I knew my parents would have objected to a long engagement.'

'The gentleman was the same gentleman to whom you became engaged on Whitsunday?'

'Yes.'

When the governess had finished giving her evidence, she rose and left the court. Mrs Keen followed her, but returned shortly afterwards. The counsel for the defence then rose and informed the judge that 'my client has placed himself entirely in my hands in regard to this matter, and, after the evidence given in court, I have advised him not to go into the witness box. Under the circumstances he has accepted my advice, and he is not going to contest the case.'

The jury, after a brief consultation, declared Mr Keen guilty on both counts – adultery and cruelty – and the judge granted decree nisi, giving Mrs Keen custody of the children. Shortly afterwards a notice appeared on the door of Northstoke church declaring that the Rev Shadwell Keen had been formally suspended pending proceedings in the consistory court.

On 5 June 1909, Mr Keen was summoned for non-payment of a year's poor rates amounting to £11-17-6. He did not appear and Mr Batley, overseer of the parish, said he was rumoured to be in London – 'rather a big place'. He also reported that Mr Keen's wife had 'put the bailiffs in' and that a sale of the contents of the house

was to take place the following Wednesday. He applied for a distress warrant, as otherwise, he said, 'there will be nothing left,' and this was granted.

The contents of the house, made up into 145 lots, were sold by Alfred Turpin, an auctioneer from Broad Street in Bath, on 9 June 1909. Despite there being 'nothing to attract an antique dealer', a sizeable crowd attended the sale. Some of the prices realised were reported in the *Bath Chronicle*: the bedsteads went for 7/- each, a settee for three guineas, a reversible carpet measuring 10' by 13' for £2, a Welsh dresser for £6-12-0. Four framed pictures, including a photograph of the late Mr Charles Hale attired in full dress as the City Sword Bearer went for 12/-. Perhaps the most poignant item was a presentation clock in a leather case with the inscription: 'Presented to the Rev

Shadwell Keen by the Parishioners of Priddy, in recognition of services rendered ... 26 June 1904'.

Mr Keen, however, despite having his possessions auctioned off and being, in his own words, 'a poor man', had not given up. He lodged an appeal against the ruling of the Divorce Court, which came before the Master of the Rolls and Lords Farwell and Kennedy. Mr Keen asked for the case to be deferred, claiming that 'he had not been able to obtain the support from his friends which could be reasonably expected later on'. When the appeal was eventually heard, he asked for a retrial on the grounds of 'surprise', explaining that the grounds given had not allowed his evidence to be placed before the court. The Master of the Rolls said it all seemed very strange and that, as the appeal was 'perfectly hopeless', it must be dismissed.

The decree nisi was made absolute on 7 February 1910, and shortly afterwards, at a Consistory Court in Wells, the Bishop decreed that Mr Keen should be deprived of the living of Northstoke. In Mr Keen's absence, the parish had been cared for by the Rev Ernest Poynton of Kelston (whose own trial, for child abuse, featured in Chapter 10), but the benefice now being declared vacant, it was presented to the Rev William Jeffcoat.

The plight of the Keens' governess highlights that of young women who went into service. Some of them came from far away and had grown up in the country. Many of the girls who worked in Bath came from Somerset or Wiltshire, where there were few employment opportunities. She came from a Cambridgeshire farm and was recommended to Mr Keen by her local vicar – probably someone he had known at university or while working in another parish.

Whatever their role in the household, governesses and other female servants were subject to authority figures, with the man as the undisputed head of the household. When he – or another male member of the family – attempted to take advantage of them they were in an unenviable position. They had been told they had to obey orders, and – far from the support and guidance of family and friends – it can hardly be wondered at that so many of them succumbed. To take one case out of many – in June 1909 a 21-year-old domestic servant was indicted for concealing the birth of a child at Midsomer Norton. She had no mother and her father had disappeared. She had managed to conceal her pregnancy from her employers and, as the child had been stillborn (how or why we do not know, but she would certainly have had no one by to help her during childbirth), she had tried to burn its body in a stove. She was bound over on promising to go into a home.

Despite the Northstoke governess's appalling experience, she had the strength of character to turn to her family and tell them what had happened. They, for their part, did not abandon her but stood by her – as did her young man. We can only hope that things worked out for them. Many others were not so lucky. Afraid to go home – or turned out if they did – and spurned by their seducers, they faced a bleak future. If they were pregnant their situation was immeasurably worse. The fate of Tess of the d'Urbevilles springs to mind – but far more common was a slow drift into prostitution and an early grave. Things had improved since the mid-nineteenth century, when the Rev Skinner of Camerton tried to prevent village girls seeking employment in Bath because of the high proportion of them who ended up on the streets, but prostitution – a last resort for girls who had no other means of supporting themselves – was still rife in the city.

Widcombe Crescent.

CHAPTER FIFTEEN

THE ABODE OF LOVE

The Bishop of Bath & Wells must have had a bellyful of priapic vicars in 1909. When Reverend John Hugh Smyth-Pigott was defrocked in Wells Cathedral on 6 March 1909, it was the culmination of a saga that had begun at Widcombe Crescent in Bath almost a century earlier.

Henry James Prince was born at 5 Widcombe Crescent in 1811. His father, Thomas Prince, was a West Indian plantation owner from Liverpool. An ailing child with a disordered stomach, he was the youngest of seven children – three boys and four girls. His father died soon afterwards and his mother took in lodgers to support herself. One of the lodgers, a spinster called Martha Freeman, the Roman Catholic daughter of one of Thomas Prince's business associates, took young Henry under her wing. She was an intensely pious young woman, and, as they read the Bible together, she nurtured hopes of converting the boy to Catholicism. It never happened: his will, even at an early age, proved the stronger and it was she who converted to the Church of England.

Prince's Anglicanism was a curious thing: for him, the central text in the Bible was the exuberantly erotic Song of Solomon. It is extraordinary to think of a mature woman – Martha was 16 years older than Prince – sitting hour after hour with a boy in his early teens studying texts like:

> *Thy lips are like a thread of scarlet, and thy speech is comely: thy temples are like a piece of a pomegranate within thy locks.*
>
> *Thy neck is like the tower of David builded for an armoury, whereon there hang a thousand bucklers, all shields of mighty men.*
>
> *Thy two breasts are like two young roes that are twins, which feed among the lilies.*

Prince went to school in Corsham. He had ideas of entering the church, as one of his brothers had done, but in 1827, when he was 16, his mother decided that a medical career would suit him better. To get him out of the way of Miss Freeman, whose relationship with her son she was by no means happy with, she apprenticed him to an apothecary in Wells. He stuck this for a while, but soon fell seriously ill and returned to Bath. His mother hadn't given up the idea of medicine, however, and, when he recovered, she sent him to London to train at Guy's Hospital. After passing his examinations and being admitted to the Society of Apothecaries, he returned to Bath, where he once again fell ill. Absence, while it had done nothing for Prince's health, had had little effect on his relationship with Martha, which was, if anything, stronger than before.

Once he recovered his health, he started working at Bath General Hospital, staying there about four years. From a journal he kept at the time, it is clear that he was more concerned with the health of his patients' souls than their physical well-being. He prayed and preached at them, describing the torments of hell and damnation that awaited those who would not repent their wickedness. Of one of his patients, a Mrs Cooper, he wrote, 'I spoke to her most solemnly of her awful state, which I put before her in the most appalling picture of death and eternal damnation.' Significantly, most of these spiritual castigations were directed at women. There was clearly a strong sexual chemistry between him and many women, but one that he sublimated, channelling his lust into spiritual longing, and in the process often making himself physically ill.

In 1834, worn out by constant gastric pain and illness, he went to London to consult a specialist who operated – without anaesthetic – on his stomach. It was a risky operation and could, had infection set in, have proved fatal. His convalescence was long and agonising; high temperatures brought on delirium and apocalyptic visions. Martha appeared to him on several occasions, clothed in white samite, mystic, wonderful, urging him to higher work. Then on 7 May 1834, at half past four in the afternoon, he received a visit from Jesus Christ.

As you do.

Once back in Bath, he resigned from the hospital and retired to Widcombe Crescent to complete his convalescence. There he prayed and made plans for the future with Martha. In the autumn of 1835 he went on holiday to try to rally his health, staying with his brother, who was the rector of a mining village in County Durham. He still wanted to go into the Church of England despite his mother's opposition, and what he saw in Durham made him more determined than ever.

On his return to Bath, he started holding revivalist meetings in his bedroom. A roomful of wailing women, however, had other lodgers complaining or moving on and, as a way of resolving the problem, Martha offered to pay for Prince to study for the priesthood. In 1836 he went to Lampeter College in Wales, which, despite its high reputation, he found distinctly lacking in the high-minded spirituality he was used to with Mary. He became a fanatical temperance campaigner; on one occasion, at a drinks reception held by the vice principal, he launched himself at his host, dashed a glass of sherry out of his hand, admonished those present for their enslavement to the demon drink and left to a chorus of boos and hisses. Lesser mortals would have been thrown out of the college for such outrageous insubordination; it is a measure of his devotion to his studies and of the charismatic effect he had, even on those who weren't taken in by him, that he got away with it.

He had not been there very long before he formed a group of like-minded religious zealots called the Lampeter Brethren. On his visits to Bath he would walk the streets terrorising friends and relations, warning them of the judgement to come. On 10 July 1838 he married Martha at St James's church. 'She is not the supreme object of my affections, nor occupies the place of an idol in my heart,' he wrote bluntly in his journal, and, whether Martha was happy with the arrangement or not, he decreed that there would be no physical consummation of their union. It was to be a spiritual partnership – and, of course, one in which her money would come to him.

In 1840 he graduated and became curate of Charlinch, five miles west of Bridgwater. Before long he was ready to acknowledge that he was the visible manifestation of God on earth. He had, he announced, cast off his ailing body, which was now occupied by God. The Rev Samuel Starky, Rector of Charlinch, who was living on the Isle of Wight, heard what was going on, returned to sort Prince out – and fell under his spell. Prince's services grew ever more bizarre; he would stand in the pulpit waving his arms about, jumping up and down, groaning and claiming that the Holy Ghost was not in him. Then one day, when the crowds who had started flocking to Charlinch to see these performances had grown sufficiently large, the Holy Ghost decided to return. The Charlinch Revival had started. He didn't just target adults – this is a description of what happened when he took the Sunday School:

In a few minutes the Holy Ghost came on the minister with the most tremendous power, so that the word of the Lord was really like fire. About 20 of the children were pierced to the heart by it, and appeared to be in great distress; but the bigger boys still continued unmoved, and some of them even disposed to laugh. In a short time, however, the word reached them too, and they were smitten to the heart with the most dreadful conviction of their sins and danger; it appeared as if the arrows of the Almighty had pierced their very veins ... In about ten minutes the spectacle presented by the schoolroom was truly awful: out of 50 children present there were not so many as ten that could stand upright: boys and girls, great and small together, were either leaning against the wall quite overcome by their feelings of distress, or else bowed with their faces hidden in their hands, and sobbing in the severest agony: it appeared as if the Spirit of God was breaking their hearts into pieces like a potter's vessel.

As people flocked to Charlinch, members of the Lampeter Brethren turned up to help out with Prince's ministry. Women's revivalist meetings began to acquire a dubious reputation far beyond the parish. Prince restricted attendance at his services to the converted – those that were lukewarm, including many of the local gentry, were excluded. This caused hostility and occasional outbreaks of violence between what Prince called the wheat and the chaff.

The Bishop tried to move Prince on, feeling that the church in Somerset had no need for a second Messiah, but he refused to budge. Martha died – at Bath – in April 1842; five months later, Prince married Starky's sister. She was even older than Martha, being well over 50, but, like Martha, she had an annuity. By then, the bishop had revoked Prince's licence to preach in the diocese, but a wealthy civil engineer called William Cobbe, who was working for Brunel on the Bristol & Exeter Railway, built him a meeting house in the parish so that he could continue his ministry.

The Charlinch Revival was, however, starting to run out of steam, and so, leaving one of the Lampeter Brethren in charge, Prince moved to Suffolk to take up another curacy. When his licence to preach was revoked there as well, he decided it was time for him and the established church to go their separate ways.

He moved to Brighton to establish his own sect, while Starky, now a fully paid-up member of the Prince fan club, set up a branch in Weymouth. The choice of genteel watering places, full of wealthy widows and spinsters, was a calculated one. Prince had served his apprenticeship and knew exactly what he was capable of. Now, unrestrained by the exigencies of established dogma, he could give full rein to his peculiar genius. Not everyone was impressed, however. A lady who met him at this time recorded that he 'made the most exhausting efforts to win my mind to his cause by quoting at length from the Song of Solomon', to no effect. Among those who did fall under his spell were the five unmarried daughters of a rich London merchant who had retired to Suffolk, each of whom was due to inherit £6,000 from their father's estate. He was implacably opposed to them having anything to do with Prince; despite this, when Prince moved to Brighton, they followed him.

Although Prince's Brighton campaign was extremely successful, what he really wanted was a secluded retreat, where he could be surrounded by the faithful converted, with no distractions. His first move was to Weymouth, where he joined Starky in a large house on Belfield Terrace. Here he set up his first Agapemone or 'Abode of Love', preaching the imminence of the last days, when sinners would be consigned to the fiery furnace. For those who believed, however, the Holy Ghost (aka Henry Prince) had manifested himself among men (and – more particularly – among women), that all who believed in him may be saved.

His fund-raising rallies would have shamed the most shameless television evangelist: The end of the world is nigh, he told his followers, and then what will be the use to you of your riches, your fine carriages, your houses and your land – so sell them all to show your true repentance – and give the money to me. The manifestation of the Son of Man took place in the unlikely setting of the Assembly Rooms at Weymouth. Prince entered to a flourish of trumpets and hymns of praise – 'Behold he cometh', 'Behold he is among us'. He blessed the assembled multitude, announced that the Day of Grace was passed, and that God had already decided who were the elect – those who had accepted the word of a charlatan from Bath.

'There is no dogma so queer, no behaviour so eccentric or even outrageous,' wrote Aldous Huxley, considering the career of Prince, 'but a group of people can be found to think it divinely inspired.' Prince was a genius at parting people from their money; he was also an inspired speaker, with an encyclopaedic knowledge of scripture that enabled him to counter any objections. He paid court only to those among his followers who could contribute financially to his dream of a greater Agapemone in the Somerset countryside, within sight of the village where his ministry had begun.

Two hundred acres was acquired in the village of Spaxton and Cobbe set about designing a new Agapemone. It is extraordinary to think that this temple to the power of one man to play upon the gullibility and superstitions of others was designed by a man responsible for building much of the railway between Bristol and Exeter. To ensure that sufficient funds would be available, Prince married off three of the daughters of the now deceased London merchant to three of his Brethren to secure their inheritances – making him £18,000 richer. None of the women were allowed

The main entrance to the Agapemone.

to consult their families before the weddings, and their new husbands were pledged to celibacy, on the understanding that their marriages were spiritual. One of the women, however, soon began to chafe at the restrictions placed upon her, suspecting that she had been conned. But the spirit of rebellion that started to kindle itself within her soon brought retribution down upon her head. She was consigned to an attic room and assigned menial tasks. Then the bombshell fell – she was pregnant. She was expelled from the community and sent home to her mother where she gave birth to a son.

The Somerset Agapemone was ready in 1846 and the faithful – around 200 by some accounts – moved in. As well as a large house, with a full-size chapel, there were cottages, stables and a farm in the grounds, all surrounded by a high wall. Here, Prince ruled with an iron hand, enforcing total celibacy and frugality, while enjoying a lavish lifestyle (including a well-stocked wine cellar, his total abstinence regime having passed). Perhaps the most bizarre detail – a hint at the sort of rock-and-roll lifestyle he may secretly have craved – was the installation of a full-size billiard table in the chapel.

He was a well-known public figure locally, addressing revivalist meetings in Bridgwater and other towns. When he and his entourage went shopping in Bridgwater, they were preceded down the High Street by a large man in purple livery shouting,

The Agapemone chapel.

'Blessed is he who cometh in the name of the Lord'. In 1851 he visited the Great Exhibition, travelling through Hyde Park in a carriage he had recently bought from the Queen Mother. Yet, despite the manifest absurdity of all this, he did actually acquire a modicum of respectability for a time. His tracts were widely read and discussed in serious magazines and theological journals. Then he went that one step too far.

One of the faithful was a woman called Mrs Paterson, a widow who had come to Prince in Weymouth with a young daughter in tow. She had died and been buried in the garden at Spaxton (upright, like the others buried there, so that they wouldn't be on their backs at the Second Coming), and her daughter was now an attractive girl of sixteen. Prince, smitten by her charms, came up with his most audacious ruse so far. Announcing that 'the Day of Judgement has come,' he told the faithful that God was about to extend his love from heaven to earth, and the Holy Ghost would take the flesh of a virgin.

And so, with the faithful assembled, a row of virgins arrayed in white linen stood before the altar in the Agapemone chapel. Prince, dressed in his finest ritual garments, entered to the sound of soft organ music. Hymns were sung as he walked up and down the row of virgins, inspected them as though judging a fashion show. Then, stopping before Miss Paterson, he ordered her onto a couch, removed her frock and, in his own words, 'the Holy Ghost took flesh in the presence of those whom he had called as flesh. He took this flesh absolutely in his sovereign will, and with the power and authority of God.'

A century and a half on, Prince's audacity and moral culpability are still profoundly shocking. Even more shocking is the tacit approval of the faithful gathered there on that day. Admittedly, some did realise he had gone too far and a few started to plan their escape. Despite Prince's assurances that it wasn't him that had ravished Miss Paterson in the chapel, but the Holy Ghost, and that the union was therefore a divine one, she found that she was pregnant. Prince, in desperation, declared that the child was the spawn of the devil, who had impregnated her when his back was turned.

Prince survived this setback, and managed to hang on to most of his followers, still asserting that the Day of Judgement was at hand and that God had already decided who would be saved. The elect, behind the high, bloodhound-patrolled walls of the Agapemone, would rise to the heavens in triumph; everyone else was damned to eternal perdition.

Victorian moralists were horrified when the news leaked out, and there were calls for a stop to be put to Prince's antics – all to no avail. Offend public decency he might have done, but he was nothing if not a shrewd operator, and with the money of the faithful behind him – amounting, according to some estimates, to several hundred thousand pounds – he was effectively untouchable. What took place at the Agapemone took place behind closed doors, with only the faithful to witness, and, unless one of them brought an action against him, nothing could be done.

As the years rolled on, Prince, the sultan of this improbable Somersetshire seraglio, clung fast to the claim that he was immortal. His early bouts with stomach trouble had evaporated, but, as the last decade of the nineteenth century drew nigh, the shades of senility began to close around one of Bath's least illustrious sons.

His death in 1899 came as a profound shock to most of his followers. He was 88 – not a bad age for a sickly child with stomach trouble, but on the other hand not good if you've gone round telling people you're immortal. When Prince succumbed to the grim reaper, the chances are that the sect he had founded, with his immortality as the cornerstone of its creed, would have succumbed as well, had there not been someone just as wily to step into his recently-vacated shoes.

In terms of dodgy vicars, the Reverend John Smyth-Pigott was right up there with the Reverend Henry Prince. John Hugh Smyth-Pigott was born in 1852 at Brockley Court in North Somerset. His family were wealthy landowners; part of their estate was the coastal strip where Weston Super Mare was in the process of being built. He was not, however, destined to inherit any of this wealth. He was the youngest of three boys and was only five his father died in a lunatic asylum – possibly as a result of contracting gonorrhoea. It was traditional for the Smyth-Pigotts to be educated at Eton, but for some reason it was decided to send young John to a far less prestigious, newly-opened boarding school at Rossall in Lancashire.

He failed to distinguish himself at school, left Pembroke College, Oxford after a year, and ran away to sea at the age of 18, signing on as a merchant seaman under the name Johnny Pigott. He also tried his hand at gold prospecting in Australia before finding God at a seaman's mission in New York at the age of 27.

In 1879 he returned to England and enrolled at the London School of Divinity, which specialised in training missionaries. After ordination, in 1882, he became a curate at St Jude's in Hackney. Within two years, however, he had given up his curacy and become a staff captain in the Salvation Army. He rose quickly through the ranks, was selected to accompany General Booth to a convention in Brighton and appointed vice-principal of the Army's training homes at Clapton. However, he lasted little more than a year before resigning amid mutual recriminations. The reason for his forced resignation is unclear, but it seems likely he was already peddling his somewhat unusual interpretation of the Christian gospel, in which spiritual love played a pivotal role.

He decided to rejoin the Church of England and went to stay with a friend who was a vicar in Cheshire. He gave sermons and helped with the work of the parish – as well as marrying the vicar's sister. In November 1886 he took up an appointment as a curate at the Church of Ireland Mission in Townsend Street, Dublin. This time he lasted a mere six weeks. 'Mr Pigott left me at my own desire,' the priest in charge wrote later, 'as he held doctrines, as I found out, which were entirely contrary to my own, and which I thought calculated to undermine the faith of my flock.'

He returned to his friend in Cheshire, who once again invited him to preach in his church, until word of the contents of his sermons reached the ears of the bishop, who banned him

The Rev Henry James Prince and the Rev John Hugh Smyth-Pigott (third and fourth from the left in the front row) with some of their followers at the Agapemone, c1895.

from the pulpit. He then decided to return to Dublin to try and poach members of the Townsend Street congregation. Here he met a former acquaintance called Douglas Hamilton, who not only shared his vision of Christianity but was also a member of Prince's Agapemone. This may have been a chance reunion; it is far more likely, however, that Prince had heard about Smyth-Pigott's less than illustrious career from Hamilton and was eager to recruit him. For his part, Smyth-Pigott would almost certainly have known about Prince, and may have been influenced by his writings in formulating his own version of Christianity.

When he walked into the Agapomene in 1887, Prince soon realised that here was someone who not only sang from the same

238

hymn sheet but also had the charisma to revive what was by now a dwindling – and rapidly ageing – sect. He appointed him pastor of a congregation of Agapemonites in North London; within months Smyth-Pigott was attracting the sort of wealthy converts necessary if the Abode of Love was to survive. Smyth-Pigott was a passionate convert to Prince's creed, and, with no superiors hidebound by orthodoxy to rein him in, he gave full vent to his religious mania. Within five years the London congregation had grown so large that he embarked on a project to build a massive church – with no expense spared – in Clapton. Called the Ark of the Covenant, it opened four years later. Representatives of Agapemonite cells that had been established in Sweden, Norway, Germany, America and India attended the service. The Agapemonite bandwagon seemed unstoppable.

The only thing that could have derailed it was Prince's death. Smyth-Pigott wasted no time in telling the faithful that Prince had appointed him his successor, and that the Day of the Lord – despite Prince's untimely demise – was still very much at hand. Even so, it was, for some, a bit hard to stomach. Prince had told them he would live for ever; they had believed him. Now he was dead, why should they go on believing the rest of what he'd said?

To maintain the movement's momentum, Smyth-Pigott realised he had to up the ante. And this he did, in a sermon preached before a full congregation at the Ark of the Covenant, on Sunday 7 September 1902. It was, to put it mildly, heady stuff:

> Brother Prince was sent ... to prepare the way for the Second Coming of Him who suffered for sin, to prepare the way for the restoration of all things. His testimony was true and the work of the Holy Ghost in Him was perfect, and I who speak to you tonight, I am that Lord Jesus Christ who died and rose again and ascended into heaven; I am that Lord Jesus come again in my own body to save those who come to me from death and judgement. Yes, I am He that liveth and behold I am alive for ever more ... I am come for the second time as the Bridegroom of the Church and the Judge of all men, for the Father has committed all judgement to me because I am the Son of Man. And you, each one of you, must be judged by me.

As news of this extraordinary outburst, which ended with members of the congregation standing up and proclaiming Smyth-Pigott to be the Lord, spread, so did the sense of outrage. By the following morning, between five and six thousand people had assembled on

Clapton Common and marched on the Ark of the Covenant, where a long queue had already formed to hear Smyth-Pigott repeat his claims. The *Morning Leader* describes what happened next:

> The police arrangements to cope with the crowd were quite inadequate, and the long queue that had been formed was broken up by a sudden and ugly rush, in which several women were bruised. The chapel was carried by assault, and dozens clambered over the railings after the gates were shut. Both on arrival and departure Mr Pigott was hissed and groaned at, but attempts to strike him were warded off by police ... When the strange service was over, the crowd rushed out pell-mell. Mr Pigott came out shortly, still smiling and calm and was seen into his brougham by police. A mounted policeman galloped a lane through the crowd ... Thousands of people ran over the common after the carriage, yelling and hissing and uttering threats.

If he'd intended to make an impression he'd certainly succeeded. He decided it would be best to leave London and head for Spaxton, where, after running the gauntlet of a hostile crowd at Bridgwater station, he was relatively safe.

Smyth-Pigott's rule at Spaxton was similar to that of Prince. He required that his followers – including his wife – should abstain from sexual relations, although, as Son of God, he was a special case. Tales of him working his way through the ranks of the female faithful – at least the young and attractive ones – are legion, but most seem to owe more to fancy than fact. What is beyond doubt, however, is that in 1904 he took a spiritual bride called Ruth Preece and enjoyed conjugal relations with her. Their union was blessed with three children, whose parenthood he was happy to acknowledge. The lack of other children at the Agapemone, either acknowledged or unacknowledged, during his reign suggests that, unless he used contraceptives (something that had hardly squares with his image of himself as the New Messiah), the stories are simply that – stories.

The birth of his first child, Glory, in 1905, seems to have evoked little reaction outside the walls of the Agapemone. When the second child, Power, was born on 20 August 1908, it was a different story – thanks to it being taken up by an indignant press. Things came to a head on the evening of 7 November 1908 when three men – one dressed as a policeman – drove up to the Agapemone and climbed over the wall. In some versions of the

The wall scaled by Michael Sale dressed as a policeman.

story they are described as hoodlums from Bridgwater who'd driven out for a bit of fun after a few ciders. They were no such thing. They had actually come all the way down from London. Michael Sale, the ringleader, was an advertising agent from Eaton Terrace in London, who had rounded up two acquaintances – Foster Pinnall, a grocer from Camberwell, and John Green, a labourer from Holborn – who later claimed to have no idea why he had driven them down to Somerset. As far as is known, Sale had had no previous contact with any of the Agapemonites. The reason he decided to drive halfway across the country may have had something to do with the presence of a reporter from the *Daily Mail*, who was seen lurking outside the grounds on the evening of the attack. Sale actually said, when he was arrested, that he was 'practically representing the *Daily Mail*', although the editor strongly denied this and no action was taken against the newspaper.

The attack itself was like something out of a silent movie. Sale had disguised himself as a policeman, he later claimed, to evade arrest, but, instead of wearing the helmet in the customary fashion, he had filled it full of tar and feathers, with the aim of planting it on Smyth-Pigott's head. The trio made so much noise getting over the wall – which was around ten feet high – that an elderly male member of the community came out to see what was going on. Sale rammed the helmet on his head and dragged him into the bushes, before trying to make a getaway when the ensuing commotion brought other members of the community rushing out. When the three conspirators were apprehended, Sale shouted that they couldn't arrest him because he was a police officer. Tried at the local magistrates court, he said that he come to teach 'old Smyth-Pigott a lesson', and was given a month's hard labour, along with his accomplices. Despite their having got the wrong man, the *Mail* – along with every other national newspaper – had its story.

As a result of the publicity, the Bishop of Bath and Wells, who'd probably been trying to ignore the goings-on at Spaxton in the hope that everyone else would, realised he had to act. Promising that 'measures of a most drastic nature will be taken', he ordered a consistory court to be held in the chapter house of Wells Cathedral. Dozens of Smyth-Pigott's colleagues and acquaintances were subpœnaed to attend, although court officers failed to penetrate the Agapemone's defences to subpœna Smyth-Piggot himself, and he was tried *in absentia*.

On 20 January 1909, he was tried on three charges of immorality – two relating to the births of Glory and Power out of wedlock and the third relating to general allegations of immorality. 'It is a lamentable thing,' the prosecuting barrister told the court, 'that this beautiful hamlet of Spaxton should be turned into a wilderness of particularly repulsive vice.' The verdict was a foregone conclusion and on 6 March 1909, the Rev Smyth-Pigott was formally defrocked at a service in the cathedral attended by no less than three bishops. Addressing the congregation, the Bishop of Bath and Wells, said,

> To some it must appear strange that no charge has been brought against the defendant for the blasphemous utterances with which he has been credited. Upon this I would observe that there is grave doubt whether under the Clergy Discipline Act, under which the last proceedings were taken, a prosecution for blasphemy could have been included. If it could have been included, it is not easy to see how any other punishment could have been imposed than it is my painful duty now to inflict.

The Bishop then pronounced Smyth-Pigott 'entirely removed, deposed and degraded from the said offices of priest and deacon respectively', before praying that 'our erring brother' should be granted 'true repentance and amendment of life'.

He was wasting his breath. Smyth-Pigott's third child, Life, was born the following year and life at the Agapomene continued on in its extraordinary way. Although the community itself was – apart from the children – slowly ageing and dwindling as its members died, Agapemonite sects in other parts of the country and abroad continued to recruit new members. But, when Smyth-Pigott died in 1927, the game really was up. To paraphrase Oscar Wilde, losing one messiah may be regarded as a misfortune; losing two looks like carelessness. Smyth-Pigott had held the cult together by the force of his personality; with him gone – and no new messiah on the horizon – its days were numbered. But, with nowhere else to go, the women at the Agapemone – they were almost all women by this stage – had no choice but to stay put. It was, for many of them, the only home they knew, and remained so until 1958, when those that were left sold up and moved on, leaving the Abode of Love to the property developers.

Compared with some more recent cult leaders, with their mass suicide pacts and other abominations, the activities of Prince and Smyth-Pigott were – relatively – benign, if more than a little unwholesome. Both men followed a similar trajectory – losing their fathers at an early age, and pursuing, for a time, an uncongenial career, before taking holy orders in a church whose creed they kicked against and from whose pulpits they were rapidly excluded. Both developed a highly individual and highly iconoclastic creed, to which, by the force of their personalities, they attracted followers. In each case, this creed involved the excitation of sexual desire, fuelled by readings from the Song of Solomon and similar texts, along with the total repression of that desire.

If natural human passions are thwarted, they will burst forth in strange and often unpleasant ways. Sigmund Freud, who was working on his theories of 'the return of the repressed' at around this time, had much, of course, to say on this score. The Victorians were particularly keen on repression, and the Edwardians, although starting to come out of their shadow, were not much better. Repression isn't all bad, of course. Civilization couldn't function without it; the fulfilment of instincts and desires without any reference to codes of conduct or morality – and most importantly their effect on other people – is quite rightly taboo. But a balance has to be struck between repression and licence: too much repression is as bad as too much licence; the greater the repression, the greater the danger it will burst forth in uncontrollable and unpleasant ways – the sleep of reason produces monsters. While there can be no final solution to the problem of how much we should repress and to how much give free rein, most people today would, I think, consider that, by and large, we have achieved a better balance than the Edwardians.

While individuals will always diverge – some markedly – from prevailing social norms, those norms will inform the lives of the majority of the population. A good example of the norms obtaining in the late nineteenth and early twentieth centuries is provided, strangely enough, by one of the Rev Smyth-Pigott's relations. Edward Smyth-Pigott was examiner of stage plays for the Lord Chamberlain's Department from 1874 until his death in 1895. He was described by Oscar Wilde as a 'walking compendium of vulgar insular prejudice', while George Bernard Shaw said that it was 'frightful' to see 'the greatest thinkers, poets, and authors of modern Europe – men like Ibsen, Wagner, Tolstoy, and the leaders of our own literature – delivered helpless into the vulgar hands of such a noodle as this amiable old gentleman'. His aim seems to have been a theatre which portrayed a world devoid of sexual desire or of anything that disturbed the calm surface of polite society. When asked, for example, his opinion of Ibsen, he replied that, 'I have studied Ibsen's plays carefully, and all the characters ... appear to me morally deranged.'

Before leaving the Smyth-Pigotts, mention must also be made of the Rev George Smyth-Pigott, Rector of Kingston Seymour near Clevedon, whose career seems to suggest that dodgy vicars ran in the family. In March 1905, he was brought before an ecclesiastical court charged with 'inadequately discharging his duties by neglect and by his conduct in the church and pulpit'. He was

> in the habit of laughing in the pulpit and otherwise behaving irreverently. His sermons were more of a mockery than sermons, lasting sometimes only a minute. He had used violent and improper language to several parishioners and had behaved rudely to the bishop on his last visit to the parish.

More like Father Ted's sidekick, Father Jack, than the leader of the Agapemone, but, all the same, not really what you want from your local vicar.

CHAPTER SIXTEEN

A LITTLE BIT OF WHAT YOU FANCY

The careers of Shadwell Keen, Henry Prince and John Smyth-Pigott, bizarre, eccentric and unsavoury as they were, nevertheless provide insights into attitudes towards women and towards sex in the late nineteenth and early twentieth centuries. Their stories are pervaded with a sense of power and dominance on the one hand, and of subservience and entrapment on the other, in a way that could not be replicated – at least not without considerable secrecy – today. These three men were establishment figures who took – or tried to take – advantage of prevailing norms to pursue private fantasies or obsessions. To what extent this was a matter of cold calculation and to what extent an abandonment to impulse is a matter for debate; what is beyond question is that prevailing sexual mores and gender demarcations provided a climate within which their deviance could develop largely unchecked.

The Edwardian era was one of enormous change on several fronts, not least in the relations between the sexes and attitudes to sex. Such changes did not occur overnight. Tectonic plates may have been groaning beneath them, but many men carried on oblivious, confident in their belief that they were the lords of creation, with women there to minister to their whims.

The Edwardian era has come down to us, courtesy of the King in whose honour it was named, as one in which the stays of Victorian propriety were well and truly loosened, and sexual dalliance with a string of mistresses was the order of the day; this sort of lifestyle would have been enjoyed (although that hardly seems the right word) by only a few thousand people at most. Many of those who could afford such extravagance led lives more or less blameless; for the middle classes and the majority of the working classes monogamy and at least superficial respectability were still of paramount importance.

The Edwardians got married, on average, later than ever before. This was not because of any reluctance; many of them had to save for years before they could afford to get married. The average age for a woman to marry was 25; for a man it was 27. For working people, wedding days were much like any other.

They often tried to get married on Sunday; if they got married on a weekday, the groom sometimes had to go to work afterwards, only having been given half a day off.

Even with this relatively late start to married life, many couples had large families. In 1900, around half of working-class households had between seven and fifteen children. As we have already seen, many women were malnourished before and after giving birth; not only did they often come near to death, their babies were weak and sometimes died as well. Add to that the pain of giving birth when the only painkiller was a bottle of cheap gin, and it is not surprising that some women would try anything to avoid the ordeal. Although, for obvious reasons, no accurate figures are available, it has been reckoned that as many as one in four pregnancies ended in abortion. Apart from illegal back-street practitioners, there was a plethora of home-spun methods involving gin, pennyroyal, turpentine, hot baths, knitting needles, jumping off tables, falling downstairs, and so on. Some women poisoned themselves by taking dangerous drugs which caused an abortion as a side effect. Others ate adhesive plasters which contained diachylon, made from lead, or mixtures such as 'hickey pickey' – made up of a pennyworth of bitter apple, bitter aloes and white lead from the pharmacist.

Contraceptives were at best rudimentary: women could use a sponge soaked in a sperm-killing substance called a pessary; condoms were available under the counter in the more upmarket chemist's, but could not be advertised or displayed and few working men used them. Awareness of birth control was slowly growing, but many in the establishment were opposed to making contraceptives more widely available. Some leading doctors argued that men who used contraceptives would suffer 'mental decay, loss of memory, mania and conditions which lead to suicide'. A book published in the 1890s recommended 'traditional' methods such as coughing, sneezing and jumping up and down after intercourse as better than contraception. For those who presumed to sit in judgement over the morals of the lower classes, birth control was anathema, as was any mention of anything to do with sex. Ignorance and old-wives' tales were the order of the day. The results were predictable: women having one baby after another, when they could neither afford to bring them into the world or to feed them; high infant mortality and women worn down by the burden of childbirth; and high levels of prostitution, as men, rebuffed by their wives for fear of pregnancy, looked elsewhere for solace.

Church leaders, doctors and moralists were united in their belief that anything to do with sex was unmentionable. The orthodoxy of the day was that 'good' women were simply not interested in sex; those that were interested were by definition 'impure'. Men from the middle and upper classes were brought up to distinguish between pure women – the ones they married and who bore them children – and loose women – generally from the working classes and therefore excluded from the code of chivalry – with whom sex was fun. While the moralists condemned many young women to ignorance and nervous fear, they encouraged young men to find release in the arms of prostitutes, strictly separating lust from higher feelings and dividing women into virgins and whores. If this all seems a trifle exaggerated, this is what Dr William Acton (1813-75) had to say on women:

> As a general rule, a modest woman desires no sexual gratification for herself. She submits to her husband, but only to please him; and, but for the desire for babies, would far rather be relieved from his attentions ... The majority of women are not very much troubled with sexual feeling of any kind.

As for men – well, you remember all those old wives' tales about it making you blind? They weren't old wives' tales – they came from Dr Acton. 'Sperms are a man's vital substance – a kind of energy,' he declared, 'and if all used up he will be unable to work to his full capacity.' Once a week was the recommended maximum. He suggested that married men should sleep with their hands tied behind their back to avoid temptation. He was also very exercised about the evils of child masturbation, believing that it could lead to blindness, baldness and consumption.

If this all seems more than a little loony – a chilling pre-echo of General Jack D Ripper from *Dr Strangelove* – it should be pointed out that Dr Acton was one of the top gynaecologists of his day and that his books were widely read and widely respected. Dr William Acton was to the 1900s what Dr Alex Comfort was to the 1970s.

There were some who opposed this sort of tosh – Henry Havelock Ellis, for example, who believed that impurity flourished behind the veil held up by a prudish establishment and launched a crusade to combat ignorance and superstition. His groundbreaking studies of the Psychology of Sex laid the foundation of a rational reassessment of the whole question, and paved the way for later reformers like Marie Stopes. For Dean Inge, one of the era's most influential public figures, however, his research could be summed up in one word – 'unwholesome'.

One of the things that soured married life for many couples was the impossibility of divorce. Despite the example of Mrs Keen, few upper or middle class people were prepared to incur the social ostracism that accompanied divorce; for working people it was a financial impossibility. Divorce cases could only be heard in a single court in London. An undefended suit cost £50 to £60, a defended one up to £500. And, while a man could divorce his wife on grounds of adultery alone, a woman had to have other grounds such as cruelty as well. In 1910 there were only 908 divorce cases in England and Wales; in 2007, by contrast, the figure was 128,534.

The system caused a lot of misery; it also meant that many upper and middle class men, trapped in loveless marriages, kept a mistress or visited prostitutes. For their wives it meant a life of quiet desperation. As for the working classes, it sometimes meant desperation of a more vocal kind. In February 1909, a Mr Wiltshire, living at 2 The Ambury, was summoned for assaulting his wife. She wanted him to get rid of a woman renting a room in the house. He refused; in the ensuing quarrel she was injured, although he maintained this was because she was drunk. He was fined 10/-, but when his wife asked the judge to grant her a separation order, he advised her to 'get a separation between yourself and drink'.

In April a miner from Peasedown St John was summoned for assaulting his wife. She was living at 3 St James's Street South, having taken her child and left her husband three months earlier to stay with her mother. She was desperately short of money and went out to look for him. She found him at a dancing class in the Assembly Rooms with another girl. When she asked him for money, he told her 'to go down the town for it'. She said he was a filthy beast to suggest such a thing, to which he replied that, if she didn't want to do that, she and the child could put themselves in the river. Some time later, she saw him coming out of a pub in Southgate Street at around eight o'clock in the evening with 15 fellows all wearing football colours. He managed to avoid her, but three hours later she caught up with him and knocked his hat off. When the case came to court, the judge said he wanted 'to put an end to this farce', dismissed it as being too trivial, but ordered the husband to support his wife and child, at which he handed her ten shillings.

The *Bath Chronicle* reported many charges brought against those living on immoral earnings during 1909. It wasn't just prevailing moral values that fuelled this trade; it was the yawning chasm between rich and poor, with some women and girls so desperate they were prepared to do just about anything. Sometimes, women were forced into casual prostitution just to support children they wouldn't have had if they had had access to reliable forms of contraception. According to an anonymous memoir, *My Secret Life*, published privately in 1888, it cost '£1 for a very good woman, 10/- for as nice a woman as you needed, 5/- for quite a nice girl, and a silk pocket handkerchief (which could be sold for three or four shillings) for a poor girl'. It is that last entry – a handkerchief for sex with an under-age girl – that really seems to sum up the hypocrisy and mendacity of the whole 'respectable' system. And, as we have seen, Louie Stride's mother was prepared to accept as little as 1/6.

Although the authorities – many of whose representatives doubtless enjoyed 'a bit on the side' – saw prostitution as a black-and-white issue, in reality it was no such thing. While there were, as there always have been, professional prostitutes, much of what went on was of a casual nature, part of a wider, and predominantly working-class, social networking, with payment for sex an acknowledgement of deep, institutionalised financial and social inequality between the sexes. Today we would probably call it promiscuity; it differed from twenty-first century promiscuity, however, in that it was customary for men to give the women they spent time with – much of it often in a pub or 'on the town' – some money to help them out. And, while there were brothels in the generally accepted sense of the term, many of the 'disorderly houses' the magistrates closed down were simply lodging houses where rooms were let by the hour. Although a sympathetic observer might have concluded that those following a disorderly lifestyle were merely apeing the morals and manners of Edward VII and his circle – the celebrities of the age – few, if any, drew such parallels. Although they undoubtedly benefited, financially or otherwise, from their relationship with him, the King's mistresses, along with those of upper classes, would never have been referred to as prostitutes; nor would their abodes of love have been termed disorderly houses. Such terms were reserved almost exclusively for the working classes.

The cases brought before the magistrates in Bath in 1909 bear this out. In February 1909, a married couple were charged with 'unlawfully and knowingly allowing 107 Walcot Street to be used for the purposes of prostitution'. The woman was dismissed but the man was given three months' hard labour, and their two sons, age six and eight, were sent to an industrial school. In May, a ship's fireman living at 49 Avon Street was summoned for living on the earnings of prostitution and given three months hard labour. A woman, also living at 49 Avon Street, was summoned for allowing 6 Beauford Square to be used for improper purposes. In her defence she said it was simply a lodging house, with each lodger paying 3/- a week. She was given a fine of £10 or six weeks in jail. In August, a woman from Howells Cottages in Southgate Street was charged with keeping a disorderly house. She admitted having been warned by police against allowing certain girls to come into her house. She told the court that one girl came 'to change into fine clothes' because her father would not let her wear them at home. She was found guilty and fined 40/- or three months in jail. Three of her four children were taken into care; one who was over 14 was sent to a home.

During the 1909 licensing session, Mr Ford from the Town Clerk's Office appeared on behalf of the Chief Constable to oppose the granting of a licence to the *Malt & Hops* in Corn Street. 'It is largely frequented by colliers and people of the rougher class,' he told the magistrates:

> On three separate occasions the licensee has been cautioned for allowing prostitutes to be on the premises. He has also been cautioned for allowing dancing and singing to take place on the premises, and finally on the 23rd of last month to permit drunkenness. The circumstances were of a somewhat aggravated nature. Two young girls visited the house on Saturday evening and remained there for upwards of three hours. One of the girls, when attempting to leave, was detained by the licence holder, who was subsequently summoned, convicted and fined. The girl who was convicted for being drunk on the premises also gave evidence. She was there from around 7.30 to 11. About 10 the lights were turned off in the smoke room but she could not say if the people were noisy.

It was decided to refuse a licence on the grounds that the house was ill conducted, but an appeal was lodged and the *Malt & Hops* survived for another two years, being finally closed down in 1911.

Looking back at relations between the sexes a century ago, it is hard to resist the conclusion that, whatever problems we may have today, things are infinitely better than they were then – and we haven't got on to the topic of female suffrage yet! Before we do, there is one further topic – rarely accorded even a footnote in most studies of Edwardian England – that throws notions of prudery – along with certain other things – into sharp relief. This is the curious case of the Edwardian 'nothing to the imagination' swimming costume.

Until the 1860s, sea bathing was frequently undertaken *sans tout* – in a state of nature. Some maintained the tradition even longer. On Thursday 24th July 1873, the Rev Francis Kilvert, from Chippenham, wrote in his diary:

> This morning Uncle Will, Dora and I drove to Seaton with Polly and the dog cart ... At Seaton while Dora was sitting on the beach I had a bathe. A boy brought me to the machine door two towels as I thought, but when I came out of the water and began to use them I found that one of the rags he had given me was a pair of very short red and white striped drawers to cover my nakedness. Unaccustomed to such things and customs, I had in my ignorance bathed naked and set at nought the conventionalities of the place and scandalized the beach. However some little boys who were looking on at the rude naked man appeared to be much interested in the spectacle, and the young ladies who were strolling nearby seemed to have no objection.

A year later, on 12 June 1874, he was on the Isle of Wight; once again he saw no reason to hide his charms from the local ladies:

> At Shanklin one has to adopt the detestable custom of bathing in drawers. If ladies don't like to see men naked why don't they keep away from the sight? Today I had a pair of drawers given me which I could not keep on. The rough waves stripped them off and tore them down round my ankles. While thus fettered I was seized and flung down by a heavy sea which retreating suddenly left me lying naked on the sharp shingle from which I rose streaming with blood. After this I took the wretched and dangerous rag off and of course there were some ladies looking on as I came up out of the water.

Not, obviously, something you'd find your average vicar doing today, at least not on the Isle of Wight.

The first bathing costumes were made of flannel or calico. These preserved the modesty of the shiest youth or most bashful maiden, but became very heavy when wet, making swimming difficult if not dangerous, and took ages to dry. They were superseded by stockingette and, later, cotton for the new one-piece costumes worn by men and women. Although these were much easier to swim in,

Edwardian bathing costumes left little to the imagination. Above, a group of young men line up for the photographer before taking a dip in the canal. This photograph was printed with a postcard back, so it could be sent to friends or loved ones. This was common practice at the time, but one can only wonder what the reaction was at the other end if any of the men featured on it were bold enough to entrust this view of themselves to the Royal Mail. On the left, women model Edwardian costumes on the steps of a bathing machine, while the comic card on the right promotes opportunities available at the seaside for the less scrupulous male sightseer.

they clung to the figure when wet, accentuating those parts of the body it was considered most essential to conceal. The admiring glances they evoked were celebrated in a 1906 music-hall song –

> Ev'ry day I do enjoy
> Bathing in the sea,
> But some stupid little boy
> Always stare at me.
> I turn my back – he get Kodak.
> Mon Dieu, que t'es bête!
> Sur la plage, on the plage,
> They are full of persiflage
> When I take my bain-de-mer,
> At what do the men all stare?
> C'est un ange quand elle plonge
> Elle a beaucoup de courage,
> Il faut la voir dans la chic peignoir
> On the plage.
>
> In the sea not far I go,
> For I might get wet,
> Just about to there, you know,
> Quite enough, you bet.
> I'm so very brave, you see,
> When I've had my swim;
> If some man he look at me,
> I look back at him!

253

More refined resorts segregated the sexes or provided bathing machines; in Bath, the Royal Baths and the Cleveland Baths had separate sessions for men and women – mixed bathing was not introduced to the Cleveland Baths till June 1913 – but in most cases men and women swam – and flaunted their charms – in front of one another. Moralists may have tut-tutted – in Bath in 1909, for example, there were several complaints that 'insufficient costume' was worn by bathers frequenting 'Mr Coombs' swimming bath at Twerton' – but nothing was done. It is an extraordinary thought that, in an age when a glimpse of stocking – or any exposed flesh – was considered shocking, going for a swim in costumes that would be considered indecent on your average beach today was perfectly acceptable. Not that Kilvert would have been too impressed, of course. Modesty was eventually restored in the 1920s when woollen costumes were introduced, leaving only fading photographs in family albums to remind us why some people really did like to be beside the seaside.

CHAPTER SEVENTEEN

HOPE FOR THE COUNCIL!

Even more shocking than the disadvantages suffered by women a century ago was the belief that such disadvantages were part of a divinely ordained scheme. It wasn't just men who held this view; many women did as well. Most of the professions were strictly men only: at the time of the 1901 Census there were 172,000 women teachers and 64,000 women nurses in England & Wales, but only six architects, three vets and two accountants. There were no solicitors or barristers. Women teachers were virtually all spinsters; with few exceptions, they had to resign when they got married. For the majority of working-class girls, domestic service was the only job open to them. One in three girls between 15 and 20 were domestics. Admittedly, things were changing, but only slowly, and not to everyone's satisfaction. 'The young working girl of today,' wrote Mrs CS Peel in 1902, with evident disapproval, 'prefers to become a Board School mistress, a post-office clerk, a typewriter, a shop girl, or a worker in a factory – anything rather than enter domestic service.'

It is hardly surprising that many women were frustrated. There has been a tendency of late – not just from those from whom you'd expect it, such as Melanie Phillips, but also from writers such as Roy Hattersley – to play down the achievements of the suffragists or to write them off – as many did at the time – as a bunch of histrionic women who retarded rather than advanced the cause of female emancipation. In a similar way, some people argue that 'strikes never achieve anything', that protest and revolution get in the way of progress, and that we would have got more or less where we are today without the industrial and social unrest that characterised much of the twentieth century. While such a resolutely non-Hegelian view may be alluring, it hardly withstands close scrutiny. No one gives up their rights and privileges willingly; sympathy for the disadvantages of others is rarely translated into a desire to share them. Women got the vote, in the same way that workers improved their conditions, by fighting for it.

After the Liberal landslide of 1906, many women assumed that the anticipated programme of social reform would include a bill to introduce female suffrage. They were wrong. Things had moved on a little since Gladstone had declared his belief that woman should not 'trespass upon the delicacy, the purity, the refinement, the elevation of her own nature' by seeking the vote, but a majority of the new government were, like the Conservatives who preceded them, opposed to extending parliamentary democracy to women.

No one was too surprised by the Conservatives' failure to give women the vote. Many advocates of female suffrage were prepared to hold fire and wait for the Liberals – whom they assumed supported their cause – to achieve power. It was the failure of the Liberals to come up with the goods that marked the beginning of a concerted campaign to achieve female suffrage by fair means or foul. This split the movement, with groups like the Conservative & Unionist Women's Franchise Association, who held a meeting at the Guildhall in Bath in February 1909, remaining strongly committed to peaceful means.

It may come as a surprise, familiar as we are with images of women chained to railings, attacking public figures, throwing stones and going on hunger strike, to realise that initially the suffragist movement was eminently respectable ('suffragist' was the name chosen by the campaigners themselves; 'suffragette' was a term coined later as a patronising put-down). In June 1909, a play advocating votes for women was performed at the Theatre Royal. The *Bath Chronicle* gave it a cautious welcome:

> The only suffrage play that may be said to have obtained popularity, *Man and Woman*, was produced at the Theatre Royal on Thursday, by members of the Clifton Women's Reform Union, under the direction of Mrs Cross. Needless to say, the play met with a good reception. *Man and Woman* is a very clever and thorough exposition of the case of the woman suffragist, and apart from the gospel it preaches it makes a far wider appeal for more equitable laws ... One can only regret that there were not more voters among the audience, which was chiefly composed of ladies.

By then, though, the battle lines had been drawn. Bath was in the forefront of the suffrage movement due to a remarkable Batheaston family – the Blathwayts of Eagle House. Mary Blathwayt had joined the Women's Social & Political Union in 1906, and, with the support of her parents, Eagle House had become a well-known meeting place and campaigning centre for suffragists from all over the country.

The violence the campaigners ultimately resorted to is the stuff of legend; less well known is the violence they suffered at the hands

Mary Blathwayt (centre) with her mother (right) and an unidentified lady on the family Oldsmobile outside Eagle House. Acquired in 1904 for £150, this was the first car in Batheaston.

of the Edwardian mob. An extract from Mary's diary for 8 June 1909 indicates the level of abuse they had to suffer:

> We went [to Bristol] on a lorry and a large crowd of children were waiting for us when we arrived. Things were thrown at us all the time; but when we drove away at the end we were hit a great many times. Elsie Howey had her lip hit and it bled. I was hit by potatoes, stones, turf and dust. Something hit me very hard on my right ear as I was getting into our tram. Someone threw a stone as big as a baby's head; it fell onto the lorry.

On the evening of Saturday 19 June, Annie Kenny, a Lancashire mill worker who was one of the leading lights of the suffragist movement, addressed an 'orderly crowd' (the *Chronicle's* description) of around 500 people, including many men, in front of the weighing machine on the Sawclose, and defended the militant methods increasingly being adopted. Less than a month later, with more and more arrests being made, Miss Wallace Dunlop began the first hunger strike in prison. Among those growing increasingly concerned with the rising tide of militancy was Mary Blathwayt's mother, Emily, who left the WSPU in September 1909. Eagle House continued to

The weighing machine on the Sawclose, scene of a large suffragette rally on 19 June 1909.

be an important centre for the movement, however, attracting both militants and non-militants, many of whom planted trees, with their names attached, in the grounds.

Because suffragists had a policy of disrupting meetings at which political leaders were speaking, women were often excluded from them. Not only did suffragists find ingenious ways of gaining entry, however; male supporters of the movement would sometimes act on their behalf. On 14 August 1909, Richard Haldane, the War Minister, addressed a meeting at the Theatre Royal on the subject of the budget. A couple of days earlier, a correspondent to the *Bath Chronicle* wrote that, 'I hope to be present on Saturday at the Theatre Royal to hear what Mr Haldane has to say on the budget. May I suggest that every effort be made to prevent any disturbance by the suffragettes. They are very resourceful and have outwitted "mere men" before.' It was, however, a 'mere man' who, after the audience had sung 'For he's a jolly good fellow', shouted out, 'When are you going to give votes to women?' Uproar ensued, until he was eventually ejected.

Although women did not get to vote in national elections for over a decade, however, the Liberals had passed the Qualification of Women Act in 1907, giving them the right to vote in local elections and to seek election as councillors. The following year, two women stood for the council in Bath, although both were disqualified. When Valentine Evans stood down as a councillor for Kingsmead in October 1909 and Miss Helen Hope came forward to take his place, a certain degree of amusement was caused in the council chamber when Alderman Phillips asked what would be done about ladies' retiring and ante-rooms if they were elected. As the laughter died down, Councillor Colmer said that if they were elected it would mean extensive expenditure – at which point the Mayor stepped in, saying that that sort of talk could prejudice their election chances. In the event, Miss Hope was returned unopposed. Her election was greeted with a poem by LB Hewitt in the *Bath Chronicle*:

> *Now shines the sun o'er golden autumn fields*
> *(I think this metaphor is rather good);*
> *Hope joined to work such bounteous harvest yields*
> *As I scarce thought it would.*
>
> *Last year Bath's ladies, who for seats did try,*
> *Found themselves ousted on a legal point,*
> *But now the vexed misogynist must cry:*
> *'The time is out of joint!' ...*
>
> *'Hope for the council!' – let us not despair;*
> *Bath now must wake: she dare not slumber more.*
> *But stay – 'Hope' now is in the council where*
> *No woman sat before ...*
>
> *Take courage, now, dames of enlightened mind!*
> *Take courage now, O Force-fed Suffragette!*
> *See here a sign that fate to you is kind,*
> *For Hope is living yet!*

Miss Hope was a well-known figure in Bath. Born in 1866, she was the daughter of William Hope of Rock House, Lansdown Road, where she still lived. Her brother was Liberal MP for North Somerset. She was a passionate campaigner on behalf of working people in Bath and worked tirelessly to improve welfare and educational facilities. She was instrumental in setting up cottage homes for children who would otherwise have had to go into the workhouse, providing special tuition and care for physically and mentally handicapped children, and for introducing free medical care, spectacles, toothbrushes, and school meals for children whose parents could not afford them.

She helped to found the Stead Hostel in Pierrepont Street for women who would otherwise have had to live in dubious lodging houses. She also established a branch of the Workers Educational Association (WEA), along with a working girls' club and an amateur

Two views of Citizen House, founded by Helen Hope.

Club Room of the Walker Girls' Club, Citizen House, Bath.

Rock House on Lansdown Road.

theatre, at 2 Chandos Buildings, which was renamed Citizen House. The *Chronicle* later described Citizen House as 'a kind of folk house or meeting place for people of all classes'. In an obituary published after her death in 1922, the paper also recorded that a year earlier she had been voted the most popular member of the council. The lease of Citizen House passed to Consuelo de Reyes, a colleague of Miss Hope's who had established the Citizen House Players there in 1915. In January 1936, Consuelo, now Mrs Peter King, opened, together with her husband, the Little Theatre – housing a theatre and a newsreel cinema – as an extension to Citizen House. Citizen House burned to the ground only a few weeks later, but the Little Theatre survives as one of the most vibrant cultural and social centres in Bath – a fitting reminder of one of Bath's most remarkable councillors.

After her death, Bath High School moved from Portland Place to her former home, Rock House, which was renamed Hope House in her honour, a name it still bears, as the Royal High Junior School, today.

Guinea Pig Jack, Bath's most famous street person, in Manvers Street.

CHAPTER EIGHTEEN

STREET LIFE

If we were able to go back a century and step out of our time machine onto the streets of Bath in 1909 what would be the first thing we'd notice?[1]

There's a fair chance it would be the smell. Drains, especially in hot weather, and in the lower part of town, would probably have been pretty nasty. Ideas of personal hygiene, even for the upper and middle classes, were far less exacting than they are today. Daily bathing or showering was regarded as eccentric – and, while the majority of working people would have had a weekly bath, many never bathed from one year's end to the next. Some wore the same clothes year in year out. Summer clothes did not feature in many people's wardrobes; they remained wrapped up through the hottest of heat waves. There wasn't a heat wave in 1909 – a particularly miserable summer – but, two years later, the heatwave of 1911 broke all records. People worked in hot airless workshops and factories with no air conditioning. And no deodorant.

It has often been pointed out that most working people never saw a doctor because of the cost. But what about dentists? When men enlisted in 1914, in some places four out of five of them had such bad teeth they couldn't eat properly. This was an age when false teeth were a sign of affluence; factories in the north of England held weekly sweepstakes, with the winner treated to having their teeth extracted and a false set fitted. On a personal level, the agony of toothache – and the rough and ready extractions used to treat it – cannot readily be imagined; on a social level, the olfactory result of widespread dental neglect – many people never used a toothbrush – cannot have been too pleasant either.

---

1 For much of the information in this chapter, I am indebted to PC Edward Smith who served full-time in the Bath Police Force from April 1919 until April 1950, and part-time till 1961. He kept a notebook in which he recorded what he saw as he walked the beat, along with memories of his childhood in Bath. Before his death in 1970, he gave the notebook to Bruce Crofts, to whom I am grateful for permission to use it here. I have also referred to *Twenty Shillings in the Pound* by Walter McQueen-Pope, many of whose recollections of Edwardian life echo those of PC Smith.

Setting aside such squeamish considerations, street life a century was a much more vibrant affair than it is today. The streets of Bath – as of every other town and city – were far more entertaining and edgy than they are today. They bore more relation to parts of Southern Europe or the Third World than anything you will find in Britain today. While, in the more refined parts of the city, street urchins, hawkers, costers and musicians were discouraged, if not prohibited, elsewhere there was a Dickensian cornucopia. It was difficult to go for a quiet walk without being accosted or pestered, and, although most of this was good-natured enough, there was a rough edge to it that many people would find difficult to cope with today.

Many people more or less lived on the street. There was little enough to keep them at home; most working-class homes were so small that mothers had to send children out if they were to stand any chance of getting the housework done. And the street was where, if you were sharp enough, you could make a bit of money. Most people wouldn't resort to outright begging – which was against the law and could land you in prison – but there were a thousand and one ways you could provide some sort of service – in the loosest possible sense of the word – and make a few coppers.

The letters of complaint quoted in Chapter Two indicate how much shouting and singing there was. Many of the old street cries could have been heard in the city in Georgian or even Tudor times; refrains of 'Sweet Lavender' or 'Ripe Strawberries' conveyed a powerful sense of an earlier age. Almost invariably, street traders were known not by their real names but by the catchphrases they called out as they wandered the streets.

The Hokey-Pokey Man, who sold cheap ice cream, was a familiar sight in many towns. His name came from 'Hocus-Pocus', a seventeenth-century name for a juggler's trick, and later applied to a drugged liquor. Bath's Hokey-Pokey Man was Mario Mancini who lived at 66 Avon Street where he made ice-cream and packed it in flat slabs wrapped in plain white paper. He kept it in a tub inside a red cylinder. Unlike most Italian ice-cream, which was soft, it was quite firm. As he pushed his red-wheeled cart along, he would invariably be followed by a group of children shouting –

> *Hokey-pokey a penny a lump,*
> *The more you eat, the more you jump!*

– although, sometimes, mischievous children would substitute 'pump' for 'jump'.

Then there was 'Oysters O' – real name Tommy Bowden – a convivial old soul with a cart that looked like a railway engine, complete with funnel. He sold small oysters called 'queenies'.

George Hull, from Coburg Place in Widcombe, was known as 'Fish and Chips' and had a horse-drawn vehicle, like a small traction engine, with a vertical steam boiler and chimney. He toured the streets at night ringing his bell and offering a complete meal for 1½d.

The Cat's Meat Man pushed a handcart and was usually followed by his feline supporters as he went from house to house calling out 'Mee-mee-meat'. He displayed boiled horse meat on skewers which he collected from the knacker's yard at Brass Mills.

'Catch-'em-alive-O' sold square flypapers, covered with strong adhesive on one side, for 1d each. He wore a top hat with a fly-laden paper hanging from each side. His cry was:

> Catch 'em alive. Catch 'em alive,
> Those tormenting flies
> Tickle the babies' eyes,
> Catch 'em alive.

'Heads or Tails' was a pieman called Batchelor who pushed his wares around on a cart with a coal-fired oven. Sometimes he would encourage customers to bet on the toss of a coin; depending on the outcome, you either paid 1d for nothing or got a free pie. If business was a bit slow, he would call out, 'Only selling tonight.'

Cokey Giles sold coke from a handcart at 1d a bucket. He collected the coke from the gasworks where one of his tricks, when no one was looking, was to put a brick under a wheel of one of the company's carts. As it drove off, some of the coke would fall onto the ground as the wheel lurched off the brick, where it was 'salvaged' by Cokey.

Shavings George – otherwise known as Tuncher Wibley – was a very large man who collected sacks of shavings which he mixed with coal dust and sold as cheap but effective fuel.

The Muffin Man was a particular favourite with children. He carried his muffins on a tray which rested on a round, flat pan on his head, with the muffins covered by a green baize cloth. His cry of 'muffins and crumpets', accompanied by the ringing of a bell, was a familiar sound on autumn and winter evenings in the streets and alleys of Edwardian Bath.

Donkey Ball was a lady called Nellie who lived at Rosebery Place in Twerton. She sold 'chumps' (or logs) from a dray drawn by a donkey; her temper and impatience were legendary. 'Get a move on!' she would shout at her donkey, as she stood on the cart with whip in hand, swaying from side to side 'with a wild look on her bespectacled face'. On one occasion – so legend has it – she grew so enraged by the donkey's refusal to 'get a move on' that she poured paraffin over it and set it alight!

Then there was Jossy Gould, sartorially resplendent in a carter's cap with ear flaps, pearl buttons on his coat and corduroy trousers. He would drive upwards of 200 ducks through Westgate Street to market where they were sold at 3/- a pair. Customers pointed out the ones they wanted and Jossy would lasso them.

Rufus Crook or 'Crookie' was perhaps the best known of all Bath's street people, even though he owned a meat and fish shop on Lower Borough Walls. His Friday and Saturday night auctions drew such large crowds that the police had to keep order. Sometimes Crookie turned up drunk, which was good news for anyone after a bargain. Many people, though, turned up just for the entertainment; his patter was a match for any stand-up comedian. 'Keep off the pavement!' he would shout. 'The police'll have me again! My fines have already paid for the Guildhall – and the police uniforms and boots!' He auctioned his meat 'by hook or by Crook', and if the bids weren't high enough he'd start swearing and abusing people in the crowd, before turning down the gas and stalking off to his fish shop next door to start selling kippers at a shilling for two dozen.

Unlike most shopkeepers, he didn't go out of his way to court the top end of the market. 'Lift up your necks and smell it – that's your share' was one of the more restrained comments he reserved for middle-class customers. With working-class customers, though, it was a different story, and he would often give away joints of meat to regular customers who were down on their luck.

He is said to have held the record for the number of court appearances; there he would regale the magistrates with the sort of non-stop patter he used at his auctions. On 23 December 1909, for example, he was summoned for assaulting a man called Wheeler who had tried to drive Crookie's horse and trap because he'd been too drunk to control it. On this occasion, he caused no end of merriment by offering to take the pledge, and adding, in his defence, that trade was bad and 'there's trouble at home'. He was fined 20/-. On another occasion, he was sentenced to a spell in Horfield Prison. On his release, he was greeted by a welcoming party, including a brass band, at Twerton station, and made a triumphal journey into town in a carriage towed by his friends.

He retired to his home, Cherry Orchard in Upper Swainswick, where he kept the last hansom cab in Bath, which he bought for a pound. He died in November 1914 at the age of 57. When his body lay in state in his shop, the queue of people waiting to pay their respects stretched to the Old Bridge. The funeral cortege was one of the longest in Bath's history.

Sal Crook, Rufus's daughter, was a well-known figure on the streets of Bath selling salt cod and haddock from a box balanced on her head – hence her nickname, 'Dry Haddock'.

There were out-of-town street traders as well. William Bolsom of Church Street in Weston was blinded by an accident at the gasworks as a young man. Such an event would be terrible today; in the days before workmen's compensation acts or disability pensions it was immeasurably worse. He had a sheepdog which led him along Park Lane, where he would sit on the wall outside Grafton Place, selling oranges from a basket covered with a net to deter thieves. He was known as Blind William, and was one of about 50 blind people living at home in Bath in the early 1900s. In 1909, an Association for the Home Teaching of the Blind was set up under the auspices of the Mayor to try to help train and care for blind people in the city.

Other well-known blind people in Edwardian Bath included Blind Alice, who lived in the Ambury, and a man called Webb, who carried a tin cup to solicit donations and was led around by one of his children. Another blind man called Hobbs often stood in the Sawclose between the Bluecoat School and the Palace Theatre. Some said that he wasn't blind at all; according to some boys who'd stood and watched him, he would wait for a while if he heard anything drop into his cup, before removing his dark glasses to see how much it was. It was also said – although this sounds like the sort of urban myth that often attached itself to these unfortunate people – that when he died he left £1,000.

Many other people ended up on the street because of physical disability. One of the best-known was Lavender Liz, who had a variety of other names, including Hoppy-Go-Giggy, Hoppy Flo, Hoppity Flo, North Parade Kate and Mrs Up & Down. Her real name – seldom if ever used – was Florence Williams. She lived in Avon Street but spent much of her time sitting on the wall of the fountain in Stall Street, selling lavender, matches and Old Moore's

Photographs of street people are notoriously difficult to find and none of 'Lavender Liz' has yet come to light. Paper Sal from Bristol, whose story echoes Lavender Liz's, featured on this picture postcard, however. She got her name from her habit of collecting old newspapers, which she would then sell. She also supplied them to a local fish and chip shop and was given bags of scrumps in return. Like Lavender Liz, she had a variety of nicknames – Sally Apple, Old Mother Pony, Coke House Sally and Hoppy – and there were numerous stories concerning her ancestry. Some said she had been abandoned on a doorstep by a rich lady; some said she had been cheated out of a fortune by evil relatives. When she died, at the age of 82, in 1926, her little house in Redcross Street near Old Market was stuffed with enough rubbish (including the skeletons of cats and dogs) to fill three carts.

Almanac. On Sundays she sat in the gallery of St James's Church. Although she kept herself tidy and always wore a clean white apron, she suffered crippling disabilities: one of her legs was shorter than the other, her face was disfigured and she walked with one of her hands cupped behind her back, into which naughty children dropped fagends. Stories about her were legion – that she was the victim of a factory explosion, that she was a 'copper's nark' or that she was the daughter of a titled lady, for example. Whatever the truth, in reality she was a poor soul trying to get by the best way she could in a harsh world, before the advent of the welfare state. She died in 1932 at the age of 78.

Shoeblacks also operated from the fountain in Stall Street. The streets – muddy when wet, dusty when dry – ensured a regular supply of customers. Some wore a sort of uniform – red coats were popular – and many had regular customers who would turn up at a particular time of day. It

was strictly 'men only' – no woman would have dared lift her leg up to the shoeblack's stand in Edwardian Bath.

There were also, as Louie Stride recalled, lots of 'totters' or rag and bone men in Edwardian Bath:

> Some of them had the proverbial handcarts, some prams and some only sacks on their backs. They sold goods on the pavements outside their houses, old clothes, pots and pans, any and everything. Many had little shops, two in particular I remember. One was a lovely lady, Aunty Clare, who made and cooked faggots and peas. If only one could get hold of sixpence, or even threepence, and took a basin, she would be most generous, and the smell of those fragrant faggots are with me to this day. Another man had a baker's and huckster shop and sold paraffin and candles, and salt fish, and everything one could imagine. His name was Mr Ollis, very clean and tidy he was. He also went out with a basket selling cooked snails and winkles, and I used to waylay him with a cup and if he had any over I would beg for some and I was never refused.

Many other tradesmen called round to people's houses; some had regular rounds and turned up on a particular day. Then there were the knife-grinders, mat menders, basket sellers, pedlars selling odds and ends of drapery – cotton, thread, darning wool, needles, tape and so on. Something we regard as a very modern nuisance – junk mail – was delivered, not by the postman, but by men walking the streets with satchels slung over their shoulders, pushing endless circulars from local tradesmen through letter boxes. The sign, 'No hawkers or circulars' was a common sight affixed to tradesmen's entrances, as were marks scratched by the tramps that were always wandering around, informing their colleagues of the welcome they could expect if they knocked at the door.

Postmen were much more in evidence than they are today. A century ago there were five postal deliveries a day in town – at 7am, 9.30am, 1.15pm, 4.30pm, 6.40pm and 8.30pm – and at least seven collections from street pillar boxes. Most local post – and much long-distance post – arrived on the day it was sent; it was possible, for example, to get a letter to Radstock the same day by posting it at the main post office before 4.10pm. You could even get a letter to London on the same day if it was in the post by 3.25pm. In the days when very few people had telephones this level of service was invaluable both for businesses and individuals. It was also used, to comic effect, by Saki in a short story called 'Shock Tactics', in which Clovis stops the mother of a friend opening his mail by sending a string of letters, implicating him in a series of ever more outrageous and implausible intrigues, over the course of a day, finishing off by revealing it to be a hoax in the last post of the evening.

There were not only many more deliveries than there are today; there were many more post offices, and they were open for longer. The main post office in York Buildings (now the Revolution Bar, although the old clock is still there) was open from 7am to 11pm on weekdays and from 8.30am to 10am and 8pm to 6pm on Sundays. Post offices could also be found at:

> 2 St George's Place, Bathwick Hill
> 35 Bathwick Street
> 77 Richmond Place, Beacon Hill
> 7 Charles Street
> Claremont Terrace
> 3 Cleveland Terrace
> 28 Victoria Buildings, East Twerton
> 1 Mile End, Grosvenor
> 1 Hayes Place, Holloway
> 7 Kingsmead Square
> 23 Belvedere
> 4 Lambridge Buildings, Larkhall
> 5 Cork Place, Locksbrook

1 Violet Bank Villas, Lower Weston
4 Margaret's Buildings
24 Moorland Road, Oldfield Park
25 New Bond Street
8 Marlborough Street
4-5 Sladebrook, Southdown
40 Southgate Street
1 Mill Lane, High Street, Twerton
1 Lymore Avenue, South Twerton
2 Westmoreland Mart
8 High Street, Weston
16 Widcombe Parade
2 Berkeley Street
Claverton Down
GW Railway Station (up platform)
Midland Railway Station

One of Bath's lost post offices – Wansdyke at Claverton Down.

Only in outlying districts was the level of service more in line with what we expect today, although all but the smallest villages supported a post office. Rural rounds were sometimes done by a postman with a horse and trap, although many were done on foot. One postman walked across Lansdown to Wick and Doynton every day. Before returning to Bath, he spent his spare time at Doynton repairing boots for the villagers.

The rural postman.

Another figure who is still with us is the milkman, although here too the passing of a century has wrought enormous changes. Milk was generally delivered either by horse-drawn carts with a churn on them or by a man pushing a churn on wheels. Milk was drawn off from the churn into pewter cans with lids which were left on people's steps or hung on their railings. Often, there was more than one delivery a day, and the milkmen would shout 'Milk-

A Bath milkman with a handcart.

milk oh!' or some such refrain to let their customers know they were coming. Milk was also delivered by men or women carrying two pails suspended from a yoke across their shoulders. Sydney Harding – better known as Milky Gallow or Skiffy Harding – was one of those who operated like this. He worked for the Abbey Dairy and sold skimmed milk at a penny a quart. He was often drunk and amused onlookers when he lost his balance and spilt the milk.

Above: Milk carts outside the Eastbourne Dairy in Camden.
Below: To streamline the supply of milk to Bath's dairies, the Bath & District Farmers established a depot in Newark Street. Here it is seen in course of construction.

On Saturdays he would go to the recreation ground and dance on the pitch in front of the rugby crowds, being forcibly removed to loud cheers before the game started. His cry, although well-known to Bathonians, had the disadvantage of being totally meaningless:

> *You won't always have it,*
> *You can't always get it,*
> *I've got mine to get!*

Watercress sellers were also a familiar sight. Watercress was grown in beds behind the *Cross Keys* at Combe Down. Rabbit sellers walked around with a pole slung over their shoulders from which wild rabbits dangled. Rabbits were cheap and a staple of the working-class diet; the middle-classes, however, although they would buy Ostend rabbits from a provision merchant, looked down on wild rabbits as peasant food.

Some door-to-door tradesmen were after buying rather than selling. The rag man, for example, would offer pieces of china for old rags, while the iron man would give you a few pence for old iron. In an age of subsistence, recycling wasn't just an ecological desideratum but an economic necessity. One of Bath's rag ladies, known as Kitty Doll Rags, was notorious for using language that 'would make a donkey blush'. A man-and-wife team who went from door to door repairing umbrellas were known as Adam and Eve. Apparently, she looked like a 'female Punch' and they were famous for being 'constantly in argument'.

With most children leaving school at eleven, there were many more youths hanging around the streets than there are today. Girls generally found some sort of menial indoor work, but many boys from poor families took to the streets, living by their wits to earn a few coppers. They collected horse manure to sell to gardeners and held carters' horses when they nipped into the pub; they swept crossings, cleaned shoes – and sold newspapers. At the time of the 1911 Census, there were 30 newsboys in Bath (along with 73 costermongers), although the figure, given the casual nature of the work, was almost certainly much higher. Victor Rosenburg, writing in the 1960s, remembered the daily race between the various newsboys in Bath to be first on the streets with the early edition of the paper. They dashed around yelling out sensational headlines – ''orrible murder' was a favourite one – sometimes with only the most tenuous connection to any of the stories in the paper. Paperboys, though, were unpopular with certain sections of the community – and not just because of the noise they made. Councillor Charles Long was particularly exercised about them, exclaiming at a meeting in 1909,

> I deplore the number of unemployables that are being bred in the city. If you look at the railway stations you will see they are being grown by the dozen. They are mostly newspaper boys. I confess I know of no remedy except persuasion, and I have persuaded a number of them to go into the navy or army. But I fear the unemployables are increasing alarmingly.

A Chronicle newsboy in Sydney Road announces the Relief of Mafeking in 1900.

It wasn't just boys who hung round the streets to carry out menial duties in the hope of raising a few coppers. Some men worked as crossing sweepers as well, exercising a sort of squatters right over their particular crossings. Walter Macqueen-Pope recalls that they were 'a strange race of men, often half-witted or afflicted, and always in advanced sartorial decay'. One of Bath's most notorious crossing sweepers was the 'Terrible Turk', who terrified old ladies if they failed to provide a reward after a way had been cleared for them through the dust or mud. There were other issues with crossing sweepers as well. One letter in the local paper complained of 'crippled crossing sweepers standing some distance off the roads purposely in the hope of being struck by the poles or shafts of passing vehicles and then claiming compensation'.

Other letters complained about the number of costers on the streets of Bath. Fred Goad, a second-hand bookseller at 2-3 Bath Street, wanted something done about the costers who stood outside his shop on Saturdays, obstructing the pavement, pestering his customers and affecting his takings. Unlicensed pedlars were constantly getting picked up by the police, although one, a homeless man called Harry Franklin, arrested at Weston in July 1909 for selling needles without a licence, clearly wasn't going to make a killing. When arrested, he was found to have only one penny on him and two packets of needles. He was still fined five shillings or three days' imprisonment.

There were even more complaints about the number of beggars. Many of these, such as one called Shammer, were well-known characters. He was a melancholy old man with a shaggy beard, greasy overcoat and battered bowler who looked for sympathy as he played his penny whistle. He had a crutch which he forgot to use when chasing abusive children. On one occasion he went to prison for throwing a stone at a boy, which smashed a window of Tuck's drapers in Kingsmead Square. In 1909, he was charged with striking a fellow lodger in his digs at 5 Avon Street with a poker, and the question that all Bath wanted answered was asked in court. 'Is he a cripple or not?', the magistrate wanted to know; after a thorough examination, the doctor pronounced him 'weak generally but fit to do hard labour' – so he got one month! The trial also revealed that his real name was Henry Rose.

Bun-Eater wasn't a beggar but a character who dressed in a frock-coat and silk hat and carried an umbrella. He is said to have got his name by gate-crashing parties and chowing down as many buns as he could before being thrown out. Then there was Mother Quack-Quack, an old lady with short legs and a duck-like walk who brandished a walking stick at abusive youths. William Jones – known as Billy Madoo – repaired boots with odd bits of cobbler's leather, with which he 'made do', hence his nickname. He was also a perpetually hopeful and invariably disappointed candidate at local council elections. His speeches always began: 'Ladies and gents and females. I am here to undress you!' You can't help feeling that he would have made a valuable contribution to council debates. He died in April 1909.

William Linney's nickname – Billy Look-Up – was the result of his habit of walking round staring up at the sky. This came in handy, though, when he got a job as a lamplighter. Walter Macqueen-Pope describes why the lamplighter held such a special place in the memories of those who grew up in Edwardian England:

> He came along the road at dusk walking briskly, with his pole over his shoulder. That pole had a brass container on the end, something like a cartridge case, but perforated by holes. Inside was a flame, but how it was kept burning was apparently a trade secret, for nobody seems to know. He came to the lamp-post, he pushed the pole through a small hole at the bottom of

the gas-lamp and the pole turned on the tap, which set the gas coming through the jet. Then out of his pole darted a little flame, and the gas-lamp flared merrily. Down the road he went, as one watched from a window, and lamp after lamp sprang to life. He left a firmament of flickering stars behind him, illuminating the growing dusk and twilight.

Children watched him eagerly and with a touch of sadness too, for it meant another day was over, and bedtime loomed near. And yet he was a friend of theirs, although unknown. His coming was a daily event, part of the life of their youth. To the grown-ups it meant that night time had come – and it brought relaxation, or the pursuit of pleasure.

Lamplighters disappeared when automatic timers – invented by Horstmann's in Bath – were fitted to street lights. Horstmann's Patent Gas Controllers were already fitted to many of Bath's street lamps by 1909, although there was some resistance to their introduction elsewhere – and not just from sentimentalists. In January 1909, the *Bath Chronicle* reported that Horstmann's controllers were being fitted to 250 lights in Glasgow, saving on gas and lamplighters' wages. Labour members on Glasgow council tried to block the scheme, however, because the redundant lamplighters would swell the ranks of the unemployed. After Billy was replaced by Horstmann's controllers, he kept on his other jobs, pumping the bellows of the organ at Percy Chapel and running errands for people, before ending up in Frome Road Workhouse.

Long Horn Jack lived in a grotto tunnel near Hamilton House on Lansdown – part of the garden built by William Beckford, which stretched from his house on Lansdown Crescent to his tower on Lansdown. Although he didn't ride a horse, he attended hunt meets wearing a huntsman's long green coat and black cap, and often wandered up and down Milsom Street in the same garb. He too died in the workhouse.

There were many other street people in Edwardian Bath who are known to us only by their names – Jimmy Woods, Gentleman Joe, Gentleman Dick, Cabby Old, Magpie Smith, Mizzen, Biddy, Farmer One Cow, Whistle like a Bird, Monk, Juicy Lemon, Cushy, Kick-up George, Irish Jack, Fishy Lee, Combe Down Willy, Harry Jam Jar, Salty Jimmy, Gaffer Hughes and Butler Bill. The most celebrated, though, was undoubtedly Guinea Pig Jack. He achieved celebrity status when a photograph of him, taken by Captain F J Nash, MBE, from Lancashire, was turned into a postcard, with a poem on the back, one verse of which read:

> *Who is that quaint little man down the street, Sir?*
> *He with the coat that's too big for his back?*
> *Not many folk that I happen to meet, Sir,*
> *Haven't some knowledge of Guinea Pig Jack.*

Over 20,000 of these postcards were sold, turning him into such an international celebrity that, when the American writer WD Howells came to Bath to write a feature for *Harper's Magazine*, he sought him out:

I myself used often to meet in Bath a little queer plinth of a man, whose nationality I could not make out, but every inch of whose five feet was suggestive of Dickens. His face, topped by a frowsy cap, was twisted in a sort of fixed grin, and his eyes looked different ways, perhaps to prevent any attempt of mine to escape him. He carried at his side a small wicker box which he kept his hand on; and as he drew near and halted, I heard a series of plaintive squeaks coming from it. 'Make you perform the guinea pig?' he always asked, and, before I could answer, he dragged a remonstrating guinea pig from its warm berth within, and stretched it out on the cage, holding it down with both hands. 'Johnny die queek!' he commanded, and lifted his hands for the instant in which Johnny was motionlessly gathering his forces for resuscitation. Then he called 'Bobby's coming!' and before the policeman was upon him, Johnny was hustled back into his warm box, woefully murmuring to its comfort of his hardship, and the queer little man smiled his triumph in every direction. The sight of the brief drama always cost me a penny; perhaps I could have had it for less; but I did not think a penny was too much.

Jack could also be seen, wearing his trademark bright red waistcoat and seaman's cap, selling oranges at four a penny and the *Bath Journal* in Manvers Street. He came from Genoa and his real name was Dominic Como. He lived with the Pierano's at 84 Avon Street; when the house was pulled down he moved to 6 St John's Place where he lodged with a Mrs Wall. On one occasion he was seriously ill and gave all his worldly goods to the Catholic Church, only to make a miraculous recovery and demand them all back. He finally succumbed to an attack of bronchitis in 1907 and died at the age of 76, which, strictly speaking, puts him outside the scope of this book – although memories of Bath's most famous street person would undoubtedly have lingered on.

Musicians – to the delight of some and the despair of others – made their own contribution to the street life of Edwardian Bath. The most sophisticated were the members of the Rhine String Band – always neatly turned out and with music stands which they set up when they stopped to perform. They played throughout the season in Bath for many years – decamping to resorts like Rhyl during the summer – but their appearances came to an abrupt end, like much else, in 1914, when, on the outbreak of war, many of the performers were interned as enemy aliens.

There were hundreds – possibly thousands – of German bands in England a century ago. Many, like Bath's German Band (which, unlike the Rhine String Band, was restricted to performing in the suburbs) were something of a joke. Its line-up was variable and it was known to all and sundry as the Huffum-Puffum Band, which tells you everything you need to know. It consisted of half a dozen or so solemn, bearded, bespectacled Germans, one playing an 'oom-pah-pah' on the bassoon, accompanied by cornets and flutes – and a cavalier disregard for what is normally understood by the term 'melody'. They were, like all German bands, widely believed to be spying on behalf of the Kaiser – why else would such an unmusical group persevere in the face of overwhelming odds? – and those that didn't make it back to Germany before the outbreak of war were, like the members of the Rhine String Band, interned.

Also consigned to the suburbs were the one-man-bands. These – because of their spectacle, showmanship and noise – were especially popular with children. A drum on the performer's back was played by drumsticks strapped to his elbows. Cymbals on the top were operated by a boot strap, while the other boot was connected to a triangle. With bells on his hat, pan-pipes fastened under his lips and a cornet in one hand, he still had another hand free for a tin whistle, flute or even, on occasion, bagpipes. A Mr Grant from Frome was one of the most celebrated one-man-banders around Bath in the early twentieth century.

An Italian lady called Tina Tinkalina and her daughter operated a piano-organ or hurdy-gurdy made by Pasquali. These were heavy instruments and, while others used donkeys or ponies to pull them, they hauled them around Bath by leather straps over their shoulders. The daughter performed cartwheels as they went from door to door asking for money. Some hurdy-gurdy men performed balancing acts, running with cartwheels or large stone jars balanced on their heads as the music played. Often, hurdy-gurdies had dancing dolls on top, which revolved in a simple waltz-like dance no matter what tune was being played. Hurdy-gurdies were also hired out for a few shillings to bazaars and garden parties, but not with the players. They popularized the tunes of the day; getting a song on the organs was equivalent to getting one on a radio playlist today.

The Melodia or barrel-organ was a small pipe organ, with a handle turned to pump air and revolve a spiked cylinder which played tunes. Most organ-grinders had a small monkey, dressed in a red coat and fez, which held out a bag or cup to passers-by. An organ-grinder and monkey from Milk Street used to entertain people queuing outside the Palace Theatre.

There were many other solo performers and singers roaming the streets. The favourite instruments were euphoniums, trombones, cornets, violins, tin whistles, flutes, mouth organs and concertinas. Many were dismal, others were as good as many of the buskers in Bath today. Marie Hall, for example, who later became a famous violinist, played in Brock Street for a while around 1900.

A rather different kind of performer was an Italian woman in 'contadina' costume, with raven tresses and flashing smiles, who told fortunes in the High Street opposite the Guildhall. She had a large cage of love birds which she wheeled around and, when you gave her a penny, she would put a stick into the cage and tell one of the birds to hop onto it. She would then take it out of the cage and set it in front of two trays of cards – one for ladies, the other for gentlemen. It took one of the cards from the appropriate pile and presented it to the customer before being returned to the cage. On the card was printed your fortune – and it was always good.

One performance artist whom everyone knew – and most tried to avoid – was Badger Pope. Cyril Beazer, in his autobiography, described him as a rowdy, ginger-haired man who drank too much and exhibited his physical prowess on Saturday nights on Broad Quay. He ran knitting needles through his biceps, or held a glass containing burning paper against his bare chest so that the vacuum held it fast. Another of his tricks was holding a concrete slab against his chest and getting people to hit it with a sledgehammer. These sorts of stunts earned him free drinks from the crowds that gathered, although his drinking bouts often ended with him being arrested and sent down for seven days to cool off. He was said to have saved many people from drowning in the Avon – including some he pushed in himself. After conscription was introduced in the First World War, he was approached one night by two military policeman who asked him why he wasn't in uniform, to which he responded by picking them up and chucking them into the river. On another occasion, he was presented with £5 for bravery when the river was flooded and cattle were being swept downstream; he dived from the Old Bridge and secured ropes round their horns so that they could be hauled ashore at the Midland Bridge. He was also famous for biting the heads off rats; when Widcombe Lock was emptied for maintenance and full of thick mud, Badger grovelled in it to catch eels weighing up to two pounds each, which he killed by biting their heads off as well.

There was also a female flame-thrower who performed feats with red-hot pokers and finished her act by taking a young rat and, with a cry of 'hello my pretty, give me a kiss', biting off its head. Other memories include a West Indian who performed in Kingsmead Square, snapping thick copper wire on his arm muscles and performing vanishing tricks with wooden sticks. An escapologist could regularly be seen in the Sawclose, extricating himself from chains, while Little Tom Thumb, only three feet tall, drove round town in a brougham drawn by two tiny ponies. There was much, much more – Punch and Judy shows, one-man Merry-Go-Rounds, acrobats, tumblers, strong men, ventriloquists, banjo-playing stilt-walkers ... the streets of Edwardian Bath were, as long as you weren't too squeamish or timid – and didn't take things too seriously – a magical place.

Unfortunately, some people did take things very seriously indeed – unfortunately because they were the ones whose opinion mattered most. We met some of them earlier, complaining about the noise and the dirt and telling Bath to 'Wake Up'. They were busy, in 1909, trying to improve Bath's image and clean the place up. Street performers, beggars, costers and anyone living by their wits was well and truly in their sights, but what they seem to have been most exercised about in the summer of 1909 were the paraders.

Parading – the Anglo-Saxon equivalent of the passeggiata – has largely died out in this country, but a century ago it was still very much alive. In eighteenth-century Bath, well-to-visitors had spent a good deal of their time parading up and down, seeing and being seen, exchanging idle gossip, making assignations and sorting out who they would dance with at that evening's ball. North and South Parades were designed for precisely this purpose, hence their names. By 1909, well-to-do visitors tended to stroll round the park or sit and look at the view rather than indulge in anything so frivolous as parading, but the tradition was kept alive by the working classes – and not just in Bath. Hannah Mitchell, who was brought up in the industrial north, describes the etiquette of parading, Edwardian style:

> The procedure was to parade the principal streets on Saturday and Sunday evenings, each sex in groups or couples until some adventurous male would make the first advance with some fatuous remark such as 'Can I see you home, miss?' If the girls responded this constituted a sort of introduction. The same groups would meet for several weeks and chat together before ultimately pairing off. Sometimes it all ended with nothing definite, and the groups began to parade again. But in some cases couples who met in this way became engaged and later were happily married. It was most innocent and pleasant and in a sense was the working girls' equivalent of the London season.

Alas, not everyone was so convinced of its innocence. Under the heading, 'Bath Streets on Sunday Evenings: An Evil and its Remedy', the following letter, signed 'A Visitor', appeared in the *Bath Chronicle* on 13 May 1909:

> During the last four weeks I have noticed with interest the attention that has been drawn to the crowded state of Southgate Street and Stall Street on Sunday evenings, and the numerous suggestions for remedying the evil that have come from ministers and public men ... As one who has noted a similar state of affairs in other towns, and followed the efforts, successful and otherwise, of corporate bodies to deal with the evil, I should like to offer a few suggestions as to steps that might be taken in mitigation of the trouble. First of all, however, it might be as well to adopt a logical course by diagnosing the complaint, and thus administering the prescription.
>
> Man is a gregarious animal, Addison has somewhere remarked, and that, I take it, is at the bottom of the whole affair. Is it inconceivable that young people, domestic servants, factory hands, or any of that vast army who are employed indoors during the whole week, and possibly a part of Sunday, should desire to promenade in the open air, exchange greetings and make friendships during that time which is probably the most pleasant of the whole week? At any rate, such is the custom of our young working folk in every town, large or small, that I have visited. It

has always been so, and will continue so until our Corporations take the necessary steps to secure its prevention. 'Street crawling', if I may so term it, becomes a habit as smoking and will cling to the infected one until some stronger habit eradicates it. Though a practice apparently harmless in itself – so long as the peace of the community is not disturbed – it is nevertheless to be deplored, for it leads nowhere, and the effect on the individual is a general aimlessness of purpose and deterioration of character more far-reaching in its results than may be imagined at first sight.

How has the problem been met in other towns? In one town that I know of, the inhabitants were faced with a difficulty similar to that in Bath. The main thoroughfare became almost impassable on Sunday evenings owing to the large crowds that promenaded there, especially during the winter months. A prominent minister took the matter in hand, and a large place of worship was placed at his disposal. It had previously been suggested that the theatre should be utilised, but this was found impracticable. It was arranged to hold after the evening service a popular service such as would appeal to all denominations, bright music being the dominant feature. Local vocalists came forward, the building was crowded every night, and at the concluding service of the winter 400 people were turned away.

Of course, it will be objected that indoor services are of no use for summer evenings, but all the same the idea may be useful in future, and it goes to prove my first point, ie that it is only necessary to offer a counter attraction to draw people from the streets.

I am quite convinced that the class of people that patrols Southgate Street and Stall Stret would not enter a building on a summer evening, however attractive the fare provided might be. What then is the remedy? Undoubtedly, to my mind, it is an open space for promenading and music.

And now to clear away some of the difficulties and apprehensions that have been raised, and to frankly criticise part of what has already been said and done. In the first place it is useless to approach the Watch Committee on the state of the two streets before mentioned. I personally visited those streets last evening and saw nothing in the nature of disorderliness or anything that could be construed into a breach of the law or public discipline. The Watch Committee have, apparently, done all that lays within their power, and accomplished it effectively. The street is well lighted and perfectly policed. Of all the objections raised to public music I have not found one that will hold water. The main one seems to be that people will be drawn from the ordinary church services. That difficulty can be easily met by arranging your musical programme after church hours. A contention that music, or a musical service, is not an act of worship, or is 'dishonouring God', as it has been put, cannot be regarded seriously. The problem at issue is not so much a religious one as a question of public order, and the solution I am trying to evolve is the one best calculated to attract these young people from the streets, and place them in an environment more healthy both from a physical and moral standpoint. It is absolutely useless to attempt anything in the nature of a crusade, for your proletariat as well as your patrician resents bitterly anything that seems to him to interfere with his sacred rights of citizenship, and will go to any length and take a pride in circumventing opposition. It is useless also to propose distractions, either in the way of open-air services or concerts, simultaneously at different parts of the city. The effort would be unfruitful and disappointing, because it does not attack the root of the evil which is, I take it, the innocent and natural desire to congregate at some fixed spot. Up to the present, I believe, no other suggestion worthy of consideration has been made. There are, of course, many details that will have to be considered and arranged, such as the venue and the form the music should take. I do not for a moment suppose that it would be possible to utilise the Recreation Ground, as has been mooted, for any large gathering would at once inflict considerable injury upon delicate turf.

To my mind a grand opportunity is offered by the churches, who by concerted action could strike a magnificent blow for Christianity and public service. Will they let it slip? The vicar of St James's Church, from whose vestry the complaint has to some extent come, holds very broad-minded, sensible views upon the subject, and a similar attitude has been displayed by many of the local clergy. The Mayor and a number of councillors too, are earnest in their endeavours that something should be done in the way of sacred open-air concerts but the matter must be followed up or it will fizzle out ... If the churches do not seize this occasion to not only demonstrate their usefulness, but to perform an act of public service, it will devolve upon the municipal body to take action. It will come to this sooner or later, and the earlier the better for Bath and its citizens.

The Bath Songsters Brigade of the Salvation Army – the sort of morally uplifting open-air entertainment approved of by those who wanted to clean up the streets.

As agitation for something to be done about the Sunday promenaders intensified, Councillor Thomas Plowman argued for a little moderation:

> In common with my brother magistrates and councillors, I was recently asked by Mr Lavington to state my views with respect to Southgate Street on Sunday evenings, and I have written to him accordingly. The excellent and well-thought-out article upon the same subject in your issue of Monday has induced me, although I am not entirely in agreement with the views expressed therein, to place at your disposal ... such observations in relation to the matter as have occurred to me ...
>
> In most good-sized cities and towns large numbers of persons, of the class to be found in Southgate Street, are in the habit of congregating in some public thoroughfare on Sunday evenings. This is accounted for by the fact that the leisure enjoyed by many on that particular evening of the week affords an opportunity for the gratification of those gregarious and social instincts common to most human beings, and we must not be too hard upon them for this. It is quite true that you will not find in Southgate Street the staid decorum and the dignified deportment of the Sunday paraders in Hyde Park, but we have no right to expect it, and, moreover, it would be an unnatural and artificial condition of things if it existed, in view of the very different circumstances in which many unfashionables live. Their life is too often a fight

for existence in a rough-and-tumble world, and this does not conduce to the cultivation of a calm exterior at all times or of a rigid suppression of any emotional displays. We must take the world as we find it and make the best of it, with a due regard to the varying conditions under which different sections of the community exist.

I do not think that, as has been suggested, you are going to help matters by providing open-air concerts with or without religious services sandwiched in between the pieces. That would simply mean taking the promenaders out of the street – supposing that they were willing to go, which I very much doubt – into a park or field, where, as they would necessarily be less under surveillance, whatever evils exist at present would be intensified. Nor do I think you are going to regenerate the promenaders by multiplying street preachers …We must have patience. I verily believe that the world is moving on in a right direction and towards a higher appreciation of the moral and social virtues. You cannot, however, hurry the pace too much, for poor human nature is not to be hustled all in a minute into that idyllic condition of mind which conforms to the highest standards … I would say – keep the street properly policed and well-lighted – as it seems to be at present – and then let it alone for a bit as a subject for writing and talking about, for these constant references to it only advertise its attractions and form an additional inducement for folk to congregate there.

His plea was to no avail. The Mayor called a public meeting, which was organised by HC Lavington – not a temperance campaigner, as might be supposed, but the licensee of the County Wine Vaults in Westgate Street (now Flan O'Briens). The Rev Titley, Vicar of St James's said that the crowds around his church were 'a disgrace to the city', even though he sympathised with people 'who had no place but the streets in which to meet their friends'. The first united evangelical service was held on Broad Quay on Whit Sunday 1909; the *Chronicle* reported that it was 'thronged with people', and that the streets were 'almost clear' while it was on.

A few weeks later, meetings were held in the city in support of the Sunday Closing Bill that was going through parliament. At a meeting in Lower Weston, Herbert Chivers argued that the 'Sunday closing of public houses is right in principle and successful in operation' and that the condition of Southgate Street on Sunday evenings was largely due to the pubs being open.

It is a risky business, making value judgements regarding things that happened a century or so ago. So much has changed that we may as well be looking at a foreign country, whose culture, beliefs, expectations and morality are profoundly different from ours. A foreign country, though, which condemned the majority of its citizens to arduous, poorly-paid labour, allowed them only a few hours leisure a week, and then tried to stop them passing that leisure time in a lawful manner of their own choosing, would not, I suggest, be one we would rate too highly.

Elephants are led along Darlington Street in Bathwick.

CHAPTER NINETEEN

ANIMAL MAGIC

When asked to recall her childhood in Edwardian Bath, one of Rose Maslin's vividest memories was playing in Pulteney Road – then a quiet, tree-lined backwater. If a train stopped on the bridge waiting to get into Bath station, the children would call out to the engine driver to throw them pennies, and when he did they would all scramble for them. One of her biggest thrills, though, was to see the animals being brought up out of the field to be fed and watered when the circus came to town.

It was the third week of February 1909 when Bostock & Wombwell's Royal No 1 Menagerie came to Bath Cricket Ground, bringing with it 'a colossal amalgamation of strange and curious animals from the uttermost parts of the universe'. These included:

A lion and a leopard cub living together;
A litter of young porcupines;
Young pumas (the first ever seen in Bath);
Mr George Ferebee, proprietor of the New Inn, Southgate Street,
will enter a den of lions for a wager – and receive a handsome gold
medal;
Lions, tigers, leopards, bears, hyenas, wolves, jaguars,
A wagonload of monkeys;
Aviaries of foreign birds;
A white kangaroo carrying its young;
Tasmanian devils;
The smallest horse alive;
Wild boars from Windsor Great Park presented to Mr EH Bostock by
HM the King as a mark of esteem;
Herds of elephants, camels and dromedaries for children to ride.

Everything went off splendidly, although when the circus moved on to Newport, some of the animals turned poorly. The *Bath Chronicle* reported that Lily, a 15-year-old elephant, needed six pails of old ale and four bottles of hot gin and water to bring her round, while a gorilla with a temperature was 'embedded in straw' and given coffee laced with rum and hot whisky with lemon. It may not have been up to the standard of *All Creatures Great and Small* but it seemed to have done the trick.

When Boswell's Circus came to town in November 1909, it set up not on the Cricket Ground but in the Assembly Rooms:

The circus ring has been installed in the largest of the suite of rooms – the ballroom – but before the performance commenced the popular parts were filled and a good many at the back of the room were compelled to stand ... The animal performers include 16 ponies, a donkey, several dogs and a monkey. 'Extra turns' are plentiful. Undoubtedly, the reception of the evening was accorded to Little Togo, 'the Wonderful Little Jap'. His performance commenced with a capable demonstration of that pastime so popular two years ago – Diabolo. This was followed by a top-spinning performance, and then came the most sensational feat of the evening. A rope was stretched at an angle of about 45 degrees from the ring to a point in the roof in about the centre of the ballroom. Little Togo then proceeded to climb this rope in a practically erect posture, relying for his grip on his prehensile toes alone, and carrying a large Japanese umbrella the while. On reaching the top, he slid down the rope backwards, still in a standing position, and thus regained the

The ballroom in the Assembly Rooms – venue for Boswell's Circus.

stage. Of course, during the performance of this sensational feat, Little Togo is walking literally over the heads of the audience, and as a precautionary measure a belt is attached to his waist, from which depends a loop of cord which encircles the rope. This ensures that in the event of a mishap, Little Togo would not use the audience as an emergency mattress. This turn was deservedly popular, quite the most appreciated during the evening, in fact, and it seemed as if the audience would never have done cheering the performer. As an encore, Little Togo climbed the rope again, but this time blindfolded and with his head in a sack. Thus garbed, he looked like a mixture of a diver and a victim of a Spanish auto-da-fe. Again he accomplished his feat successfully, and again was the recipient of hearty applause. The Luigi Brothers perform some remarkable springboard leaping over a number of ponies. The number of animals is gradually increased from one to twelve, so that at last the acrobats had to spring across practically the width of the ring. One of the pair concluded this turn by turning a forward somersault over the whole dozen gee-gees. This feat is claimed to be without parallel in the acrobatic world. There are 19 turns in all, and these include a smart conjuring turn by 'Coma' and a ventriloquial display by Professor Andrews.

Other acts included: a performing pony ridden by a dog; a clown called Comical Walter wrestling with the ponies; another clown having supper with two ponies while a monkey acted as waiter; and a donkey executing 'some very amusing rough and tumble business'.

How different, how very different from the genteel entertainments in the Assembly Rooms today! But, before we start to descant on the superior state of culture in the city today, it is worth reflecting that a century ago they at least refrained from staging wrestling bouts in the city library. And the Assembly Rooms certainly did see more elevated entertainment: Clara Butt sang there a week before the circus came to town, for example, and a few weeks later Sir Ernest Shackleton gave a talk on polar exploration.

For wrestling – which generally formed part of strong-man acts – and boxing you had to go down to Broad Quay, where there were regular fairs. Boxing booths were generally run by the Gratton family, who were, according to Victor Rosenburg, 'some tough exponents of the noble art'. Particularly tasty was 'One Round Gratton', so called because nobody lasted more than a round with him, who was billed as 'a legend from Poole to Penzance'. A Tom Gratton, who described himself as a travelling showman, was living at 108 Locksbrook Road in 1909, but whether he was 'One Round' or not I have been unable to establish.

Animals played a much bigger role in fairs and circuses a century ago than they do today. Often, the treatment meted out to them was, by today's standards, cruel. Nevertheless, the Edwardian era did see an increasing awareness of animal welfare. In January 1909, the Bath Cats' Home & Shelter for Lost & Starving Cats moved to larger and more convenient premises at 4 Thomas Street, 'where stray cats will be welcomed at any time'. In April, the local branch of the RSPCA announced that it had obtained 26 convictions for cruelty to animals in the previous twelve months. Some of those prosecuted were guilty of little more than ignorance of changes to the law: in June 1909, Fred Wilkey, a shoemaker from 30 Charlton Buildings in Twerton was summoned for having two thrushes in a cage outside his house. He told the court they had been given to him and he did not know the Wild Birds Protection Act made it illegal. He was dismissed with a caution. Some, however, were straightforward cases of cruelty. In March 1909, for example, William Philpott of 31 Milk Street was summoned for ill-treating a sheep by beating it on the head while going up Lyncombe Hill, as well as taking it by the tail and throwing it several times against a wall. When apprehended, he said, 'I'm going to get it up the hill somehow'; he got one month in prison instead.

On the other hand, performing bears were still a common sight, as their owners wandered the length and breadth of the country, stopping in towns and villages for a show or two. The men who wandered the country with these bears were almost always foreigners. One troupe which regularly turned up in Bath with their Russian master – who addressed them in his native tongue – were known as the Three Bears. They lodged in Avon Street and would pace the streets tied to a chain attached to a long pole. As well as performing a shambling dance, they would catch the pole when it was thrown to them. Although there are no known incidents of the bears turning violent whilst in Bath, this was apparently an occupational hazard: they were notorious for being among the most dangerous animals in captivity. As far as cruelty went, they were always trained abroad, out of the jurisdiction of the English courts. Despite their less than scintillating performances, and the safety and welfare issues, however, children adored the bears and

Above, unloading performing bears from carts.

Right, a chained bear stands with the aid of a pole while his master carries the tambourine played to make it dance.

news that the Russian had turned up in Bath again was sure to bring them flocking to Avon Street.

Bath also had a private zoo. Known as the Little Zoo, it was at De Montalt Cottage on Lyncombe Hill. Unlike conventional zoos, its main aim was selling birds and kangaroos that had been captured in Australia to collectors in this country. It was set up by Messrs Payne and Wallace, both of whom had spent many years working in remote cattle stations in Australia before turning their hand to animal trapping and trading. They established their headquarters at Wyndham in the Kimberley region of Western Australia. From here they set out with bands of aborigines, striking camp at watering holes, where they set up traps and waited for kangaroos to turn up. Once inside the traps, the hunters would rush in, grab them by their tails and bundle them into sacks. Dogs were also used to hunt kangaroos; once they had cornered them, they would hold them at bay until the hunters arrived. Only the more unusual species were captured, with younger animals generally preferred over older kangaroos, which were more difficult to tame. If a female was trapped with a 'joey' in her pouch, the baby was taken and the mother released. The zoo in Bath was surrounded by stone walls, too high for the kangaroos to jump over, although at least one did manage to escape. A keeper pursued it through the streets on his bicycle before managing to recapture it.

An account of a visit to the zoo appeared in *Bird Notes: The Journal of the Foreign Bird Club* in 1909:

> Being an ardent aviculturist, the prospects of a visit to Messrs Payne and Wallace at the Little Zoo, Bath ... was eagerly looked forward to. These gentlemen (the Bushmen, as they term themselves) make a speciality of importing Australian birds and animals, and they make it a boast that all their stock are caught by themselves, and not bought second-hand from natives or sailors. In addition to this, I have had many dealings with this firm and can honestly say that better or fairer treatment could not be desired. Should it be possible, I would strongly advise intending purchasers of Australian birds or animals to visit the Little Zoo at Bath. One great drawback to this is that very often one is tempted to speculate more than was originally intended, by being influenced by seeing so many beautiful birds.
>
> The first thing that attracts attention upon entering their grounds is the outdoor aviary in which are kept Parakeets,

Doves and Pigeons. This is highly suggestive of the aviary of a private fancier, and is divided into two portions ... Alongside this were a few cages apparently just as they had

Kangaroos at Payne & Wallace's Little Zoo on Lyncombe Hill. The middle picture shows the kangaroo that escaped being returned to captivity.

left the ship, containing several small kangaroos. A few steps away was the admirable structure built expressly for the finches and the more valuable specimens. Entering here the aviculturist is simply amazed – a feast for the eyes worthy of the trouble and expense incurred in travelling a long distance to see them. Leaving aside many comments which ought to be made upon the admirable manner in which these birds are kept, which is far in advance of anything the writer has ever seen upon dealers' premises, one is immediately drawn to a cage containing a most perfect specimen of the Pileated or Red-capped Parakeet (Platycercus spurius) a bird of uncommon beauty. Extremely rare, Mr. Payne informed me, that excepting a pair they brought over with their last year's consignment, which were the first to be brought over to this country, these are, as far as his knowledge goes, the only specimens in Europe. Is it needless to add that there is only one thing that prevented the writer from bringing this bird and its mate back home with him – price.

Very comfortably housed ... were kangaroos of different varieties, apparently very happy in their environment. Leaving here we were conducted to what appeared to us an exaggerated poultry run, containing some very fine Spotted Emus. All seemed exceedingly tame and very fit. Lying in the grounds were the packing cases which had brought these large birds over, and Mr Payne pointed out to us how the cases had been enlarged as the birds grew during the journey. He informed us that when they left the depot at Wild Dog Creek, NW Australia, they were only the size of ordinary fowls, but as we saw them they stood upwards of five feet high. We could see for ourselves how the cases had been added to in the manner described.

It was indeed a pleasure to chat with Mr Payne on the wild habits of all these species, and the methods adopted for catching and transporting them, and we must confess ourselves greatly indebted to him for the courtesy and trouble taken to make our visit pleasant and interesting. Apart from this one must admit that words fail to adequately describe the generally superb condition of the birds and animals, after such a trying journey of forty days. The consignment, by the way, came via the Cape and reached here on Good Friday, and we saw them on the following Wednesday. After wishing Mr Payne good-day, we hurried down Lyncombe Hill to catch our train after one of the most enjoyable and instructive afternoon holidays I have ever spent.

All of which makes Mr Wilkey's two thrushes in a cage pale into insignificance. As an aside – seeing that we've got onto the topic of birds – it might also be worth mentioning that one of the most significant differences between Bath in 1909 and Bath in 2009 is the number of seagulls. A century ago they were about as rare as emus. There were plenty of them 20 miles or so away, of course, along the Bristol Channel coast, but in Bath not a one. So rare were they, in fact, that when, during the bitterly cold winter of 1917-18, a few turned up in Twerton scavenging for food, the *Chronicle* treated their arrival as a major news story. They are still in the news today, albeit for somewhat different reasons. There are now so many, in fact, that, just as this book was going to press, Don Foster, Bath's MP, called for an adjournment debate on controlling the menace of urban seagulls in the House of Commons.

CHAPTER TWENTY

THAT'S ENTERTAINMENT

The Edwardian era was the first in which recorded performances reached a mass audience. Music could be recorded onto wax cylinders or records; drama – or any other human activity – could be recorded on film. As yet, the two couldn't be synchronised, but it was pretty earth-shattering all the same. Throughout history, if you weren't there, you couldn't see or hear what happened. Every performance, every action, was quite literally unrepeatable. Now every great performance, every momentous event could be captured and played back time and again – for ever.

Admittedly, the quality of much of what was produced was fairly ropey – even allowing for the fact that singers couldn't be seen and actors couldn't be heard. Equipment was primitive, and, while suitable for a fairground sideshow or an accompaniment to an al fresco picnic, what was produced was a pale reflection of the real thing. The films of Mitchell & Kenyon, in which crowd scenes captured on the streets of a town or city were played back to the people who featured in them later the same day were part of the vaudevillean nature of Edwardian entertainment. With anything more ambitious, you soon ran into trouble. Deprived of speech, early filmmakers adapted and amplified the impassioned gestures of stage melodrama, creating, in the words of one critic, 'an extravagance of grimace and gesture that had hitherto been foreign to the British character'.

JB Priestley, who grew up in Edwardian Bradford, had little time for early films, which were generally shown to round off variety shows:

> The final act in most of these variety shows when all the glory of the programme had vanished, was a few minutes of jerky film, generally called Bioscope. But we rarely stayed to discover

what the Bioscope was offering us. Now that we have so many accounts of the early history of films, we know that men in various places were taking them very seriously indeed. But that was true of very few people. My friends and I waved them away. Apart from halls where films were occasionally shown, I seem to remember – as my first genuine cinema – a certain Theatre de Luxe, where for sixpence you were given an hour or so of short films, a cup of tea and a biscuit. I tried once, and once was enough. Not until the First World War, when I was in the army, did I begin to look for films ... in search of the early Chaplin shorts that were arriving then. Before that, in the Edwardian years, like most other people I spent very little time looking at films, which were just so much prolonged Bioscope.

Films were very popular with children, however, and special screenings were put on for them. This led to one of the saddest tragedies of the Edwardian age. In 1908, a show was put on for 400 children in Barnsley Civic Hall. In the rush for admission, 16 children – some as young as four – were killed in a crush on the stairs. Legislation was passed the following year requiring local authorities to inspect premises and issue safety certificates before venues were used for screening films. The 1909 Cinematograph Act – which was not just concerned with the issue of safety – was the first legislation regulating the film industry in Britain, and paved the way for the establishment of the British Board of Film Censors in 1912.

It is surprising that it took so long for the government to wake up to the potential danger of films. This wasn't a question of moral danger: early film was highly flammable. When combined with the limelight illumination used in variety theatres, it was potentially lethal, and did result in a number of fatal fires. Films were also shown in fairground booths and converted shops called 'penny gaffs'. The 1909 Act did away with most of these at a stroke and paved the way for the purpose-built cinemas that soon started appearing in ever-increasing numbers. As late as 1906, when films had been around for a decade, there was still only one cinema in the whole of London; by 1914 there were 308. In Bath, the Picturedrome in Southgate Street opened in June 1911, the Vaudeville Electric Theatre in Westgate Street six months later.

The extent of the 1909 regulations can be gauged from the modifications needed at the Palace Theatre on the Sawclose. An 'additional box of sheet iron' had to be installed round the 'cinematograph box' and the cavity filled with asbestos; in addition, extra fire hoses and stand pipes had to be provided. A new box also had to be built round the projection booth at the Assembly Rooms before it was granted a licence to carry on showing films.

Above: The Assembly Rooms, one of the first places to show films in Bath.
Below: Among the principal outlets for early films were the bioscopes that toured with travelling fairs. Arnold's Electric Bioscope & Theatre of Varieties was one of the grandest in southern England.

The cricket ground was the most popular venue for travelling fairs and circuses. This was the fair held during Carnival Week in 1911.

In pre-cinema days, when live performances were all there were, performers had Sunday off. They were happy and, perhaps more importantly, the Sunday-observance lobby were happy. With cinema, all that changed. Instead of performers, all you needed was someone to crank the projector, someone to take the money and someone to bash away on a piano. As soon as Sunday performances started, the Lord's Day Observance Society organised protest meetings. After staging a protest meeting in November 1909, they sent a deputation to the council 'objecting to the Sunday evening living picture exhibition performances at the Palace Theatre' which were 'very crowded with young people'. Although they didn't suggest that anything improper went on,[1] they felt it wasn't good that they should spend their Sunday evenings 'witnessing that kind of entertainment'. After due deliberation, in January 1910 the magistrates renewed the licence 'for cinematographic exhibitions at Palace on Sundays', explaining that the only grounds they were able to take into account were those of public safety. Not that that satisfied the protestors. Their campaign continued.

Before leaving the subject of early cinema, it is worth quoting another contemporary who wasn't too struck by it – not because he was bored with it, like JB Priestley, nor because it was an affront to his religious and moral sensibilities, but because he foresaw where it would lead. In 1913, the French critic Louis Haugmard, said of

---

1 They obviously hadn't heard about the back row of the stalls.

the cinema that 'Through it the charmed masses will learn not to think any more, to resist all desire to reason and to construct, which will atrophy little by little; they will know only how to open their large and empty eyes, only to look, look, look ... And we shall progressively draw near to those menacing days when universal illusion in universal mummery will reign.'

Given that he couldn't have known about reality TV, soap operas and all the other appurtenances of modern 'family entertainment', to come up with such a prescient analysis of where we were headed as early as 1909 is pretty impressive.

In terms of musical entertainment, Bath seems to have been well provided for in 1909. On 25 September, the Pump Room Orchestra embarked on a 33-week season. Its conductor, Max Heymann had wanted to form a choir. To achieve an appropriate balance with the orchestra, he needed 45 singers, but the council only agreed to funding for 25, so the idea was dropped. Every Thursday during the season there was a concert featuring a different symphony, starting with Beethoven's first eight, then Brahms's four, and continuing with Tchaikowsky's six. Soloists – especially pianists – also appeared regularly in major concertos.

It was, by any standards, a punishing schedule, leaving one to wonder what the quality of the performances was like. Perhaps, one might assume, with recording in its infancy, and exposure to world-class performances less common than today, expectations were not so high. But, had performances been routinely

second-rate, there can be little doubt that those complainers who moaned about anything and everything – and especially about what went on in the Pump Room and Concert Hall – would have been quick to draw unflattering comparisons with concerts they had attended in London or wherever. The only conclusion we can draw is that standards were consistently high – after all, a similar municipal orchestra in Bournemouth was to grow into the

The Post Office Band was among those which played regularly in Bath.

internationally acclaimed Bournemouth Symphony Orchestra. And Max Heymann, although forgotten today, was a well-known and respected musician. The soloists were pretty good as well. In February 1902, for example, a 19-year-old Australian pianist called Percy Grainger came down to perform Tchaikowsky's 1st Piano Concerto. He also played in a chamber concert, with Max Heymann on violin.

Music was a staple feature of the Theatre Royal's repertoire as well. In the first four months of 1909, it staged three musical comedies – *The Girls of Gottenberg* by George Grossmith Jr and LE Berman, with additional lyrics by PG Wodehouse, *The Catch of the Season* by Seymour Hicks and Cosmo Hamilton, and *Butterflies* by William Locke, TH Read and JA Robertson – as well as *Tom Jones*, a comic opera by Edward German. It also staged two 'romantic comedies' – *Diana of Dobson's* by Cicely Hamilton and *Robin Hood* – a French farce called *Toddles*, an American farce called *Mrs Wiggs of the Cabbage Patch* (based on a novel by Alice Rice and later made into a film starring WC Fields), *The Silver King*, a celebrated melodrama from 1882 by Henry Arthur Jones and Arthur Herman 'with a villain to be hissed', *You Never Can Tell*, a comedy by George Bernard Shaw, and a local production called *Dingley Dell*.

Most of these productions – with the exception of the play by Shaw – seem to have been the sort of light, frothy, undemanding entertainment we tend to associate with the Edwardian era. But there is one other exception: *Diana of Dobson's* was, in Edwardian terms, a challenging – even shocking – piece of theatre. Its author, Cicely Hamilton, founded the Women Writers' Suffrage League in 1908, and her other plays from this period – *Women's Votes, Marriage as Trade, How the Vote was Won* and *A Pageant of Great Women* – leave us in no doubt as to where her sympathies lay. Diana, the heroine of the play, works in a department store called Dobson's. The dormitory scene, in which five shop girls undress and unfasten their stays while moaning about the drudgery of their 'five bob a week' life, shocked many critics. Diana is saved from this life by an unexpected £300 legacy. Instead of opting for a secure future, she sets off, after cheeking the boss to the cheers of her colleagues, to blow the lot on a sumptuous month's holiday. Booking into a grand alpine hotel, her fellow guests assume she is a rich widow in search of a husband – thus setting the scene for a glorious romp in which she brushes off two fortune-hunting suitors. Although never less than entertaining, the play also ruthlessly exposes the sexism and inequality at the heart of Edwardian society. When revived at Richmond's Orange Tree Theatre in 2007, it received rave reviews, one critic describing it as 'the best production in the Orange Tree's admirable season – sparklingly fresh and tremendous fun'.

Dingley Dell was a production by the Bath Amateurs, founded in 1894 to present an 'amateur week' at the theatre. Amateur weeks continued until 1902, but then there was a break, with only an occasional concert, until 1908, when a comic opera called *Bladud* was performed. The words were by Edwin Fagg and Samuel Poole, with a score by Lewis Thomas and Charles Wright, all of whom were Bathonians. The cast included Sidney Vaughan, FW Fry, Graham Simmons, Arthur Taylor, Bertram Fortt, Stanley Russ, Harold Fortt, Mrs FW Fry, Miss Nancy Evans and Hilda Blake. The dramatis personæ included Bladud, Pitchkin J Cluster (a Chicago millionaire who thinks Bath 'quaint' and wants to buy everything in sight) and his daughter Sadie, the Duke of Shamcastle ('a seedy nobleman'), Sir Hampton Rox, Beau Belvedere, Baroness Beechen de Cliffe and Gertie Greenpark. The play is a rollicking comedy with Gilbert-and-Sullivan-style songs and assorted intrigues, featuring, as its main dramatic twist, the coming-to-life of the statue of Bladud in the King's Bath when water is sprinkled on it and a light-hearted spell uttered. Bladud's first song after his reawakening will give an idea of the script:

When I was Prince I came to Bath,
In the year eight hundred BC
But found the head that wears a crown
Did truly lie uneasy,
A grievous ailment I acquired
For a Prince that 'infra dig' is,
So left the court and found myself
Custodian of piggies.

Chorus: *He left the court and found himself*
Custodian of piggies.

Thus bad begins, but worse remains,
One morning I detected
It wasn't I alone that ailed,
The pigs became infected,
'My lot is truly hard,' I said,
'My troubles are fair corkers,'
The cuticle complaint I'd caught
Broke out among the porkers.

Chorus: *The cuticle complaint he'd caught*
Broke out among the porkers.

I took my piggies for a walk,
We one day Bath arrived in,
We passed a warm and muddy pond,
The pigs they squealed and dived in,
I thought that I had seen the last
Of what was once a fine herd,
When out they came completely cured,
Which staggered me, their swineherd.

Chorus: *When out they came completely cured,*
Which staggered him, their swineherd.

I followed suit and was amazed,
At the turn that things had taken,
The wondrous water cured me quite,
Just as it cured the bacon.
Throughout the world the water's known,
Its reputation big is,
I think it's due, the credit's due
To Bladud and his piggies.

Chorus: *We think it's true, the credit's due*
To Bladud and his piggies.

Sadly, Fagg and Poole were not given the opportunity of writing any scripts for the following year's Pageant – not serious enough, my dear! – although they did have a hand in designing the costumes. Fagg did, however, write *Dingley Dell*, the Bath Amateurs' 1909 production, based on an episode from *The Pickwick Papers*. In the following year, the Bath Amateurs became the Bath Operatic Society, presenting Gilbert & Sullivan's *The Sorceror* and Oliver Goldsmith's *She Stoops to Conquer*. In 1939, the company became the Bath Operatic & Dramatic Society, under which name it continues today.

Above: Edwin Fagg and Samuel Poole's libretto for Bladud.
Below: The Bath Operatic Society's 1912 production of Veronique.

The revival of the company in 1908 and the staging of *Bladud* could have been among the factors that led to the idea of staging a Pageant. As we shall see, Bladud was originally intended to be the presiding deity of that entertainment as well. In the absence of any reference to the play by the Pageant organisers, however, the extent of that influence must remain speculative.

One other play from later in the Theatre Royal's season also deserves a mention, mainly because it bears out WC Fields' dictum about never working with children or animals. In a musical comedy called *The Dairymaids*, staged in August, two of the performers had to cross the stage in a donkey cart. On the first night, the donkey reached the middle of the stage and refused to go any further, despite being tempted by offers of sugar lumps. Eventually it had to be manhandled off 'to the huge delight of the audience'.

Music played a very important part in the Edwardian theatre, with over half of the works staged at the Theatre Royal billed as musical comedies, comic operas, operettas or such

like. The most popular show was Franz Lehar's *Merry Widow*, the surprise hit of 1907, which went on to inspire countless imitations and establish the Ruritanian style of musical comedy as a standard for years to come.

Elizabeth Firth and Robert Evett in the original West End production of The Merry Widow.

Tunes from the operetta were everywhere – as background music in restaurants, at garden parties, or churned out by organ-grinders in the street. It had two runs at Bath's Theatre Royal in 1908 – in January and December.

For lovers of popular music, 1909 was something of a vintage year. The Cockney school was particularly well represented, with 'Boiled Beef and Carrots' and 'Let's All Go Down the Strand' (Have a Banana)'; other classics that first appeared in 1909 included 'By the Light of the Silvery Moon', 'Has Anybody here Seen Kelly?' and 'I Do Like to be Beside the Seaside'. The marches of John Philip Sousa were also very popular; many could recall the sell-out concert he gave in the Assembly Rooms when he toured England with his band in 1901. The cakewalk had started to creep into dance-band repertoire, but rag-time –

PUBLIC FIXTURES.

PALACE THEATRE, BATH.

| Proprietor... | ... | ... | MR. FRANK MACNAGHTEN. |
| Manager ... | ... | ... | MR. CHAS. SCHUBERTH. |

| **7.** | **TWICE NIGHTLY.** | **9.** |

Seats may be Booked at C. Milsom & Son, Milsom St.
MONDAY NEXT, and during the Week,
FELDMAN'S BEAU-IDEAL, Talented Juveniles.
BERNARDO, Comedy Juggler.
RAYMOND'S BIO-TABLEAUX.
MDLLE. SIDY NIRVANAH, Presenting Artistic
Poses in Colours, introducing her STATUE HORSE.
NORAH DESMOND, American Song Illustrator.
JIM CHEETHAM,
King of Boy Whistlers and Bird Mimicry.
AVON & CREST, Speciality Comedy Artistes.
SABLE FERN, a Singer whose Words you can hear.

Attractions at the Palace Theatre on the Sawclose in January 1909.

although popular in America – had yet to hit England. That was to come in 1911, when the ersatz but phenomenally successful 'Alexander's Ragtime Band' would be the hit of the season.

As far as England was concerned, the greatest living composer was Sir Edward Elgar – a bluff, four-square, roast beef and plum pudding character, with a military moustache that caused him to be mistaken for the Duke of Connaught, Edward VII's brother. Just like Edwardian society, though, the façade hid something much more complex and troubled. Elgar was a profoundly sensitive, self-conscious man, his music full of cadences forever unresolved. He was the master not of the confident gesture, as many would have you believe, but of longing and never-to-be-consummated desire. Compare, for example, his marches with those of Sousa, whose exuberant delight in harmonic and melodic invention whirl the listener irresistibly along. It's difficult to listen to Sousa without smiling, but Elgar's first *Pomp and Circumstance March* (the one Arthur Benson fitted the words of 'Land of Hope and Glory' to) – not bawled out by an Albert Hall full of promenaders, but played as originally intended – is a profoundly melancholy piece. Elgar – to use a modern turn of phrase – didn't do cheerful, and when he tried to do confident he achieved only an empty, unconvincing swagger.

The *Pomp and Circumstance Marches* have been taken as a musical expression of everything that was wrong with the Edwardian age – brash, insensitive, vainglorious and militaristic. But the name Elgar bestowed on them should at least give us pause – 'pomp' is straightforward enough – but 'circumstance'? What no one seems to have spotted is that the phrase is charged with a meaning far removed from what the incautious listener, picking up on the word 'pomp', might assume. It actually comes from Shakespeare's *Othello* – from the turning point of the play, in fact, just after Iago has convinced Othello that Desdemona has been unfaithful to him. Othello's world has come crashing down around his ears, and he bids farewell not only to marital but also martial bliss:

> *I had been happy if the general camp,*
> *Pioners and all, had tasted her sweet body,*
> *So I had nothing known. O, now, for ever*
> *Farewell the tranquil mind! farewell content!*
> *Farewell the plumed troop and the big wars*
> *That make ambition virtue! O, farewell,*
> *Farewell the neighing steed and the shrill trump,*
> *The spirit-stirring drum, the ear-piercing fife,*
> *The royal banner, and all quality,*
> *Pride, pomp, and circumstance of glorious war!*
> *And, O you mortal engines, whose rude throats*
> *The immortal Jove's dread clamours counterfeit,*
> *Farewell! Othello's occupation's gone!*

It was an odd choice, summoning up – for those who knew their Shakespeare – loss, betrayal, fading glory, a world on the brink of collapse. All of which fits the Edwardian age perfectly – but not for the reasons generally assumed.

There was another reason why Elgar should have been especially attracted to Othello: he was the ultimate outsider – a Moor, tolerated because of his military prowess, but socially adrift in a society whose mores and politics Iago understood so well. Elgar too, despite all his bluster and military – even regal – bearing, was an outsider – born a Catholic in a nation that still distrusted them, his father a small-town tradesman, selling instruments and tuning pianos, in an age when birth and breeding were everything. Unable to afford any formal training, it took him years of unremitting struggle and penury before he was recognised. And, in an age of philistinism, when sport and indulgence were seen as the mark of a gentleman, he was an intensely sensitive soul, driven at one point to suicidal despair at the death of one of his closest male friends. JB Priestley, a teenager during the years of Elgar's greatest triumphs, had no illusion where the real heart of his music lay – 'the kind of passage, for ever recurring, when strings are quietened and the

Above: No middle-class home was complete without a piano; they could be found in many working-class homes as well.

Below: Edith Clarke of 10 Bloomfield Avenue was a 'teacher of pianoforte and harmony'. She drew this vignette on her business card and sent it to a Mr G Davey at Taunton on 19 September 1906 with the message: 'Many happy returns of the day. When shall we have our next recital?'

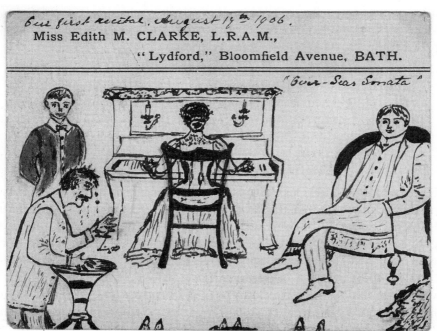

jagged thunder of his brass has gone, and, like a purple and sepia sunset suddenly revealing patches of purest cerulean or fading apple green, it is all different, strangely beautiful as music and catching at the heart because the man himself, no longer masterful, seems to be staring out at us out of a sorrowful bewilderment.'

In terms of literature, when we think of the Edwardian age today we think of EM Forster, Joseph Conrad, Henry James, and, perhaps, Rudyard Kipling, John Galsworthy, Arnold Bennet and HG Wells. At the time, though, the two most popular authors were Henry Seton Merriman, said to have invented the strong silent Englishman, and Marie Corelli, described by a critic in the *Spectator* as 'a woman of deplorable talent who imagined that she was a genius, and was accepted as a genius by a public to whose commonplace sentimentalities and prejudices she gave a glamorous setting'. She was also interested in astral projection, reincarnation and similar topics; her books on these subjects continue to inspire today's New Age devotees.

Bath, immortalised in earlier times by Smollett, Jane Austen and Dickens, also had its Edwardian chroniclers. Alice and Egerton Castle produced a series of very popular novels set in Bath; like Georgette Heyer, who turned to the city for inspiration a few years later, it was Georgian Bath they cast their gaze upon. Walter Macqueen-Pope, writing in the 1940s, when their novels had fallen from favour, recalled

> Alice and Egerton Castle's delightful and fragrant tales – with titles scented to match, of Bath in the days of Nash and eighteenth-century romance – pleased the middle classes. They could not have enough. *Mistress Kitty Bellairs* was much to their taste – and good judges too – and so was *Young April*, a very charming story which has been very lucky in escaping the doom of being filmed.

Unfortunately, their novels, although using the 'folly and noise of the great world of Bath' as a backdrop to tales of passionate liaisons, sword fights and villains, where the hero always gets the girl, convey very little of the spirit of the place. The most popular was *Sweet Kitty Bellairs*, set in Bath in 1793. Kitty, who declares that 'in spite of 30 or 40 affairs, I've not lost a bit of my honour' was rather like those raunchy ladies who provided the star turn in the saloons of the wild west. The novel was made into a film in 1916 and a musical, starring Claudia Dell and Walter Pidgeon, in

1930. Pictures of Claudia Dell in the title role actually show her looking as though she's walked off the set of a Western – which is what the film might as well have been – with highwaymen taking the place of 'Red Indians', the Master of Ceremonies taking the place of the sheriff and the Pump Room taking the place of the town saloon.

Above: The Victoria Art Gallery, designed by JM Brydon, nearing completion.
Below: Sollis's friterer's on the corner of Bridge Street and Newmarket Row, pulled down to make way for it.

As for the visual arts, the Victoria Art Gallery had recently opened and the Holburne of Menstrie Museum, a small private collection, was planning to move from Charlotte Street, where it occupied the old savings bank, to the disused Sydney Hotel in Great Pulteney Street. The museum was open daily from 11am to 4pm, with free admission on alternate days. The nucleus of the collection had been formed by Sir Thomas William Holburne, a bachelor friend of William Beckford, who lived just down the road from Beckford at 10 Cavendish Crescent. Although Holburne wasn't short of a penny or two, he was not in the same league as Beckford, and the choice of items for his collection was dictated by what he could afford.

In 1906, the curator of the Holburne of Menstrie Museum invited Horace Buttery, an experienced and well-respected conservator, restorer and dealer, who had worked for most of the country's major art galleries, to make an assessment of the paintings in the collection. His verdict was recorded bluntly in the minutes: 'Very Good – 11; Good – 23; Fair – 59; Bad – 155'. Buttery also seems to have disputed the attribution of many of the paintings, which were taken off public display; it is unclear how many have subsequently been reinstated.

Sydney Hotel, built in 1796-97, had seen many changes of fortune. In 1845, 'a set of baths on the hydropathic system' had been installed, but these lasted only a short time and the building reverted to a hotel. In 1856 it became Bath Proprietary College, commonly known as Sydney College. The proprietary interest was represented by 120 shares: one pupil could be nominated for each share. Lord William Powlett was the first president. Sydney College formed the basis upon which Bath College was founded in 1880, and the building was later sold. Somerset College, another proprietary college, based at 11 The Circus, was also merged into Bath College. In the eighties and early nineties, there were several schemes for dealing with the hotel and gardens, and several prominent citizens became interested in the property. The winding-up of the old proprietary interest was a very involved process, owing to the many people who had a right to a share in the proceeds.

Around 1892 a Bath hotel proprietor acquired the estate, but in 1893 it was offered for sale by auction at the Grand Pump Room Hotel. It was thought the city might acquire the property, but it did not, and there was no purchase in the room. Subsequently, however, it passed into the possession of Mr David Jones of Bristol, who attempted to float a new Sydney Hotel scheme. Plans for a magnificent new building were prepared, and a prospectus was issued in 1896. The project did not materialise, however, and shortly afterwards Mr Jones sold it to the Gordon Hotels Company Ltd for £6,700.

Above: Sydney Hotel as Bath Proprietary College.
Below: In the early 1900s, untenanted and untended, with its windows smashed and ivy growing up its walls.

Sydney Gardens continued to be used for flower shows and fetes, but the old Sydney Hotel slowly deteriorated, its lawns untended, its paintwork peeling and its windows broken. William Howells, who stayed in Bath in 1905, was very taken with its atmosphere of dereliction. A seeker after the Bath of Beau Nash and Jane Austen, he declared himself an opponent of any development in the city, lamenting the fact that 'there was indeed only too little ruin in it'. However, he was cheered by there being

> at least one gratifying instance in the stately mansion at the end of our street, falling or fallen to decay with its Italian style rapidly antedating the rough classic of the Roman baths, in the effect of a sorrowful superannuation, which I could not have rescued from dilapidation without serious loss. Whose the house was or why it was abandoned I never learned, and I do not know that I wished to learn; it was so satisfying as it was and for what it was.

Having failed to redevelop the site as a hotel, in 1908 Gordon Hotels approached the council to see if they were interested in buying it. They intimated they might be prepared to accept less than they had paid for it. They told the council that they had held negotiations with the Holburne of Menstrie Trustees, who wanted to acquire the college 'and sufficient land adjoining', but, as they did not want to sell just a portion of the property, the deal had fallen through. The council offered to pay £5,150 and sell the college and adjoining land to the trustees for £2,650.

At a council meeting in July 1909, it was agreed that the purchase should go ahead, with the proviso that 'the Education Committee may have a portion reserved for educational purposes'. When Councillor Charles Long asked if the site would be available for building, the Town Clerk replied that Captain Forester had 'said that they could build an educational establishment or some other public building that would not be detrimental to the property in the neighbourhood'. It was accepted that the grounds were in a poor condition, but that, if a gradual programme of repair was adopted, within three or four years it could be in first-class order. Part of the gardens could be used for a bowling green and part of it could be leased out.

There was some debate as to whether the Sydney Hotel should be demolished and replaced with a new building, but, given changing attitudes to eighteenth-century architecture, it was felt that reconstruction, keeping the original façade, would be a better option.

The artistic event of the year, however, was not the Holburne of Menstrie trustees' decision to move to Bathwick but an exhibition at the Assembly Rooms, which consisted of a single painting – *Despised and Rejected of Men* by Sigismund Goetze. Originally exhibited at the Royal Academy, it was, for a time, the most famous painting in Britain, and toured the country attracting large crowds. In Glasgow 98,000 people paid sixpence each to see it; 77,000 people saw it in Manchester; in Newcastle a religious fanatic punctured it with a walking stick. According to the *Bath Chronicle*, Goetze was 'an Englishman of deep spiritual conviction' who had

created 'a veritable sermon on canvas … drawing attention to the growing indifference of the world to the claims of Christ'. The painting shows Christ tied to a pagan altar in front of St Paul's Cathedral as a motley collection of worldly Londoners file heedlessly past. It is a strange, disturbing painting by any reckoning – the suffering Christ, the central image of Christianity, surrounded by modern-day representatives of the humanity he died for. The bustling crowd is not like those in William Powell Frith's famous social panoramas; Goetze's satire was not that of a confident man of the world, viewing his contemporaries with patrician disdain mingled with wry humour. His work looks forward to the bloated grotesques of George Grosz, with all humanity squeezed out, and only a ghastly, piglike carapace left. The success of his painting betrays not so much an unease with material values as a revulsion from them; not so much a wish to rediscover spiritual values as a desperation at their absence. The impact of this frightening painting tells us more about the concerns and preoccupations of society in 1909, and the erosion of old certainties, than mere words could hope to.

Fiedling's Lodge, Twerton.

CHAPTER TWENTY-ONE

LET US NOW PRAISE FAMOUS MEN

Many of Bath's historic buildings acquire much of their lustre from an association with famous people. Indeed, a appreciation of their literary and historical associations seems to have preceded an appreciation of their architectural merits. The plaques that adorn so many buildings in Bath were unveiled at lavish ceremonies by celebrities who often had similar professions to the people commemorated. Some of the buildings graced with plaques have since disappeared, although few with so little justification as one in Twerton.

Sir Henry Irving unveiling a plaque to the eighteenth-century actor James Quin in Pierrepont Street.

On a dull February afternoon in 1909, a small group, wrapped up against the bitter cold, gathered outside an house on the Lower Bristol Road to witness the chairman of the parish council unveil a plaque to one of England's greatest writers.

The house had long been known as Fielding's Lodge; it was one of Fielding's friends, the Rev Richard Graves, who, shortly after the novelist's death, identified it as the place where *Tom Jones* was written – 'the first house on the right hand with a spread eagle over the door'.

Actually, it wasn't a spread eagle, it was a phoenix, but others were happy to perpetuate the error, and, as the posthumous fame of their temporary resident grew, the people of Twerton accorded a special place to the old house on the edge of the village. It was Robert Naish, a local engraver and historian, inspired by the bicentenary of Fielding's birth in 1907, who designed the plaque unveiled that day.

Fielding was born near Glastonbury on 22 April 1707 and knew Bath from an early age. Although he never settled in the

Above: Unveiling the plaque to Henry Fielding. Those present are, from left to right: AW Andrews, C Butler, C Powell, W Gosling, T King, Mrs G Luton, W Luton, Mrs King, Robert Hope, RG Naish, WH Naish, RJ Sansome and CJ Hopper.
Below: The phoenix over the door.

city permanently, from his mid-twenties he spent part of each year – generally the late summer – in the city. On 28 November 1734, he was married in the church at Charlcombe by Walter Robbins, Master of King Edward's School. Fielding was a friend of Robbins, and, on at least one occasion, stayed with him at his house in Abbey Green.

Fielding's reasons for visiting Bath were, like those of most visitors, twofold – health and pleasure. He suffered from gout, for which 'the vivifying effect of the waters' had a 'good and immediate effect'. Bath he found a 'pleasant city', although 'full of nothing but noise, impertinence and confusion'. He regarded Beau Nash, whom he dubbed the Great Snash, as particularly tiresome. And, although he sometimes found convivial company, at other times he was not so lucky. On one occasion, he wrote sourly to a friend that there were 'few men of any consequence and fewer women of any beauty' in the city. For a comic novelist, however, Bath offered unparalleled opportunities for people watching.

It also provided him with an entrée to a man whom he came to idolise as a pattern of benevolence. Fielding seems to have been taken up by Ralph Allen in 1741. Thereafter, he and his sister Sarah – also a novelist – were regular guests at Prior Park. Fielding's sister also moved into a cottage in Widcombe, provided for her, according to local legend, by Ralph Allen.

In 1743 Fielding took a house in Twerton – or Twiverton as it was then known. His wife was recovering 'from a very dangerous illness in which she was given over' and the semi-rural location suited him better than the bustle of town. He wrote to a friend, asking him to 'fill a vacant room in my house at Twiverton', adding, in a postscript, 'my small beer is excellent'.

It was here, nursing his wife, that he started work on *Tom Jones*. There is an abiding legend that he based the character of Squire Allworthy on Ralph Allen. But, while there are many points of similarity between Fielding's patron and his fictional creation, the portrait of Allworthy is by no means a flattering one. Although benevolent and well-intentioned, he is so high-minded that he frequently fails to see evil in others, and is easily duped by them, with disastrous consequences. Allworthy may resemble Allen in certain ways, but, whatever else Allen might have been, he was nobody's fool.

By the following year, Fielding had given up the house at Twerton and taken lodgings in Bath, where, a few weeks after his arrival, his wife died in his arms. According to his friends, his grief at her death 'approached to frenzy' and they thought him 'in danger of losing his reason'.

The back of Fielding's Lodge

He continued to visit Bath – and Prior Park – on a regular basis – either staying with his sister in Widcombe or in lodgings in the city. By the early 1750s, his health was failing. In 1754 he wrote that he 'was no longer what is called a Bath case', and, on his doctor's advice, set out for Portugal to try and regain his health. He died there on 8 October 1754, at the age of 47.

His sister Sarah stayed on in Bath, later moving to a 'little cottage' in Walcot. She died on 9 April 1768 in her 57th year and was buried in Charlcombe. A memorial was also raised to her in the abbey.

Sarah's cottage in Widcombe still survives, as, of course, does Prior Park. Sadly, Fielding's Lodge, one of the earliest Georgian buildings in Bath, was bulldozed to build a factory, which is itself now threatened with redevelopment. Even if it hadn't been one of Bath's most hallowed literary shrines, its demolition would have counted as one of the worst excesses of the Sack of Bath. Perhaps the powers that be considered that, as it was in Twerton, it didn't matter too much.

A century ago, Twerton wasn't part of Bath at all; it was, as it had been for centuries, fiercely independent. Victor Rosenburg recalls that 'the city boundary ceased at Brougham Hayes, and all East and West Twerton was outside the city, and included in the Frome constituency for political purposes. Elections were a little more exciting and a little rougher than those in the city. John Barlow carried the Liberal banner, and Charles Foxcroft the Tory banner. At that time Twerton was overwhelmingly Liberal, and it was a brave Tory who wore his party's blue colours.'

Twerton not only had its own railway station, built by Brunel; it was an important industrial centre. The major employers in the town were the Carr family, who owned the mills that lined the river. Victor Rosenburg recalls that 'the Carr family had much influence in Twerton. They presented Innox Park to the villagers and also allowed use of the grounds of Wood House on August Bank Holiday for the annual Twerton Flower Show, which was a main event in Twerton's calendar. The trams took many workers from Bath to Twerton for their jobs in the cloth trade. The fare from the Guildhall to Twerton was one penny; before 8am it was a workman's return at one penny.'

Innox Park was laid out on five acres of land given to the people of Twerton by Thomas Carr. The opening ceremony, presided over by the Vicar of Twerton, Rev HL Maynard, took place on 26 June 1909 in atrocious weather. In this photograph, Robert Hope, Chairman of Twerton Parish Council, is seen thanking Mr Carr, on his right.

Above: Bath City Secondary School Football Team, 1907-8.
Below: East Walcot Reserves AFC, 1907-8.

CHAPTER TWENTY-TWO

PLAY UP, PLAY UP . . .

Sport was as important, in its own way, in 1909 as it is in 2009. For the aristocracy, Ascot, Lords, Henley, Cowes and Goodwood were the lynchpins of the social calendar, after which it was off to the grouse moors for a spot of shooting. Sport was also central to the public-school ethos, while university life, for many, consisted of little more than rowing, cricket, rugby and other sports.

Britain was supreme in sports. It held practically all the championships, except the heavyweight boxing title. No other country, apart from America, devoted itself to sport so wholeheartedly. In the 1908 Olympic Games, held at the White City in London, Britain won 56 gold, 51 silver and 38 bronze medals; America, second in the rankings, won 23 gold, 12 silver and 11 bronze; other countries' totals were virtually all in single figures. Although it was an extraordinary achievement, host countries had a habit of sweeping the board; four years earlier, in St Louis, America had achieved an even more remarkable record, while in Paris in 1900, France had led the field. Sport was far from being the *lingua franca* it is today; athletes from the host country had an overwhelming advantage simply because most of their foreign competitors couldn't afford to travel abroad. Only 22 countries participated in the 1908 Games; all, with the exception of America, Canada, Australia, New Zealand, South Africa, Turkey and Argentina, were European. CB Fry, the well-known sportsman and writer, suggested that future games should be even more exclusive, restricted to contestants from the Empire.

For the majority of people, though, sport basically meant three things – football, cricket and – in certain places such as Bath – rugby, but the greatest of these was football. The middle classes, although many of them were keen cricket fans, could be quite patrician about this. FE Smith, the 1st Lord Birkenhead, wrote that 'The poorer classes in this country have not got the tastes which superior people or a royal commission would choose for them. Were cricket and football abolished, it would bring upon them nothing but misery, depression, sloth, indiscipline and disorder.'

As far as professional football went, 1909 was notable as the year in which Bristol City played for the first and only time in the FA Cup Final, losing 1-0 at Crystal Palace to Manchester United. The run-up to the final was remarkable, as far as City was concerned, for the number of replays. In the first round they drew 1-1 at home with Southampton, beating them 2-0 in the replay. In the second round they drew 2-2 at home with Bury, beating them 1-0 in the replay. The third round saw a 2-0 home win over Norwich City, but in the quarter final they drew away 0-0 with Glossop North End, beating them 1-0 in the replay.[1] In the semi-final they drew at home 1-1 with Derby County, beating them 2-1 in the replay. Ten games in the last six rounds of the FA Cup is not a record, however – that honour goes to Fulham, who played twelve games in the last six rounds in 1975.

Down the road in Bath, Bath City didn't get to play the likes of Bristol City or Rovers, although they did play both teams' reserves on a regular basis. Bath City had been founded in 1889 but folded soon after, before being revived in 1900. They played on a ground owned by the Midland Railway behind the Belvoir Castle pub, which had originally been used by the railway cricket club. Drainage of the pitch was a constant problem, despite over 100 yards of piping having recently been installed so that water could drain away into culverts. The *Bath Chronicle*, somewhat cruelly, reported that City's ground was 'not in bad shape, verdant in midsummer, with only large puddle on it'.

Among the teams Bath City played in the 1908-09 season were Kingswood Rovers, Radstock Town, Welton Rovers, Camerton, Trowbridge Town, Staple Hill, Street, Weymouth, three Welsh teams – Barry District, Aberdare and Treharris – and the Old Newportonians from Leytonstone, whom they played on Easter Monday. Reporting on this match, which ended in a 1-1 draw, the *Chronicle* said that 'Bath would have piled up a heavier score had they accepted an iota of their chances.'

Bath was in Division Two of the Western League, winning six out of 22 matches, drawing six, and ending eighth (out of twelve) in the league. In the 1909-10 season, the Western League was expanded to include another team (Ton Pentre); Bath played 24 matches, won five, drew six and ended the season ninth in the league.

---

1 Glossop North End was founded in 1886 and still exists, despite being disbanded twice. In the 1890s, they gained promotion to the First Division before dropping back to the Second Division, where they stayed until 1914-15. In the 2007-8 FA Cup, they were beaten 3-0 in the preliminary round by Malvern Town.

Ascension Church AFC played in Division One of the Bath League. Here the 1912-13 team are seen after winning the Portway Cup. Back row: G Masters (committee), F Bryant (committee), CJ Horler (Ass Sec), J Aplin (Chairman), WG Ward (committee), L Hayes. Middle row: W Hope, A Ashley, S Ponfield, PF Ingram (Vice Captain), LT Cook (Captain), S Lippiatt, E Bellringer (Hon Sec), EH Summers, JT Crouch. Front row: S Marquiss, G Newman, A Mills, L Cook.

Bath City Reserves played in Division One of the Bath League; the other teams in the league included Bath Rovers, Twerton St Mary's, Bath Abbey, St James's, Ascension Church, Weston Rovers and Manvers Street Institute. Victor Rosenburg recalls that, 'in addition to Saturday soccer, there was a Thursday League. Jolly's of Milsom Street were represented by Hartley FC,[2] while Colmers of Union Street named their club Victoria FC. The newspaper boys had a club of their own called the *Daily Mail*; it received some assistance from that newspaper.'

For many Bathonians, then as now, football meant rugby football, played on the Recreation Ground – known universally as the Rec. Victor Rosenburg recalls that 'the Somerset Rugby Cup Competition was instituted during this decade. Bath were, I believe, beaten by Bridgwater Albion in the first final. On a later occasion Bath and Weston Super Mare were drawn together. The

2 Jolly's owned Hartley House on Belvedere, which is presumably where the name came from – even though the house was a women's dormitory.

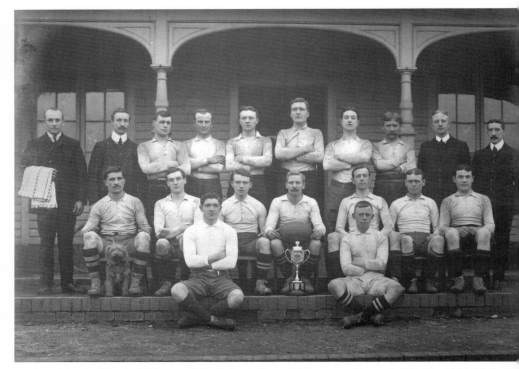

Bath 'A' Rugby Football Team, 1908-9. Back Row: H Bristow (Trainer), W Cleall, E Holvey, Bristow, S Graves, B Wakefield (Vice Captain), B Hurst, W Dainton, EF Simpkins (Committee), C Clement (Hon Sec). Middle Row: L Hatherill, P Brooke, HJ Lewis, AE Cleall (Captain), H Cross Bushnell, G Chivers. Front Row: J Phipps, E Toop. Played 24. Wone 12, Lost 7. Drawn 5. Points F 193. Against 90.

game had to be replayed three times before a result was obtained. These replays caused many outbursts of temper on the field, and because of this both clubs agreed to discontinue fixtures for a few seasons.' At the time, Bridgwater Albion were renowned as just about the most formidable club in the West Country; Bath's 3-3 draw with them at Bridgwater in 1909 was the first time they had avoided defeat there. 1909 also saw Bath adopt the official playing colours – blue, white and black – which celebrate their centenary in 2009. Another footnote to Rugby Union history – at a meeting in London in May 1909, GA Roberts, speaking on behalf of Bath, proposed that the value of a drop goal should be reduced from four points to three. The proposition was agreed by a vote of 44 to 27 and a recommendation was made to the international board, although the change does not seem to have been implemented until 1948.

Astonishingly, the topic that dominated Bath Rugby in 1909 was the same one that dominates it a century later – whether or not the club should stay at the Rec. The club had been formed in 1865, and its first ground, later acquired by the cricket club, was at North Parade; from there it had played at a variety of venues – Claverton Down, Lambridge Meadows, Kensington Meadows, and Taylor's Field on the Warminster Road – before moving to Henrietta Park in 1892. A couple of years later, Captain Forester, who owned the Bathwick estate, applied for an act of parliament to develop the Recreation Ground. Grandiose plans had been drawn up in 1889 to build an enormous luxury hotel on the site, but these had come to nothing; the Bath & County Recreation Ground Company had since acquired the land and were seeking to develop it. They approached the rugby club, who agreed to move to the new site on the understanding that the company would erect barriers and a grandstand in return for a share of the gate.

By 1909, however, when the rugby club had been there for 15 years, the company was struggling. The annual general meeting of the company was held at the Castle Hotel in Northgate Street in early November. The Mayor presided, and opened his remarks with the hope that the proposed lease of a site on the land would turn out satisfactorily; this, presumably, was the plot on which

The Castle Hotel on the corner of Northgate and New Bond Streets, where the future of the rugby club was discussed in 1909. The Castle closed in 1924 and was demolished to make way for the main post office.

the skating rink – now the Pavilion – was built the following year. Then it was on to the main topic of the evening – who should use the Rec. It was started by Mr Pope, who voiced 'a complaint about football':

The association people are very anxious to get down to our ground. They say it is quite possible for the ground to be divided by a moveable fence during the football season, and allow association to be played on one side and rugby on the other. There are others who think it might be possible to arrange matches on alternate Saturdays – a first-class association match on one Saturday and a first-class rugby match on another Saturday. There is no doubt that association football is very popular with a great many people, and it is possible it could work. Those who have been shareholders ever since the company was formed are getting a little hungry and they would like to have a little dividend if it is possible.

Mr Ambrose echoed Mr Pope's comments:

One or two members of the association club have been speaking to me during the past few weeks and went into the question of the Recreation Ground. On average about 800 people go to their first-class games at Twerton. They think some arrangements could be made with the rugby club to have alternate Saturdays. They fully realise that it would not be possible to divide the ground as first suggested into two pitches, because it might happen that there would be two first-class matches going on on the same day and it would be impossible to carry it on in that fashion. If the clubs in the early part of the year knew that they only got the ground on alternate Saturdays they would be able to make their fixtures fit in ... In dealing with this matter we will have to get the two clubs together and make a mutual agreement. I fancy it has been recognised that rugby is going down all over the country and that association is coming to the fore. At least that is what I am told.

Mr Mundy disagreed, pointing out that 'Last year in Bath, rugby showed a great advance, and gates are going up. This year they are well up to the average. It is a question whether a club is successful. A winning club always brings good gates.'

Mr Gandy said that he did not see 'how we could run the two games together. The arrangement now is that there is a first-class rugby match one Saturday and perhaps the A team the next Saturday, so they are really running three teams, and have not

The Recreation Ground from the Abbey tower in the early twentieth century.

enough room for them now. I do not see how they could, in any way, give up a Saturday.'

Mr Lewis added that

the matter of association football on the Recreation Ground has not been lost sight of by the directors. About two years ago, I, with the late Mr Mundy, met Mr Hoskins on behalf of the association club. We went over the ground and Mr Hoskins suggested dividing the ground for the playing of two matches at the same time. It was pointed out to him that that was impossible and he afterwards saw that it would be. If we took the piece of ground now used by the rugby club and a piece of ground for association football, we would be practically on the outfield of the cricket ground. The directors are very anxious in every possible way to encourage sport, but some considerations must be given to county cricket. To do away with county cricket would be a great loss to the city, and to arrange football matches on alternate Saturdays seems to be impossible.

Mr Pope was less concerned about the cricket, however, saying that the company didn't get enough out of it: 'We get £80 and our expenses are over £52. I think we ought to get a better return, especially when we get good gates.'

Mr Lewis pointed out that the £52 included the cost of erecting the stand: 'I am afraid we will not get any more out of the county cricket committee. It is as much as they can do to make ends meet after exercising strict economy. We have got the very best terms we

329

can get with the county. It must be remembered that the Taunton ground is their own and they don't have the expenses there as when they come to Bath.'

One of Somerset's top cricketers was Len Braund, who had a sports shop at 13 Argyle Street. He was a versatile batsman and a leg break bowler who played 23 tests for England and was regarded as the best slip fielder of his generation. Whenever Somerset was playing, he would send the lunchtime score to his shop, where the telegram, eagerly awaited by the schoolboys who hero-worshipped him, was pasted up in the window. In January 1909, at the Bath Cricket Club dinner, he made a speech advocating moving the headquarters of the Somerset Cricket Club from Taunton to Bath. 'The attendance when the county side appear at Taunton is lamentably poor,' he told the audience. 'What is needed to improve Somerset cricket is a nursery, which should be established at Bath. Scarcely anyone is seen at practice on the Taunton ground but the professionals; the corner of the field formerly used for nets has been released to the local bowling club.'

Above: Len Braund
Below: Somerset County Cricket Club Week at the Recreation Ground.

The move never took place – one of the possible reasons being the poor showing of the county side

S. MCAULEY (SCORER)   NORTH   F. M. LEE   ROBSON BRAUND H. F. MONTGOMERY.   P. R. JOHNSON.   W. H. EDWARDS
                                H. MARTYN   L. C. H. PALAIRET   S. M. J. WOODS.   A. E. NEWTON   (SCORER)
PHOTO HAWKINS, BRIGHTON   SOMERSETSHIRE.   (CAPTAIN)   CRANFELD   COPYRIGHT

at the Rec. Of the 33 matches they played there between 1906 and 1914, they won only two – losing 21 and drawing ten. In 1909 they drew with Yorkshire and Hampshire and lost to Lancashire and Australia. They lost against Australia by two wickets; Somerset scored 93 and 111, while Australia scored 139 and 69 for 8. After playing at Bath the Australians went to Lords where they beat England by nine wickets. The Australians' visit to Bath was marked by a fête in Sydney Gardens, featuring a firework display ending with 'a kangaroo at the wicket surrounded by Hail Australia'.

The summer of 1909 was – with the notable exception of Pageant Week – a miserable one, and takings at Bath Cricket Club's big matches were down on previous years. The Pageant

Another possible reason for the Somerset County Cricket Club's failure to move to Bath: the Recreation Ground under water during Cricket Week, July 1903.

obviously took its toll as well – not only during Pageant Week, but in the run-up, with thousands of Bathonians too busy to watch cricket. The club's announcement that it needed to boost its income if it was to survive was met with constructive – and not so constructive – criticism from correspondents in the local press. There were complaints that sixpence was too much to charge for entry without a

331

seat. It was suggested that more people might go to matches if seats were available at a penny or twopence, but then it was pointed out that this would probably reduce the receipts for the enclosure and the stand. The *Chronicle* didn't mince its words: 'Provide for the masses is the progressive policy of the day,' it thundered, 'and the one that pays.' The club, which celebrated its 50th anniversary in 1909, survived, however, to celebrate its 150th in 2009.

If anyone was in any doubt that the Edwardian age was indeed the age of the masses, they only had to look at the roller-skating phenomenon. At its peak, there were three large covered rinks in Bath – one of which survives as the Bath Pavilion – but the peak didn't last very long. The first was the Empress Rink, which opened at the Drill Hall on the Lower Bristol Road on 22 March 1909. The *Chronicle* celebrated the opening a few days later:

'Are you a rinkite?' is a question everyone is asking. There is no doubt that the fascinating pastime of roller skating has 'caught on'. Not that it is a new idea – far from it – but it is many years since it was taken up with such enthusiasm as at present. It is a revival of an old sport, and perhaps never before have such facilities for indulging the graceful art been offered to skaters … The excellent rink opened at the Drill Hall … is one of the finest floors in the country … The rink has been brought to a very high pitch of perfection. Experts will find it beautifully smooth and easy-running, while there are no rough bits, which might spell disaster to the novice.

Although skating was portrayed as a glamorous recreation, the reality – with inexperienced skaters hurtling round the rink – was often very different.

Outdoor skating on meadows such as those at Kensington, which were specially flooded during icy weather, was also popular during the Edwardian period.

It was open from 11am to 1pm, 2.30pm to 5.30pm and 7.30pm to 10.30pm. A military band played at all sessions and there was always an instructor in attendance. Admission was sixpence for the morning session and a shilling for the others. Within weeks of opening, it was regularly attracting around 200 people to the afternoon sessions and around 350 in the evenings.

The next rink to open was on the corner of James Street West and Norfolk Buildings. Plans for it were laid before the Surveying Committee at the end of August 1909 and it opened – incredibly – just over three months later. On 16 December, the *Chronicle* reported that it was doing good business, with a military band always in attendance, a lounge for spectators and first-class refreshments. The building was 107 feet wide and 179 feet long, with a skating area measuring 80 feet by 160 feet.

The third rink – on the Rec – was approved by the Surveying Committee on 25 October 1909. A few weeks later, Alderman Oliver voiced his concern at the effect all this roller skating was having on one of the council's top attractions:

> There is a craze at the present time for roller skating. We are going to have three rinks in Bath, and while the craze remains I am afraid that a great deal of money that we ought to take at the Roman Promenade may go to other sources.

West Elevation.

Above: The west elevation of the skating rink – a homage to John Wood the Younger?
Below: A view of the newly-built rink.

The skating rink on the Rec, designed by an architect called H Dan from Enfield, opened on 17 September 1910. It had a rock-maple floor, music at all sessions, 'dainty refreshments' and 'an exhibition of fancy skating during the afternoon and evening sessions by Miss Merry Martha, the only skater in the world who dances the sailor's hornpipe on skates'. To encourage people to use it, skaters were allowed to cross North Parade Bridge toll free to reach the rink. From the beginning, it seems to have been used for other events – for example, in November 1911, Lloyd

Bath Y.M.C.A. Gymnasium,
Largest and Best Equipped in the City.

SCIENTIFIC PHYSICAL TRAINING.
Educational and Recreative Gymnastics & Calisthenics.
EVENING CLASSES FOR MEN, LADIES AND
CHILDREN.
Private Lessons in Fencing, Club-Swinging, and Apparatus
Work (Ladies or Gents).
Special Day Arrangements to suit Schools and Private Classes.

Medical Gymnastics at George Street House, George Street.
PRIVATE ROOMS for the Treatment by
MECANO-THERAPY of BODILY
DEFORMITIES and DISEASES, CHEST, LUNG
and DIGESTIVE DISORDERS.
For full information Apply
Mr. P. C. COTTLE, Professor of Physical Education.

One institution still going strong today is the gym at the
YMCA, featured here in an advertisement from 1909.

George addressed a Liberal rally there. Essentially, the Pavilion, as it is now known, was a large shed. John Betjeman called it an 'unworthy building'; many would agree with him, although an echo of the west front of John Wood the Younger's Assembly Rooms in the west front of the Pavilion suggests that Mr Dan was inspired by the example of his great predecessor. Inside, the addition of a stage and the extension of the lobby forward into the hall have changed the internal appearance of the building, but it is still possible to imagine the swathes of roller-skaters rumbling noisily around the room, with the occasional novice coming unstuck and careering off into the crowd, while Merry Martha danced the hornpipe and the band played on.

Money was also being spent improving swimming facilities at Cleveland Baths. In the summer of 1908, 45,000 people used the baths; at times they were seriously overcrowded. Unemployed workers were drafted in to work on an extension which cost £700 and was unveiled in April 1909. This eastern extension, which increased the length of the baths from 80 to 120 feet, was 30 feet wide and four feet deep. Extra dressing rooms were also provided. So successful did it prove that in December 1909 it was proposed to spend a further £200 on improving the baths; the *Chronicle* reported that 'the work is desirable more especially as the larger portion of the money will be spent in wages and the whole of the labour will be selected from the unemployed.'

Bath Cycling Club was one of the largest and most prestigious in the country; in 1908 many of the competitors in the Olympics had come down to Bath for the August Bank Holiday meeting. The main event of the year was the Whit Monday sports day on the Rec; the hotly-contested five-mile race for the Dunlop Gold vase attracted top riders from all over the country. Cycling, though, was beginning to lose its allure. At the club's annual general meeting in February, it was reported that the numbers turning up for club runs was falling 'owing to the clouds of dust caused by motorists'.

For those who could afford it golf was becoming increasingly popular. It certainly did not have the popular appeal it has today, however. The annual subscription fee to Lansdown Golf Club, founded in 1894 as a nine-hole course, for example, was £1-11-6. One of those who came to Bath to play golf, in April 1909, was the Prime Minister, who, while staying with Sir John Dickson-Poynder, MP for Chippenham, motored over to play at the Sham Castle links. There was also a Bladud Golf Club at Stirtingale Farm in Southdown, whose club house was at Woodfield in Bloomfield Road.

Bowls was also attracting an increasing number of players. The Bath Bowling Club had been formed at a meeting in the pavilion on the Rec two years earlier and plans were being discussed to build bowling greens in Royal Victoria Park and Sydney Gardens.

When the two golfers seen in these photographs came to Bath in 1909 to play at the Lansdown Golf Club, they rented a 'bungalow' – converted from a railway carriage – near Brockham End, which features in the pictures on the opposite page.

"Our Bungalow" Bath

"After lunch & recreation.
Bristol Channel can be seen from
hammock, 6 miles off."

"Ye resting place for ye weary"

Tennis and croquet courts were also planned, the idea being that unemployed men could be paid to build them.

One of the biggest annual events in Bath's sporting calendar was the Bath Horse Show, held at Lambridge in early September. Victor Rosenburg recalls that 'it was a great social occasion, and generally drew large crowds of the hunting fraternity. The Liberal party also held its annual fete on the horse-show ground and many balloon ascents were made.' The 1909 Horse Show,

Two postcard views of the 1909 Bath Horse Show.

Above: The horse-show ground was host to many other events, such as the Somerset County Show, held there in May 1905.

Below: As this photograph of the Bathwick Boating Station demonstrates, rowing was also a popular sport in the Edwardian period, with two clubs — the Avon Rowing Club and the Bath Rowing Club — based there.

held on 1 and 2 September, was hit by the unsettled weather that blighted so many events that year and attendance was down as a result. The event was covered not only by local newspapers but also by the *Times*, which reported that, 'as usual, the strongest feature of the exhibition was the hunter section. Captain Forester, in accordance with custom, gave a trophy for the champion hunter, and this was, after much deliberation, awarded to Mr Hinchcliffe of Harrogate.'

CHAPTER TWENTY-THREE

MEMORIES OF LARKHALL[1]

'I left school in 1909. There were no playing fields. There were watercress men in the streets. The roads were mud in wintertime, dust in the summer. We played marbles in the cart tracks. In summer there were outings to Kensington Gardens ... Magic lantern shows were put on by Ernest Crawford – Larkhall's father of cinema. Along with Roebuck Rudge, he invented the Bianthoscope – slides were rotated in a projection device to produce the effect of moving pictures.'

Mr Dangerfield, Brooklyn Road

'I remember the first playing fields at Plain Ham with swings and a seesaw. If we wanted to play cricket or football we had to carry the gear to the top of Little Solsbury. Francis Garraway, the schoolmaster, ran a club for boys over 14 in a building behind the White Lion in the square. He started a bible study class there, and it was there I saw the

1 The accounts in this chapter were recorded by Bruce Crofts and are given here verbatim as a valuable social record of a part of Bath that has changed, like the rest of the city, beyond recognition. They also demonstrate the importance of oral history and of recording memories such as these before they are lost forever.

first aeroplane fly over Bath. Among the characters I remember was Mr Lodge, the baker, who also broke in horses. I can also remember Tinker Rawlings, Copper Steele, and Mr Crawford who pushed his 100-year-old mother around in a Bath chair.'

Mr Harold Horsell

'Mr Short was the village cobbler. He was a Methodist preacher who sold toys for a halfpenny and a penny in his shop. He would give a halfpenny to boys who could remember and recite their prayers.'

Mr Holbrow

'There was a greengrocer called Mr Coles who had a wooden peg-leg. It meant he had to sit down while customers helped themselves – the first self-service shop in Bath! There was a gardener at the bottom of Charlcombe Lane who grew delphiniums with an elaborate system of drainage pipes. The diocesan school stands there now. Mr Smith mended boots and played the violin at the Larkhall Inn. Where the bus shelter is now was Mr Singer's blacksmith's shop. At one time, spare horses were stabled there to pull the trams to town. The Queen Inn is now a house opposite St Saviour's on the corner of Beaufort East. The best sweets cost fourpence a pound and you could get a good cinema seat for threepence.'

Mr Wall

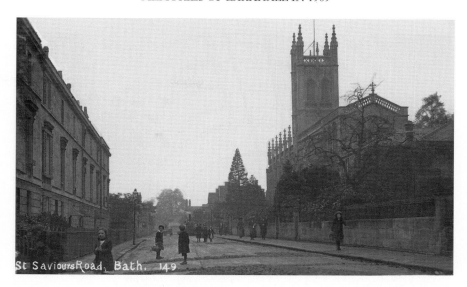

St Saviours Road. Bath. 149

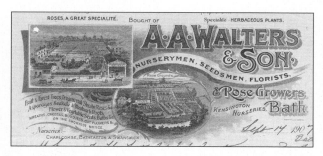

Lambridge, Bath.

CHAPTER TWENTY-FOUR

RETAIL THERAPY

The number of shops in Edwardian Bath was astonishing. In 1909, there were 56 bakeries, 49 butchers, 56 dairies, 27 fishmongers and poulterers, 93 greengrocers and 99 grocers in Bath (not counting those in Twerton and Weston). There were also 31 antique shops, 56 boot & shoe makers, 43 coal merchants, 18 cycle agents & manufacturers, 13 ironmongers, 51 tobacconists and 42 wine merchants. Some had several branches but most were small independent stores. Although one-stop shopping was starting to make inroads, specialisation was still the order of the day, largely because, in an era before pre-preparation and pre-packaging were the norm, shopkeepers needed a high level of knowledge and skill. Lack of refrigeration also meant that shopping for perishable items had to be done on a daily rather than a weekly basis; this was only possible if shops were close to where people lived.

Some specialists survive, but, in the face of competition from supermarkets and convenience stores, their numbers dwindle every year. Bath still has several excellent butchers – one right in the heart of the city – but while there are greengrocers, selling local produce, in the suburbs, in the city centre there is just a single (but very well stocked) fruit and vegetable stall in Kingsmead Square, while the only fishmonger's is attached to an upmarket restaurant in Green Street.

Bakeries, too, have been pushed out to the suburbs; a century ago, the smell of freshly-baked bread would have wafted along most of Bath's main shopping streets. Until the 1880s, bakers used coal-fired ovens, which carried the risk of contamination; the advent of gas ovens did away with this risk, and by the early twentieth century almost all bakeries had switched over to gas. Cottage loaves were the most popular, but tinned loaves were slowly gaining in popularity.

Bakeries didn't just sell bread, of course: a mouth-watering array of cakes and pastries were displayed in their windows to tempt passers-by – iced cakes, marzipan cakes, seed cakes, tennis cakes, pound cakes, madeira cakes, sultana cakes, fruit cakes, sponge cakes, shortbreads, fruit tarts, jam tarts, rock cakes, almond cakes, cheesecakes, maids of honour, doughnuts, jam puffs and, of course, Bath buns. William Howells, visiting Bath in 1905, was unimpressed by these epicurean delights. 'I do not know,' he wrote, 'whether it is the tradition of the Bath bun which has inspired the pastry shops to their profuse efforts in unwholesome-looking cakes, but it seemed to me that at every third or fourth window

J. R. GODDARD, Fruit Salesman & Commission Agent, High Street, Bath.

Postcards issued by JR Goddard to celebrate the arrival the arrival of the first major consignment of bananas in Bath. Starbuck's now occupies the building on this site.

W. G. Lewis,   J. R. GODDARD, Fruit Salesman & Commission Agent, High St., Bath.   Photo, Bath

I was invited by the crude display to make way entirely with the digestion which the Bath waters were doing so little to repair.'

Displays of poultry at Rice's at the Balustrade on the London Road and Broadhurst's in York Buildings. Broadhurst's is now Prey Lifestyle Boutique; Rice's was, until recently, the Beaufort Stores — better known as Mrs A's.

Xmas Show, 1907.

E. BROADHURST,
Fishmonger, Poulterer, and Game Dealer,
3, York Buildings, Bath,
TELEPHONE No. 71   Pub. by H. Foster, Bath.

Although much of the meat sold by butchers was imported, most greengrocers' produce was local, with the obvious exception of items such as oranges and bananas. Bananas were a luxury until 1901, when Fyffes brought the first consignment of unripe bananas to Britain in a refrigerated ship. Soon, ripening sheds were established across the country and bananas were on their way to becoming one of the nation's favourite fruits.

Kippers and bloaters were the staple fare in fishmonger's. Fishmongers wore straw hats and their shops sometimes had aquariums with goldfish swimming in them – not for sale but as a kind of advertisement.

Provision merchants sold a variety of goods. The fronts of their shops were often obscured

347

by rank upon rank of whatever game or poultry happened to be in season at the time. Pheasants were expensive – at six shillings or more a brace – while hares were hung upside down with little buckets over their noses to ensure that they would 'jug' well, and Ostend rabbits would be skewered up, skinned and purple. A dozen new-laid eggs could be bought for a shilling, while 'cooking eggs' – unguaranteed – cost around sixpence. Bacon was generally cut by hand – slicers came later – and butter was cut from large slabs and moulded into shape between butter pats, before being wrapped up. Pre-packaged goods were slowly coming in, especially in the larger grocery stores, but virtually everything could still be bought loose. Tinned goods – with the exception, for some reason, of tinned tongue – were regarded with suspicion, and were very much a last resort. Biscuits came in large tins and cost so much a pound, with broken biscuits sold at cut price. Most things were sold in pounds and ounces, although certain items, such as flour, were sold by the peck.

The smell of Edwardian grocer's was made up of many things: spices, dried fruit, foil-lined tea chests, loaves of sugar, almonds, sultanas, flour, candied peel, cheese, vinegar, marmalade – but above all the heady aroma of freshly-ground coffee. In ironmonger's it was the smell of paraffin, sold for lamps, that was most prominent, mingling with the whiff of soda, sold in lumps for cleaning, and the bracing tang of green soap, which was cut off large blocks and wrapped in newspaper.

Tobacconist's had a distinctive aroma as well, each subtly different according to the special mixtures of tobacco made up on the premises. Each made their own brands of cigarettes which were kept in glass cases and sold by weight. Proprietary brands came with cigarette cards, eagerly collected by boys, whose oft-repeated request – 'Got any cigarette cards, mister' – became one of the catchphrases of the age. Among the brands that have long since disappeared were Ogden's Guinea Gold, Bandmaster and

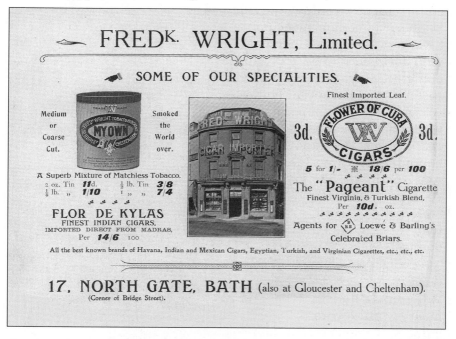

Cinderella. Turkish and Egyptian cigarettes were also popular with the more well-heeled customers; brands included Quo Vadis, Neb Ka, Au Bon Fumeur, Snake-Charmers and Du Perfex. Most cigarettes, though, were still relatively cheap. Players cost 2½d for ten, Gold Flake cost 3d for ten, and Woodbines were five for a penny. You could buy them in packets, in cartons, in cardboard boxes and in flat or circular tin boxes.

Alcohol too was only just beginning to be seen as an easy way for the government to raise money, and was relatively cheap. The middle classes generally drank at home, rather than going to the pub, and few ladies ever stepped into a pub at all. Beer and wine were bought from wine merchants or the larger grocery stores. A surprisingly large variety of wines was on offer. Bottles of claret generally cost from 1/6 to 2/6, while burgundies cost from around

4/-. A cheaper alternative was Emu burgundy from Australia, which came in flagons. Whisky cost around 3/6 a bottle, or 4/6 if you wanted twelve-year-old. Beer, such as the ever-popular Oatmeal Stout from Bath Brewery, which carried an endorsement from 'Granville H Sharp FCS, late principal of Liverpool College of Chemistry', who declared it to be 'a product of high class quality and purity', cost 3/- for a dozen pint bottles.

Although supermarkets would not appear for another 50 years or so, the move towards having everything under one roof had already started. Cater, Stofell & Fortt, who described themselves as 'grocers & provision dealers, druggists, fruiterers & florists, meat purveyors, game dealers, poulterers & fishmongers, wine & spirit merchants, ironmongers and pastrycooks & confectioners' occupied premises at 19-20 & 25-27 High Street, 1-4 Northumberland Place, 27-28 Upper Borough Walls, 4-5 Milsom Street, 4-5 John Street, 8

FAIR CONNOISSEURS.

CATER, STOFFELL & FORTT, Ltd., (18 Departments).
Largest and Cheapest Stores in the West of England.
3 SPECIALITIES.

BEAU NASH   FORTT & SON'S   SULIS WATER
"FAMOUS"
BATH OLIVER BISCUITS

Scotch   Whiskey

CATER, STOFFELL & FORTT, Limited,
BATH, BRISTOL and CLIFTON.

Above: Staff at the Home & Colonial Stores in Westgate Street.

Below: A Twerton Co-Operative Society delivery cart in Westhall Road, Lower Weston.

Southgate Street and 8 Margaret's Buildings. National grocery chains with outlets in Bath included the Home & Colonial Stores at 34 Westgate Street and Lipton's at 1 New Bond Street, 21 Green Street and 12-13 Westgate Street. Boot's, which arrived in Bath in 1896, had 'cash chemists' at 21-22 Union Street, 4-5 Union Passage and 56 Southgate Street.

The Twerton Co-operative Society, founded in 1889, had also introduced centralised shopping, along with a radically new business model. By 1909 it had stores at 6-8 St Peter's Terrace, East Twerton; 32 Claverton Street, Widcombe; 16 & 18 Lyndhurst Road, South Twerton; 46-48 Moorland Road; and 6 Augusta Place, Lower Weston. The Bath Co-operative Society, which was founded later, had a store at Chelsea Buildings on the London Road.

Then there were the department stores – Colmer's at 5-11, 17 & 20 Union Street and 6-9 Union Passage; Ealand's at 1-4 New Bond Street and 2 Northgate Street; Evans & Owen's in Bartlett Street, St Andrew's Terrace and Alfred Street; and the great survivor, Jolly's,

Above: Colmer's on the west side of Union Street; WH Smith's, the Disney Store, Jane Norman, Clark's, and Wallis occupy this range of buildings today.

Right: Ealand's in New Bond Street was one of Bath's most elegant stores a century ago.

Below: An 1909 advertisement for Jolly's echoes the peacock motif used in the store. The 100-year claim seems a rather generous interpretation of the store's history, however.

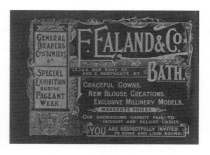

at 11-14 Milsom Street, 9-11 Old King Street and 8-10 John Street. Bath also had two Marks & Spencer's – in the Market and at 8 Stall Street – although these penny bazaars, which had originated on a Leeds market stall in 1884, were a far cry from the stores we know today.

Department stores had their origins in the bazaars of the early nineteenth-century, in which space was rented out to traders selling a variety of goods to well-heeled shoppers. The first was the Soho Bazaar in London, which opened in 1816; less than ten years later, a bazaar – now the Eastern Eye restaurant – opened in Quiet Street in Bath. The first department stores appeared in the 1860s. Evans & Owen's opened in 1864, Colmer's in 1871. Jolly's, Bath's most famous department store, started off as the Bath Emporium – a high-class milliner's – at 12 Milsom Street in 1831, before diversifying and opening departments in the shops on either side in 1879.

It wasn't just economy of scale that gave these stores an advantage; they spearheaded changes that would see the virtual disappearance of many small independent shopkeepers. Ready-made, off-the-peg clothes and shoes were increasingly popular, threatening the livelihood of the city's tailors, dressmakers and bootmakers. Lipton's produced the first mass-produced tea in 1889 at 1/7 a pound, heralding the start of a retail revolution. As more and more items came pre-packaged, shop assistants needed far less knowledge and skill. Traditionally, shop assistants were boys who served apprenticeships; in the Edwardian era, it was increasingly girls who worked in shops. Often, they didn't have to serve apprenticeships, and they could be paid far less than their male counterparts as well.

Shop work may have required less skill, but working in a large store in the early 1900s was one of the most soul-destroying jobs imaginable. Hours were appallingly long – at least 65 hours a week, sometimes as many as 90. Shop assistants were on their feet the whole time; anyone found sitting down risked dismissal. Tea breaks were the exception rather than the rule. It was not until 1909 that the Shop Assistants' Union started campaigning for a 60 hour week. Many large stores stayed open till seven, eight or even nine at night. Wages were low and many employers ruled with a rod of iron. Many shop assistants lived in, sleeping in barrack-like dormitories, spending their free time in communal sitting rooms that made station waiting rooms look cosy. Percy Allott, later a prominent trades unionist, has left us this account of his time as a shop assistant in London in the early twentieth century:

I worked at a big London drapery store. We lived in. This system meant that you slept and had your meals on the firm's premises. The food was poor and we were always hungry at the end of the day. We slept four in a room on hard beds. The conditions in crowded, dingy, and ill-ventilated dormitories were appalling. There was no heating and no covering on the bare boards. Occasional visitors were rats. There were only five bathrooms for

Working as an Edwardian shop assistant was one of the most soul-destroying jobs imaginable.

several hundred employees. We washed each morning in cold water in zinc basins, in a room with a concrete floor. The shop assistant in those days was virtually a wage slave, and fear of the sack prevented protest and virtually imprisoned him.

Things may have been better in Bath, of course, although on balance this seems unlikely. On 2 September 1909, for example, *John Bull*, a national magazine that sought to redress the grievances of its readers, attacked Colmer's in Union Street for the treatment meted out to its employees.

1909 saw two developments in the retail industry with far-reaching consequences, however. On 15 March, Harry Gordon Selfridge, an American who had already amassed a fortune at home, opened his first store in Oxford Street in London. His aim was to make shopping a pleasure rather than a chore. His stores had elaborate window displays and operated on the basis that – in his own words – 'the customer is always right'. He treated his staff differently as well, rewarding them for good sales figures rather than fining them for breaking rules. People could examine the goods on display before deciding to buy. He aimed to give customers a glimpse into a world of glitz and glamour; in putting the perfume counter centre-stage at the front of the store he pioneered a cornerstone of department-store layout still in place a century later.

But, although Selfridge's was the shape of things to come, as far as department stores were concerned, an even more significant opening took place a few months later, on 5 November, in Liverpool – the first British Woolworth's. Here too shoppers could handle goods before buying them; the difference was that nothing cost more than sixpence. This was a department store for the masses: democracy in action. The *Daily Mail* was unimpressed, comparing Frank Woolworth to Barnum and suggesting that Liverpool had been chosen so that, when the business failed, its managers could jump on a ship for America, leaving their creditors behind.

The store was an instant success, however, with the counters virtually stripped bare by the end of the first day's trading. Woolworth's secret was bulk ordering of mass-produced items – china, glassware, children's clothes, paper patterns, haberdashery, tin toys, sheet music, Christmas decorations, pots and pans and stationery. But, although it was cheap, it wasn't dowdy. Like Selfridge, Woolworth was a showman; his store openings had all the glitz and glamour so conspicuously lacking in the lives of so many of his customers. The stores themselves, and the items arranged on their mahogany counters, glittered and gleamed as if in an Aladdin's Cave.

Other stores soon followed, although Bath did not get a Woolworth's – at 13-14 Stall Street – until the 1920s. It is hard for us to appreciate the glamour Woolworth's had – especially for the young – as late as the 1970s. When they first hit these shores, they introduced a level of consumer choice most people had never imagined possible. Woolworth's was glitzy, democratic – and American. It introduced the British public to what has become almost universal today – self-service.

A century ago, the idea that self-service would become the order of the day was unthinkable. Although the first self-service grocery store opened in the USA in 1915, with the first supermarket following in 1930, it was only after the Second World War, when food packaging had become standard, that the practice spread to grocery stores in Britain. Marks & Spencer's, which started selling food in 1931, was one of the first to introduce self-service to its food departments, on a trial basis, in 1948. Nevertheless, the principle had been established, and it was Woolworth's which established it. It is ironic that, months short of its UK centenary, it should have fallen victim to the retail revolution it initiated.

Today, the retail revolution is entering another phase – one the Edwardians would have had even more difficulty getting their

A baker's boy with his delivery cart in Moorland Road, Weston-Super-Mare. Scores of similar carts could have been seen on the streets of Bath a century ago.

heads around. Self-service is one thing; shopping online something else entirely. By a curious irony, however, internet shopping is reintroducing something that was commonplace a century ago – home delivery. Middle-class shoppers rarely carried their purchases home, unless the items were very small – that was the job of the errand boy. Although, after the Great War, many errand boys started to use bicycles, before the war most of them pushed carts or carried trays on their shoulders.

Working-class shoppers wouldn't have wanted to pay a premium to have their purchases delivered – not that they had to walk very far with them. Apart from hundreds of corner shops throughout the city, dozens of streets were, in effect, small shopping centres. Today, virtually all the everyday businesses on those streets – fishmongers, butchers, tobacconists, confectioners, greengrocers, post offices – have vanished. Shops have either been converted to houses or specialist businesses – interior design consultants, therapists, furniture makers, antique dealers – while local residents go to convenience stores or supermarkets for their everyday needs.

Visiting streets such as Belvedere, just north of the city centre, and comparing what is there today with what was there a century ago is to appreciate the full impact of this social and commercial revolution. Belvedere isn't a particularly long street – 40 buildings, more or less, many of which have always been houses, flats or lodging houses. Yet a century ago you would have had the choice of two confectioners, three stationers (one selling newspapers, another doubling as a post office), a fishmonger, two butchers, a milliner and dressmaker, a tobacconist and hairdresser, a chemist, two greengrocers, a dye works, two pubs, a dairy, a bootmaker, and a grocer. With the exception of the two pubs – one now converted to a wine bar – all these businesses have gone. They have, however, like echoes on the wind, left traces of their existence behind.

Starting at the bottom of Belvedere on the left-hand side, Nos 1 & 2 were the Bath Eye Infirmary, founded in 1811 and absorbed into the Royal United Hospital in 1973. Next to it, at No 3, was the *Beehive* pub, which closed in 2001 and is now the Grappa Bar. Next door, at No 4, was EFS Tucker, 'hairdresser, tobacconist and fancy dealer' – long gone, and the shopfront replaced by a pair of smaller windows. The shopfronts at 5 and 6 – No 6 with a flying bay and undersill railings over its area – both survive, although neither is now a shop; Oscar Ashley was a blind maker at No 5, while No 6 was William Black's confectioners. Moving on to No 23, many people will remember when this was a post office. All that remains to remind us today is a pillar box on the pavement outside. Up on the corner, the *Belvedere Wine Vaults* is still open and still bears its original name.

The Eye Infirmary at 1-2 Belvedere.

Crossing over, No 25, on the corner, was WR Fletcher's, Family Butchers. The old shopfront has been replaced, and the shop is no longer trading. Round the side, at the back of No 26, was Fred Mill's fishmonger's, while at 26½ (now Anne le Coz's curtain shop) was Miss Ellen Guy, milliner and dressmaker. The curious numbering system indicates the haphazard way this side of the street was built, as does the frontage of No 27 – built onto the side of 26½ and facing downhill with only one window above ground floor – at attic level – on the side facing the street. Today occupied by Flooring Works, a century ago it was Herbert Price's butcher's; many of the external fittings survive to give an excellent idea of what an Edwardian butcher's looked like. The curved brackets supporting the canopy wrapped round the corner of the building doubled as hooks from which meat was hung; the grilles to carry cool air into the shop also survive, as does the long sash window round the corner, which would have been open during business hours, with the meat displayed on a slab behind it. The grilles, the open windows, the canopy and retractable blinds kept the temperature in butchers' shops several degrees below than that outside.

On the other side of Ainslie's Belvedere was Miss FM Smith's confectioners – now the Sofa & Sofabed Company. The shopfront

Above: Looking down Belvedere, with Fletcher's butcher's on the left.

Opposite: A postcard of the Beehive sent to Bridport on 28 April 1909 and believed to show the landlord, Ernest Nudds, leaning on the railings. The story of his tragic death eight years later can be found on page 310 of All Roads Lead to France; *the story of the Beehive can be found on pages 86-87 of* Bath Pubs.

survives, with modifications, but of greater interest is the legacy of an earlier owner – a painted sign, still visible, for 'Bosley: House, Sign & Decorative Painter', between the windows on the first floor. This type of sign was common in the nineteenth and early twentieth century, but later fell out of favour; when houses were spruced up, the opportunity was generally taken to remove them. The few that survive are a fading reminder of a time when Bath's buildings were covered with words on walls in the most vibrant colours available.

Next door, No 28 still retains its original, rather fine porch, but beyond that, at No 29, change from domestic to commercial use has been celebrated with extraordinary exuberance. The building is now occupied by Tina Engell, a contemporary jeweller, but its original purpose is still proclaimed by words chiselled

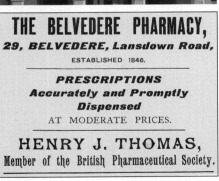

into a superb, classically-inspired Victorian shopfront – Harding's Belvedere Pharmacy. Mr Thomas, who ran the pharmacy a century ago, also worked as a dentist.

Next door but one, tacked onto the side of a five-storey building, a modest two-storey structure, which still retains its shopfront, was home to Edwin Mead's newsagent's and stationers. Curry Mahal, at No 31, beside the archway leading down to Wellington Terrace, one of the streets that disappeared in the Hedgemead landslip, was E Bailey's greengrocer's. No 32, next door, which also retains its shopfront, was Walter Mallard's dairy. Frank Dux's antique shop, at No 33, was home to Edwin Hopkins, a decorator, while No 34, now Antique Textiles, was home to a plumber called Charles Rich.

On the other side of the entrance to Hedgemead Park – once a street that led into the warren of alleys and closes that covered the hillside – a gateway leads to the front door of Hartley House, built in the early eighteenth century when everything else around here was fields. In the 1890s, Hartley House was the home of William Harbutt, who invented plasticine in the basement. By

1909, he was living out at Bathampton, near his newly-opened plasticine factory, and Hartley House had been acquired by Jolly's as lodgings for its staff. The building to the right of the gateway now forms part of Hartley House, but was originally separate and in 1909 housed a branch of Brook's Dye Works. Brook's had started up as dyers and cleaners at Castle Street in Bristol in 1819; ninety years later, they had numerous branches. In Bath, they could also be found at 11 Argyle Street, 73 Lower Bristol Road and 18 Chelsea Road. The imposing shopfront has been replaced with a domestic-style frontage.

Next door, the charming two-storey gabled building, with a nod in the direction of half-timbering, long familiar as Ann King's antique clothes shop, was Thomas Taylor's bootmakers. Today, there is no indication that No 39 was ever a shop, but a century ago it was Arthur Ashman's greengrocer's. Next door, Challenger International Letting Agency, with an impressive frontage wrapped round the corner of Guinea Lane, was Percy Batten's grocery and provision merchant's. This was a grocer's as recently as the 1980s, when it was famous as S Johnson's West Indian Grocer's.

So ends our tour of a fairly typical out-of-town shopping street a century ago. We could have continued on up Lansdown Road, past the Old Farmhouse pub – still trading – where there were more shops – a dairy at No 2, a baker and confectioner at No 3, a grocer and wine merchant at No 4, a greengrocer at No 9, another grocer at No 18 … or carried on down Belmont … or along Julian Road …

Edwardian shoppers may not have been as affluent as today's, but they had a seemingly unlimited choice of traders to patronise – and any who were off-hand or pricey, or whose goods failed to come up to the mark, would not have survived very long.

One reason for the number of out-of-town shopping centres, as mentioned earlier, was the lack of domestic refrigeration, which made it necessary to shop for perishable items on a daily basis. It wasn't practicable – either for servants shopping for their employers or housewives shopping for their families – to walk any distance on a daily basis just for a few items. Lack of effective refrigeration was a problem for shopkeepers as well. Turnover had to be quicker than it is today, and in the height of summer the items most likely to go off were simply not available – hence those half-forgotten strictures about only eating certain foods when there was an 'r' in the month.

We will end this walk up and down Belvedere with a couple of short diversions to look at some words on walls advertising businesses that were there in 1909. Down Guinea Lane, at No 17, the bressemer bears the legend 'William Cottell, Furniture Remover', while over at the end of Rivers Street can be seen, behind the small

white building on the corner – once a branch of the Red House Bakery – a red-painted reminder of this long-gone business.

Many out-of-town shopping centres have totally disappeared. Peter Street, for example, which a century ago boasted a greengrocer, three butchers, a poulterer, a wood merchant, a dressmaker, a fish-monger, a wheelwright, an undertaker, a coal merchant, a bootmaker, a blacksmith, two pubs and a coffee house, lies underneath City of Bath College. Kingsmead Street, largely destroyed by bombing in the Second World War, was one of the busiest streets in the city. Over in Widcombe, Holloway, almost totally demolished in the late 1960s, had four pubs, two dairies, four grocers, two newsagents, two coffee houses, a fishmonger, a fancy draper, seven bootmakers,

The bottom of Holloway in the early 1900s.

three butchers, two confectioners, two greengrocers, a hairdresser, two antique dealers, an oil store, two coal merchants, two bakers, three dressmakers and a brewer. On the rebuilt Holloway, there is not a single shop.

Similar lists could be drawn up for many other streets. In a few places, where the hand of progress has not fallen so heavily, reminders of the retail trade that once flourished can still be found. Take one of the most atmospheric parts of the old city, Queen Street, that byway leading northward through an arch from Trim Street. Its air of faded gentility and olde-worlde shop fronts give it the feeling of a place Jane Austen may have wandered down while pondering the intricacies of one of her plots. As indeed she might have done: in 1805, she lived for a few months just around the corner in Trim Street. By 1909, though, it was a gritty, no nonsense neck of town, echoing to the sounds of machinery, shouts of workmen and carts rattling over uneven setts.

At No 1, at the bottom right-hand corner under the arch – now the Bo Lee Gallery – was Brooks the Bakers, which many will still

remember. No 2 was home to two bootmakers, a coach-smith and a plate and silver polisher, while at No 3 was Robert Castle, clock maker and antique dealer. Today Nos 2 and 3 are the Restaurant de l'Arche, although many will still remember a previous incarnation – the Canary Café. No 4 – offices today – was a warehouse in 1909. No 5 – home to the recently-closed Mary Shaw Studios – was Room's Gasfitters. At 6 and 7 – now the *Raven* – was HR Fuller's Wine Merchant's.

Harington's Hotel now occupies Nos 8 to 10 on the other side of the road. A century ago, only No 9 was business premises, occupied by William Paisey, a cutler. The shopfront looks to be a later addition, possibly put in when the Little Kitchen Restaurant was at 9 and 10 (at the same time that the Piccolino Coffee Bar was at No 8).

No 10a, on the southern corner of Harington Place – until recently Blackstone's Kitchen – was part of Lee's Bag & Box Works, the main entrance of which was on Trim Street. The shopfront of

No 11, like those across the street at Nos 2 and 3, dates from around 1760. Today, No 11 is Vintage Kit, a children's clothes shop; a century ago it was Richard Meden's tailor's. Fred Duck, a packer was at No 12 in 1909; today it is home to an interior design business. The shopfront is a twentieth-century addition. Next door, under the archway, at 4 Trim Street, was the *Cabinet Makers' Arms*.

Most of Trim Street was given over to workshops and factories. West of the archway, on the north side of the street, was Lee & Sons' Bag & Box Works (which extended back to Harington Place and later took over the *Cabinet Maker's Arms*) and EJ Adams, Engravers, Letterpress & Lithographic Printers. Trimbridge House (the council planning office) now occupies the site of both businesses.

Facing it, the large eighteenth-century buildings with the shell porches were home, in 1909, to Drew, Son & Butcher's staymaking factory. On the corner of Trim Bridge, the shop with a bay window dating from around 1800 – now Wisteria Nails, but until recently Needful Things Interiors & Gifts, and before that Secession Books[1] – was the offices of Copestake, Crampton & Co[2], warehousemen.

Today, these streets, where some of the shops seem to be ever changing, may be one of Bath's most atmospheric corners, but a century ago they housed the sort of businesses that have since migrated to industrial estates. Even the local pub took its name from the cabinet making trade.

Queen Street not only provides a fascinating glimpse of how the city has changed over the last century – it also stands as a memorial to people power. If the plan to build a road tunnel under Bath in

---

1 Its stalactite-encrusted cellar, mired with the dust of centuries, was the venue, as recently as 2005, for one of the most celebrated subterranean celebrations of recent years, the launch of Stanley Donwood's *Slowly Downward*, with selected lugubrious and atmospheric readings by Mr Ric Jerrom.

2 A Donwoodesque name if ever there was one.

1972 had gone ahead, as it very nearly did, it wouldn't be standing at all. In its place would be a busy road in a 20-foot cutting, leading to the western portal of the tunnel. So, instead of walking down Queen Street, you'd have walked over a patch of weedy grass, to be brought up short by a high fence and a panoramic view of the roaring traffic below.

The tunnel was to run from the Upper Bristol Road to the London Road. Traffic interchanges at either end would have involved the demolition of large numbers of buildings in the New King Street and Walcot Street areas. Some did indeed disappear, so convinced were the planners and politicians that it would go ahead; many more were bought and boarded up. It was the local government elections of 1972, in which independent and tunnel-action-group candidates shifted the balance of power decisively away from supporters of the scheme, that effectively killed it – hopefully for ever.

The legacy of that bitter struggle was the areas earmarked for the transport interchanges being left in a right old state – many buildings empty and running to ruin, businesses that had traded for generations closed, the communities that had supported them scattered to the four winds. Although, by and large, they escaped wholesale redevelopment, they still bear the scars.

It is almost as if they are forgotten parts of the city, which is odd when you consider how many people drive through them on a daily basis. For those who take the trouble to get out of their cars or off the bus and take a look at these areas, though, they have much to offer. Neglect has meant preservation – and not in aspic. There is, here and there, dereliction, it is true, but for the most part, buildings have been adapted to new uses by people who have created new communities and new businesses out of the ashes of the old. They are probably too close to the city to escape gentrification for ever – even though the current recession may stave it off for a while – but, for the moment, they provide some of the best opportunities to understand what life was like a century ago, not because they've been tarted up to look Edwardian, but because they're a century older and not that much has happened to them.

Monmouth Place, on the Upper Bristol Road, not only has some early shopfronts; it also has some of the oldest buildings in the city, predating anything (except the Abbey and the Roman Baths) the tourists flock to Bath to see. Despite having Norfolk Crescent at the back and the Royal Crescent across the fields, this was never a fashionable purlieu. No 11 Monmouth Place, just west of Little

Stanhope Street (the west side of which was largely demolished for the tunnel) is one of the older buildings; the curious extension at the front, with windows only covering enough of the frontage

Coles' bootmaker's in Monmouth Place – an extraordinary survival.

to admit light and let people see in, housed the business of William Coles, a shoemaker, a century ago – an extraordinary survival. The shop on the corner of Nile Street, currently boarded up – a good example of unostentatious nineteenth-century design – was Hill's grocer's in 1909. The sign above the door has unfortunately been painted out.

Back towards town, at 8 Monmouth Place, the sign of the *Royal Oak*, which closed in 1961, can still be seen – probably looking much as it did in 1909. It's also worth walking round to the back of the *Royal Oak*, in a court that, a century ago, would have been full of children playing and washing strung from windows, to look up at its crazily-pitched, off-kilter roof – originally thatched – and wonder what refrontings and changes it has seen.

For a real sense of the number and variety of shops a century ago we need to head across town to the top of Walcot Street. Here the shadow of the tunnel had an unexpected effect; the vacuum created by people moving out and businesses closing down was filled by a grassroots resurgence of community action, spearheaded by groups such as the Bath Arts Workshop, and culminating in day-long street parties and the declaration – à la Passport to Pimlico – of Walcot Nation in 1979.

Since then, gentrification has crept on apace, with Walcot Street rebranded, by someone with a curious line in irony, as Bath's 'artisan quarter' – just as the craft workshops and industries that had been there for centuries started to be pushed out to make way for upmarket residential developments behind locked gates, to keep the artisans out. It's still, for the moment at least, the liveliest street in Bath, thanks largely to the continued survival of the *Bell*, even though its erstwhile bedfellow, the ever-edgy, ever-unpredictable, ever-varied *Hat & Feather* has gone.

The story of Walcot Street is far too large and far too inappropriate a subject to be dealt with here – and to get an idea what this part of town was like a century ago we need to head up to the top of the street, where the tide of gentrification has, for the moment, faltered. Today, where once butchers, bakers and grocers held sway, antique shops, furniture emporia and takeaways predominate; many of the old shopfronts survive, however, to give a flavour of a world long gone.

We will start, just past the old mortuary chapel, at 138 Walcot Street, with its modest, but very attractive double-fronted bay windows – Davis's Rag Merchant's a century ago but now the Moghul Takeway. Next door is the Fine Grime Gallery; beyond that the Advertising Shop. A century ago, they were Henry Batham's bootmaker's and Fred Bean's confectioner's respectively. Nothing much seems to have happened to these shopfronts, but something has happened to the level of the street – note how the doorway of the Advertising Shop is below street-level, with the pavement sloping up past it.

Next door, however, at No 146 (a bookshop for many years, but Joseph Kelly's clothes store a century ago), the entrance is on the level. This is a much grander affair, double-fronted, with large windows, an entrance lobby and book-end consoles at each end of the sign board, indicating that the shopfront dates from the 1890s or 1900s. If we look up to first-floor level, the gable-end indicates that, unlike the buildings to the right, it dates not from the eighteenth or early nineteenth century, but from the same time as the shopfront. Looking at late nineteenth-century maps, we can piece together what has happened here. The original building on this site stood several feet further forward than the one that is there now, as did the ones further up the street. It would have made the street very narrow – and that is why the council ordered the whole block to be set back around 1900. In 1909, 146 Walcot Street and the whole of London Street was an example of state-of-the-art commercial development.

The three- and four-storey Bath-stone terraces that make up London Street were, unlike the gabled building at the end of Walcot Street, built to harmonise with the Georgian terraces nearby. They were, to Edwardian Bath, what the new Southgate is to twenty-first-century Bath. London Street does not, however, consist of what Jonathan Glancey, the *Guardian's* architectural correspondent, has termed 'bulky concrete boxes pasted over with little more than a veneer of Bath stone ... dolled up in a style you might call Las Vegas Georgian for its soulless imitation'. It was built of Bath stone by builders and craftsmen who understood Georgian design and proportion. A particularly pleasing touch is the ramped cornice and string course on the buildings leading uphill, a device used extensively by John Pinch. And, perhaps more importantly, a hundred years on it looks as though it will be good for a least another hundred.

Many of the shopfronts in London Street have been altered, but a few look as though nothing has happened to them since the day they were built – providing a useful indication of how much the restored ones have changed. London Street is still a vibrant shopping street, but the businesses there today are far more eclectic, exotic and – in one case at least – mind-blowing than they were back in 1909.

No 1 seems never to have been a shop. No 2 – which was unoccupied in 1909 – is no longer a shop, but still retains its original glazing, recessed lobby, security grille and a canopy bearing the name of 'The Artistic Blind Company, Bath'. No 3 – once George Maslen's bakery – is Jack & Danny's Vintage Clothing Store, the

No 4 London Street – once Wake's newsagent's and tobacconist's, now purveying somewhat more heady wares, but with its original shopfront little changed.

upholder of a long-standing Bath tradition. There were ten second-hand clothes shops in Bath in 1909 – seven of them in the Monmouth Street area. At No 4, which wasn't occupied in 1909, but subsequently became – as the old sign indicates – FW Wake's Newsagent's & Tobacconist's, is the Appy Daze Hemporium – not something you'd have found in Edwardian Bath, although use of cannabis for medical and recreational purposes was still legal back then. Even Queen Victoria was prescribed it as a painkiller.

At No 5, where William Flint worked as a tailor and

Street music, 21st-century style: Nick Cudworth entertains passers-by outside his gallery during the 2009 Bath Fringe Festival.

his wife sold stationery, is a gallery featuring the wonderfully atmospheric and occasionally surreal paintings of Nick Cudworth, which celebrates its tenth anniversary in 2009. In contrast to Nos 2-5 – double-fronted, with entrance lobbies – No 6 is single-fronted and only half the width. Today it's Walcot Sandwich Bar; in 1909 it was John Spencer's boot and shoe shop.

The remaining shopfronts in the row – with one honourable exception – have either been replaced or altered. No 7 – W & J Warren's greengrocer's in 1909 – is Zeitgeist Eastern Textiles; No 8 isn't a shop today and wasn't in 1909. No 9 was also unoccupied in 1909, while No 10 was CO Davis's china & glass shop; today Terry & Sons' butcher's can be found at 9 and 10.

The shopfront of No 11 – formerly Scott Antiques but Albert Glisson's greengrocer's in 1909 – is gloriously unrestored, splendidly untinkered about with, so that we can readily imagine what it was like a century ago, when the paint was hardly dry. Not only does it still have its sash windows, which would have been rolled up to

A. Glisson, Commission Agent, 11, London Street, Bath.
Telephone 475.

F. G. Goodall, Bath.

369

display the goods inside; the old bracket for the gas light above the entrance has survived as well.[3] The shops at this end of the row, unlike those at the other, have no entrance lobbies. There are other differences too: the ramped cornice and string course disappear as the street levels out; the consoles at either end of the signboards are more prominent, and, if we lift our eyes skywards, we will see that the buildings have an extra storey.

The last two shops in this row – 12 and 13 – were CW Jones' pork butcher's and William Brimble's oil & colour warehouse a century ago. Today, No 12 is part of TR Hayes' furniture store, while at No 13 is the Fine Art Print Co.

The row that makes up the rest of London Street was built with a pub at each end and three shops in between. At the west end was the *Hat & Feather*; at the east was the *Three Crowns*, with some superb terracotta moulding and a capacious entrance lobby. In between were Miss R Johnson's hardware store, a shop which was unoccupied in 1909, and HA Newport's tailor's, hatter's & outfitter's. Today, everything except the old *Hat & Feather* (now the *Hudson Bar*) is part of TR Hayes' furniture store.

Some of the much older buildings that survived the redevelopment of London Street can be seen behind the old *Three Crowns*, giving an idea of what the area might once have looked like. The shop on the corner of the next row – Nelson Place East – is another part of the TR Hayes empire. It is also another superb example of an old butcher's shop, with grilles, canopy, hooks, shutter keeps and shutter slots all intact, and the old shutters converted to windows – an example of how original features can be incorporated into a new shopfront without being ruined in the process. The butcher here in 1909 was Fred Young. As at 27 Belvedere, the corner site meant that windows could be opened on two

Young's butcher's on the corner of Nelson Place East – now part of TR Hayes' furniture store.

sides, helping to create the through draught so essential to keep temperatures down in hot weather.[4]

---

3 A Glisson's delivery cart can be seen outisde the Castle Hotel in the photograph on page 327.

4 The most ornate and unusual former butcher's in Bath can be found in the covered entrance to St James's Place from St James's Square, where an intricately decorated gable leads into a passageway lined with hooks.

Next door, No 2 has a classic Edwardian shopfront – curved windows creating a lobby with art-nouveau tiling, book-end consoles and a clerestory with small square lights stretching  the length of the frontage. Currently closed, in 1909 it was Reginald Richards' watchmaker's and jeweller's. The three remaining shops in Nelson Place East – Rapid Repairs, the Yummy House Takeaway and Laptop Repairs – all retain their old shopfronts, albeit modified. A century ago, the businesses here were S Boon's hairdresser's, George Stone's bakery and Henry William's stationer's.

On the far side of Walcot Methodist Church comes Cleveland Terrace, and a splendid display of words on walls – 'Nestle's Swiss Milk: Richest in Cream: Sold HJ Archard' is still legible, but nearer the street it gets a bit more tricky. The insertion of a window and earlier lettering showing through underneath don't help, but 'Devonshire Dairy', with 'depot' showing through from an earlier sign, and 'Bovril' below it, can be just about  made out, along with other tantalising letters and blocks of colour. The shopfront of the building on the corner – much earlier than those further up the street – has survived, albeit much altered, and with tiles overlaying the original design. As indicated by the  Nestle's sign, a century ago the shop here was owned by HJ Archand, and, as the other sign indicates, it was a dairy. What neither sign tells us, however, is that it was also a grocer's, provision merchant's and post office. Today, it is Walcot Upholstery.

The four shops below Walcot Upholstery, with a superb iron balcony running along at first-floor level, are filled today with antiques. Several shopfronts have been replaced, but No 4 is a particularly fine and particularly well-preserved early quadrant-ended shopfront

4 Cleveland Terrace.

from around 1830, with some original glass, shutter keeps, and recessed panels for door shutters; in 1909, JT Bath, a watchmaker, and Herbert Hart, a photographer, operated from here. At the far end of Cleveland Terrace – Martin & Cos Estate Agent's today – was Norris's chemist's. The old shopfront has gone but the splendid bracket that once held the sign still survives.

Next door, at 13 Cleveland Place West, the canopy studded with hooks tells us that this was once a butcher's, even though the old shopfront has been replaced by the modern façade of the Golden Plaice. The butcher here in 1909 was Benjamin Shaul.

Before crossing over – a far more protracted affair than it would have been a century ago – and heading down London Road, a few features of Cleveland Place East and West in 1909 are worth looking

out for. The *Curfew* pub was a wine merchant's; over the road, the Dispensary, its name still chiselled into the stonework, but its function long since taken over by doctors' surgeries and hospital outpatients' departments, was where the 'sick poor' from the east of the city went for medical treatment. They were charged sixpence for their first visit, but subsequent visits were free, as long as they could produce a recommendation paper signed by one of the dispensary subscribers. There were two other dispensaries in the city – at 1 Albion Place on the Upper Bristol Road and in Claverton Street. There was also, as we will see shortly, an Ear and Eye Infirmary.

Next door but one to the Dispensary, at 6 Cleveland Place, was the Bath & West of England College of Chemistry & Pharmacy, founded in 1907. It later expanded into No 5, before moving to Bristol in 1929, where it formed part of the Merchant Venturers' College and later the College of Advanced Technology. In 1966,

Below: A 1981 photograph of the sign for the Bath & West of England College of Chemistry & Pharmacy. It is much fainter today.

This sign, advertising Pyke & Sons', who once occupied the premises on the corner of Cleveland Place East, has been painted out altogether. This is how it looked in 1981.

it moved to Claverton Down as part of the University of Bath. Today Nos 5 and 6 house a signmakers and a computer shop. The present shopfronts were inserted after the college moved to Bristol. The shopfront next door at No 7 – the Crouching Tiger takeaway – is also relatively modern.

The rather fine shopfronts to the right of the old college – Nos 1 to 4 – look to date from around 1909. At No 4, its lobby framed by curved windows, was J Sampson, pharmacist, photographic chemist and optician. At Nos 1 to 3 – London Road Stores and the former premises of the Iron Bed Company – was Pyke & Sons – Linen Drapers, Silk Mercers & Undertakers.

Beyond Cleveland Place is London Road, familiar to the thousands of motorists who drive – or more likely crawl – along it daily. Few people, unless they live hereabouts, walk along it; fewer still pause to take in the view, with the result that this is a penumbral, half-forgotten part of Bath. If it were in some unfrequented quarter, down a cul-de-sac where few ventured, it would doubtless be a place of pilgrimage for those in search of the old and picturesque; here, with cars and lorries grinding past mere inches away, it is another street on the way to somewhere else. But, just as, pulling up at the side of some busy, familiar highway, and stepping through a gap in the hedge, we would find ourselves in a landscape never before seen and never suspected, so it is – unlikely as it may seem – with London Road.

Take, for example, the ironwork on the first building we come to, 1 Canton Place, with the railings of the balcony matching those below the hanging bay. A century ago, Charles Hansford, the deputy parish clerk of Walcot, ran a tobacconist's here. At the back of the building, some indistinct words, which may date from this time, appear above the first-floor windows; at the time they would have been visible from Cleveland Bridge. Next door, at No 2, were Kate Price, milliner and fancy draper (who was fined five shillings

373

George Stuart, Semple & Sons' at 2 Walcot Terrace.

in March 1909 for sweeping the footway in front of her shop) and Coleby & Son's, builders and decorators. Both shops are now occupied by Sulis Pianos.

No 1 Walcot Terrace, currently the home of the Bath Centre for Psychotherapy and Counselling, was Mrs Raine's confectioners; at No 2 were George Stuart, Semple & Son, pianoforte dealers. At the far end of Walcot Terrace – No 8 – was Willway's Dye Works & Laundry Co. Dyeworks, once common on the streets of our towns and cities, disappeared decades ago. Luckily, however, a description of the long-forgotten business on Walcot Terrace has survived.

It forms part of a biographical sketch of Reginald Ainsworth, born at 8 Walcot Terrace on 7 July 1882, written by his sister, Lucy Wates:

This house in Bath, 8 Walcot Terrace, was the business premises of Willway's, dyers and cleaners, and had been run by his grandmother since the death of her invalid husband, James, in Australia in 1860. In this home she had brought up, with devotion and considerable sacrifice, her five children – the eldest Lydia, Reginald's mother, being only nine years old on the death of her father.

Grandmamma was small, frail and delicate but of indomitable will, and her influence over her children was such that no important step was ever taken by them without her advice, even when her two sons and three daughters had reached middle age. In times of trouble she was always their refuge.

She liked to be with them in illness and so it came about that Reginald's mother was in her old home when the baby was born. It was a terraced Georgian house. Its windows at the back looked out over the valley across the River Avon to the hills beyond, and the bedroom with curtained bed was peaceful enough in spite of the business being carried out on the floor below.

There was plenty of interest for children in the dye works – the large room behind the 'shop' littered with pieces of cloth, trimmings and cuttings from the unpicking; the old sideboard at one end of the room in which was the 'till', sometimes containing very little money, hardly enough to pay the wages of the workmen at the end of the week; and the large table in the centre of the room round which and under which a child or children were always playing in spite of the busy business life that was going on around them. There was a basement kitchen and steep narrow stairs led to it, on which one hesitated to hear the crickets chirruping in the walls.

The garden was hardly worthy of the name, but it had sparse patches of grass, a few vegetables and, at one time, some fowls. On either side were low wide walls on which it was possible to walk if one could avoid the eyes of Miss Barker, the schoolmistress next door, and a vigilant grandmother or aunt looking from the vine-covered balcony windows of the 'shop'.

The Dye House (now pulled down) was a solid stone building on two floors. On the upper one worked an ogre, Parker the presser, in an atmosphere of oppressive moist heat which was always unbearable. It was a temptation to plague him by throwing small pebbles through this window and escape by the skin of one's teeth from the enraged Parker who, armed with a flat iron, threatened with dire punishment the fleeing boy. The dye was in great steaming vats and had to be stirred with long sticks or poles and the materials dipped and lifted until they were well permeated with the dye. These huge black vats, the dark steam enveloping figures of the men and the acrid smell of the dye gave a Dante-esque impression to the scene, and it was with a somewhat awesome feeling that the children entered into it. A newly installed wringing contrivance was used to extract the moisture from the dyed or cleaned articles by centrifugal force. When not in use this was regarded as a toy by venturesome children, but the use of it for that purpose was not regarded with favour by the foreman in charge.

Beyond the dye-house was the bank of the river and the dye ran into it through pipes or channels staining the river water with wonderful eddies of swirling colour.

Across the river was the 'garden', a plot of land which had been in the possession of the family for many years and in which grew fruit and vegetables and straggling old-fashioned rose trees. This supplied the family with all they needed in garden produce and was reached by crossing the Cleveland Bridge at the cost of ½d per person or a 'season ticket'.

Next to the dyeworks, the building with a Greek Revival portico – now an undertakers – with the bust of Aesculapius, God of Healing, above the door, was the Ear & Eye Infirmary. Its former function is revealed, faintly, in words on the side wall. It only became an infirmary in 1837, however; the presence of a large cold bath underneath the floor suggests that it was originally built as a bath house, with the portico added later. Perhaps it formed part of a small complex of buildings, together with  Hawthorn Cottage and what is now the Salisbury Club, before the developers moved in and built the terraces on either side.

Although this amble along the London Road was intended to stick sedulously to the south side (the north having been comprehensively redeveloped), we can't continue without a brief glance across the road at one of Bath's lost trading empires – Longacre Secondhand (or Longacre Econdhand as the sign now reads) – and one of its most extraordinary nineteenth-century shopfronts. It's also the only shop in Bath to be immortalised in song – the Zen Hussies' *Skeleton Store Detective*:

King Louis lou aye Irie
Him got dem 20ᵗʰ century antiques
Household clearance while you wait
Done dem now at a reasonable rate.

Sadly, the '20th Century Antiques While You Wait' sign on the panels to the right of the door, which inspired the lyrics, is now obliterated by posters advertising local gigs. How long before the place is tarted up and all reminders of King Louis are swept away is anyone's guess.

Past the Salisbury Club comes Walcot Buildings, another lost shopping centre, where people could find everything they needed on a day-to-day basis. Many of the shops are closed; others house specialist furnishing or design businesses, antique shops and fast-food outlets. Modern shopfronts have replaced the old ones in a few cases, but a remarkable number have survived, many little changed since the street's heyday.

At No 1, with a shopfront projecting forward from the building, was William Hockey's grocer's. Next door – Bedsteads today – was Maria Howell's tobacconist's. At No 3 – with a canopy supported by supremely graceful brackets – was Cooper & Sons' butchers. A surprise awaits us here, for, peering through the windowpanes, we can see an array of tins, many a century old or more, and bearing images of Edwardian heroes such as Baden Powell. This specialist collectors' shop, which also stocks decorative furniture, is owned by Michael and Jo Saffell and has been here for over a quarter of a century.

Above: One of the finest butcher's shop frontages in Bath, now Michael and Jo Saffell's antique shop.

Below: A century ago, 5 Walcot Buildings was Forte's newsagent's.

Next door was a pub, the *Black Dog*; the shopfront is a modern addition. Not so the shopfront next door, at No 5, which dates from the early nineteenth century; in 1909 this was Miss Forte's newsagent's. The attraction at No 7 is not the shopfront but the words above the first-floor windows – 'Walcot Fruit & Potato Stores'. In 1909 it was run by WR Marchant. At No 7, now Bespoke Kitchens, was James Cobb & Co, Bakers and Confectioners.

Unlike the rest of the buildings in the row, which have four storeys, Nos 8 to 11 are only two storeys high, and look to have been a later infill. Nos 8 and 9, which housed Williams & Worrell, house decorators, and Mrs Williams' furniture store in 1909, have modern shopfronts. However, Nos 10 and 11 – George Johnson's bakery and Joseph Thomas's cobbler's in 1909 – have retained their nineteenth-century facades. No 10, with its original underbay railings and security grille, is particularly fine.

Nos 12 and 13, although no longer shops, retain their nineteenth-century bay fronts. Mr and Mrs Palmer lived at No 12 – he was a painter, she sold stationery; next door, at No 13, were James Pugsley, a bootmaker, and Mrs Smith, who ran a newsagent's.

The Old Bank Antiques Centre occupies Nos 14 to 17. Almost by definition, antique dealers can usually be relied upon to retain original features, and this is no exception. Nos 14, 15 and 16 are much as they would have appeared in 1909,

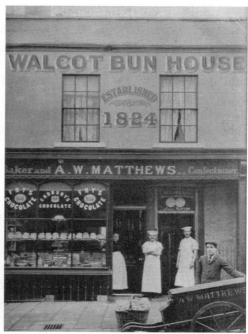

Top: A photograph of the art-nouveau shopfront at 12 Walcot Buildings around 1920 when it was Furze's café.

Above right: Before George Johnson took over the bakery at 10 Walcot Buildings it was run by AW Matthews and known as the Walcot Bun House. Here it is seen around 1906.

Above: 10 Walcot Buildings today.

378

while the old bank at No 17, which gives the antiques centre its name, sports a classically-inspired frontage added in the 1920s. It was empty in 1909, but later there was a tailor's here before it was acquired by the National Provincial Bank. At 14 and 15 was Hine & Collinson's ironmonger's, while 16 was Lydia Wyld's dressmaker's.

At No 18 was Charles Dark's dairy, with Lucy May's newsagent's and toy shop at No 19. On the corner of the row – No 20 – with a window round the side, was CB Farr's greengrocer's. Maintaining the toy connection, No 19 was, until recently, a nursery, while No 20 forms part of the Old Bank Antiques Centre.

On the other side of Bedford Street (where there was a butcher and a baker, as well as a number of other tradesmen and women) was J Batten's grocer's. Today, with a modern frontage, it is a Chinese takeaway. Another takeaway, with another modern shopfront, is at the other end of the row of six buildings, with Nixey's domestic appliance store and a courier firm in between. In 1909, Mrs Winckworth, draper and milliner, was at No 22, Miss Drabble, feather cleaner, at No 23, JA King, builder and decorator, at No 24, William Connett, butcher, at No 25, and F Riddle, greengrocer, at No 26. The roofless and derelict warehouse building tacked onto the back of No 26 is of

Above: Looking along Weymouth Street towards the back of 26 Walcot Buildings

Below: White's pork butcher's at 29 Walcot Buildings.

a type that was once common in Bath, but is now rare, especially in this unrestored and dilapidated state. It won't last for ever; the tide of redevelopment is already lapping at its feet, but for now it still stands, a mute but potent reminder of what much of working Bath looked like a century ago.

We are almost at the end of Walcot Buildings now, with three shops to go. On the corner of the last row, the Old Pet Shop Design Centre has taken its name from the painted signs, advertising pet food, at first-floor level. The signs are only around 50 years old, however. In 1909, this was Townsend's china shop, which lasted until the 1950s, when the pet shop took over.

Next to it were two butchers – Tripp's at No 28 and George White's pork butcher's at No 29. The shopfront at No 28 has been replaced by ashlar blocks and domestic windows, restoring the building to its original appearance, but No 29 has another classic butcher's shopfront. Its windows have, it is true, been replaced, but the way in which it has sagged, as if exhausted by decades of hard work, give it a charm and character all it own, and one which provides a fitting conclusion to this walk down one of Bath's most fascinating lost shopping streets.

Perhaps 'lost' is too strong a word – after all, many of the shops are still trading. But while a handful – the butchers, the second-hand clothes shop, the piano warehouse and the general stores – would be familiar to Edwardian shoppers – in many cases they would be baffled at the goods and services offered.

The shops in the main thoroughfares of the city have fared better than those in side streets and suburban areas. Although shopping habits and fashions have been transformed beyond recognition, jeweller's and clothes shops are as much in evidence now as they were a century ago. Milsom Street is still the most fashionable street in town, even if William Howells, visiting Bath in 1905, found its vaunted charms rather overstated:

> The modern handbook which was guiding our steps around Bath advised us that if we would frequent Milsom Street about four o'clock we should find the tide of fashion flowing through it; but the torrent must have been very rapid indeed, for we always missed it, and were obliged to fill the rather empty channel from the gaiety of the past. There are delightful shops everywhere in Bath, but it is in Milsom Street that most of the fine shops are, and I do not deny that you will see some drops from the tide of fashion clustered about their windows.

The buildings in Milsom Street were originally designed as lodging houses, the shopfronts being inserted later. The genteel hand of decay, which we have seen ample evidence of elsewhere, has not had chance to take hold here. Yet, although many shopfronts have been replaced – some more than once – an astonishing number have survived. The Edwardian period was one of the high points of shopfront design. The heaviness of late Victorian design – seen at its fussiest in Major Davis's 1879 design for Jolly's at 11-13

Milsom Street – gave way to a lightness of touch, with classical columns or pilasters replaced by narrow, cylindrical glazing bars in the form of colonnettes, and high windows curving into long, tapered entrance lobbies. Other characteristic features were large book-end console brackets and decorative glass in the upper part of the windows.

The supplanting of Victorian ideas of shopfront design happened over a very short period of time. A striking example of how fast Victorian modes fell out of favour can be found at 46 Milsom Street. In 1900 it was exuberantly refronted by Silcock & Reay, with a row of heavy stone columns framing the windows on the ground-floor. Just over ten years later, the columns on either side of the entrance were removed and curved windows with narrow glazing bars, leading to an entrance lobby, installed. Although the columns at either end were retained, the shopfront was totally transformed: Victorian weight and stolidity replaced by graceful curves.

No 46 Milsom Street as refronted in 1900, and (right), as altered around ten years later.

Milsom Street has several more classic Edwardian shop-fronts. No 3, now Mayther's Card Shop but Walker & Ling's fancy drapers and ladies' outfitters a century ago, was designed by CB Oliver in 1911. No 32, slightly earlier but even more elegant, was designed by Silcock & Reay in 1902. The matching side entrance (now leading to the Bengal Brasserie but originally the entrance to Lambert & Lambert's photographic studios) was added in 1909.

Walker & Ling's draper's and outfitter's, refronted with curved windows framing a tapered entrance lobby in 1911.

More functional is No 31, designed for WH Smith's bookseller's and newsagent's by J Foster in 1909. Stationery is still sold here – by Paperchase – today. The shopfront at No 25, although not running to the expense of curved glass or a deep entrance lobby, has the thin cylindrical glazing bars characteristic of the period. It was designed by J Long in 1904.

Many of the shops in George Street received an Edwardian makeover as well. Nos 6 and 11 were redesigned by Spackman & Son in 1909. No 6 has a restrained elegance, with no decorative frieze; the mosaic in the lobby bears the name of the original proprietor – Vaughan, a florist and fruiterer. No 11, although similar in outline, takes advantage of its wider frontage by having matching windows and a wider door. It is the superb curvilinear glazing bars with bevelled glass in the fanlight and the upper part of the windows and door, that catch the eye here.

Top: Silcock & Reay designed the shopfront of 32 Milsom Street in 1902.
Left: No 31 Milsom Street, a frontage designed for WH Smith's in 1909 by J Foster.
Bottom left: Vaughan's florist's and fruiterer's at 6 George Street, designed by Spackman & Son.
Below: The exuberant frontage of 11 George Street was also designed by Spackman & Son.

Other notable Edwardian shopfronts can be found at:

23 Brock Street, designed for Rawling's fruiterers by J Foster in 1907, with leaded lights in the clerestory windows on the Margaret's Buildings side. The exuberant elegance of the design is matched by the window display of Alexandra May's jewellery and gift emporium, which occupies the shop today.

12 New Bond Street, a superb design of 1906 by AJ Taylor for Tovey's watchmaker's and optician's, with large sheets of curved glass flanking the two entrance lobbies and art-nouveau mosaics.

14 Chatham Row, a modest but extremely attractive corner-shop design of 1906 by Henry West. Originally, a grocer's-cum-tailor's, today it is the Women's Aid shop.

55 New King Street (Rudge's electricians in 1909, Julian House bookshop today), dating from c1908; the photograph on the left dates from the 1930s, when it was home to Keepence's music and furniture store.

1 Burton Street (right): Lawrence's fruiterer's in 1909, Justice jewellers today, designed by J Foster in 1908.

The finest of these designs achieve an elegance, combined with utility, that has rarely been equalled since. Of those that came later, only the superb shopfront at 19 New Bond Street, with its recessed, black-and-white marble lobby surrounded by curved windows, designed in 1922 – and more a final flowering of Edwardian design than a radical change of direction – seems to match the best of what was produced in those years.

The late nineteenth century saw an attempt, spearheaded by the City Architect, Major Davis, to rebuild the centre of Bath in a style more appropriate to Bradford or Birmingham. As the council ordered buildings on many of the principal streets to be set back for road widening, so the opportunity was taken to rebuild them in a more imposing style.

The two former banks that flank the entrance to Milsom Street from George Street, in the Italian palazzo style, not only fail to blend in with the buildings around them; they disrupt the effect aimed at by the original builders in a brash and un-neighbourly way. No 24 – now a Loch Fyne fish restaurant – was built for the National Provincial Bank by Wilson & Willcox in 1865; No 23, now a bar, was built for the Wilts & Dorset Bank in 1875.

It is Major Davis's hand that lays most heavily on the city, however. Before setting the seal on his lifetime's work with the Empire Hotel, his projects included the north side of Quiet Street (1871), with its unfeasibly tall doorways, in a style more fitted to Haussmann's Paris than John Wood's Bath, and the Roundhouse building (now Pret a Manger) on the corner of Stall and Cheap Streets (1896). It was his design for the building at the corner of Cheap Street and High Street that was to prove most controversial, however.

On 15 April 1909, as debate raged over the proposed redevelopment of Bath Street, a correspondent calling himself

Excelsior wrote to the *Chronicle* denouncing

> the monstrous building at the corner of Cheap Street, glaring in its anomalous style, inconsistent with all other structures in the borough. Having completed the erection of the handsome municipal offices [the council] actually passed the plans for this unsightly building ... that would dwarf the new public offices, and was to be built of red brick! Indignant protests prevented that last outrage.

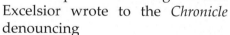

This spurred William Smith, who ran a trunk and bag shop there to leap, if not to the building's defence, at least to his own. 'My attention,' he wrote to the paper a few days later,

> has been called to a letter in your last Wednesday's issue, and, lest it be should be thought that I, as owner of the block of business premises at the corner of High Street and Cheap Street, am to blame for having caused to be erected the building that some consider unsightly, as towering above the adjacent buildings, I would ask you to insert this letter, in which I wish to point out that the elevations were prepared by the late Major Davis, and by him designed in his capacity as City Architect; and the site being corporate property, I had not much voice in the matter. As to the architectural merit of the building, I do not feel competent to express an opinion, but I can say from experience that, as regards position, accommodation and general suitability as business premises, it is admirable in every way.

The building which caused such offence in 1909 was not especially new, having been built in 1894. Today it is such an established part of Bath's streetscape that most people barely give it a second glance. Yet looked at objectively – and despite the excellence of its internal accommodation – it really is a shocker. It's not so much a case of it being an ugly design – in the right place it would be fine, but this is emphatically not the right place. It soars above the adjoining buildings (even though they are four storeys high), dominates the entrance to a narrow street and seems to be squaring up to the Abbey, as if it would like to shoulder it out of the way. It is un-neighbourly in the extreme, and, by being even more out of the human scale than the buildings around it, makes this corner of Bath that little bit more uninviting and unfriendly. It is a classic example of the effect bad architecture can have on us without us realising it. People realised it in 1909 because the building was relatively new, but even the worst buildings eventually blend in to the streetscape, however much they may degrade it. We should at least be grateful that Major Davis's original plan to build it of red brick was scotched by the council.

We can also be grateful that Major Davis was not around in 1909 when Green Street was redeveloped. Originally, the carriage entrance to Wiltshire's Yard was on the north side of the street, flanked by a pair of lodges, later home to a variety of small businesses. Dr Oliver established a bakery in the yard to make the Bath Oliver biscuits which he sold at the shop on the corner of

Above: Green Street in the eighteenth century, with the entrance to Wiltshire's Yard on the left flanked by a pair of lodges, and the Georgian St Michael's church at the end of the street.

Below: Fortt's new biscuit factory in Manvers Street, opened around 1908.

Bottom: The row of lock-up shops in Green Street, built in 1909-10.

Broad Street, which, although it is now a bar, still has his portrait above the door. The bakery was acquired by James Fortt in 1820 and subsequently expanded.

When Fortt's moved to new premises on Manvers Street, the Green Street site was acquired by Mallett's, jewellers, goldsmiths and antique dealers, based in the Octagon. In 1908, they were granted permission to demolish the lodges, set back the building line and build a row of three single-storey lock-up shops, designed by J Foster, which became 7, 8 and 9 Green Street. Nos 8 and 9 were completed in 1909 and became an antiques showroom for Mallett's, while No 7, completed a year later, was taken over by Hayward's milliner's.

Lock-up shops in the city centre were something of a novelty, but whoever decided against multi-storey buildings on this site deserves our continued gratitude. The three shops fit seamlessly into the streetscape, while providing the necessary break in the roofline that prevents Green Street from becoming a gloomy canyon. While they are not architectural showpieces, they are, taken together, a masterpiece of urban design, and one that today's town planners – such as those who designed the narrow streets and tall buildings of the new Southgate – could well leanr from.

Above: The row of lock-up shops at Lark Place.
Below: The shopping centre at Bear Flat.

Lock-up shops were built out of town, as well. The block on the corner of Upper Bristol Road and Park Lane – 14 to 16 Lark Place – were designed by Herbert Matthews in 1907. The original occupants were John Bennett, a shoemaker, Miss M Glass, a draper, and Miss Sants, a milliner. Elsewhere, where new shops were needed and existing buildings could not be adapted, traditional designs with living accommodation above were still the norm. One of the biggest developments was at the top of Holloway, at the junction with Wellsway. In 1906-7 AJ Taylor built a block of five shops (3-7 Hayes Place) on the west side of the road; in 1911-12, he eight more – one of them a bank – across the road on the site of Bruton Cottage.

CHAPTER TWENTY-FIVE
THE BUILDING OF BATH

The imposing shopping centre at the top of Holloway was built to serve one of the largest residential developments in the city. Often referred to as Poet's Corner – because its streets were named after poets – this greenfield site was transformed, over the course of about 20 years, into one of the most desirable locations in the city. There were similar developments elsewhere – on Villa Fields in Bathwick and in Oldfield Park, for example – and substantial building took place in other areas, such as Fairfield Park, Combe Down and the Bloomfield Road/Englishcombe Lane area.

It is a curious twist of fate that both 1909 and 2009 witnessed the end of sustained building booms. It remains to be seen, however, whether the buildings erected in the past decade or so will wear as well as those the Edwardians built. On balance, it seems unlikely; the early years of the twentieth century saw domestic architecture reach heights it has rarely, if ever, achieved before or since. In a city whose fame is built on its eighteenth-century terraces, squares and crescents, this may seem little short of apostasy, but, while the Georgian city may be glorious to look at, its effects were achieved by a kind of sleight of hand. To apply the epithet 'stage set' to it would be an overstatement; nevertheless, the pseudo-palatial series of lodging houses, built as a backdrop for eighteenth-century intrigue and abandonment, were in their own way as much of a sham as the castle Ralph Allen built overlooking the city. Go to the back of any of the superbly-proportioned, exquisitely-ornamented showpieces featured in glossy guides to the city, and see what an unseemly jumble lies there. These buildings were intended not as homes but as roosts where the gaily-plumaged birds of passage could settle for a while before flying on to Tunbridge, Brighton or wherever the fashion of the day decreed.

By the time Victoria came to the throne, however, Bath's brief spell in the limelight was long past. Houses now were built as homes, not lodgings. Semi-detached and detached dwellings, at least for those who could afford them, took the place of terraces. And, instead of opening directly onto the street, they were set in gardens, with all the accoutrements for a comfortable, settled lifestyle. Increasingly, people opted for the suburbs rather than the city centre. Larkhall, Weston, Lansdown, Wells Road, Bathwick and Widcombe Hills – all became sought-after retreats for those eager to escape the noise and dirt of the town. Architects such as Edward Davis, Henry Edmund Goodridge and James Wilson built Italianate mansions high above the city, transforming it, in the eyes of those with a romantic turn of mind, into an English Florence.

Although some lower-middle-class and working-class housing was built in Bath in the early Victorian period, the migration of the upper classes to the suburbs – and Bath's abandonment by the *beau monde* – met much of the demand for this type of housing stock. Many once fashionable streets and squares were colonised by the working classes. Not until the late nineteenth century, when the council decided to set about eradicating the worst of the city's slums and addressing decades of inner-city decline, did building at the lower end of the market start in earnest.

We have already visited Dolemeads to see the urban regeneration work there. A similar scheme was considered in 1909 for the Corn Street area, which was similarly low-lying and subject to regular flooding. Stage one of the plan was for a high-level road from Peter Street, across Corn Street and down Little Corn Street. Inclines 'of moderate gradient' would

> connect this high-level road with the existing low-level roadways New Quay, Back Street and Corn Street, and raised footpaths [would] give access to the houses where they stand above the level of the existing roadways of which it is impracticable to raise the level.

The development was to comprise 54 houses, to be let for between 4/- and 7/- a week, as well as six factories, workshops or stores. Stage two of the scheme was for a similar development to the east, in the Somerset Street area. Neither scheme was realised; had they been, the area immediately to the north and north-west of Churchill Bridge would wear a very different aspect to the one it wears today.

It was in the suburbs that most building work was concentrated in the early years of the twentieth century. Today, the late-nineteenth and early-twentieth-century housing stock in these areas is among the most sought after in the city. At the time, though, not everyone was so enamoured of this urban sprawl – if a letter published in the *Chronicle* on 28 August 1909 is anything to go by:

Sir,

With regard to the correspondence contributed in your paper, under the heading of 'Wake up, Bath', no one attempts to point out how the suburbs of Bath have suffered at the hands of the speculating builder. The once attractive districts have been turned into straggling streets, irregularly laid out, and lacking in almost every form of beauty.

After the opportunity of making a pleasant suburb has been wasted, we find the houses erected in the style not worthy of the skill of a builder, and in many cases the building materials used have been of the most inferior kind to avoid expense. Here and there we find houses left in an unfinished condition through the miserable system of their financial limit, and so remain for a considerable time a harbour for rubbish to accumulate, or we find a large space left in the road to remain for years an eyesore to the surrounding property, until some ingenious builder can arrange to fill the gap up with a house of a wedge-shaped description. One can meet with such queer houses in almost every road or street, and it is no wonder that these houses are nearly always to let.

It is regrettable that such sites have been left to builders to erect the houses which they thought most economical to themselves, and we also find several in the same road building houses of their own ideas, and ignoring, perhaps, the surrounding property. Through the present way of building we get quite a collection of houses in the road sadly lacking any form of interest, and it is a pity that the local authorities do not possess power to compel landowners and speculating builders to adopt some reasonable system for planning the roads and building of dwelling houses.

I venture to say that the suburbs of a city catch the eye of all visitors, and if Bath wants to wake up, a little more interest should be paid to its suburbs, which have lost their rural character.

However, when we reach the end of the letter we discover that its author was one William Steddon from Cleeve Road, Knowle, in the southern suburbs of Bristol. The lack of any other letters to the paper bemoaning the state of Bath's suburbs or the competence of its builders suggests that, whatever Mr

Steddon's problem was, it wasn't one shared by the majority of Bathonians.

The development of Bath's suburbs in the late nineteenth and early twentieth centuries is a fascinating subject, but one that is, once again, too complex and inappropriate to be dealt with in a book on Bath in 1909. We are fortunate, however, to have a record of planning consents granted by the council for the whole of the Edwardian period, which gives a comprehensive picture of building work in the city. Unfortunately, it does not include Twerton, Lower Weston and the other areas that became part of Bath in 1911; even so, it gives us a very good idea of Edwardian style and the way in which the face of Bath was changing.

Considering how short the Edwardian period was, it is remarkable how distinctive its domestic architecture was. Although it grew out of styles developed in the late nineteenth century, with the work of many architects and builders spanning the late Victorian and Edwardian eras, it is, with very few exceptions, impossible to mistake an Edwardian house for one built in the 1890s – or, indeed, the 1920s. What makes this consistency of style even more remarkable is that Edwardian domestic architecture was characterised by eclecticism and diversity. In all but the most basic developments, builders sought to vary the ornamentation or proportions of every house – sometimes subtly, sometimes not. Standardisation was – as indeed it had been to the Victorians – anathema.

The redefining of architectural styles reflected a fundamental social change – from the portentousness and high seriousness of the Victorians to something altogether lighter and more approachable. While art nouveau and the arts and crafts movement may have influenced architects at the top end of the market, most builders and architects were content to adapt tried and tested designs, making them lighter, freer, less cluttered. There are very few Edwardian houses that can be described as truly ugly; the same, sadly, cannot be said of many late Victorian ones. What did not change in the Edwardian period, though, was the standard of craftsmanship; almost all Edwardian houses were built to a extraordinarily high standard. To build today in the manner of the Edwardians would be prohibitively expensive; they were able to do it because labour was relatively cheap. Such attention to detail and craftsmanship would never again be possible, except for the seriously wealthy. The Edwardian age was indeed a golden age of domestic architecture, even though most of the people who built the houses received what would be regarded today as a pittance.

Bath stone from Hartham Park Quarry, half a mile west of Corsham, opened by Marsh, Son & Gibbs in 1905.

In terms of materials, apart from the wood used in half-timbered gables and bargeboards and the ironwork used for balconies, stone predominated. Virtually all Edwardian houses in Bath incorporated Bath stone – either smooth or rough cut, or a mixture of the two – with some using darker pennant stone for contrast. Brick, with which Bath builders had had a brief flirtation in the late nineteenth century – generally in conjunction with Bath stone dressings – had fallen out of favour for frontages, although it was still used extensively for side and rear walls. Just about the only Edwardian development in Bath that used brick exclusively was the Dolemeads social housing project.

Although there was some development on the north side of the city, especially in Fairfield Park, most building activity in the Edwardian era was to the south – a great swathe of land running from Twerton, through Oldfield Park to Bear Flat and Poet's Corner, with further development around Bloomfield Road and Englishcombe Lane, and at Combe Down. Away to the west, not yet incorporated into the city, Lower Weston and Newbridge also saw considerable building activity.

Although building continued right up to the outbreak of war in 1914 – in Poet's Corner and on Englishcombe Lane, for example – there was a sharp downturn in the number of new projects started in 1909, and hundreds of men were thrown out of work. The boom in the building industry, which had started a couple of decades earlier, had finally come to an end – and not just in the domestic housing market. Churches – Anglican and nonconformist – had been built to serve the new suburban congregations, along with church halls; there were pubs too – great barns like the *Victoria* and the *Moorfields Tavern* in Oldfield Park and the *Weston Hotel*; schools had been needed as well, and not just in the suburbs – new education legislation saw large, new inner-city schools being built. Now, most of this infrastructure was in place; the lack of new projects in the public realm combined with a downturn in the housing market to further depress the building trade.

Above: Much of the Villas Fields estate, east of Bathwick Street, on the site of one of Bath's least successful pleasure gardens, had already been built by 1909. Some of the houses on Forester Road incorporated carvings from the villa that stood at the heart of the pleasure gardens, while those in Powlett Road were built of brick. This view of Rockcliffe Road can be dated to around 1905. The houses with half-timbered gables in the distance were built by James Gould in 1904-5; he lived in the house at the end of the row (No 44). He was shortly to build another row of four houses in the gap on the left occupied, at the time this photograph was taken, by a small single-storey building, possibly dating from the time of the pleasure gardens.

Herbert Matthews was one of Edwardian Bath's most prolific architects. In 1907, for these semi-detached houses on Hampton View in Fairfield Park (above left), he opted to use pennant stone with Bath stone dressings – a common enough combination – in a remarkably original way, reminiscent of half-timbered construction. In 1905-6 he had employed a similar design at nearby Solsbury View (above right), but, because of the presence of ground-floor bays, it is less striking. Note the different materials used for the side walls – ashlar stone at Hampton View, red brick at Solsbury View.

Beckhampton Road in Oldfield Park was built around 1900. Here variety was achieved by using small ashlar blocks and dark mortar with more traditionally worked Bath stone for the dressings. Porches were also created by extending the gables of each pair of bays over the front doors. In 1909, 72 Beckhampton Road, seen here, was a police station; Eli Horler was the policeman in residence.

The lower end of Junction Road was designed by Frederick Gardiner in 1908-11. Although he used only Bath stone, partial use of dark mortar and small blocks gives varied texture to the frontages. Gardiner also designed Junction Avenue at the same time.

Less than 20 years before this photograph of Stanley Road was taken, an orchard stood on this site, with fields all around. Stanley Road, with its small front gardens, ground-floor bays and variations on a standard design, is typical of many of the streets built in Oldfield Park around this time.

This view of Moorland Road is unusual in that shows a building – at the far end of the road – in course of construction. Today it houses K & M Carpets. Clark's grocer's (which doubled as a post office) and the Excelsior Meat Co, on the left, are now the Livingstone public house. The original Livingstone Hotel is the three-storey building with a flagpole at the far end of the row. When this was destroyed by bombing in 1942, the licence was transferred to its present location.

Although not taken in Bath, this photograph of the stone-laying ceremony at the Methodist chapel at West Camel near Yeovil on 14 June 1908 is included because it gives a good idea of Edwardian building techniques. Note the wooden scaffolding poles and the equivalent of the builder's pick-up truck in the foreground. The chapel, built of local stone with red-brick dressings, is still in use today.

These imposing three-storey semi-detached houses at the top of Oldfield Road were built in 1910. Here rough-cut Bath stone has been used with smooth-cut Bath stone dressings for textural variety. Harry Erwood, of building firm, Erwood & Morris, occupied the house on the extreme left.

Maple Grove, off Bloomfield Avenue, was a creation of the Edwardian age. F Gardiner and AJ Taylor were among the architects who designed a variety of buildings – mostly semis but with the occasional detached house – along here. The lack of uniformity in style and materials – including an early use of pebbledash on the third and fourth houses down – make this short road a compendium of Edwardian design.

This pair of semis on the corner of Oldfield Lane was designed by Silcock & Reay in 1910. Here again ashlar stone dressings and bands frame pennant stone; square, full-height bays topped by gables decorated with barge boards were also common features of Edwardian design. The curvilinear design of the windows in the doors is another pleasing touch.

The most striking thing about this view of Newbridge Hill is how wide the road is. The houses on the left, with their gleaming pristine whiteness, look newly-built. Given the amount of smoke pollution at the time, they wouldn't have looked like that for long — one reason, perhaps, why builders were keen to experiment with different types of stone, rather than sticking with smooth ashlar. The buildings on the right are of red brick with Bath stone dressings, and were built a few years earlier, during the brief period when Bath's builders saw red brick as the building material of the future.

These two maps of Bear Flat date from around 1890, and show that it wasn't just semi-rural – there was a working farm at the junction of Wellsway and Bloomfield Road as well. The collapse of the agricultural economy in the last two decades of the nineteenth century, and the fall in the value of land, provided a spur to suburban developments in areas such as this. On Bear Flat, though, development swallowed up not only farmland but also Beechen Cliff Villa and its grounds, along with Bruton Cottage.

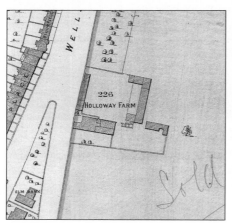

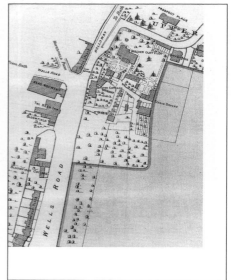

Muddy feet would have been inevitable if you had walked up Longfellow Avenue at the time this photograph was taken. The houses on the southern side of the road were built first, and their gardens were already well established when those on the northern side were added between 1907 and 1909 – hence the scaffolding poles in the road and the two gentleman weighing up the development.

400

Above: Looking down Shakespeare Avenue from Alexandra Park in 1902. The only buildings are the row later numbered 11 to 43, but at the time numbered 1 to 17. Beyond them is the place where Beechen Cliff Church would later be built.

Below: The view from almost the same spot just over a decade later. The buildings on the right were designed by F Gardiner between 1905 and 1906, those on the left by F Armstrong, who lived at 2 Shelley Road, between 1909 and 1914.

The trees in Kipling Avenue were the focus of controversy in 1909. At a meeting of the Pleasure Grounds Committee on 8 March, the residents presented a petition calling for trees to be planted, pointing out that Shakespeare Avenue had already been planted up at a cost of £25. A Mr Maule objected, saying that 'it's time this expenditure was stopped'. Councillor Jackman said he thought that the builders or residents should plant them. Theophilus Riddle, superintendent of the pleasure grounds, pointed out that the council had taken over Kipling Avenue some years earlier. Councillor Thomas objected that the builders had 'christened the estates avenues and expected the Corporation to make them so'. The committee decided against planting the trees.

On 18 March, a letter appeared in the Chronicle from a Mr T Anstey condemning the decision, and calling on the council to 'emulate Ealing, the "Garden Suburb". I remember Pulteney Street before the trees were planted,' he went on. 'How much more beautiful it is now, even though the trees might have been better selected. I also remember the plane tree planted in Abbey Green by Mr JB Yates. What about a row of trees in dreary London Road from Grosvenor to Walcot and some in Wellsway?'

The issue was raised again at the next meeting of the Pleasure Grounds Committee in early April, where it was pointed out that three out of four avenues in Poet's Corner had already been planted with trees at a cost of £55 and it was unfair to leave out Kipling Avenue. It was eventually decided to proceed with planting 'when practicable'.

THE BROTHER BUILDERS

In the late nineteenth century, four brothers, Elisha, Francis, John and Samuel Hallett, moved to Bath from Witham Friary near Frome. They all became builders and, at John's golden-wedding celebration at Beechen Cliff Church, the City Building Inspector, Mr Swain, said that between them the brothers had built 1,700 houses in Bath, of which John had built 1,300.

The first houses were built around Hungerford Road; they then moved south through Oldfield Park, the Bear Flat area and on to Southstoke Road. When Samuel was working on a development he often lived in one of the houses there, and as his wife came from Maiden Bradley he often named this Bradley House. This can be seen, for example, carved over the entrance of 119 Wellsway. He was killed in a shooting accident in 1908 and his son, also called Samuel, took over his business, building the villas on the top side of Chaucer Road.

Samuel and John were founder members of Beechen Cliff Methodist Church, having moved up from Hope Chapel (now a pet shop) on Lower Borough Walls. He laid one of the foundation stones of the church; his wife, Emily, laid one at the church hall in 1912. The architect was W Hugill Dinsley of 12 Cleveland Street, Chorley, Lancs and the church was built by William Webb of Railway Place. The building inspector passed the excavations on 1 May 1906, the damp-proof course on 20 June 1906 and the drains on 7 December 1906. The church was officially opened by the Mayor of Bath on 25 April 1907.
(Information supplied by Mr Vic Chivers, Samuel Hallett's grandson)

Nos 1-6 Hayesfield Park, leading down from Bear Flat and designed by Herbert Matthews, were built between 1904 and 1906. This terrace of large Bath stone houses with half-timbered gables had two storeys, except for No 1 – seen here – at the northern end. Here an exuberantly gabled, Arts and Crafts-influenced third storey, its large windows (the central ones canted outward) fitted with small square panes, provides a sumptuous end to the terrace and commands magnificent views over the city.

When the photograph above was taken from below the Tumps around 1912, Poet's Corner was more or less complete, although the eastward extension of Kipling Avenue and Beechen Cliff school were still way in the future. Alexandra Park was only around a decade old; the trees along its south and west sides were still little more than saplings. Although university buildings now dominate the skyline to the right, the wooded hills and many of the open spaces seen here have survived. The biggest change has occurred in the fields in the middle distance. Although the large field below Elm Place is now part of the Linear Park, most of the others are now covered by housing.

Bloomfield Park, Bath.

Above: Bloomfield Park was another Edwardian greenfield development. While the large semi-detached houses on the right – the one nearest the camera still with the estate agent's boards up – are similar to those in other parts of Bath, such as Oldfield Road, St Saviour's Road and Southstoke Road, the Gothic-style turret on Sunnycroft, on the left, seems a throwback to an earlier age. The design of the main body of the building – pennant stone with ashlar dressings to the front, and ashlar stone to the sides – is consistent with other buildings in the road, but the tower, eye-catching and delightful though it is, is not. The architect was Alfred Banks, who also designed the two sets of semi-detached houses – Nos 6 to 9 – in the distance at around the same time – 1906. The clue to the turret lies in the man who commissioned Sunnycroft – none other than Harry Hatt (right), who, as we saw in Chapter Three, used the principles established by Ruskin in the Seven Lamps of Architecture to condemn Bath Street. It is not surprising that a supporter of Ruskin should have been keen on turrets. When Ruskin bought a mansion at Brantwood in the Lake District in 1871, the first thing he did was to stick a turret on it, from

which he could survey his demesne. Is it too fanciful to imagine Harry Hatt standing in his turret like some latter-day Ruskin, surveying the city below and devising grandiose schemes of architectural regeneration?

Left: The houses on Englishcombe Lane were among the last flowerings of Edwardian elegance in Bath, setting a benchmark for elegant living never matched before or since – although that fence looks as though it could do with a bit of attention. Note also the electric street lighting, introduced in 1909. Eagle-eyed readers will also no doubt note the turret on the house in the distance. Its design in this case conforms with that of the house it is attached to – its cupola-style roof avoids any hint of Gothicism, while its more expansive dimensions suggest a bay or an extra room rather than a winding staircase.

Two of Bath's most remarkable Edwardian buildings — both masterpieces of Arts & Crafts design — can be found at Combe Down. Ormidale, on Southstoke Road, was built by Silcock & Reay in 1910, of coursed rubble, with a distinctive butterfly shape, its two wings linked by a terrace and covered

verandah. The butterfly shape may have been influenced by ES Prior, a major figure in the Arts and Crafts movement, who exhibited a model of a 'butterfly cottage' at the Royal Academy in 1895. He subsequently adapted the design for the Barn in Exmouth (1896-7) and Home Place at Kelling in Norfolk (1903-5). Ormidale was built for Robert Walker, a director of the Wolsey hosiery company and a fellow of the Royal Geographical Society. Even more remarkable was Lodge Style on Shaft Road (above). It was designed in 1909 by Charles Voysey for T Sturge Cotterell, the manager of the Bath Stone Firms, overlooking a narrow defile. It was a bungalow unlike any other bungalow before or since — built round a quadrangle (inspired, apparently, by Merton College in Oxford) and with a squat, fourteenth-century-style tower at the entrance. The stone came from a nearby quarry. It is a building of extraordinary beauty and presence, undemonstrative yet unforgettable, drawing heavily on late medieval style yet unmistakably of its time. Compared with the fussy, over-ornamented Gothicism of the Victorians, its restraint and

clearness of line and function have an aesthetic integrity that looks forward to modernism rather than back to an ersatz historicism. It is perhaps not coincidental that Sturge Cotterell was one of the driving forces behind the Bath Pageant, in which the past was, as we shall see, vigorously reinterpreted as a way of setting a course for the future.

Left: The Memorial Cottages in Weston, built in 1905, were also influenced by the Arts and Crafts movement. They achieve their effect through a combination of solidity and simplicity. Although they hark back to an earlier vernacular style and use traditional materials, they too are uncompromisingly of their time.

406

UNITED METHODIST FREE CHURCH,
BEECHEN CLIFF, BATH.

BUILDING FUND £4,000.

Architect: W. HUGILL DINSLEY, Chorley.
Minister: Rev. H. WALKER BLOTT, 28, Devonshire Buildings.
Secretary: Mr. A. P. MONKS, Cumberland Villa, Lower Weston.
Treasurer: Mr. JACOB TUCKER, Hope Cottage, Twerton-on-Avon.

The Penny paid for this Card is a Contribution to the Building Fund.

Above: Following development of the Newbridge Road/Newbridge Hill area, the Diocesan Church Building Society gave £300 to build an iron church on Apsley Road. It was called Emmanuel Church and dedicated by the Bishop on 3 October 1909. It was destroyed by bombing in 1942, but a new church opened on the site in 1956.

Left: A fundraising card issued by Beechen Cliff Methodists. The foundation stones were laid on 17 July 1906 and the church opened on 25 April 1907. Built of Bath stone – rough cut with ashlar dressings – it leans heavily towards the gothic, but with rectangular windows at the side of the tower and angular mouldings betraying its Edwardian provenance.

Above: Silcock & Reay's design for the Baptist chapel and schools in Oldfield Park, an essay in Edwardian classicism; Edward Robinson laying the foundation stone on 26 May 1902; and as the buildings appeared – minus swags, Diocletian windows and acroterial ornaments – when built.

Left: Another example of Edwardian classicism – Clan House Lodge on Sydney Road, built by Wallace Gill in 1906. Although clearly influenced by earlier models (such as the lodges on Cleveland Bridge), its clean, confident lines make it very much of its time, and contrast favourably with the ponderous gateposts, dating from the mid-nineteenth century.

Left: Laying the foundation stone of St Michael's Church Hall, Walcot Street on 2 April 1904. It was designed by Wallace Gill with more than a nod in the direction of Art Nouveau. Below left: The ornate lettering above the door is surmounted by a curved pediment broken by the figure of St Michael slaying the dragon – a study in controlled tension – while the five stepped rectangular windows above are framed within an unadorned, semi-circular headed, recessed arch. Below: Today the hall houses a restaurant.

Below: Wallace Gill also designed the school in Walcot Street. Opened by the Bishop of Bath & Wells on 29 October 1906, it closed in the 1960s and was converted to housing in 2000-2001.

A Swift motor car, made in Coventry and costing in the region of £325, by the railings that once enclosed the open space in the middle of the Circus.

CHAPTER TWENTY-SIX

THE BEAUTY OF SPEED

The Edwardian age was one of astonishing technological and social advances – and nowhere more so than in transport. It is difficult to overestimate the extent of the changes that took place in the first decade of the twentieth century. In 1909, the oldest residents could still remember a time when nothing went faster than the fastest horse, but for most people the railway – which had arrived in Bath 69 years earlier – was something they had always known. Even so, it was something that ran on dedicated tracks, fenced off and out of bounds – not on the roads and streets where people lived and worked. There, until very recently, horses had held undisputed sway. Wagons, carriers' carts, landaus, broughams, hansoms, omnibuses – all had been drawn by horses. When trams came along in 1880 they too were drawn by horses. Apart from a handful of slow, steam-driven traction engines, the streets of Bath in 1899 were – as they had been for centuries – the domain of pedestrians and horses. Ten years later, although there were still plenty of horses about, a revolution had taken place.

One of the most dramatic changes was the replacement of horse trams by electric trams. The horse trams had run from Twerton railway station, along the Lower Bristol Road, across the Old Bridge, through the city and along Walcot Street and London Road to Lambridge. Apart from a short climb near Hedgemead Park, the route was level throughout. The hills on either side of the valley were totally out of the question for horse-drawn trams. When electric trams were introduced in the early 1900s, though, the existing route was extended to Bathford in the east, with new lines to Weston, to Newbridge and the Globe at Newton St Loe, to Oldfield Park, and up the Wells Road to Combe Down. Construction began in November 1902 and the service started just over twelve months later on 2 January 1904. It is the sort of timescale today's traffic engineers can only dream of; apart from laying over 14 miles of track on some of the busiest streets and roads in the city, a new Midland Bridge was built (although, in the event, it was never used by trams). Plans were also drawn up for two lines to the

Above & left: Tramlines being laid in the High Street..

Below: A postcard celebrating the inauguration of the electric trams on 2 January 1904.

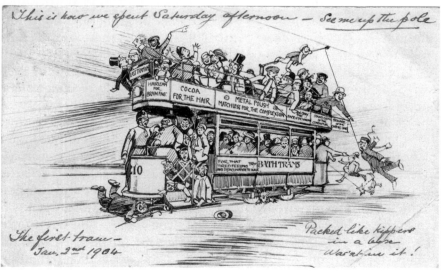

racecourse on Lansdown – one from the city centre and one across the fields from Weston, although these were never built.

The new trams sparked a suburban building boom. A 1902 Guide to the city remarked: 'Now that suburban trains have brought the country close to the town, and electric trams are about to climb hitherto inaccessible heights, street life has gone entirely out of favour, and some of the best-built rows and crescents of Bath present a melancholy array of house-agents' bills.' When William Howells visited Bath in 1905, he also found 'many fine houses [standing] empty'.

Tram routes and fares were as follows:

Route 1   *Guildhall to Lambridge 1d, to Batheaston 2d,*
             to Bathford 3d.

Route 2   *Guildhall to the Devonshire Arms 1d,*
             to Glasshouse Farm 2d, to Combe Down 3d.

Route 3   *GWR Station to Park Lane, 1d, to Weston 1½d.*

Route 4   *GWR Station to Newbridge Road 1d, to Newbridge 2d,*
             to Newton St Loe 3d.

Route 5   *Guildhall to Twerton 1d.*

Route 6   *Guildhall to Oldfield Park 1d.*

The new trams had only been running for a few months when the tramway company decided to invest in twelve open-top double-decker buses – six Milnes Daimlers (registration numbers FB02 - FB07) and 6 Straker Squires (FB08 - FB13) – which arrived the following year. Services started not from the city centre but from outlying points served by the trams. From Combe Down buses ran to Frome, Radstock and Midsomer Norton, while from Bathford they ran to Trowbridge, Devizes and Chippenham. In 1907, the Bristol Tramway Company started a bus service from Brislington (served by trams from Bristol city centre) to the Globe at Newton St Loe, from where passengers could catch a tram into Bath.

A tram heads away from the Bathford terminus for the journey through Batheaston and along the London Road to the city centre.

Trams and buses were so busy on Bank Holidays that higher fares were charged. Over the 1909 Easter weekend, 110,000 passengers travelled on Bath's trams, while 8,000 travelled on buses which made special trips to places like Burrington Combe and Cheddar. A fleet of charabancs was later acquired by the tramway company specifically for the excursion trade.

Above: One of the Milnes Daimler buses at Midsomer Norton, about to set off for Combe Down to connect with a tram into Bath.

Below: One of the Straker Squire buses at an unidentified rural location.

Above: A charabanc outside the tramshed in Walcot Street with the corn market in the background.

Below: The tramway company issued picture postcards of beauty spots visited on excursions. On this card of Wick Rocks a driver and conductor contribute to the human interest.

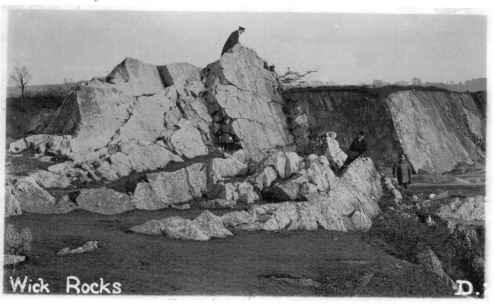

Buses could also be hired for private outings. On this postcard, sent from Bath to Chippenham by a Mr Jarvis of 5 Julian Road on 26 July 1912, a driver, wearing the uniform of the Bath Electric Tramways Ltd, is seen surrounded by a group of excursionists.

The larger hotels in the city also ran buses to and from the railway stations. Until 1909 these were drawn by pairs of horses, but in July 1909 the Empire Hotel introduced a motor bus, painted blue and 'of very neat design'. Other hotels soon followed suit. This was the bus built for the Francis Hotels by Richardson's Carriage & Motor Works on Bathwick Hill. The Moorings retirement flats now occupy this site.

When we complain about the pall of diesel and petrol fumes hanging over our streets and think longingly of the days before the advent of the internal combustion engine, we tend to forget that streets smeared with horse manure were not only appallingly whiffy and unhygienic – a Mecca for flies – but also, in wet weather, lethally slippery. Not that much stayed of it stayed on the road for long – keen gardeners kept buckets to hand, ready to rush out when a horse relieved itself and collect manure for the vegetable patch or the roses. Boys wandered around town collecting buckets of manure and selling it – there was even a group known as the Street Orderly Boys armed with dustpans and hard brushes, who dived around among the traffic scooping up the 'brown gold' and depositing it in metal pillars along the gutters, from where it was carted away and sold. And forget any notion of the streets being oases of calm before the advent of the petrol engine. The steel hoops of cart and wagon wheels rattling over setts was deafening.

Before motor cars started appearing on the roads in any numbers, there was another transport revolution – one that pales into insignificance compared to that which was to come, but important at the time all the same. Bicycles had been around for decades, but were unwieldy and dangerous. In the last decade of the nineteenth century, however, rapid advances in design and safety transformed the bicycle into the most fashionable way of getting about. The invention of inflatable tyres by a vet from Belfast called John Dunlop in 1887, replacing the heavy solid tyres in use till then, also meant that cycling required a great deal less effort. It was in the industrial towns of the English Midlands – notably Coventry and Wolverhampton – that the modern safety bicycle was developed, although Dursley in Gloucestershire can lay claim to one of the most innovative designs, the Dursley Pedersen. With its lightweight cantilevered frame, many riders thought it superior to anything else on the road. Sadly, its inventor's lack of business acumen meant that it was never a commercial success and, after the collapse of the company, he died penniless in his native Denmark in 1929.

Cycling was very much a middle-class pastime, and the ladies were as keen on it as the gentlemen. This was despite warnings of the moral danger that young women placed themselves in if they mounted one of these infernal machines – a danger that could only be mitigated, apparently, by the fitting of a well-padded seat.

The price of bicycles put them beyond the reach of most working people – the Royal Sunbeam, for example, 'a bicycle

Above & right: Cycling gave women a new-found freedom, although moralists condemned the increased opportunities it gave for unchaperoned intercourse with the opposite sex.

Bottom right: The legacy of the Marvel Cycle Company in New King Street.

of best quality at a medium price', cost £21-10-0 (over £1,600 in today's terms) – and for a short time cyclists were the kings of the road. By 1909, however, the craze was already on the wane, largely due to the increasing number of cars, which not only made cycling more dangerous but also – because of the dust they threw up – extremely unpleasant. The composer Edward Elgar was among those who took up cycling around 1900. He went on many long rides in the following years, but by

1908 his wife noted in her diary that he was 'depressed about cycling on account of motors'. In 1909, he more or less gave up cycling for good. His reaction was typical of many. Cycling would regain much of its popularity as the price of bikes came down after the Great War, but among the working rather than the middle classes. Cycling would never be so safe – or so fashionable – again. A faint echo of the early Edwardian cycling craze can be seen on the wall of 56 New King Street – a message, faint but still legible announcing: 'Marvel Cycle Co – Makers of the Marvel & Northampton – For Hire – Ladies, Gents & Tandem Repairs – Instruction in the Best Styles of Riding'. By 1909, though, the Marvel Cycle Company had moved out and the building had become the Cumberland Hall.

What brought the golden age of cycling to an end was one of the most momentous discoveries of all time – how to harness the power of petroleum. Petrol had been known for millennia – the Babylonians called the substance that seeped from rocks in what is now Iraq 'naptha' or 'the thing that blazes' – but there were few obvious uses for it. It acquired the name 'petra-oleum' (Latin for 'rock oil') in the sixteenth century. When the first oil wells were drilled in America in the mid-nineteenth century, the crude oil was boiled to produce paraffin or kerosene. This produced a by-product called petroleum or gasoline.

In Germany, inventors set to work to find a use for this apparently useless by-product. In 1886, three researchers, Karl Benz, Gottlied Daimler and Wilhelm Maybach, came up with prototype single-cylinder engines using petroleum and a carburettor. A few years later, Daimler refined his invention, substituting electric spark ignition for the original – and highly dangerous – flame-heated hot tube. In 1892-3 Rudolf Diesel invented the compression ignition engine. The motor age was born.

The rapid development of petroleum-powered, rather than steam-powered, locomotion, had tremendous implications, not just for the future of transport but for the geo-political map of the world. As soon as it became clear that oil was going to replace coal as the main source of power, at least as far as transportation was concerned, it was apparent that countries that had significant reserves of oil – or could exercise control over those countries – would grow; those that did not would decline.

Britain's pre-eminence as the world's greatest trading nation was due to a happy combination of circumstances: it had pioneered the industrial revolution because its social, economic and political framework encouraged invention, technological change and entrepreneurism, at a time when its European rivals were either racked by war or revolution, or hidebound by antiquated feudal systems; it also had vast reserves of the two minerals that fuelled that revolution – coal and iron. Despite increased competition from Germany and America, as long as coal remained the primary source of power, Britain's position was secure; if coal was overtaken by oil things would suddenly look a lot less rosy. Germany faced a similar problem, which is why it set out to build a railway from Berlin to Baghdad – which was the last thing Britain wanted. Not only was it to prove one of the most potent sources of tension between the two countries in the run-up to the Great War; AN Wilson has made a convincing case that fear of ceding control of Middle East oilfields to the Germans was the crucial factor in Britain's decision to declare war on Germany in 1914.

The motor car was introduced to the British public at an exhibition in the Crystal Palace in 1896. By 1904 there were 8,465 private cars in the country; by 1910 there were 53,196, and by 1914 the number had risen to 132,015.[1] The number of motor vehicles registered in Bath in 1914 was 636.

Motoring was very much a rich man's pastime. At the top end of the market, a Rolls Royce Silver Cloud cost £1,154 (equivalent to £86,550 today), although when Colonel Blathwayt bought the first car in Batheaston – a six-horsepower Oldsmobile – in 1904, it cost him £150 (equivalent to around £11,250 today). Petrol, which cost around sixpence a gallon (£1.88 today), came to Bath by train and was stored in the 1,000 gallon tanks of the Anglo American Oil Company at Westmoreland Goods Depot, from where garage owners collected it for resale.

The development of motor cars in Britain was hampered by government legislation. The 1861 Locomotives on Highways Act limited the weight of vehicles to twelve tons and imposed a speed limit of ten miles an hour in the country and five miles an hour in towns. Four years later, the speed limits were reduced to four miles and two miles an hour respectively, and every vehicle had to be manned by a three-man crew – a driver, a fireman and a man with a red flag (or a lantern at night) walking 60 yards ahead. Not until 1896, under pressure from early motoring enthusiasts, was the law repealed for vehicles of less than three tons, and the speed limit raised to 14 miles an hour. By then, though, the damage had been done.

---

1 The figure today is in the region of 33 million.

Britain, the home of innovation, where the steam locomotive had been developed and exported to the world, had, by the imposition of restrictive laws, allowed France and Germany to steal a march on it. In 1897, a race was staged from Paris to Bordeaux and back, with the winning vehicle travelled at an average speed of 15 mph. British manufacturers could only look with despair at what their continental rivals, unhindered by stringent regulations, had achieved.

The combative motoring journalist, Leonard Setright, has demonstrated that the Locomotive Acts, ostensibly introduced to address public concerns, were actually designed to scupper the steam stagecoach trade and later kept in place to kill off the nascent British car industry. This was to protect the interests of members of parliament and other influential persons, who had invested heavily in Britain's railway companies. Ironically, it seems to have been a similar hidden agenda that scuppered the railways just over 60 years later. By then, they had been nationalised, so there was no money to be made from them. With roads, however, it was a different story. Ernest Marples, the Minister of Transport who appointed Dr Beeching chairman of the British Railways Board, had also set up a civil engineering company (Marples, Ridgeway & Partners) which specialised in road building. This company helped to construct the M1 – which was officially opened by Ernest Marples. The Beeching Axe was the key element in a government-approved switch from rail to road – a policy whose disastrous consequences will continue

Edward VII with Lord Montagu of Beaulieu who introduced him to the delights of motoring.

to be felt for decades to come. What makes it the more galling is that it seems to have been inspired, at least in part, by self-interest.

The motor age in this country really kicked off in April 1900, when 65 cars left Hyde Park corner for a 1,000 mile run. As far as the manufacturers went, though, it was too late to snatch the lead from France and Germany. The best cars came from there, and when Edward VII, an early motoring enthusiast, ordered his first two cars, they were a Mercedes and a Renault. It was a slap in the face for the British car industry, but, then, with a name like Saxe-Coburg-Gotha, that's not too surprising. 'The motor car,' he declared, 'will become a necessity for every English gentleman' – but what he would have made of our near-universal dependence on cars is anyone's guess.

Between 1903 and 1906 car imports rose from £800,000 to £1.5 million a year. The earliest British cars, such as the Arrol-Johnston, were copied from imported Panhards and Daimlers, while the Arnold, the first British car to be produced in series, was modelled on the Benz. Between 1900 and 1913, 198 new makes of British motor car were introduced, over 50% of which sank without trace. The most successful car manufacturers were established companies with transferable skills. Bicycle makers – such as Star and Sunbeam in Wolverhampton and Swift, Rover, Humber and Singer in Coventry – figured largely. Wolseley made sheep-shearing machinery, while William Morris was an Oxford cycle dealer and Henry Austin worked for Wolseley.

In 1903, the speed limit was raised to 20 miles an hour and motorists were required to register their vehicles. Bizarrely, number-plate one-upmanship actually predated the issue of the first number-plates. Earl Russell was one of those who queued all night outside the London County Council offices to secure the coveted A1 registration. 'There has been some amount of competition for the securing of the number plate A1,' *Car Illustrated* reported, 'and this has been acquired by Earl Russell for his Napier car.' In the first year, 23,000 cars were registered, 8,500 of them in London.

Many early drivers regarded motoring as a sport rather than a serious mode of transport, and, as performance rapidly improved, trundling along at 20 miles an hour was little fun. The only answer was to go off-road. In 1907, motor racing, already established on the continent, was imported to Brooklands in Surrey. In 1912, the 100 mph barrier was broken at Brooklands for the first time in this country – eight years after it had been broken in Belgium. Hill climbing was also a popular sport; in 1911, the same year that a Model T Ford climbed to the top of Ben Nevis, hill trials were held at Upper Weston.

The love of speed was an abiding theme in the early twentieth century, with adherents as diverse as Mr Toad –

O what a flowery track lies spread before me henceforth! What dust clouds shall spring up behind me as I speed on my reckless way!

– to the Italian Futurists, who published their manifesto in *Le Figaro* on 20 February 1909:

We declare that the splendour of the world has been enriched by a new beauty: the beauty of speed. A racing automobile with its bonnet adorned with great tubes like serpents with explosive breath … a roaring motor car which seems to run on machine-gun fire, is more beautiful than the Victory of Samothrace.

Not everyone was so wild about motor cars. Octave Mirbeau, in an iconoclastic novel called *La 628 E8*, wrote:

It has to be said … that automobilism is an illness, a mental illness. This illness has a pretty name: speed … [Man] can no longer stand still, he shivers, his nerves tense like springs, impatient to get going once he has arrived somewhere because it is not somewhere else, somewhere else, always somewhere else.

We will be returning to the question of nervous energy later. Other commentators had their own issues with the infernal combustion engine. Charles Masterman saw the motor-car craze as a classic case of keeping up with the Jones's:

A large proportion of those who have employed a motor car in habitual violation of the speed limit, and in destruction of the amenities of the rural life of England, have done so either because their neighbours have employed motor cars, or because their neighbours have not employed motor cars; in an effort towards equality with the one, or superiority over the other. When every man of a certain income has purchased a motor car, when life has become 'speeded up' to the motor car level, that definite increase of expenditure will be accepted as normal. But life will be no happier and no richer for such an acceptance; it will merely have become more impossible for those who (for whatever reason) are unequal to the demands of such a standard.

Many people simply regarded motor cars as an unmitigated nuisance. The novelist EM Forster described them as 'pestilential', and believed that technology, 'instead of freeing man [had] enslaved him to machinery'. In *Howard's End*, Henry Wilcox is introduced as the prophet of a new age in which 'the fields will stink of petrol and airships shatter the stars'. He takes his wife by car to Hertfordshire:

A motor-drive, a form of felicity detested by Margaret, awaited her … It was not an impressive drive. Perhaps the weather was to blame, being grey and banked high with weary clouds. Perhaps Hertfordshire is scarcely intended for motorists. Did not a gentleman once motor so quickly through Westmoreland that he missed it? and if Westmoreland can be missed, it will fare ill with a county whose delicate structure particularly needs the attentive eye. Hertfordshire is England at its quietest, with little emphasis of river and hill; it is England meditative … The chauffeur could not travel as quickly as he had hoped, for the Great North Road was full of Easter traffic. But he went quite quick enough for Margaret, a poor-spirited creature, who had chickens and children on the brain.

'They're all right,' said Mr. Wilcox. 'They'll learn – like the swallows and the telegraph-wires.'

'Yes, but, while they're learning –'

'The motor's come to stay,' he answered. 'One must get about … Look out, if the road worries you – right outward at the scenery.'

She looked at the scenery. It heaved and merged like porridge. Presently it congealed. They had arrived.

Although Margaret Wilcox hated motor cars, many women were keen motorists. Clothes designed to withstand the rigours of the road, such as the coat seen here, had a significant impact on fashion. One of the most noticeable effects of the motoring craze was a vogue for smaller hats that were less likely to blow away. The car is a Swift, made in Coventry by a company that switched from making cycles in 1902.

One of the reasons early cars caused so much aggravation was the state of the roads. In the days before roads were tarred, dust was always a problem in dry weather, but, when the only vehicles travelling along them were horse-drawn, water-carts managed to contain the nuisance. Water-carts consisted of a metal tank on wheels, drawn by a horse. At the back was a large metal pipe with holes in it, through which the driver could spray water by pushing down a lever as he drove along. Walter Macqueen-Pope recalled that

> the smell of that water on the dust, a real smell of bygone summers, was one of the best things of the time and an ineffaceable memory. They don't use watercarts now. There is no need. It may be better or it may be worse, but one of the best summer scents has gone, and the stink of petrol does not make up for it. Nothing so fresh, so clear or so vitally of the true earth can be smelt today.

When cars came along, however, spraying water was soon found to be an inadequate solution. In Bath, as in other cities, tar spraying was introduced, but even this failed to cure the problem. At a meeting of the Surveying Committee on 10 May 1909, there were numerous complaints about the state of the roads. The worst road in the city was, by general agreement, Wellsway between the Bear and Devonshire Buildings. The City Surveyor said that there was no better way of keeping the dust down than by spraying tar. The

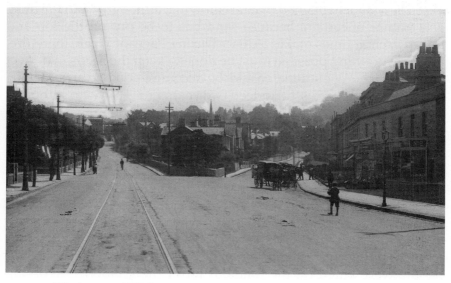

The bottom of Wellsway was the most notorious road in Bath for dust.

425

This was the state of one of the busiest thoroughfares in Bath, the Lower Bristol Road just west of the Royal Oak pub, around 1909. None of the houses in the photograph, with the exception of those in the far distance, have survived.

city already had two tar-sprayers and a third, costing £90, had been authorised. He also announced that the Rural District Council had decided to buy a tar-spraying machine for use in suburbs like Batheaston 'to mitigate the terrible dust nuisance, which becomes more aggravated as motors multiply'.

The Mayor explained that tar-spraying, although it laid the dust, was 'rather uncertain, because sand has to be put on the top and this in itself at times makes a dust'. During Pageant Week, therefore, 'when everything possible must be done to keep the roads in perfect condition, the committee would be recommended to use akonia, which was very successful indeed two years ago'. However, although akonia was far superior to ordinary tar, it was much more expensive, and its use at other times, therefore, could not be sanctioned.

One of the most hotly-debated topics at the time was road safety. The first death due to a motor vehicle in this country occurred in 1899. Ten years later, in 1909, 1,070 people died on the roads. Not all of these were due to motor vehicles, however; it was not until 1910 that fatal accidents involving motor vehicles outstripped those involving horse-drawn vehicles for the first time. As far back as 1875, when motor vehicles weren't even at the design stage, 1,589 people were killed on the roads. A lot of the accidents involving horse-drawn vehicles involved excessive consumption of alcohol.

Driving a vehicle or being in charge of animals on the highway while under the influence of alcohol was only made an offence in the Licensing Act of 1872. Carting or driving horses was thirsty work and the culture of drinking at work wasn't killed off by the 1872 act. The term 'roadside hostelry' was not just a idle turn of phrase. Even if those in charge of horse-drawn vehicles were sober, there were plenty of people wandering around under the influence, only too liable to fall beneath the wheels of a carriage or be crushed against a wall by a cart.

Road safety is still very much an issue today, but, while there are over 600 times more cars on the road than in 1909, the number of road traffic deaths in 2007 was 2,943 – less than three times the figure back then. Road traffic deaths peaked at 9,169 in 1941 (many due to cars driving without lights in the blackout – 4,781 of those killed were pedestrians). As recently as 1966, 7,985 people died on the roads, since when the figure has steadily fallen, due to the implementation of safety measures, improvements in vehicle technology and an increased awareness of potential dangers. We have, after all, had over a century to come to terms with the motor car – although there are still people who consider it a good idea to drive under the influence of alcohol. A century ago, determining whether or not someone was under the influence was less straightforward, as this report from December 1909 indicates:

At Bristol on Saturday the charges against Mr AD Hatch of this city which had been adjourned from an earlier hearing were further investigated. Mr FP Tyrell, who conducted the prosecution, intimated at the first inquiry that he would not proceed with the indictable charge of wilful misconduct which caused bodily harm, but would rely on the charge of being drunk while in charge of a motor car and with driving recklessly. Mr Hatch totally denied the charge of drunkenness and called a number of witnesses included Dr James Lindsay and Dr WH Duncan of Bath, who agreed that the effect of such an accident as that the defendant met with would be to render a man dazed and peculiar, and the last named mentioned that Mr Hatch was naturally excitable. Other witnesses called were Sidney George Smith, a sculptor of Bath, who said that after the accident the defendant seemed dazed and frightened, Frank Hill, a chauffeur, Arthur Thomas Wordell, a motor mechanic, Mr EH Atchley, a solicitor, and William Whiting, a Bath motor engineer. Mr Weatherley proposed to call Mr Arthur Robertson, Registrar of the Bath County Court, to give evidence of the defendant's general sobriety and good character, but Mr Tyrell suggested this was unnecessary, as no allegations of previous drunkenness had been made; and Mr Robertson was not sworn. The Chairman of the Bench (Mr Samuel Lloyd) said the justices thought that the solicitor for the prosecution had elected wisely in preferring the charges of drunkenness, apart from that of reckless driving. They entertained no doubt that the defendant was drunk while he was driving his car on the Bath Road at the time of the collision. Defendant would therefore be convicted and fined £1 and costs (the costs amounted to £5). Mr Weatherley said that the defendant would appeal.

Many accidents in 1909 were due to horses being startled by motor vehicles. Just after eleven o'clock on the morning of Wednesday 6 January, a runaway horse pulling a milk cart collided with a brougham in New Bond Street. The horse had been frightened by a motor car at the bottom of Milsom Street and bolted off in the direction of the High Street. Just outside the Red House Bakery, it collided with Dr Hardyman's brougham which was going in the opposite direction, throwing the coachman, George Gingell of Sydney Wharf, off his seat, and smashing a wheel and a lamp on the brougham. The brougham was empty at the time but the horse was injured and the coachman suffered shock.

At 6.30pm on Tuesday 6 April, a horse driven by Henry Evry, and owned by Thomas Evry of Sandybank Farm, St Catherine's, bolted in Julian Road, while drawing a 'spring cart' carrying vegetables. It 'bumped' into a motor car as it shot across Lansdown Road and continued down Guinea Lane. At Cleveland Bridge it collided with and damaged a tramcar before eventually being brought to a standstill along the London Road at Grosvenor Place. Nobody was injured.

The following case, of a taxicab causing a pony to bolt on the road to Radstock, is quoted at length, not only because it gives a good idea of traffic conditions and regulations at the time, but also because it conveys a vivid sense of social life and attitudes:

At the Bath County Court ... William Thomas Weaver sued the Provincial Motor Cab Company for damages sustained as the result of an accident. The plaintiff was represented by Mr Hookway, who explained that the action was for damages caused on 14 October. Mr Weaver was driving a pony and trap from Bath in the afternoon, and when about a mile and a half past the

Burnt House towards Dunkerton a Provincial motor cab flashed past at a high speed without giving any warning. The pony was frightened, dashed to the opposite side of the road and fell down and overturned the trap. Mr Weaver and two young men with him were thrown out. Mr Weaver was badly cut and unable to follow his occupation as a butcher for about a month ... On the return journey witness's son-in-law stopped the defendant and asked him to come into the *Crossways Inn*. He did so, and witness identified him as the driver of the car. He knew the man by sight before he became a motor driver, and had done business with him. They took his name and address.

Cross-examined by Mr Vachell, witness said he never heard a sound of the car until it was up to the horse's head. If witness's horse had heard the horn it would not have bolted.

Fred Bolter, one of the men in the cart with the last witness, estimated the speed of the car at over 20 miles an hour. No horn was sounded. When witness afterwards saw the taxi driver in the inn he said he remembered passing the trap, but saw no accident.

Mr Pollard, a representative of the Dunkerton Collieries Ltd, of Newbridge Road, Bath, stated that, when cycling along the road to Dunkerton, a car, which he thought was a red one, passed him at about 20 miles an hour. After travelling about a mile along the road he came across an overturned cart and three men. Witness noticed that the car was an open one, and that a boy was inside.

George Snook, son-in-law of the plaintiff, licensee of the *Crossways Inn*, Dunkerton, stated he waited for a taxi and stopped it. The driver came into the witness's house, and said he passed the plaintiff on the hill. He had been to Downside College with a fare. He said he knew nothing about the accident. Witness saw the taxi going on the outward journey, and the cab was then closed.

Mr J Welch, veterinary surgeon, stated the value of the pony had depreciated nearly £10 in value since the accident. Henry Yelling, another witness, stated he considered the speed of a car that passed him near the *Crossways* to be about 30 miles an hour.

Mr Henry Bence of Twerton stated that on the afternoon of 14 October he was driving a pony cart towards Bath. Another pony trap was coming towards him when a taxicab went between them like a flash. Witness saw the accident.

Taxis at the rank in the Orange Grove.

Dennis Daly, a pupil at Downside, stated that he went to Downside College from Bath on the afternoon in question in a taxi. They did not travel at a great speed, and passed traffic, the horn being sounded from time to time. Witness saw no accident.

Arthur Usher, driver, in the employ of the Provincial Motor Cab Company, stated that he started from the Empire Hotel, Bath, at 5.10, to take the last witness to Downside College. It took 50 minutes to do the 11¾ miles. Witness did not remember passing plaintiff's cart. Coming back, witness was stopped at the *Crossways* by plaintiff's son-in-law. He told them he knew nothing of the accident and did not remember passing the trap. Cross-examined, witness knew the road. He could not recollect what vehicles he passed on the three mile hill. He would certainly sound his horn if he passed a vehicle. Witness had been driving for six months …

Mr Vachell contended that there was not the slightest evidence of negligence. His Honour found it as a fact that the defendant did not blow his horn as it was his duty to do when going downhill with his clutch out. Considering also the traffic and the position of the two carts, the car was going at a greater pace than it ought to have done. He thought that if the proper notice had been given, and even then the horse shied, an accident could have been prevented. He therefore found a verdict for the plaintiff for £19 1s 6d.

As far as scaring horses went, though, cars were nothing compared to steam lorries. Although steam-powered haulage vehicles had been around for decades, it was only in the mid-1890s, when the Thorneycroft Steam Wagon Co in Basingstoke and Leyland's in Lancashire both launched new designs more or less simultaneously, that steam lorries really caught on. Although they dispensed with the need to keep a team of horses, they shared the horses' thirst for water, the difference being that, if horses weren't watered, they stopped co-operating; if steam lorries weren't watered they blew up. Drivers had to stop every few miles to fill up from streams, ponds or horse troughs. Despite these drawbacks, steam lorries remained more popular than petrol lorries, which were introduced from Germany around 1901, throughout the Edwardian period. Problems with steam-lorry design were gradually resolved and they continued to be produced up to the outbreak of the Second World War, some remaining in service until the 1960s. In the early days, however, there were problems a-plenty.

On the afternoon of Saturday 30 January, 26-year-old Tom Bedford from 53 Locksbrook Road, who worked for Bath Brewery, was delivering beer to the *White Lion* in Batheaston. The dray was standing outside and, having finished his delivery, he was standing on the step of the pub. A Midland Railway steam delivery lorry was standing nearby. The driver started to pump water from the brook into the engine. As he shut off steam, the safety valves blew off, startling the horse, which bolted. Tom Bedford ran to its head to try to stop it but it stood on his foot, knocking him down, and one of the wheels of the dray went over his chest. He was rushed to hospital where he died four days later from internal injuries. At the inquest the lorry driver was asked if the regulations permitted him to 'blow off' in the public highway. He replied that he didn't know. The coroner, however, said it was against the law. In this instance, he wasn't prepared to declare the driver guilty of manslaughter, 'but it was very near it and hoped he would be careful how he conducted himself in future'. A verdict of accidental death was recorded.

Early steam lorries were not only guilty of startling horses – they could be dangerously unpredictable as well. In early April, William Hooper of 4 Poplar Place, Dolemeads was firing up another – or possibly the same – Midland Railway lorry when two tubes burst. He was badly scalded about the face and arm. The following morning, George Kingston of 15 Victoria Road, Oldfield Park, 'was called to attend his motor lorry when by some means it ran over his ankle, fracturing it'. He was taken to hospital in the police ambulance.

Many road accidents were due to people – especially children – not being aware of the dangers posed by the new forms of transport. Many picture postcards from the early twentieth century are full of children standing around or playing in the street; often there was nowhere else for them to go – their homes were too small, too overcrowded, with no gardens, and the local parks or playing fields were too far away.

Early motoring was fraught with difficulties and dangers, some due to the state of the roads or the inexperience of the drivers, but many due to the technical limitations of the vehicles themselves. Above, on a postcard captioned 'trouble at Bath', we see the result of a broken axle on the road near Corsham. Below, an Edwardian greeting card turns the unreliability of early cars to comic effect.

Just after midday on Friday 9 April, a man was driving his wife into town along the Lower Bristol Road 'at around four miles an hour'. As they came

through East Twerton, a lad on his bike turned in front of the car to go up Brougham Hayes. Not only was the lad knocked off his bike – as the driver swerved to try to avoid him, he knocked over a small girl and ran into the wall of the Weights and Measures Office, 'upon which his wife was thrown over the top of the car'. Fortunately there were no serious injuries – it's a good job he was only travelling at four miles an hour! Even at low speed, though, early cars could be death traps – to take just one example, early windscreens were made of ordinary glass, which, with a high incidence of sudden stops and an absence of seat belts, caused many horrendous injuries.

To enforce the speed limits, speed traps – and prosecutions – soon became commonplace. A typical case was heard at Devizes Petty Sessions on 25 August 1909. Robert Membery of 11 Percy

Place, Bath was charged with 'having driven in excess of 20 miles an hour – to wit at 30 miles an hour – near Devizes'. PC Goodson had been timing cars on the Bath road 'with an electrical apparatus' and Mr Membury's car had covered a measured furlong in 15 seconds – equivalent to 30 miles an hour. The policeman confirmed that the number of the car was FB 214, but said that he could not tell if it was a two-seater because he 'was lying low behind a hedge and could only see the wheels'. The accused was fined £2-10s with 9/- costs.

Speed traps were as unpopular a century ago as they are today, so much so, in fact, that on 29 June 1905 a group of motoring enthusiasts met at the Trocadero Restaurant in London to form an organisation to support members caught by police speed traps. And so the Automobile Association was born. Members were supplied with badges for their cars and AA patrolmen saluted anyone displaying a badge. It was illegal for patrolmen to warn drivers of speed traps, but, if they did not salute, members were advised to stop and ask the reason why – a handy way of circumventing the law. In 1909 the AA also introduced free legal representation for members summoned to appear in magistrates courts. By 1914, with only just over 132,000 cars on the road, the AA had 83,000 members.

Motorists were routinely prosecuted for breaking other regulations as well. On 27 March 1909, Thomas Hill of 2 Lorne Road, Twerton was fined 10/- for descending the hill at Combe Park with the wheel locked without using a skid-pan. On 17 April, Sidney Horstmann of 10 Norfolk Crescent was convicted of driving a motor car at Weston at 4am on 11 April without a lighted lamp at the rear. He had already been convicted twice under the Motor Car Act of 1903 and was fined 10/- in his absence.

It wasn't just motor vehicles that fell foul of the law. In the first summons against a council employee, George Slip of 4 Millbrook Buildings, Larkhall was summoned for driving a 'street-sweeping brush' in Southgate Street at 12.55am on 17 October without a light attached. With him on the vehicle was Charles Milton of 23 Calton Road. Both men said that the lights were lit when they left the yard, but they each had two horses to attend to and 'could only see the lamps when turning a corner'. He was dismissed with a caution.

Traction engines, which the Locomotive Act had been designed to control in the first place, also continued to generate a steady stream of convictions. On 23 January 1909, Beaumont Kennedy & Co, colliery proprietors, of 5 Queen Square, Bath, were summoned for failing to comply with Section 5

A 1909 advertisement from Moore & Sons, one of Bath's long-established firms of carriage builders, shows how they were having to keep up with the times.

of the Locomotive Act. PC Hembury said that on 9 January he had witnessed a traction engine being driven along Wellsway at 7.05pm drawing four empty trucks, with two men on the engine and one in the rear truck. As there should have been four men, the company was fined 5/- with costs. In September 1909, Fred Mitchell of Weston Super Mare was accused of driving a traction engine through Batheaston at over two miles per hour, with three furniture vans attached. A policeman had timed it covering half a mile in ten minutes and the driver was fined £1 with costs.

Bath actually played a small but significant role in the early development of the motor car. Coach building had long been one of the main industries in the city – hardly surprising with the Bath Road being one of the busiest in the country. Even after the railway had killed off the coaching trade, there were still plenty of people in and around Bath who could afford their own carriages. The development of motor vehicles in the early twentieth century, although it ultimately spelt the demise of the coach-building trade, actually stimulated it for a while. Many early motor manufacturers provided chassis rather than finished cars, leaving coach builders to add bodies tailored to customers' requirements.

This 1909 advertisement suggests that Richardson's coachbuilders on Bathwick Hill were already concentrating solely on the motor-vehicle side of their business.

S&A Fuller's Carriage Works on Kingsmead and Monmouth Streets and Richardson's Carriage Works on Bathwick Hill not only provided this service but also developed engineering expertise to build and service motor vehicles. Even after motor cars came ready-finished off the assembly line, both firms continued to build customised bodies for commercial vehicles.

In February 1909, the *Chronicle* reported the introduction of a 'Royal Mail motor van' between Warminster and Bath – 'the first time in the history of cross-posts in this part of country which are not served by rail'. The van replaced 'a stud of seven horses' owned by Mr RC Cooke of Clevedon, who held the contract. The body of 'this smart-looking motor van' was made at Richardson's Carriage Works, while the chassis was a Panhard & Levassor from France, which was reconstructed at the Central Garage in the Sawclose. The van, enthused the *Chronicle*, 'carries every conceivable kind of spare and the chauffeur is an accomplished engineer'. A month earlier, Bath Corporation had acquired its first motor lorry – a Foden, registration number FB 018, with 'City & County Borough of Bath' painted on its side panels.

Fuller's had started as coachbuilders in Bath in 1737, moving to premises in Kingsmead Street around 1820. The first car body they made was in the form of a four-wheel back-to-back sporting dog cart, which was fitted onto a six-horsepower Daimler chassis for Ernest Pitman in 1898. In 1903, the Bath Motor & Garage Company, a wholly-owned subsidiary of Fuller's, was formed in association with a motor engineer called Sidney Horstmann (whom we've already encountered driving without a rear light). The company also acted as an agent for larger companies, starting with Siddeley in 1903 and later including Singer, Humber, Oldsmobile, Citroën, Willys Overland, Austin, Ford and many others. The motor business struggled in its early years, often trading at a loss and bailed out with injections of capital from people convinced that cars would soon drive horse-drawn vehicles off the roads. By 1909, it was clear their faith had been well-placed and the business was starting to prosper.

By then, the traditional coachbuilding side of the business had all but collapsed. This seems to have happened quite suddenly, affecting not only Fuller's but also other companies in the city. Roy Fuller, who was working for the company at the time, recalls that

Interior and exterior views of S & A Fuller's in Kingsmead Street. The building was destroyed by bombing in 1942.

the slump in the carriage building trade started about 1908. New carriages became unsaleable – very much money was lost, and gradually the business came to a very low state. The motorcar business then being done by no means covered the losses in carriage building. New carriages had to be broken up and disposed of for a few shillings, and no more were built. In 1913, we did, however, at the special request of a customer in South Wales, build a new brougham. We quoted £250 for a new one – £174 being the price a few years earlier. It cost us well over £300. When it was finished it was not wanted. It was paid for – never delivered, and finally we gave the owner £5 and took it over and broke it up. The pieces did not realise even the latter amount.

Fuller's, because they had diversified into motor cars, survived. Vezey's, an equally venerable firm, which hadn't, closed down:

In 1908 S&A Fuller purchased the stock-in-trade and goodwill of the old-fashioned firm of Vezey & Company, Coach Builders, Long Acre, Bath. They had a very good name and built high-class lighter types of carriages than S&A Fuller. They held the royal warrant as coachbuilders to Her Majesty Queen Victoria, and counted amongst their customers the Kings of Norway, Sweden and Denmark, and had also exhibited carriages at the Great Exhibition of 1851. Mr Henry John Vezey joined the staff of S&A Fuller and remained with them until he died. Vezey & Cos's large stock of carriages, coach goods of all description and plant were sold by auction. The auctioneer was a well-known London man who brought down with him many London trade buyers. The sale, which was held on 10 March 1908, was a success, realising slightly more than what was paid for the whole business as a going concern.

It was the end of an era. Meanwhile, the car-body side of Fuller's business continued to prosper. In 1910 they exhibited a limousine and a landaulette body on an Italian Rapide body at the Motor Show in Olympia. However, this success, at least as far as the luxury-car market went, proved short-lived. When it was resumed after the disruption caused by the Great War, the company found itself competing against the rise of mechanised assembly-lines producing ever more luxurious vehicles at a fraction of the price. Fuller's continued to build bespoke commercial-vehicle bodies

Above: Three of the motor bodies built by Fuller's, photographed in Royal Victoria Park.

Below: An advertisement from December 1909.

until after the Second World War, but ceased production of motor-car bodies in 1924.

It was Sidney Horstmann, however, who really put Bath on the motoring map. Born in 1881, the youngest son of Gustav Horstmann, a German watchmaker and engineer who had come to England in 1854, he had started his career as an apprentice to the research engineer Commander Bayntun Hippisley at Ston Easton. After spending three years making clocks and bicycles in his brother's workshop, he helped set up the Bath Garage & Motor Company in 1903. A year later, following his invention of a variable-speed gear, his three brothers set up the Horstmann Gear Company to manufacture it, and appointed him managing director. This was not a commercial success, however, and although the company

Top: A commercial vehicle built by the Kingsmead Motor Company with a Fordson tractor in tow in Seymour Street. The Seymour Hotel, facing the entrance to the Midland Railway station at Green Park, is on the left.

Above: A delivery vehicle built for Duck, Son & Pinker, a company still trading today.

Right: When the Kingsmead Motor Company proclaimed that 'Possibly in the distant future the Ford van will become obsolete', it couldn't have seemed too likely. A century later the phrase has an ironic ring to it.

439

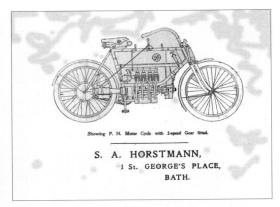

The two-speed gear for the FN Motorcycle – Sidney Horstmann's first commercially-successful invention.

continued in business, making time switches for gas lights, Sidney returned to the Bath Garage & Motor Company.

In 1906, he branched out on his own again, setting up as a motor engineer and salesman at 22a Monmouth Place. Much of his income at this time came from an invention which did prove commercially viable – a two-speed gear for the FN Motorcycle, which retailed at ten guineas. He sold the Monmouth Place premises in 1908 and the following year set up a new business – also in Monmouth Place – in partnership with Raymond Doudney.

Sidney Horstmann's next invention, the Road Spring Wheel, was an attempt to solve the problems associated with early pneumatic tyres – in particular, the numerous punctures they were subject to. He developed a solid tyre mounted on a rim 'sprung' on

Many early cars were very basic and three-wheelers were common. On the left a Swift tourer is seen with a one-seater AV monocar or cyclecar, built by Ward & Avery in Farnham, Surrey. On the right is a side-starter by Crouch of Coventry, which also appeared in a three-wheeled version. Driving on untarmaced Edwardian roads in cars like this was not for the faint-hearted.

440

Horstmann's works on James Street West, converted from a skating rink.

spokes radiating from a hub. This never got beyond the prototype stage, and in 1912 he turned to his next project – a light car based on the FN motorcycle. He had been trained in engine construction by Commander Hippisley and made a tricar as long ago as 1901. He took over and converted the former skating rink on James Street West – the skating craze was already on the wane by this time – and the first Horstmann car appeared in the 1913 Motor Show at Olympia. With the outbreak of war, production was put on hold, but later resumed. By the time production of Horstmann cars ceased in 1928, around 2,000 had been sold, nine of which survive, including a 1914 coupé, preserved at the Museum of Bath at Work. Meanwhile, Horstmann Controls, now based in Bristol, remains the country's leading designer and manufacturer of controls for domestic-heating systems and advanced metering equipment.

By 1909, the death knell of motoring as a rich man's pastime – as well as the future of bespoke car bodies – had been sounded On 13 November 1908, the first Model T Ford was unveiled at the Motor Show at Olympia. It cost $825 (£170), but by 1916 this had dropped to $360 (£75) In 1911, an assembly plant was set up in Manchester. By 1913, it was the biggest-selling car in the UK with 30% of the market. According to Ed Pilkington, the chronicler of the Model T's centenary, Henry Ford's 'most revolutionary insight

Above: An early Model T Ford drives through Warwick. The girl standing in the middle of the road is an image that conjures up a world we have lost, a world destroyed by Henry Ford's mass-motoring revolution.

Below: The car seen here in front of Wells Cathedral was a Willys-Overland, built in Indiana, and one of several American models popular with British motorists.

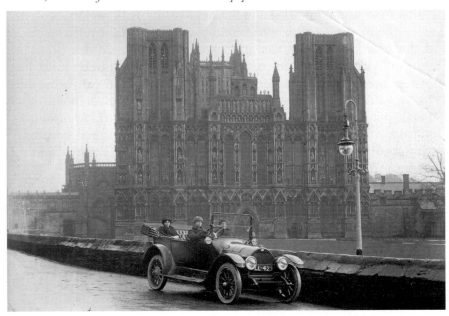

was to make the unit travel to the appropriate worker, rather than making specialised workers go to every unit'. The Ford plant in Highland Park – a city within the city of Detroit – opened in 1910; three years later the world's first car-assembly line was set up there. By 1925, the plant was churning out 9,000 Model Ts a day – all identical. 'Any customer,' said Henry Ford, 'can have a car painted any colour that he wants so long as it is black.'

Highland Park's importance is recorded on a green-and-gold heritage plaque by the main entrance: 'Mass production soon moved from here to all phases of American industry and set the pattern of abundance for twentieth-century living.' 'Pattern of abundance' – even knowing nothing of the Highland Park plant, the phrase now reads like a sick joke. The Ford factory today is a monument to a dream turned sour – in the words of Ed Pilkington, 'the windows are broken or boarded up, its ceilings have gaping holes, the floor is covered in broken lumps of fallen plaster. On the roof, the flagpole that for years flew the Stars and Stripes is rusty and bare.'

'They paved paradise to put up a parking lot' – a line that could have been specially written to accompany this photograph of the gardens in front of St John's Church – now the site of Manvers Street car park, one of the ugliest corners of modern Bath. One instance among millions of the impact of mass motoring.

Unwittingly, Henry Ford provided the most fitting epitaph for the motor age a century ago: 'History is more or less bunk. It's tradition. We don't want tradition. We want to live in the present, and the only history that is worth a tinker's damn is the history we make today.' In *Brave New World*, Aldous Huxley invented a new calendar, substituting AF (After Ford) for AD. Today, ACC (After Credit Crunch) seems more appropriate.

Despite the rapid growth of motor transport, hundreds of people in Bath in 1909 were still dependent on horse transport. There were 50 fly proprietors, 28 blacksmiths, 16 saddlers & harness makers, twelve livery stable keepers, eight wheelwrights and five farriers. Although some companies and tradesmen had acquired motor vans or lorries, most continued to use horse-drawn – or man-drawn – vehicles. Among the most impressive were the brewery drays. The Bath Brewery, next to the Midland Railway at Lower Weston, on the site now occupied by Hartwell Motors, was the city's largest, and its drays were a familiar sight, delivering not only to pubs but also to private houses. Walter Macqueen-Pope describes how impressive Edwardian drays were:

Twenty-eight carriers ran from various inns in Bath to outlying villages on a regular basis. The Sherston carrier left the yard of the Bell in Walcot Street every Wednesday and Saturday at 4pm, calling at Pennsylvania, Tormarton, Badminton and Acton Turville. Here it is seen near Badminton.

Your beer was delivered to your door by the barrel in a brewer's dray with big powerful horses; big powerful men of might and brawn, matching those dray-horses, carried the beer to your cellar ... They wore corduroy trousers and white shirts, like overalls, sleeves rolled up to their elbows displaying huge

Above: There were 28 blacksmiths in Bath in 1909, with many more in outlying villages such as Newton St Loe.

Below: The funeral of ex-PC Brimble of 2 Cleveland Terrace in April 1913. To the right of the footbridge in the distance can be seen the entrance to Hampton Row Halt, opened by the Great Western Railway in 1907.

forearms. They had brewers' caps on their heads, knitted caps of colour made of stockingette tapering to a point and betasselled. Across their leather aprons was a leather crossbelt. On this they carried an inkwell and a pen with which they signed your receipt.

He also recalls 'one occasion when the horse had a very big show, and that was at a funeral. Funerals then were very solemn occasions, they were pageants.' Horse-drawn hearses survived long after most businesses had switched to motor vehicles and are still occasionally seen on the streets of Bath even today.

Nowhere was the conflict between horses and petrol engines in Bath more bitter than in the taxi business. When the first taxicabs were introduced they were considered so chic that there was a music-hall song – somewhat in the manner of the Divine Comedy's *National Express* – about them:

> *Oh, the car! The taximeter car!*
> *It's better than taking a trip to Spain,*
> *Or having your honeymoon over again;*
> *If you're out with your sweetheart,*
> *Your mater or papa,*
> *Do it in style for eightpence a mile*
> *In the taximeter car.*

Unfortunately, some taxi drivers – hard though it may be to believe today – fell foul of the law. In April 1909, Albert Austin of 3 Old King Street was fined 10/- for driving a taxicab in such a reckless manner on Lansdown near Hamilton House that 'he could not pull up within a space of 15 yards when directed by PC Hansford to stop.'

Naturally, there was opposition to the taxicabs from horse-cab drivers. Sometimes this took the form of ill-advised bloody-mindedness. On 22 January 1909, George Lambourne of 37 Avon Street was charged with wilfully obstructing the public highway. PC Crane had asked him to move his hackney carriage from the front of 9 Gay Street, so that a taxicab could draw up, but he refused. As a result, the taxicab had to draw up behind him and the people who had ordered it 'had to walk three or four yards to get in'! He was fined 12/-.

The horse-cab drivers sought in vain to get the backing of the council. At a meeting of the Sanitary Committee on 5 April 1909, a deputation of 54 horse-cab drivers asked the committee

Two views of the rank in Laura Place, showing the changeover from horse to motor cabs.

not to licence any more taxicabs in Bath, claiming they had the backing of many residents. Councillor Fortt said that, 'We are sorry for the cab drivers but they are asking for the impossible. The railways drove old coaches off the road and now taxicabs are driving off horse-cabs. In the near future taxicab drivers will be asking for protection against airships.' The committee agreed that the licensing of taxicabs should go ahead, and pointed out that some horse-cabs would still be required.

447

In July 1909, however, as Pageant Week approached, a more serious threat emerged – cab drivers from outside Bath had applied for licences. At another meeting of the Sanitary Committee,

> the Chairman read a memorial from 23 local cab proprietors in which they stated that they understood application had been made to obtain licences for a number of carriages and motor cabs to ply for hire during Pageant Week. They had plenty of carriages with which to supply the demand, and as they paid rates and taxes in the city, they considered it would be hard upon them to allow strangers to step in. The past season had been a very disastrous one, and they trusted the committee would give the memorial serious consideration.
>
> The Chairman said that Inspector Bence informed him on Wednesday last that he had had application made to him from two companies to allow their cabs to ply for hire. He asked Inspector Bence how many cabs were at present licensed, and he said there were 60 horse-cabs and 14 motors ... He thought it would be sufficient if they only licensed six extra cabs. He thought that would give the horse-cabmen a chance. They had come, he thought, to their last days, and it was his wish to give them any benefit there might be during Pageant Week. However, several councillors disagreed, asking that as many cabs as possible should be licensed. The Chief Constable's opinion was asked for, and he said that there was no doubt they could do with a great many cabs. They had a preliminary experience last Friday, when there was a rehearsal, and it rained. The performers could not get cabs for love or money, and one of the local managers told him that he had 120 orders by telephone. He did not think the additional licences would hurt the local cabmen. It was agreed to leave the decision as to how many extra licences should be granted to the Chief Constable.

Horse cab and taxicab fares were generally the same – a shilling for the first mile and pro rata thereafter. However, horse-cabs could also be hired by the hour – at 2/6 an hour; horse-cab drivers were also entitled to charge an extra sixpence if they had to go up any of the hills around the city. The principal taxi ranks in the city were in Laura Place and the Orange Grove. Each rank had touts hanging around who watered the horses and ran errands; they also had little shelters for the cabmen, which, in September 1909, the Sanitary Committee threatened to close down because of their

'disgracefully dirty' state. There was – if travelling by horse or taxi cab was a bit too exciting – one further option in 1909 – Bath Chairs, available for hire at a shilling an hour from the Abbey Church Yard.

Although the railways experienced fewer changes than the roads in the Edwardian era, they did see some significant developments. The Great Western Railway, which had arrived in Bath in 1840, was, despite the arrival of the Midland and Somerset & Dorset Railways a few decades later, still the major player as far as Bath was concerned. Despite being the first on the scene, though, its subsequent performance had left much to be desired. ET Macdermot, the company's historian, criticised the 'prolonged lethargy, which … made it the most backward of all the great companies north of the Thames in matters affecting the public'. It was only in the 1890s that it started to shake itself out of this torpor.

Above: Building the West of England Direct Line near Somerton.

Below: The newly-opened line sweeping across Somerton Viaduct.

It soon made up for lost time. Its initials – GWR – were often said to stand for Great Way Round, with good reason. Trains from London to South Wales and the West Country had to travel via Bath and Bristol, while trains from London to Birmingham went via Oxford. Not only were these routes very circuitous; there were bottlenecks, of which Bristol was the worst.

Between 1903 and 1910 the GWR opened a series of direct lines, transforming the service out of all recognition. The first of these was the South Wales direct line, from Wootton Bassett to Patchway via Badminton,

449

which opened in 1903, taking South Wales services away from the Bristol area and cutting journey times by 25 minutes. The second was the West of England direct line from Reading to Taunton via Westbury – a combination of 33 miles of new line and upgraded branch lines – which was over 20 miles shorter than the old route. The opening of these two lines cut the amount of traffic travelling through Bath considerably. It wasn't just the number of passenger trains that were cut; before the Badminton line opened, all coal trains between South Wales and London had had to travel via Bath as well.

The GWR's bid to cut journey times by shortening its routes was part of a frantic attempt, indulged in by most of the major main-line companies, to outdo the competition. As Philip Blom points out, 'one of the favourite words of the time was "hustle". The most approved of all ambitions was to break a record, preferably for speed. Railway companies eagerly competed against each other for the longest and fastest runs.' Two years before the West of England direct line opened, the GWR achieved one of the biggest publicity coups of the decade by breaking the 100-mile-an-hour barrier. The locomotive that broke it – *City of Truro* – still occasionally runs on the main line today, over a century later. The location – Wellington Bank, south of Taunton – was significant as well, lying as it did on one of the most hotly-contested routes in the country.

Not only were there a large number of railway companies in the years leading up to the Great War; there were many duplicate routes. You could, for example, travel from London to Birmingham on the London & North Western Railway via Rugby, or on the GWR via Oxford; from London to Sheffield you had the choice of three different routes and three different companies – Great Central, Great Northern or Midland. If plans drawn up in 1902 for a Bristol, London & Southern Counties Railway had gone ahead, Bath and Bristol would have had an alternative route to London as well. Rivalry between railway companies for the prestigious London-Scotland traffic gave rise to what became known as the 'Race to the North', with vital minutes shaved off schedules by the introduction of lighter trains and more powerful locomotives, and new record times published in the press.

Hardly less prestigious was the Boat Train traffic between Plymouth and London. Although Southampton was the principal south-coast port for transatlantic liners, passengers who were in a hurry could pay to go ashore at Plymouth, where they could catch an express to London. Dubbed 'the route that cuts the corners off', steamship companies made great capital of the time thus saved. The trouble was that there was a choice of routes from Plymouth, operated by the GWR and the London & South Western. Rivalry between the two companies meant that ever-faster journey times were needed if they were not to concede the traffic – and the prestige that went with it – to the competition.

It all ended in tears when, in the small hours of 1 July 1906, a London & South Western Boat Train hit the sharp curve through Salisbury station – with a speed limit of 30 miles an hour – at around

Above: City of Truro, the first steam locomotive to travel at more than 100 miles an hour.
Below: The aftermath of the Salisbury disaster.

70. In the ensuing crash 24 of the 43 passengers, and four railwaymen, were killed. It was alleged that passengers had bribed the driver to get them to London as quickly as possible but this was never proved. It did, however, bring the races between Plymouth and London to an end.

The GWR also built a new line from Cheltenham to Birmingham and knocked over 18 miles off the distance between Paddington and Birmingham by the construction of a cut-off between Ashendon and Aynho. 1906 also saw the opening of an upgraded route between Swansea and Fishguard. This was part of a plan to capture a greater share of transatlantic traffic, which came to fruition three years later, when Cunard decided its liners would call at Fishguard. The first, on 30 August 1909, was the *Mauretania*, then the biggest and fastest liner afloat. The *Bath Chronicle* declared that

> the successful inauguration of Fishguard as a port of call for the mammoth Cunard boats the *Mauretania* and *Lusitania* undoubtedly ranks as the most notable feature in transatlantic travel of 1909. Great interest was displayed by the public in the event on the momentous day ... when the first Great Western Ocean Specials were run from Fishguard, and the route of the expresses was practically lined from the shores of Pembrokeshire to the London terminus by crowds of expectant onlookers.

The inaugural Ocean Special pulls out of Fishguard.

The GWR ran nine daytime expresses from Bath to Paddington – at 8.02am, 9.28am, 9.54am, 12.35pm, 2.32pm, 3.20pm, 4.15pm, 6.13pm and 7.45pm. There were also two night expresses – conveying sleeping carriages from South Wales and Penzance – which called at Bath on their way to London at 12.42am and 4.05am. Two of the daytime services – the 9.28am and the 2.32pm – ran non-stop from Bath to London, making the journey in just under two hours. Three of the services – the 8.02am, the 9.54am and the 2.32am – conveyed slip coaches which were detached at Reading. Slip coaches, introduced in the mid-nineteenth century and used until 1960, were specially-designed coaches attached to the rear of trains and uncoupled on the approach to stations; they rolled to a standstill under their own momentum, with a brakesman to bring them to a gentle halt. This meant that passengers could alight at intermediate stations without the train having to stop.

The fastest journey time from Paddington to Bath was, in fact, via a coach slipped from the 11.00am Penzance express, which arrived in Bath at 12.48pm – an average speed of 59.3 miles an hour.[2] This was the service often chosen by visiting dignitaries, as it got them into Bath just in time for a civic lunch in the Guildhall.

Journey times varied considerably. The 12.35pm and 3.20pm to Paddington both took 2 hours 40 minutes – over 40 minutes longer than the fastest service – despite having to make only two or three stops en route. For passengers who were in even less of a hurry, there was a service at noon from Bath to Paddington over the now closed line via Devizes, which took almost three hours for the journey.

The 4.15pm to Paddington also included coaches which were detached at Swindon and went forward to Oxford and from there over the now-closed Great Central line to Leicester, Nottingham, Sheffield, Leeds, Huddersfield and Halifax.

Sunday services were lean, to say the least. Apart from a night train at 12.42am, there were only three expresses to London – at 9.18am, 12.15pm and 6.08pm. A single ticket from Bath to Paddington cost 17/10 first class, 11/2 second class and 8/11 third class; second class was, however, withdrawn by the GWR on 1 October 1909. Ordinary returns, valid for six months, and weekend returns were also available at less than the price of two singles. There was also a large number of excursion tickets available; one of the most popular was an evening trip to Weston Super Mare, leaving Bath at around five and returning

---

2 This was one of several West Country expresses that continued to run via Bath and Bristol, despite the opening of the West of England direct line.

Above: In 1903, in a bid to improve locomotive performance, George Churchward, the GWR's Chief Mechanical Engineer, commissioned a locomotive from a French company to compare it with the company's own locomotives and see if he could pick up any ideas. Here it is seen standing in the station at Bath with a down express.

Below: A down goods train trundles through Oldfield Park around 1909.

about ten-thirty, which cost between ninepence and a shilling. Combined train and steamer trips – train to Clevedon, steamer to Bristol and back to Bath by train – cost three shillings. There were also frequent excursion trains to London for special events.

On 8 December 1909, for example, it cost 5/6 to travel up to London for the day to the Smithfield Cattle Show.

The GWR also made many improvements to local services in the first decade of the twentieth century. The most innovative was the introduction of railmotors – passenger coaches incorporating a steam locomotive, with a cab at each end, so that they did not need to be turned round at the end of each journey. The first railmotors were introduced between Stonehouse and Chalford in Gloucestershire in 1903; within five years there were over a hundred across the network. The problem with railmotors was their lack of capacity; this was solved by the introduction of autotrains in 1905. These were push-and-pull trains with a small locomotive at one end and a coach, with a cab from which the driver could control the engine, at the other. To increase capacity, extra coaches – known as trailers and also fitted with driving cabs – could be added.

As autotrains were introduced, so new halts – very basic and often at ground level, so that passengers had to climb up to and down from the train – were opened. Avoncliff, between Bath and Bradford on Avon, opened on 9 July 1906,

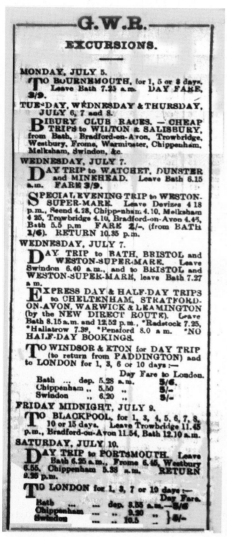

A selection of Great Western Railway excursions from Bath in July 1909.

Avoncliff Halt

455

and is one of the few that still survive. There was another at Hampton Row in Bathwick, which opened on 18 March 1907; unfortunately, this useful little station closed just over ten years later, as part of cutbacks forced on the railways by the war.

The most significant event in terms of rail services around Bath in 1909, however, was the construction of a line from Limpley Stoke to Camerton. This, once again, was the product of inter-company rivalry – although the goal was not passengers but coal. The Somerset Coalfield was served by two companies – the GWR and the Somerset & Dorset, jointly owned by the Midland and London & South Western Railways. The GWR had opened a branch from Hallatrow, on the Bristol-Frome line, to Camerton in

Above: Hallatrow, junction for Camerton and Limpley Stoke.
Below: A train of empty coal wagons near Paulton.

1882. In 1907 they extended this just over a mile to the new colliery at Dunkerton. Although this gave the colliery rail access, it was less than satisfactory, as all the coal had to go west, to Hallatrow, before going on to Bristol or Frome. Not only did this cause congestion; if the coal was destined for Bath or Southampton, it had to go via an extremely circuitous route. As the GWR line from Bath to Westbury was just over six miles to the east, and the abandoned Somersetshire Coal Canal ran from there to the colliery, the obvious solution was to build a railway along the canal bed. Which is what – given a few major deviations here and there – they did.

Combe Hay Tunnel on the Somersetshire Coal Canal – later a railway tunnel on the line between Camerton and Limpley Stoke.

Work started in 1905, and by 1909 was well advanced. On 21 January 1909, the *Bath Chronicle* announced that the bridge carrying the Warminster Road over the railway by the *Viaduct Hotel* at Limpley Stoke had been completed. On 27 May, it reported that 'Notable progress is being made with the Camerton and Limpley Stoke Railway and several of the more important works present quite a finished appearance.' The viaduct and bridge at Midford were complete, the bridge at Dunkerton near the *Swan* was finished and the station approach roads well advanced. Track had been laid from Dunkerton towards Combe Hay. Although there was still a great deal of work to do building embankments between Midford

Top: Although much of the Camerton & Limpley Stoke Railway was laid on the course of the Somersetshire Coal Canal, major earthworks were needed at Midford. Here the embankment and viaduct are seen in course of construction, with two of the contractors' locomotives on temporary tracks laid to carry materials to the site.

Above: A view from the high ground to the west, looking into the cutting and across the embankment and viaduct seen in the previous photograph. The Somerset & Dorset Railway viaduct is in the distance.

Facing page top: A closer view of the digger used to excavate the cutting at Midford.

Facing page bottom: Building the line near Monkton Combe.

and Monkton Combe, the bridge over the Monkton Combe brook was complete. It was at Limpley Stoke, though, that signs of progress were most evident:

Here, the bridge over the brook, consisting of two arches, one over the stream and one over the footpath, has been completed, and the embankment leading to the existing railway is well in hand. The upper course of the road leading from the Warminster Road to Limpley Stoke is to be diverted. In the near future those desirous of reaching Limpley Stoke by road from Bath will first cross the bridge carrying the Warminster Road over the new line, and then proceed over the new portion of the road having the new railway on their left throughout.

The legacy of this complicated arrangement is the awkward staggered junction at the bottom of Brassknocker Hill, and the narrow, steep and dangerously curved approach to it from Limpley Stoke. By the time the *Chronicle* published another update, on 16 December 1909, the new road layout was complete:

> Very substantial progress is being made at Limpley Stoke and Freshford with the construction of the Camerton & Limpley Stoke Railway. For some time now the new portion of the road from the *Viaduct Hotel* to Limpley Stoke station has been open to vehicular traffic, and the bridge conveying the Warminster Road over the new line is also completed. Persons journeying by road from Bath to Limpley Stoke have to cross the new line before entering the diverted portion of the roadway. For the remaining portion of their journey to Limpley Stoke the new railway lies on their left hand. The brook is crossed at this point by a single-arch bridge in blue brick, with an adjoining occupation arch to accommodate the footpath. To the west of Limpley Stoke station a good deal of embankment work has been necessary, and some massive, but hardly beautiful, retaining walls have been erected here.
>
> The actual junction of the new line with the existing Great Western metals will be close to Limpley Stoke station, so as to be under the supervision of the signalman there. For some little distance before this junction is effected the two lines will run parallel. A new signalbox has been built at Limpley Stoke, and the platforms at the Bathampton end of the station are being lengthened. A bay will be constructed on the down platform to accommodate the railmotor, which will work the passenger traffic over the new line, and suitable connections will be provided to enable the coal traffic to be worked through in the direction of Salisbury, and thence on to Southampton.
>
> Between Limpley Stoke and Freshford two new up and down running loops, each about half a mile long, will be provided, and an additional signalbox has been erected at the Freshford end of Limpley Stoke station. Four lines of new sidings are also to be provided here, and the work of excavation necessary for them is now proceeding.

Opposite: The stations at Limpley Stoke, Monkton Combe and Dunkerton.

The line opened on 9 May 1910. Passenger traffic – very light from the start – was withdrawn as a wartime economy measure less than five years later. It was resumed briefly in 1923, but ceased completely in 1925, after which the line was used for goods only. The original line from Hallatrow to Camerton closed in 1932, but the Camerton-Limpley Stoke section survived until 1951. Its

Two views of the station at Camerton. Above: an autotrain calls shortly after opening, with Camerton Old Pit, closed in 1898, but retained to provide an airway to and escape route from Camerton New Pit, in the background.

Below: The station in its heyday, with coal wagons in the siding and milk churns on the platform – but not a passenger in sight.

moment of glory was yet to come, however. The line had already been used to film Arnold Ridley's *The Ghost Train* in 1931, but in 1952 it starred in one of the greatest Ealing Comedies of all – *The Titfield Thunderbolt*. Monkton Combe station was renamed Titfield and the abandoned colliery at Dunkerton was used for the famous duel between a train and a steamroller.

One of the most memorable scenes in the film is the opening sequence, with a Somerset & Dorset express whistling over Midford Viaduct as the Titfield Thunderbolt trundles along below. A century ago, the idea that the Camerton & Limpley Stoke Railway, which had only been built to carry coal, would close when the collieries did, would have seemed perfectly reasonable; the notion that the Somerset & Dorset, only completed, at tremendous expense, 45 years earlier, would last just 57 more would have seemed preposterous. The line was not without its problems – the long climb at 1 in 50 out of Bath, long, narrow tunnels and long stretches of single track. But it not only carried coal; it formed part of an express route between the Midlands and the South Coast. Automatic token-exchanging equipment had recently been introduced on the single-track sections, so that trains did not have to slow down

The Somerset & Dorset signalman at Midford with the automatic token-exchanging equipment introduced by Alfred Whitaker, the company's locomotive superintendent, in 1904-5.

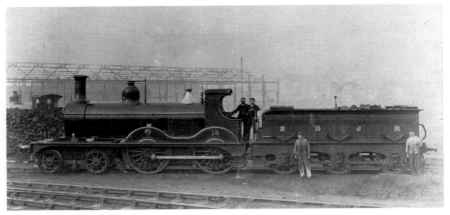

S. & D.J.R.

A Special Service of Express Trains

RUN BETWEEN

BATH, BOURNEMOUTH, and the L. & S.W. RAILWAY, *via* Templecombe, Wimborne, Broadstone and Poole ; also SCOTLAND, the NORTHERN and MIDLAND COUNTIES, NEWCASTLE, YORK, LEEDS, BRADFORD, SHEFFIELD, MANCHESTER, LIVERPOOL, DERBY, BIRMINGHAM, GLOUCESTER, CLIFTON DOWN and BRISTOL.

Through Carriages between Bath, Bournemouth, Bristol, Clifton Down, Gloucester, Cheltenham, Birmingham, Derby, Leeds, Bradford, Sheffield, York, Newcastle, &c.

Breakfast and Luncheon Cars between Bath, Bournemouth and Derby.

SALOON, FAMILY and INVALID CARRIAGES of the Newest Pattern and replete with every Modern convenience, supplied on Two Days' Notice being given.

NOTE.—DURING THE WINTER SEASON.

Tourist and Week-end Tickets, Bookings and Cheap Tickets for Pleasure Parties, Football and Hockey Teams are issued.

DURING THE SUMMER MONTHS

(MAY 2nd to OCTOBER 31st),

DAY EXCURSIONS

Are run from BATH to BOURNEMOUTH, GLASTONBURY, WELLS, BURNHAM, PORTSMOUTH, WEYMOUTH, SOUTHAMPTON, SEATON, &c., &c., and other places of interest.

HALF=DAY EXPRESS EXCURSIONS

Are also run frequently DIRECT from BATH to **BOURNEMOUTH** and **WEYMOUTH**.

Tourist and Week=end Bookings are issued to all popular resorts.

Bills, Programmes, and all information can be obtained at the Stations, the Midland Company's Offices, 24, New Bond Street, or from

GEORGE H. EYRE,

Traffic Superintendent.

Above: Details of Somerset & Dorset services in 1909.

Opposite page top: A 4-4-0 tender locomotive built for the Somerset & Dorset Railway at Derby in 1891, seen here at Bath. Its livery, like all Somerset & Dorset locomotives at the time, was Prussian blue, with black and edging and yellow lining.

Opposite page centre and below: The Somerset & Dorset stations at Radstock and Midsomer Norton, on the line to Bournemouth.

to exchange tokens by hand. Although most trains were semi-fast or slow, by 1909 the fastest expresses between Bath and Bournemouth took only around 1 hour 50 minutes. The Somerset & Dorset was, for generations of Bathonians, the holiday line, even if all that holiday amounted to was a day by the sea. In 1909, August Bank Holiday excursions to Bournemouth over the Somerset & Dorset cost 3/9, while for 2/9 you could take a trip to Burnham – changing at Evercreech Junction.

Above: An Edwardian view of the Midland and Somerset & Dorset station in Bath, now Sainsbury's car park.

Below: Weston station on the Midland line from Bath to Bristol.

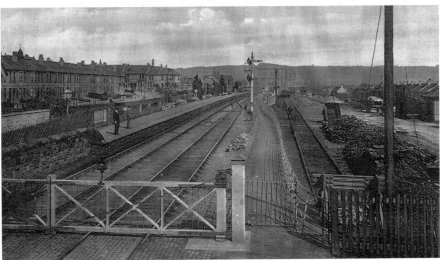

For generations of Bathonians, their annual holiday was a Bank Holiday trip to the seaside. Many went to Weston Super Mare, but for those who could afford a bit more there was Bournemouth or Weymouth. Bournemouth was served by the Somerset & Dorset, Weymouth, seen here on a postcard from around 1909, by the Great Western.

All long gone – as is St Philip's Station in Bristol, near Old Market. Today, the site is covered by a trading estate, but in 1909 it was the terminus for all but a handful of Midland Railway services from Bath to Bristol. The Midland station in Bath has fared somewhat better, although what Edwardian travellers would make of its transformation into a car park is anyone's guess.

A transport link whose days were clearly numbered in 1909 has, however, come back with a vengeance. The Kennet & Avon Canal, one year short of its centenary, was an all-but-forgotten waterway in 1909. Nevertheless, it was expensive to maintain; the section between Bath and Limpley Stoke caused especial problems, with embankments giving way and water breaking through on a regular basis. The pumping station at Claverton was also expensive to run; major work had had to be carried out there in 1902. Although tolls on the canal were much higher than on other waterways, it had been losing money for 30 years or more. The deficit for 1907, for example, was over £5,000. The GWR, which had acquired it in 1852, dearly wanted to see the back of it, and it seemed that abandonment was only a question of time. By 1909, it was carrying virtually no through traffic: the Reading to Newbury and the Bristol to Bath and Devizes sections were still in regular use, but the stretch between Newbury and Devizes saw little traffic. In 1905, only 62,147 tons were carried on the canal, around half the tonnage

Above: Sydney Wharf around 1909: a half-forgotten backwater.
Opposite: A horse-drawn barge near Bathampton.

carried 20 years earlier and less than a fifth of that carried before the GWR opened.

In January 1909, Bath's Inspector of Nuisances – a wonderful job title – reported that he had made 106 inspections of canal boats in the previous year. Several boats previously recorded as dwellings were now used only for cargo. The number of people living on boats was decreasing every year and it was now very unusual to find families living on board. Boats, the inspector added, were unsuitable for women and children; only three of the boats he had inspected had women and children on board.[3] Although many of the boats were very old, the standard of cleanliness and comfort was improving. He concluded his report with the observation that no infectious diseases had been recorded among people living on the canal during the year.

No new boat registrations were taken out in Bath in 1909; of the 56 boats registered, twelve had been destroyed. Another 30 could not be traced and it was felt that at least half of these had probably been broken up, although some were probably working in other parts of the country. The Sanitary Inspector, summing up the situation, stated his belief that 'the number of boats registered by this authority and plying on the local waterways does not exceed 20. Most of the boats passing through the city are registered elsewhere.'

3 Living accommodation on boats at this time, of course, was confined to small cabins, with the majority of space used for carrying goods. Conversion of boats to provide living space throughout was some way in the future.

CHAPTER TWENTY-SEVEN

O BRAVE NEW WORLD

It wasn't just in transport that major technological advances were taking place. The Edwardian period saw gas lighting, which had been around for as long as anyone could remember, begin to give way to electric.

The first gas lights had been installed in Bath in 1819 and their range had been gradually extended. It wasn't until 1909, however, that gas mains reached Saltford. By then Bath's gasworks covered a twelve-acre site on either side of the river, served by the Midland and Somerset & Dorset Railways. A new gasholder had been installed only a year earlier. Initially, gas was used for street lighting, then for lighting houses, and finally, in the 1870s, for heating gas stoves and other household appliances. Gas was made by heating coal to a temperature of over 1000°C in a sealed retort that stopped it igniting. The thick gas that resulted was passed through a series of condensers to remove tar, ammonia and other impurities before

Above: Purifiers at Bath gasworks.

Opposite page top: The offices of the Bath Gas Light & Coke Company on the Upper Bristol Road, built in 1858.

Opposite page bottom: The gas showrooms at 2 Cheap Street,

471

'I met my love by the gasworks wall, Dreamed a dream by the old canal.' Ewan McColl was writing about Salford but he may as well have been writing about Edwardian Widcombe. The canal is still there but the site of the gasholder, which once supplied gas to Widcombe, is now covered by student accommodation.

being pumped into a gas holder. The coal was reduced to coke which, when removed from the retort, was watered down to stop it catching fire; this created the smelly smoke complained of by nearby residents. The gas company sold the coke, as well as other by-products; ammonia was used to make fertiliser, while the tar was taken to Bristol by barge for creosoting timber.

Electricity was a much more recent innovation. In 1889 a boot and shoe dealer called Henry Massingham was contracted to supply electricity to Bath City Corporation. He considered adapting Bathwick Mill for electricity generation but opted for Kingston Mill, near the Great Western station, instead. The City of Bath Electric Lighting & Engineering Company's supply was switched on in June 1890. The supply was largely DC at first but a new AC system was introduced in 1906.

The Corporation took over the company in 1897, but by 1909 were trying to dispose of it to a Mr Schenk. After lengthy negotiations, at the end of January, the Board of Trade ruled that they couldn't sell it and told them that 'the ratepayers must settle down to the idea that it is a permanent possession for good or ill. Whitehall feels that commercial considerations must be waived and a long-sighted policy followed.' The *Chronicle* added that 'generations to come may thank the Board of Trade for their intervention'.

Electricity, like gas, was initially used just for street lighting. In June 1909, electric lights, hitherto confined to the main streets, were installed in Bloomfield Park, showing that suburban streets could be lit at reasonable cost. 60-candlepower gas lights were replaced by 100-candlepower electric lights which, although vastly superior, cost much the same. In September 1909, it was announced that electric lights would be installed on Wellsway between the *Bear* and Bloomfield Road, in Walcot Street, on Bathwick Hill as far as Cleveland Walk, and in Marchant's Passage off Southgate Street.

An increasing number of homeowners were converting to electricity as well. Cables were strung from poles along the street and fed into individual houses – a far quicker and cheaper system than the underground pipes needed for gas. By 1909, electricity was powering the city's trams, factories and workshops, and the relative ease with which new consumers could be 'plugged in' made it clear it would be the power supply of the future. The substitution of tungsten for carbon filaments in electric light bulbs from 1909 created a much brighter light. The days of gas lighting, already unpopular because of its smell and the sooty marks it left on ceilings, were clearly numbered.

Although electricity was starting to take over from gas, both systems relied on the same source of energy – coal, most of which came from the Somerset coalfield. The gasworks were supplied with coal by the Midland and Somerset & Dorset Railways, while the electricity works were supplied by the Great Western. Although so much has changed in the last century, some things – superficially transformed beyond recognition – have, in essence, changed surprisingly little. Electricity may no longer be produced in Bath, nor coal mined in Somerset, but much of the electricity we use still comes from coal.

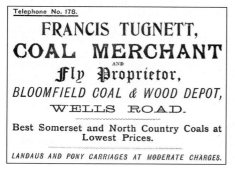

In 1909, there were over 40 coal merchants in Bath, several of them operating from a number of different locations.

In the early 1900s, over 250 million tons of coal was mined in Britain every year. By 2007, that figure had fallen to 17 million tons (over half of which came from open-cast collieries), while 43 million tons was imported. A century ago, coal from North Somerset was taken by train to Kingston Mill in Bath to make electricity; today, imported coal is taken by train from Avonmouth to Didcot power station for the same reason. The principle is the same. One thing that has changed is our awareness of the effect of burning coal. When you consider that, a century ago, Bath in the wintertime was smoky beyond anything we can imagine (look at all the chimneys on those multi-storied Georgian buildings and you'll get some idea of how bad it could get), it seems strange that we, in our smokeless city, should be the ones concerned about global warming.

Another innovation was the telephone. It had been invented in 1877; Bath's first telephones were installed in 1884 by Davis & Sons, gasfitters and plumbers of Walcot Street, who were agents for the United Telephone Company. A national directory published by the company in that year listed just 7,000 numbers, most of them businesses. Two years later, when Bath's first telephone exchange was opened by the Mayor in Union Passage, there were 40 subscribers in the city.

The United Telephone Company merged with several other companies to form the National Telephone Company in 1889. In 1912, all private telephone companies were nationalised to become part of the General Post Office. A larger telephone exchange opened at 11 Northgate Street in 1893, and stayed there until replaced by an automatic exchange in the new central post office in 1929. This was replaced by the Kingsmead exchange in 1967.

Although telephones had been around for 25 years by 1909, and were regarded as standard in the world of trade and commerce, very few homes had them. Public call offices (the forerunner of the telephone box, which appeared after the First World War) were established in post offices, shops and public offices. In Bath, several call offices were situated in the various offices of the tramway company

The first time many young people encountered a telephone, however, was when they started work. Walter Macqueen-Pope describes how daunting such an encounter often was:

> The new office boy, on being told to ring up 'So-and-So', was in a real dilemma. He was shown how to do it but he was afraid of the machine ... The usual telephone then was a wall instrument –

made in Sweden mostly – and it had a hook bearing the receiver on one side and a handle to turn on the other. You turned the handle a few times, removed the receiver – and waited.

It took a good time to get the exchange, and then a female voice said 'Number, please' – and you gave it in and waited again. Altercations between subscriber and the mysterious operator were constant affairs ... The 'number engaged' signal was a hooting noise, as of tugs befogged in the Thames. The young middle-class beginner took quite a time to master the 'phone, but he did so in the end, even to using the spare earphone provided if the line was indistinct, as it mostly was.

The erection of telegraph poles, as the network slowly spread over the city, was often a cause of friction, although rarely so entertainingly as in a meeting at St Michael's Church, Twerton in April 1909. Mr FJ Blackmore complained that two 'telephone poles', which he considered a 'disfigurement', had been erected near the church. Those present tut-tutted their disapproval, until the vicar, the Rev Henry Maynard, intervened, saying that he felt 'a little delicacy in this matter – it is my own telephone'.

Many technological advances had no immediate impact on the lives of ordinary people, although it must have been clear that it would only be a matter of time before they would. Take wireless, for example. The first transatlantic message had been transmitted from Cornwall to Newfoundland in 1901; in 1907, regular telegraphic communication – available, at a price, to the general public – was established between Britain and Canada. By 1909, around 200 ships carried wireless sets. One of them, the *Republic*, collided with an Italian steamer in the Atlantic in fog. The radio operator, Jack Binns, sent an SOS and followed it up with over 200 messages, before the *Baltic*, alerted by radio, arrived to rescue around 1,800 people off the two ships. Shortly afterwards, the *Republic* sank. Only six lives were lost and Binns was a national hero. The following year, Dr Crippen, attempting to flee to Canada with his mistress in disguise, aroused the suspicions of the ship's captain, who alerted the authorities by telegraph. As the ship entered the St Lawrence Seaway, a detective came aboard and arrested him. Crippen's is still one of the most famous crimes of all time, largely due to the manner of his arrest. Perhaps its most extraordinary aspect was that, while everyone in Britain with access to a newspaper was aware of Crippen's forthcoming arrest – there were even songs about it in the music halls – he was blissfully unaware of the net closing around him until the last minute.

Meanwhile, Rutherford, Freud, Einstein and the Curies, along with many others, were busy redefining the world and our place in it. One discovery that Bath really took to its heart, though, was radiation. Madame Curie discovered radium in 1900, and for a long time it was seen, not only as a potential elixir for all ills, but as totally safe. X-ray and radium therapies were all rage. The cosmetics industry jumped on the bandwagon, developing creams containing traces of thorium and radium. One of them was called Tho-Radia – 'stay ugly if you want to' was their slogan. Each 100g of cream contained 0.5g of thorium chloride and 0.25mg of radium bromide.

Bath, too, was keen to boast of the radioactive properties of its healing springs. During a debate on the baths in 1909, Alderman Oliver said he knew 'the Bath waters possess much radioactivity, and we ought to do all in our power to bring that fact prominently before the public.' The hint was taken up, and the radioactivity of Bath's healing springs featured prominently in many advertisements in the ensuing years.

To us, this blind faith seems alarming, if also a little touching. But, reviewing what has happened over the last century, the Edwardians were surely right to feel optimistic about scientific advances. Those advances may have brought us the atom bomb, along with a lot more we could have done without, but they have also consigned many once virulent and fatal diseases to the rubbish bin of history. And, combined with advances in technology, they have freed millions from the drudgery of domestic service. It may be fashionable to sneer at labour-saving devices, but how many of us would wish to return to Edwardian days, when virtually everything had to be done by hand?

It has been a long time since anyone extolled the radioactive properties of the water that bubbles up from below Bath. It was still mentioned in guidebooks as late as the early 1960s, but all reference to it ceased in or around 1963, possibly in response to the Cuban Missile Crisis. In such a way is the 'bad science' of our ancestors conveniently forgotten about. This has been the fate of another scientific theory dear to the hearts of many Edwardians. We don't hear much about eugenics these days, but a century ago you wouldn't have been able to avoid it. It's not surprising we don't hear much of it; not only has it been discredited, it runs counter to all current ideas of human dignity and equality. If you ever had any illusions about how bad things could get a century ago, prepare to

An Edwardian advertisement extolling the radioactive properties of Bath's hot springs.

shed them now; this is a journey to the black heart of Edwardian England.

During a council meeting in Bath in January 1909, it was agreed that Bath should contribute £2,883 to the county lunatic asylum at Wells. This prompted Councillor Evans to say he thought a lot of people were in lunatic asylums who ought not to be, adding, 'To my mind all chronic cases of lunacy should be done away with.'[1] Alderman Phillips replied, 'I don't know whether I can say anything to that. I don't think I should go as far as Councillor Evans. I think they should be sterilised.' There was laughter around the council chamber before the meeting continued with other business.

This is, on any reading, profoundly shocking, but, unless you know what lay behind these remarks, it is actually far more disturbing than at first appears. It sounds no more than an unpleasant joke in the worst possible taste; it actually reflected a major strand in social and scientific thought at the time.

Eugenics was largely the brainchild of Francis Galton. Taking ideas from Charles Darwin, among others, he believed that eugenics would be 'introduced into the national conscience like a new religion ... What nature does blindly, slowly and ruthlessly, man may do providently, quickly and kindly.' Many influential people subscribed to this pseudo-science that had as its aim nothing less than perfecting the human race by a process of selective breeding and the eradication of deficient genetic strains. They saw eugenics as the salvation of the human race at a critical point in its history. Among those appointed honorary vice presidents of the organisation were Winston Churchill, the President of the Royal College of Physicians, the Lord Chief Justice, and Alexander Graham Bell. In 1910, when he was appointed Home Secretary, Churchill tried – and narrowly failed – to introduce compulsory sterilisation laws.[2] There was an overwhelming fear that the British race was becoming enfeebled, that the working classes were breeding more while the birth rate among the upper and middle classes, with their superior strength and intelligence, was falling.

1 Nine months later, Valentine Evans stood down as councillor for Kingsmead and was replaced by Helen Hope, whose attitude to those less fortunate than herself was in marked contrast to that of her predecessor.
2 Compulsory sterilisation programmes were, however, introduced in several US states and two Canadian provinces, as well as elsewhere. The last compulsory sterilisation in the USA was in Oregon in 1981.

One of the things that galvanised public opinion was the number of Boer War volunteers from the working classes who were turned down for active service because they were physically unfit. This was, of course, a classic case of reaching a false conclusion by failing to look at the whole picture. It was true that, by and large, the working classes were physically inferior to the upper and middle classes. But to then say that this was due to breeding ignored the crucial role played by diet and nutrition. It beggars belief that the proponents of eugenics were too blinkered to see what any gardener could have told them – seedlings that are nurtured grow into healthy plants, those set in poor soil and left to their own devices will, if they survive, be stunted and weak.

Montague Crackanthorpe, KC, President of the Eugenics Society from 1909 to 1911, summed up the organisation's position succinctly:

> In England it is among the upper and middle classes that the birth rate shows the most serious decline … The great danger lies in the fact that if the birth-rate of the middle-classes continues to decline as it is now doing, the majority of the British race will be recruited from the physically unfit people of the slums and lower classes.

To many, eugenics was a matter of common sense – cattle and chickens had been improved by selective breeding – why couldn't the same thing be done with people? This raised not only ethical but also practical questions – which features should be developed, and, more important, who should make the decisions? Henry Havelock Ellis neatly summed up the dilemma many chose to ignore: 'Animals,' he pointed out, 'are bred for specific purposes by a superior race of animals, not by themselves.'

The importance of eugenics as a tool for rescuing humanity from a descent into imbecility, however, was accepted by scientists and laymen in the same way that, say, global warming is accepted today.[3] To question the scientific basis for its conclusions was not merely eccentric but morally culpable. Many felt that unless drastic action was taken immediately, a tipping point would be reached, beyond which progressive racial degeneracy would be irreversible.

Some, however, were prepared to take a stand against the prevailing orthodoxy – Arthur Balfour, Conservative PM from 1902 to 1905, for example:

3 This isn't to imply that concerns over global warming aren't justified – the analogy is intended to indicate how much of an orthodoxy eugenics was a century ago.

We say that the fit survive. But all that means is that those who survive are fit. The idea that you can get a society of the most perfect kind merely by considering certain questions about the strain and ancestry and the health and the physical vigour of various components of that society – that I believe is a most shallow view of a most difficult question.

Balfour's injection of a bit of sanity into the proceedings was sorely needed. It wasn't just sterilisation that some eugenicists proposed – for them, nothing less than a cull was good enough. A German scientist called Ernst Haeckel – one of the most influential eugenicists in Germany – wrote in 1904 that, 'rationally speaking, the killing of a crippled newborn child ... cannot be subsumed under the notion of murder, as our modern law books would have it. Instead, we must see and approve of it as a sensible measure, both for those concerned and for all society.'

Terrifying, yes, but then, he was German, and Britain wasn't too keen on Germany at the time, so that doesn't really count, does it? Perhaps not – but DH Lawrence wasn't German. He wrote – to a girlfriend! – in 1908:

> If I had my way, I would build a lethal chamber as big as the Crystal Palace, with a military band playing softly, and a Cinematograph working brightly; then I'd go out in the back streets and main streets and bring them in, all the sick, the halt, and the maimed; I would lead them gently, and they would smile me a weary thanks; and the band would softly bubble out the Hallelujah Chorus.

All right, but that was DH Lawrence, and he always was a bit of a maverick ... Here is Virginia Woolf, writing in her diary on 9 January 1915:

> On the towpath we met and had to pass a long line of imbeciles. The first was a very tall young man, just queer enough to look at twice, but no more; the second shuffled, and looked aside; and then one realised that every one in that long line was a miserable ineffective shuffling idiotic creature, with no forehead, or no chin, and an imbecile grin, or a wild suspicious stare. It was perfectly horrible. They should certainly be killed.

And this is George Bernard Shaw, a no-nonsense rationalist if ever there was one:

There is now no reasonable excuse for refusing to face the fact that nothing but an eugenic religion can save our civilisation from the fate that has overtaken all previous civilisations.

'The past is another country; they do things differently there.' Nothing underlines how far we have come in the last hundred years and how deep is the gulf that separates us from the Edwardians than these appalling extracts – the views not of deranged extremists but of figures generally regarded as among the most enlightened and progressive of their age.

It wasn't just class and mental deficiency that came into the eugenicists' line of fire. Sadly, race came into it as well. Racial prejudice wasn't new, of course, but eugenics took it to a new level. Prejudice that proceeds from ignorance is terrible enough; prejudice that dons the cloak of pseudo-scientific justification is infinitely worse. Here is another writer, HG Wells, on his vision of the future:

How will the New Republic treat the inferior races? How will it deal with the black? How will it deal with the yellow man? How will it deal that alleged termite in the civilized woodwork, the Jew? Certainly not as races at all. It will aim to establish, and it will at last, though probably only after a second century has passed, establish a world state with a common language and a common rule. It will ... make a multiplication of those who fall behind a certain standard of social efficiency unpleasant and difficult ... The Jew will probably lose much of his particularism, intermarry with Gentiles, and cease to be a physically distinct element in human affairs in a century or so. But much of his moral tradition will, I hope, never die ... And for the rest, those swarms of black, and brown, and dirty-white, and yellow people, who do not come into the new needs of efficiency? Well the world is a world, not a charitable institution, and I take it they will have to go.

The utopian visions of a fantasist like Wells were given scientific justification by people like Henry Goddard, an influential American eugenicist who conducted a research experiment at the Ellis Island immigration station in New York and concluded that 83% of Jewish, 80% of Hungarian, 79% of Italian and 87% of Russian immigrants were 'feeble minded'. How much this had to do with their inability to speak English, the traumas of separation from their home-land and family, the privations of a transatlantic crossing and the impertinent probings of a unsympathetic authority figure is not recorded. As a result of his research, Goddard concluded that severe cases of 'feeble-mindedness' should be sterilised to prevent them impeding the development of a 'pure, American, superior race'. In such a climate it is hardly surprising that President Theodore Roosevelt could say that he believed African Americans were 'as a race and in the mass ... altogether inferior to whites'. What would he have said if he had known that, a century on, America would get its first president of African descent?

One of the keenest advocates of eugenicism was, of course, Adolf Hitler; its discrediting is largely due to the implementation of his theories of racial purity. What happened in Germany had been prefigured by writers such as Lawrence and Wells, who embraced the half-baked orthodoxy of eugenicism. The tragedy is that the eugenicists needed to be confronted by the consequences of the orthodoxy they had created for it to be discredited.

It is unfortunate, however, that the eugenics movement has been airbrushed out of history. Only by confronting the darker side of our history can we hope to understand it – and to guard not only against rose-tinted views of the past but also against the blind acceptance of other dodgy orthodoxies in the future.

A century on, sterilisation of criminals and those with low IQs may no longer be on the agenda, but the implications of genetic engineering – far more complex and far-reaching than the would-be social engineers of a century ago could ever have imagined – and the choices we, as a society, make as to its use will have profound consequences for those living a century hence. History is an ever-evolving process; some of the routes we will take may – as they have been in the past – be dangerous dead-ends. We can but hope that, a century hence, we will be judged less harshly than we now judge the Edwardian advocates of eugenic engineering.

It is with a great sense of relief that we turn from the murky world of eugenics to a scientific development that was not only wholly benign but has brought pleasure to millions of adults and children worldwide. Plasticine, uniting science and art, was one of the great successes of Edwardian Bath; the story of how William Harbutt developed and marketed it remains an inspiration to this day.

Harbutt was born in North Shields in 1844 and came to Bath to teach art in 1874, eventually establishing his own college in Bladud

Plasticine — one of the great success stories of Edwardian Bath.

Buildings. In 1876, he married Elizabeth Cambridge, an artist from Royston who had painted miniatures for Queen Victoria.

He felt the need for a modelling medium better than anything then available, so set about making some in the basement of his home, Hartley House on Belvedere. Using calcium salts, petroleum jelly and aliphatic acids, he made a non-toxic putty-like substance, which could not be hardened by firing and did not dry on exposure to the air. So pleased was he with the results – and the demand for it once he started supplying it to local art shops – that in 1900 he bought an old mill at Bathampton to produce it on a commercial basis.

Harbutt was not only an inspired inventor; he was also a great communicator, a great marketing man and a great graphic designer – and he had a single-minded ambition to tell everyone just how good Plasticine was. In 1909, for example, he went to Australia to spread the word over there. With that combination, he couldn't fail – nor did he.

William Harbutt was also a family man – with a large family – and his company was very much a family business. He was one of the highest profile entrepreneurs in Bath in the early 1900s – comparable to Aardman Animations in Bristol today, whose success owes so much to the product William Harbutt developed over a century ago.

Above: William and Elizabeth Harbutt leaving the factory in Bathampton.

Opposite above: William Harbutt, on the left, and members of his family outside their home at the Grange, Bathampton.

Opposite below: Walking from church, Sunday, 14 October 1906.

One of the better-known photographers who recorded Edwardian Bath for posterity was TC Leaman, whose studio was at 7 The Corridor. Harry Hatt's hairdressing saloon can be seen to the right at No 8. This recessed entrance has been swept away and replaced by a modern frontage flush with the line of the Corridor.

486

CHAPTER TWENTY-EIGHT

DAYS OF WINE AND ROSES

Edwardian society was institutionally racist, homophobic, xenophobic and sexist; add to that the ritual flogging of children, elitism and exclusivity of the worst sort, and you've got a fairly unpleasant mix. But, for all that, it was an exciting time to live and things were changing fast – not only the obvious things like transportation and technology, but also attitudes. There was a very real sense that the lid was going to be blown off the whole business in short order – whether people liked it or not. For the old guard, with vested interests, the prospect must have been terrifying, but for those who were forging a new identity after what seemed centuries of repression, they were heady times – if a little scary. In politics, transportation and social organisation – not to mention music, literature and the arts – the old world was being torn apart; it would soon be torn apart in rather more unpleasant ways as well.

But the myth of the Golden Age persists. This wasn't something invented long after the event, by people who'd never been there. It was propagated by those gilded beings who didn't have to endure hunger or the daily grind and who looked back on the Edwardian age, after the cataclysm of the Great War, as a sort of paradise lost – Dame Irene Vanbrugh, for example, star of the London and New York stage, who recalled summer evenings, with 'bicycles piled outside the old Star and Garter Hotel at Richmond and the strains of a waltz [tinkling] across the darkening river, when Chinese lanterns caught the gleam of bright dresses and bright faces as Cockney clerks and their girls drifted by in punts and rowing boats. It was a gentle scene. There was a sort of unconscious acceptance of a beautiful world – and it *was* a beautiful world in many ways.'

But, even if many privileged Edwardians later saw the period before the war as a Golden Age, at the time such a view would have seemed distinctly odd. A leader in the *Times* on 19 January 1909, discussing the threat of socialism, was of the opinion that contemporaries 'place the Golden Age behind them, and assume that no generation ever had to deal with evils so great and perplexing as those of the present day'.

The two main things that militated against Golden Ageism were the escalation of the arms race and the problems generated by social inequality. If we were to be transported back to Edwardian England, we would find the extremes of wealth and poverty as shocking as those in, say, India today. Many found them shocking even then. In 1909, CF Masterman, wrote that 'again and again the foreigner and the colonial, entering this rich land with too exuberant ideals of its wealth and comfort, have broken into cries of pain and wonder at the revelation of the life of poverty festering round the pillars which support the material greatness of England'.

Inequality wasn't anything new, of course; what had changed was the attitude of the ruling classes. Compare King Edward, his life given over to a round of pleasure, with Prince Albert, who wore himself out in service to his adopted country. The reaction against the high seriousness of the Victorians had become an obsession. Along with a distrust of the arts and anything smacking of intellectual endeavour went a fanatical devotion to manly sports – hunting, shooting, fishing, racing, yachting – and the pursuit of the ladies. Well-bred idleness and the ostentatious display of wealth were elevated to art forms. All scruples about flaunting wealth were abandoned. 'Money, the supplanter of birth,' wrote Esmé Wingfield-Stratford, 'had at last with good King Edward come into its own; Cassels and Sassoons, Rothschilds and Lawsons, were such men as he delighted to honour.'

Many found this headlong pursuit of pleasure profoundly disturbing. 'The young,' wrote Masterman, 'look forward with foreboding, wondering how long the artisan, the shop assistant, the labourer, the unemployed, will be content to acquiesce in a system which expends upon a few weeks of random entertainment an amount that would support in modest comfort a decent family for a lifetime.'

Edwardian England can be characterised as a fast car raising the dust and scattering lesser mortals in its wake; on its leather seats reclines a portly, top-hatted gentleman, clad in astrakhan and puffing on a cigar, his arm round a showgirl, en route to a weekend's shooting in the country, while in the gutter a girl in rags roots for a crust. The Edwardian age had more in common with the eighteenth century than the nineteenth, but there was one importance difference – a hysteria, absent from the court of Beau Nash, underpinning all. Masterman called it 'delirium', adding that it 'would seem to be the fate of all societies which become content in secured wealth and gradually forget the conditions of labour and service upon which alone that security can be maintained'.

At the root of this hysteria or delirium was a feeling that society as presently constituted was doomed. Much of the popular music and poetry of the time expressed a curious sort of nostalgia – curious because it was for a time that had not yet passed away, but was instead trembling on the point of dissolution, like a rose glimmering in a breathless twilight, whose petals will fall with the next gust of wind.

> They are not long, the days of wine and roses :
>   Out of a misty dream
> Our path emerges for a while, then closes
>   Within a dream.

That was Ernest Dowson writing in the 1890s, striking a note of melancholy that runs through Edwardian literature. So many Edwardian novelists seem to have been chronicling a civilisation in its death throes; ennui is the dominant emotion. The old order, based on the life of aesthetics, intellect, taste, good breeding, was being swept away by the force of material progress. Some writers, such as HG Wells, seem to have believed that material progress would sweep away not only society but also civilization and possibly life itself. Others, reviewing the state of the world, thought that total annihilation was, on balance, probably a good thing. Thomas Hardy's 'Before Life and After', published in 1909, expresses a wish not just for personal but cosmic oblivion:

> A time there was – as one may guess
> And as, indeed, earth's testimonies tell –
> Before the birth of consciousness,
> When all went well.
>
> None suffered sickness, love, or loss,
> None knew regret, starved hope, or heart-burnings;
> None cared whatever crash or cross
> Brought wrack to things.
>
> If something ceased, no tongue bewailed,
> If something winced and waned, no heart was wrung;
> If brightness dimmed, and dark prevailed,
> No sense was stung.
> But the disease of feeling germed,

And primal rightness took the tinct of wrong;
Ere nescience shall be reaffirmed
How long, how long?

Looking back at the Edwardian age in the early 1930s, Esmé Wingfield-Stratford wrote that 'It was a cliché of the time that it was one of transition. But this rather implied that there was somewhere to go, whereas all that was really certain was that the old order of things had been left definitely behind. In a surprisingly short time after the old Queen's death, the reaction against everything Victorian had completely triumphed.' The Edwardians felt themselves to be, in a phrase coined by Matthew Arnold as long ago as the 1850s, 'wandering between two worlds, one dead, the other powerless to be born'.

The Edwardian age was the crucible in which the modern world was born – and crucibles are not very pleasant places to be. It was a time of profound dislocation and discomfort; change was inevitable, but there seemed no way it could be accommodated within the parameters of the world people knew. And, of course, it couldn't. The Edwardians felt themselves to be sitting on a powder keg for the very good reason that they were. The upheaval of cataclysmic proportions they knew was coming came in the form of the Great War; if it hadn't come in that form, it would have come in another – civil war in Ireland, civil unrest and strikes on the mainland, a worker's revolution, a military coup, who can say? All people knew in 1909 was that what was coming would not be pleasant. Esmé Wingfield-Stratford captured this feeling of impending doom:

> No one, surely, who remembers that time, can have forgotten, unless he is abnormally insensitive, the apprehension, never very far below the threshold, of some approaching peril – it might be German, it might be Red or even Yellow, but in any case destined to break the continuity of the safe and prosperous life of those who could afford to live it ... It was a gay age, but with something of the hectic gaiety that one can imagine in the latter stages of Belshazzar's Feast ... The astonishing thing is that the catastrophe should have hung fire as long as it did.

The sense of ennui and a fear that their privileged lifestyle was going to be swept away was, of course, confined to a relatively small number of people. The majority of the population was too busy trying to earn a living, to put enough food on the table, to keep warm, to bother about such highfalutin ideas. One thing did unite rich and poor, however – an increasing excitability. Esmé Wingfield-Stratford characterised this as a

> tendency to get wildly excited on the least provocation … In the nineties came the outburst of music-hall patriotism and Empire boosting, many of whose recorded utterances read to us now like the ravings of lunacy … England was becoming a nation with nerves, a nation morbidly responsive to mass suggestion and extravagant in its responses. The day was already beginning to dawn of what was known, with accuracy, as the craze. The 1900s were to see many such outbursts – ping-pong, treasure-hunting, diabolo, and all sorts of more or less honest competitions, harmless in themselves … but unmistakably symptomatic of the ease with which mass suggestion could be applied. There were other ways which were not harmless at all. It might be a paying journalistic proposition to work up hysterical excitement and panic against the imaginary beings who were supposed to represent foreign nations. It might be possible to inflame already existing hatreds to the pitch of civil war.

Left: Jean Aylwin, a celebrated Edwardian actress, demonstrates a diabolo.

Right: A comic postcard suggesting that even those who declared such things beneath them were caught up in the craze.

This over-excitability was accompanied by the advance of neurasthenia. The term neurasthenia was first used by George Beard in 1869 to describe a condition characterised by fatigue, headache, anxiety, impotence, neuralgia and depression. This seems a particularly modern malady, something the Edwardians – according to the costume-drama interpretation of history – wouldn't have worried their heads about. And, if they had felt it coming on, they would, according to another myth, have stiffened their upper lip, put a brave face on it, and played the man. The fact is, however, that neurasthenia – which was believed to be a reaction to the stresses of modern life – was rampant in the Edwardian age, and was just as typical of it as displays of impassive bravado. The Second Symphony of Edward Elgar contains a third movement suffused by a neurasthenic breakdown of order, with insistent drumbeats, screaming brass and disjointed rhythms; it provides just as apposite a signature tune for the age as his more conventional and popular works.

Neurasthenia was the great disease of the age. Many believed it indicated a radical shift in human nature, but of course it didn't. It was a response to an unprecedented wave of technological innovation and the social changes that followed in its wake. While we should not forget that there was much optimism in the Edwardian era, it was generally confined to those on the side of change – scientists working on cures for some of mankind's most virulent and deadly diseases; artists breaking away from hidebound tradition and developing new ways of seeing the world; engineers creating ever faster, ever more powerful machines; social reformers and revolutionaries confident that the end of inequality was finally in sight. For those who clung to the old order, all this optimism just confirmed them in their belief that the world was going to hell in a hand cart.

One of the most high-profile and tragic victims of neurasthenia in Bath was Mr Campbell Cory, and it is with the report of his death from the *Bath Chronicle* that we end this brief but undeniably gloomy survey of the Edwardian state of mind:

> One of the richest men in Bath, Mr Saxton Campbell Cory, caused consternation when it was revealed that he shot himself at his home, Cranwells, on Sunday 5 September 1909. He was 54 years old, the eldest son of Richard Cory JP of Cardiff, who with his brother was the founder of Cory Bros the shipping line.

Mr Campbell Cory had been suffering from depression for some time. The circumstances surrounding his death were revealed at the inquest. On the advice of his physician, Dr Forbes Fraser of the Circus, Mr Cory had travelled to Hampton Court where a nerve specialist recommended that a medical attendant should be constantly present with Mr Cory, and so he engaged the services of a Dr Coomber and stayed in London for three weeks.

Mr Campbell Cory

On the fateful day Mr Cory, having decided that the air of Bath would do him good and promote sleep, drove in his own motor with Dr Coomber and a solicitor friend, Mr Fothergill Evans of Chepstow. There was a puncture ten miles outside Bath. They eventually reached Cranwells where Mr Cory introduced Dr Coomber to the housekeeper, Mrs Harford, and a cousin, Miss Matthew, who was staying in the house. After he went up to the bedroom Mrs Harford followed to ensure that all was well. Mr Cory 'looked so strange I went to call his cousin'. She took two steps, heard a shot and found him on the ground.

The medical evidence revealed that Mr Cory 'didn't want to do anything but lie about' and 'took no interest in anything'. A Dr Tweedie said he suffered from the eye disease corodotis and was apprehensive that it would get worse, He was taking 7½ - 9 grains of the recently discovered barbiturate veronal at night for sleeplessness, He was planning to get a nurse in. He died within three minutes with a 1½ inch wound in the temple.

Mr Fothergill Evans said Mr Cory was obsessed with the notion that his friends were planning to put him into a home. Mr Cory was aware that discussions had taken place with a Dr Johnson who kept a mental home in London. Dr Stewart said there had never been signs of suicidal tendency.

It emerged during the inquest that Mr Cory's wife, Constance, and their only daughter had resided for some years at St. Leonards. They did not appear in court.

The verdict of the Coroner was: Suicide during a period of temporary insanity.

Campbell Cory with his retinue outside Cranwells in happier times.

The mansion, Cranwells, had been built for Sir Jerom Murch – seven times Mayor of Bath. It stood in 15 acres and originally cost £16,000. Mr Cory spent vast sums on the estate; it was said to be the first house outside Bath to have electric lighting. The grounds were opened up to the YMCA and temperance organisations for money-raising fêtes. He supported the war-wounded during and after the South African war with money and jobs. He was Vice-President of Bath Rugby Club but would not participate in the administration of political or social bodies, though he had been a JP when resident in Chepstow.

He was frequently asked to stand for parliament and to become mayor but steadfastly refused At his death his estate was estimated to be worth £250,000. The house and contents were eventually sold by auction, with antique dealers attending from all over the country. The house was bought by the Pitman family and later became Summerfield School.

CHAPTER TWENTY-NINE

THE HUN IS AT THE GATE

Perhaps the most blatant expression of the hysteria that bubbled away below the surface of Edwardian society was the panic over fears of German invasion. Admittedly, the Germans have to bear some of the blame for this, especially the Kaiser, a man 'who couldn't sit still for a moment' – another victim of neurasthenia – and who was obsessed with building a navy to rival Britain's.

The strange thing is that Britain should have been anti-German at all. The Kaiser was Queen Victoria's grandson. He had been present at her death and headed the procession at her funeral. France was Britain's traditional enemy and remained so until around 1901, when the Conservative government was still exploring the possibility of a formal alliance with Germany. True, Edward VII didn't like his imperial nephew and was a regular visitor to France, but the first real dent in Britain's relationship with Germany came when it applauded the Boers in their fight against the British – although, to be fair, most other countries expressed similar anti-British sentiments, if only because of instinctive feelings of sympathy towards an underdog. It was the Kaiser's determination to build a first-rate navy that really rang the alarm bells, though.

At the risk of stating the obvious, Britain had a powerful navy because it was an island and needed to defend itself from attack by sea. For countries on the mainland of Europe, defence relied more on land than sea forces. Britain's navy also protected its trade routes and imperial possessions. For Germany, which had little coastline, relatively few overseas possessions and no seafaring tradition to speak of, the desire for a world-class navy could mean only one thing – they were planning to invade.

The Germans were busy building ships long before Britain started to get worried – 14 large battleships between 1893 and 1903, plus many more cruisers, torpedo boats and other craft. It was Jackie Fisher, appointed First Sea Lord in 1904, who really awakened the country to the scale of the threat. 'Only a congenital idiot with criminal tendencies,' he declared, 'would permit any tampering with the maintenance of our sea supremacy. Once beaten the war is finished. Beaten on land, you can improvise fresh armies in a few weeks. You can't improvise a new navy. It takes four years.' To cope with the German threat, he insisted, the only answer was a fleet of battleships that could blow anything else out of the water – battleships that would fear nothing, or 'dread nought'. The first of them was launched at Portsmouth on 10 February 1906.

The Conservative government had decided that four Dreadnoughts would be built a year. When the Liberals came to power in 1906, however, they cut the figure to three a year. In 1908, only two were built. The Germans, meanwhile, had not slackened the pace of their relentless expansion, launching two new classes of battleship – Nassau in 1907 and Helgoland in 1909 – in response to the Dreadnoughts. When, early in 1909, it seemed that the British government was going to cut back on naval expenditure yet again, the nation was gripped by fears – fuelled by statements from naval and military leaders – not only that the country's naval supremacy was slipping away but that Germany was planning to invade. There were reports of a secret plan to land 70,000 men on the east coast, of 'an enemy in our midst' ready to poison water supplies and cut transport links as a sea-borne army swept ashore, supported by bombs dropped from Zeppelins.

A lot of this fear wasn't rational – but, at the risk, once again, of stating the obvious, fear very often isn't rational. It is also easy, for those in a position of authority, to manipulate public anxiety for their own ends, and it seems likely that this was going on here. Certainly, the build-up of the German navy gave justifiable cause for alarm, but invasion never really seems to have been a serious threat. The need to confront German forces, on sea and, quite possibly, on land, seemed increasingly likely. At sea – so long as naval building didn't slip disastrously behind – there wouldn't be a problem; that would come on land. Compared with Germany and other European powers, Britain's army was tiny, and was mainly committed to keeping the peace in India and other parts of the empire. Military leaders were desperate to build up the strength of the army so that it would be capable of fighting, if necessary, on the mainland of Europe. The most effective way of doing this would be to introduce conscription, as Germany had done. The problem was that the government, as well as public opinion, was firmly opposed to this. The only way that advocates of conscription could bring public opinion round to an acceptance of the need for it was by convincing the public that invasion was imminent. And so fears of invasion were whipped up for all they were worth. The strategy didn't work – conscription was only introduced, with some reluctance, over a year after the outbreak of war in 1916 – but at least the government capitulated on the Dreadnoughts and decided that four should be built in 1909.

One of those committed to warning the public of the threat of invasion was the Bishop of Bath & Wells. Speaking at Claverton in March 1909, he told the congregation that 'It is our duty to resist

The Edwardian arms race focused on naval supremacy: the dreadnought HMS Neptune was launched at Portsmouth on 30 September 1909, four days after the Kaiser launched Helgoland, Germany's first super-dreadnought, at Kiel.

Territorial forces such as the North Somerset Yeomanry made up a good part of Britain's army. Here members of the Yeomanry are seen riding along the Paragon.

invaders from taking our land and overcoming it.' At a confirmation service at St James's in Bath, he talked again of the 'likelihood of invasion' and urged the congregation 'to think about our own land and homes and see what can be done to strengthen the nation'.

Some were brave enough to condemn this sort of scaremongering, but they were few and far between. In a council meeting on 5 October 1909, a letter from Commander Critchley, the Secretary of the Navy League, was read out, asking the council

> to co-operate with the coming anniversary of Trafalgar and make it general throughout the country. On all sides we see preparations being made to wage war upon the sea and to destroy the maritime supremacy of the country ... In this celebration there is no desire to indulge in 'flag wagging' but to recognise that the existence of the British Empire depends on our superiority at sea ... You are asked to hoist municipal flags.

Councillor Evans moved that the letter be thrown in the wastepaper basket, but there was no seconder and it was agreed to fly municipal flags on 21 October.

The 'enemy in our midst' was another constant theme. Colonel Clayton, guest of honour at the Bath Licensed Victuallers Annual

Dinner, told his audience he was 'afraid the people of this country do not yet realise to the full the necessity for our home defence. I believe I am safe in saying that our intelligence departments are aware that at this very moment there are in the United Kingdom no fewer than 5,000 spies in the pay of the continental government.' Colonel Clayton's estimate was conservative compared with Lord Roberts, who stated his belief that there were 80,000 trained German soldiers in Britain, while the Conservative MP Sir John Barlow said he knew of 68,000 German reservists in the London area alone.

The *Daily Mail* instructed its readers to 'refuse to be served by an Austrian or German waiter. If your waiter says he is Swiss, ask to see his passport.' In 1906, the novelist William Le Queux fuelled the hysteria with a best-selling tale called *The Invasion of 1910* in which Germans who have served in the army come over to England to work as waiters, clerks, bakers, hairdressers and private servants, while continiung to honour their oath to their fatherland and operating as spies. In 1909, he published a follow-up, *Spies of the Kaiser: Plotting the Downfall of England,* whose hero manages to frustrate German attempts to steal plans of British battleships, submarines and planes and obtain information about Britain's coastal defences. In his introduction to the book, Le Queux affirmed his belief that 'England is the paradise of the spy, and will remain so until we can bring pressure to bear to compel the introduction of fresh legislation against them'; he also told his readers that, 'as I write, I have before me a file of amazing documents, which plainly show the feverish activity with which this advance guard of our enemy is working.'

Although there is no evidence that any such documents existed, soon after the book was published, Le Queux started to receive letters describing 'the suspicious behaviour of German waiters, barbers and tourists in the vicinity of telephone, telegraph, and railway lines, bridges, and water-mains on the east coast and near London'. He passed these on to Lieutenant-Colonel James Edmonds, a counter-intelligence office, who 'used them to construct a picture of what he supposed was the German intelligence organization in Britain'. By such means did a work a fiction come to influence British foreign policy. Two years later, the 1889 Official Secrets Act was revised, effectively shifting the burden of proof from the prosecution to the defence in cases of alleged espionage.

It wasn't only invasion by sea that the public was growing anxious about; fears of aerial invasion – or at least bombardment

– were fuelled by novels such as HG Wells' *The War in the Air*, published in 1908, in which Germany bombs New York. A short film by Walter R Booth, *The Aerial Torpedo*, in which the hero brings down a Zeppelin dropping bombs on England with an experimental aerial torpedo, was one of the most popular cinematographic entertainments in 1909. In June 1909, the *Morning Post* appealed for donations to build an airship for the nation; a correspondent in the *Bath Chronicle* drew attention to the appeal, adding that, 'While France and Germany are making extensive trials, little is being done here. I appeal for larger support to this appeal … If we do not retain our supremacy of the sea and obtain a supremacy of the air, we shall have to bow to a foreign flag.'

However, airship trials were taking place near Bath, as the *Chronicle* reported on 27 May:

> With a hundred or so of captive airships hovering over Britain by night, emitting terrifying whiz and whir, and sometimes accompanied by men who talk in guttural tones, it must give a certain amount of satisfaction to known that, despite accusations of indifference to the defensive needs of the country, the War Office is alert as to the danger which is present. Away in the wilds of Wiltshire … a battery of field artillery, and a balloon company and searchlight company of Royal Engineers have been engaged in exciting experiments. They have sent up captive balloons, not too large, and therefore not too easy targets. In strong winds the balloons have described circles in the air, and generally made things as difficult as possible for the gunners below. A field gun is not a very handy article, but, judging from reports, the gunners have succeeded in making such excellent practice on the balloons that they have been demolished in the air at a range of about 1,200 yards. This is excellent and proves that the artillery can shoot straight. But, after all, the problem of destroying airships is by no means solved. An airship which can be manoeuvred, which can mount much higher than the 800 feet these captive balloons attained, is a very difficult object to strike. Mr Wells, in his fanciful *War in the Air*, pictures the great guns defending New York Harbour as being quite ineffective against the German airships. There is at present little doubt that his view is correct; but it is comforting to know that the War Office has the matter in hand, and, doubtless, from the small beginnings of Wiltshire and the captive balloons will come greater experiments to

master the greater problems of high angle-fire against airships with more power of evading the aim of the gunners.

The same edition of the paper carried a report of an unidentified flying object that had been seen by children in Bathwick:

A sensation was caused in the neighbourhood of Bathwick on Monday afternoon between half past four and five, by an object resembling an airship, which came in a westerly direction and travelled towards Bathford. Several children on their way home from school witnessed its passage, describing it as of cigar-like shape. It was distinctly outlined against the clear sky. The appearance of the object created a great impression in the minds of those who saw it.

Amid the general panic, those who counselled moderation and refused to concur in the general perception of Germans as barbarians intent on invasion found it hard to make their voices heard. In a meeting at New King Street Methodist Church in December 1909, the Rev Stephen Burrow submitted resolutions passed in Berlin and London by the churches of Germany and Britain during interchange visits in 1908 and 1909, appealing to all classes in both nations to promote a mutual spirit of goodwill and friendship, and denounce that section of the popular press that was trying to foment strife between the nations. The meeting supported the resolutions and expressed a desire that the bond of peace between the two peoples might be preserved and strengthened. It was a plea that fell on deaf ears.

One of the most disturbing aspects of Edwardian jingoism, to modern eyes, is the extent to which children were corralled into demonstrations of patriotic and military fervour. One of the most potent examples of this was Empire Day, celebrated on Queen Victoria's birthday, 24 May. Its aim was 'to remind children that they formed part of the British Empire, and that they might think, with others in lands across the sea, what it meant to be sons and daughters of such a glorious Empire'. Processions and rallies, at which the union flag was saluted amid the singing of patriotic songs, instilled into them the belief that 'the strength of the Empire depended upon them, and they must never forget it'.

In Bath, the Victoria League, an organisation devoted to instilling the importance of the empire in all its citizens, decided that Empire Day in 1909 should outdo all previous ones. They announced that there would be a fête in Royal Victoria Park, with all elementary school children – and their teachers – expected to attend. Initially, the teachers' association objected, saying that they had no objection to children being invited to the fête and being addressed by a member of the League, but, as Empire Day was a holiday, they did not like being ordered about. When they were told that Lord Roberts was going to speak, however, they 'took a more favourable view'.

On the great day, the streets were decorated, people wore rosettes and many houses flew union flags. Major Simpson's house in Queen Square was, the *Chronicle* noted, especially striking. Even the pulpit of St Luke's Church sported a union flag, although here the *Chronicle* was forced to point out that 'There is no foundation for the rumour that some members of the congregation objected.'

'I think,' said one of the speakers at the fête, 'it will be conceded by everyone that this is a most memorable day in the history of Bath.' It certainly must have been an impressive sight, with a 'vast concourse' of around 5,000 boys and girls on a sloping lawn before a military orchestra, watched by thousands more spectators. At eleven o'clock, 5,000 voices sang the National Anthem, followed by *The Flag of Britain*, with 5,000 pairs of arms waving flags. Then came the feeding of the 5,000 as each child was given a bun; the celebrations ended with half the children heading towards Queen Square behind the Somerset Industrial School Band and half following the Sutcliffe Industrial School drum-and-pipe band along Brock Street.

The first decade of the twentieth century saw the establishment and rapid growth of several organisations for boys and young men, all of which sought to instil a sense of duty, obedience and resourcefulness into their members. To what extent they promoted military ideals is debatable. Certainly, some unease was felt in certain quarters at the time. The oldest of these organisations was the Boys' Brigade, founded in Glasgow in 1883. At a Boys' Brigade demonstration at the Guildhall on 20 May, Captain FN Orr, clearly responding to adverse criticism, said the organisation was unjustly accused of fostering a spirit of militarism. They were not trying to prepare boys for the army; they were training them to lead a dutiful life.

Others had no such qualms. The Church Lads' Brigade, founded in 1891, was one of several organisations inspired by the success of the Boys' Brigade. When Field Marshal Lord Grenfell wrote to the *Bath Chronicle* in April 1909 soliciting subscriptions for the local battalion, he said that the brigade strove to make its lads God-fearing

Above: The 4th Bath Company of the Boys' Brigade, whose headquarters were at Victoria Hall in Larkhall.

Below: Demonstrating prowess with Indian clubs in Sydney Gardens. These boys look to have been eleven or twelve when this photograph was taken around 1909. That would have made them 20 or 21 by 1918, more than enough time for them to have been conscripted and sent off to war. Although we have tried, in the words of John Cleese, not to mention the war, images like this make speculation, with the dubious benefit of hindsight, almost inescapable and almost unbearably sad.

men and teach them to do right for conscience' sake. He went on to say, however, that 'They are trained for national service and to be fit for any duty to the state which the emergency of the moment might call upon them to fulfil.'

During the Siege of Mafeking in 1899-1900, Colonel Robert Baden-Powell organised the town's boys into a youth corps. After the war, he decided to set up a youth organisation on similar lines in Britain. He wanted boys to be 'scouts' rather than miniature soldiers, and so the most famous youth organisation of all was born. The first scout troops were established in 1907; soon, there were over 100,000 scouts in the country. In 1909, 11,000 scouts attended a rally at the Crystal Palace; some, to Baden-Powell's surprise, were girls, whom he handed over to his sister to form the nucleus of the Girl Guide movement. In July 1909, the *Bath Chronicle* reported that 'Major Baden-Powell's movement is making good progress in Bath. "Troops" have been established with the YMCA in Widcombe and Wells Road districts and at Weston.' At a Sunday evening church parade at All Saints, Lansdown – the first in Bath – hymns included *Onward Christian Soldiers, Soldiers of Christ Arise, Fight the Good Fight, Stand Up, Stand Up for Jesus* and *The Son of God Goes Forth to War.*

In the first week of 1909, a branch of the National Service League, which advocated that all men between 18 and 21 should receive military training, was formed in Bath, with Lord Roberts as president. At a meeting on 18 March at St Peter's Hall, Twerton, the chairman, WJ Cook, explained that the aim of the League was to encourage patriotism and make men and boys smarter by physical training. Lieutenant-Colonel HP Dalzell-Walton said that all other European countries had ceased to rely for their defence on voluntary enlistment. He proposed that every British boy and girl should be taught patriotism at school, and that all boys should undergo physical training and be taught how to use a rifle. Boys should also undergo six months' compulsory military training at the age of 18 and attend annual camps for the following three years. Colonel HV Hunt of St George's Hill, Bathampton, the secretary of the local branch, reinforced his comments, adding that 'Nothing but a nation in arms, with the whole manhood of the country trained to defend their homes will be sufficient to secure England from the ruin and misery which is at least possible.'

Few voices were raised in opposition. At the YMCA Debating Society on 6 April, the motion 'that compulsory military training is unnecessary and unwise for England' attracted a large audience, including many women, and was overwhelmingly defeated, with only twelve votes in favour.

At a meeting of the council Education Committee on 15 January, it was proposed to establish a rifle club at the Technical School; several objections were lodged and a decision was deferred. The same month, however, Lord Roberts opened the Bath Rifle Club's new miniature range in Monmouth Place. The club, which had been founded in 1898, had folded in 1908, largely

Lord Roberts of Kabul and Kandahar

because the cost – fourpence for seven shots – put many people off. When it was reformed in January 1909 the price was reduced to twopence and 130 members signed up. In his opening speech, Lord Roberts said that shooting practice should be compulsory, but until such time as it was he would give all the support he could to rifle clubs. His speech over, he fired the first shot and scored a bull's eye.

Two territorial army units were based in Bath – the 4th Battalion The Prince Albert's Somersetshire Light Infantry and the Wessex Divisional Royal Engineers. In addition, many men from Bath were in the North Somerset Yeomanry, which was based in Shepton Mallet. In March 1909 the *Chronicle* reported that the 4th Battalion of the Somersetshire Light Infantry was 'now up to strength, being one of the first regiments in the kingdom to achieve that distinction', with 34 officers and 980 other ranks. It added that 'smart young men will be welcomed as recruits to replace those who signed on for only one year.' In October, the *Chronicle* covered a Royal Engineers exercise that failed to go according to plan:

The local company of Engineers had an exciting experience at their drill on Saturday. The company, with the wagons and pontoon equipment, had proceeded via Warminster Road to Bathampton, their intention being to bridge the canal and return by the London Road. The bridge was well constructed in good time at a spot near the schools, but the available site presented a very difficult approach on both sides, there being a considerable bank, in addition to the canal bank itself, followed on the exit side by a very sharp turn between a belt of trees into the roadway. The two tool-carts made the crossing safely, but the leaders of the trestle wagon had never before crossed a military bridge, and the rattle and sway often proves trying to horses until used to it. In addition to this, these bridges are not wider than necessary, and great care has to be taken to keep in the centre, as there are no rails at the side, only a six-inch riband to keep the planking down. However, this wagon had safely reached to within a yard or two of the far bank, when the near leader inclined too much to the left, and placed one forefoot quite over the edge, causing it to overbalance and fall into the canal, taking its rider with it; he, fortunately, dropped the rein of the other leader, which gained the bank all right; but in falling the first horse pulled over the two wheelers, with their driver, and in less time than it takes to tell there was a confused mass of men and horses struggling in the water. As they were only walking, the wheels did not jump the riband,

The 4th Battalion The Prince Albert's Somersetshire Light Infantry outside their Drill Hall on the Lower Bristol Road.

otherwise wagon and all must have toppled over. But everyone kept splendidly cool, and no time was lost in helping the two drivers to the bank and liberating the horses, one of which, as soon as free, seemed in no way disconcerted, but made its way down the centre of the canal towards Bath, and had gone some half a mile before a driver was enabled to persuade it towards land by a grappling iron thrown to catch in its collar. The other two proved much more difficult to extricate, owing to the steep banks, but eventually all – men and horses – were safely landed, and apparently little the worse for their involuntary immersion, although it seemed impossible that they could escape injury. The bridge being dismantled, the company returned to Bath, everyone thankful that such slight inconvenience had followed the accident, which afforded considerable excitement, if not alarm, among a large crowd of onlookers.

Fears of German invasion were fuelled, in 1909, by what by all accounts was the theatrical sensation of the year. *An Englishman's Home*, written by Major Guy du Maurier, was described by the *Annual Register* as 'a forcible and cleverly-written argument in favour of universal military training'. In June, Bath audiences had the opportunity to see 'the play over which such controversy has raged and which has attracted record houses. Those who are in sympathy with the object of the play,' reported the *Chronicle*, 'are keenly delighted with it and those who strenuously oppose what they call a tendency to militarism cannot help being stirred to admiration at the brilliant stage realism that is its outstanding feature.' The play took the convention of middle-class drawing-room drama, but added an unexpected twist. Into the cosy world of diabolo, afternoon tea and tennis parties, some soldiers intrude, ask questions and leave. It isn't long, though, before a detachment of cavalry is spotted camping on the lawn and the house is captured by black-bearded dragoons. Put like that, it sounds like farce – and, indeed, some members of the family take the whole thing very lightly, but comedy soon turns to tragedy when the master of the house is shot by a firing squad.

One person who didn't take all this very seriously was PG Wodehouse, who wrote a spoof called *The Swoop*. Wodehouse starts the novel with a disclaimer designed to lull the unwary reader into a sense of false security – or should that be insecurity – with an assurance that it was written to rouse England to a sense of her peril. It isn't long, though, before any illusions are shattered. The hero of the novel is Clarence MacAndrew Chugwater, a 14-year-old Boy Scout whom Wodehouse describes as a 'Boy of Destiny'. Among his accomplishments, he can gurgle like a wood pigeon, low like a bull, imitate the cry of the turnip 'in order to deceive rabbits', smile and whistle simultaneously in accordance with Rule 8, fell trees, read people's character from their boot-soles and – his most prodigious achievement – 'fling the squaler'.

While walking down the street one afternoon he hears a newspaper boy declaim, amid the cricket results, a German invasion. It soon transpires, however, that it isn't just the Germans who've landed: no fewer than eight other armies have chosen the same day to invade. The Russians have landed at Great Yarmouth, the Swiss at Lyme Regis and the Chinese at Lllgxtplll in Wales; the Mad Mullah has captured Portsmouth, the army of Monaco has taken Auchtermuchty on the Firth of Clyde, the Turks have seized Scarborough, while a band of Moroccan brigands has come ashore at Brighton and 'dark-skinned warriors from the distant isle of Bollygolla', whom the Bank Holiday crowds initially assumed to be a 'troupe of nigger minstrels on an unusually magnificent scale' have landed at Margate.

Most of the armies soon leave – the Swiss to be home in time for the hotel season – leaving only the Germans and the Russians. Clarence comes up with a plan to offer music-hall engagements to the leaders of the German and Russian armies; when they fall out, jealous at the fees the other is receiving, Clarence leads the Boy Scouts in a rout of the invaders.

For anyone unaware of *An Englishman's Home* and the fear of German invasion in 1909, *The Swoop* may seem a rather odd story; it was very much of its time and fed, like Du Maurier's play, off popular anxieties. Unlike Du Maurier, though, Wodehouse turned them on their head, to show how silly many of them were. Sadly, like those whose enthusiasm for Empire Day junketings was less than wholehearted and those who wanted stronger fraternal links

Opposite page: In the West End production of An Englishman's Home, Geoffrey Smith, the central character, was played by Lawrence Grossmith (son of George Grossmith, co-author of The Diary of a Nobody). His mockery of the preparations taken by local territorials in response to the threat of a German invasion let the audience know that he is the one who will come a cropper. After an unhappy encounter with German dragoons he pays the ultimate price for his hubristic impertinence in possibly one of the most unconvincing death scenes ever seen on the London stage. No wonder PG Wodehouse saw the play as ripe for lampooning; it is a pity more people didn't take the same view.

with Germany, he was very much in the minority. It is for the apolitical adventures of Psmith, Lord Emsworth and Jeeves and Wooster that Wodehouse is remembered today, not his quixotic attempt to make his fellow countrymen come to their senses as the world slipped towards war.

CHAPTER THIRTY

THE GREATEST EDWARDIAN?

Ill news hath wings, and with the wind doth go;
Comfort's a cripple, and comes ever slow.
      Michael Drayton, The Barons' Wars (1603)

To select, from the figures who have appeared in the preceding chapters, the one who exercised most influence on the future course of history is not easy. Lloyd George, the driving force behind the creation of the welfare state, and Henry Ford, who ushered in the age of mass motoring, are two obvious candidates. Given the influence he was to continue to exert for another 40 years or so, many may plump for Winston Churchill. Casting the net wider, others may choose Sigmund Freud or Albert Einstein. Some may opt for the Kaiser, whose naval and territorial ambitions did so much to lead the world to war. Others again may go for Edward, the King who stamped his character – and his name – on the age.

There is, however, another candidate: a man, born in poverty near Dublin in 1865, who became one of the most influential figures in Edwardian England – Alfred Harmsworth. After leaving school, he worked as a journalist on an illustrated magazine for boys called *Youth* before going on to edit *Bicycling News*. It wasn't long before he spotted a gap in the market. It was *Tit-Bits*, founded by George Newnes in 1881, that provided the initial inspiration. 'The Board Schools are turning out hundreds of thousands of boys and girls annually who are anxious to read,' he declared. 'They do not care for the ordinary newspapers. They have no interest in society but they will read anything which is simple and sufficiently interesting. The man who started *Tit-Bits* has got hold of a bigger thing than he imagines.'

In 1888, he and his brother Harold set up a magazine with the self-explanatory title, *Answers to Correspondents*. This, at least to start with, was something of a con. For answers to be given, questions had to be asked, and, as the magazine was starting from scratch, there weren't any. So the two brothers made a load of questions up and, to cover their tracks, started not with issue one but with issue three. Although all this may sound a bit dodgy, the public loved it. Within a year the Harmsworths were making an annual profit of £30,000. Then came *Comic Cuts* and a range of similar titles such as *Marvel*.

Six years later, Alfred was ready to move into the journalistic mainstream, acquiring the London *Evening News* which was in financial trouble. Two years later, on 4 May 1896, he launched the *Daily Mail*, which cost ½d, against 3d for the *Times*. The age of the popular press had arrived. Harold ran the business side and Alfred was the editor. In his first editorial, he boasted that he would not feature long leading articles, pages of parliamentary reporting or columns of speeches. The first issue did contain, however – like most issues since – a story about the rising crime wave, as well as a feature extolling the virtues of motoring. From the start, he took

Alfred Harmsworth, Lord Northcliffe

a strong editorial line, proclaiming that the *Mail* would be 'the champion of the greatness, the superiority of the British Empire … the embodiment and mouthpiece of the imperial idea'. Alongside the campaigning journalism there was plenty of the sort of stuff Harmsworth had cut his teeth on in *Answers to Correspondents* – social gossip, household hints, DIY features, fashion and even a children's corner. The City page was not a dreary summary of prospectuses, like that in the *Times*, but a practical guide for the small investor.

Lord Salisbury may have sneered that the *Mail* was 'written by office-boys for office-boys', but there were a lot of office-boys around, who up till then had been ill-provided for. The first issue of the *Mail* sold 397,215 copies; by the turn of the century circulation had risen to a million a day.

In 1903 Harmsworth launched the *Daily Mirror*, initially conceived as a newspaper for and largely produced by women. This proved less successful and, after running at a loss for a time, was relaunched as the first tabloid newspaper – a downmarket version of the *Mail*. No story in the *Mirror* was more than 250 words long, and celebrity gossip featured alongside debates on whether Mr Balfour should play golf on Sunday or whether it was all right for a girl to enjoy a mild flirtation on her summer holiday.

The Labour politician Norman Angell said of Harmsworth that 'he possessed the common mind to an uncommon degree', while the Liberal journalist, AG Gardiner, described him as

An Edwardian Daily Mirror reader.

the type of 'the man in the street'. There is no psychological mystery to be unravelled here, no intellectual shadowland. He is obvious and elementary – a man who understands material success and nothing else. He has no other standard by which to judge life ... He not only wants success himself; he admires it in others. It is the passport to his esteem. It is the thing he understands. If you will watch his career you will see that, as far as he has any philosophy at all, it is this, that merit rides in a motorcar.

Yet this straightforward, no-nonsense approach, while it may have struck a chord with his readers, had worrying implications. Harmsworth's biographers, Reginald Pound and Geoffrey Harmsworth, spell out the problem:

Harmsworth journalism changed the relationship of press and public. It destroyed the old, enlightened view that reason would prevail.

Many of Harmsworth's readers had been taught to read but not to think. If this sounds pompous or patronising, it isn't meant to be. Mass education was established in the nineteenth century to teach what was dubbed (presumably by someone who couldn't spell) 'the three Rs' – Reading, Writing and Arithmetic – and that, apart from a bit of basic history and geography, was about it. The establishment certainly didn't want the working classes questioning the status quo. Educating the working classes was, as much as anything else, a way of inculcating respect for authority.

When the Bishop of Bath & Wells opened a school under the railway arches in Dolemeads in Bath in 1856, he expressed the wish that it would produce 'people who should be hereafter an honour to their country, and who would fulfil their duty in that station of life in which they would be placed'. That was still the prevailing view –

> The rich man in his castle,
> The poor man at his gate,
> God made them, high or lowly,
> And ordered their estate.

They were taught to obey their betters, to believe what they read – which gave anybody writing for them an awesome power. Sadly, when it comes to selling newspapers to the masses, it seems, someone presenting a balanced view, with a commitment to encouraging readers to think for themselves, will inevitably lose out to someone with a basic grasp of psychology, strong views and a talent for sensationalism.

In the late 1890s, spurred on by the *Daily Mail* and imitators like the *Daily Express*, founded by Arthur Pearson in 1900, a wave of popular emotion, amounting almost to hysteria, swept across the nation, culminating in the extraordinary outburst of jingoism that greeted the Boer War. In the Edwardian period, as Esmé Wingfield-Stratford later recalled,

> A generation was coming to maturity whose minds had been nourished on the titbits and stunts of the new journalism. And the journalese habit of relying on repeated and disconnected stimuli had, in an astonishingly short time, come to prevail. It was a time for sensation and not reflection ... The intensive cult of national egotism, that had already, on the Continent, come to prevail absolutely, and even in England was fast superseding the old Liberal idealism, had the effect of limiting sympathy by frontiers.

Harmsworth did not want people to think for themselves; he wanted them to think as he thought. He also believed in the right of a rich and successful man to exert a political influence commensurate with his commercial power. When he was created Baron Northcliffe in 1905, he decided that, to wield real power, he needed to take the citadels of the establishment by storm. His first move was to buy the *Observer*, which was in financial difficulties; three years, later, when the *Times* was going through a rocky patch, he acquired that as well, although not without a struggle. Its circulation had fallen to 38,000 a day, but it was still the establishment newspaper, with its reputation as a two-way channel between the top people in the country and the government intact.

Fears that he would take it downmarket proved unfounded; he was far too astute for that. It was the power that went with ownership of the *Times* he wanted, not a change in its editorial style. His takeover of the *Times* came at a critical time, with the Dreadnought programme being cut and funding diverted to social reform. Northcliffe was an implacable opponent of the welfare state and of progressive taxation. 'The Liberal Socialist theory of taxation,' he wrote, 'is that one million citizens are to serve as milch cows of the rest of the community.' He also saw himself as the chief standard bearer (or rabble rouser, depending on your point of view) of anti-German sentiment. In this he showed all the zeal of the convert. In 1901, he wrote in the *Mail* that 'it would be impossible to find in the records of our history a foreign sovereign who has so much endeared himself to the British people as has the Kaiser.'

Within months of writing that, he had convinced himself that Germany was preparing to invade, and set about trying to convince everyone else. He made a series of fact-finding visits to Germany to confirm his fears; during a visit in 1909, he declared that 'every one of the new factory chimneys here is a gun pointed at England.' In the same year, an article in the *Mail* contained the statement, 'I believe that Germany is deliberately preparing to destroy the British Empire.'

Not only did Northcliffe know war was coming; he knew how it could be won – in the air. He urged the government to invest in the 'motor car of the air', telling them that 'aerial power will be an even more important thing than sea power.' He did all he could to encourage the development of aeroplanes. In 1906, he offered a prize of £1,000 for the first cross-channel flight and £10,000 for the first flight from London to Manchester. Rather wickedly – but with a confidence in the unfeasibility of air travel that would very soon be dashed – *Punch* offered to match this sum for the first flight to Mars.

All this, of course, exercised an enormous influence on British perceptions of Germany in the years leading up to the Great War. In 1913, when Northcliffe was urging the British Government to build airships to counter the Zeppelin threat,

Daily Mail readers started seeing phantom Zeppelins in the night sky over Yorkshire. To ascribe to Northcliffe a major share of responsibility for the outbreak of the Great War would, perhaps, be to share his exaggerated egotism, but it is interesting to speculate what would have happened if the political direction of Northcliffe's papers had been entrusted to Norman Angell, Paris editor of the *Daily Mail* from 1905 to 1912. In 1909 he published a pamphlet, *Europe's Optical Illusion,* later published as *The Great Illusion*, in which he argued that the economic harmonisation of the major European countries had grown to such a degree that war between them would be entirely futile. And it is also worth noting a comment from the editor of *Star*, a Liberal newspaper, shortly after the outbreak of war: 'Next to the Kaiser, Lord Northcliffe has done more than any living man to bring about the war.'

Northcliffe didn't let up once the war had started. In May 1915, the *Mail* led a campaign against Kitchener's handling of the war. After he was lost at sea in June 1916, the *Mail* turned its attention to Asquith, who resigned six months later. Lloyd George, who took over as prime minister, with the help of lobbying by the *Mail*, had no illusions about Northcliffe, whom he regarded as 'one of the biggest intriguers and most unscrupulous people in the country'. Partly to reward him, but partly also to get him out of the way, Lloyd George sent him to America as head of the British War Mission, promoting the aims of the war and raising money for the war effort. More than one American newspaper hailed him as 'the most powerful man in Britain'. On his return he was offered the post of Minister of Aviation. When he refused it, the post was offered to his brother; in March 1918, however, he became Minister of Information.

The Great War, and Northcliffe's role in it, lie well outside the remit of this book, but are mentioned briefly here to indicate the enormous power he wielded over both public opinion and the government. Although war was still five years off in 1909, Northcliffe's conviction that it was coming not only set the agenda for public debate but also made its outbreak that much more likely.

Northcliffe was undoubtedly a genius, one of the most influential men of the twentieth century. Whether you regard that influence as good or bad – or a mixture of the two – will come down, in the end, to personal conviction, and, perhaps, to the newspaper you read. He tapped into a rich vein of lower-middle and working-class aspiration, establishing, for example, the Daily

Mail Ideal Home Exhibition in 1908 and promoting the motor car as an instrument of upward mobility, going so far as to forbid details of car accidents to be reported in the *Mail*. I will leave the last word on Northcliffe and the popular press he created to CFG Masterman:

> At the end this newspaper world becomes – to its victims – an epitome and mirror of the whole world. Divorced from the ancient sanities of manual or skilful labour, of exercise in the open air, absorbed for the bulk of his day in crowded offices adding sums or writing letters, each a unit in a crowd which has drifted away from the realities of life in a complex, artificial city civilization, he comes to see no other universe than this – the rejoicing over hired sportsmen who play before him, the ingenuities of sedentary guessing competitions, the huge frivolity and ignorance of the world of the music hall and the yellow newspaper.

The popular press, a new relatively phenomenon in 1909, is still, of course, with us, and still recognisably the same. The same cannot be said about the local press. In 1909, many people never read a national newspaper; the standard of the best provincial journalism – on the *Manchester Guardian* or the *Birmingham Post* – was a match for that of any national daily. And virtually all newspapers were independent; there were very few combines, especially in the provinces. The papers, as W McQueen Pope says, 'were free and independent, like the people they served'. As recently as 30 years ago, according to Nick Cohen in *Cruel Britannia*, one third of British journalists still worked in the provinces; today it's down to one tenth.

The *Bath Chronicle* may not have been up to the standard of the *Manchester Guardian*, but an educated man in 1909 would have been able to keep reasonable track of national as well as local affairs by reading it on a regular basis. While it was partisan – supporting the Conservative cause – it did not go in for the gimmicks of the tabloids, nor did it pander to the public's delight in sensationalism – and if its politics didn't suit there was always the *Bath Herald* to turn to for a Liberal perspective. The *Chronicle's* coverage of national and international affairs was comprehensive if not exhaustive; Victor Rosenburg recalls that although 'tape machines were then in their infancy, we Post Office lads used to deliver up to 100 telegrams a day to each paper from the Press

---

THE BATH HERALD

Every Evening ½d., Weekly (Saturday) 1d.

WILL CONTAIN THE

FULLEST AND BEST ACCOUNT

OF THE

BATH HISTORICAL PAGEANT.

Order of your Newsagent, or of

The Publishers, NORTH GATE, BATH.

Association'. Its coverage, at its best, was considered, rather than just following the winds of public opinion or reflecting the imperatives of the council. A century on, it is possible to piece together, from its reports, a reasonably rounded picture of the tensions that informed life in Bath. Perhaps most important of all, it did not try to pass off political opinion as news, not did it ignore developments that ran counter to the interests of the party it supported.

In June 1909, the *Chronicle* came under new management and applications were invited for 10,000 shares at £1 each. In December 1909, the paper moved out of its offices in Kingston Buildings, which were due to be redeveloped, to new offices in Westgate Street. The new offices were officially opened by Lady Kathleen Thynne on the afternoon of Saturday 18 December, with staff entertained to dinner by the directors in the Assembly Rooms in the evening. After the loyal toast, Lord Alexander Thynne rose to speak:

The paper in connection with which we are assembled has a record extending back for 150 years, and during the whole of that time had never wavered one iota in its loyalty to the cause which, from the first, it has made its own. That is a record of political consistency of which any paper might well be proud. This afternoon, when admiring the complex ingenuity and perfection of mechanical invention, which enable you to turn out at the rate of I dare not say how many thousands an hour a 16-page newspaper, I could not help wondering what Mr Barber's predecessors of 100 and 150 years ago would have thought if they could have seen it. And I suppose that if you could look forward 150 years you would find engines and machines still more wonderful to the eyes of the present generation than these would have appeared to your predecessors of a century and a half ago. I invite you to drink to the success of a paper which has gone through a process of rejuvenation … You drink to a paper with a great history, a great past, and also to a paper with a great future (cheers). It is a paper that has kept a very high standard and ideal in the journalism of this city, and, as I look around this room, I feel that ideal will be maintained in the future as consistently as it has been maintained in the past, and that whether it is recording the great deeds done abroad, incidents in the world's history, or whether it is conducting a political campaign, its records will always be marked with accuracy and its criticisms always tempered with fairness. As a member of

After the Bath Chronicle moved out of the buildings south of the Abbey in 1909, they were demolished and a large pedestrianised square created. Although many parts of modern Bath are less pleasant than they were a century ago – largely thanks to the motor car – this is one instance where the Bath of today is immeasurably better than it was in 1909.

the great party whose cause it advocates …I feel confident that, influential as the *Bath Chronicle* has been in political circles in the past, under Mr Barber's able management it is going to be still more fruitful. In conclusion, it affords me peculiar pleasure to take part in this gathering. It is a splendid idea to have this dinner, and let everybody feel, from the chairman of the paper down to the smallest boy, that this is one great enterprise in which they all have a common interest, that they belong to a great community, that they have one great object to keep up, the honour of the paper and to promote its success.

The editor, Mr Barber, then declared that

it has been a wonderful day for the *Bath Chronicle*. No newspaper in England has ever had a better send-off, whether starting on a new career or whether it has been rejuvenated … It undoubtedly has a wonderful past, one of which we all feel proud. I see no reason why it should not become one of the finest provincial papers and I believe I have the men around me to help it attain that position. When I came to Bath and looked at the old offices in Kingston Buildings, I was absolutely taken aback at the possibility of producing an evening paper in such antiquated and restricted premises. I believe the new premises in Westgate Street are equal to any used for the production of a similar paper in the country.

A century on, the *Chronicle* still survives, albeit only as a weekly publication. It is now owned – as is the *Western Daily Press*, the *Bristol Evening Post*, *Venue* magazine and over a hundred other local titles – by Northcliffe Media, an offshoot of the Daily Mail and General Trust. Lord Northcliffe would no doubt be most gratified.

CHAPTER THIRTY-ONE

PAGEANTITIS

The Edwardian nostalgia for the past manifested itself in various ways. The recreation of idealised village life in garden cities and suburbs such as Bournville, Hampstead and Letchworth, like Cecil Sharp's and Ralph Vaughan Williams' revival of a folksong tradition on the point of extinction, can be seen as an attempt to recapture the organic feeling of community lost with the transition from a rural to an urban civilization.

The Battle of Bath Street reflected a fundamental shift in attitudes to conservation. Preservation of the old suddenly became an imperative. In 1907, the National Trust, which had been founded twelve years earlier, was recognised by law; there were similar initiatives in Germany, France and Austria. At the 1900 World Fair in Paris, every country – with the notable exception of Finland – chose to build its national pavilion in a pastiche of an earlier style. England was represented by a mock-Jacobean confection designed by Edwin Lutyens, closely modelled on Kingston House at Bradford on Avon. This was, in Philipp Blom's words, 'symptomatic of the lack of confidence in the aesthetics of a new world, of a need to cover up the manifestations of tomorrow in a cloak borrowed from yesterday'.

The retreat into historicism was primarily a response to the insecurities engendered by social change – a sort of cultural comfort blanket. It is ironic – but not surprising – that this interest in a shared history came at a time when old values and associations seemed to be finally unravelling, when the traditional ties that had bound communities together were coming irrevocably apart, and when the traditional subservience of women and the working classes was coming, despite everything that could be done to maintain it, to an end. History was looked to not as something to enrich the present but as something to shore up the flood gates as the forces of modernity threatened to overwhelm all that had, up to now, been held sacred.

The pageant mania that overtook England in the early years of the twentieth century started almost by accident. Louis Napoleon Parker, born to wealthy American parents at Calvados in France in 1852 and brought up in Europe, had, on graduating from the Royal Academy of Music in London, been appointed music master at Sherborne School in Dorset. He was not only a talented musician but also of a theatrical bent, and tried on several occasions to persuade the school authorities to let him stage a large-scale 'folk play', celebrating the historical associations of Sherborne, in the school grounds. After teaching at the school for almost 20 years, and having failed to realise his dream, he left in 1892 to pursue a career as a playwright. While at Sherborne, he had married the daughter of a local merchant and, despite moving to London, maintained a close connection with the school and the town.

In 1905, having achieved success in his new profession, he tried again to interest the school in his idea, pointing out that, as 1905 marked the 1200th anniversary of the founding of the school and the appointment of Aldhelm (later St Aldhelm) as first Bishop of Sherborne, it would be an ideal time to stage an historical celebration. Despite their reservations, they agreed, but insisted that the event should be referred to as a pageant rather than a folk play. It was by no means an obvious name to choose – at the time the word 'pageant' was more likely to be associated in people's minds with the great naval pageants at Spithead in 1897, 1901 and 1902 than with anything of an historical nature. Nothing indicates more clearly the success of the historical pageant phenomenon initiated by Parker than the abandonment of the word 'pageant' for subsequent demonstrations of naval superiority in favour of 'review' – after all, they were

Above: Bishop Aldhelm as portrayed in the Sherborne Pageant of 1905.

Below: An Edwardian Lady Godiva about to set off for a ride through the streets of Coventry.

intended to demonstrate how up-to-date the fleet was, not to look back at the past.

Parker's idea was not as revolutionary as may be supposed. Many towns and cities, Bath included, staged annual carnival processions featuring large numbers of local people dressed in a variety of costumes, many of them historical. In some places, local events or legends were celebrated, such as Lady Godiva's naked ride through the streets of Coventry. In terms of the logistics of gathering a large number of people together, kitting them out in costume and getting them to perform, Parker was treading familiar ground. Where he differed was in attempting to stage something altogether more serious – a series of set pieces celebrating the growth of a community, more akin to a play than a carnival.

He set to work recruiting 900 people from the school and town to perform eleven episodes covering aspects of the town's history from 705 to 1593. Far from the idea being hailed as the 'coming thing', however, the Sherborne Pageant very nearly sank without trace. Robert Withington, a friend of Parker's who later chronicled the pageant phenomenon, takes up the story:

> The pageant at Sherborne – the first of a long line – was some-thing new; it met with opposition and ridicule from outsiders; given in a small out-of-the-way town, under a pageant-master who himself hardly knew what he meant to do, the first modern pageant struggled into life. As the preparations for the festival went on, great difficulty was found in interesting the press … The grandstand was erected, yet everything seemed to have been done for nothing, because no audience was in prospect. Ten days before the performance, the dress rehearsal took place; and by accident two newspaper men were present. Their notices brought 50,000 people to the little Dorset town. All England took fire.

Two scenes from the Sherborne Pageant, with the ruins of the castle as a backdrop.

Parker was made. The following year, he staged a pageant at Warwick. Others, such as Frank Lascelles, who organised a pageant at Oxford, picked up the idea. When FR Benson staged a pageant at Romsey, the *Romsey Advertiser* declared that 'there can be no doubt that pageants have caught on very badly in England. Nearly half the towns with anything of interest in the history of England affecting them are preparing to celebrate the fact with a pageant.'

'Pageantitis', as it soon came to be known, affected Bath as well. Among those who saw the pageant at Sherborne was David Evans of 6 Milsom Street. He wrote to the paper urging Bath to stage its own pageant. Twelve months later, he wrote again, with a similar lack of success. The idea was taken up by the Rev Charles Shickle, Master of St John's Hospital and a noted local historian, but even he failed to rouse the great and good of Bath.

Above: Two postcards showing scenes from the Warwick Pageant of 1906.

Below: In some pageants historical accuracy was sacrificed to entertainment value.

Elsewhere, though, the pageant craze seemed unstoppable. The *Times* remarked that, 'It is possible that the philosophical historian of the future will see in their sudden popularity one of the most significant instances of a great change in tastes and ideas to which, he will say, the people of England were subject at the beginning of the twentieth century.' Pageants weren't just confined to England: New York and Quebec also jumped on the bandwagon. In 1908, Cheltenham, Bath's great rival, was chosen as the venue for the Gloucestershire Pageant. George Hawtrey, who was appointed Pageant Master, admitted that the choice

*Postcard views of the 1908 Gloucestershire Pageant. The photograph of the Georgian
episode was clearly taken at a rehearsal with people milling around in modern dress; note
how they have been inexpertly airbrushed out.*

was less than ideal. 'In selecting Cheltenham as the home of the
Gloucestershire Historical Pageant,' he wrote, 'some difficulty
was felt, because the town is not one that possesses many
historical associations.' Despite this, the Gloucestershire Pageant
was a great success. Bath, with the advantage of more historical
associations than almost anywhere else in the kingdom, was
beginning to look as though it would be left behind. When
Bristol announced it was going to stage a Pageant, Bath finally
roused itself and decided that enough was enough.

On 10 December 1908, several prominent citizens arranged a
public meeting in the Guildhall to discuss the idea of a Pageant. It
was not an auspicious occasion. The Banqueting Room was less than
half full, the Mayor didn't attend because he was ill and several of
the speakers – even those who supported the project – seemed to
have grave reservations.

In the absence of the Mayor, Major Simpson, the Master of
Ceremonies, took the chair. Despite his absence, the Mayor put the
council's view in a letter read out by Mr T Sturge Cotterell:

I am writing to ask you, in my utter inability to be present
at the Pageant meeting, to say there are one or two points I

want to make perfectly clear. First, that the meeting has in their hands the absolute decision of whether we shall or shall not have a Pageant for Bath in 1909; second, that the city shall not be pledged to any expenditure or responsibility in the matter. Further, that if the meeting shall decide to carry on the Pageant, I will do everything in my power to help to make it the brilliant success I believe it would be.

A letter from the Marquess of Bath was similarly non-committal:

From what I have heard there seems to be some doubt whether the Pageant would be a financial success, but if the opinion of the citizens is in favour of the holding of a Pageant I will be pleased to accept the office of president.

Major Simpson added his own words of warning, which, he stressed, were 'made in the kindest manner':

I think we might have had a far larger body of members representing the citizens of Bath than we have present. I know that many residents and others are taking a strong objection to the Pageant simply on financial grounds ... I feel that in the coming year we have what I will call two spectacular plays to be staged. The first is now being rehearsed, and there will be a full dress rehearsal on Thursday in this hall. This I will call 'My Neighbour's Landmark' or 'The Extension of the Boundaries'. But that is on quite a different basis from that which we are here to consider. The expenses of that play will be met from what we might call a body of 'standing guarantors'

Major C.H.Simpson. M.C.

– the ratepayers. But in regard to the other pageant we will have to look further than the ratepayers. I will call that play 'The Dream', for it is certainly a vision of beautiful conception, and we are waiting now so that we might sleep again and try to realise the scenes that will be depicted. Those scenes will be the old, old stories of Bath. They will be sweet and soul-inspiring; they will be beautiful but evanescent. We all want to do everything we can for the benefit and the welfare of the beautiful city of Bath. I am in favour of progress, and I want to see that something will be done that is not evanescent. We might be able to form a nucleus which could be utilised some day for the purpose of providing a place where we can gather the visitors together and enjoy far more recreation than at the present moment. If the Pageant of 1909 is to be a success, and to leave a fund behind it which can be utilised in starting something that will be of permanent benefit, we must work.

While the assembled company were scratching their heads over Major Simpson's speech, another letter, from Thomas Plowman, Secretary of the Bath & West & Southern Counties Society, was read out:

May I venture to suggest that the meeting should seriously consider whether the time is sufficient between now and the date when the Pageant will probably be held to carry out so large an undertaking as it will be, especially in view of the fact that little or nothing can be done in the way of preparation until the book of words is completed. The book will have to be written with extreme care, probably by two or three different people, who will take different periods of history, and it will involve a great deal of antiquarian and archaeological research, as any anachronism would draw attention to the Pageant in a way which it would be very desirable to avoid. Another point for consideration is to ascertain, before going too far, what amount of support will be forthcoming from the county and neighbourhood surrounding Bath, as the amount required to be guaranteed will, I think, be more than Bath alone can face. It is the more desirable that this should be ascertained in view of the fact that the boundaries question may to a certain extent influence outside feeling during the current year. I am not offering these suggestions with any desire to discourage anything that may be to the advantage of the city, but only with a view of putting the meeting into possession of points to which it occurs to me its attention may fairly be directed.

Mr Sturge Cotterell then told the meeting that he had been busy canvassing opinion and that the replies received and the calls made should in my opinion encourage us in the belief that support, both financially and in the working of the episodes, is sufficient at this stage to warrant proceeding with the arrangements for the Pageant. I would like to reply to the following criticisms that have been passed upon the movement: firstly, as to whether pageants have not lost their attractive power; secondly, that there is not sufficient enthusiasm to ensure success: and thirdly, that there is not sufficient time to organize a Pageant in 1909. With regard to the first, I would point out that the drawing power of pageants held in 1908 exceeded those of 1907. At Cheltenham the receipts totalled £7,000, and the profit will probably reach £1,500. In 1910, Bristol, Exeter and Plymouth intend to hold pageants, and those responsible for the proposals certainly do not consider that pageants are on the wane. England has witnessed during the last few years about 20 pageants, whilst in Belgium and Holland hundreds have taken place. Therefore with proper organization I have come to the conclusion that pageants have not lost their drawing power. As to the second point, there are in every town plenty of pessimists, but I do not believe in Bath that this opinion is largely held. I believe there are a sufficient number of citizens loyal to their city who are anxious to see it progress, and I believe that when the time comes there will be plenty of those ready to give their services to make the episodes successful, and that it will reveal talent unknown to exist. At Cheltenham there was no difficulty in that direction, people coming forward in a remarkable manner. As to the third criticism, I believe there is ample time to write the book and fully organize and equip the episodes. To ensure success the first important point is finance. We will require a certain number of subscriptions to meet out-of-pocket expenses and these should be the first charge on the profits. Then a guarantee fund must be behind us. There is every reason to believe that the guarantee will not be required, as it is quite possible to insure the gate. It is proposed to have eight episodes. As to the date, the general opinion is that the month of July will be the most convenient. It appears to me that a pageant is calculated to attract a large number of people to Bath.

He then proposed a motion to go ahead with the Pageant, which was seconded by the Rev C Hylton Stewart, Rector of Bathwick, who then went on to qualify his support:

I am one of those who believe we ought to have a Pageant in Bath, but the question is whether this meeting is sufficiently representative to determine the fact or no. I am sorry not to see the Guildhall packed with people, but I am afraid that the circular announcing the meeting has been treated by a large number as circulars are generally treated. If we are going to make the Pageant a success we will have to devise means whereby every class of person can be touched, and we must induce people from outside Bath to come and put their shoulders to the wheel. I know

The Rev Hylton Stewart.

that Cheltenham had the greatest difficulty to get people to send in their names, and we must be awake to that fact. I am thoroughly in favour of having a Pageant, but it is not the slightest use to look at the Pageant unless we first look at the tremendous difficulties which surround it. If the episodes are to be properly done, great care and time must be expended. They must not be done in a hurry. The great difficulty to my mind is the time, and I think we would carry it out on a very much better scale if we had more time in which to do it.

There were other dissenting voices. Thomas Miller, of Clan House in Bathwick, said that, 'I don't want to say anything discouraging, but I witnessed the pageants at Winchester and Cheltenham, and though I do not like to disagree with Mr Cotterell, I know that at both places there were difficulties. The Mayor of Cheltenham told me that they very nearly gave it up altogether. Bath and Cheltenham are socially very much alike, and the difficulties of one place will be those of the other … Another point is whether enough is known about Bath's municipal history.'

Russell Duckworth of the Cloisters, Perrymead, was similarly dubious about the prospect of the Pageant's success: 'I do not want to throw cold water on the scheme – even though I am a teetotaller – (laughter) – but when you consider that pageants are to be held next year at London, Plymouth and Glastonbury, and that 22 pageants have been held already, it seems that the pageant is overdone nowadays.'

It was left for Mr AM Broadley to make an optimistic speech. In it, he indicated that an informal approach had already been made to Frank Lascelles, who had staged pageants at Oxford and Quebec. Despite being committed to organise the London Pageant in 1909, he had agreed to organise Bath's as well:

> From my experience of the Sherborne Pageant I am of the opinion that the time available is ample ... It is doubted by some whether the disease of 'pageantitis' is still prevalent. Well, we are going to have in London first the ecclesiastical pageant, which will lead the eyes of the foreign visitor to dwell on the great ecclesiastical history of Bath. Then there will be the London Pageant, which will occupy the first week in June. What could be more profitable for Bath than for the visitors to the London Pageant to leave it feeling that they were now coming to Bath, that city which was at one time the epitome of English social and historic life. Mr Lascelles has been called to New York to manage the pageant there, and fourteen cities in America have invited him to superintend the production of their own pageants. If the Pageant is advertised throughout the kingdom and America, and if it is managed in a businesslike way, as I am sure it will be by my friend Mr Cotterell, I am confident that it will be a success. Of course, Mr Lascelles will not be able to be in Bath all the time, but he will be able to put the finishing touches. If we work well at this project it will be the means of encouraging American visitors to make their pilgrimages to Bath with the same faithfulness that they now visit Warwick or Stratford-on-Avon, and make the year 1909 mark an eventful period in the annals of this city.

Mr Broadley's speech was greeted with loud applause and the resolution to hold the Pageant was passed with only two dissentients, one of whom was Russell Duckworth. A general committee 'to make all the necessary arrangements for carrying out the Bath Historical Pageant', consisting of all those at the meeting plus several notables (including the Marquess of Bath and the Mayor) was then appointed.

A 17-member Finance and General Purpose Committee was set up under the chairmanship of Mr Sturge Cotterell. Among the venues considered for the Pageant were Alexandra Park, the horse-show ground on Grosvenor Meadows, the grounds of Bath College, the fields off the Warminster Road and the Upper Common; in the end, it was the Middle Common in Royal Victoria Park that was chosen. 'It is believed,' said a representative of the committee, 'that this site will prove most suitable, and the absence of "practical" water is not considered in any way a drawback. In fact, it is stated that the presence of water is not required.' Unfortunately, he did not explain what 'practical' water was, nor how it differed from 'impractical' water.

Performances were scheduled to be held at 2.45pm daily from Monday 19 to Saturday 24 July. Pageant sermons would be preached

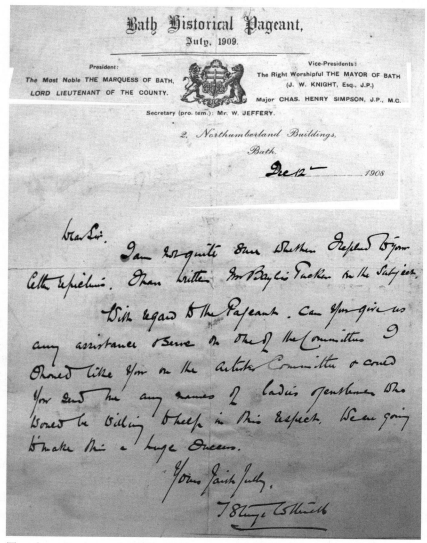

Two days after it was decided to hold a pageant in Bath, Sturge Cotterell was writing to potential committee members on specially-headed paper.

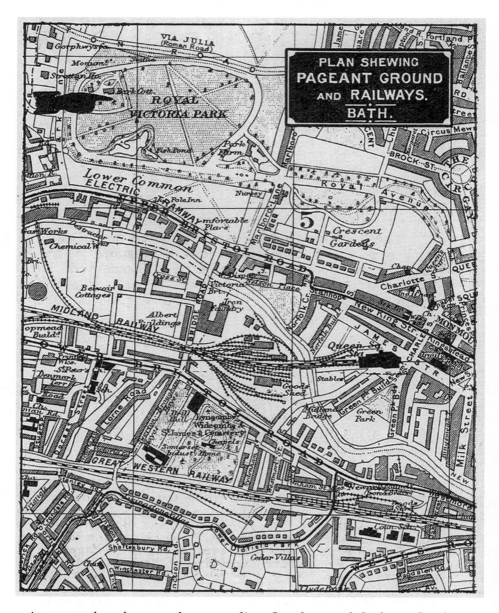

in most churches on the preceding Sunday, and Sydney Gardens
would host a series of 'fringe events'.

On Monday 11 January, a meeting, presided over by Lady de
Blaquiere, who lived in the Circus, was held in the tea room at the
Assembly Rooms, for the purpose of forming a Ladies' Committee.
In contrast to the meeting at the Guildhall, the room was filled to
overflowing, and, according to the report in the *Bath Chronicle*, 'a

large number of ladies had to remain standing'. As anticipated, Lady de Blaquiere gave a rousing speech:

Pageants are no novelty, but those who have been to pageants that have been held in different cities know how very interesting they are, and what an attraction they are to a town. Mr Lascelles, who is taking charge of the Bath Pageant, only last year organized a pageant in Quebec. He had only 300 years behind him in which to find episodes, but the pageant, as you all know, was of immense interest in all parts of the British Empire. This year he has almost 2,000 years to go back to for episodes, and they ought to be very successful … There has been a great deal of correspondence recently as to making Bath more attractive. Bath of itself is a most attractive place. Its wonderful architecture, its old-world streets are wonderful, and apart from that it has a fascination of its own which holds people and makes them want to come, time and again, back to it, and always with pleasure. But it wants life and it wants to be made attractive, and now is our opportunity (applause). We must not be content to read in the papers what is being done. We are easy-going citizens, and inclined to take things as they come, unless it is a question of the boundaries, which touches us rather nearly (laughter). I put it down to the climate, which I believe makes us sleepy (laughter). Visitors complain of it, and I think they must feel it. But now there is work for all. No more unemployed (renewed laughter). All sects, all politics, all classes must meet and work for the common good of Bath. You will remember when the Prince of Wales came back from his tour in the colonies his advice to England was 'Wake up, England'. Now we must apply it personally, and say 'Wake up, Bath'. This is a citizens' movement – not a council movement – though I hope the council will show their appreciation in a very practical manner by supporting the Pageant, but it is for the honour of Bath, and everyone must lend a hand and make it a success.

Besides this it will be of great advantage to the city. The orders for the costumes will be given in Bath; all materials will be purchased in Bath; anything that has to be hired will be hired through Bath tradesmen.

Then the local talent must come forward. A great many ladies present have taken part in private theatricals, and we depend on those ladies to come forward and take part in the Pageant. There will be about 150 speaking parts and about 2,000 non-speaking parts, besides the musical parts, and we want to be able to say 'All Bath talent' (applause). So we require volunteers. The ladies who cannot act, or are not able to, can give their services at Pageant House in Pulteney Street. There will be a lot of costumes to be made, and if they cannot act they can sew. The men have come forward nobly. Captain Prowse is to be Master of the Horse, and we have the offer of volunteers and yeomanry to take part in the Pageant, and the ladies now must do their parts. As a matter of fact, the men have nobly owned up that if the ladies do not join in, the Pageant will not be a success and it must be (applause).

After thanking Lady de Blaquiere, the Rector of Bath added his own thoughts on the Pageant, stressing that it

must not be looked upon in any kind of way as a merely business enterprise … Our hope and belief is that we will be able to present a thoroughly beautiful spectacle. We will have lovely colours, taking care that the grouping of those colours is as artistic as possible. In this we need the help of everybody of artistic taste. There are many who have been lamenting for years past that the public aspect of affairs of life in England is grave and monotonous. The introduction of a Pageant like the one proposed is to correct that condition of things. I cannot understand people who say that the day of pageants is over. It is only beginning, and we are moving, and we will secure a lovely spectacular effect. But it will not appeal to the eye only. We also need to appeal to the ear. A great deal of the charm of pageants is in the music that accompanies the scenes. I have been told by one who was there that the music at the Winchester Pageant was glorious. I certainly hope that the music of the Bath Pageant will be glorious. I do not see why it should not be, for Bath is rather famous and popular for its music. What we hope to do and must do is to bring the past history of Bath into life again. We have a magnificent history, and one could hardly imagine a place with a richer, fuller, more variegated or more picturesque history than the ancient city of Bath. But it is not everybody who knows it, and what we propose to do is to make those stirring and glorious episodes of Bath history live again. If this is to be, it is essential that there should be the very widest co-operation!

Mr Cotterell, who had been appointed chairman of the executive committee, then talked about the work of organising the Pageant. He started off by putting the ladies firmly in their place, before qualifying Lady de Blaquiere's comments about all the costumes being made in Bath:

> In the early stages, the gentlemen had to take a prominent part, but now that the financial position is practically assured (some £1,500 having been subscribed or guaranteed), the time has come for the ladies to join in the organisation, and help with the 'great work'.

A pageant brings together all classes, all sections of society, all creeds, all shades of political opinion, in one common effort. It is a great historical drama, acted in the open air, in some beauty spot

The Bath Historical Pageant, 1909.
Chairman:
T. Sturge Cotterell, Esq., J.P.

where, or close to where, the events represented actually took place, and acted by the successors of the ancient heroes. A pageant fulfils other purposes. We have decided, as a matter of principle, that everything necessary for the Pageant should (as far as possible) be made in Bath. I hope to see the book of words written locally; perhaps some of the Bath composers will supply some of the music required; local artists will design the dresses and properties, and local hands will make them. Only items such as plate armour, wigs, and the richest and most elaborate of the dresses will be obtained outside Bath. Local choral societies and choirs will, we hope, furnish the singers; local people will play the principal parts; local people will play the crowds; local ladies and children will perform the dances. One does not expect to get a complete orchestra of 199 performers at a moment's notice, but with one of the bands as a nucleus and many local musicians to swell it, and with a leading local conductor to conduct, I have no anxiety on that score. Even the grandstand and the thousand and one accessories, including the electrical installation, should be provided by local men. Then, the Pageant will be not merely a living picture of the town's history, but an exhibition in the most interesting conceivable form of its arts and crafts, and of all the talent in it ...

There will be a general Ladies' Committee, from which several committees will be elected, including an executive of 20, who will organize and conduct the various working properties for the making of the costumes. There will be special accommodation at 53 Pulteney Street (Pageant House) for weekly parties. There will be fully 1,000 costumes to make. The Pageant Committee will provide all material, and place expert advice at the disposal of the voluntary workers, by the appointment of a professional lady, as costumier, a lady of considerable experience, who occupied the position in 1907 at Bury St. Edmunds and in 1908 at Cheltenham. A Mistress of the Robes has also to be appointed (who should be a local lady with a good knowledge of costuming), and a further appointment will be the Mistress of the Headdress, who will conduct that important branch of the costuming at Pageant House. The Ladies' Committee will recommend to these appointments.

I cannot stress the importance of the working parties too highly, and we intend to make Pageant House comfortable for the workers, and afternoon tea and refreshments will be provided free of charge. Principals will usually provide their own dresses, but the material will be found, and the cost thereof will be small, and often represented by the work that the wearer puts into it. Much thus devolves upon the ladies, but I can assure you of the support of the gentlemen's committees.

Eight episodes have been provisionally selected after very great care, the real difficulty of the committee being in the direction of what to leave out rather than what to adopt. It is intended to open the performance with Prince Bladud, who will not only narrate his own mythical experience, but who will be the narrator to each episode. Thus the audience will be told briefly the particulars of the episode about to be represented. The first episode will take them back to the early Roman period, and a market scene will be represented, followed by the re-dedication of the temple. Episode Two will bring them to the year 577 when the West Saxons sacked the Romano-British City of Bath amid a scene of much desolation. The crowning of King Edgar in 973 will be Episode Three, being one of the prominent incidents in early Bath history. The fourth episode will probably be the founding of the Norman cathedral by John de Villula, the first Bishop of

Bath. Episode Five will bring in Henry VII and his visit to Bath accompanied by Bishop Oliver King. This episode will probably consist of two tableaux, the last one being the recitation by Oliver King of his famous dream. Episode Six will be a popular one with the ladies, being the visit of Queen Elizabeth to Bath. The Queen is usually accompanied by a number of ladies-in-waiting, Raleigh and other distinguished personages, and quite 250 ladies will be required for this episode. In addition, there will be morris and maypole dances, in which about 300 children will be utilized. The seventh episode will not interest the ladies very much, because it will be a representation of the Battle of Lansdown, in which it is hoped to have some hundreds of soldiers. But the crowning glory of the Pageant – especially as far as concerns the ladies – will be the eighth and last episode – Bath in the days of Beau Nash. In this brilliant scene it is hoped to have 400 or 500 people engaged, mostly ladies, and the costumes should be perfect. We are all very keen in having this episode, which represents Bath at the height of its eighteenth-century triumphs. In addition, it is proposed to have a representation of the presentation of the colours to the Bath Volunteers, illustrating the whole Volunteer movement which commenced in Bath. As a finale it is proposed to have something quite unique, and I have endeavoured to keep it a secret until this meeting. There are twelve places, large and small, in America called Bath, all of which have directly or indirectly derived their names from Bath, England. In the finale it is proposed to represent these towns and places by twelve American girls, selected as representatives from the state in which the town of Bath is situated, and the governors of each of the twelve states will be asked to nominate the ladies. They will be received in Bath as guests, and there are several citizens already willing to act as hosts. In the finale they will be costumed with the state coat of arms of their country and received by a lady to represent the mother city. This will, I feel sure, appeal to all, and be immensely popular on the other side of the Atlantic. The duty of receiving these daughters and granddaughters will be most graciously performed by Lady de Blaquiere. I wish to impress upon all of you that if the Bath Pageant is to be the success which it should be – and we want it to be the best and most artistic pageant yet presented in England – we must have unanimity in our ranks. This Pageant of ours must be thoroughly representative of all sections in Bath. Please bear in mind this fact – no performer in any one department of the Pageant can take part in any other. I mean that each episode must be absolutely independent of the others. So much for the performers. But for the general work, several of my oldest friends in the city have not seen quite eye to eye with me in this matter, but now that we have really decided to go on with the project, and have actually put our hands to the plough, I ask, with all the sincerity I possess, for every person interested in our ancient city to join in this movement, and raise the proposal to the dignity of complete unanimity, and make the Pageant worthy of our past history and traditions. I can guarantee good and faithful service on the part of the gentlemen with whom I am associated on the various committees, and after the generous attendance of the ladies today I have but little fear of the result of the Bath Historical Pageant of 1909.

As the cheers that greeted Mr Sturge Cotterell's remarks died down, a resolution to form a Ladies' Committee with Lady de Blaquiere as president was passed unanimously and the meeting came to an end.

CHAPTER THIRTY-TWO

FROM DRAWING BOARD TO OPENING DAY

In Bath Record Office are four large cardboard boxes containing some of the designs for the costumes worn in the Bath Pageant. They were originally owned by the Victoria Art Gallery, but it

Edwin Fagg

was decided they were not really art, and in 2003 they found their way to the basement of the Guildhall. It is true they are not great works of art, although some are by Bath artists held in considerable esteem at the time, including one – Edwin Fagg – who went on to be a senior member of staff at the Tate. They tell us a good deal, however, about how the costumes were researched, how the designs were created, and how they were finally used by the sewing parties which actually stitched them together. From notes attached to them, we can also gain an idea of how meticulously the properties were researched – even if the results were not entirely accurate. Given the time it took for the project to go from drawing board to opening day, it was an extraordinary achievement. How was this logistical triumph achieved?

Some of what happened we know from contemporary accounts, while some has to be deduced from circumstantial evidence. The collection of designs is far from complete. Many designs are repeated with minor variations; many of the drawings are rough copies of the originals and are often quite crude and childlike.

The design process seems to have begun with the formation of committees – so many and so large, that it is surprising that anything was achieved at all. For the costumes and properties alone, there was a Colour and Design Committee, a Head-dress Committee, a Properties Committee and finally a Sewing Committee. The function of the Colour and Design Committee was to 'assist the Master of Design in his arduous task of design and colour of a very large number of costumes'. Given that Nat Heard, the Master of Design, was a highly talented artist and headmaster of the Art School in Bath, one wonders how he felt about having his efforts overseen by Bath luminaries such as the Rector of Bath Abbey, who succeeded in having a finger in most of the Pageant pies. He also had to put up with letters to the *Bath Chronicle* complaining about the accuracy of the Roman costumes. It was the committee which determined the colour scheme, although they had trouble making decisions. All the indications are that Nat Heard and his able lieutenant Edwin Fagg just got on with the work, gently persuading the committee that certain colours would work well. The committee arranged for other professional artists in Bath to help, which explains the presence of Samuel Poole. His name was probably put forward by Cedric Chivers, for whom Poole worked as an illustrator. As he was older and better known than Heard or Fagg, it may not have been a very comfortable working relationship; he is given no credit in the reports, although he was clearly responsible for some of the more elaborate designs.

To assist with making the costumes, the artists worked with a professional costumier, Mrs Edwards, who had been involved with other pageants. She too had to work with an overseeing amateur: the Mistress of the Robes, Mrs Dominic Watson.

The Bath Historical Pageant, 1909.
Costumier:
Mrs. F. Edwards.

Mrs Dominic Watson

The designs for the Roman costumes caused controversy in the Bath Chronicle

When everything had been decided, the designs were given to the sewing parties. It soon became evident that much more work was involved than originally thought – Sturge Cotterell's estimate of 'fully 1000 costumes to make' turned out to be wildly inaccurate. In fact there were over 3,000. The women of Bath and district rose magnificently to the occasion, however.

Sturge Cotterell's plan was that weekly working parties would be held at Pageant House, with free afternoon tea and refreshments. His intention seems to have been to keep control over what was happening, but, as the number of parties grew, many ended up being held in people's homes. From the start, Lady de Blaquiere thought this a good idea. She described how one lady who contacted her had 'secured the services of twelve others, who were going to start work at Easter. They believed that by working one day a week for three months they would do marvels.' Lady de Blaquiere supported this idea, for she could see what Cotterell apparently could not: firstly, that arrangements like this would make the working parties a pleasurable social event, and, secondly, that far more effort was required than he had envisaged.

In mid-February, Lady de Blaquiere reported that over 30 parties were working away: 23 at Pageant House, where there were twenty sewing machines, and the rest in private houses. She felt that more support should be given to groups working in private houses, to bring them 'into sympathy with the movement'. By the end of February, the number of working parties was up to 38, including three evening ones at Pageant House. These were often attended by working girls. Still the number increased. On 11 March the *Chronicle* reported that there were 46 working parties, 32 of them at Pageant House. The others included two groups at Hinton Charterhouse, two at Weston and one at Mount Beacon House. Over 500 ladies were now involved. But how did they know what to sew?

One clue is given by Lady de Blaquiere's report on how to help groups working in private houses.

One of the many sewing parties at Pageant House

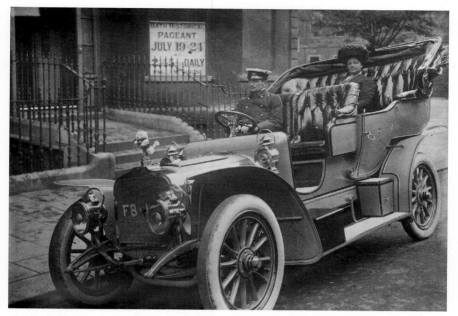

Lady de Blaquiere outside Pageant House, 53 Great Pulteney Street, now Dukes Hotel.

She suggested that before each group started work 'one of the assistant mistresses of the robes would go out and visit [them] or else a model of the costume that was being made would be sent out as a guide'. However, the remaining designs suggest there was another method of illustrating what the designers intended. At least one of the pictures has been hung up – the string is still in the punched holes at the top. It appears that the drawings were hung up or displayed around the room. This explains the crude copies – as the number of working parties expanded, more designs had to be produced in a hurry. The drawings often have helpful notes on them, concerning colour, design or how draperies were to be fastened. This also explains why so many designs are missing – they would have been spread across the working parties, and never returned. Why should they have been? If people knew the performer who was going to wear the costume, they may have kept the drawings for them – or kept them themselves as a souvenir of their contribution to the Pageant. No one could ever have guessed that a hundred years later they would be studied with interest. The designs would also have been used by Nat Heard's students at the Art College, who were employed in stencilling the designs onto the tunics and robes in the early episodes. We should perhaps be surprised that so many have survived, given the way in which they must have been dispersed.

Some of the principal characters supplied their own costumes, or at least paid for them to be made. One report says that a costume in the Beau Nash episode was 200 years old, although photographs suggest it was not that of the Beau, who was played by Dr Leslie Walsh. Dr Walsh does not seem to have attended the Pageant Fancy Dress Ball, at which performers wore their costumes, which was just as well, since AM Broadley, the author of the episode, appeared as Nash, in a costume specially made for him. The Fancy Dress Ball was a way of ensuring that those who attended would buy their costumes, but not everyone did – or could afford to. A scheme was drawn up which encouraged the purchase of costumes, but allowed working people to take part without undue expense. 'Every working man and woman' – by which one assumes the committee meant blue-collar workers – had their costume provided free of charge. For others, the cost of hire was roughly half the cost of making the costume, which made sense if the part was to be played by different people at different performances. The cheapest costumes were those for the lady peasants in Episode I and the British girls and warriors in Episode II, which cost 3/6 each; most crowd-scene costumes cost between 7/6 and 10/-. At the other extreme, a court costume for Episode VII cost £3.10.0 – over £250 in today's money. What is intriguing is what happened to the costumes after the Pageant. Did people keep them as souvenirs? More to the point, what was

Above: This sketch of a Roundhead musketeer, with string through the punched holes at the top, includes a detailed drawing of an ammunition belt and a note of the cost of hiring – '5/6 without arms'.

Below: The decorations on this costume for Queen Farinmael in Episode Two would have been stencilled by art students. The final design did not include the dramatic sleeves – perhaps they were felt to be too medieval.

The properties, from swords, shields and armour to large set pieces such as King Edgar's throne, were made at Long Acre.

done with those that were hired and returned after the Pageant? So far, not one of over 2,000 costumes has surfaced – nor any of the missing designs. We only have the charming set of watercolours preserved in the Guildhall and the many postcards to indicate what the costumes looked like.

The price of costumes did not include properties and accoutrements such as armour and weapons. These were made at the former Vezey's Carriage Works on Long Acre. Here, too, women made flowers and jewellery; among them were girls from Lee's cardboard box factory, who came in three times a week and put in 'valuable work'. There was also a carpentry shop, where furniture, such as the chair for King Edgar's coronation, was made. Considerable attention was paid to getting the details of armour and military uniforms right. Attached to the back of a sketch for the uniform of a yeomanry officer is a letter from RSM Holwill of the North Somerset Yeomanry in response to queries from Edwin Fagg regarding the colour of the helmet and cut of the jacket. One of Nat Heard's assistants was J J Witcombe, curator of the Victoria Art Gallery in Bath. He was not only an artist, but also had an interest in interior design. In September 1900, he submitted a wallpaper

Beside this picture of a Roundhead horseman were written the hiring and buying costs – 8/6 to buy, 4/3 to hire, but that did not include breastplate and arms.

design to a national competition held at South Kensington. Esther Wood, in *The Studio*, considered it one of the 'one of the best … a strong and well-balanced design, broadly conceived and sober in colouring, in a scheme … of clay-browns and Indian red'.

Sadly, none of the sketches for the properties has come to light, nor do any of the properties seem to have survived. Yet, however ephemeral the pageant may have been, it was a triumph of community effort that so many costumes and properties went from drawing board – via endless committees – through the hands of the working parties to be ready on the opening day. It seems unlikely that such a thing could be achieved today. It involved hundreds of people not only from Bath but also from the outlying districts, and realised Lady de Blaquiere's aim of bringing together, if only for a brief time, 'all sects, all politics, all classes'.

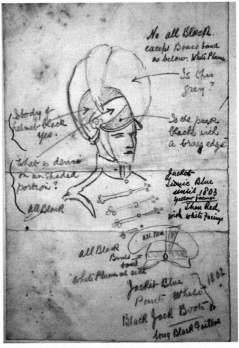

Above: The sketch Edwin Fagg sent to RSM Holwill.

Below: RSM Holwill's reply.

Right: The final design.

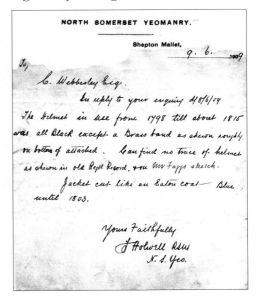

Silver facings
and shoulders
chains R

Cut like
Eton coat

EF.

North · Somerset · Yeoman ·

The Bath Historical Pageant, 1909.
The Master of the Pageant: Mr. FRANK LASCELLES.

Lewis Bros., Official Photo.]

548

CHAPTER THIRTY-THREE

FOOTPRINTS ON THE SANDS OF TIME

As preparations got underway, the London Pageant, which had already been postponed from 1908 to 1909, was postponed yet again, to 1910. This was good news for Bath: the city's Pageant would not be overshadowed by the much larger Pageant planned for London; more importantly, Frank Lascelles could devote more time to directing proceedings at Bath.

Early in the New Year, though, Mr Lascelles was in America, visiting Mark Twain, who, in a letter of 18 January 1910 to Sir John Henniker Heaton, revealed himself to be a pageant enthusiast:

> After seeing the Oxford Pageant file by the grandstand, picture after picture, splendor after splendor, 3,500-strong, the most moving and beautiful and impressive and historically-instructive show conceivable, you are not to think I would miss the London Pageant of next year, with its shining host of 15,000 historical English men and women dug from the misty books of all the vanished ages and marching in the light of the sun – all alive, and looking just as they used to look! Mr Lascelles spent yesterday here on the farm, and told me all about it. I shall be in the middle of my 75th year then, and interested in pageants for personal and prospective reasons.

Sadly, he never made it to the London Pageant. It was postponed yet again – to 1911 – when it formed part of the Festival of Empire at the Crystal Palace,[1] but Mark Twain had died on 21 April 1910.

Frank Lascelles had been born Frank Stevens in 1875, the son of the vicar of Sibford Gower in Oxfordshire. After studying at Oxford, he became an actor, changing his name to Lascelles. Although successful, appearing regularly at His Majesty's Theatre, where Sir Herbert Beerbohm Tree was actor-manager, it was with pageants that he found his true metier.

---

1 To which Bath contributed the Temple of Sul Minerva, later moved to Sydney Gardens in commemoration of the Bath Pageant, but that is to get ahead of ourselves.

After his formal acceptance of the post of Master of the Bath Pageant, he addressed the committee, outlining his philosophy and tracing the origin of pageants back to the early days,

when the clergy found it difficult to impart the truth of the gospel to their hearers. People were unable to read, and it became expedient to introduce living tableaux for the presentation and teaching of Bible history. In the result the churches became crowded, and resort was had to the churchyards, and this in turn gave place to processions through the streets, the living pictures being placed on trolleys. In course of time these miracle plays lost their religious feeling, and developed into what is now found on the continent, and at Nice in particular. In England the demonstration has continued on the lines of the Lord Mayor's Show. A revival of the second stage has recently taken place in England – has gone back to the times when these great scenes were given in the open air. The scope, however, has been enormously enlarged, and they now deal with English history from the earliest times. The value of the pageants themselves in a country town or a large city is very great. First of all, there is the historical interest; they knew so little of the deeds of those great men who were their predecessors and had gone to their rest hundreds of years before.

It is essential that there is entire accuracy in regard to everything in connection with the Pageant. Suitability as well as correctness has to be studied. It is essential that the costumes, properties, carriages, and trappings should appropriately contribute to the ultimate spectacular effect. Costumes are a particularly essential part, both as to blending and historical accuracy. As regards the selected site, the position in Victoria Park is one of the most beautiful for the purpose I have seen in England. It gives a glimpse of water and several distant vistas, down which horsemen can ride in procession and come into view with much effectiveness. It is also capitally situated as regards the sun, which, if shining, will give a most excellent effect on the colours.

From my experience, it is absolutely impossible to adequately indicate to anyone who has not seen one of these pageants the curious feeling engendered in seeing people, as it were, in the flesh and blood of their ancestors. Another advantage is the bringing together of a variety of people in a way never experienced before.

The greatest importance attaches to the taking up of the Pageant in the right spirit. The effect such a celebration has upon a place which undertakes it is of an unique description, lasting long after it has become but a memory, while opportunities are provided of intercourse and appreciation of each other to an extent which has previously not existed and might not present itself again. Above everything, it enables us to realise those telling lines of Longfellow:

> Lives of great men all remind us
> We can make our lives sublime:
> And, departing, leave behind us
> Footprints on the sands of time.

Stage managing a great pageant is the most fascinating work in the world. I cannot talk about it without growing poetic. There are some lines by Mr Rudyard Kipling that describe it exactly. You remember them:

> They shall sit in a golden chair,
> And splash at a ten-league canvas
> With brushes of Comet's hair.

Those words give the fascinating idea of bigness. In a pageant one does splash at a ten-league canvas; the colours are rainbow masses of living people, and the picture is painted on green grass with a ready-made background of nature's foliage and the blue dome of the sky to frame it.

That realism may sometimes be carried to too great a length was demonstrated by an incident at Quebec that was too exciting to be pleasant. A fort was to be bombarded and I sent a man out before the performance to obtain the needed supply of blank ammunition. The scene was very successful, and was carried through with heaps of warlike energy. When it was all over, some of the Red Indians who had taken part came to me and said that some of my men had been firing real bullets at them. They actually produced some of the bullets. When I called up the man who had bought the ammunition, he said, with perfect innocence, 'Oh, yes, sir, I went to the shop you told me about, but they had not got enough cartridges without bullets, so I thought it would not matter if I took a few ordinary ones.'

Authors were appointed to write the eight episodes, but, as the Pageant started to take shape, tensions began to surface within the committee. In late January, the *Bath Chronicle* announced that 'an important alteration has been made in the programme ... involving the introduction of an entirely new episode. It had been felt by many that an episode dealing with the history of Bath in the early nineteenth century ought to have been included ... The history of the city during that period is rich in pageant material and it was felt that such an episode would give ample scope for the provision of an exceedingly brilliant spectacle.' To make way for the new episode, the one dealing with the founding of the Norman Cathedral by John de Villula was dropped. The decision, according to the paper, was unanimous, although it seems certain clergymen were less than happy with the substitution.

They got their revenge a few weeks later, when another change – this time affecting the whole shape and character of the Pageant – was announced. Prince Bladud was to be relieved of his role as compere and narrator and demoted to acting out a masque in front of Queen Elizabeth in Episode Five. The reasoning behind this was that Bladud was not a real person and therefore had no place in an historical pageant. It was claimed, moreover, that his presence in the Pageant 'would mislead our youth'. The dethronement of Bladud, although reluctantly agreed to on account of the impeccable logic of the clergy, was to be a running sore throughout the course of the Pageant. So much for Mr Cotterell's hopes of unanimity.

Prince Arthur, Duke of Connaught, brother of King Edward VII, accepted an invitation to open the proceedings. The US President, Theodore Roosevelt, was invited as well, but declined. Invitations to ladies from the two Baths in Canada and the twelve in the United States were taken up eagerly, however. Sir Charles Villiers Stanford accepted an invitation to compose a choric ode although Sir Arthur Quiller Couch declined an invitation to write the words.

Over 3,300 performers were needed, plus a large choir and orchestra, and innumerable helpers. Some episodes required more performers than others – over 450 in the Battle of Lansdown for example, and over 650 in the Elizabethan episode. Despite early concerns that women would be reluctant to offer their services, it soon became apparent that it was men who were in short supply, and a call was sent out to the districts around Bath for help.

The episode which had the most serious manpower shortage was the first; Bathonians volunteering to portray ancient Britons were conspicuous by their absence, probably because of the distinctly unglamorous design of the costumes. Lloyds Bank was approached but declined to urge their staff to apply. Fortunately the gasworks was more co-operative. However, there was still a shortage so

THE MARQUESS OF BATH.

THE LADY DE BLAQUIERE.

President:
The Most Hon. the Marquess of Bath.
Vice=Presidents:
The Rt. Worshipful the Mayor of Bath.
J. W. Knight Esq., J.P.
Major C. H. Simpson J.P., M.C. of Bath
Ladies' Committee:
President: The Lady de Blaquiere.
Vice-President: Mrs. S. A. Boyd
Hon. Sec.: Miss Hill
Executive and Finance Committee:
Chairman: T. Sturge Cotterell, Esq., J.P.
Master of the Pageant:
Frank Lascelles Esq.
Director:
E. Baring, Esq.
Mistress of the Robes:
Mrs. Dominic Watson
Assistants:
Mrs. J. A. Hancox and Mrs. Macintire

Master of Properties:
A. G. Franklin Spurr Esq.
Masters of Grand Stand:
H. W. Matthews, Esq., M.S.A.
A. J. Taylor, Esq., M.S.A.

Master of the Horse:
Capt. C. B. Prowse
Assistant:
Major F. B. Beauchamp J.P.

Costumier:
MRS. F. EDWARDS.
Mistress of Dancing:
Miss Rolfe
Master of Designs:
Nat Heard, Esq.

Committees:

Performers'
Chairman: Geo. Northey, Esq. J.P. (Box)
Hon. Sec.: A. Bertram Fortt, Esq.
Grand Stand:
Chairman: W. E. Hatt, Esq.
Hon. Sec: H. W. Matthews, Esq., M.S.A.
Properties:
Chairman: Rev. C. E. Doudney, M.A.
Hon. Sec.: A. G. Franklin Spurr, Esq.
Colour and Design:
Chairman: Rev. Preb. Boyd, M.A., B.C.L.
(Rector of Bath)
Vice-Chairman: A. Trice Martin, Esq.,
M.A., F.S.A.
Music:
Chairman: Rev. C. H. Hylton-Stewart,
M.A. (Rector of Bathwick)
Hon. Sec.: J. S. Heap, Esq., M.A.
Horse:
Chairman: Capt. C. B. Prowse
Hon. Sec: W. Charles, Esq.
Episodes:
Chairman: Rev. Preb. Boyd, M.A., B.C.L.
Publicity:
Chairman: J. D. Allen, Esq.
Vice-Chairman: W. W. Bell, Esq.
Reception and Housing:
Chairman: The Mayor of Bath.
Vice-Chairman: Rev. Preb. Norton
Thompson M.A.

Fancy Dress Ball:
Chairman: Major C. H. Simpson, J.P.,
M.C.
Vice-Chairman: Dr. C. Curd
Hon. Sec.: P. B. Ford, Esq.
Evening Entertainments:
Chairman: B. R. F. Pearson Esq.
Hon. Sec.: J. S. Carpenter, Esq.
Lecture Committee:
Chairman: Rev. C. W. Shickle, M.A.,
F.S.A.
Hon. Sec.: Rev. A. Scott-White.
Head=Dress:
President: Mrs. Stanley Wills.
Hon. Solicitor:
Austin M. King, Esq.
Hon. Treasurer:
Col. H. F. Clutterbuck, V.D., J.P.
Bankers:
The Union of London and Smiths
Bank, Ltd.
Managers:
Messrs. Baring Bros.
Secretary:
Mr. W. Jeffery, F.S.A.A.
Official Photographers:
Messrs. Lewis Bros., Seymour St., Bath
Studio on Ground.

Convenors of Working Parties

Lady de Blaquiere, Lady Martindale,
Mrs. E. Baggs, Mrs. Begg, Mrs.
Bannatyne, Mrs. Boyd, Mrs. G. F. But-
cher, Mrs. Candy, Mrs. Chivers, Mrs. Cot-
terell, Mrs. Curd, Mrs. Dorman, Mrs.
Downes, Miss Drake, Mrs. Dugdale, Mrs.
Fitzhugh, Mrs. A. H. Fortt, Miss Foxcroft,
Mrs. C. H. Gooding, Miss Greenwood,
Mrs. Hawling, Mrs. Hensley, Mrs. Knight,
Mrs. Lawrence, Mrs. Macintire, Mrs.
Mackenzie, Mrs. Mason, Mrs. Matthews,
Miss Moody, Mrs. H. Brice Mundy, Mrs.
Newman, Mrs. Pagden, Mrs. Pinkney,
Mrs. Robinson, Miss Rogers, Mrs. Shep-
herd, Miss Sheppard, Miss Timbrell, Mrs.
Townsend. Mrs. Allon Tucker, Mrs.
Langfield Ward Miss Scott-White, Miss
Hill Wickham.

THE MAYOR OF BATH

THE REV. PREB. BOYD

The list of organisers was a long — and prestigious — one.

the council press-ganged the corporation dustmen into filling the vacancies on the understanding that they could keep the underwear 'specially designed for then, by Mrs Dominic Watts, Mistress of the Robes'. This, however, provoked criticism from employees at the gasworks, who didn't see why the dustmen should get preferential treatment.

It was decided to have two 'heads' – a lady and a gentleman – in charge of every episode. Below them were a number of deputy heads in charge of between ten and twenty performers each. Each episode had its own committee, consisting of the heads and deputy heads, with responsibility for recruiting people to fill speaking and non-speaking roles.

Direct recruitment by heads and deputy heads would, it was claimed, mean 'that the groups will consist of personal friends working together in loyal co-operation, and so far from the rehearsals being looked upon in the light of drudgery, they will be rightly regarded as delightful recreations, and the prediction may be ventured that before many rehearsals have been held, those taking part will be enviously regarded by their friends who lacked the initiative to send in their names'. As far as rehearsals went, it was obviously an advantage if the members of various groups knew, lived or worked near each other, although this occasionally provoked criticism. The Roman second legion, for instance, all came from Combe Down. As the date of the Pageant approached, they had to march down to the Middle Common to take part in rehearsals. The Temperance League objected to this on the grounds that they passed eleven public houses on the way.

As for rehearsals, the Pageant Master (or someone standing in for him) would first rehearse the episodes with the heads, who would then rehearse the groups. Early group rehearsals, consisting of no more than 20 or so people, took place in private houses and church or village halls. Gradually, with the advent of spring, forces were combined and larger rehearsals were held outdoors, but not until mid-June were there any full-scale rehearsals. A recurring problem, according to group leaders, was that, despite being instructed to adopt distinctive personas when taking part in the crowd scenes, many of the performers 'bunched together like sheep'.

Such was the enthusiasm that Captain Prowse, Master of the Horse, announced that the Battle of Lansdown episode 'would outshine the event of 1643'. He already had offers of 56 men with horses and a squadron of yeomanry from the Marquess of Bath,

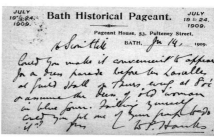

Above: Two postcards sent by the Rev WP Hanks (below) to Miss Padden of 2 Upper Church Street (below left), a group leader in Episode VII. The first, sent on 7 May 1909, asks her to enrol Miss Irene Smith of 24 Queenswood Avenue into her group; the second, sent on 14 June, asks her — or one of her group — to attend a dress parade in the Guildhall before Mr Lascelles 'and assume the form of old woman in blue gown'.

plus 15 men without horses and 23 horses without men. Over-enthusiasm seems also to have been to blame for a half-baked scheme to print special postage stamps, bearing the head of King Edgar, for use during Pageant week. Needless to say, the Post Office vetoed this idea at an early stage.

By 10 March some £2,300 had been promised by over 70 guarantors in sums varying from £5 to £30, but once the sale of tickets began it was clear that their money was safe. There were 4,000 seats priced from 3/6 to 21/-, while entry to the standing enclosure cost 2/-.

An abiding concern was the weather. The organisers would have looked to the heavens with no less anxiety than that with which Michael Eavis scans the skies over Glastonbury today. We are so accustomed to the myth that the sun always shone on Edwardian England, it comes as something of a surprise to learn that the summer of 1909 was, for the most part, a washout. According to WH Hudson,

> a long, cold winter and a miserable spring, with frosty nights lasting well into June, was followed by a cold wet summer and a wet autumn.

The prospect of the Pageant Ground being transformed, by the passage of thousands of historical feet, into something resembling Bladud's swamp, was the stuff of nightmares. The thought of all those historical costumes clinging to bedraggled bodies, of pratfalls in the mud, and a meagre complement of spectators hanging onto their hats under billowing awnings was too awful to contemplate.

Seven full dress rehearsals were held in the week before the Pageant. Security was on hand to 'rigidly exclude the non-paying public', although selected audiences were admitted on the following basis:

Saturday 10 July	*Bristol schoolchildren at 6d each*
Monday 12 July	*Bath schoolchildren at 6d each*
Tuesday 13 July	*Husbands, wives & sweethearts*
Wednesday 14 July	*Members of charitable institutions at 1/6 each*
Thursday 15 & Friday 16 July	*Bath citizens at 1/- to 5/- each*
Saturday 17 July	*Correspondents from the local, national and international press.*

Bath Historical Pageant.

— IMPORTANT. —

Calls for Full Rehearsals

On PAGEANT GROUND.

Every Tuesday and Thursday, UNTIL JULY 8th (INCLUSIVE).

EPISODE	II.	-	at	5.30	o'clock	p.m.
	III.	-	at	6.30	,,	
	IV.	-	at	7.30	,,	
	I.	-	at	8.30	,,	

Every Wednesday and Friday, UNTIL JULY 9th (INCLUSIVE.)

EPISODE	VIII.	-	at	5.30	o'clock p.m.	
	VII.	-	at	6.30	,,	
	V.	-	at	7.30	,,	
	VI.	-	at	8.30	,,	

N.B.—The Rehearsals on Thursday, July 8th, and Friday, July 9th will be for the purpose of Dress Parades.

FULL DRESS REHEARSALS.

IN PROPER ORDER OF EPISODES

To which Schools, Colleges, Societies, and others will be admitted at reduced charges.

SATURDAY,	JULY	10th	-	at	3	o'clock p.m.
MONDAY,	,,	12th	-	at	5	,,
TUESDAY,	,,	13th	-	at	6	,,
WEDNESDAY,	,,	14th	-	at	6	,,
THURSDAY,	,,	15th	-	at	6	,,
FRIDAY,	,,	16th	-	at	6	,,
SATURDAY	,,	17th	-	at	3	,,

PUBLIC PERFORMANCES

JULY 19th to 24th each day at 2.45 p.m.

NOTE:—Leaders are requested to see that their Groups attend all Rehearsals and are fully prepared with costumes and properties in time for performance. Tickets for Admission to ground and for obtaining reduced Train and Tram Fares may be obtained at Pageant House.

A. BERTRAM FORTT,   FRANK LASCELLES,
Hon. Sec. Performers Committee.   Master of Pageant.

Printed at the "Bath Chronicle" Offices, Bath.

No less than seven full dress rehearsals, to which schoolchildren and members of the public were admitted at reduced rates, were held in the week preceding the Pageant.

The London newspapermen travelled down in a special saloon attached to the eleven o'clock from Paddington which was slipped to arrive in Bath at 12.48pm. They travelled to Royal Victoria Park in motor cabs and were treated to lunch in the royal marquee. After lunch, Mr Lascelles addressed the visitors:

557

This is an age of records, and the Bath Pageant certainly establishes two records – that in it representatives of Canada and the United States come for the first time to England in a Pageant, and they are sent officially by the governors of their states; and not I think less important – certainly to us here in Bath – is that this Pageant has been organised in less time than any other pageant ever produced in the United Kingdom. Bath is a beautiful city, and one does not, perhaps, in some ways associate artistic beauty with the strenuous life. But it is not more than a month since, at the invitation of the citizens of Bath, I came to reside here to take in hand the artistic and dramatic production of the Pageant. The committees themselves have been at work on costumes and properties since February, when I had the pleasure of visiting Bath for the first time in my life. The episodes themselves had already been written by then.

Last month Bath welcomed me with her usual grace and hospitality. The last four weeks have been full of work for many willing heads and hands from early morning till late at night. At night we have even worked so late that we have rehearsed by the light of the moon, and we have seen as we acted the stars twinkling on those distant lovely hills. I am proud to say that today we are ready except for a few minor details. As I have said, four weeks ago we had not even begun the organisation of the dramatic side of the Pageant. This fact is, I think, interesting in comparison with the seven months which I have spent in the stage organization of the English Church Pageant, which I found myself reluctantly compelled to relinquish – leaving all my organisations completed – a few weeks before the actual performance. But principle is the basis of conduct, and important fundamental differences of opinion with certain clergy of the executive committee as to my absolute authority in matters connected with the stage left me no other course to pursue.

And this brings me to what I want particularly to note this afternoon – my gratitude to the people of Bath for their loyalty, their strenuous labour, and their splendid devotion to work for the good of the Pageant and the honour of their city.

Mr Meltzer, from the *San Francisco Examiner*, responded, thanking the committee for inviting the press and treating them to lunch, before going on to stress the importance of pageants in bringing England and America together:

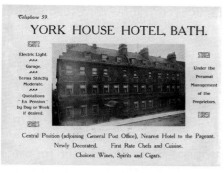

Above: Bath's hotels, along with other businesses in the city, found the Pageant a useful way of promoting themselves, although, as the Francis Hotel was in Queen Square, the York House's claim to be the closest to the Pageant Ground was more than a little dubious.

Below: Railway companies offered special fares to those visiting the Pageant.

Bottom: The Somerset & Dorset also laid on special trains.

RAILWAY FACILITIES

ON production of Pageant Tickets within 150 miles of Bath, the Railways will issue Return Tickets to Bath at about a Single Fare and a Quarter (minimum 1/-) for the Double Journey.

Tickets for distance up to 50 miles are available for return on day of issue, or up to and including Monday, July 26th.

Tickets from Stations between 50 and 150 miles of Bath are available from Saturday, July 17th, to Monday, July 26th, inclusive.

THE BOOK OF WORDS OF THE PAGEANT, 1/- and 2/6 (Edition de Luxe). Post 3d. extra. Orders should be sent to Pageant House, Bath.

BATH HISTORICAL PAGEANT.
JULY 19, 20, 21, 22, 23, 24.

Excursion Trains leave	Each Day.		July 19, 21, 22.		July 24.	
	A.M.	P.M.	P.M.	P.M.	P.M.	P.M.
Mid. Norton	11.2	12 53	2.33	5.26	3.10	5.26
Radstock ...	11.9	1 2	2 39	5.34	3.15	5.34
Wellow ...	11.16	...	2 45	5 42	3.26	5.42
Midford ...	11.21	...	2.53	5 47	3.30	5.47
Returning at	8 p.m. and by Special Late Train July 19, 21, 22, 24.		10.45 p.m.		10.45p.m. for Mid. Norton 11.10p.m. for other stat'ns	

Special facilities are also offered to persons holding Pageant admission tickets. For full particulars see bills.

GEORGE H. EYRE, Traffic Superintendent.

The more pageants we have, the more we will find that the two great English-speaking nations, which ought to be one people, will be drawn together. There is a moral as well as an artistic side to pageants, but I think the most important side is the moral. If these pageants only bring England and America into closer relationship – as I am convinced they will – the pageant movement will have accomplished a very great work, and Mr Lascelles will be the person to whom we will owe our gratitude.

They then made their way to the Pageant Ground, where it was announced that the tournament in Episode IV would be omitted so that the reporters could witness the Grand Finale before catching their train back to London. The weather was fine and 'ladies were able to sit with heads uncovered in the auditorium without suffering any inconvenience'. Given the size of some of the hats then in vogue, this was an important consideration. Ladies who didn't remove their hats could block the view of several people, so it is not surprising that they were 'earnestly requested' to divest themselves of their headgear while watching the Pageant.

The *Bath Chronicle* reporter considered the event a resounding success:

> All the performers threw themselves heartily into their work, and the result was that the rehearsal was an unqualified success. Interviews with one or two of the most prominent London critics showed that they were delighted with what they had seen. The London visitors were highly delighted with the beautiful park in which the scenes are being enacted, and expressed the opinion that no setting could be more appropriate than that chosen for the episodes. Everybody was charmed with the singing of the large choir. The lady visitors were loud in their praises of the beautiful costumes worn, the effect, while correct as to the period, being also highly artistic.
>
> The two episodes, 'The Crowning of King Edgar' and 'The Reception of Queen Elizabeth', made a great impression today, and the later episodes called forth the warm admiration of all. Some said there were indications that this would be the best of all the pageants.

His only reservation concerned the music:

> The chorus are doing their work valiantly, artistically, and successfully, their attack and balance, even under the most trying circumstances, being noticeably good, while the orchestra, finely led by Mr JW Duys, do all that is possible to support the singers. That it would have been better for the orchestra to have occupied a position in front of the stand, as originally intended, is the opinion of many, but in a matter of detail of this sort we would prefer to bow to the decision of those who looked all around the question before coming to a decision. There now only remains one further thought for us to suggest, and that is that, as the intrinsic value of the music can hardly be properly exemplified at the Pageant, that at some future date it should be given on the concert platform, when the singers and orchestra would be enabled to display to greater advantage the wonderful amount of original composition which has been scored by willing writers, both of national and local repute, and for which it is believed that there is a permanent future. We trust that this suggestion may meet the eyes of those competent to give effect to the same.

The national papers, on the whole, were impressed by what they saw. The *Daily Chronicle* thought it 'one of the prettiest, most impressive, varied and dramatic that has been devised even in this era of pageantry ... The result was something beyond mere success. It was a series of pictures that will haunt and enrich the imagination of each one among Bath's myriad pilgrims.' The *Daily Telegraph* declared that, 'from the first the scene upon the Pageant Ground was one of animation and well-ordered movement.' The *Daily News* opened its remarks with a comment that must have been particularly galling to some of the more progressive elements on the council: 'In spite of all the efforts of its citizens to prove otherwise Bath lives in the past.[2] Therefore the Bath Pageant was bound from the first to be an artistic success. As for the people, nine-tenths of them seem to be tasting with a sweet sense of proprietorship the past glories of what they will tell you is the Modem Athens.' The *Daily Express* was particularly taken with the setting, which it described as 'one of the beauty spots of the west. The site is a charming one containing acres of rich meadowland, with a gleaming lake in the background, and several avenues of trees down which the gaily dressed performers and cavalcades of soldiery come gradually into view.'

There were criticisms, however. The *Standard* thought there should be 'a judicious shortening of the Elizabethan episode and the last portion of the Battle of Lansdown episode'. The *Morning Post*, while admitting that, 'on the whole, Mr Lascelles has employed with striking success his intimate knowledge of stagecraft in presenting with the aid of 3,000 performers a series of scenes of amazing animation and artistic beauty', added that 'the Pageant fails here and there, just where other pageants have failed. The action is too often delayed by the introduction of speaking. Even if the words spoken were of the highest quality, they can be heard only by very few people in the auditorium, and weariness ensues. Design, movement, colour should be the dominating factors in pageantry.'

Inability to hear the words was to be a recurring complaint. Books of words, in versions ranging from cheap paperbacks to lavish hardbacks, were available, but reading along meant taking your eye off the action, which rather defeated the object. Even with Frank Lascelles in charge, it took some time to appreciate the scale of the problem. Speeches were repeatedly cut – no doubt to howls of outrage from the various authors – not only during rehearsals but also during the week of the Pageant itself.

The *Times*, however, while it found the amount of (inaudible) speech acceptable, had much more serious reservations:

2 It probably wouldn't go down too well today either.

One effect of studying a pageant is to put one out of conceit with the senses. Experience proved several years ago that the ear was not to be trusted. Dialogue, even of the most dramatic, and verse even of the strongest, were found to go for little or nothing. Action was all. And now at Bath we learn that the eye, at which action is aimed, is sadly limited in capacity. The action must be concentrated, intensified, forced upon the vision. Bath having learned the lesson about the ear, has, very wisely, pinned her faith to action, and treats the dialogue of the episodes ... in rather summary fashion. But her Pageant Ground is so wide, of her 3,000 performers there are so many in each episode, and they all have so much to do that the eye is kept too busy. Could Mr Lascelles, the Pageant Master, have concentrated the action a little more closely, it would have been more effective and the impression it conveys less vague.

This criticism seems to have hit home, for the *Bath Chronicle*, after reporting these remarks, added that, 'since this critique appeared the action of some of the episodes has been distinctly concentrated, and we think if the *Times* critic paid another visit he would be prepared to admit his comments have lost much of their force.'

BATH HISTORICAL PAGEANT

1909.

CORONATION OF KING EDGAR
IN BATH ABBEY, 973.

JULY 19 to 24 at BATH

CHAPTER THIRTY-FOUR

POMP AND CIRCUMSTANCE

On the Sunday preceding the Pageant, special church services were held throughout the city. A hymn was written by LB Hewitt,[1] with the tune – a cross between 'Eternal Father, Strong to Save' and 'Come, Ye Thankful People, Come' – by HJ Davis. It ran to six verses (the fifth of which could be omitted 'if the hymn be thought too long'). Curiously, given the clergy's opposition to Bladud's role in the Pageant, the first verse refers to his miracle cure as though he was a real historical figure:

> *O God of Nations, deign to bless*
> *Our city in her festal hour:*
> *We plead not our own righteousness,*
> *But humbly own Thy hand of power.*
> *Thou didst of old our healing spring*
> *To leprous prince in mercy show;*
> *Still guide us, and our footsteps bring*
> *Where crystal streams life-giving flow.*

The theme of Bath's healing springs continues in the second verse:

> *Our city of the Healing Stream*
> *Long years has stood by Avon's side.*
> *Her thousand lamps at evening gleam*
> *Like gems that deck a royal bride.*
> *Thy good hand hath our hill-throned queen*
> *In her dominion firmly set;*
> *And through the ages men have seen*
> *Her healing waters flowing yet.*

After three more verses in a similar vein, the hymn concludes with a reference to the angels on the west front of the Abbey which were to feature in Episode Four of the Pageant:

> *And teach us, Lord, to read aright*
> *How carven on Thy House of Prayer*
> *Are sculptured forms of angels bright,*

1 The author of the poem about Helen Hope quoted in chapter 17.

And Heav'n and Earth are meeting there.
O may Thine angels give us strength
To climb the steep from earth to Thee,
That so we may behold at length
Thy throne upon the crystal sea.

Above: This decorated tramcar outside the Guildhall invites passers-by to 'enquire within'
for details of the tours and excursions advertised in its windows.

Below: Pageant organisers gave due prominence to the dignitaries who graced the event with
their presence.

BATH HISTORICAL PAGEANT

(President—The Most Hon. The MARQUESS OF BATH)

Will be held in the ROYAL VICTORIA PARK, BATH
——— MONDAY, JULY 19th, 1909, till ———
SATURDAY, JULY 24th, 1909, DAILY at 2.45 p.m.

3,000 Performers.   Grand Orchestra.   Large Choruses.
Beautiful Spectacle.   Stately Dances.   Gorgeous Costumes.

COVERED AUDITORIUM FOR NEARLY 4,000 SPECTATORS.

——— **Royal Day** ———

On Monday the Pageant will be opened by
Their Royal Highnesses The DUKE AND DUCHESS OF CONNAUGHT,
accompanied by
The PRINCESS PATRICIA OF CONNAUGHT.

——— **Mayor's Day** ———

On Friday The MAYOR AND CORPORATION OF BATH will Entertain The LORD MAYOR
OF LONDON and SHERIFFS, who will attend in State; and also The LORD MAYOR
AND SHERIFF OF BRISTOL and other Provincial Mayors.

SEATS may be booked at C. MILSOM & SON'S MUSIC WAREHOUSE, BATH, also at BRISTOL and SWINDON;
and in London at THOMAS COOK & SON'S OFFICES (Town and Country), and all District Messenger Offices.
SEATS—**21/-, 10/6, 7/6, 5/-,** and **3/6** (Numbered and Reserved). Standing Enclosure 2/- Pageant Book free from
BARING BROS., MANAGERS, PAGEANT HOUSE, BATH; Telephone: 610 Bath; Telegrams: "Pageant, Bath."

At a civic service in the Abbey, the Bishop of Bath & Wells, perhaps still mindful of the substitution of the Queen Charlotte episode for one celebrating the foundation of the Norman cathedral, asked the congregation to reflect on the godlessness of Georgian Bath – 'the personal vanity, the apparently absolute indifference to the wants of others, the satisfaction in the selfishness of life, no recognition of the claims of people of other classes, or of their merits, or of their rights'.

Finally, on Monday 19 July, the opening day of the Pageant arrived. The Duke of Connaught, brother of Edward VII and Grand Master of the United Grand Lodge of England, who was staying at Hartham Park as a guest of Sir John and Lady Dickson-Poynder, attended a special masonic function at the Assembly Rooms. About 600 freemasons, representing all of Somerset's 28 lodges, were present.

At 12.40pm he proceeded to the Guildhall, where he was joined by the Duchess, who had travelled separately from Hartham Park. The Mayor and Lord Bath, the Lord Lieutenant of the county, along with several other dignitaries, greeted him at the entrance, in front of which an awning had been erected. The *Bath Chronicle* described the transformation that had overtaken the Guildhall for the Duke's visit:

Entering the building, the visitors walked beneath huge towering palms, and everywhere in the corridors the air was heavy with the fragrance of choice flowers. Every little nook and cranny which affords facilities for treatment had been utilised with charming effect. The grand staircase had in the corners on its two landings choice groups of flowers set about tall overshadowing palms, the flowers represented being begonias, with carnations, geraniums, gloxinias, etc, and foliage plants in dark and light shades. The window sills overlooking the staircase contained banks of carnations, a pale yellow marigold, with smaller palms and lichens and creepers depending. At the end of the corridor by the Mayor's entrance to the council chamber there was a very handsome group to which the scarlet salvia and moss provided a dainty edging. Stately delphiniums were used with striking effect with marguerites, palms, etc. The council chamber proper was handsomely fitted up as the reception room, and here again the floral decorations were the acme of taste. Opposite the entrance was grouped an exquisite bank of carnations and roses in several tints, edged with maidenhair fern and hydrangea paniculata, and surmounted by some fine palms of the Kentia Balmoralma variety. Other palms of the same variety were dispersed about the room, and in the galleries. The Mayor's Parlour and Committee Room No 2 were set apart as the private apartments of the Duke and Duchess of Connaught, and each was specially furnished by Messrs Powell & Powell, while the Town Clerk's outer office served for the retirement of the ladies of the royal party, and the Town Clerk's Assistants' Room for the gentlemen.

A curtain marked the junction of the old and the new buildings, and here began red felt carpeting which Messrs Horton had laid throughout the Banqueting Chamber and the old council chamber (which served as the luncheon apartment). The large apartment had been turned into a temporary council chamber by Mr Silvanus White, under the direction of Mr JH Colmer (Chairman of the Corporate Property Committee). Nearly one half of the floor space was occupied by a slightly raised platform approached from the floor of the hall by broad, easy steps, on which a super-carpet of purple looked well. Seats were provided for the six prominent participants – the Mayor and Mayoress, the Town Clerk (sitting at a little table apart), the Duke and Duchess and their daughter, and for the Lord Lieutenant of the county. Behind them were provided seats for the members of the Corporation ... and some special onlookers. In all the platform accommodated 159 persons, and the seats on the floor of the house were just over 300 in number. Some 50 of these were at the disposal of the public after a really representative gathering had been assured and these were disposed of by ballot among the applicants. The decoration of the room was specially undertaken. The platform had an edging of palms and red begonias and the fireplaces and other coigns of vantage all had their floral treatment, the most conspicuous blooms being those of the petunia, begonia, gloxinia, etc. The minstrel gallery was occupied with palms, ferns, and Chinese shrubs, and the effect of the whole could not have been better.

A small orchestra relieved the waiting for the royal procession, whose departure from the reception room was signalled by the upturning of the electric light, and they entered to the strains of the national anthem. The Mayor, preceded by the sword bearer and maces, walked first with the Duchess, and the Duke next with the Mayoress who was charmingly robed in heliotrope liberty silk handsomely trimmed with passementerie with bonnet to match. She wore the Mayoress's chain of office. The Princess Patricia with Lord Bath, and the Lady and Gentleman-in-Waiting, with the Town Clerk, completed the procession ... The foremost seats on the platform were occupied by Lord and Lady de Blaquiere, the Bishop and Mrs E Kennion, Mr and Mrs Donald Maclean, and others.

The official position was that a special council meeting was to take place, and this involved the formal adoption of the minutes of the last meeting and the calling of the roll. The Mayor, in welcoming the Duke and Duchess, recalled the Duke's last visit to Bath, in 1881, 'to promote the interests of the Royal School for Officers' Daughters'. After assuring him of Bath's loyalty to the crown, he went on to extol the virtues of the Pageant – and to have a dig at the clerical killjoys who had deposed Prince Bladud:

> The performance which you will kindly witness is the culminating point of an enormous amount of anxious thought, of many months of steady work – given freely and ungrudgingly by thousands of our citizens. It is no light thing for any city to set itself to prepare a pageant, but it is quite possible to carry it through successfully when every man and woman engaged in it devotes all his or her time and attention to promoting it. Bath, guided by Mr Cotterell and Mr Frank Lascelles, has responded most nobly to the invitation, and I feel that your Royal Highness will agree that the brilliant spectacle that will be displayed before you is a real reward for the pains taken to produce it.
>
> It is worth noting that every episode is our own, and was enacted in this very place. Every detail is historically correct, and may be relied on as a true representation of the period. I am not sure that the promoters have not been overscrupulous in dealing with the history of Bath. The discovery of the healing properties of our hot springs by Prince Bladud's pigs should not have been so lightly discarded and treated as a fable. I daresay your Royal Highness will have noticed the overwhelming influence of the clergy in the list of our Pageant makers, and I quite believe they have subjected the history of Prince Bladud to that higher criticism that has been fatal to many of the church's ideals of our youth.

The Town Clerk then read a formal address, and, after the Duke had responded, the royal party retired, along with the Mayor and selected dignitaries, to the old council chamber for lunch. There was 'a variety of the choicest vintages to accompany the courses,

including the local Beau Brummel whiskey and Sulis Water from the famous springs of Bath'.

Shortly after 2.30, the royal party left the Guildhall and the Duke inspected the guard of honour of the 4th Somerset Light Infantry, drawn up under the command of Major Noke. Lieutenant Fortt was also on parade, carrying the King's colour recently presented to the regiment. The Duke also walked up the line of cadets drawn up along the west side of High Street,

before walking back to the Guildhall door with Captain Bland, the officer in command of the corps, and getting into his carriage. The procession then formed up, escorted by the Bath troop of the North Somerset Yeomanry and headed by the Chief Constable on horseback and the Bath mounted police.

The city through which the procession made its way had been transformed just as dramatically as the interior of the Guildhall. A century ago, Bath, with its thousands of chimney pots still belching forth smoke, was, for the most part, a soot-black city. Almost a century earlier, when Anne Elliot's carriage had arrived in Bath, her 'first dim view of the extensive buildings, smoking in rain', left her 'without any wish of seeing them better'. By 1909, factories and railways had made things, if anything, worse; the only buildings which glowed as Bath stone should glow were the ones that had just been built. Those that dated from the days of Bath's glory were as black as a fire back. But, as the *Morning Post* reported, strenuous efforts had been made to hide the fact:

> The ashen face of the ancient city [is] half hidden in the brilliance of banners and bunting that scatter rich colour in almost every street ... The people of the Parade and Milsom Street have thrown aside the reverential restraint of age, and decorated their houses and shops with splendid hues that recall the joyous days when the uncrowned King of Bath drove along those thoroughfares in his gaudy chariot, with his prancing cream-coloured ponies and gold-laced flunkeys, while the blare of French horns brought out the youngsters to wonder and cheer. Bath was then the 'cradle of age, and a fine slope to the grave'. The Pump and Assembly Rooms and the streets were thronged with the wit, folly, and decrepitude of England.

Above the Guildhall the Union Flag fluttered from a newly-erected flagpole, with other national flags hanging from the pediment. Each windowsill had been transformed into a 'bank of the choicest and brightest flowering plants, artistically intermingled with foliage, and from this horticultural adornment arose heraldic shields'. Across the road, Cater, Stoffell & Fortt's had mounted a similarly extravagant display, with, as centrepiece, a crown and the royal monogram in coloured electric lights.

Ealand's drapery store, on the corner of Northgate and New Bond Streets, had, as the centrepiece of its display, 'a noble shield of the Bath arms, with the supporting lion and bear having a background of Union Jacks, and the 'Floreat Bathon' prominent on the scroll'. Coming up New Bond Street, 'the gay adornment of the houses in Old Bond Street' was no less striking, while Milsom Street had been transformed into a horticultural showpiece:

> Very sensibly the occupants of this popular thoroughfare co-operated to have a uniform decoration for the whole street, and extremely refreshing and beautiful is its appearance. On

each side the edges of the pavement and the gutters are laid with turf, and, despite the unnecessary trampling to which it was subjected on Saturday night, it has retained much of its verdant green. At intervals striking floral borders are contrived with coconut fibre. Several of these are aglow with that brilliant scarlet geranium, 'Paul Crampel' edged with the richly variegated 'Mrs Collins' and 'Mrs Pollock'. In the central beds,

however, are pink and white hydrangeas, with geraniums of the same shades – 'Hortense Grandiflora Alba' and 'Dr Hogg'. For edging the curious rubra ice-plant is employed. At intervals are ornate vases containing flowers, and a series of flourishing bay trees, conifers, maples, etc. At the top of the street, against the steps of Edgar Buildings, is a deliciously contrived fountain with rockery, climbing plants, white roses, and palms being principally used for its floral garniture.

After the restraint of Milsom Street, George Street, with 'multitudinous lines of flags and streamers stretched from one side to the other', was an eye-blitzing extravaganza of patriotic fervour. The *Bath Chronicle* was especially taken with the decoration of Edgar Buildings, which, it considered,

> compares most favourably, if it does not excel, any rank in the city for the richness and effect of its Pageant decorations ... Above each house floats a large flag. There is continuous draping of red, white and blue, effectively looped, running the length of the building, in two rows, and the space between each window on the second floor is filled with a shield and device of flags, with garlands of flowers below.

It was less impressed with the decorations in Gay Street, the Circus, and Brock Street, which 'were not on what might be termed a lavish scale', although 'a brave show of flags was made':

> There was hardly a single house that did not display a flag or some sign of decoration in the way of effective window flower-boxes. In Gay Street two houses exhibited the motto 'Success to the Bath Historical Pageant', while several occupants of dwellings had gone in for a somewhat complete scheme in the shape of coloured shields, flags and bunting. The most noteworthy house decoration in the Circus was the residence of Lord and Lady de Blaquiere. Here flags, banners, flowers and Venetian streamers had been employed with the most pleasing effect. Flags made a distinctly brave show in Brock Street, and almost every house in the street displayed a Union Jack, while outside the main entrance of Trinity Presbyterian Church was exhibited the following words: 'Bath Presbyterians bid you welcome'. The Brock Street entrance to the park was also made gay by a liberal display of flags ... The residents in the Royal Crescent evidently believe with the poet that 'Beauty is, when unadorned, adorned the most'. Rightly judging that no effect could be finer than the majestic grandeur of the Crescent, they did not resort to artificial embellishments, and the only decorations were the floral displays in many of the window recesses. Brightly tinted flowers, set off against the backgrounds of green, furnished refreshing touches of colour. On the magnificent lawn in front of the terrace a Union Jack, attached to a flagstaff, floated in the breeze, and oblique streamers were suspended from the top of the staff.

The distaste for excess exhibited by the refined residents of the Crescent were – as might be expected – not echoed in the main commercial streets of the city. It is a pity the route to Royal Victoria Park did not take the royal visitors through Cheap Street and Union Street, 'streaming with flags of the miniature and monster type [and] occasional Chinese lanterns of the large and many-coloured variety', where the displays rivalled those in George Street.

The procession continued down Marlborough Buildings, where 'a brave display of flags, bunting, standards, bright art muslin, real and artificial flowers, festoons, ornamental shields, etc, was made', before turning into Royal Victoria Park, where a guard of honour was provided by the 1st Wessex Field Company Royal Engineers. The seven carriages, led by the Chief Constable and his mounted men, proceeded up the roadway at the rear of Marlborough Buildings before heading across the park:

> The oncoming of the party was in full view of the crowded grandstand, as the Pageant processions are, and a pretty sight it was. The carriages were driven right across the 'stage' to the entrance to the royal box, where Major CH Simpson, as Master of Ceremonies, was waiting with Mr T Sturge Cotterell, Chairman of the Executive, to receive the distinguished guests.

The royal enclosure was in the centre of the stand,

> a special extension awning being employed to afford the shelter that was so happily requisite from the brilliant sunshine. The enclosure was covered with red felt, and surrounded with an edging of flowering plants … There was no ceremony whatever by way of opening – the royal party having taken their seats and acceded to Messrs Lewis Bros request for a photographic view of the occupied enclosure, the telephone commenced its activity, and the Bath Historical Pageant of 1909 was opening with the pretty Romano-British scene.

The *Bath Chronicle* declared the opening performance a resounding success:

Facing page top: The Marquess of Bath and Major Simpson (with his back to the camera) greet the Duke of Connaught.

Middle: The Duke and Duchess walk to the grandstand.

Bottom: Major Simpson formally welcomes the Duke and Duchess.

Arrival of T.R.H. The Duke & Duchess of Connaught at Pageant Grounds.

Lewis Bros,
Official Photographers.

After seven months of the hardest labour and nearly a month of anxiety about the weather, that the opening day should have been favoured with weather so glorious seemed an abundant reward. The general anticipation of a fine week ahead moreover raised everybody's spirits.

The performance went without a hitch, and the enthusiasm of the company of visitors was unbounded. Experienced pageant-goers declare that Bath has beaten all records for the beauty of the dramatic scenes presented, and Bathonians themselves know that, while breaking all records for rapidity of preparation, they have observed historical exactness before all things. There can be nothing but a succession of triumphs during the remaining days that are to come, and the best word that we can add to those not yet provided with seats is they are purchasable still, but should be secured promptly. The Bath Pageant has been gloriously inaugurated.

Sadly, the opening day was marred by tragedy. A 20-year-old woman from Twerton had come down to Marlborough Lane, with her four children, to see the people coming out of the Pageant. She crossed the road with three of her children, leaving her six-year-old son on the pavement with a friend. He decided to run after her just as a car was approaching and the front wheels ran over him before the driver could stop. He was taken to the hospital but was dead on arrival. The chauffeur said that the car was doing no more than eight miles an hour. And, in case you're wondering, the ages quoted above are correct.

On Friday it was the turn of the Lord Mayors of London, Bristol and Cardiff, together with the Mayors of 24 other towns and cities to come down for Civic Day. Like the journalists six days earlier, the Lord Mayor's party came down by the 11am from Paddington. On this occasion, however, they were met by the Mayor and Mayoress. It was just before 12.30, with the Abbey bells ringing, that six carriages left the Guildhall for the station, where a large crowd had already gathered. The Great Western had entered into the spirit of things, and the station was decorated, inside and out, with flags and finery.

Arriving back at the Guildhall, whose decorations had been refreshed for the occasion, lunch was served in the Banqueting Room. In a speech after the meal, the Lord Mayor of London approached the subject of Bath's decline as a health resort by means of a rather clumsy analogy:

I am glad, sir, that you have placed the arms of Bath and the City of London side by side on your menu card today. The two cities have been united together from a social point of view certainly for centuries, and then you know we both owe our prosperity to one source – water. The water which has secured the importance and prosperity of London is drawn from the west. It arises in the western hills and it flows to the eastern shore of our island, and there it opens up such a wide river with such a wide mouth that the Romans – who knew what they were about – decided to make the chief city of England on its banks. But, sir, in Bath you have taken care not to allow the water which is underneath your town to flow to London; you have retained it for your own prosperity, and I am delighted to know that while Bath is a most historic city, and has had a most prosperous past, it has a very prosperous present, and I believe that it is destined in the future to enjoy ever increased prosperity.

We all know of the old days when Bath was visited for the benefit to be derived from its water. Well, for a time that fashion waned. The introduction, I suppose, of increased facilities of travel led people to turn their thoughts to the continent, and for some years the fame of Bath was not so great as it had been. But I cannot help thinking, and I think it is borne out by facts, that Bath is now becoming freshly a fashion. People are beginning to appreciate that they need not run abroad in order to obtain the benefit of medicinal waters, and therefore I think I am right in prophesying for your city a fresh increase of prosperity, and that is the devout wish I express on behalf of the city of London today.

He concluded his speech by admitting that

there is one thing that might cause a little friction in connection with our visit to Bath today. I am afraid there is a spirit of jealousy arising in the mind of the Lady Mayoress of London on seeing so many of her sisters in office decorated with chains. Well, the only thing I can say is this – that up to the present we have not found it necessary to chain our Mayoresses.

In reply, the Mayor recalled Sir Malcolm Morris's criticisms of the city a few weeks earlier:

He told us we were almost a wicked Corporation in allowing the blessings of our waters, the blessed waters we have, to run to waste through the whole of the summer. Bath is a city which has an autumn and winter season, and Sir Malcolm Morris thought we were doing a great injustice in allowing the waters of the city to run away in the summer months. Sir Malcolm was good enough to inaugurate an open-air fountain, situated in one of the prettiest spots in Bath, through the agency of which we hope Bath will be assisted in the regaining of its ancient glories. The drinking fountain will not only be a means of health, but in such pleasant surroundings it will be an attraction to those who are not invalids. We are incurring just now a great deal of expenditure, and we look for its justification in increasing popularity and prosperity in the future.

He could almost be talking, a century on, about the Thermae Bath Spa building – although the drinking fountain, now sadly disused, cost, of course, somewhat less.

As the luncheon drew to an end, the fine weather which had blessed the Pageant started to break up, and heavy rain began to fall. The streets outside the Guildhall, which had been closed to traffic, were, nevertheless, filled with spectators. Shortly before the procession was due to set off, a bodyguard of Cavaliers and Roundheads, from the Battle of Lansdown episode, began to line up.

The rain intensified as the civic party, led by the mace bearers, emerged from the Guildhall. Then the dignitaries entered the carriages, the hoods of which had been closed against the rain, and the procession set off. The route was slightly different to that taken on Monday – it had probably been pointed out that

two of the most lavishly decorated streets in the city had been missed out. Instead of heading north along Northgate Street and turning down New Bond Street, it headed down Cheap Street and up Union Street before continuing up Milsom Street.

Cheap Street and Union Street decorated for the Pageant. Above can be seen William Smith's bag & trunk store, described by a correspondent in the Chronicle as that 'monstrous building at the corner of Cheap Street', while below, on the left, is Alderman Peacock's fish and game dealer's.

Above: The Lord Mayor of London's coach drives through the Circus in the rain.
Below: The Lord Mayor of London and other dignitaries wait for the afternoon's entertainment to commence.

On the following day, the rain had passed over and, in brilliant sunshine, seven Members of Parliament from Bath and nearby constituencies, together with the Agents-General for Western Australia, the Commonwealth of Australia, Tasmania and South

Australia, were entertained to lunch, followed by a procession to the Pageant Ground.

So much for the dignitaries. What would ordinary members of the public have found as they made their way to the Pageant Ground? The main entrance was on Weston Lane, just past the *Marlborough Tavern*. Carriages and motors entered from Marlborough Lane, past the obelisk. Only a handful of people had their own transport, so, despite there being around 3,000 performers and 4,000 spectators at each performance, parking was not a problem.

The Pageant was staged in part of the park that was absorbed into the Botanical Gardens in the 1920s. What was then largely open grassland is now covered by flower borders and the network of paths threading through the rockeries and ponds below the temple built for the 1924 British Empire Exhibition at Wembley. The grandstand stood roughly where the temple stands today, although it was, of course, much larger. Tickets for the grandstand started at a guinea (for which you got to see – although not hear – everything) and went down to 3/6 (for which you got to see very little). Even those in the expensive seats, however, were not guaranteed a good view, if the ladies in front of them refused to take their hats off. Although the 'polite request of the stewards that hats should be removed' met with a 'ready and gracious response' from 'nearly every lady who sat at the grandstand for the inaugural presentation of the Pageant', some refused. At the opening performance,

> one party who arrived late and obstructed the view of many while they were finding their seats, when accommodated declined to take off their headgear, although it was of the most obstructive description – picture hats of formidable dimensions. When the much-tried steward was appealed to by those in the rear he exclaimed, 'They have refused to take them off'. Those 'ladies' heard such remarks from onlookers in their immediate vicinity that they left the stand after watching two episodes – with their hats on.

For those unwilling or unable to pay for seats in the covered auditorium, there was a standing enclosure a little way to the east, admission to which was 2/-.

Taking their seats in the grandstand, the audience would have been able, as they listened to music from the orchestra, and looked across the park, to take in the somewhat minimalist props. Down to

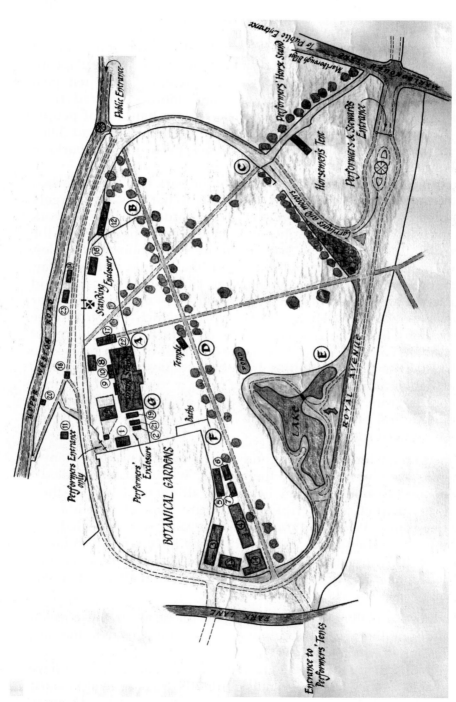

A plan of the Pageant Ground based on the original by the architects Herbert W Matthews and Alfred J Taylor.

A key to the numbers appears on the opposite page.

REFERENCE for TENTS etc.

1 MR LASCELLES.

2 Secretary to Performers and Heads of Scenes.

3 Lady Performers.

4 Gentlemen Performers.

5 Ladies' Quick Change.

6 Gent's Quick Change.

7 Properties.

8 Executive and Press.

9 Ladies' Cloaks and Lost Property.

10 Gents' Cloaks and Lost Property.

11 Ladies' Lavatory.

12 & 20 Gents' Lavatories.

13, 14, 15, 16 Refreshments.

17 Telegraph, Post Office, Photographs, and Chocolates.

18 Ambulance.

19 Royal and Reception Tent.

21 Colonial and American Tent.

22 Wheel Chair Stand.

23 Souvenirs.

24 Post Cards.

✸ Public Main Entrance.

✠ Entrance to Grand Stand and Standing Enclosures.

A   B   C   D   E   F   G

Performers' Stage Entrances . . . .

their left, where the paths that still lie outside the Botanical Gardens crossed, was a Temple of Minerva. To their right was a representation of the Roman baths, while far off, through the trees, was a picturesque gateway.

Above them, on the roof of the grandstand (and therefore out of sight), was the nerve centre of the whole operation – a box from which Frank Lascelles

> directs the proceedings, makes ... trifling alterations, gives an occasional reminder to the performers of what is expected from them but more often a word of encouragement through the megaphone, or indicates his approval of their efforts by clapping his hands and in other ways.

The uninitiated may have assumed that this was as far as stage direction went once the Pageant was under way. Far from it – that marvel of modern technology, the telephone, was vital to the success of the enterprise – so vital, in fact, that it is hard to see how a spectacle such as this could have been organized before its invention. The *Bath Chronicle* explains how it was employed:

> From his position in the tower, Mr Lascelles is in communication with every entrance to the ground used by the performers, and with all other points to which it is possible he may wish to send directions. At each of these points there are stewards who have certain definite orders to carry out, and certain duties for which they are held responsible. Every group of performers has its leader, who is looked to to produce them at the proper moment, and properly attired. Above them again are others with more general responsibilities. A pageant differs from other dramatic performances in that the size of its stage makes it impossible for those engaged to take up their own cues. They have first to be warned by telephone from the conning tower when to be ready, and then the cue for their entrance is given them in the same manner.

> Mr Lascelles could not, of course, undertake all this himself, but he has a most able lieutenant in Mr DS Kennedy, who is in charge of the telephone, and proves a most reliable operator. His position is a particular onerous one. The whole scheme of each episode is before him and throughout the whole of the three hours or more that the Pageant lasts he has few moments of relief. Long before one episode is over he is telephoning instructions for the assembling of all the characters in the next and at the same time giving the cues for that being enacted.

Not only do the characters and the 'crowd' come within his scope but the properties also. It is not a position that anyone would lightly undertake, and yet it is a further evidence of the voluntary side of the work which we have already spoken of, for Mr Kennedy's labours, as well as those in charge of the various instruments with which he communicates are all purely voluntary. It is very essential that this side of the production should be fully understood, since it says so much for the local effort which has contributed to make the Pageant so great a success.

The telephone which Mr Kennedy controls with its intricate switchboard, is, however, not the only one on the roof of the grandstand. Mr Heap occupies a similar position to Mr Kennedy with respect to the music, and has an instrument at his disposal by means of which he conveys the necessary instructions to the orchestra and choir. It is in this way that the trumpets sound at precisely the right moment, when the state trumpeters who precede King Henry VII sound a fanfare, for, of course, it is no secret that the instruments they carry are ornamental rather than useful. As they advance Mr Heap 'rings up' the real trumpeters, then gives the order for them to be ready, and finally (for they are standing in sight of the roof of the grandstand) by a hand signal he indicates the precise moment when they are to sound their instruments. This is only mentioned as an instance of the detail which has to be observed throughout.

One of Mr Lascelles' great troubles has been to keep people, some of them who apparently have no business near the place at all, from calmly walking on where they are visible to the spectators. Even those engaged occasionally transgress in this manner, but Mr Lascelles' quick eye speedily detects them, and a message is promptly telephoned to stewards at the particular spot to seize the delinquent, and – well, we will not repeat the sentence he passed upon a small choirboy who so transgressed yesterday. Now that everything is going so smoothly, and his attention is not obliged to be fully concentrated upon the scene in front of him, Mr Lascelles is able to receive a few privileged visitors at his exalted post, and one of these yesterday was Lord Northcliffe, but even while conversing with them his sharp eye is ready to detect any little flaw in the performance – a little thing which could certainly pass unnoticed by the ordinary spectators, and his megaphone is ready to his hand to make a suggestion, or to urge the performers to increase their efforts. The enthusiasm of the crowd after the coronation of King Edgar and Queen Elfrida yesterday did not altogether satisfy him, and he quickly put up his notice 'Cheers', and cried through the megaphone, 'Louder, Louder'.

But those not privileged to share Mr Lascelles' box would have been blissfully unaware of all this. All they would have known, as the clock ticked closer to 2.45 and the tension mounted, was that they were going to see a spectacle – involving scores of people they knew – the like of which Bath had never seen before – and would never see again.

CHAPTER THIRTY-FIVE

A CAST OF THOUSANDS

A century on, we can count ourselves fortunate, in trying to imagine what those thousands of spectators would have seen on those long-gone summer afternoons, that the Pageant took place at the height of the Edwardian postcard boom. Dozens of different postcards were printed so that those attending could write and show their friends what they had seen – or indeed, what they had taken part in. Sifting through them today, however, one rather unfortunate feature soon becomes apparent. The publishers naturally wanted to have cards ready for sale on the opening day, if not before. This meant that photographs had to be taken at rehearsals; many were not action shots but standard group portraits. In many cases, the stage sets were not ready. Despite these drawbacks, however, the photographic record of the Pageant, together with the books of words and comments of those who saw it, make it possible to get some idea of what it was like. Here, then, is an illustrated account of what happened.

Episode I: The Dedication of Sul's Temple AD 160

A beggar, as played by Mr Little,

As the Pageant opens, a motley band of peasants, including several children, gather, buying and selling 'trinkets, pottery, skins, cloth and the usual market produce'. A procession of priestesses enters, carrying a figure of the goddess Minerva. On one side is a character familiar to many members of the audience – 'a beggar, making a hearty meal from the contents of his wallet, and drinking copiously from a horn'. Another figure familiar to many – a female invalid – is brought from the baths, not in a Bath chair but carried on a litter. She is accosted by the beggar, who claims that he has been 'two days without bite or sup'. After upping it to three days and being rebuffed, he turns his attention to a centurion who appears on the scene, claiming that he has been without bite or sup for four – and then five – days. In the first of many Pythonesque touches, the centurion kicks the beggar's crutches away. As his food and money roll in all directions, the crowd scrambles for it eagerly.

The centurion delivers his opinion of this 'pestilent island where no grape ripens ... fog and mist and snow and an evil journey overseas from Gaul'. A Greek trader, selling charms and potions, arrives, and is handled roughly by the crowd, until a herald arrives to announce

The Bath Historical Pageant, 1909.

The Greek Trader

Lewis Bros, Official Photographers.

The Bath Historical Pageant, 1909.

Episode I. Roman Soldiers.

Lewis Bros Official Photographers.

the rededication of the temple. He orders all trading to cease and declares a public holiday, with everyone invited to attend the games to be held after the rededication ceremony. The crowd discourse on the healing properties of the baths and the efficacy of praying to the gods, until the arrival of a troop of soldiers from the second legion, led by a standard bearer singing a curiously unmilitary song:

> *The long white road is leading us*
> *(Going northward to the wall)*
> *Wherever Rome is needing us*
> *(With your pack on your back*
>   *and your armour and all, O)*
> *Every road leads Romewards*
> *(Going southwards across Gaul),*
> *Will we never be marching homeward?*
> *To return again, we pray. (In vain.*
> *O Emperor, hear our call!)*

He declares himself so dry that he could 'relish even the abominable corn-liquor brewed by these hairy islanders', but is interrupted by a hue and cry. The Greek trader has snatched the invalid's purse, but the crowd manages to catch him and retrieve it. At this point a magistrate appears with his retinue and announces that Antoninus, Emperor of Rome, has charged the priests to rededicate the altar to Sul Minerva. The incense-fuelled ceremony that follows ends with a chant sung by another procession of priestesses:

The Bath Historical Pageant, 1909.

Episode I. Magistrate dedicating Temple.

Lewis Bros, Official Photographers.

O Goddess, deign with us to dwell
In thy new-hallowed fane,
And as thy healing springs dispel
All suffering and pain,
So let our ancient enmities
By thee be pacified,
That for thy peaceful mysteries
Within thy sight we may unite
Two nations side by side.

A total of 339 performers took part in this episode, including 51 soldiers, 37 British children, 35 Roman boys, 17 Roman girls, 29 priests, 11 priestesses, 13 female slaves and 10 hucksters. There were 22 speaking parts, including Captain Daubeny as a Magistrate and the Rev Hylton Stewart, Rector of Bathwick, as a Standard Bearer. The priestesses, though few in number, were important not only in terms of action but also in terms of spectacle. 'There was', according to the review in the *Bath Chronicle*,

no escape from the presence of a legion of armoured soldiers, and Mr Heard's business was to clothe the priestesses and others who were not already limited to a certain colour so as to make a beautiful picture. In this instance the Master of Designs was particularly happy in alighting upon the inspiration to robe the priestesses in a pale blue, which imparted an ethereal air to their motions, and made the scene one of the most striking of the

The Bath Historical Pageant, 1909.

Miss English as "Rusonia Avenna in Dedication of Sul's Temple.

Lewis Bros,
Official Photographers.

tableaux ... The priestesses, who with their wreaths, cymbals, and tibecenae, chant so effectively Mr Tapp's People's Hymn, are in white stolas, with blue, long, broad and flowing togas, silver fillets, and armlets.

Miss English, who on her litter occupies the forefront of the striking picture with which the Pageant opens, is seen wearing a cream dress with a gold fringe trimming, and she has a striking red headscarf very much jewelled ...

The standard bearer to the Roman legion wears a wolf skin over his head and a buff over white tunic. Mr Vaughan, as the first centurion, is a striking figure in his white Roman tunic with blue tab and white ornaments. He has a gold cuirass, and the Roman armour bands with a striking flowing crimson cloak, caught at the shoulders with correct Roman clasps, the whole figure being set off by the brazen Roman helmet, surmounted with long white plumes. The second centurion is arrayed hardly less gorgeously in scarlet and white, and with a silver scale-armour tunic. The early Britons supply effective contrasts in their coarse canvas dresses, and a notable figure to which attention should be directed, since he attains no prominence in the episode, is the slave dealer in tiger skin, with armlets, leg rings, earrings and a knotted whip, to emphasise his brutal vocation. The group of women slaves he is vending is another of the many groups that contribute to this telling scene.

Music for the episode was provided by a local composer, FH Tapp, whose score, according to the *Bath Chronicle*, was 'felicitous without being pedantic':

It is scored in the two modes which were in vogue in the period in question, while the peculiar intervals also preserve the illusion of the Roman period. He has been consistently successful – take, for instance, that wonderfully effective yet sedate solo sung by the standard bearer of the Roman legion, close the eyes for a moment, and listen to the unison chorus of the soldiery, and then glance at the warriors as they complete their march, and if the effect conveyed is not to carry the mind back to the Roman period, then the listener must be devoid of imagination. Still more striking in its way is the deeply beautiful flowing chant of the picturesquely-garbed priestesses of Minerva as they glide across the grassy slopes in the vicinity of the temple, some of them accentuating the rhythm by the clashing of cymbals, while others hold aloft double flutes of the sort to be seen represented in Etruscan mural paintings ... A stirring march from the pen of Mr JW Duys acts as a prelude to the episode.

One of things that most delighted Frank Lascelles about the staging of this episode was 'the natural manner in which the British children play on the ambulatory of the Roman Bath. The difficulty in coaching performers for pageants,' he told a reporter, 'is to get them to be thoroughly natural, but the youngsters of Bath, who are allotted this part, cannot be chided for any lack of freedom.'

British peasants, including the children whose performance so captivated Frank Lascelles.

Episode II: The Sack of Akeman after Dyrham Fight, AD 577

The second episode was, according to the reporter from the *Western Daily Press*, 'less spectacular than the first but immensely more dramatic. There was a lack of the bright colouring of the earlier scene, but the concentrated horror of a grim tragedy incidental to the defeat of the British by the Saxon invaders.'

As it opens, the temple has become a Christian church, although the extent of the transformation is unclear. All we have to go on is a passing reference in the *Daily Chronicle* –

> There is but little artificial scenery. To one side is the ancient Temple of Minerva, transforming itself later, by an ingenious device, into Bath Abbey – surely the first transformation scene of its kind in any pageant –

and a photograph taken during one of the rehearsals showing half of the temple portico covered by what appears to be the top of a gothic window (see facing page top). As the portico consisted of painted canvas, it is possible that canvas screens were also used to cover the pillars, thus transforming the temple into the west front of the Abbey. However, photographs of the closing ceremony, which took place on the steps of the temple, show the pillars unadorned. In the absence of firmer photographic or descriptive evidence the extent of the transformation must, therefore, remain speculative.

Another innovation in Episode II (presuming it wasn't there in Episode I, when it would have looked decidedly out of place) was a representation of the west gate which appeared to the left of the baths.

The Queen comes out of the temple (or church), where she has been praying for victory and is saluted by the aged captain of the guard who tells her he has seen men running from the battle. She is confident they bring news of victory, but two messengers arrive and tell her that the battle is lost and that she must flee to the caves of Mendip. Then comes news that the Saxons have broken through the north gate. She is urged to flee through the south gate, but she declares she will stay and fight.

The Saxons swarm into the city, taking the British soldiers hostage. The Queen picks up a sword and holds them off for a while, but when she learns that her husband is dead, she turns the sword on herself. The Saxon King orders her body to be taken into the temple and for the building to be burnt as a funeral pyre. Smoke is soon seen coming from the building, and then, with a curt 'Burn me Akeman', he orders the whole city to be put to the torch. As smoke begins to pour from the baths, an aged priest is brought before him. The King promises to spare him if he tells him what he foresees, and the episode ends with the priest's prophecy

> that here, where I alone am left to pray, many shall worship. That here where a Queen died, a King shall be crowned. That here in Britain, where nation fights against nation, there shall be one people, of one faith, having one peace, under one King.

Queen Farinmael, played by Miss Somerville, makes a dramatic exit.

596

A total of 340 performers took part in this episode, including a crowd of 140 women and children, a 72-strong British garrison and 91 invading Saxons, all of whom worked at the Post Office. There were 12 speaking parts, including the Rev Hylton Stewart, who had already appeared as a Standard Bearer in Episode I, taking the part of Ceawlin, the Saxon King. So much for Sturge Cotterell's insistence that no performer should appear in more than one episode. 'The groups in the second episode', according to the report in the *Bath Chronicle*,

> give as much satisfaction to the Master of Designs as any part of his work. There is a barbaric atmosphere about the whole which precisely fits the story. The 'ornaments' – rings, skins, bones, and even skulls – all suggest, as one spectator was heard to say, 'a real heathen lot'. The Queen in the second episode (Miss Somerville, daughter of the High Sheriff of Somerset), whose tragic death thrills the company, has a petticoat of blue Bolton sheeting, and an overdress of deep red, stencilled with white and gold in ancient British designs. A bright green cloak edged with gold fringe, a toque, and an old British belt, set with daggers and jewellery, make one of the most effective costumes of the Pageant. Miss Somerville is attended by 16 women of Akeman, all wearing various coloured costumes in the same style as the Queen's, and stencilled by the students of the Bath City Art School, who have in their leisure hours done this splendid service. The King and the invading Saxons are in ring armour tunics, with red under-tunics and jewelled belts.

Saxon warriors – from the Post Office.

For another reviewer, it was the realism of the episode that was most memorable:

> The end of the British Queen, who plunged a dagger in her heart rather than be taken captive, was intensely realistic. Another striking feature was the rush, first this way and then that, of the hundreds of British women alarmed at the conquerors' approach.

According to the report in Tuesday's *Chronicle*, one of the performers – an early proponent of method acting perhaps – seems to have taken things rather to extremes:

> Everyone who has seen the Pageant remarks on the wonderful fall which is done by one of the Saxon soldiers, who endeavours to seize the body of Queen Farinmael on the temple steps and is stabbed by one of the dead Queen's maids. The man drops with a terrific thud and rolls down half the flight of steps onto the grass. It is said that the performer's body is black and blue owing to the realistic way in which this piece of acting is carried out.

Two days later, the *Chronicle* updated readers on the result of this overzealousness:

> The weather was splendid again today, for the westerly breeze most obligingly had blown away the ominous clouds that threatened to drop moisture earlier in the day. The attendance was most gratifying, for not only was the grandstand full, but the

enclosure was well patronized. Mr Wilkey, who stunned himself by falling down the temple steps when he is killed by one of the Queen's women on Tuesday afternoon, had quite recovered from the mishap, and took the part of the dead Saxon with the same realism which rendered him insensible the other day.

Episode III: The Coronation of King Edgar, AD 973

The priest's prophecy is realised in Episode III, the coronation of King Edgar. In contrast to the frenzied action of the previous scene, it is ceremonial and stately, only relieved by the jostling and cheering of the crowd, through which a path has to be made for the King, at the start. Long speeches from the King and Archbishop are followed by the coronation, the singing of the Te Deum (during which the King prostrates himself before the altar), and prayers. Finally, the King and Queen take their seats on the coronation thrones. It seems that, during rehearsals, it was decided that all this went on too long. A note in the books of words on sale at the Pageant informed readers that 'the prayers will be omitted in the performance, and the subsequent anointings will be performed in dumb show'.

Apparently the author of this episode, Edward Tylee, was told to ignore the King's predilection for chasing nuns. He did, however, make a passing reference to his more disreputable side, by having the Archbishop describe him as 'pious Edgar, our sometimes erring but obedient child'. You can't help feeling that a spot of nun-chasing

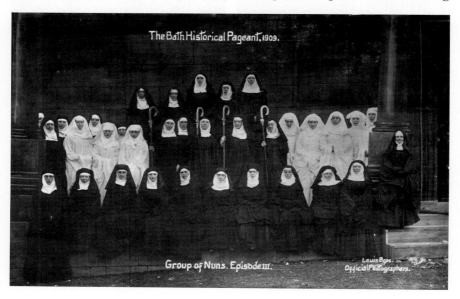

The Bath Historical Pageant, 1909.

Group of Nuns. Episode III.

Lewis Bros.
Official Photographers.

would have provided some light relief in an episode that sorely lacks it.

There were only eleven speaking parts in this episode; astonishingly, the Rev Hylton Stewart popped up yet again, as the Archbishop of Canterbury, along with three other clergymen: the Rev VCA Fitzhugh, Curate of Christ Church, the Rev CEB Barnwell, who lived at 1 Lansdown Place West, and the Rev EW Poynton, Rector of Kelston (who was to be charged with assaulting a minor a few months later). Colonel Clayton, who had warned Bath's Licensed Victuallers to

Alfred Thornton as King Edgar.

Kathleen de Blaquiere as Queen Elfrida.

keep a lookout for German spies, played a thane called Godric; Alfred Thornton played King Edgar. The other 382 performers included 73 children, 46 acolytes, 41 nuns, 38 Saxon warriors, 20 thanes, eight bishops, seven abbots, six abbesses and a dog. Queen Elfrida, played by Lady de Blaquiere's daughter, Kathleen, wore

> a comparatively simple Saxon robe of cream composed of heavy linen, but the costume is beautifully embellished with stencil work and jewelled, and caught up with a jewelled girdle. She also wears a long flowing saxe-blue cloak of linen, stencilled and jewelled. King Edgar approaches his coronation in an alb, over which is worn a blue dalmatic. After the anointing he is vested with a very full cloak, with a large appliqued eagle on the shoulders worked in black and red. This is considered the most gorgeous raiment in the Pageant, and was worked by Miss Edith Sheppard and her co-workers in the ecclesiastical section. The court ladies are arrayed as effectively as any group in the Pageant, the stencilled decorations and jewels being very fine. Archbishop Dunstan wears chasuble and dalmatic, the former being red on account of the ceremony occurring on Whit Sunday ... The loose altar cloth [has] the characteristic Celtic border and the standards displaying the White Horse of Avebury and the Green Dragon of Wessex.

The *Daily Chronicle* reporter found a 'peculiar beauty' in the 'peaceful ritual of the coronation of King Edgar and Queen Elfrida. With its incense and its roses, its chanting monks and gracious young King and Queen, it has about it a true touch of medieval poetry.

It is like some old illumination come to life.' The *Court Journal* was especially taken by the Queen's costume:

> The Hon Kathleen de Blaquiere as Queen Elfrida, clad in silken raiment of the glorious blue tone that we associate with celestial skies, was a vision of regal beauty, and her lady-in-waiting, with her gentle hound held in leash, was a harmonious note in a magnificent tableau of living moving beauty, that was further heightened in its reality by the dignified air of the King and the sonorous tones of the stately ecclesiastical dignitaries as they chanted the odes incidental to the ritual.

The music, by Dr HP Allen, which had already been performed earlier in the year at the Church Pageant in Fulham, does not seem to have been greeted with the same enthusiasm as the music in some of the other episodes. The *Chronicle* reporter, for example, while admitting it was 'impressive', went on to damn it with faint praise:

> The effect of the singing is quite as it should be, and never do the voices rising and falling in soothing harmony tend to destroy the illusion of an ecclesiastical ceremony. Dr Allen quite sustains his reputation as a scholarly composer, who seeks his effects and obtains them by legitimate methods.

Abandoning all pretence of historical verisimilitude, the episode also included Handel's coronation anthem *Zadok the Priest*, written over 750 years after Edgar's coronation.

The Bath Historical Pageant, 1909.

King Greeting Queen after Coronation.

Lewis Bros.
Official Photographers.

Episode IV: King Henry VII Visits Bath, AD 1497

The action in Episode IV is also slow-paced. It opens with a shepherd boy singing of the joys of spring and assorted rustics setting forth for their day's labours. As the angelus rings, they uncover their heads and the voices of monks float over the greensward. The Prior crosses towards the Abbey and meets the Bishop coming out. Their conversation, although its historical credentials may be impeccable, is the sort of thing that normally comes with copious footnotes:

PRIOR   *The humble greeting of thy lowly flock,*
      How fares it with my Lord?

BISHOP   *Why tired I am, good Prior, tired.*
      What would you have?
      Those journeyings over sea, that embassage
      To Spain! To serve the King and Christ at once
      Too much for one strength.
         I am Issachar.
      The ass between two burdens.

PRIOR   *Dare I then*
      Venture? We all would gladly see you eased
      Of one, to bear the other burden light.

BISHOP   *Thanks for your loving care, and yet, my son,*
      You err. Again my case is Isaachar's.
      For load, one pack upon a single flank
      Of your poor beast, and look! you overswing
      And break the weary, patient back of him.

PRIOR   *My Lord, I cannot read your parable.*

– an observation many of the audience might have concurred in – if they could have heard what was going on.

  By now, the Pageant had been going on for nearly an hour. Punctually at 3.40 – assuming everything was running to time, King Henry VII, in his horse litter, 'with the steeds brightly caparisoned in blue and gold', ascends the slope between the trees. Preceding him are the heralds, marching in stately formation and then blowing a mock fanfare on their mock trumpets, at precisely the same time as a real fanfare is blown off to the side – 'a triumph in stage deception' effused one reviewer.

  The King approaches and the Bishop tells him of a dream he has had 'this very morn':

I dreamt I saw
The ladder of Jacob and the Angels on it.
Beneath there sprang an Olive, and it held
A crown up; then from Heaven it sounded down
'The Olive props the Crown; the King shall prop
The House of God.'

A choir takes up the theme, before a guard of bowmen enter and a group of maidens step forward to sing in honour of the King. The Bishop tells the King of the ruinous state of the Abbey, and the King agrees to finance its rebuilding. As the Bishop pours blessings on the King's head, the episode ends with a joust – if you're lucky.

Luck, in this instance, depended on visiting the Pageant on Monday. Tuesday's *Chronicle* informed readers that 'for the first time yesterday the joust prescribed in the book to be introduced into Episode IV was given, Sergeant-Major Shakespeare and Sergeant Vincent, clad in armour cap-a-pie, had a capital and rousing set to with lances.' Their set-to seems to have been a little too rousing, however. On Thursday, the *Chronicle* reported that 'no tournament was possible today, and this has only been seen

on one occasion (Monday). Its absence is to be regretted, but the fact is that Sergeant-Major JW Vincent, North Somerset Yeomanry, who was one of the knights in the charge, was really hurt in the ribs by the armour being forced into him. It is hoped he will be well enough to enter the lists again before the Pageant concludes.' There are no further mentions of the joust, however, suggesting that the wounded sergeant-major had decided enough was enough.

There were seven speaking parts in the episode, and a relatively modest corps of 242 other performers, including 54 soldiers, 43 ladies, 35 traders, 22 scholars, ten monks, eight

Bishop Oliver King, played by Arthur Godfrey Day, director of studies at the Technical School.

heralds, a falconer, a goat keeper and a dog man. Costume-wise, the aim was, according to the *Chronicle,* to 'keep the scene as bright and rich as possible':

> The King, who is borne in on a horse litter, with the animals gaily caparisoned, makes a commanding figure in his tabard of resplendent armour with the coat of arms. The trumpeters, who head the King's procession, are wearing tabards of the brightest hues, all glorious with their coats of arms, and the heralds

Trumpeter to Henry VII
Bath Pageant. July 1909

immediately behind, while of more subdued array, make an excellent group in gold tunics with green slashings. The army leaders have surcoats of different colours, with coats of arms worked in, and their chain armour, swords and belts make up a fine martial uniform. The courtiers are gay in stencilled velveteens, very much jewelled, and they have quaint hats with long plumes. The court ladies are in costumes of the period and quite up to date, while the country ladies are a little less forward in their fashions, as might be reasonably expected.

The episode, although 'not overladen with music', had, according to the *Chronicle*, one work 'quite worthy of extended reference'. This was a 'chorale for equal voices' by JS Heap, organist of St Mary's, Bathwick, which the *Chronicle* commended 'to the attention of all interested in this description of music'.

Episode V: The Visit of Queen Elizabeth to Bath, AD 1590

Episode V is much more lively than the two previous episodes. It opens with townsfolk milling around as the final touches are put to preparations for the visit of Queen Elizabeth. In the pillory is a local character called Benjamin Grimkin, who has been put there for drinking 'the Great Queen's health o'er loyally, and in sack of the vilest'. As he is pelted with flour, eggs and vegetables, he complains he's hungry. A teenage girl leaps upon the pillory

and thrusts a pasty into his mouth.[1] She berates the crowd, who not only stop throwing things at him but grab the keys off the sergeant and release him.

Shakespeare wanders on with Christopher Marlowe. Their attention is distracted by a 'band of fair West Country girls in flowing white dresses', one of whom throws Marlowe a rose. His ebullient mood is soon shattered, however, when a fortune teller takes his hand and foretells his death in a tavern brawl three years later. The Queen enters, to the strains of

The Bath Historical Pageant 1909.

Episode V. Queen Elizabeth & Court.

Lewis Bros.
Official Photographers.

a madrigal sung by the boys of the grammar school, and is greeted by the Mayor. After he has introduced Shakespeare to her, she grants St John's and Magdalen Hospitals to the Corporation.

Then comes what was for many the highlight of the Pageant – the Masque of Prince Bladud. The idea may have come from the Chelsea Pageant of 1908, when the Masque of the Faery Queen was performed before Queen Elizabeth, but this was of a different order entirely. It was intended as a bit of light-hearted fun – and perhaps, despite being written by a clergyman, as a riposte to those who saw the Pageant as primarily an educational tool. Some were dismissive of it, claiming that it only really appealed to children, but I suspect that most people, after a surfeit of inaudible history, were only too glad of a bit of silliness.

1 Pasty shops weren't as thick on the ground a century ago as they are now, but it's heartening to note that a pasty still seems to have been the busy man's No 1 choice of comestible.

It would be impossible to recreate the Pageant today, even if the Pageant Ground had survived in its original form. It relied on a large number of people with lots of time on their hands – and an even larger number of servants and retainers to do their bidding. Not only that, present-day tastes are, if not more sophisticated, very different. Cinema and television have familiarised us with costume drama and historical epics – as well as reducing our attention spans – but, if any part of the Pageant is worth reviving, it is surely this glorious piece of tomfoolery. And, as it's quite short, we'll quote it in full:

A MASQUE OF PRINCE BLADUD

Characters
PRINCE BLADUD
THE FAIRY OF THE HEALING SPRING
FAIRIES OF THE SPRING
KING LUD HUDIBRAS
HOBBY HORSES
BOYS

The Scene: A wood to the North of Bath.
Enter seven boys chasing several pigs toward a swamp, around which grow many aquatic plants. The pigs plunge into the pool.
Enter PRINCE BLADUD, as a Swineherd.

BLADUD   *This loutish garb fits not with my degree,*
I am a King's son, smit with leprosy.
Alas! that son of King Lud Hudibras's
Should e'er chase swine, as Saul his father's asses.
From Canesham and my master I must fly,
For now my pigs have ta'en the leprosy!
O Lud ! – Hudibras, where have my swine gone?
(Shouts to his pigs)
Slender snout! Bacon born! Come ye on.

Enter seven boys. They shout: 'How now, pig prodder?'

BLADUD   *No swineherd I! Son of King Hudibras,*
I've lost my throne, and now my pigs, alas.

FIRST BOY   *Thy pigs are bathing yonder in the stream*
That warms our valley. Mark the rising steam.

SECOND BOY   *Come, we will drag them forth.*

The Bath Historical Pageant, 1909.

King Bladud & Pigs.

Lewis Bros.
Official Photographers.

The boys and BLADUD rush towards the pool. The Fairy of the Stream rises from the long river grasses, with her fairies, who, dancing, make a ring about the pigs, cutting off the approach of the boys. The boys rush at them, but are driven back by fairy wands.

FAIRY   Lay not your impious hands upon these swine
That seek the healing of my magic spring.
Know that the Blissful Virgin Queen Benign
Hath blessed these waters, and they succour bring
To all diseases. Lo ! The swine are Clean.

BLADUD *(falling on his knees)*.
O blessed Sprite!
Do I behold my piglings pure and white?

FAIRY   Even thus, sweet Prince, our healing powers are seen!

BLADUD   O healing Spring
Now for a springing heel. I'll yet be King!
Here's for a ducking, this muck in,
This blessed puddle heals all my muddle;
One thorough rinse
Cures pig and saves Prince

Dives in with uproar. The pigs rush neglected away, pursued by the children. The Fairies group themselves about the Spirit of the Spring.

FAIRY   Potent medicated mud

610

The Bath Historical Pageant, 1909.

Miss M. Clutterbuck as Queen of the Fairies.

Lewis Bros,
Official Photographers.

Heal Prince Bladud!

As BLADUD scrambles out, KING LUD HUDIBRAS approaches, in state, with Hobby Horses, and embraces his son

KING LUD   *Marvellous Springs of Bath, that can restore*
                   My son to health, and to my arms once more

The boys now restore the pigs to BLADUD, and the whole body of mummers advance towards QUEEN ELIZABETH, KING LUD HUDIBRAS leading the Fairy of the Stream, while the Knights swing up each a Fairy upon the Hobby Horse in front of him. The FAIRY OF THE STREAM addresses the QUEEN

FAIRY   *Thus, puissant Sovereign, thy healing eyes*
               Shine on Time's waters with their glorious light,
               And the world's ills are cured, and men arise
               To bless the dawn that erstwhile was their night.
               Earth to thy favour owing every boon,
               Shines in thy light as in the Sun's the Moon.

Although we cannot be sure, it seems likely that the pond that Bladud and the pigs cavorted in lay beyond the main arena, just above the lake. Photographs of the masque seem to show this pool – although they were, of course, taken at rehearsals, and the photographer may have used this pool in preference to a temporary one nearer the main arena. If this was the pool used, it would have been over 100 metres from the grandstand, and, although the audience would have been able to see the action, they would have been able to hear very little. Sadly, the pool – perhaps our last real link with the Pageant – was filled in, having been extended and altered in the interim, around 20 years ago, thus destroying any chance of recreating this particular bit of history – although, when it comes to pools, one is probably as good as another, especially if it's got a liberal complement of mud.

The Bladud interlude seems to have captivated everyone – except, of course, for the killjoys who wanted him removed from the Pageant entirely. Lord Northcliffe, from his vantage point in Frank Lascelle's box, marvelled at how well the piglets behaved, failing to notice the harness that kept them together. Prince Bladud was played by George Worrall, a house decorator from 8 Belgrave Crescent, who not only trained the piglets, but also played Benjamin Grimkin, the character who was pelted in the pillory at the beginning of the episode. The *Daily Telegraph* declared his performance 'perhaps the finest piece of acting displayed in all the Pageant', while the *Court Journal* reported that 'Mr Worrell, with a true spirit of ancient comedy, evoked shrieks of laughter by his clever acting as the prince'. He must have been a master of the quick change as well; reviewing one of the performances, the *Chronicle* reported that the bags at flour thrown at him in the pillory were aimed with such precision that his head and face 'were soon as white as Queen Elizabeth's palfrey'. Cleaning off a liberal dusting of flour before wallowing in a muddy pool required a performer of rare calibre. At least – with that pasty – he wouldn't have gone hungry.

Initially, when Bladud was going to play a more prominent role in the Pageant, the masque in Episode V was going to feature St George and the Dragon. One of the souvenir booklets sold to visitors at the Pageant still actually billed it as such.

At the end of the masque, the Rector of Bath is presented to the Queen, who tells him to amalgamate Bath's four parishes into one,

The Bath Historical Pageant, 1909.

Scene in Episode V.

Lewis Bros,
Official Photographers.

with the Abbey as the parish church. The episode concludes with revels, madrigals, morris dances and a maypole.

Episode V had by far the most performers – 654. Most were just members of the crowd, although there were 53 court ladies, 20 court gentlemen, 14 riders, 56 maypole dancers, ten fairies, four pigs and two members of parliament. The *Daily Telegraph* described it as 'one of the best of all the scenes', praising especially the vividness of its costumes:

> Queen Elizabeth wears one of the most elaborate costumes of the Pageant. It is composed of old cream tapestry, trimmed with silver pearls, and jewels. What is known as the 'Tilbury' dress in the Tower of London has been reproduced with much care. She wears an elaborate crown of pearls, and her cloak is of brocade lined with silver and trimmed with silver lace. Silver gauze 'wings' complete a striking robe. Her ladies-in-waiting are arrayed in costumes of various shades, ranging from a mulberry red to a strawberry tint; all are in farthingales, and the whole episode is completely characteristic of Elizabethan days. The variety of headgear does much credit to the ingenuity of the milliners. The hawking party in dark greens and browns are a picturesque group. Their horse trappings are of white and gold, and they have hawking hats with drooping feathers, and are accompanied by two pages in costumes of white and gold with purple cloaks. The bevy of fair maids of Somerset include some of the

Some of the 654 performers in Episode V in a tableau that offers an uncanny pre-echo of Peter Blake's Sergeant Pepper cover.

The Bath Historical Pageant, 1909.

Rev. W.P. Hanks. M.A. as William Shakespeare.

Lewis Bros
Official Photographers.

Shakespeare was played by the Rev WP Hanks, who also wrote Episode V.

fairest of Bath's daughters, who become their simple costumes of grey and white. The dressing of the masque deserves a word. Bladud is clad only in skins, and the boys also, but the nymphs make a pretty group in green and gold dresses composed of torn shreds of materials.

In the fifth episode the music is naturally very noticeable, for the Elizabethan period conjures up of itself visions of dancing and melody. Throughout the scene there are dotted many sparkling tunes, such as those which accompany the dances and the maypole revels, while there is also a truly admirable madrigal, scored in the accepted medieval

The Fair Maids of Somerset included 'some of the fairest of Bath's daughters'. There were 19 Maids – Miss EM Beere, Mrs Dainton, Miss Harper, Miss D Barnwell, Miss Thring, Miss Davey, Miss Vallings, Miss E Gibbs, Miss H Gibbs, Miss Dingle, Miss Waite McClean, Miss L Kennard, Miss Wilson, Miss Cotton, Miss E Fry, Miss S Lansdown, Miss Saxty and Miss Simms – 17 of whom appear on this postcard.

style for five voices by Mr ACL Hylton Stewart, the gifted son of the Rector of Bathwick. It is in contrapuntal form, and has had an equally favourable reception from the public as it had on its introduction to the chorus. During the course of an episode which is bound to be somewhat noisy and boisterous it may be that such a beautiful piece of madrigal writing as this does not obtain the best of chances, but for all that the faithful chronicler will not omit to rank it as an altogether worthy addition to the Pageant music.

The review in the *Bath Chronicle* noted that, at the end of the episode, 'even Shakespeare caught the spirit of joyousness and [was] dancing gaily in a ring with the grand dames of the court in their velvet farthingales, rich jewelled stomachers, and quaint head dress'. As the author of the episode – the Rev William Hanks, Curate of Christ Church – had cast himself as Shakespeare, we can take it that he was happy with the way things had gone.

Episode VI: The Battle of Lansdown, AD 1643

Episode VI was the most spectacular and had the least dialogue. It also most closely resembled what we think of as historical re-enactment today. The difference is that it was a one-off event, involving the whole of the community, whereas present day re-enactors are members of societies and perform on a regular basis.

There were 19 named parts – 13 Cavaliers and 6 Roundheads – and 445 other performers – 290 Cavaliers and 155 Roundheads.

The Bath Historical Pageant, 1909.

Episode VI. Group of Battle Lansdown.

Lewis Bros, Official Photographers.

The Cavaliers were made up of 67 horsemen, 186 Cornish pikemen, 36 musketeers and a master gunner; the Roundheads were made up of 58 horsemen and 97 musketeers and pikemen. The battle – between the Roundheads under Sir William Waller and the Cavaliers under Sir Ralph Horton – including the Cornish Foot commanded by Sir Bevil Grenville – begins with stirring charges of horses, in which the Royalists are routed. The tide is turned by the Cornishmen, but Sir Bevil falls mortally wounded. His young son is placed on his charger and, with a cry of 'a dead rebel for every hair of our Sir Grevil's beard', the Roundheads are

The Bath Historical Pageant, 1909.

Episode VI. Fall of Sir Bevil Grenville

Lewis Bros,
Official Photographers.

The Bath Historical Pageant, 1909.

Episode VI. Funeral of Sir Bevil Grenville.

Lewis Bros,
Official Photographers.

BATH HISTORICAL PAGEANT
Episode VI. The Battle of Lansdown
John, son of Sir Bevil Grenville, Master I. J. Pitman

Photo, Lewis Bros.

Sir Bevil Grenville's son was played by James Pitman, Sir Isaac Pitman's eight-year-old grandson. Many people will remember him as Conservative MP for Bath from 1945 to 1964 and chairman and joint managing director of Pitman Press. As chairman of Pitman & Sons, he wrote several books on teaching English and invented the Initial Teaching Alphabet. He was also a squadron leader in the RAF in the Second World War, a director of the Bank of England and a senior Treasury official. He died in 1985.

driven from their position. The episode ends with Sir Bevil being borne off on crossed pikes.

On Thursday, Captain Prowse, who played Sir Bevil Grenville, was invited into Mr Lascelle's box. His part was taken by Horace Mann from Farleigh Plain and, according to the *Chronicle*, he 'had the satisfaction of seeing the combat carried through with the utmost success, and his deputy killed in the most approved fashion.'

The *Times* called the battle 'the sensation of the Pageant ... by far the best mimic battle we have yet seen ... The manoeuvring of the troops in the distance is especially effective; the firing and cavalry-charging are persuasively actual; and it is hard to say which is the more moving – the final rush of the white-clad Cornishmen, with their huge pikes, which carries the Parliamentary breastworks, or their slow departure, with pikes reversed behind the body of their leader.' The *Court Journal* was equally enthusiastic, judging the episode 'possibly the most effective in its power of rousing the vast body of onlookers to great enthusiasm'. So convincing was the action that, during one performance a foot-soldier who was 'shot' was attended by worried ambulancemen. 'Go away you fools,' he snapped, 'I'm doing this every day till Saturday.'

In an interview with the *Bath Chronicle*, Captain Prowse, who also wrote the episode, outlined the difficulties he had faced:

> When the question of having a Battle of Lansdown was first of all discussed, it was thought to be impossible, but it was decided to try. Nothing in the way of a complete battle had ever been attempted at a pageant before. I explained that it was a very big thing to undertake, and the men would all have to be taught the various drills. However, we made a start, and in May we began to get the men into squads. They were awfully keen and picked up their work very quickly.
>
> The great difficulty in arranging a battle scene is that there is such a small margin between the ridiculous and the sublime. The idea is to give a true representation of the fight, in which every man has to act as though he were an actual performer in the real event. The battle is a true account of what happened on 6 July 1643. The space, of course, is very limited, being curtailed considerably by the temple and other buildings. We should have liked the whole park in which to give a more realistic effect. The room for horses was very small. A hundred horsemen in that narrow space takes a great deal of good horsemanship to avoid serious accidents.

As the *Chronicle* pointed out, in this all-male episode, action took the place of colour:

> So far as the colour scheme in the Battle of Lansdown episode was concerned, the instruction was to keep the colours as sad as possible. Designs, and colours too, were largely governed by the very detailed information which Captain Prowse's enthusiastic researches secured. The Roundhead musketeers in russet brown and orange, and the pikemen in all white arrayed themselves as it were. The Cavaliers are richly clothed, and in much variety, for their masters chose what colours they would for their fighting men, and the result was a brave show. The large number wearing breastplates and morians served to make the ensemble very impressive. The bright standards used, including the 'One and All' of the Cornish Pikemen, the Bristol and the London banners, and that of Sir Bevil Grenville, were faithfully imitated by Miss Williams of Bathwick, who did excellent work in making all the banners required for the Pageant.

Despite the action-packed nature of the episode, it did feature some music, including

> the ancient psalm, 'Let God Arise' … chanted with subdued but undoubted effect by the Puritan soldiery, as they lie ensconced behind their earthworks. Then when the gallant Cornish pikemen swing bravely into sight, their feet keep time with the famous 'One and All March', which is the special quick-time of troops associated with Cornwall. Before leaving this episode it is certainly germane to the subject of this article to pay a passing tribute to the excellent trumpet calls which are sounded in various portions of the ground, and add a vivid touch of realism to this the finest battle depiction in the history of pageantry.

The Roundheads and Cavaliers trained by Captain Prowse not only provided a guard of honour for the Lord Mayor's visit on Friday but also paraded through the city on Saturday evening as part of the closing ceremony.

Episode VII: The Glorious Times of Beau Nash and Ralph Allen

The seventh episode brings us to the eighteenth century, and to a fête in Harrison's Gardens attended by the Duke of Cumberland and Princess Amelia on 25 September 1752. A string band plays and a choir sings an 'Ode to the Bath Gardens' as Beau Nash wanders up and down holding a long stick 'with a large knob in his hand'. The Earl of Chesterfield greets him with the words, 'Welcome back to Bath, your Majesty', and, as various celebrities

The Bath Historical Pageant, 1909

Episode VII. The Glorious Times of Beau Nash.

Lewis Bros.
Official Photographers.

Above: Beau Nash, played by Dr Leslie Walsh.

Below:: Dr Oliver, played by Frederick Sare, a chemist at 14 New Bond Street.

– including the Duchess of Queensberry, Edmund Burke, Henry Fielding, Dr Oliver and James Quin – indulge in witty banter, a civic procession enters, headed by 25 of the Bath Volunteers raised by Ralph Allen in 1745. The procession not only includes the masters of the city companies – masons, carpenters, joiners & cabinet makers, tilers & plasterers, bakers, barbers & peruke makers, grocers & chandlers, mercers & drapers, shoemakers, and tailors – but also boys from the grammar and charity schools and 'the Mayor's band, composed of horns and other brass instruments, playing lively airs'.

As Beau Nash greets the Mayor, seven guns are fired to welcome the arrival of the Princess Amelia in a sedan chair, attended by four footmen, two Negro pages, six ladies-in-waiting and 'two or three gentlemen'.

No sooner has she been greeted by Beau Nash than 14 guns are fired to greet the Duke of Cumberland. Amid mutual congratulatory speeches, the Duke is made a freeman of the city and a special minuet is danced in his honour by 22 couples, before Ralph Allen takes the Duke and Princess to dinner at Prior Park. The playing of 'God Save the King' and 'other patriotic airs' brings the episode to an end.

In all, 428 performers, including no less than 81 named characters – 34 ladies and 47 men – took part in this episode and, as the *Chronicle* records, great care was taken to make the costumes as authentic as possible:

The costuming of Episode VII is most interesting, for, observing closely the date, the designer was able accurately to introduce the 'donkey hip' in quite a number of cases. We believe that only in reproducing a scene of the year 1752 would it have been correct, for the fashion did not outlast that year – and small wonder! The 'donkey hip', the uninitiated may like to know, was a term applied to a style of dress from which the crinoline may have descended. A cage was worn beneath the skirt that

had the effect of making the dress stand off square from the figure so much as to somewhat resemble a donkey carrying panniers on each side for children, as the custom used to be; probably the similarity suggested the description of 'donkey hip'. The townspeople are attired in greater variety, the license being permissible because the fashions of the visitors would be somewhat in advance of those of provincials; and so the scene in a very realistic way depicts the fashions of the time. The great MC's court dress is of white with gold ornamentation and the costumes worn in the minuet are delicately graded; the ladies from palest primrose to deep orange, and the gentlemen from palest mauve to deep purple; the whole makes a charming piece of dressing. The Princess Amelia wears a white brocade dress, with silver panel, and she has a white court train lined with silver, and carried by two black pages in red coats, yellow facings, waistcoats of gold, and white turbans. The maids of honour are in white and silver dresses of the time, and the Duke is gaily clad in dazzling regimentals. Delicacy is throughout the keynote of the colour scheme in this scene, and a marked contrast may be noted to the prodigal display of colour say in Episode IV.

The *Chronicle* reviewer was suitably impressed;

The Gainsborough hats of the ladies were rather disturbed by the wind which was flowing, but the gay scene passed off admirably. From above, the wonderfully harmonious blend-ing of the colours could be fully noted, and the toning down of some of the glaring gowns by the more subdued shades worn in their proximity is a proof of the artistic minds who have planned the whole colour scheme.

Mrs Anstey as the Duchess of Portland

Musically, too, great attention was paid to getting it right:

The seventh episode lends itself with particular grace to musical accompaniment, and apart from the Roman episode, it is probably the richest of all in this respect. There is, for instance, a very effective piece for male voices from the pen of Mr AE New, the accomplished conductor. Then there is the original Ode to the Bath Gardens, which comes from Mr AM Broadley's collection. The well-known strains of the traditional Somerset Regimental March, played by the 4th Somerset Light Infantry Band, serves to introduce the volunteers ... Most delightful of all, however, is the dainty music for the minuet, played by a small corps of musicians in drab costumes, composed of instrumentalists not unknown in the orchestra at the local Theatre Royal. To listen to the dulcet notes of the minuet, and to watch the gaily-dressed belles and their beaux dancing with stately grace, is to reconstitute a page from Bath's past history very pleasingly.

The pretty and graceful dances in the Pageant composed by Miss Rolfe of George Street are recognised as being one of its chief attractions, more especially the stately minuet in the Beau Nash episode, which invariably draws forth a hearty round of applause. There are many charming slow movements in this dainty dance, and the numerous rehearsals and the immense amount of trouble and pains to which the 22 couples engaged had willingly placed themselves found fruit in a perfect performance ... Miss Rolfe has composed the minuet to pretty music from Mr A M Broadley's fine collection.[2]

MISS ROLFE.

The reporter from the *Daily News* was also bewitched by this evocation of eighteenth-century Bath:

From the grandstand Bath gleams through the trees like a cameo set among the hills. As for the people, nine-tenths of them seem to be tasting with a sweet sense of proprietorship the past glories of what they will tell you is the Modern Athens. Into this setting and this company step Beau Nash and all his brilliant court out of the days of powder and patches, sedan chairs and minuets ...Then they dance a dainty minuet upon the lawn – Edmund Burke and Fielding, and Mr Pitt and Mrs Montagu and all the fair ladies and gallant gentlemen who met at Bath in the glorious days of Beau Nash – until you fall head over ears in love with the age and its Dresden porcelain belles and beaux.

The china analogy was also used by the reporter from the *Court Journal*:

The costumes were exquisite, and the ladies without exception were charming, while in their grace of movement and dainty appearance they gave an impression of rare china figures come to life at the bidding of the dancing-master.

2 Sadly, photographs show that the minuet bore no relation to any minuet danced in Beau Nash's day, but more to Miss Rolfe's imagination.

The dubious authenticity of the minuet performed in Episode VII was underlined by the swords brandished by the gentlemen. In the glorious times of Beau Nash, the wearing of swords was outlawed in Bath.

Episode VIII, The Visit of Queen Charlotte to Bath

The subject of Episode VIII is similar to that of Episode VII – a royal visit, in this case that of Queen Charlotte on 5 November 1817. The visit this time is not for pleasure, but for health, and the setting is the Pump Room. Once again, the audience's imagination has to compensate for the discrepancy between the scene in front of them and that in which the action is supposed to take place.

There are twelve speaking parts and 477 other performers in the episode, including a 50-strong 'civic party', 53 authors and literary characters, assorted court ladies, gentlemen, stewards and maids of honour, and three choirs. The episode starts with long speeches from three famous ladies – Mrs Piozzi, Madame d'Arblay and Hannah More – harking back to the days when Bath's pre-eminence as a fashionable resort was unchallenged. The Queen

The Bath Historical Pageant. 1909.

Episode VIII. Procession. Queen Charlotte Visit to Bath.

Lewis Bros. Official Photographers.

enters and is introduced to prominent society figures, including several poets, who each read a few lines in her honour. An ode is then sung by members of the Bath Harmonic Society, after which Her Majesty expresses the hope that members of the royal family will continue to visit the city from whose waters she hopes to receive so much benefit.

The *Standard* recorded that, on the opening day, the royal guests took an especial interest in this episode, 'in which the Duke of Connaught saw his great-grandmother, Queen Charlotte, who visited Bath in 1817, represented in a most striking manner by Mrs Mackenzie. A great hit was made by the parodies of congratulatory verses by Bowles, Crabbe, and Tom Moore, and the good acting of Miss Blackstone as Mrs Piozzi, Miss Dodington as Mme D'Arblay, and Mrs Cedric Chivers as Hannah More, while Mr Mallory made an ideal Bath Mayor.'

As far as the costumes went, 'quaintness' was 'the most noticeable feature of the dressing of the last episode', according to the *Bath Chronicle*:

Queen Charlotte wears the palest shade of mauve with pearl trimmings and real Honiton lace. She has a velvet cloak lined with purple, and a very curious headdress of white and purple, with purple plumes. Mrs Kitson (the Mayoress) is gaudily arrayed in yellow satin, with pearl trimmings, and a quaint yellow cap, and her little daughter is in white and gold. Mrs Russell, the lessee of the Pump Room, stands behind the bar in blue and white, and, like her assistants, wears a curious white muslin cap. Miss Draper, whose school contributes a large group of young performers, is attired in pink and black; Madame d'Arblay is in plum coloured brocade with light green scarf; Mrs Piozzi wears black; and Miss Hannah More assumes terra cotta with old gold facings, a gold scarf and a mob cap. The Queen's maids of honour are in charming costumes of white satin, and there should be noticed the distinct groups of ladies costumed in pink, green, mauve and blue. Only in the sunlight can the full beauty of this scene be realised.

Episode VIII. "Queen Charlotte", Mrs Mackenzie. Lewis Bros, Official Photographers
The Bath Historical Pageant, 1909.

The final episode is also not wanting in musical interest and is mainly remarkable for the melodious part-song composed by Mr HT Head, FRCO, the popular organist of St Andrew's Church. It is a finely conceived composition, and shows that Mr Head has a distinct talent for composition in madrigal form. It is given with real feeling by the picturesquely attired members of the Bath Harmonic Society. This is a suitable place to add, that as regards the incidental music Mr WFC Schottler has given much ready assistance, and Mr HJ Davis, organist of Christ Church, has lent valuable aid in setting some Somerset folk songs for the orchestra, while music by Purcell, Gounod, and Edward German also finds a place in the episodes.

The Bath Historical Pageant. 1909.

Bath Historical Pageant Harmonic Society

Lewis Bros, Official Photographers.

Mr Broadley, who wrote the seventh and eighth episodes, was a well-known historian; in 1908 he had published an account of Napoleon's plans to invade England a century earlier. This proved very popular, due in large part to fears of German invasion, but was nevertheless a sound piece of scholarship, last reprinted as recently as 2007. The costumes for these two episodes were based on plates in his collection, while much of the music came from the same source, and was adapted from rare original compositions of 1752 and 1817.

As the episode draws to a close, 'the River Avon appears from the water beyond the stage'. This was not, however, some grand aquatic spectacle bringing the Pageant to a triumphant close, but a man dressed up as a river – none other than the Rev JC Skrine, the author of Episode IV. And, as the stage fills with 'the representatives of Bath throughout the ages', he recites a Choric Ode, written by – you've guessed it – the Rev JH Skrine. It opens with a reference to Bladud – an echo, perhaps, of the original plan to cast him as narrator. This time, unfortunately, there are no comic rhymes or rampaging piglets – this is serious stuff:

Mortals, when your Bladud fed
  Swine beside the magic pool;
When upreared their lordly head
  Halls that housed a Roman's rule;
When to rob your island nest
  Came the keels of Teuton foe;
Avon I on changeless breast
  Mirrored all the changing show.

Then the band – 'the usual modern orchestra with glockenspiel' –
strikes up and the harmonic society join in with a chorus set to music
by Sir Charles Villiers Stanford:

Where my wan waves onward streaming
  Wind and winder,
Where the glooming heavens or gleaming
  O'er them ponder,
Towards the stately town and dreaming
  West beyond her,
  Silent I in urgent flow
  Avon I for ever go.

This goes – or should that be flows – on in a similar vein for three more
verses – and three more windy, wandering choruses that, according
to the *Chronicle*, 'enchanted its hearers from start to finish'.

During the ode the stage fills with representatives of Bath
throughout the ages. Nine authors associated with Bath –

The Bath Historical Pageant, 1909.

Literary Group.

Lewis Bros.
Official Photographers.

629

The Bath Historical Pageant. 1909.

Masters Lewis, Gardiner & Davis as Cupid & The Sonnets. Lewis Bros. Official Photographers.

Chaucer, Smollett, Fielding, Christopher Anstey, Sheridan, Fanny Burney, Jane Austen, Lord Lytton and Dickens – emerge from among them, drawing out 'by silver cords the characters of their books', while Shakespeare receives his two 'Bath' sonnets – 153 and 154 – from Cupid.

Left: Robert Wall, an accountant from 27 Crescent Gardens, played two roles in the same costume: Dr Pearce, an eighteenth-century physician, in Episode VII, and Squire Allworthy, from Fielding's Tom Jones, in the literary parade in Episode VIII.

Grand Finale: Homage from the Western World

As a Grand Finale, 'Ladye Bath, who personifies the city' makes her way to a throne which has been set up at the top of the steps of the temple-cum-abbey, accompanied by a sword-bearer and a soldier with the Union Flag. Two maidens, wearing dresses 'of scarlet and gold maple leaves, crowned with golden corn and carrying fruit and sheaves', make their way towards her, attended by pages bearing golden banners on which are emblazoned the arms of Ontario and New Brunswick. As they approach the throne, the choir break into the Canadian national anthem. Ladye Bath then asks what, under the circumstances, seems a fairly redundant question:

> *Lo! Who are these, in virginal array,*
> *Brilliant with banners, bearing evergreens?*

The sword-bearer replies:

> *Ladye, they are the Maidens who have come,*
> *At thy most noble bidding, o'er the sea –*
> *Daughters of those confederated States*
> *That hold in unity a high ideal;*
> *And thine imperial Daughters of the West.*

The Bath Historical Pageant, 1909.

Miss Powell (Ontario) } Canadian
Miss Taylor (New Brunswick) } Representatives.

Lewis Bros.
Official Photographers.

Ladye Bath then bids them

> *Welcome! dear Daughters of brave Canada;*
> *All honour to that loyal-hearted land*

To which one of the maidens replies:

> *Hail – Ladye Mother, Bath the Beautiful,*
> *Majestic in white loveliness! We come*
> *To bring thee tribute from our far-off home*
> *That lies between the oceans, girt about*
> *With sunset splendour and with golden dawns,*
> *Washed with vast waters, mountain-crowned and glad.*
> *There, 'mid our forests, we have dreamed of thee;*
> *But all the waiting dreams we dreamed are merged*
> *In fairer vision, when we see thy face.*

The Bath Historical Pageant, 1909.

Procession of American Representatives Mother Bath.

Lewis Bros. Official Photographers.

Then, to the sound of trumpets, twelve more maidens, all dressed as the Statue of Liberty, led by heralds and pages carrying banners with the arms of the states of Maine, New York, Illinois, New Hampshire, North Carolina, South Carolina, South Dakota, Ohio, Kentucky, Missouri, Pennsylvania and Michigan, approach the throne. The 'Star Spangled Banner' rings out; this time even Ladye Bath guesses who they are and comes forward to welcome them with outstretched arms:

> *Hark! 'Tis the coming of the white-robed Maids,*
> *Your neighbours in that wondrous Western World.*

Daughters of England, stand at our right hand
The while we give them greeting to our shores …
Illustrious maidens of America,
We welcome you to England and to Bath.
The lintels of our doors are wreathed for you,
The bread is broken, and your place prepared.

'Ladye', one of the maidens replies – a splendidly American form of greeting –

we thank thee for thy courtesy.
O'er the wide way of the unfathomed sea
We come to bring thee homage from our land,
And share thy tryst with mighty memories.
Strangers we come – to find within thy gates
An open-hearted hospitality.

The rousing conclusion to Ladye Bath's next speech –

You are not strangers; we are kin –

is taken up by the American maiden:

Thy speech is our speech, and thy heroes ours;
We hold a common heritage and hope;
We serve the common God our fathers served.

Mrs Moger as Ladye Bath, surrounded by the Canadian and American representatives.

634

The maidens then lay garlands at the feet of Ladye Bath, who makes the final speech of the Pageant:

> *Maidens, we read the symbol in the gift.*
> *Now will we break fresh branches from our oaks*
> *To twine them with your evergreens. Today,*
> *The goal of all humanity looms clear;*
> *O may the immortal Word of Brotherhood*
> *Be a memorial of this festival,*

at which the band strikes up the National Anthem, and the chorus joins in with specially-written words:

> *All folk upon the earth*
> *Spring from one common birth,*
> *Children of God.*
> *Lord of Humanity,*
> *Teach us Fraternity,*
> *Peace let the watchword be*
> *In all the earth.*

With bells ringing and cannons booming, doves are released and Ladye Bath is covered 'with a shower of roses from the thousands of her sons and daughters of all time'. Then, as she is borne away, the strains of 'O God our help in ages past' float over the Pageant Ground.

Unlike the other characters, who had, at best, an understudy to take over the role if the performer was indisposed (or if, like Captain Prowse, they got an invitation to Mr Lascelle's box), the kudos of playing Ladye Bath was so great that it fell to no less than six ladies to receive tributes from their transatlantic cousins – Lady de Blaquiere, Mrs Mackenzie, Mrs Fitzhugh, Mrs AGD Moger, Mrs HW Tugwell and Mrs TS Cotterell.

It was a stirring spectacle, albeit one that nearly lacked a key ingredient. The sheaves of corn carried by the Canadian representatives symbolised the wealth of the prairies, upon which Britain was now heavily dependent – but, when they tried to obtain some locally, none was available. The problem was not so much a lack of wheat as a lack of golden wheat – all the wheat round Bath was still green. The day was eventually saved by a farmer who had some left over from the previous year.

The Ladye Bath episode was written not by one of the worthies of Bath, but by Katrina Trask from New York, the wife of a prominent Wall Street banker and President of the Edison

Illuminating Company. She and her husband set up the Yaddo community on a 400-acre site in Saratoga Springs, New York to offer residences for creative artists and writers where they could work in a supportive environment. It is still going strong today and more than 6,000 people – including many internationally-known artists and writers – have benefited from the facilities. Katrina Trask was also a prolific writer; her output included two controversial works dealing with love and marriage and a vehemently anti-war play, published in 1913, which was taken up by pacifist groups during the Great War. Her personal life was beset by tragedy; her four children died in infancy or childhood and her husband was killed in a railroad accident in 1909, a few months after the Pageant.

Katrina Trask.

The Pageant ended with a march past of all the performers, during which the audience were 'particularly requested' not to leave their seats. '3000 performers – c' était magnifique', as the sender of a postcard showing the grand march past scribbled on it when he

C'était magnifique BATH HISTORICAL PAGEANT, 1909. GRAND FINALE (3000 performers).

sent it to France a few days later. The *Court Journal* was similarly ecstatic:

> The scene was one never to be forgotten, as the whole mass of the performers (3,000) grouped themselves amid classic pillars (garlanded with roses) bearing on each apex flaming fires, the concluding moments of a most entrancing *coup d'oeil* ended amidst harmonious sounds of music, bells ringing, voices uplifted in glorious melody; while to crown the whole scheme of beauty a flock of doves winged their flight into the skies from the background of Minerva's Temple. It was a glorious moment.

As indeed it must have been, especially on Saturday afternoon, when one of the pillars, linked by festoons of paper flowers and topped by burning braziers, blew over, 'with the result that the paper flowers were set alight and burned away fiercely until the scene-shifters beat out the flames with their hats'.

The Bath Historical Pageant, 1909.

Episode V. Queen Elizabeth.

Lewis Bros
Official Photographers.

638

CHAPTER THIRTY-SIX

FASHION, FEMINISM AND THE PAGEANT

For all the insistence that Pageant costumes would be absolutely accurate, a quick glance at the postcards of the Pageant shows that they were very much of their time. They bear at best only a passing resemblance to what a visitor to the Fashion Museum would see when looking at genuine costumes. Whereas today's re-enactors and early dance companies have a wide body of research to consult when recreating their costumes, the study of fashion barely existed in 1909. True, Charles Paget Wade, who lived at Snowshill Manor in Gloucestershire, had started collecting by then, but he was widely regarded as eccentric. Influenced by her friend, the historian and biographer Carola Oman, the novelist Georgette Heyer wanted her historical novels to be factually accurate. Hence she was forced to do her own meticulous research, and the devotion to detail shown in her famous notebooks was quite unusual. Perhaps the only authors who paid much attention to antique clothes were those writing books on art – which might explain the involvement of artists in the designs for the Bath Pageant. It was not really until the 1950s that the history of fashion began to be taken seriously.

The nineteenth-century illustration to The Marriage of Figaro used as a basis for the designs in the Beau Nash episode rather than an original print.

It is not too surprising, then, that some of the fashion research undertaken for the Pageant seems, to modern eyes, curious to say the least. The designs for the Beau Nash episode, for example, were taken not from eighteenth-century illustrations but from late-

The dresses worn by Princess Amelia and her maids of honour in Episode VII owe more to the fashions of 1900 than 1750. Eighteenth-century century corsets had straight boning, not curved – but far more bosom was shown then than is on display here.

Victorian designs for *The Marriage of Figaro*, in which the countess wears a gown unlike anything worn in the Georgian period, as well as what looks like a large doily on her head. The remarks in the *Bath Herald* about 'the donkey hip' – a fashion which, we are told, died out in 1752 – are another case in point. 'Donkey hips' – a term that does not seem to have been used in the eighteenth century – were, in fact, side hoops. While it is true that these became less extreme and more rounded as the years passed, they certainly lasted well beyond 1752, especially at balls.

In some episodes there were attempts to reproduce costumes exactly. In Episode V, the visit of Queen Elizabeth, at least one of the designers knew that Tudor ladies wore farthingales beneath their dresses, holding their skirts away from their bodies. Four of the designs – three by Heard and one possibly by Edwin Fagg – show this. But it was Samuel Poole who did the designs for Elizabeth and the ladies of her court, and, although he based the Queen's dress on a contemporary sketch showing her wearing an enormous farthingale, he not only reduced it considerably but altered the outline of the costume, with the result that it owes more to late-Victorian corsetry than Elizabethan.

Samuel Poole seems to have had an eye for fashion – many of his delicate watercolours of Bath show elegantly dressed women. For students of fashion, the early twentieth century is particularly

Above: These two designs, by Nat Heard and Edwin Fagg respectively, show accurately the Tudor straight front to the robe – like eighteenth-century corsets, the boning did not allow for any body curves – and the enormous farthingale holding out the skirts around the body.

Below: In Samuel Poole's final designs, the farthingale has shrunk dramatically, and the bodices have the curvaceous body shape made popular in the early 1900s by Charles Gibson's illustrations. As the illustration on page 638 shows, when Queen Elizabeth's costume finally appeared, the farthingale had been reduced almost to nothing, and the dramatic – if inaccurate – draping around the bosom had also gone.

interesting, because design was taking a new direction, linked closely to the emancipation of women. The heavily-boned corsets which women had worn for over three centuries to create a distorted silhouette were about to disappear. The last extravagant flowering of the corset-maker's art was the strange S-bend fashionable in early Edwardian days, inspired by the illustrations of American artist Charles Dana Gibson. In this country, the Gibson Girl, as his ideal woman was known, was personified by Camille Clifford. Yet this contorting corsetry was already in retreat as women took up sporting activities, such as cycling, tennis and golf. And it was not just women's shapes that were changing. There were radical advances in what women could wear. In 1895, 50 years after Mrs Amelia Bloomer had invented them, trend-setting women

Above: An 1902 advertisement for corsets.

Left: Camille Clifford, with her S-bend shape, epitomised the Gibson girl for the English.

Below: Costume historians dispute whether the extreme body shape suggested in this sketch by Gibson, with its handspan waist, was ever actually obtained The picture has an unlikely link with the customs of 2009: incredibly, it shows an Edwardian hen party.

Above: The popularity of tennis encouraged women to wear garments which gave more freedom — though the lady spectator on the left with the hat seems to be giving a disapproving glance at her more liberated friends as they sprawl happily on the grass.

Below: These two young ladies on a cycling picnic near Bath were not audacious enough to wear bloomers, although they may have been wearing trousers beneath their skirts. In those days, just going cycling and then sitting cross-legged at a picnic would have been considered daring by some.

Above: The women in this picture, taken at Ilfracombe in 1909, *appear to us today to be hopelessly over-dressed for a day at the beach. However, a closer look shows a more serviceable tailored style, based on men's clothes, becoming fashionable.*

Below: The fashion for sea-bathing brought even more daring garments on show — though beaches were often segregated. Most of the girls in this picture are unashamedly wearing leggings. The woman holding the child's hand appears to be wearing a little dress. There is an almost identical version of this costume in the Fashion Museum in Bath, which shows that the skirt was detachable — it was just there to hide the leggings from male passers-by. It is hard for us to imagine today how liberating these clothes must have been.

cyclists decided her knickerbocker suits were the ideal garment. Corsets were not suitable for playing hockey or tennis, either. As for sea-bathing, women quickly realised that full length garments were inconvenient and here too the knickerbocker suit appeared, often dashingly based on the sailor suits worn by small boys, with the breeches ending just above the knee. However, decorous little skirts were added to hide the anatomical indelicacies revealed when the costumes got wet, as well as masking the fact that – shock horror – ladies were wearing trousers.

French fashion plates of the late nineteenth century show how designers were beginning to look towards men's clothes for inspiration. The male impersonator, Vesta Tilley, showed how elegant a woman could look when dressed as a man. Predictably, some cartoonists poked fun at this, drawing increasingly masculine women smoking cigarettes and wearing trousers. Little could they have guessed how soon their vision would come true. The trend

Vesta Tilley seems an unlikely heroine of the feminist movement, yet many women admired her stage act as a male impersonator, as she sported men's clothing with aplomb – showing how smart it could look on a woman. Her songs poked gentle fun at men's pretensions and deceits. When not dressed as a man, she was a trend-setter in elegant women's wear. In the photograph on the right she shows off the new soft lines of the early 1900s. This style was sometimes known as the lingerie dress.

Above: Two examples of the slightly masculine tailored style, which also brought in a more casual look for women.

Below: Male cartoonists such as Gibson, alarmed by what they perceived as the masculine trend in women's clothes, poked fun at it. Here Gibson imagines an army regiment composed of women. A century on, many army regiments have women soldiers and officers.

About 1909, Mlle Agier of Paris struck back at the anti-corset movement. She used research intended to show how damaging corsets were to the body to prove not only that her anatomical corset was superior to all others but better than not wearing one at all.

did not just touch high fashion. Girls' schools started to introduce school uniforms, and these too tended to be tailored and serviceable.

Some of the change was due to the realisation that distorting women's bone structure could not possibly be good for them. As early as 1880, reformers such as Karl Jaeger and, perhaps surprisingly, Oscar Wilde, were advocating healthier, comfortable clothing for women. The Rational Dress Society was formed a year later by Viscountess Harburton and Mrs King to free women from corsetry and confining clothes. In Canada, another dress reformer was Dora de Blaquiere, the second wife of Lady de Blaquiere's father-in-law. A prolific author, she wrote on a variety of subjects, including dress, for women and girls. The corsetiers struck back, first of all by declaring that damage was being done to women by not wearing corsets, then by inventing anatomical corsets, which purported to improve on nature. Finally, after bowing to the inevitable, some introduced boneless corsets. The more enterprising looked for other markets. The Leicestershire company Symington's invented the Liberty bodice, and for nearly 70 years small children were protected from chill winters by this cosy garment with its unforgettable rubber buttons. Apart from a brief return to the wineglass silhouette after the Second World War, women's underwear moved towards comfort and freedom.

One of the most influential figures in the movement away from restrictive clothes was the American dancer, Isadora Duncan. In 1909, Mariano Fortuny created for her the Delphos gown, after experimenting with pleating material and draping it on the human form. He used natural dyes, and the clothes were often stencilled – a

The designs of Paul Poiret seem to have had as much influence on the Regency dresses in the Pageant as the original fashion plates of the period.

Above: The costume of Princess Elizabeth was strikingly similar to the Poiret design on the left, if a little more modest. Princess Elizabeth, played by Miss Norton Thompson, is seen with the Duke of Clarence, played by Mr E W Hylton Stewart.

Below: Edwin Fagg, however, stuck closely to the original fashion plate on the left for his design for a Maid of Honour or Lady in Waiting.

technique used in the Bath Pageant. Another designer inspired by Isadora Duncan was Paul Poiret. First, he persuaded his clients to abandon the S-bend in favour of a straight corset, and then to give up corsets altogether in favour of the bra. At first, this was not a support garment at all, but merely covered the bosom. His designs show tunics, sometimes layered, and coats based on loose gowns with draped sleeves, such as the kimono. Art, too, was following this trend, as the desirable but well-upholstered ladies of Pierre-Auguste Renoir gave way to the loosely draped, sensuous women of Gustav Klimt's jewel-like paintings.

There is no doubt that the change in fashion is reflected in the costumes for the Bath Pageant, and the pleasure with which they were worn. From an historian's point of view, perhaps the Regency costumes for Episode VIII were the most successful. However, the Empire line had been revived in 1908 by Paul Poiret, and some of the ladies' costumes owe more to his reinterpretation of it than the original designs. The dress for Princess Elizabeth is strikingly similar to a Poiret design, with an overdress fastened with a single button just below the bust line. However, Edwin Fagg once again designed costumes based on period clothes; for one design an original fashion plate was preferred to an artist's drawing. His historically-faithful designs for Queen Charlotte and her maids of honour were just as faithfully followed by the sewing parties, only to be dismissed as quaint by the *Bath Herald*.

Bath Historical Pageant, 1909.

Queen Charlotte & Maids of Honour

Lewis Bros. Official Photographers.

The Bath Historical Pageant, 1909.

Episode I. Group of Priestesses.

Lewis Bros.
Official Photographers

The enthusiasm with which the genteel young ladies of Bath embraced the draperies of Roman priestesses, and the loose robes of British and Saxon women, may at first seem surprising. Sturge Cotterell must have been astonished. He thought women would only be interested in wearing Tudor and Georgian costumes, yet here they are, the daughters of some of the leading families in Bath, literally letting their hair down and wearing their togas and tunics with enthusiasm – even, in the case of the Roman priestesses, gay abandon. The fairies in the masque

The Bath Historical Pageant, 1909.

Episode VII. Group of Fairies.

Lewis Bros
Official Photographers.

THE MOTHER OF BATH

in Episode V wore extraordinarily imaginative costumes of loose, sleeveless under-tunics hung about with strips of material, ropes and flowers.

One might have expected these nicely brought-up young ladies to have recoiled from such costumes in horror – but no, they seem to be having a wonderful time. In fact, these designs not only represented the cutting edge of Edwardian fashion but were very liberating. Although it may be difficult for us to appreciate, from start to finish the Bath Pageant had an undercurrent of women's empowerment.

It is tempting to see evidence of this in the Ladye Bath sequence which closed the Pageant. Pageants from Sherborne on had often featured a mother figure representing the

Above: The splendid robes Poole designed for Ladye – or Mother – Bath. The influence of the latest fashions can be seen by comparing the design with the illustration on the right from the fashion notes in a 1909 Bath Chronicle.

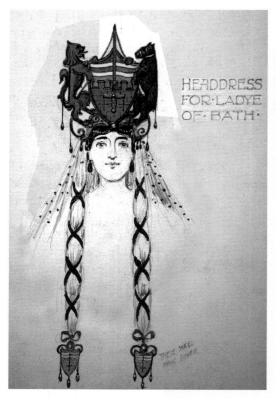

HEADDRESS
FOR·LADYE
OF·BATH·

Left: Edwin Fagg designed an alternative headdress for Ladye Bath. This formed the basis for the final design, although the various Ladye Baths seem to have drawn the line at having their hair in plaits.

Below: By the time of the Pageant, Faggs' head-dress had metamorphosed into something simpler, while simplified versions of the sunrays Poole intended for Ladye Bath were worn by the representatives of the other Baths. As for Poole's wonderful robe for Ladye Bath – here played by Lady de Blaquiere – that had been rejected in favour of something resembling Queen Alexandra's coronation robes (facing page top).

The Bath Historical Pageant, 1909.

Canadian & American Representative.
Lady de Blaquiere, as Mother Bath (England).

Lewis Bros.
Official Photographers.

652

town or city. The original design for Ladye Bath by Samuel Poole was magnificent. Again, the robes were influenced by Paris fashions, with a headdress from which emanated the rays of the sun. In the event, Poole's splendid flowing gowns were replaced by something closer to Queen Alexandra's coronation robes, while the headdress, redesigned by Edwin Fagg, incorporated the arms of Bath. The various Ladye Baths, however, being mature ladies, chose not to wear their hair in the plaits Fagg envisaged to complement this design, with the result that they looked faintly comical.

Women threw themselves into preparations for the Bath Pageant with an unanticipated enthusiasm. As we have seen, plenty of women volunteered to perform; it was men that dragged their feet. The work parties were made up of women – and, if an irreverent sketch on the back of one of the designs is anything to go by, they were very cheerful events. It shows a lady in a large hat happily holding a glass in one hand and a bottle marked 'Old Tom' in the other. This was almost certainly a reference to Old Tom gin, which had been around since the eighteenth century and was the 'Gin of Choice' in the nineteenth century. Was it sketched from life, one is forced to ask, at the end of a busy needlework session?

This irreverent little sketch on the back of one of the designs suggests that it wasn't always tea that was drunk at the working parties.

It was not just the great, good and genteel who got involved. Girls from Lees' cardboard factory went straight from work to help out at the properties workshop on Long Acre. Sturge Cotterell had thought that making properties was men's work, but Lady de Blaquiere appealed for 'all sects, all politics, all classes' to join in, and women took her at her word. They formed committees and were appointed heads and deputy heads of the various episodes. Despite Sturge Cotterell's attempt to assert men's role as leaders, some strong-minded women even succeeded in serving on committees which were normally male

Mrs Moger

preserves. One such was the Finance Committee, where Mrs AGD Moger and Mrs Cedric Chivers were to be found. They also

served on the Ladies' Committee, which was headed by Lady de Blaquiere, and included ladies from other prominent Bath families, such as the Silcocks and Horstmanns, and, perhaps, to keep an eye on the enthusiastic Lady de Blaquiere, Mrs Sturge Cotterell.

Lady de Blaquiere was undoubtedly an inspirational figure. Her speech at the first ladies' meeting in January put most of the male orators at the previous meeting in December to shame. She used what today are regarded as classic speech-making techniques. Her sentences were short and punchy, she was not afraid to use humour, nor to be emotive. Her rallying cry – 'Wake up, Bath!' – reached out to her audience. How different she sounded to her pompous, turgid male counterparts, many of whom offered only half-hearted support for the Pageant. It was no wonder that women took to the idea.

Lady de Blaquiere was born Lucianne Desbarats, the daughter of Georges-Edouard Desbarats, a French-Canadian. He was a highly talented man who could have made a career in several fields, but who threw his energies into publishing books, journals and newspapers. He pioneered the use of photographic images in magazines and newspapers and was also involved in the development of a new printing process which, in 1875, bankrupted him. Lucianne, who was eleven at the time, had been brought up to enjoy a comfortable lifestyle. Two years earlier, her second youngest brother, Jean-Robert-Alexandre, had died at the age of five. The family picked themselves up from these setbacks, however, and by the time Lucianne married William de Blaquiere, an Irish baronet, in 1888, Georges Desbarats was once again at the top of his profession and leading a busy public life.

Lucianne de Blaquiere was, therefore, a woman who had seen good times and bad. Her father, while inherently conservative, was a humane man who believed in working for the community, and his beliefs had rubbed off on his daughter. She and her husband had a family home at Brinkworth in Gloucestershire – a Tudor manor house extended in later centuries – as well as a town house at No 3, The Circus, yet she was by no means the average titled lady. Her vigorous, no nonsense, populist style clearly rattled Sturge Cotterell, who rather liked to be in charge himself.

She was not the only woman on the committee with radical views. Mrs Cedric Chivers was the wife of a man who was not just a local philanthropist; he was also involved in trade union activities in London, and was widely regarded as a model employer. Another woman with a liberal outlook was Mrs AGD Moger. She had married into a family which included several Liberal councillors, council officers and Mayors, and was on the radical wing of the party. Another Mrs Moger, who seems to have been her sister-in-law, was a noted Bath suffragette.

During the first half of 1909, as Bath's ladies worked away at the Pageant costumes, or learnt their parts, they did it to the background of the feminist events described in Chapter 17. There were debates about women's suffrage, with, on one occasion, a woman speaker on each side of the argument – not all women wanted the vote. This debate took place at 46 Great Pulteney Street, just down the road from Pageant House. Meetings were also arranged by the Bath Women's Local Government Association, which, in October 1909, saw years of campaigning and hard work rewarded by the election of Helen Hope to the council.

In April, there was a talk at the Assembly Rooms by Mrs Cazalet Bloxam on 'Woman and her New Sphere'. The *Chronicle*, not noted for its liberal views, remarked sarcastically that there was 'a moderate attendance in the Card Room, and women were decidedly in the majority'. However, it is worth looking at this meeting and the lecturer in some detail, for it demonstrates a different style of campaigning to that espoused by Emmeline

Pankhurst's Women's Social and Political Union, and deals with some of the suffragists' other concerns.

The meeting was chaired by Mrs Vaughton-Dymock, the widow of Lt Col Theophilus Vaughton-Dymock, JP. She was born Sabina Letitia Bell in Tasmania. Her grandfather, George Meredith, had gone out to Tasmania after the death of his first wife, taking with him his young family, and the children's nanny, who became his second wife. Sabina's father was Captain John Bell, who owned ships taking cargo and convicts out to Australia; he too became a settler. Both the Meredith and Bell families were involved in some shady dealing. Sabina's Uncle George was speared by Aborigines in what George Robinson, protector of the Aborigines in Victoria, described as just retribution, after he had seized their women and carried them off as slaves and prostitutes. Nevertheless, Sabina came from a family where women too could be independent and ready to face vicissitudes. In her introductory remarks, she told the audience that, while the nineteenth century had seen the emancipation of woman, the twentieth century needed to build on that achievement.

The lecturer, Mrs Ursula Cazalet Bloxam was born Sophia Ursula Gardner, the daughter of a doctor. Her marriage to Reginald Cazalet Bloxam may have been one of convenience, to escape living with her much older married sister, the wife of a retired colonel in the Indian Army, and another sister, also in her forties, who shared the same house. It may have been in this house that her future sister-in-law, Rosa Bloxam, met her future husband Ronald Ross, who discovered that mosquitoes transmitted malaria. Sophia was 38 when she married, and was 44 when she had her only child, Julia Mabel Cazalet Bloxam. Two years earlier, she had written a book called *Temperance Talks with the Children*, which is surprising for the immediacy of its writing. We may laugh today at some of her sentiments, but her style is confident and pithy.

While Emmeline Pankhurst felt that women needed to concentrate solely on female suffrage, to avoid dissipating their energies, other women, such as Mrs Cazalet Bloxam, believed that temperance, social reform and education were related issues and campaigned for them as well. Her speech at the Assembly Rooms was wide-ranging; her calm, logical approach – combined with heady sentiments – found a more appreciative audience than the Pankhursts' confrontational style would have done. She referred to women's education, and how, since medieval times, when 'young ladies wrote to Boniface in Latin hexameters', women, unless highly born, were deprived of schooling. She quoted extracts from the writer Olive Schreiner, a South African born free-thinker, pacifist, and campaigner for women's rights, who had worked with Henry Havelock Ellis.

Her political heroes were all Liberal peers. Lord Coleridge, as she reminded her listeners, had pronounced that 'the slavery of women had no authority in law and was founded only upon tradition'. He had represented the women of Manchester in 1868 when they had registered as voters under the Representation of the People Act (1867). He had not, however, managed to convince the judges of their case. The Grand Old Man of Liberal politics, Gladstone, had been adamantly against women's suffrage and for a time the Conservatives seemed to offer a better option for women. Mrs Cazalet Bloxam failed to acknowledge Conservative champions of female suffrage. Instead she said that Liberal peers such as Lord Rosebery and Viscount Goschen had in 1904 'sounded the war-cry' by suggesting that women should influence men's decisions. In the light of this, she called on women to 'devote themselves in their new liberty to social and educational questions' and called for them to be granted the franchise.

She explained that there were four million working women in the country, most of whom were unprotected by any employment legislation. Not surprisingly for a temperance campaigner, she was particularly exercised by the plight of barmaids, among whom, she said, suicide was terribly frequent. She particularly condemned the way in which accounts of their deaths were generally dismissed with the words, 'Only a barmaid!' This aspect of her speech shows how closely temperance was linked in her mind with improving the condition of women. She ended with a surprisingly modern sentiment – one still under discussion: that a woman need be no worse as a wife or mother because she has sought a 'fuller and wider life' in employment.

'A brief discussion followed,' noted the *Chronicle* 'and the usual votes of thanks were recorded.' We do not know how many of the women present were also members of those busy sewing parties who had created the costumes and properties for the Pageant. Did they, one wonders, go away and spread the word as they stitched? The event throws an interesting light on the activities of women's campaigners during the year of the Pageant, and demonstrates how ideas once considered outrageous were fast being accepted by women of all classes.

𝕭𝖆𝖙𝖍 𝕳𝖎𝖘𝖙𝖔𝖗𝖎𝖈𝖆𝖑 𝕻𝖆𝖌𝖊𝖆𝖓𝖙

JULY 19TH TO 24TH, 1909

EVENING ENTERTAINMENTS

During Pageant Week Bath will be *en fete*, and the Entertainments and Fancy Dress Ball Committees have made the following evening arrangements :—

MONDAY—Gorgeous Illuminations, Display of Fireworks on a scale never before attempted in Bath, by J. Pain & Sons, and Band, Promenade Concert, Sydney Gardens at 8 p.m., 6d.

TUESDAY—Besses o' th' Barn Band, at Sydney Gardens, at 8 p.m., 6d.

WEDNESDAY—Children's Fairy Play and Band, Promenade Concert, at Sydney Gardens, at 8 p.m., 6d.

THURSDAY—Living Chess, Animated Pictures of the Pageant, and Band, Promenade Concert, at Sydney Gardens, at 8 p.m., 6d.

FRIDAY—Fancy Dress Ball at Assembly Rooms, Tickets (including Supper), 10/6. Pierrots at Sydney Gardens, at 8 p.m., 6d.

SATURDAY—Battle of Flowers, Decorated Motor Cars and Vehicles. (Prizes for best Decorated Vehicle.) Band, Promenade Concert, Sydney Gardens, 8 p.m., 1/-.

MANY OTHER MINOR ATTRACTIONS

FANCY DRESS BALL

WILL BE HELD ON

Friday, July 23rd, in the Assembly Rooms, Bath

Catering by Messrs. Fortt & Sons. Supper served in the Tea Room, and both buildings elaborately decorated and illuminated.

Specially organised Band by Messrs. C. Milsom & Son, Ltd. Tickets may be obtained at Messrs. C. Milsom & Son, Ltd., Milsom Street, Bath :—Ladies and Gentlemen, 10/6 each (including Supper and Refreshments). N.B.—Fancy Dress optional.

The Committee are indebted to the National Telephone Company, Ltd., for kind assistance in making the necessary telephonic arrangements.

CHAPTER THIRTY-SEVEN

FRINGE AND FINALE

Like today's Bath Festival, the Bath Pageant had a 'fringe'. A display of 'ancient manuscripts, wills, chantry bequests, rare books, and many other articles of interest from 1266 to 1664', together with a 'model in cork of Bath Abbey … by a deceased military officer (Colonel Rome)' was held at Gregory's Imperial Book Store at 5 Argyle Street.[1] From Monday to Saturday during the week of the Pageant, lavish entertainments were staged in Sydney Gardens. However, although many more people enjoyed these events than saw the Pageant – up to 25,000 on one evening alone – not one picture postcard or photograph of these spectacles has come down to us. We have to rely solely on contemporary newspaper reports to try to recapture what they must have been like.

The extraordinary scenes in Sydney Gardens on Monday night were described the following day by the *Bath Herald*:

Probably never before have the gardens been so crowded as they were last evening (at one time the queue … stretched as far up Pulteney Street as Pageant House), and a more fascinating scene has certainly never been witnessed there. Thousands of tiny electric lamps of a variety of delicate tints had been specially installed by Messrs R Kendall & Sons. They were used chiefly to line the paths, nestling among the luxuriant foliage of the trees, and under these novel and entrancing conditions, visitors were able to admire the natural charms of the beautiful grounds to the utmost … From the brilliantly illuminated bandstand the Bath Military Band, conducted

---

1 Although 5 Argyle Street has long been a restaurant, the trompe d'oeil window on the side wall, at which a Victorian gentleman sits reading, recalls its earlier career. According to an advertisement in 1909, 'the Imperial Book Store contains one of the largest and finest stocks of second-hand books in the world; it comprises upwards of a quarter of a million volumes, carefully arranged on the alphabetical principle, and classified under subjects and languages, and displayed in 30 convenient rooms … Next to the Roman Baths and remains, and the Abbey Church, the Imperial Book Store is the most interesting of the attractions of Bath.' George Gregory's can now be found in Manvers Street.

Lewis, Photo

BATH MILITARY BAND.
Mr. W. F. C. Schottler, Conductor.

by Mr WFC Schottler, discoursed an excellent programme of music, while in another part of the grounds Mr Carl Fredricks' Costume Concert Party catered for hundreds of appreciative listeners with song and dance and patter. The party have returned from their seaside tour with quite a number of new items which were very popularly received. Elsewhere a tent was provided for dancing, and there were many who availed themselves of the opportunity, the music being provided by a string orchestra, supplied by Mr Schottler. The country-fair amusement grounds were under the management of Messrs Fredricks and Larcher, and throughout the evening they were thronged with crowds of people. The electric switchback, and the 'slipping the slip', a novelty which caused a good deal of merriment, seemed to be especially popular ... Late in the evening there was a gorgeous display of fireworks by Messrs Pain, and for half an hour the sky was brilliantly illuminated and the foliage of the trees assumed a variety of lovely tints. There were several novel features in the display. One was like a fairies' maypole – a revolving horizontal wheel, with dangling ropes of many colours crowned by a fountain of fire; and another fascinating spectacle was the outline of a burning house, with a fire engine madly working close by, and the firemen playing on the building with their hose.

How many of the audience were moved, by this spectacle, to reflect on the debate regarding the future of Bath's fire brigade is a moot point.

The following evening, at which the star turn was the Besses o' th' Barn Brass Band, was equally successful. The *Bath Herald* seems to have been under the impression that its readers would be unfamiliar with the concept of brass bands and included the following explanation in its report of the proceedings:

> The instruments are wholly of brass, and for every one present who missed the softening influence of reeds there were scores who revelled in the astounding effects the composition of the band rendered possible.

The programme included classics such as the March from Wagner's *Tannhauser*, the Overture to *Zampa* by Herold, selections from Weber's *Oberon* and the *Yeomen of the Guard* by Gilbert and Sullivan, as well as pieces, such as Rimmer's *Titania*, which have stood the test of time less well.

Wednesday night saw around 60 girls from Harley Street School take centre stage, performing a play specially written for them by their headmistress, Miss Bessie Hawkins. The *Bath Herald* reported that 'the performers might well have had a second night in the week's programme, for more wanted to see it than could do so, and the committee were considerably embarrassed to find seats for those who had bought tickets in order to secure them'. The play, called *In my Lady's Garden* was a 'simple little comedy'. In a prologue it was explained that, 'because of the Pageant, these children, "Bath's fairest, sweetest flowers", have formed a fairy garden to while away an hour':

> My lady and her maid attend and exact loving homage from the assembled flowers, tended by the Spirit of the Flowers, and before her they pass through a floral alphabet, so that there are some 31 'speaking parts', after which the second chorus of much smaller children appear as butterflies with their Spirit. In due course the Spirit of the Night sends all to sleep, and the Spirit of the Past speaks an epilogue which brings the play to an all too early conclusion.

Dances were 'agreeably frequent', as were the glees and choruses written by the headmistress's brother. In terms of spectacle this little play seems to have compared favourably with the Pageant:

The children were charmingly costumed – the spirits as fairies with wands, the butterflies with wing attachments of gauze, and the rest of the children to represent their particular flower. The resemblance of the child to the flower had not to be aided by a powerful imagination; each child was easily identified, and the manner in which the costumes were made to suggest each a flower was clever designing. The make up of Night, in dark raiment, spattered with shimmering stars and carrying on her wand a moon, was specially good. The children had to address themselves to an audience of 3,000 people, not half of whom could possibly have heard the little voices, but nearly all spoke out bravely, and there was no sign of nerves. The dances … were all good. That of the Spirit of the Night was a slow, dreamy step, to the favourite melody, 'Narcissus'. The dances in which all the flowers, and later on all the butterflies took part, were equally correctly done, and the training of the girls, alike in regard to their words and their singing, had been so thorough that they conducted themselves through the play unguided.

Thursday saw a game of living chess – which some of the organisers seem to have been rather unhappy about – in Sydney Gardens:

There was some fear of a slump in the minds of the committee, and when rain set in at 7.30 it did seem that comparative failure must result, but the consistent good fortune which has so far attended the Pageant and all that belongs to it did not desert. The rain held off, and the attendance was again numbered in thousands … It is many years since a game of chess with human pieces has been played in Bath, but the diversion is familiar enough to enable costumes to be hired, and so neither the performers nor the committee were troubled on this score. Very fine costumes were sent, and the little armies of 16 a side looked well in them … The queens and kings were becomingly majestic in apparel and in bearing; and to them all the minor pieces paid homage, and no opponent checked the opposition king without an apologetic bow, nor did a piece come to the king's rescue without a similar exchange of courtesies. And when at the 52nd move the red king was effectively checkmated by a little red boy pawn (the white pawns in contrast were girls) he surrendered his crown with kingly dignity to the fair queen of the conquering side … Mr EP Mallory acted as director,

Edward Mallory, who owned the jeweller's in Bridge Street, not only appeared as John Kitson, Mayor of Bath, in Episode VIII of the Pageant, but also directed the living-chess game on Thursday evening.

calling the moves, and Mr SW Baster and Mr F Melluish, both well-known players, were stewards, their office being to conduct the pieces from one square to another. Their intervention seemed to detract somewhat from the effect of the game, and it should have been possible with a little more rehearsing for the pieces to have moved themselves, but any way, it was a pretty spectacle, and one well suited for a week when pageantry is all-absorbing.

Mr William Hatt and Mr LC Seymour were the players. It is no secret that they played a standard game from the book – a sound exhibition of French defence which occurred in a tournament a quarter of a century ago. It had the spectacular advantage of retaining the principal pieces a long time on the board, and it was interesting because the end came prettily after a sustained attack had collapsed ... The stately movements of the more valuable pieces were heralded by Mr J Russell on his cornet. At the close the pieces took their original places on the board and the rival queens had bouquets bestowed upon them by the opposition kings.

After the game of chess came a 'cinematograph display', at which a film of the Pageant taken at the final rehearsal on Saturday was shown for the first time. It was preceded by a series of photographs, including those of Lady de Blaquiere, Mr Sturge Cotterell, the Rector of Bath, Mr Bertram Fortt, Mr Nat Heard, and Mr Frank Lascelles. According to the *Bath Herald*,

the living pictures were unexpectedly good, and the fact that the episodes had got a bit mixed – literally they were at sixes and sevens – served to amuse the crowd. A bit of the Battle of Lansdown came to light when Henry VII was expected, and the rest was given after Beau Nash, but these little things were merely accidents. If the pictures are going on tour it will be an excellent after-result of the Pageant, of which they give a very fair idea. Onlookers felt the enormous adjuncts that the colour and music are as they looked on the first episode and saw the priestesses apparently all in white, and the Roman legion without hearing Mr Tapp's delightful music, and some in the crowd feeling this began themselves to supply what was missing by starting the people's hymn, which has become so popular. Mr Worrell descanting on his troubles and bemoaning his lost pigs, and Mr Wilkey's splendid fall in Episode II came out exceptionally well. It was a windy evening, and the bulging of the curtain sometimes turned grave to gay; the humorous effect on the saddened warriors after the battle was to suggest that the whole were suffering from a very bad form of intoxication, and it made everybody roar with laughter. The rare privilege of 'seeing ourselves as others see us' was given to not a few present, and it was credibly reported that Lord Roberts was among those who were delighted at the pictorial representation of a magnificent spectacle. The crowd cheered more vociferously than ever when the operator repeated Mr Lascelles' portrait as his finale.

The film was also shown all the following week at the Assembly Rooms, after which it did indeed go on tour. It was also shown to pageant organisers in Bristol and Carlisle to help them prepare for similar events in 1924 and 1928. The committee in Bath had received similar assistance earlier in the year when film of the Oxford and Bury St Edmunds Pageants had been shown at their meetings. Sadly, although footage of several pageants – including Bury St Edmunds and Sherborne – survives in the archives of the British Film Institute, the film of the Bath Pageant has disappeared without trace – unless anyone knows different.

ASSEMBLY ROOMS, BATH.

ANIMATED PICTURES OF THE BATH PAGEANT.

FOR ONE WEEK ONLY, commencing MONDAY NEXT, July 26th, at 3 and 8 p.m. daily.

OTHER FIRST-CLASS COMEDY FILMS

AND

MR. JAMES CHILCOTTE

IN HIS HUMOROUS ENTERTAINMENT.

Doors open 2.30 and 7.30. Carriages 6 and 10. Early Doors 2 and 7. Ticket-holders Free. Reserved and Numbered Seats, 2s. 6d.; Second, 1s. 6d.; Third, 1s.; Admission (limited), 6d. Children Half - Price to Matinees. Plan and Tickets at Assembly Rooms Office.

Friday night's entertainment was less well attended than the others because of the counter-attraction of a fancy dress ball at the Assembly Rooms. Music, provided by the Bath Military Band and the

Vivandieres, included Tchaikowsky's *1812 Overture* and a 'clarionet' solo, 'In Cellar Cool', by Mr W. Shay, which was 'enthusiastically applauded'. There was also a concert on the Queen of the West Lawn which included a variety of popular songs:

> After a concerted number, 'Anabella', by Wilfred Dane and Co, Miss Marie Bonner sang 'When the Ebb Tide Flows' remarkably well. Mr Eddie Noble's song, 'I Couldn't Keep from Laughing', had that effect on the audience. 'Four Delightful Little Men' is a dainty little song and was very daintily presented by Miss G Russell and Co. 'Love Me, and the World is Mine' is a song that takes a good deal of singing – properly – but Miss Dora Jaye contrived to get quite the proper expression of the song. The vivacious Miss Della Fredricks was delightful in 'A Little Bit of Fun'. Mr Carl Fredricks and Mr Allan Wright also contributed, and Mr Fredricks, in the part of the Registrar, was well appreciated by the audience. Character songs and monologues by Messrs Carl Fredricks, Eddie Noble and Wilfred Dane made up the greater portion of the second part, which was concluded by a fine dance by Mlle Cordelia. Special arrangements had to be made for this, and these were very satisfactory.

The proceedings concluded with another lavish firework display.

Tickets for the fancy dress ball in the Assembly Rooms cost half a guinea each – equivalent to around £40 today. At first, take-up was slow; with only a day to go, only around 300 had sold – well short of the target. On Friday, however, an 'astounding boom set in' and another 200 went, ensuring the event's success. Music was provided by Milsom's Orchestra, and dancing, which commenced at 9pm, went on till the early hours. There were 17 dances in all – including the 'Teddy Bears' Picnic Two Step', the 'Vision of Salome Valse', the 'Rooster Strut Two Step', the 'Dollar Princess Waltz' and the 'Post Horn Galop'.

Many people wore their Pageant costumes, although there were plenty of others that had not been seen on the 'greensward stage'. The talk of the ballroom was Mr AM Broadley, the author of Episodes VII and VIII, who appeared as Beau Nash in a costume based on a pastel of Nash by William Hoare and created by Mr Clarkson. The *Bath Herald* reported that:

"BEAU NASH".
A.M. BRODLEY ESQ

Many felt instinctively that here *was* Beau Nash, and no more delightful comedy has ever been watched within these historic walls than to see the MC of Bath that is Past making profound bows to the MC of Bath that is Present, and to watch him take a dignified leave to walk and talk with the quaintly garbed Madame d'Arblay and Hannah More, through the crowded ballroom.

Another costume that created a good deal of interest was that worn by the architect Mr Bligh Bond, who came as Avonmouth. He had been involved in the development of the new docks at Avonmouth, and originally wore the costume at a fancy dress ball at Shirehampton to celebrate their inauguration. In the absence of a photograph, the *Bath Herald's* description must suffice:

> There was in the centre of the costume a mouth, from which were traced symmetrical lines to the shoulders, representing the course of the Avon and the straighter Severn, terminating at the shoulders in medallions of the arms of Gloucester and Bristol. About the skirt was traced the course of the channel, and the ports and towns on the Welsh and English sides were all cleverly worked into the design. From each were blue lines proceeding up the back of the coat, representing the sinuous course of the several rivers on which they stand, while below

the mouth was a pictorial representation of Dunball Island, with its gibbet all in the illustration. Generally Avonmouth was pictured in its half-developed state, suggested especially by the green background of the design, and green velvet cap with buttercup decorations.

Before the company took supper, the minuet that had proved such a success on the Pageant Ground was danced by the same performers. And then came the highlight of the evening – a moment of high camp that would have had the Village People eating their hearts out:

> The ballroom quickly filled, and scores of delighted people stood round and saw the dance executed under ideal conditions. While everything was in full swing, the tall figure of a redskin, feathers around head, entered and made his way to the ballroom. It was Mr Frank Lascelles, the Master of the Pageant, who attended as Chief of the Iroquois Indians, of which he and the Prince of Wales are the only English chiefs. His make-up was perfect, and his movements were closely watched as he passed along to where Beau Nash was standing and was formally welcomed. Many, of course, failed to recognise the popular Pageant Master in such a get-up.

MR. FRANK LASCELLES
AS A CHIEF OF THE IROQUOIS INDIANS.

CHAPTER THIRTY-EIGHT

OUR REVELS NOW ARE ENDED

'In the long years of one's life there are days that fix themselves indelibly on the memory.' So began the *Bath Chronicle's* coverage of the last day of the Pageant. It continued in similar vein:

BATH HISTORICAL PAGEANT 1909.
GRAND PARADE OF PERFORMERS.

Never to the final stage of this earthly journey is one likely to forget that last glorious picture in the park, with the sun casting its lengthening shadows across a green sward, peopled with thousands of gorgeously attired performers and thousands more gaily-dressed spectators in a vast grandstand. On the faces of the amateur actors and actresses was the flush of pride – the pride of achievement—and in their breasts was a feeling of something attempted, something done. The sweets of success were theirs, for both Pageant workers and performers. The great task was over, the labour of long months was ended, the concomitants of the players were about to be put aside, the end was near at hand.

At the top of the temple steps stood the Lady Bath (Mrs T Sturge Cotterell), surrounded by her daughter Baths; at the foot was the Lady de Blaquiere, a beautiful silver rose bowl filled with choice blooms in her hand. She was the chosen instrument in the hands of that great crowd of performers to thank Mr Lascelles for his guidance ... They crowded round him in a great circle, with smiling faces, eager to catch the gracious words of the Lady de Blaquiere, and to hear once more the voice of their leader.

Then, in the words of the *Bath Chronicle*, Lady de Blaquiere made a 'nice little speech':

Before we put aside our borrowed dignities and characters and return to our ordinary everyday life, I have been asked to express to the Master of the Pageant our appreciation of the courteous, kindly – though firm – manner in which he has drilled and trained the characters (cheers) and brought each episode to such a point of perfection as has made the Pageant a great success – an honour to him and an honour to Bath – and also to ask his acceptance of this souvenir from the performers (cheers). In Quebec, where Mr Lascelles held the

The Bath Historical Pageant, 1909.

F. Lascelles Esq. (Pageant Master) replying to Presentation.

Lewis Bros, Official Photographers.

Mastery of the Pageant last year, he was made a chief of one of the Indian tribes, who gave him the name of Tehonikonraki, which means a man of infinite resource and lightning ideas (cheers) and we must congratulate ourselves on having had as Master of the Pageant a man of such resource to lead us through all our difficulties to such a very good end (cheers).

As she presented him with an engraved rose bowl, loud cheers and a rendition of 'For he's a Jolly Good Fellow' rang out. As soon as he could make himself heard, he replied:

Lady de Blaquiere, ladies and gentlemen, and, may I say, my friends the performers (applause). It is not very much over a month since I came to live among you, and I hope I may go away considering that every one of the performers is my friend (cheers). Ladies and gentlemen, and all you children too, you have been simply splendid. You have put up with me and my many corrections in the spirit I know in which I made them. I am sure that never was any pageant organised that has gone so smoothly, or with such general good feeling, as the Bath Historical Pageant, and this is due not to me or to any of us individual workers, but to all of you performers, who have taken your rehearsals, your instruction so splendidly ... Ladies and gentlemen, Bath will have a place very near my heart, and let my last words be 'God protect Bath' (loud and prolonged cheers).

Other speeches, presentations and thanks followed, after which the orchestra struck up 'Auld Lang Syne', Mr Lascelles was placed in King Edgar's coronation chair, and, as the old song was sung by thousands of voices, lifted shoulder high and borne by sturdy Saxons to the grandstand. This done, the crowd of performers and spectators dispersed in all directions, and the park was soon left empty – the Bath Historical Pageant was over.

As for Frank Lascelles, he went on to even greater success. Among other glittering extravaganzas, he would mastermind a pageant in 1910 to celebrate the establishment of the Union of South Africa, the 1912 Coronation Durbar at Calcutta, with over 300,000 participants, and the 1924 Pageant of Empire at Wembley.

Frank Lascelles' valedictory letter, written on the last day of the Pageant.

He built a mansion in his birthplace, Sibford Gower, where he held legendary house parties, and became lord of the manor. Then, somehow, it all went wrong. When he died in 1934, the mansion had long been sold, and he was living, beset by financial worries, in rented accommodation at Brighton.

That all lay in the future, though. For the moment, he was the toast of Bath, and the evening's festivities were about to begin. First came a banquet at the Guildhall in honour of the Canadian and American representatives, at which Lady de Blaquiere, after proposing a toast to the Canadians, explained the significance of their visit:

> For many years efforts have been made to bring about more friendly relations between the mother country and her daughters over the seas, and I am proud, as a Canadian, to think that this occasion has been made use of as an opportunity for bringing together the Canadian Baths and the Mother Bath.

Miss Powell from Ontario replied that

> Miss Taylor [from New Brunswick] and I have been overcome with the overwhelmingly kind way in which Bath has received us We have not been made to feel strangers, but daughters coming from the dominions over the seas. Bath has been much too kind to us, and we will always treasure the presents we have received as mementoes of a very happy week and an historic occasion. As Canadians, we are most happy to be associated with our American neighbours from the south on this occasion (applause). We have all grown very fond of each other in our comfortable tents, and I hope we will all meet again in friendship at the next pageant.

Miss Taylor, who admitted that she had never spoken in public before, added a few words of thanks, and then Mr Sturge Cotterell proposed a toast to 'Our American Guests':

> It is very difficult for me to follow after such an eloquent speech from our Lady President, the Lady de Blaquiere, who has so won our hearts during the whole of the Pageant Week (applause). Our Pageant is over. The labours of months, labours of life and loyalty for the most part, are at an end, and the Bath Pageant has become part and portion of Bath history. When the story of our Pageant comes to be told there is one feature of it which will stand out prominently and distinctly, and it will do this because it is unique ... I refer to the international

character of our great poetic finale, and the fact that I am now about to ask you to toast the representatives of America, who played so important a part in it. For the first time in the history of pageantry the governors of American states have accredited delegates from amongst the inhabitants of the daughter Baths, in their respective territories to represent the cities and towns bearing the same name in the closing scene of what I venture to call our great human drama ... The toast I have the honour of proposing is one which is singular in the history of our city. Many of us will remember the visit last year of his excellency the American ambassador, who came to Bath to perform the ceremony of unveiling a tablet to Edmund Burke, a name revered by American and English alike, and whose visit will ever be remembered by the citizens of Bath. Tonight we part with our fair daughters from America, who have won our hearts. We do not intend to allow them to leave us without saying one word of what our aspirations are for the future. From this day forth we hope to keep in close touch with our daughters in the far west, and I have discussed several schemes, which, I believe, will be taken up enthusiastically by the citizens of Bath, as heartily as by those who I may describe as our lineal descendants on the other side of the broad Atlantic. First, that in every library there shall be a corner devoted to the literature of Bath, and, in addition to this, it is our desire to give every year a prize to the children in the schools, to be awarded to those students who show the greatest proficiency in the history of the Mother City and its surrounding country, 'Wonderful Wessex'. I trust our Pageant has done something to promote the mutual love and good understanding of the Anglo-Saxon race on both sides of the ocean. I trust it will bring many more Americans to our beautiful city, associated as it is with countless American memories of the mighty past. I trust it will knit the two great nations closer together, and, on behalf of the citizens of Bath, I thank you one and all for the service you have rendered the great mother of all the daughter Baths, throughout the world.

Miss Clifford was the first to respond:

I find it very difficult to say everything that I should like to say on behalf of the American girls who have been entertained at Bath during Pageant Week. Before we came we were advised by Mr Clemens (Mark Twain) not to marry, drink, or smoke (laughter)

– that is, to excess (renewed laughter). We have been simply overwhelmed with kindness and this week has been as much a record in our lives as it has been in the history of the old city. I am sure we all love this old city, and we should like to take it all back with us. I am making a little list of the nice men we have met during our visit here, and I think Mr Cotterell's name is very nearly at the top.

She then presented a Georgian-style silver cup to Mr Cotterell, 'with the kind regards and appreciation of the American and Canadian girls', and, 'in the words of Uncle Remus', said, 'We all wish him well'.

Miss Heinaman from Bath, New York, said she felt there was very little left for her to say, but she would like to thank everyone for the kindness they had shown and the many little gifts they had received. 'Your city is very delightful,' she added, 'it is far better than ours, being so quaint, and we thank one and all for their kindness and attention.'

Miss Ward from Bath, North Carolina, said there was even less for her to say after Miss Heinaman's speech, but, 'in the words of Tiny Tim', she would simply say 'God bless you every one'.

Mr AM Broadley, to whom it now fell to propose a toast to Mr Cotterell, began by saying that he would resist the inspiration afforded him by his surroundings, and keep his remarks brief. Such introductions often strike fear into audiences – and with good reason. Mr Broadley's speech, which included references to William Shakespeare, the Hudson Bay Company and the portraits on the walls of the Banqueting Room, was, as befitted a man of his erudition, the longest of the evening. In it he too mused on the significance of the Pageant:

My memory goes back to the dreary month of November, when at the other end of this room I pleaded, with somewhat feeble accents I am afraid, the cause of the Bath Pageant.[1] I pointed out to those present what results would accrue to Bath from the carrying out of the idea of a Pageant, which had been propounded to us by my good friend, Mr T Sturge Cotterell. I said that if the idea was adopted great good would accrue to Bath for the reason that no city in the United Kingdom possesses so great and glorious opportunities as those which

1 Mr Broadley's memory was playing tricks on him; the first meeting held in the Guildhall to discuss the Pageant was on 10 December 1908.

present themselves to this city. Now, we are here this evening to celebrate what I venture to characterise as a great and striking and complete victory (applause) ... The Pageant is over – the consequences of the Pageant are now to begin, and I do not think that anything which this city could have done, or that any scheme which this city has propounded, that any idea which this city could have carried out, will do more good to the city in the immediate future than the splendid Pageant so beautifully worked out by my friend, Mr Frank Lascelles, and which has become during the last six days to many of us almost a second life.

Bath has always been, as regards the old world and the new, somewhat of a travel centre. From this day it will become a travel shrine. It will take, and must take, the position, both as regards America, and the colonies, which is occupied by places like Oxford and Stratford-on-Avon. There will be no more question of the American who comes to London, of the colonial who comes home, thinking his visit complete until he has paid his respects to the great city associated not only with the days of the Romans and with Edgar, but, coming down to later times, with the glorious periods of Georgian history – a city which has a history no other city can boast.

No one knows more than I do the important part which Mr Cotterell has played in carrying out this scheme (applause). Had it not been for the tact, for the energy, and for the popularity of Mr Cotterell, the Pageant would never have been (hear, hear) and I think it is in the fitness of things that in the hour of victory, of a brilliant success ... that we should drink his health with the enthusiasm which he deserves. Mr Cotterell has the interest of Bath at heart and he lives for the good of the city, but he has never rendered a greater service to his fellow citizens than in assisting, as he has done, to carry through this wonderful Pageant which has been from start to finish a march of triumph to everyone concerned in it ...

As Mr Cotterell has pointed out, the Pageant has had the international feature of the co-operation of the charming daughters of Canada and America, which for all time will distinguish it from every other pageant and every other spectacle of the kind ... You have heard of certain mementoes and certain gifts, which we hope the fair daughters of Canada and America will take back with them across the Atlantic. I am happy to say that my friend, Mr George Gregory, intends to present each lady with a copy of that now rare book, Warner's *History of Bath*, a copy of which I hold in my hand – which will always be a reminiscence of the eighth episode of the Bath Pageant, in which that book was presented to Queen Charlotte by the author. Then they are to have the lighter and more satirical side of Bath, and Mr Gregory also intends to present each lady with a copy of Anstey's famous *Bath Guide*, written by the gentleman whose benign countenance smiled upon the distinguished and charming representative of Queen Charlotte.

After more effusions of this nature, the toast was most heartily drunk, accompanied by the singing of 'For He's a Jolly Good Fellow'. Mr Cotterell, in thanking Mr Broadley, added to the pile of books to be presented a specially bound copy of *Bath as a Health Resort*.

The banquet over, it was time to repair to Sydney Gardens for the grand finale – the Battle of Flowers. The *Bath Chronicle* sets the scene:

It did not require the deductive powers of a Sherlock Holmes to discover that something of more than usual interest was happening in Bath on Saturday evening. In the

Great Pulteney Street slumbers on a sunny Edwardian afternoon, and a dog ambles slowly across the road. It presented a very different face as preparations got under way for the grand finale of the Pageant.

677

crowded streets, figures clad in all the varieties of garbs of the past nineteen centuries jostled one another, while on the pavements and grouped at the corners of the principal thoroughfares, staid citizens in more sober raiment watched the progress of this strange mingling of many generations. Cab ranks were deserted, and down Pulteney Street there was a continuous, steady procession of every kind of vehicle. All roads led to Sydney Gardens, where a wind-up to the week's festivities was promised in the shape of a magnificent fête of unprecedented brilliancy ...

The Sydney Gardens have been the scene of many a gorgeous gathering, but never has it been thronged with such a mass of colour and movement as on Saturday night. Pageant performers, in costume, and everybody else were there. The proceedings commenced with a parade of the decorated vehicles ... Undoubtedly the most popular of the exhibiting vehicles were the motor cars, which had been garnished in every conceivable way. Probably the most effective and novel was that above which a swing was erected, a young girl occupying the seat, and gently swaying to and fro as the car proceeded. Another effective car was decorated in a prevailing colour of red, and latticed with gold round the body. Three cars, not for competition, represented as many episodes. No 1 was arranged by Mr Vaughan, No 5 by Mrs Owen, and No 7 by Miss Dora Sants. These were occupied by characters taking part in the episodes which the cars represented. Among the bicycles an amusing exhibit was a prehistoric pattern of cycle, built of wood on the most approved ET Reed lines.

Unfortunately the crowd was so dense that a comparatively small number of people were able to see the competitive vehicles. All now awaited the coming of the Colonial and American ladies, and, to relieve the tedium, a number of the Pageant characters present entertained the spectators in a novel manner. In the intervals between the band music, a number of ladies who figured at the dedication of the temple in Episode One, and were present on the decorated car, raised that beautiful and haunting melody that so captivated all who heard it. When the band struck up a march, a continuous circle of Anglo Saxons in their war paint, Romans in their armour, and a number of literary and other characters kept up an impressive parade in front of the bandstand, while the Elizabethan ladies held a revel round the car.

At last the expected party arrived and took their seats in the orchestra. Among those present besides the Colonials and Americans were the Lady de Blaquiere, the Hon Kathleen de Blaquiere, Mrs Pagden, the Judges, Mr Lascelles, Mr Bertram Fortt, Mr Pearson, Mr HW Matthews, and Mr Cotterell. A bouquet was given by Mr Pearson to Mrs Campbell Cory, who presented the prizes, these being represented by dainty little bannerettes, blue signifying first prizes, red second, and white third.

At the conclusion of the prize-giving, five calls were sounded upon a bugle, the signal for the Battle of Flowers to commence. The ladies on the bandstand accordingly began to pelt everyone near at hand with the flowers, mostly made of paper, the American girls seeming to particularly enjoy this form of mimic fighting. Soon the firework display was in full swing, the whole concluding with a fine set piece, wishing 'Prosperity to the American Baths'.

It is estimated that there were between eleven and twelve thousand people in the gardens, and £300 was taken in cash.

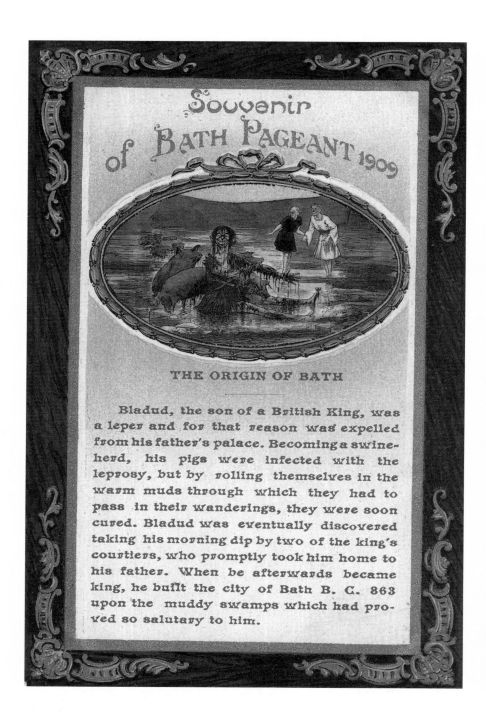

Souvenir
of Bath Pageant 1909

THE ORIGIN OF BATH

Bladud, the son of a British King, was
a leper and for that reason was expelled
from his father's palace. Becoming a swineherd, his pigs were infected with the
leprosy, but by rolling themselves in the
warm muds through which they had to
pass in their wanderings, they were soon
cured. Bladud was eventually discovered
taking his morning dip by two of the king's
courtiers, who promptly took him home to
his father. When be afterwards became
king, he built the city of Bath B. C. 863
upon the muddy swamps which had proved so salutary to him.

CHAPTER THIRTY-NINE

LIKE A HAWK OR A HELMETED AIRMAN …

Many of those who were at the last-night celebrations would only have been in bed a few hours when the sun came up. At the end of one of the most extraordinary weeks in Bath's history, they could be forgiven, as they dreamt of kings and courtesans, peasants and priors, and Bladud and his pigs, for being unaware that

> *This royal throne of kings, this sceptr'd isle,*
> *This earth of majesty, this seat of Mars,*
> *This other Eden, demi-paradise,*
> *This fortress built by Nature for herself*
> *Against infection and the hand of war,*
> *This happy breed of men, this little world,*
> *This precious stone set in the silver sea,*
> *Which serves it in the office of a wall*
> *Or as a moat defensive to a house,*
> *Against the envy of less happier lands*

was about to lose its inviolability.

Bladud, although celebrated in Bath for his pig-inspired leprosy cure and for founding the city, is as well known elsewhere for constructing a pair of wings and trying to fly, an aeronautical experiment that ended, Icarus-like, in a crash-landing on the Temple of Apollo in Trinovantum (or London, as it is more commonly known). Bladud featured as a failed aviator in Geoffrey of Monmouth's *History of the Kings of Britain*; recent retellings of the story include Iain Sinclair's prose poem, *Bladud*, and Moyra Caldicott's novel, *The Winged Man*.

People had dreamed of flying for millennia; Leonardo da Vinci had designed flying machines that lacked only the means to power them. The Montgolfier brothers invented balloons that could carry people up into the atmosphere, but, for all the refinements developed during the nineteenth century, this wasn't so much flying as drifting along with the wind.

The problem was that, although inventors could design ingenious flying machines, before the development of the petrol engine there was no practicable means of powering them. In the

1890s, Sir Hiram Maxim, the inventor of the Maxim gun and the mousetrap, designed a massive steam-powered aircraft, but it never got off the ground. Steam may have powered the industrial revolution, but steam engines were too heavy to conquer the air. With the development of ever smaller and more efficient petrol engines, however, it was, whatever the doubters said, only a matter of time before someone achieved powered flight.

It happened on 17 December 1903 at Kitty Hawk, North Carolina, when Orville Wright took to the air for twelve seconds. It could, had things turned out differently, have happened much closer to home.

The Wright Brothers were not working in isolation. Hundreds of people across the world were devoting their energy and ingenuity to a frantic attempt to build the first powered flying machine. One of them was Patrick Young Alexander. He was born in 1867 and, after a spell at sea, settled with his parents at 8 Portland Place in Bath. By 1890, both his parents were dead, leaving him with a fortune of £60,000. As well as being a keen balloonist, he was convinced that powered flight was a practical possibility. In 1893 he wrote that 'aerial navigation is not an *impossibility* but a *difficulty*, which may be mastered by careful study and perseverance.' His ambition was to be the first man to fly; freed from the necessity of earning a living, he could devote his time and money to achieving that end. He set up a workshop at 24 Ballance Street and moved out of Portland Place to the Lansdown Grove Hotel. His next move was to De Montalt Wood, Combe Down, where he set up a workshop in an old mill, before moving again, to the Mount at Batheaston, where he established another 'Experiment Works'. He became an internationally-known and respected figure on the aeronautical

scene, and was invited to the launch of the first Zeppelin in 1900.

In 1902, he organised celebrations to mark the centenary of the first manned balloon ascent from Bath, inviting many prominent figures, including Major Baden Powell, Samuel Cody, and Charles Rolls of the Aeronautical Club to the city. The centenary ascent – a twelve-mile trip from Sydney Gardens to Chew Magna – was not the highlight of the celebrations, however. What Alexander had really invited his fellow aviation enthusiasts down to Bath for was a demonstration of the aeronautical and meteorological equipment he had developed at Batheaston.

In the event, of course, it was the Wright brothers who won the race, consigning Alexander and his works at Bath-easton to historical oblivion. Which, especially in Bath, is a little unfair. His experiments made an important contribution to the development of aviation in its formative years; he was well known to the Wright brothers, both before and after their inaugural flight. They were, however, a little wary of him; while visiting them, there were concerns that he was spying for the British government – which he may well have been.

In the years that followed the Wright brothers triumph, vast strides were made – many of them ending, sadly, in Bladud-like disaster. Early aviation was one of the most dangerous pursuits imaginable. But still they persevered. And, as the sun rose on that summer Sunday morning, high above the English Channel – or, as he would have known it, La Manche – hung a helmeted airman, denizen of one of those 'less happier lands', chilled to the bone, peering into the mist:

I am alone. I can see nothing at all. For about ten minutes I lose all orientation. It is a curious situation: without guidance, without compass in the air, above the Channel. My hands and feet rest lightly on the levers. I let the plane choose its own course. And then 20 minutes after having left the French coast, I see the cliffs of Dover, the castle, and further to the west the point where I should have landed.

The small crowd that had gathered to welcome Louis Bleriot to England took some time to make their way from the spot where he should have landed to the golf course where the only witness to his momentous touchdown was Police Constable Stanford, who happened to be on duty in the vicinity. Bleriot removed his helmet and climbed, with difficulty, out of the plane – his right foot had been severely burned in an accident a month earlier and he bore the scars of around 50 other crashes – and asked, pointing to the fuselage where they had been strapped before take-off, 'would you be so kind as to hand me my crutches'. It is recorded that, as he enjoyed a celebratory breakfast in a nearby inn, three customs officers questioned him as to whether he was carrying contraband

or infectious diseases.

When Bleriot's plane was exhibited at Selfridge's in Oxford Street the following week, no less than 120,000 people came to see it in the first four days. Opinion as to the significance of the event was divided, however. RD Blumenfeld, managing editor of the *Daily Express*, noted in his diary:

> Last week M Bleriot flew the Channel in half an hour – 33 minutes to be exact ... These things represent a foolish waste of money. Besides, flying across the Channel means nothing after you have done it. You can't carry goods or passengers.

Lord Northcliffe had no such doubts. It was he who had put up the prize money of £1,000 for the first man to fly across the Channel, in the hope that it would be an Englishman. In May 1908, he had written to Winston Churchill:

A man with a heavier-than-air machine has flown. It does not matter how far he has flown. He has shown what can be done. In a year's time, mark my words, that fellow will be flying over here from France. Britain is no longer an island.

With fears of a German air invasion so prevalent in the summer of 1909, it is curious that Bleriot's achievement was greeted not by cries of foreboding but with delighted applause. Perhaps it was because photographs of the crippled Frenchman standing by his diminutive craft, with its bicycle wheels and a propeller that snapped off on landing, were calculated to evoke feelings of pity rather than alarm.

Nobody knew then that airships were not destined to be the flying machines of the future; nobody in Bath on that July morning, as they began to clear away the debris of the weeklong Pageant could have known that, on a spring morning less than 33 years later, they would be clearing away the deadly debris of a mass aerial bombing raid.

One
Shilling
Nett.

SOUVENIR OF THE BATH HISTORICAL PAGEANT
19ᵀᴴ TO 24ᵀᴴ JULY, 1909.

WILLIAM LEWIS & SON.
The Bath Herald Office.
BATH.

The "Pageant Bouquet."

An ENTIRELY NEW PERFUME of DELIGHTFUL FRAGRANCE. A CHARMING SOUVENIR OF THE PAGEANT.
In Bottles at 2/3, 2/9, 6/6 and 11/6 each.
Bijou Sprinkler Bottles at 6d. each.

The "Pageant Bouquet Toilet Soap."
In Dainty Boxes containing 3 tablets, at 2/6 per box.
Single Tablets, 1/- each.

FROM STEELE & MARSH, Chemists and Perfumers,
6, MILSOM STREET, BATH.

Ye Old Gates of Bath, 1650.

THE OFFICIAL
BATH PAGEANT SOUVENIR SPOON
IN STERLING SILVER AND FINE ENAMEL.

THE SPOON Illustrates: Coat of Arms of Bath, Bath Abbey, Sword of King Bladud, Fountain of the Large Roman Bath, Statue of the Angel of the Pool; and in the Bowl is a Portrait of Beau Nash.
PRICES: Plain Silver, Silver Gilt, or Oxidised, 7/6   Ditto ditto Enamelled, 8/6

MANUFACTURED AND SOLD BY

W. G. Dickinson
GOLD AND SILVERSMITH
19, NEW BOND ST., BATH

E. J. Vokes
GOLD AND SILVERSMITH
16, MILSOM ST., BATH

BATH PAGEANT   SOUVENIR KNOCKER.

CHAPTER FORTY

FLOREAT BATHON

Once the Pageant was all over, what was to be made of it? There was the inevitable lost property, of course – a fur boa, five fans, two odd gloves, six umbrellas, two parasols, six hat-pins, two field glasses and some coppers. It transpired that not everyone had been touched by the spirit of benevolence that characterised the proceedings. Pickpockets had inevitably found the crowds a handy source of revenue. Several 'substantial hauls' had been reported; one man had had his pocket cut off with over £3 in it. There had been thefts from the performers' tents as well, with one vicar having his cassock stolen. It transpired that 'a few persons of doubtful character' had enrolled as performers, but were promptly dismissed on being recognised by 'detectives from Bristol'.

There had been suggestions that the performers should parade through the city to round off the celebrations, but the committee did not consider that 'such as display would be consonant with the dignity of the Pageant'. The editor of the *Chronicle* was disappointed: the idea had struck him 'as being a charitable one, as many of the poor people in the city cannot afford to pay to see the beautiful Pageant', but he accepted that 'the committee undoubtedly saw insuperable difficulties in the way'. In the end, it was only the Roundheads and Cavaliers from Episode VI who paraded through the city on Saturday evening. There was also talk of using the grandstand and Pageant Ground for an open-air service on the Sunday after the final performance, but this too was ruled out because of 'the difficulty of controlling the crowd which would have been likely to assemble'.

But, as the dust settled, the costumes put away and the postcards filed in albums, what was Bath to make of the extraordinary, unrepeatable extravaganza that had taken place? There were plenty of people ready to descant on the wider implications of the pageant phenomenon – GK Chesterton, for example, who took the

Opposite page: Souvenirs of the Pageant came in many shapes and sizes. Apart from books and postcards, pipe holders, perfume, soap, spoons and door knockers were among the objects produced to cash in on 'pageantitis'.

role of Dr Johnson in the Church Pageant at Fulham, and saw in it an antidote to a meaningless, commercialised modernity. Louis Parker described the phenomenon in similar terms:

The modernising spirit which destroys all loveliness and has no loveliness of its own to put in its place is the negation of poetry, the negation of romance... This is just precisely the kind of spirit which a properly organised and properly conducted pageant is designed to kill.

According to Ayako Yoshino, who has studied the subject in depth, 'English pageantry was often described by contemporaries as an quasi-mystical act of collective social healing, bringing people together outside the narrowing and dirtying confines of a commercialised modernity.' In a pamphlet published for the Romsey Pageant of 1907, Parker described the event as 'a great act of thanksgiving for the mercies of the past'. This spiritual dimension was underlined by the special church services routinely held on the Sunday before a pageant started.

Pageants were, therefore, according to their most articulate apologists, a way of promoting unity and reasserting traditional values against the fracturing forces of modernity. In essence, pageants were about communities talking to themselves and reinforcing social bonds by looking back at significant events in the past that had involved the whole community. This was, after all, the time of the English folk song revival and the Arts and Crafts movement, when people were trying to re-engage with their roots in a variety of ways.

While this elucidation of the roots of the pageant phenomenon might explain the passion with which pageants were staged, however, it only tells part of the story. It ignores not only the commercial but also the promotional aspects of pageants. Pageants were profitable: the Winchester Pageant, for example, made around £2,500, and while the £1,100 profit at Bath was less impressive, it was still a respectable sum in 1909. The commercial aspect of pageants, while it may have dismayed some contemporaries, was unavoidable when, as at Bath, pageants were staged not by the civic authorities but by a group of local citizens.

The need to make a profit, or at least break even, inevitably meant that pageants had to be promoted – and, in the case of Bath, that promotion was inspired to the point of genius. Organising three special trains from London, inviting national and international journalists, royalty, colonial representatives, the Lord Mayor of London, various members of parliament ... wining and dining them, driving them in procession through flag-bedecked streets, and sitting them in a VIP box in the grandstand – all this was a public relations exercise of a high order. This had nothing to do with a community talking to or bonding with itself, this was all about Bath selling itself to the world. What was being promoted was not the Pageant, but the City of Bath.

The organisers had a very clear idea what the Pageant was for – to raise the profile of the city and to attract visitors – especially foreign visitors. Instilling a knowledge of and pride in the city's history in its residents was not only desirable in itself; it also made them ambassadors for what we call 'heritage tourism'. Heritage tourism would have come to Bath without the Pageant, of course, but it is by no means certain it would have become as central to the city's economy – or that Bath would be so firmly on the international tourist trail – if the Pageant had not kick-started the process a century ago. The open-top buses that trundle round the streets today are direct consequence of that initiative, which prepared the way for a fundamental shift from Bath as health resort to Bath as tourist Mecca.

Although the Pageant's promoters sought to steer a course for the future, they held firmly onto traditional models of social organisation. The Edwardian period was one of immense social and technological changes, yet the Pageant, by its very nature, looked to the past. More significant, however, was its attempt to reinforce a sense of community by reference to shared heritage and to define contemporary society in terms of values enshrined in past events. It was also inescapably hierarchical, organised by the great and good of Bath, with roles and functions allocated according to rigidly defined social classes. There is no way it could be described as democratic. So, while it sought to initiate a new direction for Bath – as an international tourist destination – it reinforced, by implication, a hierarchical view of society that was rapidly crumbling.

Bath was not alone in making its Pageant a tourist attraction – nor, despite all the protestations of the organisers, was it the first to hit on the idea of attracting Americans. The very first pageant, at Sherborne, featured a character called Mother Sherborne, representing the town, with a daughter representing the American Sherborne, surrounded by girls dressed in English frocks and Native American costumes. At the end of the 1908 Dover Pageant,

Dover entered with the 44 American and colonial Dovers, while at the end of the York Pageant (held a couple of weeks after Bath's) a personification of the city appeared on a raised throne, with all the Yorks from every part of the world, led by New York, at her side rendering homage to the Mother City. In the 1906 Warwick Pageant, no less than 30 American girls took part. This international aspect

York Great Historic Pageant July 26-31, 1909.

J YORK HISTORIC PAGEANT   THE MEETING OF ALL THE YORKS AT YORK.   OFFICIAL PHOTOGRAPHERS LANE-SMITH, AND DEBENHAM & CO LENDAL   YORK

of the English pageant should not surprise us too much – Louis Parker, who got the ball rolling in the first place, wasn't English, but an American born and brought up in Europe.

Almost all the early-twentieth-century pageants were staged in towns and cities that have come to be regarded as heritage tourist destinations. They marked the coming-of-age of something we now take for granted – visitors from America, Canada, Australia and other commonwealth countries coming in search of history. Some places, like Stratford-on-Avon, were already on the American tourist trail, but what the pageants did was to take a fledgling industry and transform it into one of this country's biggest assets. A century ago, Bath was primarily regarded as a health resort – and a somewhat faded one at that. The corporation were still focused on this – they wanted to pull down Bath Street, one of the city's most attractive eighteenth-century thoroughfares, to improve bathing facilities. But the future lay not in Bath as a health resort but in Bath as a heritage tourist destination. The success of the Pageant marked the true beginning of this.

The Bath Pageant also marked a turning point in the historiography of Bath. Traditionally history had been the preserve of the middle and upper classes. Only with the advent of education for all was any thought given to educating the working classes in the history of their country and of the world. There was a strong feeling afoot that teaching history would boost national pride, patriotism and love of country; obviously this depended on a particular view of history, in which great men – kings in particular – achieved noble deeds. It wasn't a history in which stuff like the Peasant's Revolt or the Chartist Movement figured largely – unless they were condemned as 'bad things'.

There was a strong feeling that teaching history in the right way would foster a sense of national identity and purpose. History was not being democratised but used as a tool by the ruling classes to mould and guide society in accordance with what were seen as universal, timeless values – in which love of God, King and Country were the lodestones.

Apart from all the illustrated souvenir books, programmes and books of words that accompanied the Pageant, two history books were published in connection with it; these give an even clearer idea of the uses to which history was put in the Edwardian era. The first was *Bath Episodes*, a slim paperback published in 1909 by John Meehan, a writer and journalist who also had a bookshop at 32 Gay Street. Although not referring to the Pageant and not illustrated by photographs from it, it follows a similar structure, consisting of eight 'episodes' – brief descriptions of notable events in Bath's history. It begins – as the Pageant was originally intended to – with King Bladud and the Pigs, and then follows the order of the episodes in the Pageant, the only difference being that an extra episode is devoted to the Roman temples and there is no Henry VII episode.

Meehan says little about historical method or the uses of history, although he does mount a spirited defence of Bladud. If the reason for his exclusion from Bath's history were to be applied universally, he argues, it 'would close the pantheons of Greece and Rome, deprive fable of all its moral teaching, and extend its severe sentence to works of fiction, even when founded on fact'. Warming to his theme, he quotes an unnamed local historian:

If legendary lore; if the war song and lay of the minstrel; if the soft, simple ballad of trouver or troubadour, or the plaintive pleadings of minnesinger and mastersinger, are to be rejected, then national annals will lose much of their length, and more of their lustre; and those foundations, on which the adventurer into the twilight of prehistoric times rests his hope of interesting the heart, will be loosened, if not effaced.

The most revealing thing about Meehan's attitude to history comes not in the text, however, but in an advertisement inside the back cover, where he offers 'personally conducted tours of Bath ... for the benefit of visitors from a distance'. A variety of two-hour walks, for parties of no more than six people, are offered, including tours of literary, theatrical, artistic and American interest. Meehan was a pioneer of what has become ubiquitous today – the guided tour, whether on foot or by open-top bus or coach. For him, as for the Pageant's promoters, history was primarily a tool for promoting the city to visitors – not that this is intended as a criticism. Without the tourists, what would Bath have become?

Meehan does little more, however, than reinforce the view of history as a sequence of significant events featuring great men peddled by the Pageant. Of far more significance was a book by Alfred Trice Martin called *The Story of Bath*. Trice Martin was

headmaster of Bath College until its demise in 1909 and the book was published at the instigation of and under the auspices of the council, for distribution to schoolchildren in the city. The idea for the book arose at around the same time as the Pageant, although it was not published until two years later. Sturge Cotterell referred to it in a council meeting in 1909, expressing the wish that 'some of us will have the opportunity of perusing it before it is published', and adding that 'the American ladies are anxious that copies of the book might be obtained for the children in the schools of the American places called Bath'. Councillor Sydney Bush added that 'it is of the utmost importance that the book should be of the highest possible standard.'

692

PERSONALLY CONDUCTED TOURS

around the Historic Houses of Bath and District.

MESSRS. MEEHAN will be pleased to arrange, for the benefit of Visitors from a distance, a few personally conducted tours around the places of interest in Bath and District.

The Parties must be small, limited to six in each party, and on days and at times convenient to Messrs. Meehan. The fees charged will be **2/6** per person per hour. The chief Circular Tour is that of about two hours,—"the Literary Associations of a Walk round the Historic Houses of Bath."

Other Tours are of Theatrical, Artistic, and American interest.

PUBLISHERS OF:—

The famous Houses of Bath and District,''
By J. F. MEEHAN, with introduction by the late Marquis of Dufferin, 1901.

" More famous Houses of Bath and District,"
by J. F. MEEHAN, with introduction by Egerton Castle, Author of " The Bath Comedy,', 1906, 12/6 net.

" The famous Houses of Bath and their Occupants,"
by J. F. MEEHAN ; a Handbook, **6d.**, post free, **7d.**

" Famous Buildings of Bath and District,"
a Series of upwards of 120 illustrated articles, by J. F. MEEHAN, at **1d.** each.

" OLD BATH," Six unique Pictorial Post Cards,
from Drawings by DAVID COX. [Period 1820]. **6d.**, post free **7d.**

'Six Pictorial Post Cards, of the Famous Houses of Bath,
from Drawings by H. V. LANSDOWN, 18th Century Period, **6d.**, post free **7d.**

693

The Story of Bath, then, can be taken as a reflection of the official view of Bath's history, served up to educate and inspire young Bathonians. One of the most striking things about the book, to modern eyes, is the amount of space devoted to pre-Georgian Bath. Many books have been written about Bath's history since 1911, but most have concentrated on the Georgian city. The Bath Pageant may have launched Bath's career as a heritage destination, but – with the notable exceptions of the Roman Baths and the Tudor Abbey – today's visitors are concerned almost exclusively with the Georgian city. This is hardly surprising, given that there is precious little to see from the pre-Georgian period. Despite Trice Martin's – and the Pageant's – coverage of this period, it came to be almost totally forgotten, until books published in the last decade by Peter Davenport and John Wroughton started to redress the over-emphasis on the city's Georgian history.

In terms of scholarship, *The Story of Bath* is far better than its remit – and its pre-echoes of *1066 and All That* – might suggest. Yet it is irrevocably of its time. Here, for example, is Trice Martin on the Roman occupation of Britain:

> The Roman invasion was rather like the English occupation of India or Egypt, where, though we govern, we have never settled in large numbers as we have in America and Australia, and where we have certainly made no attempt to drive out the native inhabitants ... In India we honestly try to make the native population happy and prosperous, the better and not the worse for our rule.

And here he is, in *1066 and All That* mode, dealing with the thorny issue of Bladud: 'The word legend means a story that has little or no foundation in fact, so it is the right word to use here, for I am sorry to say there never was such a person as Bladud.' This, he tells us, is all the fault of Geoffrey of Monmouth, who 'set to work to write a history at a time when no one knew how to write a good history, and the result was that his book is a very bad history'.

History, for Trice Martin, was a source of inspiration:

> As the centuries move on, history teaches us to look back, and we see the beautiful things mankind has let fall in its haste; and so the future becomes an object of intense interest to us, and we learn to aim at making the city we live in full of hope, the disciple not the slave of the past.

Noble deeds of great men were also held up as examples. Having described the Battle of Lansdown and the death of Sir Bevil Grenville, he adds that, 'I hope you will go and read what is written on the monument put up to his memory by his grandson, and if ever you have to fight that you will be as brave as he was.' Coming just three years before the outbreak of war the words have a chilling ring to them.

Not surprisingly, he has little time for the morally-delinquent Georgians. His strictures extend to their buildings. Sham Castle, for example, 'to us ... seems rather an absurd building, but it was in accordance with the taste of the age', while St Swithin's Church in Walcot 'is an ugly building, but interesting because of the monuments it contains'. His antipathy to eighteenth-century society was so strong that he seems to have found Bath's nineteenth-century decline a good thing:

> ... a great change had come over Bath. It was no longer merely a city of inns and lodging houses. It had become a permanent place of residence for people of leisure and refinement, who held aloof from the giddy, foolish crowd of pleasure-seekers. Gradually the latter class of visitor deserted Bath and sought fresh scenes. At first the number of empty houses alarmed the authorities and it was thought that ruin was descending on the town. But the houses were soon filled again by persons who, attracted by the beautiful scenery and the reputation of the city as a restorer of health, became permanent residents.

In every point of comparison between Georgian and modern Bath, modern Bath comes out on top:

> In 1820 the old Assembly Rooms, the first built at Bath, were destroyed by fire, and four years later the Royal Literary and Scientific Institution was erected on their site in the Walks. This contains a museum and lecture hall, a library of more than 18,000 volumes, a reading room, a smoking room and a chess room; in the grounds is a meteorological observatory, where records are made of the state of the weather. The contrast between modern Bath and the beaux' Bath is well illustrated by the difference between the purpose of this centre of culture and refinement and the object of the rooms it replaced. The museum contains a splendid geological collection made by Mr Charles Moore, and purchased in 1878.

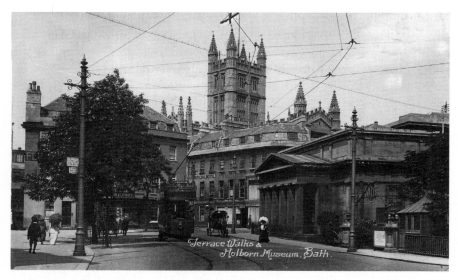

An Edwardian postcard packed with long-forgotten delights – the Twerton tram, the rustic entrance to Institution Gardens, a horse-drawn delivery wagon, the old Literary & Scientific Institute with its Greek Revival façade designed by William Wilkins (who was also responsible for the National Gallery), parasols raised against the sun. One thing it doesn't show – despite the caption – is the Holborn – or even the Holburne – Museum, which announced a move from Charlotte Street to the old Sydney Hotel in 1909.

Terrace Walk, the site of the old Assembly Rooms, is still a barometer of changing values. In the 1930s the Institution was pulled down to widen the road and replaced by subterranean public toilets. Bathonians responded to the change by renaming the spot Bog Island. The toilets were later converted to a night club, which has since closed. In the early twenty-first century, the site briefly hit the headlines when plans were mooted to build a casino there, although nothing has been heard on this head for some years. What next, one wonders?

Although Trice Martin does admit, albeit reluctantly, that eighteenth-century Bath possessed a certain allure, he is quick to stress the illusory nature of this appeal:

Although the romance, or what we may look upon after all these years as the romance, of Bath may seem to have disappeared, yet our city is a very much pleasanter, brighter and more comfortable dwelling place than she could possibly have been even in the days of her highest renown ... A gratifying token of the increasing prosperity of the city and the improvement in the habits of thought of its residents is the great amount of attention which has paid in recent times to church restoration and to the building of new churches and chapels.

It is the last section of the book, where he deals with contemporary Bath, that is most fascinating, revealing as it does what amounts to the official view of the city, addressed to its future citizens. For this reason – and for its detailed analysis of the employment and educational opportunities open to its readers, it is worth quoting at length.

With regard to Bath's growing reputation as a tourist destination, he suggests – somewhat bizarrely – that visitors are likely to be 'impressed no less with the importance of the industries located here than with the beauty of the city and its environs':

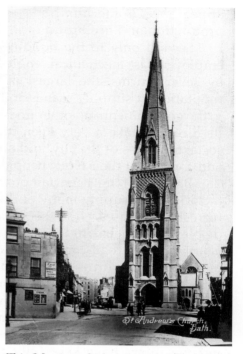

Trice Martin no doubt approved of St Andrew's Church in Julian Road, which dominated the area, its spire poking above the roofline of the Royal Crescent. It fell victim to the Luftwaffe in 1942; Nikolaus Pevsner, in his 'Buildings of England' survey of Bath, described it as 'happily bombed'. You can see where he was coming from, but you'd think, being German, he'd have been a bit more tactful.

First among the local industries must be placed the building and its allied trades, which give employment to thousands of men, and form one of the staple industries of the city. Several of the larger firms have achieved reputations extending far beyond our city, and are frequently engaged in large undertakings at considerable distances from their headquarters.

In the immediate locality cloth weaving is carried on. The mills at Twerton produce West of England broad-cloth, which, although not so much worn now as in former times, is noted for its durability, its fast colours and its general appearance. Some hundreds of workers are engaged in its production and are proud of its character.

Second only to the building trades in the number of its employees is mechanical engineering, which is carried on by several firms, the largest of which enjoys a well-earned reputation. It supplies cranes and other mechanical appliances to the government and other dockyards in all parts of the world. Its directors take a very keen interest in the educational and social activities of the city, and are fully alive to the well-being and comfort of their work-people.

Bath has long been famous for cabinet-making, and her factories now supply many of the most famous of the London furnishing houses with the goods which are so temptingly displayed in their windows. The city has also been for several years noted for road-carriage building. The vehicles constructed by our leading firms are considered models both in beauty of design and excellence of workmanship. This decade and its predecessor have, however, witnessed the coming of the automobile, or self-propelled motorcar, which is gradually but surely superseding the horse-drawn carriage. But the local manufacturers have kept fully abreast of the times, and the bodies which they place on the chassis of the cars are at least equal to the carriages that gained them so great a reputation.

Another trade deserving mention is that of printing, which furnishes occupation to a very considerable number of persons and in which Bath holds a special position as the home of phonographic printing, whence not England alone but America and all our colonies are supplied with publications of all kinds executed in shorthand characters.

Closely connected with the printing of books is their binding, and Bath is the home of a very large number of bookbinders, and possesses a method of binding which is acknowledged to be unique. It is well known throughout the whole country; almost every public library in England has adopted the method; and in America so flourishing a business has been developed that the firm has established itself in New York, and constantly recruits its staff in that city from among its employees in its original home.

The postal service provides many opportunities to the youths of our city for securing permanent and, on the whole, fairly paid employment with a prospect of promotion. Bath serves as a 'forwarding office' for a very wide area, embracing two or three counties, the correspondence of which is dealt with by the Bath officials. Consequently the staff is much more numerous than would suffice for simply local requirements; and its members form a very useful portion of the community in other than their official capacities.

A similar remark may be made of the railwaymen. Served by two great lines and their extensions, Bath is the home of hundreds of railway employees of all grades, who form a very important and skilled section of the population and add very considerably to the intellectual and moral character of the city.

Smaller, but not unimportant industries located in our midst are organ-building and the manufacture of coarser kinds of pottery. The former is conducted by two firms, one of which has been well known for a long time, and the other is rapidly acquiring the good opinion of those who are qualified to judge of accuracy and beauty of tone, and delicacy and precision of workmanship.

In the main the above industries give employment to the men and lads of the city and district and although two noted and successful corset factories provide occupation for several hundreds of female workers, it remains now, as formerly, that domestic work, millinery, dressmaking, shop-assistantships and clerkships are the main sources of employment for our women and girls.

But however much we may rejoice in the industrial and commercial advance made by our beloved city, the fact still remains that the hot mineral springs are the greatest factor in her stability and prosperity. Rightly and naturally, therefore, the corporation has been assiduous in its care for the development and improvement of the buildings and appliances devoted to either the external or the internal use of the waters and so successful have been its endeavours that a leading medical journal, the *Lancet*, asserts, 'It is doubtful whether at any spa such a complete and well-appointed bathing establishment can be found.'

He then goes on to describe the city's educational facilities:

The Act of Parliament, passed in 1902, empowered local authorities to maintain all grades of schools. The Bath City Council has taken advantage of the act, and has arranged a system of schools and classes in which pupils may follow an advanced course of instruction in art, science, industry,

BATH CITY
TECHNICAL SCHOOL,
GUILDHALL.

Director of Studies: A. GODFREY DAY, A.M.I.M.E.

School of Art.
Head Master: NAT. HEARD, Assoc. Royal College of Art.
**DRAWING, PAINTING,
FIGURE AND LIFE STUDIES,
DESIGNING. MODELLING.**
Art Crafts including Repoussé, Woodcarving, Leather Work, &c.

School of Cookery and Domestic Sciences.
Head Mistress: Miss HEYGATE, First Class Diplomée.
**Artisan, Household and High-Class Cookery.
Laundry Work. Dressmaking and Needlework.**
Students are also trained as Teachers of Domestic Subjects.

Science and Technical Classes.

Ambulance,
Botany,
Brickwork,
Carpentry,
Cabinet Making,
Chemistry,

Decorators' Work,
Electricity,
Engineering,
Geometery,
Hygiene,
Masonry,

Mathematics,
Mechanism,
Physics,
Plumbing,
Sanitation,

Classes for University Examination.

School of Commerce.
Head Master: J. STOTT, A.C.P.
Mercantile Arithmetic, **Commercial Correspondence,** **Shorthand,**
Book-keeping, **Geography,** **Typewriting.**

Berlitz School of Languages.
CLASSES AND PRIVATE LESSONS.

Secondary Day School.
FOR BOYS AND GIRLS.
Head Master: F. C. HOLMES, B.A., Lond.
A Continuation Day School for those who have received Primary Education.
The Curriculum includes SCIENCE, DRAWING, MATHEMATICS, ENGLISH,
LATIN, FRENCH, WOODWORK, DOMESTIC ECONOMY, &c.
For particulars of the various Classes, apply to the Director of Studies.

Courses offered by the Technical School, housed in the northern extension of the Guildhall, in 1909.

700

commerce or domestic science at a small cost, or, when scholarships are won, free of cost altogether. Pupils from the primary schools can enter the evening continuation schools without fees, whence they may, as a result of regular attendance and attention, pass on to the Technical School, and take up any course of study which they may desire. Selected pupils may also compete for numerous exhibitions and scholarships tenable at the City Secondary School, or at King Edward VI's Grammar School, or at the Girls' High School. Scholarships gained at the Grammar School may lead the clever student to the university; and thus a ladder, which has more than once been climbed, is reared from the infants' school to the university. It is a pleasure to recognise that this scheme of schools is appreciated and warmly supported by several of the largest employers of labour in our city, who insist that the younger employees in their various works shall attend the classes organised for their instruction, and shall thus study the principles underlying the practice and processes carried out in the workshops. So successful has been the application of this system, that it has become necessary to provide additional facilities for the thousands of pupils who desire to avail themselves of its advantages and, in September 1910, a branch Technical Institute was opened by the Countess Waldegrave at Long Acre, Walcot.

As a coda, he turns to the Pageant, photographs from which illustrate many of the chapters in the book. Many readers would, of course, have seen the Pageant – some would even have appeared in it – but the book seems to have been written with half an eye on posterity, and Trice Martin goes back to first principles, describing what a pageant is, how it came about and what the episodes consisted of. Writing of the rehearsals watched by local schoolchildren, he notes that

> The youthful spectators were keenly interested in each episode, but the representation of the 'Legend of Bladud' aroused the greatest display of approbation and mirth. The drollery of 'Bladud', the antics and capers of his well-trained pigs evoked boisterous merriment, which clearly showed the gratification of the juvenile audience.

Not surprisingly, it is 'the value of the Pageant as a visual lesson in the history of the city' on which he places most emphasis. The episodes, he declares, 'conveyed to the spectators much clearer impressions than they had previously possessed of the manners

701

and customs, dress and arms of our ancestors' and were 'a source of much instruction and great pleasure to everyone who was so fortunate as to witness them'. He concludes his description with a rousing, if somewhat laboured, valediction, which brings the book to an end:

> The memory of the Pageant will linger in our minds for many years to come; but it must ultimately happen that the curtain will be 'rung down' and the recollection pass away. May no curtain ever be 'rung down' over our beloved city; but may her motto, 'Floreat Bathon', be realised for ever.

TEMPLE MINERVA,
SYDNEY GARDENS, BATH.

In the same year that Trice Martin's book appeared, the Temple of Sul Minerva, Bath's contribution to the Festival of Empire Exhibition at the Crystal Palace, was re-erected in Sydney Gardens to commemorate the Pageant. Unlike the Temple of Sul Minerva erected in Royal Victoria Park for the Pageant, it was of Bath stone rather than wood and canvas. Nevertheless, it bears a striking resemblance to the earlier structure, which has led many to assume it is the temple that appears in postcards of the Pageant. From this, not surprisingly, has sprung the widespread belief that the Pageant took place in Sydney Gardens. It is ironic that this fine structure, whose archaeological accuracy has been confirmed by modern research, should be not only the sole tangible reminder of the Pageant – despite post-dating it by two years – but also the source of such widespread misapprehension.

As regards Royal Victoria Park, all trace of the Pageant seems to have disappeared – not surprising given the ephemeral nature of the structures built for it. Bladud's pond has gone and the site comprehensively redeveloped, the main arena being absorbed into the Botanical Gardens in the 1920s. However, there is a slim chance that a relic of the Pageant does survive. On 15 April 1910, Sir George Reid, High Commissioner of Australia, planted a Cedrus Atlantica Glauca (or Blue Atlas Cedar) at the spot where the royal box had stood the year before. Compared with the ceremonies associated with the American and Canadian representatives, this was low key, but perhaps inevitable given the Australians' oversight in not calling any of their towns Bath. Attempts to find this tree have unfortunately proved fruitless. It stood somewhere on what is now the lawn in the extension to the Botanical Gardens, but, although there are several Cedrus Atlantica Glaucas in this area, none appears to be in the right place or of the right age, and the only one to carry a label is dated 1840. But it is just possible that one of them is a bit more special than appears at first sight.

The legacy of the Pageant amounts, though, to more than a tree which, if it has survived the upheavals of the last hundred years, will shortly be celebrating its centenary; more, too, than a temple built two years later and put in the wrong place. The open-top buses that trundle through the park, full (on a good day at least) with visitors from around the globe, listening to tales of Bladud, Beau Nash, Jane Austen and Minerva, are its true legacy. The Mayor's Guides, who daily take parties of visitors round the city, have an even stronger claim as inheritors of the spirit of the Pageant, founded as they were by one of its prime movers, Sturge Cotterell; in terms of apostolic succession, it doesn't get much better than that.

Although the look of Bath – or at least the Bath that the tourists come to see – may not have changed much in the last century, the city has undergone a profound transformation. In 1909, it was a faded health resort, desperately trying to revive its fortunes; today, as a World Heritage Site, it is an international tourist destination. In 1909, it was a town of ageing spinsters; today, while still a popular place for the well-heeled to retire to, the establishment of two universities has created a large student population.

The citizens of 1909 could look back at the Bath of 1809 and congratulate themselves on a century of progress. Today, things may not be perfect, but advances in medicine and in the general standard of living have been beyond anything imaginable a century ago. Hygiene – both personal and social – has been transformed beyond recognition. Other benefits are more dubious – we have extensive personal mobility, for example – but at the cost of pollution, congestion and reliance on a dwindling fuel supply. A century ago, the threat of German invasion hung over the nation like the Sword of Damocles. The Germans didn't invade, of course, and probably never intended to, but people were right to be concerned about the Kaiser's ambitions; the war that broke out five years later was worse, far worse, than anything anyone could have imagined. Today, we live with the far greater threat of global warming; how that will pan out, a century hence, who can say?

Progress is not inevitable – and, in the onward march of civilization, there have been some savage reversals. The audiences at the Pageant would have seen ample evidence of one of the most dramatic of these – the collapse of the Roman Empire and the descent of Western Europe into the dark ages.

Bathampton Meadows, one of the most important open spaces in the Bath area – to be sacrificed for an unwanted Park & Ride scheme?

For the moment, many of our concerns for the future focus, as they always have, on more local issues – will an unwanted Park and Ride facility be built on Bathampton Meadows, will the Newark Works building find a new and sympathetic use, will the Central Library be converted to a wrestling arena? A century hence, however, battles over such issues will probably be long forgotten – only to be unearthed by some diligent delver into times long gone, curious to see what life was like in 2009. In the meantime, other, far more significant changes, most of them unforeseen, will have occurred.

While a question mark hangs – as it always has – over the future of life on earth, the overwhelming odds are that the human race will still be around in 2109 and will still live in the place we know today as Bath. Whether its residents will be a tribe of latter-day Bladuds musing upon the fall of empire or gilded creatures, holidaying on Mars, who knows? The chances are, though, that, however much changes, some things will stay resolutely the same.

Perhaps there will still be – as there were in 1909 – debates about whether rugby should stay on the Rec or whether the Holburne of Menstrie Museum needs a new gallery; perhaps conservationists will still be campaigning to save iconic buildings such as the Hilton Hotel or that masterpiece of early-twenty-first-century design, the gleaming coil of the omnibus station. Who can say? One thing we can be certain of, though: if Bath survives, in whatever form, someone somewhere will feel impelled to pick up whatever they use instead of a pen to write to the twenty-second-century equivalent of the *Bath Chronicle* and complain about something.

POSTSCRIPT

THE 2009 BATH PAGEANT

On several occasions in the preceding chapters we have stated that the 1909 Bath Pageant could never be repeated. However, just as the book was on its way to the printers, we discovered that there were plans to mount a Pageant in Bath in 2009, with Bladud as the central character. And so, at the risk of missing our deadline and at considerable expense, on 7 June 2009, we despatched a roving reporter to the streets of Bath to report on

☞ *King Bladud's Pageant 2009* ☜

The report, unedited, unshriven and unannealed, apperars below. A selection of specially commisioned photographs of the event appears on the opposite page.

Had you been in Milsom Street one Sunday in June 2009, you might have seen a tall man carrying a long wooden staff leading about 30 people, including one carrying a banner, towards the Abbey. This was Richard Carder, under his bardic name of Sulyen Caradon, who had conceived a celebration of the 1909 pageant with this 2009 version. Behind him was a band playing mainly early music , but which occasionally broke into more recent pieces such as the Gay Gordons and the Match of the Day signature tune – which sounded a little strange on shawms and sackbuts.

At the Abbey they were greeted by King Bladud, Beau Nash, a toga-clad Roman and Queen Elizabeth I, played by members of the Natural Theatre Company. After Kevan Manwaring, also known as Talyessin, had read out in full Queen Elizabeth's charter to the city of Bath, the Queen and her companions circulated among the residents and bemused tourists.

All at once, a trumpeter, clad in coloured motley and wearing a deer's head, complete with antlers over his own head, sounded a fanfare and the party – now accompanied by another banner – headed for Parade Gardens, where they were greeted by the Mayor and Mayoress and where Rose Flint read her poems to the admiring crowd.

In the afternoon there was a concert at Chapel Arts Centre, where the main participants were joined by local chanteuse Jennifer Crook, who played the harp for them.

This was the city's only commemoration of the 1909 pageant, but, if somewhat smaller than the original, was enjoyed by all its participants.

BIBLIOGRAPHY

Annual Report for 1909 to the Bath Urban Sanitary Authority by the Medical Officer of Health & Sanitary Inspectors, Bath, 1910

Adams, Carol, *Ordinary Lives a Hundred Years Ago*, London, 1982

Baily, Leslie, *BBC Scrapbooks: Volume One, 1896-1914*, London, 1966

Barlow, Kate, *The Abode of Love: A Memoir*, Edinburgh, 2006

Barstow, Harry W, *Gladiators of a Roman City: A History of Bath Football Club*, Corsham, 1986

Beazer, Cyril HG, *Random Reflections of a West Country Master Craftsman*, Bath, 1981

Bell, Lady Florence, *At the Works: The Study of a Manufacturing Town*, London, 1907

Berriman, Algernon E, *Aviation: An Introduction to the Elements of Flight*, London, 1913

Betjeman, John, *Ghastly Good Taste*, London, 1933

Blom, Philipp, *The Vertigo Years: Change and Culture in the West, 1900-1914*, London, 2008

Bobbit, Malcolm, 'A Motoring Medley', in *Archive: The Quarterly Journal for British Industrial and Transport History*, 57-59

Borsay, Peter, *The Image of Georgian Bath, 1700-2000*, Oxford, 2000

Brown, W Henry, *The Jubilee History of the Bath Co-operative Society Ltd*, Bath, 1939

Burnett, John, *A History of the Cost of Living*, Harmondsworth, 1969

Cecil, Robert, *Life in Edwardian England*, London, 1969

Chislett, Steve, *Buses and Trams of Bath*, Bath, 1986

Crofts, Bruce, 'The Historical Pageant of 1909', in *Guidelines: Newsletter of the City of Bath Mayor's Honorary Guides,*, 54-56 (March & September 1996, June 1997);

Cullingham, Gordon, *Patrick Young Alexander, 1867-1943: Patron and Pioneer of Aviation*, Bath, 1984

Davis, Graham & Penny Bonsall, *A History of Bath: Image and Reality*, Bath, 2006

Dobbie, BM Willmott, *A Nest of Suffragettes in Somerset: Eagle House, Batheaston*, Bath, 1979

Down, CG & AJ Warrington, *The History of the Somerset Coalfield*, Radstock, 2005

Drummond, JC, *The Englishman's Food: Five Centuries of English Diet*, London, 1939

Ensor, RCK, *England 1870-1914*, Oxford, 1936

Finch, Graham, *Bath Shopfronts: Guidelines for Design and Conservation*, Bath, 1993

Finlay, Victoria & Martin Palmer, *A Brief History of the Church of St Martin, Northstoke, Somerset*, 2nd edition, 2007

Forsyth, Michael, *Bath: Pevsner Architectural Guide*, London, 2003

Fuller, Roy, *History of the Firm of Fuller's, Coach & Harness Manufacturers, Bath*, Bath, 1955

Goddard, Shirley, 'Helen Hope', in *Guidelines: Newsletter of the City of Bath Mayor's Honorary Guides*, 54 (March 1966);

Gould, Shane, *The Somerset Coalfield*, 1999

Harper, Duncan, *Bath at Work*, Bath, 1989

Hattersley, Roy, *The Edwardians*, London, 2004

Hill, Dennis, *Bath Fire Brigade and Ambulance Service: 1891 to 1974*, Bath, 2003

Hockman, Hilary, *Edwardian House Style*, Newton Abbot, 1994

Howells. William Dean, 'A Fortnight in Bath', in *Harper's Monthly Magazine*, CXI, Nov 1905

Jackson, Neil, *Ninetenth Century Bath: Architects and Architecture*, Bath, 1991

Kelly, Patrick, 'The Gas Industry in Bath', in *Guidelines: Newsletter of the City of Bath Mayor's Honorary Guides*, 62, June 2003

Kelly, Patrick, 'Water Supply in Bath', in *Guidelines: Newsletter of the City of Bath Mayor's Honorary Guides*, 62, June 2003

Kelly, Patrick, 'Waste Disposal in Bath', in *Guidelines: Newsletter of the City of Bath Mayor's Honorary Guides*, 62, June 2003

Kidner, RW, *The Steam Lorry*, Tarrant Hinton, 1948

Laver, James, *Edwardian Promenade*, London, 1958

Lawrence, Felicity, 'Britain on a Plate', *Guardian*, 1 October 2008

Macdermot, ET, *History of the Great Western Railway*, 2 vols, 1927-31

McKernan, Lucy, 'The Battle of Waterloo: or, Why Can't We Film Such a Thing if We Won the War in the First Place', Talk at the National Film Theatre, 30 March 1996

Macqueen-Pope, Walter, *Twenty Shillings in the Pound*, London, 1948

Mander, Charles, *The Reverend Prince and his Abode of Love*, Wakefield, 1976

Martin, Alfred Trice, *The Story of Bath*, London, 1911

Masterson, CFG, *The Condition of England*, London, 1909

Matin, A Michael, '"The Hun is at the Gate!": Historicizing Kipling's Militaristic Rhetoric, from the Imperial Periphery to the National Center', *Studies in the Novel*, 31 (Winter 1999)

Meehan, JF, *Bath Episodes Illustrated*, Bath, 1909

Melville, Lewis, *Bath under Beau Nash*, London 1907

Miller, Kerry, *Stars in Stripes: The Official History of Bath City Football Club*, Bath, 2003

Millsum, O, 'A Visit to the Little Zoo, Bath', in *Bird Notes: The Journal of the Foreign Bird Club for the Study of all Species of Birds in Freedom and Captivity*, Vol VII, Brighton, 1908-9

Mitchell, Hannah, *The Hard Way Up: The Autobiography of Hannah Mitchell, Suffragette & Rebel*, London, 1968

Mitchell, Malcolm, *The History of Bath Bowling Club 1907-2007*, Bath, 2007

Payne, WH, 'Kangaroo Farming', in *Wide World Magazine*, Vol XIX, April-September, 1907

Penny, John, *Up, Up and Away! An Account of Ballooning in and around Bristol and Bath, 1784 to 1999*, Bristol, 1999

Petrie, Sir Charles, *Scenes of Edwardian Life*, London, 1965

Pilkington, Ed, 'The Road to Ruin', *Guardian*, 3 December 2008

Priestley, JB, *The Edwardians*, London, 1970

Reeves, Maud Pember, *Round About a Pound a Week*, London, 1913

Roberts, Robert, *The Classic Slum*, Harmondsworth, 1973

Routh, Guy, *Occupation and Pay in Great Britain: 1906-79*, London, 1980

Sealy, Elsie B, *My Memoirs*, Bath, nd

Stapley, Ron, *History at Source: Britain 1900-1945*, London, 1992

Streatfield, Noël, ed, *The Day Before Yesterday*, London, 1956

Stride, Louie, *Memoirs of a Street Urchin*, Bath, 1985

Thomas, Edward, *In Pursuit of Spring*, London, 1914

Trivett, Keith, 'The 1908 Norton Hill Mining Disaster,' in *Five Arches: The Journal of the Radstock, Midsomer Norton & District Museum Society*, 61(Spring 2008)

Vernon, James, *Hunger: A Modern History*, Cambridge, Massachusetts, 2007

Wilson, AN, *After the Victorians*, London, 2005

Wingfield-Stratford, Esme, *The Victorian Aftermath*, London, 1933

Withington, Robert, *English Pageantry*, Oxford, 1920

Yorke, Stan, *The Domestic Revolution Explained*, Newbury, 2008

Yorke, Trevor, *The Edwardian House Explained*, Newbury, 2006

Yoshino, Ayako, 'The Modern Historical Pageant: Commodifying Locality', Paper delivered at the 2005 Modern Language Association, Washington DC

INDEX

BOOKS ON BATH FROM FROM AKEMAN PRESS

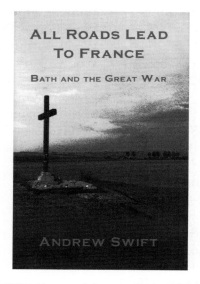

Five years on from 1909, the world was plunged into a devastating war in which over 1,800 men from the Bath area died. Drawing on letters, diaries, newspaper reports and personal testimonies, *All Roads Lead to France* tells the story of those who fought – and those who stayed at home. While soldiers fought and died in the mud of Flanders, their families battled against poverty and hunger. There were battles between jingoists and conscientious objectors, industrial unrest and fears of a breakdown in public order. After the war came peace, but not the prosperity the soldiers had dreamt of. They returned home to a land where nothing would ever be the same again.

'Highly recommended.' Michelle Young, Western Front Association

'An immensely readable account.' Sonia Batten, Centre for World War Studies, Birmingham

'I was profoundly moved by this book … A tragic and compellingly beautiful tapestry.' Hylda Holden, The Regional Historian

'Describes in amazing detail the devastating effect the war had on the Bath area… All Roads Lead to France has brought an unprecedented amount of scholarship to local Great War research.' Jonathan Harlow, Avon Local History Association

£30 Hardback
From all good bookshops or post free from:
Akeman Press, 58 Minster Way, Bath BA2 6RL

BOOKS ON BATH FROM FROM AKEMAN PRESS

Pauline Forrest's account of a working-class childhood in Bath in the 1920s and 1930s is a vivid evocation of a city changed almost beyond recognition – a city of tramcars, lodging houses, street vendors, midwinter dips in the flooded river and charabanc trips to the seaside. It was a time of 'making do', of getting by as best you could, when small pleasures counted for a lot. But, although firmly rooted in a particular time and place, her story reminds us, above all, of what it is to be a child, with all the hopes and dreams, all the adventures and tribulations (and occasional naughtiness) that entails. By turns funny, uplifting and sad, it is a classic account of childhood between the wars.

'Gives a very real sense of what the city was like for ordinary people in the 1920s and 1930s.'　　　　　Best of British Magazine

'Anyone who has ever wondered what it was like to live in the centre of Bath between the world wars ... should read this vividly colourful picture of life.'　　　　　Bath Chronicle

£6.50 from all good bookshops or post free from:
Akeman Press, 58 Minster Way, Bath BA2 6RL

ALSO FROM AKEMAN PRESS

Philip Whitmarsh, a lively four-year-old, was playing in the garden with his brother and sister when he fell over – and found he couldn't get up. Life would never be the same again for Philip. He had been struck down by the 'summer plague' – poliomyelitis. So began a nightmare of isolation wards and surgery, lying for months on end strapped to a metal frame in the Bath Orthopaedic Hospital – followed by the long slow climb to recovery. Years of missed education saw him consigned to the dunces' class, prey to the school bullies – but he fought back and, thanks to a life-changing comment from a sympathetic teacher, ended up with academic success and an award for outstanding achievement. His refusal to accept second-best saw him achieve success in a range of different careers before setting up his own business and becoming Mayor of Frome, his home town. Now he has achieved another long-standing ambition – to set it all down as an inspiration to others and proof that it's not the hand life deals you that counts, but the way you play it.

As featured in the ITV Series A West Country Childhood: Reaching for Dreams

'Impressive, moving, frequently funny and always relevant' Robert Giddings

'More than just a simple tale of triumph over adversity ... contains heart-rending anecdotes about how he battled to build inner strength.' Polly March, Western Daily Press

'A treat to read.' David Heath, MP for Somerton & Frome

£10 from all good bookshops or post free from:
Akeman Press, 58 Minster Way, Bath BA2 6RL

OTHER BOOKS FROM AKEMAN PRESS

BATH PUBS
by Andrew Swift & Kirsten Elliott   £12.99

AWASH WITH ALE:
2000 Years of Imbibing in Bath
by Andrew Swift & Kirsten Elliott   £12.99

THE LOST PUBS OF BATH
by Andrew Swift & Kirsten Elliott   £15

THE MYTHMAKER:
John Wood 1704-1754
by Kirsten Elliott   £10

SOMERSET PUBS
by Kirsten Elliott & Andrew Swift   £8.50

THE RINGING GROOVES OF CHANGE:
Brunel & the Coming of the Railway to Bath
by Andrew Swift   £12

SOMERSET FOLLIES
by Jonathan Holt   £10

Available from all good bookshops or post free from Akeman Press
58 Minster Way, Bath BA2 6RL   www.akemanpress.com